8086

INDIAN DELIGHTS

a book on Indian cookery

by ZULEIKHA MAYAT

Design and Illustrations:
Andrew Verster

Photography:
Dennis and Nalin Bughwan

Published by
WOMEN'S CULTURAL GROUP Durban

First Edition 1961 ....17 500 copies
Second Revised Edition...85 000 copies
Enlarged Super Edition 1982 ....25 000 copies
Second Impression 1983.....................................25 000 copies
Third Impression 1985..25 000 copies
Fourth Impression 1987......................................10 000 copies
Fifth Impression 1989...10 000 copies
Best of Delights 1988..10 000 copies
Sixth Impression 1990 ....20 000 copies
Seventh Impression 1993....................................20 000 copies
Eighth Impression 1996......................................10 000 copies

Printed and bound by
INTERPAK NATAL
22 Willowton Road, Pietermaritzburg
Republic of South Africa

DEDICATION

"This book is dedicated to all husbands who maintain that the best cooking effort of their wives can never compare with what 'mother used to make'."

First Published 1961
ISBN 0 620 05688 6

Acknowledgements

SABERA DESAI, NADIA MAYAT — Typing

NURJEHAAN RABOOBEE — Proof reading

KHORSED S. NADVI — Index and arranging team for proof reading

HAWA E. MOOSA, MARIAM A. H. MAHOMEDY — Loan of utensils and collating recipes

MARIAM E. E. G. PARUK, MANJRA BEEMATH, AYESHA E. A. MAYAT — Recipes for mass cooking

ZULEKHA KADWA, ZULEIKHA BOBAT, FAWZIA KAJEE — Help with metrication of recipes

TAJ COMPANY — Ingredients for spice tray photograph and sponsorship of metric chart

LEILA ALI, KHADIJA MALL, FATIMA MAHOMEDY, ZUBEIDA, FAZILA SHAIK and FARIDA JHAVERI — Help with trying out recipes

GORI PATEL — Paper cut-outs, garlands of flowers.

BIBI SHAIK — Paper Flowers and Decor.

SHAMEEMA MAYAT — Re-checking Index.

The 1st edition of 25 000 copies was sold out within one year. There can be no greater testimony to the popularity of Indian Delights and we wish to thank the public for their support.

PREFACE

Acknowledgements of Editor

Since it first appeared twenty years ago, users of Indian Delights have sent in valuable criticism and suggestions. This has been of incalculable value to me in compiling this Super Edition. It has not been possible to countenance all the suggestions for it should be remembered that Indian Delights was never intended to be a primer of Indian cooking. It aimed rather at preserving the richness of a well established culture. Nevertheless the A.B.C. of Curry, Dear Beginner and the introductory notes in various sections should aid newcomers in the field. Again with the step by step explanations of the more specialised dishes, no difficulty should be encountered by the average person.

This super edition has been long in the making. One reason is that new categories of dishes have been introduced, not all of them strictly Indian in origin. However, they have been so naturally integrated on the Indian table that they cannot be left out. Some of these dishes I have picked up on my travels to various parts of the world, but mostly they have been passed on to me by persons ranging from ordinary housewives to the super cooks that abound in our community. This is why Indian Delights remains — as it always has been — a representation of the collective culinary knowledge of our Community. To all these contributors I wish to express my sincere gratitude.

To name everyone who has contributed recipes for this edition will make tedious reading, therefore I convey my gratitude in general terms knowing that they will understand. Help with preparation of dishes for photographs, trying out recipes, proof reading etc., has been acknowledged on different pages. If anyone has been left out, I hope that they will attribute it to lapse of memory and forgive me. But what I cannot forget is the help of several persons who have been deeply involved with this project and foremost among these is my housekeeper Mildred Mdladla whose quick grasp of procedures and mastery of even quaint gadgets never fails to astound me. She has spared me many valuable hours which were so sorely needed for recording and writing. Then there are my friends and colleagues from the Womens Cultural Group (see list on back pages) under the leadership of Zohra Moosa — without them a book of this nature could just not be possible. Two of the members who also happen to be neighbours have shouldered a very heavy task load. These are Hawa Bibi Moosa and Nur-Jehan Raboobee who were virtually on "tap" for my frequent needs.

My thanks also to the supercooks in the Paruk, Mahomedy and Mayat families, who have increased my expertise in cooking to the extent that at last I feel myself a worthy disciple. In this respect I must mention Mariam (Foibibi) Essop E.G. Paruk and Mariam (Choti Bhabhoo) A.H. Mahomedy. Their profound experience gives this edition a professional touch.

In acknowledging contributions from the Transvaal, I must not fail to mention the help of a sister organisation — the Mehfile Nisa of Potgietersrus. Their chutney and biscuit recipes have added lustre to the pages, just as have the recipes of Lutchmi Pillay and Savvy Ramkisoon to the vegetarian section. To Mohtarama Fatima Ahmed Mehtar my thanks for the home remedies.

In his involvement with the printing Tony Pienaar has gone well beyond the bounds of business courtesy. His help has been highly appreciated as is that of Dennis and Nalin Bughwan whose photographs highlight our culinary efforts.

Obviously the credit for design and layout goes to Andrew Verster but apart from his artistic skill he helped in many other ways, some of which even he may not have been conscious of. And as for Sabera Desai and Nadia Mayat only I know how many hours you two have laboured at the typewriter.

To my parents and their generation, I am indebted for the stories that I heard at their knees never realising in childhood that it was but one more manner of passing on the legacy of both Islamic and Indian Culture. In appreciation thereof I hope that through Indian Delights, some of the Community values and folk lore will be transmitted to the younger generation.

Finally my thanks to my own family for their sustained help and encouragement and who since the loss of my husband encompass me with their warmth and love.

To the users of Indian Delights in so many parts of the world, the lovely warm letters you have written to me have been highly appreciated. To all of you and many more who in future years will be using Indian Delights I wish you happy working and eating sessions. Please feel free to write to me should you encounter any problems.

May we all give thanks to our Creator for His having so richly endowed Mother Earth with the good things of life.

Zuleya.

IF RECIPE CALLS FOR

1½ tsp Falooda Pdr (agar agar) = 1 Tblsp gelatine
1 Cube compressed Yeast (20g) = 4 tsp dry yeast
500g honey or ghor = 1½ cups
1 fresh Coconut = 2½ cups grated
                (250g)
1 pkt dates = 1 cup chopped
                (250g)
1 cup mawa (1¼ litre milk
   reduced to mass) = 225g
1 kg mawa (5½ litres milk
   reduced to mass) = 1 000g
1 carton yoghurt = 500ml
1 carton cream (small) = 125ml
1 carton cream (large) = 250ml
1 onion = 1 cup sliced or
                ¾ cup grated
1 tomato = ½ cup chopped
1 bunch Dhunia = 1 cup leaves
                loosely piled

Fluids
(Milk and Liquids)

1 cup	= 8 fl oz	= 250ml
½ cup	= 4 fl oz	= 125ml
1/3 cup	=	= 80ml
¼ cup	= 2 fl oz	= 60ml
1 Tablespoon		= 12.5ml
1 Teaspoon		= 5ml
1 bottle Vinegar		= 750ml
1 cup Oil		= 250ml

Length

3 mm		= 1/8 inch
5 mm		= ¼ inch
10 mm	= 1 cm	= ½ inch
2.5 cm		= 1 inch
5 cm		= 2 inches
10 cm		= 4 inches
20 cm		= 8 inches
30 cm		= 12 inches

Tinned Products

Small Tin Cream	= 155g
Large Tin Cream	= 310g
Tin Condensed milk	= 397g
Tin Tomato Puree	= 410g
Small tin canned fruit	= 410g
Large tin canned fruit	= 825g
Tin Baked Beans	= 410g
Tin macaroni in tomato sauce	= 410g

Temperatures

Farenheit	Centigrade	
250	120	very slow
275	140	slow
325	160	moderately slow
350	180	
400	200	moderate
475	240	moderately hot
500	260	hot
550	280	very hot

AT A GLANCE

Liquids	250ml	125ml	60ml	80ml	12.5ml	5ml	100g
Cup measure	1 cup	½ cup	¼ cup	1/3 cup	1 tblsp	1 tsp	
Ingredients Breadcrumbs	120g 4 oz	60g 2 oz	30g 1 oz	40g	6g	2,5g	200ml
Butter, Marge, Solid Ghee	230g 8 oz	115g 4 oz	60g 2 oz	80g	10g	5g	90ml
Cheese, Cheddar etc	100g 3.5 oz	50g	25g	33g	10g	5g	90ml
Cheese, Cottage	250g 9 oz	125g 4.5 oz	60g 2 oz	80g	12.5g	5g	100ml
Coconut (Dessicated)	80g 3 oz	40g	20g	30g	4g	1.5g	300ml
Flour, (Cake, Gram etc).	120g 4 oz	60g 2 oz	30g 1 oz	40g	6g	2.5g	200ml
Milk Powder	100g 3.5 oz	50g	25g	33g 1 oz	5g	2g	250ml
Oats	90g 3 oz	45g	22g	30g	4.5g	2g	275ml
Rice	200g 7 oz	100g 3.5 oz	50g	65g	10g	4g	125ml
Fresh, pounded Chilli Ginger, Garlic etc	200g 7 oz	100g 3.5 oz	50g	65g	10g	4g	125ml
Sugar (granulated)	200g 6.5 oz	100g 3 oz	50g	65g	10g	4g	120ml
Icing Sugar	130g 4 oz	65g 2 oz	30g 1 oz	40g	7g	2.5g	200ml
Nuts	125g 4 oz	60g 2 oz	30g 1 oz	40g	6g	2.5g	200ml

INGREDIENTS USED IN THIS BOOK

(And Their English Version)

VEGETABLES

Indian Names	English Equivalents
Aaloo	Potatoes
Adrak	Ginger (fresh root)
Ajwain ajmo	Celery or tymol seeds
Baingan or vengra	Brinjal or eggplant or aubergine
Bhaji	Green leaf vegetable
Bhaji (methi)	Fresh fenugreek leaves
Bhaji (wara)	Mfino or red leaved spinach
Bhaji (suwa)	Fresh dil leaves
Bhindi	Okra or lady finger
Chirchira	Snake gourd (thin whitish)
Chori Hing (Sing)	Indian type beans
Dodhi	Indian gourd
Dhunia	Coriander leaves
Dhunia/Jeera	Coriander and cummin powder
Gajar	Carrots
Goovar phalli (or Sing)	Flat Indian beans
Koru or Kodu	Pumpkin or calabash
Kuripulya (neem patta)	Curry leaves
Kakdi (kakri)	Cucumber
Kakdi leembo	Limes
Kalonji	Onion seeds or mangrel
Karela	Bitter gourd
Laba or Aaso Palav	Jonesia Asoca (edible cacti
Lauki	Thin dark green gourd
Lasan	Fresh garlic
Mattar	Peas
Methi bhaji	Fenugreek herbs
Mircha	Chillies
Mircha lal	Red chillies
Mircha leela	Green chillies
Mircha mota	Peppers or capsicums
Moong harga	Sprouted moong (chinese peas)
Moora	Radish
Palak	Spinach
Papdi	Sem or Indian type beans
Patra, paterwella or patta	Madumbi leaves (calocasia)
Piyaj	Onions
Piyaj leela	Spring onions
Phoodina	Mint
Sekta sing (saijan)	Drum sticks
Sekta na phool	Drum stick flowerettes
Suwa bhaji	Dil leaves
Torai	White ridge gourd
Toovar sing	Fresh Toovar peas (unshelled)
Toovar bakra	Toovar peas (same as above but shelled)
Varda	Freshly sprouted seeds of goovar
Vengra	Brinjal or eggplant or aubergine

MEDICINAL SPICES

Ajmo	Tymol seeds
Array or awray	Myra balon
Aheryo or aseryo	Indian linseed
Char magaj	Seeds of Indian specie of melon
Ganthora	
Ghor	Jaggery
Gokharoo	Caltrope
Goondar	Edible gum
Hancher	Rock salt
Hing	Asoefaetida
Karyata	Chiretta
Karijiri	Fleebane
Kharak	A dry date
Kari moosli	Nelaphanny root
Koringee or mangrela	Onion seeds
Laba or Aaso Palav	Jonesia Asoca, an edible aloe
Saaker or misri	Sugar candy
Salaum moosli	Root of salem
Singhora	Water chestnuts

Continued on Page 10

ASSORTED SPICES AND HERBS IN COLOUR PHOTO (Opposite page)

Note also:
1) Curry leaves (kurripulye)
2) Mint (phoodina)
3) Dhunia (coriander)
4) Fresh root ginger
5) Garlic
6) Saffron
7) Fresh pounded chillies

SPICES AND INGREDIENTS

Indian Names	English Equivalents
Aamli or imli	Tamarind
Ajmo or ajwain	Tymol or celery
Aaloe bokhara	Damson or plums
Arad or haldi	Turmeric
Araroht	Arrow root
Adrak	Ginger (fresh roots)
Badam	Almonds
Chana	Whole gram (chick peas)
Chana Flour	Besan or gram flour
Charoli	Chirongee nuts
Dahi	Yoghurt
Dhunia	Coriander
Elachi	Cardomom
Falooda Grass	China grass or agar-agar
Falooda seeds	Tookmarian (ocylum pilosum tulsi)
Ghor or ghur	Jaggery (dark brown sugar)
Gosht	Meat
Hing	Asoefaetida (Duiwels Drek)
Javatri	Mace
Jeero or jeera	Cummin
Jhaiphal	Nutmeg
Jinga	Prawns or shrimps
Kalonji	Onion seeds
Kabaab	Meat balls
Kaju	Cashew nuts
Karipulya or neem patta	Curry leaves
Kesar or zafran	Saffron
Kevda arak	Essence of paradanus ordorstismus
Khus-khus	Poppy seeds
Kofta	Another name for meat balls
Lasan	Fresh garlic
Laapsi	Crushed wheat
Lavang	Cloves
Mari	Pepper
Mircha	Chillies
Methi	Fenugreek
Misri	Sugar candy
Pista	Pistachio nuts
Piyaj	Onions
Shah jeera	Caraway
Soji or suji	Cream of wheat or semolina or farina
Soonth	Dry ginger
Soowa	Dil seeds
Saumnf	Fennel seeds
Sev or sevian	Vermicelli
Tandra	Kernel (of coriander, etc)
Til or tal	Sesame seeds
Tuj	Stick cinnamon
Zaitun	Olives

LENTILS AND CEREALS
(Also see in Spices and Ingredients)

Indian Names	English Equivalents
Ata or maida	Flour
Bajra ata	Millet flour (also known as Sorghum)
Chana	Whole gram (chick peas)
Chana dhal	Split gram (chick peas)
Chana Ata	Gram flour (interchangeable with pea flour) Besan
Chori	Dry beans or special type of Indian fresh beans
Dhal	Various types of lentils that are split
Urad dhal	Black gram lentil (split)
Dhal toovar	Oil dhal (split)
Dhal Moong	Green Chinese pea lentil
Dhal Masoor	Pinkish lentils (split masoor)
Ghav	Whole wheat
Harga	Fresh sprouted moong
Juwaar	Barley or millet
Juwaar ata	Flour of millet (also known as Sorghum)
Khowse	Noodles or macaroni
Laapsi	Crushed wheat
Maizena	Maize flour
Makkai	Mealies (corn)
Makkai ata	Mealie meal
Mattar ata	Pea flour
Mattar dhal	Split peas
Moong	Green Chinese peas
Moong ata	Flour of moong
Moong dhal	Green Chinese peas (split)
Saabo chokha	Sago
Sev or sevian	Vermicelli
Soji or suji	Cream of wheat or semolina
Vaal	White dry beans
Vaal dhal	Split dry beans
Varda	Sprouted beans etc

GLOSSARY

ARAD: Arad, or haldi, is turmeric powder. This is a colouring with strong preservative quality and should be used carefully. Minimum quantities given here are sufficient to tint your curries the required shade and lavish use must be avoided in order to prevent garish colouration.

ALOE BOKHARA: Dried Damson, for which prunes may be substituted.

BAGHROO: The residue that is left after butter is boiled for ghee is known as baghroo. The economical housewife will not waste baghroo but will use it up for smearing her rotis or use it as thickening for khuri.

BHINDA, KARELA, DODHI, BHAJI, ETC.: Indian type of vegetables available from all Indian green grocers or Indian market stalls in Durban.

BHATAKYAS: Spiced scones or rotis made of flour or ground lentils for use in curries. (See page 102).

BLANCHED SLIVERED ALMONDS: Almonds are blanched by pouring boiling water over them and peeling off the skins after they have been immersed for a while. To sliver the almonds, as called for in recipes from time to time, it will save a lot of inconvenience to keep a bottleful ready for use on the pantry shelf. The blanched almonds must be shaved thinly lengthwise, (thin slivers) and left to dry in a low oven, till they are crisp but not brown. Pack in airtight bottles when cold.

CHILLIES: Chillies used in recipes are fresh ones, either the red or green variety as stated. Chillies are pounded up in a kundi (mortar), or minced and stored in bottles in a fridge, and used as required. A tablespoon of oil mixed-in with ground chillies, makes for better preservation.

If red fresh chillies are not available then the red dried crushed ones are an excellent substitute. Red chilli powder may be used but care should be taken that they are not coloured artificially, since these give the curries an unattractive colour. As chillies vary in sharpness, the housewife will adapt her measurements accordingly.

COCONUT MILK: Fresh coconut is dehusked, cleaned and grated. The grated coconut must be steeped in hot water, then strained through a wire sieve. The thick extraction of milky liquid is then used in curries as specified. An easier method is to put the steeped liquid (after it has cooled down) in a liquidiser and pulverised till the liquid is thick and creamy. This is an economical method of extracting coconut milk. Dessicated coconut may be used by steeping in cold water, then liquidising and straining.

DAHI: Dahi is the cultured sour milk obtainable from any dairy and we recommend the maas or yoghurt varieties. If sour milk is made at home then use a little old dahi as culture and in curries and biryanis use only the curds and not the thin watery liquid. In Kurhi the liquid part may be used together with the curds.

DHUNIA: This ingredient is used in all its stages. Dhunia (fresh coriander leaves) are used for garnishing or in mince and savouries. Pounded dhunia leaves are important for some types of chutneys.

Dry dhunia seeds are used coarsely crushed for some types of savouries and meat dishes. Dhunia/jeero is a finely powdered combination of both ingredients used for subtle flavouring and thickening in curries. Two parts dhunia to one part jeero is used in this instance.

DOKRA: Small round disc made of spiced flour. For further elaboration see page 102.

ELACHI, TUJ, CLOVES AND WHOLE PEPPERCORNS: Elachi are whole cardomom pods bruised open and added to pot of curry or rice. Tuj is stick cinnamon. Elachi, Tuj, etc., are not absolutely essential and many homes have discontinued use of same. However, they lend that subtle distinctive flavouring for which Indian foods are famous, so, for exotic flavours, we strongly recommend that the minimum quantities specified, be used.

FALOODA GRASS: This is a sea weed commonly known as china grass or agar agar. It is obtainable from chemists and Indian grocers. A teaspoon is equal to a dessertspoon of gelatine.

GINGER/GARLIC: For every 400g of fresh root ginger, use 200 g of fresh garlic. Carefully scrape, clean and wash the two ingredients and drain off moisture. Grind through mincer twice and store in bottles in fridge for use as required. With the addition of a little salt, ginger/garlic compound can be stored for a long time. Besides its distinguished flavour, it is also a wonderful tenderiser and for tougher cuts of meat use a little more than specified in recipes. Mince and vegetables calls for lesser amounts whilst fish dishes taste much better when only garlic is used. Ground ginger/garlic freezes very well.

GARLIC OR GINGER SLIVERED: When recipes call for slivered garlic, then the carefully scraped and washed ginger and garlic must be cut in thin slivers, like almonds.

GHEE: This is clarified butter or margarine. Butter is put to boil and when it is crystal clear, the scum is drained off through a muslin cloth. The ghee is stored in tins or enamel bins. Indian housewives store as much as six months' quantity at a time. Ghee keeps indefinitely. Many Indian grocers stock ghee. Most people use margarine for ghee.

Ghee can be dispensed with in curries and sunflower oil only used if desired. In desserts we recommend that ghee be used as indicated in recipes.

Ghee/oil will be used by most housewives in proportions to suit individual tastes. We recommend oil only in meat and vegetable dishes. In poultry and beef, ghee definitely makes a difference.. Rice, of course, calls for pure ghee only. Our quantities are minimum but we feel that this is both economical and healthy, as very rich dishes are difficult to digest and in any event ghee floating on curries is unsightly. Skimming off after dishes are cooked is uneconomical.

GHARUM MASALA: After curries are done, they are "pepped" up with a last minute addition of mixed spices. This blended spice is known as Gharum Masala. (See page 53).

GHOR: Jaggery. (Sugar obtained from toddy palm, dark brown sugar may be substituted).

INGREDIENTS FOR CONVALESCENT SECTION: English equivalents for the medicines and herbs in this section (see page 9).

JINGA: Prawns or shrimps may be used when jinga are called for.

JEERA OR JEERO: This is whole cummin seeds obtainable in all grocery stores. Whenever jeero is mentioned the seeds must be used whole. Coarsely crushed jeero means the seeds are coarsely crushed up and not powdered.

KACHUMBAR: Relishes served with either rice dishes or curries (also known as Sambals).

KUNDI: The pounding mortar stone, used by Indian housewives is known as a kundi. The pestle that goes with it is made of a hardy type of wood and both are obtainable from stockists of Indian utensils. In most instances a mincer can be substituted for a kundi, and people who own blenders will hardly have to resort to a kundi at all.

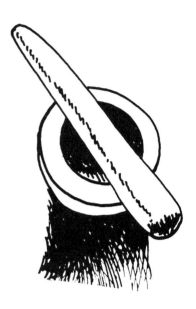

MALAI: Boiled milk, if left standing, collects a thick creamy skin after a while and this must be rescued for use in curries. The addition of malai in curries makes for a creamier and tastier consistency and although we have not directed use in our book, it should be used whenever posible. Malai is also excellent for making cream scones and in rotis.

MASALA (SPICES): Wherever the term Masala appears it indicates the collective spices in that particular recipe, either blended together and then smeared, or added to main ingredient. The Western equivalent of masala is marinade.

MAWA, KHOYA MITHAI: In sweetmeats and desserts the use of mawa is often called for. To make mawa boil ½ litre of milk at a time in a thick based enamel saucepan. The milk in the initial stages will have to be stirred continuously but once it starts boiling the heat can be slightly lowered and watched for scorching and discolouring.

The lump of fudgy mass to which the milk has been reduced is known as mawa. Mawa keeps very well in the freezer in plastic containers.

ONIONS: Sliced onions, means onions sliced in paper thin rings. Chopped onions are finely sliced and chopped across. Onions, to a large extent, control the texture of your curries, so in both slicing and braising follow directions minutely.

PANEER OR PANIR: Indian cheese which is sold in bazaars can be made at home. Ricotto cheese may be substituted.

PURIS: Roti dough is fried in hot ghee or oil and the resulting beautifully puffed out discs of crisp bread are served with pattas, mango juice, cutlets or curries.

PAPADS: Thin discs of savoury lentil flour dough is sun dried and packed away for use as required. These discs are fried or toasted and served with rice dishes. They are also known as papadams.

ROLLER OR VEHLAN: The rolling pin used by the Indian housewife is obtainable from stockists of Indian type utensils. It is a long wooden one, tapering off thinly towards the ends, and is essential in making rotis and the thin pastries. Unpainted ones of brown wood are strongly recommended.

ROTI: Unleavened Indian type bread, also known as chapatis. (see illustration below)

ROTLAS: Unleavened Indian type bread made from sorghum flour or mealiemeal.

SAFFRON: This very expensive and exotic pistil of a flower, from the snowy mountain ranges, is a must in Indian cooking. The flavour and aroma is so distinctive that it cannot be mistaken. It is also a colouring and tenderiser that cannot stand comparison with any other ingredient. It should be used whenever specified, but if for reasons of economy one does not wish to use it, then add a little more turmeric to the recipe. Saffron has been given in teaspoon measurements. TO POWDER: Heat some strands of saffron over very low heat. Crush fine, mix with little hot water and strain through sieve, or soak strands in hot milk. Steep for 10 minutes.

TAMARIND JUICE: This exotic product has a tang and sourness peculiar to itself. to extract juice, steep tamarind, after cleaning and washing, in hot water till it is soft and mushy. Thereafter sieve the pulp through a wire sieve and use as required. (Aamli or Imli).

TAVA OR GRIDDLE: A tava is the iron griddle over which rotis are made. Beautiful cast-iron or teflon covered one can be bought in any hardware store and the rimmed one in our illustrations is strongly recommended. (See illustration alongside). Electric frying pans makes lovely rotis.

TOMATO: Unless otherwise stated in specific recipes, we have given tomato measurements in cupfuls as sizes vary so much. We recommend that tomatoes be pulverised in a liquidiser, if you possess one, or otherwise grate or mince them to use in curries, etc. This avoids loose tomato skins floating in gravies which many people detest, and it also ensures a smoothier consistency.

TOOVAR BAKRAS: Fresh toovar beans for which fresh green peas may be substituted.

VAGAAR (TEMPERING): As specified in particular recipes, vagaar can either be the prelude or the final touch in curries or rice dishes. Onions fried in ghee till they are gold and crisp is known as vagaar. In some recipes onions together with mustard seeds or chillies or slivered garlic, etc., are called for. For the really luxurious dish slivered almonds alone are fried in ghee for a vagaar over rice dishes.

WHERE TO FIND IT

Persons not familiar with Indian terms will welcome this guide to the various category of dishes in this book.

Section 1
Rice Dishes   Pg 22-50

Rice dishes served as the main course look under:
Pilaaus — which is plain rice dressed up with some other ingredient.
Yakhnis — Rice and meat cooked together in one pot and mixed in.
Biryanis — Rice with meat/fish etc., cooked in one pot but each ingeniously kept separate in layers.
Khitchris — Rice cooked with some lentil and served with a yoghurt gravy (khuri)
Bhoonji Khitchris — Rice and lentil cooked in same pot but the layers remaining undisturbed

Section 2
Tarkaris (Curries)   Pg 51-159

Haleem, Haressa, Khichras — Heavy broths which are a meal in themselves. Basis being meaty bones with wheat, barley or lentils.
Khowse — Soups with noodles, macaroni etc.
Russum — Clear soup like consommé
Exotic Soup — With Coconut milk, almonds etc.
Fish Soup — Have been put in the Fish Section
Serva Curry — Meat cooked in thick gravy to serve with rice or breads.
Dhal Curry — Meat and lentils cooked together in thick gravy to serve with rice or bread and rotis.
Dhal Curry — Lentils cooked dry to serve with rotis — these may be the lentil alone or with meat such as chana dhal curry etc.

Section 2a
Roasts, Grills and Dry Meat   Pg 74-99

Kurma, Pasinda and Tikkas — Are all dry meat either roasted in oven or pot roasted or grilled.
Murghe Musallam — Whole roasted chicken
Tanduri Chicken — Originally meaning a chicken basted in a clay brick oven, but now any roast chicken qualifies for this.
Fried Chops, Chargas etc — Meat marinated and then fried or sometimes par-boiled and then fried after dipping in egg.
Kabaab Curry — Meat balls cooked in thick gravy
Khowse Curry — Meat cooked with noodles, macaroni etc.

Section 2b
Lagans or Casseroles   Pg 101-119

Moothia/Dokra Curry — When dumplings are added to curries and allowed to stew therein — these are known by the type of dumpling in the curry.

In this section many traditional dishes have been converted into lagans. Meat, mince, macaroni, vegetable on their own or a combination of these are cooked with egg or in a curry sauce with very interesting toppings.
For the unusual dish, try our lagans.
Meat/Veg Curry — Double beans and chicken, Sekta Singh with meat. Bhaji/Khima Stews, or any meat/veg combined curry will be found in curry section. Name will give indication of main components.
Harga/Varda — Sprouted bean, moong, methi etc.

Section 2c
Vegetarianism   Pg 120-137

While no egg or meat has been used in these recipes, all Indians whether they partake meat or not love their vegetable curries. Many vegetarian curries will be found in main section of Tarkaris as well, so vegetarians, please take note.

Vegetable and Lentil Curries
Also Pawpaw, banana and mango Curries
Bhaji — Green leafy vegetables cooked on their own or with meat.

Section 2d
Stuffed Vegetables   Pg 138-142

Rawayya — Stuffed brinjals with mince, meat or shrimps
Stuffed Dodhi, Bhindi, Karela — All these with meat, mince on lentil filling.

Section 2e
                                                        Pg 143-149

Exotic or Gourmet fare — Tripe, liver, brains etc., look in this section.

Section 2f
Tarkaris Curries (continued)   Pg 150-159

Mealies and their By-Products
Curries cooked with fresh or frozen mealie (corn) kernels, mealie meal, porridge, curried mealie rice, bhurkoo, mealie rice biryani etc., will be found in this section.

Mealie bhajias, moothias and lagans will be found in savoury section.

Unexpected guests — to improvise quick meals with eggs, tinned foods and what have you.

Section 3
The Deep Freeze
& Freezer Delights   Pg 160-162

How to make the best use of your freezer.

Section 4
Fish and Sea Foods   Pg 163-176

Baked, fried, curried, souped, pickled will be found in this section.

However brinjal stuffed with prawns will be in found in curry section 2d

Section 5
Mass Cooking   Pg 177-181

To cook for the large wedding receptions etc.

Section 6
Savouries   Pg 183-250

That extra bit to serve at formal dinners or for parties and buffets. Our wide selection of savouries will dazzle you.

Bhajias — Chilly bites or spiced flour or lentil fritters in all their varieties.

Chaats — Masala puris, farsi puris etc. These are fried discs of spiced dough.

Chana Puris, Kachori — Lentil, vegetable or meat fillings enclosed with dough and then fried.

Chevda — Savoury spiced noodles, rice crisps, nuts, potato flakes etc.

Cutlets — Minced meat, flaked fish or pureed vegetable shaped in flat round discs (like hamburgers) then grilled or fried.

Dosai — Pancakes filled with savoury fillings.

Gaanthias — Spiced flours in noodle shapes — fried crisply

Kabaabs — Rounded balls of mince, fish or vegetable fried and served hot.

Khima — This means mince — and in savoury section frequent use is made of spiced braised mince for fillings in various type of savouries.

Lagan — Instead of individually filled pastries. The larger family sized pie etc., are known as lagans. Also look in Section 2b where Lagans are the main course and not a savoury.

Pies — Pastry dough with savoury fillings.

Puris — Flat discs of dough (either plain or spiced) served with some savouries.

Moothias — Spiced dough shaped in the fist and fried and served as a savoury.

Moorkhoo or Murukka — Spiced gram or rice flour pushed through gadget — very crisp and tasty.

Pattas — Madumbi leaves stuffed with spiced batter and rolled.

Pakoras — Plain dough with a savoury filling.

Samoosas — Tissue thin strip of dough filled with mince filling into a triangle shape.

Varhki Samoosa — Indian flaky pastry with savoury filling.

Vadde — Spiced ground lentils fried crisply.

Section 7
Chutneys, Pickles and Papads   Pg 251-281

Achars (pickles) all types, Bharads, Chutneys, Salad Dressings, Kachoomers or Sambals and Sauces.

Section 8
Papads (Papadums)   Pg 282-285

Section 9
Roti, Bread, Naan and Puris   Pg 286-298

Bread, Bread Rolls, Naans, Puris, Rotis, Rotlas, Breakfast gruels, Parathas, etc.

Section 10
Convalescent and Remedial Foods   Pg 299-305
Also Home Remedies

Bor, Dhuwa, Ghor Papdi, Karyatoo, Kaahyo, Naah, Paaks, Phaakis, etc.

Section 11
Health, Diet & Calories (Kilojoules)   Pg 306-307

Section 11a   Pg 309-315
Ice Creams, Fruit Juices, Punches and Milk Drinks

Lassi, Faloodas, Ice Creams, Kahwa, Milk Drinks, Panis, Sherbets, etc.

Section 12
Sweets and Desserts   Pg 316-384

Biscuits, Cakes, Desserts, Faloodas, Ghawlas, halwas, Jardo, Kheers, Lagans, Malidos, Mithais, Puddings, Pastries, Phirnis, Sikhund, Sev, Soji, Sohla, Sweet Samoosas, Shahi Tukras, etc.

Faloodas — Indian Jelly

Ghawlas — Pancakes

Halwas — Rich desserts containing milk, nuts, cereal, carrot etc.

Jarda or Zarda — Rice dessert

Kheers — Milk puddings with rice or some cereal.

Lagans — Baked desserts

Mithais — Very rich sweets — the Indian confectioners art.

Phirnis — Milk and cereal desserts

Sikhund — Yoghurt dessert

Sev — Vermicelli sweets

Soji — Cream of wheat desserts

Mitha Samoosa — Indian varkhi. Pastry with sweet filling

Shahi Tukras — Bread pudding

TABLE OF CONTENTS

The History of Cooking

The art of cooking was born the day when Adam's chop fell into the fire over which he and Eve were huddled to warm their numbed bodies. Again after a quarrel Eve found the chop over which her salty tears had splashed much improved in taste. These experiences they passed on to their children and so was launched culinary art.

Trying to preserve foodstuffs during the season of abundance to provide for leaner days to come, has always challenged the ingenuity of man. Early in the history of mankind, it was discovered that products which were slowly dried in the sun, kept for a longer interval. Also that rapid deterioration could be prevented by sprinkling certain powdered roots over meat. Hence spices were initially used to combat deterioration and that the palate soon acquired a taste for them was secondary.

It is not by sheer accident that highly spiced dishes have originated from countries with tropical and equatorial climates. Nature has a way of compensating for its own drawbacks. In colder climates where food does not deteriorate so rapidly, spices do not grow in the abundance as they do in those climes where their need is imperative. For the masses who rely on the products of their environment, this easy access to spices soon lays the foundation for 'typical dishes'. What had been initiated from sheer necessity soon moulded national appetites.

Religion and culture play a great part in the dishes of a people. The kosher of the Jewish people, the halaal and haraam injunctions of Muslims, the vegetarianism of Buddhists, the gourmandism of Chinese dishes are all due to restrictions (or lack thereof) imposed by religion.

Some dishes have attained an international status. Travel, emigration and transportability of products have all been contributory factors. The rice dish known as pilaau, pilaf, paelle or pulaau, is a case in point. So is the curry whether it be known as curry, tarkari or goulash. With speedier modes of transportation one can safely predict that croissants, halwa, biryani and bhajia will soon enjoy an international reputation.

The History of Indian Cookery in South Africa

The history of Indian cookery in South Africa dates with the first boat-load of indentured labourers that arrived in the year 1860. Dispossessed and displaced persons, they clutched at any straw that promised a relief from conditions which under a Colonial Power had become untenable.

Indentured labourers all — yet in no way a homogenous people, for linguistic, Geographical and religious differences existed amongst them. Thrown together in an environment that in no way proved to be a Promised Land the skilled craftsman, the seamstress, the weaver and the peasant, bent their backs to tend the sugar fields of the masters. Alongside their sleeping quarters in the little apron gardens, they sowed the precious seeds of vegetables and herbs that they had brought with them from home.

Soon after were to follow the merchant class Indians from Gujerat and the North of India. Economically on a higher rung, here too there were divisions of Hindu and Muslim which in terms of cookery immediately implies vegetarianism of some sort, and a more varied diet which includes meat. The merchants soon established themselves in business and imported for the benefit of their compatriots the foods, clothing and spices which were intrinsically a part of their culture.

The confidence of the Indian housewife in her skill as a cook, allowed her to improvise whenever a basic ingredient was not available and the result has been that Indian cookery in South Africa, though typically Indian, is yet different from that of India or Pakistan. Despite the close-living of the various communities it would be true to say that each stream remained true to its own cooking traditions, and though to the uninitiated they may appear to be the same, to the connoisseur, the dishes cooked in the homes of the various Indian communities are distinct in taste and appearance.

It is because of the rigid adherence of the Indian to his cultural traditions, that the Biryani, Bhajias (chilly-bites), Samoosas, Curry and Rice, and Achars have become familiar fare to all racial groups in South Africa. For Durban at least it would be true to say that the curry and rice is a National Dish.

Introduction to the Art
of Indian Cooking

As a cook the South African Indian housewife is second to none. From childhood the daughters are taught to be economical with food stuff and they are gently disciplined to appreciate the characteristics, nutrient values and flavours of all ingredients. It is worthwhile to observe how children are given pieces of dough and encouraged to make perfect round rotis. It is of no consequence if after a while the dough becomes grubby; what is of importance is that an idea of perfection has been inculcated in the little mind. An idea, that will as the years roll by, be fostered till perfection is achieved in every dish presented at her table.

In the handling of food, the Indian woman finds fulfilment for her talents. Much of Indian art being functional, cooking is therefore one more means with which she expresses herself. All her creative instincts are brought into play and this is visible when her labour of love appears on the table. Symmetry of line, colour combinations, shape, choice of serving dishes and garnishes, all contrived with much thought.

Twenty years ago when Indian Delights was first published, I had stated that the cookery book as such was something foreign to Indian women; that each dish was taught down the generations till daughters became as proficient as their mothers; but that the need of a reliable cookery book was beginning to be felt since daughters were spending more time with studies and acquiring careers. Also owing to the break-down of the extended family system of living, daughters-in-law were called upon to manage their own houses at a much younger age.

That has come to pass. The earlier stigma attached to a family whose grown-up daughters could not cook has fallen away. With the mother-in-law or aunt no longer around, a good reliable cookery book has become essential for despite the trend of working wives, Indian husbands still insist on meals as mothers prepared them.

Indian Delights has proved a boon in the, changing circumstances. Both Indians and non-Indians have found cooking with it easy and satisfactory. Even super Indian cooks which abound in the community refer to it. However, let us remember that good cooks are not born, they are made after lengthy periods of hard work; that a good recipe book will not yield good results unless care is exercised during all stages of food preparation and presentation. Selecting ingredients, balancing menus, blending flavours, correct accompaniments, all this and much more has to be taken into consideration. No one is born with all this knowledge and each one has to learn from the tedious school of experience. When in doubt ask a friend or neighbour who is more experienced. There is no shame in asking and remember Grandpa's adage:

"BY ASKING, ONE CAN REACH CHINA"

The new home makers must be aware that the health of her family is in her hands. Shortcuts and improvising may be resorted to, but vital principles are not to be compromised. The can or junk food is good in an emergency, but for daily fare, good wholesome products must be used. If you love your family you will love cooking — It's as simple as that!

Dear Beginner

Welcome to the club of homemakers. Yours will be a great responsibility, for in your hands rests the health and welfare of the persons for whom you will be preparing meals. For the Indian daughter, cooking is not a chore it is a labour of love and if this attitude is maintained you will find half the battle already won.

Mother, sister or neighbours are still the best people to learn from but should this not be possible, then Indian Delights is going to be most handy. We suggest seriously that before attempting your first dish you spend some hours reading through the introductory notes, for they contain a wealth in tips and information. It will also be an opportunity to get familiar with the terms and procedures employed.

ABSOLUTE CLEANLINESS

Not only your hands, clothes and general appearance, but also the kitchen and the utensils that you will be using must have that scrubbed look around them. In Indian cooking nothing is merely wiped dry. Vegetables and meat are picked clean, then immersed in water, washed and rinsed a couple of times. Start off with a clean working area and continue to mop and wipe clean as you proceed. This way the kitchen with its delicious aromas will entice the most indifferent to venture in. It is your workroom. Treat it with love and respect.

UTMOST ECONOMY

Remember the adage: "A women's savings are equal to a man's earnings". To live up to this motto you must learn to make do, improvise and substitute. If egg white is lying around, then use that to paste down your samoosas, other-wise the tablespoon of flour made into a paste with water is more economical.

Don't buy bread crumbs, rather put the stale slices into the oven from which you have just taken out your cake. The remaining heat will make the bread crisp and you can then crumb it fine.

Which reminds us, do switch off the element a little before baking is done or the pot of curry stewed. The remaining heat will do the job for you at no cost.

What about the squeezed out lemons and oranges? Grate the peel, then dry in shade and use it for garnishing pilaus and desserts, instead of the expensive slivered almonds. And remember that almonds, saffron and cardomom are just for festive occasions. They are not for everyday cooking. In everyday cooking they can be omitted from any recipe.

Use only the actual amount of meat that you want for the day's meal. Even the two pieces of bones or mutton can be stored in the feezer, and this added to tomorrow's two pieces will be sufficient for the pot of soup or stew on the third day.

A cent saved here and a bit pinched there comes to an astonishing amount at the end of the week. So do collect your own tips as you gain experience and swop these with friends and neighbours. You will be bringing down the cost of living. We promise.

GHEE AND OILS

This is a big item in Indian cookery. Use minimal quantities even if it means watching the pot more closely, for excess fat is wasteful and detrimental to health. Also vegetable oils are excellent for all meat and vegetable curries. Use your precious supply of ghee (and we do mean margarine ghee and not butter for it is cheaper and as good) for those special halwas, rotis etc. By using your oven for cooking meat and fish dishes you can cut down ghee and oil by 50 percent.

SPICES

Use sparingly. Resist that temptation to put in a bit more for it will not improve the taste, it is harmful and it will spoil the appearance of your food. Remember that some spices are for colouring, some for tenderising, and some for flavouring. Find out the qualities of each and use to improve the inherent flavours, not smother them.

DESSERTS

With the varieties of fruit available all the year round serve them instead of time and money-consuming desserts. Have you tried a mango cut in half, de-pitted and the centre filled with icecream? Absolutely delightful.

HOW MUCH IS SUFFICIENT?

You will know your family better than us. Unless otherwise stated, our recipes are based around the family of six. Father and mother and four children and we have taken into calculation that fathers and growing sons and daughters will eat more than mother and the younger kids so use the following as a general guide when in doubt:

For a family of 6 you will require:

500 grams of meat to cook the curry to be served with rice, or which is to be served with a side dish of vegetables or lentils.
750 grams of meat for the drier curries like roasts, grills, fried chops
500 grams of mince for the family servings of kabaabs, lagan, meat loaf, cutlets etc; This will also be sufficient for

3½-4 doz. samoosas.
2-2½ cups of uncooked rice for pilaus, biryanis etc.
2 cups of peas, diced beans, papdi, okra, etc.
1½ cups of dhals, moong, gram, etc for the pot of dry lentil curry.
1 dozen methi bhaji if you intend adding eggs or mince to it.

Do remember that the more courses you serve at a meal, the lesser amounts you will require all round so do cut down accordingly.

If you allow meat to marinate in the spices for a little while before actually putting it on to the stove, it will require lesser turning and tossing afterwards. This conserves heat and also results in better taste for the juices will have penetrated into the fibres.

HOW LONG DOES IT TAKE?

We are not specifying the time it takes to cook the meal. This depends so much on the type of pots you use, or the tenderness of your vegetables, or the age of the lamb, or the toughness of the cut of your meat. You can go ahead and cook on high heat but this will just spoil the taste and appearance of your dish so why not be patient and learn to gauge how long it takes to prepare and cook a dish. Our advise is to start off at a high heat for frying onions, for bringing a pot to boil and so on, but the moment this is done, switch down to low heat, close the lid tightly, and allow it to simmer till done. Resist the temptation to open the lid frequently.

Rather learn to use your head and ears and nose for the more frequently a pot is opened, the more steam escapes, and you really want to conserve it to finish your cooking for you.

Good wishes and God speed.

Zuleikha

Section I
Rice Dishes

To Cook Rice

It is virtually impossible to spoil a rice dish. If the following instructions are followed, you will be able to turn out fluffy, loose grained rice dishes, which all good cooks aim at.

Soak the well washed rice in cold water while the pot of water is being put to boil.

Allow 3 cups of water for each cup of rice to be cooked. Add salt and a stick of cinnamon and if you can afford it, a pod of elachi (cardomom).

Add the washed rice to the rapidly boiling water. Close lid of pot and lower heat but do maintain a fairly rapid pace of cooking.

Avoid boiling over for this just results in messy stove surfaces. Cooking time will vary with the different varieties of rice available so test a grain of rice between forefinger and thumb and when it is soft then rice is done.

Drain off in colander. Should the rice be slightly overdone, then it is advisable to slosh a jug of cold water over it to reduce steam immediately.

When well drained, return the rice to the pot, sprinkle a few tablespoons of cold water over it and put over heat. Close lid and allow to simmer gently for ten minutes.

Meanwhile braise a tablespoon of finely sliced onions in a tablespoon of ghee and when onions are gold in colour pour over rice.

Close lid again and keep warm till ready to serve.

Rice

Rice has been the staple food for the inhabitants of Asia from very early times. India, China, Java each claim that it was first cultivated in their land and many beautiful myths are woven which aim to prove that it was a gift of the gods to their particular country. That it is a blessing from God like all food products, is undoubtedly so.

Rice is mentioned as early as 2 800 B.C. in Indian writings and it is perhaps the country of its original culture. Known by different names throughout the country an endless variety of dishes can be prepared from rice.

The story of pilaaus is an ancient one. The name is of Persian origin and is known throughout the world in some form or other. The Arabs spread it far and wide, introducing it to Africa and Spain, where it is known as paella and the Spaniards, in their turn introduced it to the Latin American countries which were once part of their Empire. The Moghul Kings introduced it to India and over the centuries the Pilaaus of India took on a distinctive form. In South Africa rice was first introduced by the Dutch from Java, and the Malay slaves cooked tasty dishes in the kitchens of their masters. The pilaaus came with the Indian immigrants and here it is known by its common name "Curry and Rice".

Although retaining the classic Pilaaus of India, we have here in South Africa — because of experimenting with different ingredients — added to the rich legacy of Pilaaus, and created some dishes unique in taste and flavour.

Biryani

BIRYANI is the royal dish amongst all the exotic rice dishes of India, and remains "the dish" to serve on all best and auspicious occasions. Whether one serves it to welcome house guests on their first day, or whether it be the main course of the menu in formal entertaining, or a gala festivity, the painstaking care which the housewife will take in the preparations of Biryani will commence when she selects her ingredients.

Nothing but the best will do. Although there are numerous variations of Biryani, our carefully compiled recipes are fit to serve Royalty.

The pride and care that goes in the making of Biryani is a story in itself. We remember nostalgically, the day when grandma used to make Biryani. The frying of the onions just to that particular goldness; the weighing of the saffron with the precision of a goldsmith; the marinating of the meat in the spices and curds; the sealing of the pot with dough and clean white cloth; the weighing down of the lid with a brick; the listening in, in order to ascertain whether it is ghee or moisture that is sizzling, plus a lot of other rigmarole.

We must confess that in those days the pot of Biryani, when finally opened, announced itself to the whole neighbourhood, and the aroma and fragrance that emanated was sufficient to make the most fastidious smack their lips in anticipation.

Whilst we cannot indulge in all these time consuming activities, here is a recipe which even grandmother will be hard put to improve upon.

Biryani

(KEY RECIPE) for 6-8 persons

1 chicken (1½ kg) washed and disjointed
2 cups masoor (whole black lentils)
2 cups rice
2 pieces cinnamon sticks (tuj)
4 elachi (cardomom)
1 tsp jeero (cummin)
4 green chillies (slit)
1 cup yoghurt
2 tblsp fresh tomato (grated or pureed)
1 tblsp lemon juice
2 sprigs mint
¼ tsp saffron
¼ tsp turmeric (arad)
1 tsp salt
1 tsp dhunia/jeero (coriander/cummin)
1½ tsp red chillies
6 small potatoes
3 hard-boiled eggs
¾ cup oil and ¼ cup ghee
2 fair sized onions
1½ tsp ginger/garlic

Allow saffron strands to become crisp over very low heat. Crush fine with back of spoon. Steep in a tablespoon of hot water.

Keep some saffron aside for tinting, 3 or 4 tblsp of the cooked rice. This must be spread on top of other rice, in streaks.

Fry onions in oil to a pale golden colour. Drain and cool. Leave aside 1 tablespoon of fried onions and crush rest coarsely. Wash and drain disjointed chicken. Place in large bowl. Add saffron and smear ginger/garlic over meat pieces by tossing it around meat, with spoon. Add yoghurt, tomatoes, spices, fried onions, whole green chillies, sprigs of mint and allow to marinate for at least 1 hour.

Meanwhile, boil masoor in salted water till done. Drain off in colander. Boil rice with 2 elachi and 1 piece tuj, the rest of elachi, etc., must be added to marinating meat. Rice must be drained when only half done. (Boil rice as for Pilau but leave slightly underdone). Fry potatoes to light yellow colour in oil used for frying onions. Remove from ghee and set aside.

In large flat bottomed pot (2-3 litre size) put in oil that was used for frying, plus half of ghee. Sprinkle a handful of rice and masoor over the bottom. Now arrange the marinating chicken and masalas carefully over bottom of pot. Now spread masoor over chicken, then the potatoes and then half of the rice. Place peeled hard boiled eggs over rice. Now spread rest of rice over eggs. Many people prefer to tint a little of the white rice with a tinge of saffron. This looks very attractive and puts the finishing touch to the Biryani.

Decorate with left-over fried onions, and sprinkle rest of ghee and half a cup of cold water over the top. Close and seal lid of pot tightly. Place over high heat for 5 minutes and as soon as it starts sizzling, lower heat and let simmer for 1 hour. By this time all moisture should have evaporated. Serve with fried rice papads, onion kachoomers, and its essential accompaniment, spiced dahi (see recipe on next page)

NOTE: If mutton is used, then add 1 more teaspoon of ginger/garlic, as well as ½ cup more of yoghurt. Pot should be allowed to steam half an hour or so longer depending on the toughness of meat. Remember to crack elachi pods open by pressing between fore-finger and thumb, but take care that seeds do not spill out.

Crushing Fried Onions for Biryani etc.

1. Onions fried in oil alone is much more crisp than that fried in ghee.

2. Instead of slicing onion and frying them to become crisp enough for crushing, a great time saver is to grate the onions, fry them and just before they turn golden brown, to strain them through a sieve. You already have fried crushed onions!

ALTERNATE OVEN METHOD

Busy hostesses will welcome this method as it can be prepared well in advance and kept in the fridge and put in the oven to cook just an hour and half before serving time.

After rice and masoor has drained and the chicken has been marinating for an hour or two arrange the meat in an oven-proof casserole thus:

Grease bottom of casserole with the ghee/oil in which the onions have been fried as well as any oil that is left-over, but not the ghee.

Spread a handful of masoor over bottom of casserole and arrange meat pieces attractively.

Pour all the masalas over the meat. Now put in egg and potatoes and cover with the masoor.

Remove three tablespoons of rice and tint it delicately with a little saffron. Spread white rice over masoor and lastly sprinkle the tinted rice over.

This makes a beautiful colour picture. Pour the remaining ghee over the rice and wrap the whole casserole with a thick sheet of foil.

Put in preheated oven 180°C and cook for one to one and a half hours. By this time the biryani will be cooked. Remove foil, garnish with fried onions that were kept aside and serve Biryani straight from the casserole.

Mutton Biryani will need 1¾ to 2 hours of cooking in oven.

Spiced Dahi
(YOGHURT DRESSING)

In 1 box (500 ml) of sour milk curds (yoghurt) add salt to taste and 2 teaspoons of Dhunia Chutney (see page 274). Whisk and serve in individual bowls.

Khatyoo
(MADE FROM LEFT-OVER BIRYANI)

To 1 litre size pot of left-over Biryani. Add 3 cups yoghurt to pot and allow to simmer gently till sour milk is absorbed, but not completely dried out. Serve in bowls with spoons. Serve with kachoomers and papads.

Khima Biryani
(PHOTO PAGE 49)

1 kg mince (chicken or mutton)
2 cups of any of following: chana, dhal, masoor, fresh peas or fresh toovar.
2 cups rice (boiled in salted water) but drained when half done.
Boil fresh peas or the type of dhal till nearly done (drain dry).
2 small onions
¼ tsp turmeric
½ cup yoghurt
1 tsp pounded red chillies
2 whole green chillies
½ tsp dhunia/jeero powder, (cummin/coriander)
A few potatoes (halved if big).
¼ teaspoon saffron
¼ cup tomato juice (fresh) grated or pureed
1 lemon (juice)
1 tsp salt
1 tsp ginger/garlic
1 cup ghee/oil
¾ tsp jeero (cummin)

Braise mince with ginger/garlic, salt, pounded chillies and dhunia/jeero. When dry, remove from fire and cool. Now add the saffron, dahi, tomato juice, lemon juice and the whole jeero. Add a few elachi, tuj and cloves.

Fry onions in ghee/oil. Remove when a light golden colour. drain from the ghee and when cool crush with the back of a spoon and add to mince (saving a little whole fried onion for decoration on top of rice).

Fry potatoes in same ghee/oil to a pale yellow colour. Put ghee/oil in pot or heat-proof glass casserole (in which event it is served straight from casserole at table). Sprinkle a little rice and masoor over ghee/oil.

Now distribute the mince over the floor of casserole. Place potatoes over this, then the masoor or whatever has been used instead. Lastly, add the rice to cover all.

Sprinkle left-over onion over rice, add a few tablespoons of ghee, sprinkle with a little cold water and steam gently in 180° oven till done (about 30-45 minutes).

NOTE:
Any rice dish that is to steam in the oven must have either more moisture or must be well covered with foil to prevent rice drying out.

Fish Biryani

6-8 PERSONS (PHOTO OPPOSITE PAGE)

1 kg fish (cleaned, sliced and smeared with masala)
1 grated tomato
2 cups masoor (black lentils)
1 large onion
4 hard-boiled eggs
1½ cups ghee/oil
2 cups rice
6 small potatoes
Few cloves and peppers
2 pieces cinnamon
½ teaspoon saffron (optional)
4 green chillies (whole)
4 elachi (cardamon)
¼ teaspoon turmeric (arad)
1 teaspoon jeero (cummin)
1 cup dahi (yoghurt)
MASALA:
1 tablespoon dry coriander seeds (dry dhunia)
6 or 7 cloves of garlic
6 red chillies (or green if preferred)
1 tablespoon jeero
Juice of 1 lemon
1 teaspoon turmeric
1 teaspoon salt
1 tablespoon oil
1 tablespoon tomato juice

Pound chillies, garlic, jeero and coriander. Add dry spices and mix into paste with oil, tomato and lemon juice. Smear fish slices and let them marinate for at least one hour. Or keep in fridge and fry when required.

Boil rice and masoor as in Biryani Key Recipe. Fry onions and potatoes as in Biryani Key Recipe. Fry smeared fish just enough to give it a bit of firmness.

In large bowl, add dahi, grated tomato, spices and the crushed onions, and dip fried fish in this masala for one minute. In flat-bottomed pot, pour 5 tablespoons of ghee/oil plus all that had been used for frying onions and potatoes.

Sprinkle ½ cup masoor over bottom, then arrange the fish slices and the masalas evenly over masoor. Add rest of masoor over fish. Now arrange potatoes and over them the rice. Next add fried onion and remaining ghee over rice.

Sprinkle ¼ cup cold water and close lid of pot tightly. Put on heat and when pot starts sizzling lower heat and allow to steam for ½ an hour Keep pot for about 15 minutes in 180°C oven to allow for proper cooking. Serve with spiced dahi, papads and kachoomers (shredded salads).

Jinga/Rice Biryani (Prawn)

(6 PERSONS) (COLOUR PHOTO PAGE 99)

1 kg prawns, shrimps, or rock lobster
2 cups rice
2 green chillies
1 tsp garlic (pounded)
2 tsp garlic (slivered)
2 onions
Juice of 1 lemon
1 tsp salt (or more)
6 tblsp oil
2 tblsp ghee
1 tsp jeero (cummin)
1 bunch dhunia leaves (coriander)
½ tsp turmeric
1 tsp red chillies
¼ cup sour milk (yoghurt)
½ cup tomato (juice)
1 piece tuj (cinnamon)
2 elachi, a few cloves

Shell the sea foods. Braise in a tablespoonful oil till salmon pink in colour. Braise onions in ghee and when a beautiful pale golden colour, remove from ghee and cool. Crush with back of spoon. Retain shells of some prawns.

Boil rice in salted water till nearly done, then drain in colander. To bowl of jinga add sour milk, lemon juice, tomato and spices. Pound dhunia leaves and add to jinga. Fry slivered garlic and jeero in a tablespoon of oil. Add to jinga.

In pot arrange over ghee (keeping aside 1½ tablespoons) the marinating jinga and place the whole green chillies in them. Spread rice over this. Sprinkle the left-over ghee and 2 tablespoons of water over rice.

Decorate with fried onion. Steam pot very slowly till jingas cooked and masalas dry (about 30-40 minutes).

NOTE:
If preferred, 1 cup shelled boiled peas may be arranged over jinga and rice. To make it more colourful add quartered peppers, peas and half a cup of cut corn.

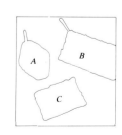

A Bhoondi Raaitha —
  spiced yoghurt (280)
B Fish Biryani (27)
C Pancakes in sauce (117)

NOTE: Oil used for frying the fish should on no account be used in Biryani. The quantity ghee/oil in recipe does not include that used for frying the fish itself. Ghee/oil to be used in proportions as preferred, but it must be noted that with fish more oil is used than ghee. Over rice, naturally, only ghee will be sprinkled.

Chana Dhal Biryani
(GRAM DHAL)

Instead of masoor (black lentils) use gram dhal (chana dhal) for biryani. Add some par-boiled carrots to the meat.
This is a delicious variation from the usual biryani.

Cornish Chicken or Pigeon (or Partridge) Biryani

(SERVES 8)
(COLOUR PHOTO 33)

4 pigeons or cornish chickens
1 doz baby carrots (par-boiled)
1 doz baby potatoes
2 cups rice
1 cup oil
1 ⅓ tsp salt
4 elachi (cardamom)
2 tsp ginger/garlic
2 tsp freshly pounded red chillies
⅓ tsp saffron (powdered)
2 sprigs mint
2 green chillies
1 doz dried apricots
12 prunes
½ cup whole blanched almonds
¾ carton yoghurt
4 tbsp ghee
Juice of 1 lemon
⅓ tsp turmeric
⅓ cup tomato puree (or fresh)
2 onions (grate 1½ and slice ½)
1 cup sunflower seeds (optional)
2 sticks cinnamon
1 tsp crushed cummin

Wash birds after splitting them in halves. Powder saffron (see page 13) and pour a tablespoon of boiling water over it. Allow to steep for a few minutes. Keep liquid aside.

In the oil and half of the ghee, firstly fry the sliced onions. Remove from oil when gold in colour and keep aside for garnishing. Next fry the potatoes and remove when pale gold in colour. Fry dried fruit for just a few seconds.

Finally fry in same oil the grated onions, and strain through sieve when they turn gold in colour. Cool onions in sieve.

Put yoghurt in a large mixing bowl. To this add lemon juice, tomato puree, half of saffron water, salt and all the spices except a stick of cinnamon and two cardamom pods.

Mix spices well in yoghurt and then add the fried (grated) onion. Smear inside and outside of birds liberally with this spiced marinade and place them in a broad, heavy based casserole.

Pour all left over marinade and oils over the birds. Place potatoes, prunes and apricots in-between birds, taking care that they have their share of the marinade. Allow to marinate for two hours.

Meanwhile boil the rice in salted water to which has been added the cinnamon stick and elachi. When rice is nearly done, drain dry in colander.

In the 2 tablespoons of ghee that was kept aside, fry the sunflower seeds and blanched almonds and remove from oil when they turn a pink colour.

Sprinkle sunflower seeds and half of almonds over pigeons in the marinade. Cover the entire contents of the pot with the cold rice.

Take half a cup of rice and streak it yellow with the left-over saffron. Spread this over the top of the white rice.

Finally, sprinkle the ghee in which the almonds were fried over the rice. Sprinkle 1/3 cup of milk over the rice and cover lid tightly.

Place over high heat for 5 minutes and when pot begins to sizzle, lower heat and simmer for about an hour. By this time chickens will be cooked and Biryani done.

This is a very attractive dish for 8 persons. So take care when serving. Take out rice first and keep aside a few tablespoons of the yellow tinted portion. Arrange the white rice on a large platter. Lift each bird out carefully and arrange carefully over the rice. Place the prunes, carrots etc. inbetween to make a pretty colourful arrangement.

Streak with the tinted rice and decorate with the fried almonds and onions.

Serve with papadums, kachoomers (preferably onion and tomato relish or cucumber and yoghurt relish) achars and spiced yoghurt.

Kokani Pilaau

2 cups rice
2 onions
2 tblsp ghee
2 tblsp oil
A few elachi pods, cloves, peppercorns
Sticks of cinnamon
¼ tsp turmeric
½ cup nuts (split cashew or almonds)
Salt to taste
2 sprigs curry leaves
1 tsp methi seeds
4 green chillies

Steep rice for 30 minutes in cold water after washing.

In pot, fry the onions in the oil together with whole spices, when onions are a gold colour, remove a quarter of onions for garnishing.

To pot with onion, add rice, turmeric and fry till rice grains are well coated with ghee — add boiling water and cook over gentle heat till rice nearly done.

Fry nuts in ghee till they begin to darken, remove from pan and now fry green chillies, curry leaves and methi seeds.

Pour over rice and toss rice with a fork.

Serve garnished with almonds, some chopped dhunia and ½ cup of fresh (long shredded) coconut. Serve with fish curries.

VARIATION:

Instead of boiling water, cook rice in thin milk extracted from 1 fresh coconut.

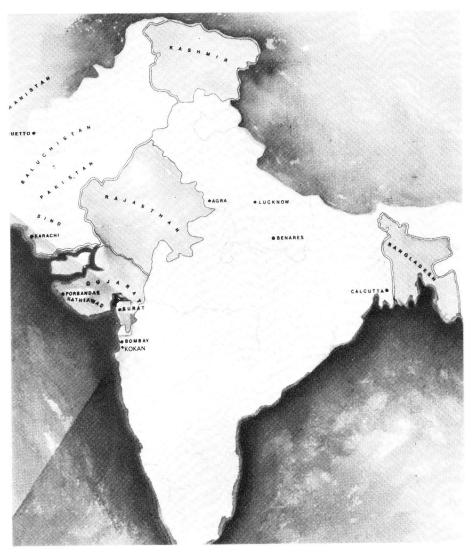

Map showing some of the areas in India from which most of our recipes originate.

Lucknow Ki Biryani
MEAT AND KABAABS IN RICE

500 g mutton (cubed)
½ tsp strands of saffron soaked in 2 tblspoons of hot milk
1 tsp salt
1 tsp ginger/garlic
1 tsp red chilli
1 piece cinnamon, a few elachi and cloves
½ tsp jeera seeds (cummin)
2 onions grated
1 onion (sliced)
1 tsp slivered ginger
⅔ cup oil
½ cup yoghurt
2 tblsp tomato puree
Juice of 1 lemon
2 cups rice

For kabaabs:
500 g mutton mince
1 tsp salt
Good pinch of fine elachi and tuj. (cardoman and cinnamon)
½ tsp black crushed pepper
1 tsp crushed garlic
1 tblespoon chopped mint
1 tsp red chilli
1 tblespoon of fried onion
2 tblespoons bread crumbs soaked in a little milk
½ tsp crushed jeera

Wash rice and soak in cold water for 30 minutes.

To washed pieces of mutton add chillie, ginger/garlic, salt, lemon juice and half of saffron milk. Allow to marinate for an hour.

Fry sliced onions in ghee/oil and remove from oil when gold in colour. In same oil fry the grated onion and sieve through strainer when gold in colour.

Add kabaab ingredients to mince and form into balls.

In same oil in which onions were fried now fry the slivered ginger, stick cinnamon and jeera seeds for a few seconds, then add to it the marinating mutton and cook slowly until mutton starts darkening in colour.

To pot add crushed onions. Mix tomato puree, yoghurt and a cup of water together and add it to pot of Biryani. Cover lid and steam gently until meat is half done.

Carefully lower kabaabs in between the meat. Shake pot at intervals and cook slowly until kabaabs begin to harden and there is no danger of them breaking.

Drain rice well. To pot of Biryani add a cup of water (or more) the rice and a teaspoon of salt. Sprinkle a teaspoon of gharum masala over contents then cook slowly (without stirring pot) with lid tightly closed.

Just before serving make a vagaar by frying 2 tablespoons of sultanas and half a cup of mixed blanched nuts (pistachios, almonds, cashews, etc.) in 2 tablespoons of ghee. Pour this over pot of Biryani.

Serve on a large platter garnishing with the fried onions.

Vegetable Biryani
(6 PERSONS)

2 cups rice
1 cup masoor
½ cup double beans
½ cup diced carrots
½ cup green peas or toovar (Indian beans)
¼ cup stringless beans (2cm pieces)
6 potatoes
1 large onion, 1 tomato

Boil rice as in Biryani Key Recipe.
Boil masoor as in Biryani Key Recipe.
Add spices to fresh vegetables but in lesser quantities.
Use more tomato and lesser amount of dahi (sour milk).
Arrange vegetables in curd and spices at bottom, sprinkle masoor, then rice. Steam for only 35 minutes.
Frozen vegetables can be used with perfect results.

Biryani to Freeze

Marinate meat in marinade and freeze in airtight container. Thaw at room temperature when required.
Boil masoor and rice while meat is thawing.
Arrange and cook as explained.

NOTES:
Rice and masoor can be frozen but it will take lots of space in freezer and the freshly boiled product definitely gives better results. Any rice dish when cooked in the oven should be well protected by thick foil on sides, top and bottom to prevent drying out of rice.

Moghlai Biryani

½ cup ghee
2 cups rice
1 kg mutton (small chops or leg mutton cut in chop sized pieces)
*1½ tsp salt
*1 onion sliced
*1 onion grated
*1½ tsp ginger/garlic
*1½ tsp red pounded chilli
*3 tbsp freshly ground almonds
*2 tsp poppy seeds
1 tsp jeera seeds (cummin)
*1 tsp crushed jeera
*½ tsp elachi powder
*1/3 tsp white crushed pepper
½ cup yoghurt
1 tblsp lemon juice
½ cup oil
1 tsp rose essence
*¹/₃ tsp powdered saffron
*125 ml cream
½ cup mixed nuts (charoli, quartered pista and almonds or cashews)
1/3 cup sultanas
Dried rose petals for decoration

Soak rice in cold water for 30 minutes then drain dry.
Wash meat and put in mixing bowl.
Blend fine half of onion, lemon, poppy seeds and other ingredients marked with * and marinate meat in this.
Fry remaining sliced onion in hot oil and remove when gold in colour.
In same oil fry the grated onion and as soon as they begin to turn gold in colour add to the marinating meat and marinade. Over low heat stir and cook until meat begins to darken in colour.
Beat yoghurt in half a cup of water and pour into pot. Cover lid and simmer gently until meat is nearly done.
In separate pot put half of ghee and fry two cinnamon sticks, some bruished elachi pods, a few cloves and peppercorns. Then add rice and fry a minute longer. Add water and salt and bring to boil.
Close lid tightly and simmer gently for about 20 minutes.
Dissolve the saffron in 2 tablespoons of boiling milk and add this to the cream. Roast the whole jeera on a tava until nearly black and add to cream.
Grease a large corning ware type of oven casserole with half of the remaining ghee, and spread half of the rice over it. Over this spread half of the cream marinade. Then spread the mutton over the marinade. Spread remaining rice over mutton and finally spread all of left over marinade over the last layer of rice. Close lid of casserole.
Cover entire casserole with a thick layer of foil and bake in a moderate oven for 40 to 50 minutes.
Just before serving fry nuts and sultanas in remaining ghee and garnish Biryani with this and the sliced fried onion. For a really exotic touch sprinkle some rose petals over the dish.

Pilaau

Plain white boiled rice (Indian fashion) is known as dhaan, and if a distinctive feature is added to it, it is known as a pilaau. Rice for Pilaaus are always the long grained variety. In Indian cooking the rice is washed in several rinsings of water, till all traces of cloudiness disappear. Water is brought to boil and the washed rice is thrown in. To the boiling water is added salt, a stick or two of cinnamon and a few elachis and cloves. When the rice is nearly done (to test, pinch a grain of rice between forefinger and thumb and if no hard core is felt, the rice is done) it is drained in a colander. When completely rid of moisture, the rice is returned to the pot, sprinkled with a little water and gently steamed for about fifteen minutes, a vagaar is added. Vagaar is made by frying a few rings of sliced onions in two tablespoons of ghee and carefully poured over rice in pot. With the handle of a long spoon, the rice is delicately tossed inside in order to ensure proper distribution of ghee. This procedure is essential in order to separate each grain of rice, which is a distinctive feature of Indian cooked rice.

Moghal Pilaau
6 SERVINGS

2 cups rice
3 tblsp ghee
1 tblsp sultanas or 5 prunes
2 tblsp blanched and finely slivered almonds
Cinnamon, elachi and cloves

Boil rice and steam as for Pilaau, but sprinkle ¼ cup of milk instead of water.

Fry prunes or sultanas in ghee till they start to swell. Remove fruit from ghee, now fry the slivered almonds in ghee and when they are pink in colour, sprinkle almonds and ghee over rice.

Toss prunes inside and slightly cover with the rice. Delicious with chicken curry.

Basic Pilaau
(WHITE RICE)
6 SERVINGS

2 tblsp finely sliced onions
2 tsp coarse salt
2 tblsp ghee
2 cups rice
1 stick cinnamon
2 elachi (whole) (cardomon)
2 whole cloves
½ tsp jeero (cummin) to be fried with onions
5 to 7 cups water

Put water to boil. As it comes to boil rapidly, add well washed rice, salt and spices. Test a grain of rice and if there is just a suspicion of hard kernel, drain off rice in colander, let it stand till completely dry. Add ¼ cup of cold water and return to pot and lower heat, and steam gently for 12 minutes.

Just before serving fry onions in ghee and when golden brown sprinkle over rice. Lid of pot must be shut tightly so that aromas do not escape and moisture is not evaporated too rapidly.

Rice in Coconut Shells

This is a most attractive way to serve rice dishes at dinners or buffets. Many of our recipes can be used to make rice in coconut shells and recipes that lend themselves well for this are Jinga Biryani, Afriki akhni, moong dhal akhni or even mince or chicken biryani. Of course when making biryani in coconut shells the meat portions will have to be cut smaller.

If desired the dishes can be first cooked in a pot and then just piled into the halved coconut shells which must be covered with tin foil and allowed to steam in the oven till required.

Instead of boiling the rice in water, cook in a few cups of coconut milk and this will give your dish a distinguished flavour.

For larger helpings, two coconut halves may be put together after filling with rice, etc., the joint sealed tight with flour paste and finally the whole coconut wrapped in foil.

Gosht Pilaau
(MEAT PILAAU)

2 cups rice
400 g mutton or chicken (cut in pieces as for stew)
2 tblsp ghee
½ cup chana dhal (gram)
1 tsp jeero (cummin)
2 green chillies
Salt, cinnamon, cloves and cardomon

Cook meat in pot with salt, pepper, spices and green chillies till tender (only sufficient water must be used to allow for cooking).

Boil chana dhal in salted water till done. Drain. Boil rice as for pilaau.

In a pot, fry a little sliced onion with jeero in ghee. Save a little of the onion for decoration on top.

Add rice to browned onion with the cooked meat and dhal and gently toss together to ensure even distribution.

Pour another tablespoon of ghee over top with the remaining onions. Sprinkle a few tablespoons of water and steam till done.

Variations of Pilaau

(1) For every 2 cups of rice, use one-third cup of chana dhal. Boil dhal separately till soft. Add to cooked rice and steam as in pilaau.

(2) Peas, diced carrots, moong dhal can each be boiled separately and steamed with rice.

(3) Instead of slices of boiled eggs, they can be grated coarsely and sprinkled over the top of rice.

(4) Fry slivered almonds or a handful of sunflower seed kernels, whole blanched almonds or cashew nuts and sprinkle over pilaau just before serving.

(5) Grated peel of lemon or orange.

Vegetable Pilaau

2 cups rice
½ cup shelled peas
½ cup diced carrots
2 hard boiled eggs
1 teaspoon jeero (cummin)
1 small onion
1 tsp salt
Cloves, cinnamon or cardomon

Boil rice as for Pilaau. Boil carrots and peas separately in salted water and remove from heat as soon as done and before they lose colour.

Boil eggs, shell and slice when cool.

Place half rice in pot, then arrange a layer of peas and carrots (half quantity) and one sliced egg.

Cover with rest of rice, sprinkle three tablespoons of water and steam till done. Just before serving, fry 1 teaspoon jeero and 1 finely sliced onion in 2 tablespoons of ghee.

When onion is a beautiful golden brown drain off ghee and sprinkle it over rice.

Serve rice in a large platter, and decorate with remaining peas, carrots and eggs. Sprinkle the fried onion and jeero over attractively. This is a beautiful platter of rice and the colour combination looks most appealing.

Orange/Rice Naranji/Dhan

2 cups rice
3 tblsp ghee
½ cup cashew nuts
2 eggs (hard boiled)
Few elachi, cloves and tuj (Cardamom pods, whole cloves and cinnamon)
2 oranges
1 tblsp seedless raisins
2 onions
Salt to taste

Extract juice of oranges. Cut the peel of ½ an orange into thin match-stick sized strips. Slice onions and fry in ghee and just as it starts to get a golden colour, add nuts, raisins and orange rind. Stir for a minute.

Add spices, oranje juice, the washed rice and salt. Add up to 3 cups of water and cook slowly till all moisture has evaporated. Garnish with a few strips of orange peel. Serve with chicken curry.

Chicken/Seafood Paella
Jinga/Murghi Pilaau
(COLOUR PHOTO 196)

2 cups rice
2 elachi
1 stick cinnamon
salt

(1) Boil rice with above ingredients and drain when done.

(2) Fry 2 grated onions in ½ cup oil. Drain off oil when gold in colour. Cool onions.

(3) **Marinate chicken thus**

500 g chicken (cut in small pieces)
1 tsp ginger/garlic
1 tsp red chilli
1 tsp salt
1 tsp crushed jeera (cummin)
2 green chillies
½ tsp saffron strands steeped in boiling water. (Keep ½ of
   this aside.)
½ tblsp lemon juice
2 tblsp tomato puree
½ cup yoghurt
1 sprig mint
½ of fried onion

Add all ingredients to bowl of chicken and marinate for 1 hour.

(4) **Marinate Prawns thus**

1 kg seafoods (prawns, langoustine tails, pieces of sole
   etc.)

Shell and devein seafoods but keep a few in shell. Wash and braise shellfish in 2 tbsp of oil till they are a flamingo pink in colour.

When cold add to bowl of fish the following ingredients:

¼ cup oil
2 tbsp tomato puree
2 tbsp lemon juice
2 tbsp yoghurt
rest of fried onion
¼ tsp black crushed pepper
1 tsp crushed garlic
1 tsp slivered garlic
1 tsp salt
1 tsp chilli
½ tsp jeera (cummin)

Marinate for 30 minutes while chicken is cooking.

(5) In large flat based pot, put in oil in which onions were fried plus 2 tbsp of ghee. Add chicken and marinade then close lid and simmer for ½ an hour.

Put seafood and marinade in separate pot and bring to boiling point. Switch off immediately but leave on stove. To seafood add 1 dozen pickling onions.

Add rice to chicken and over it spread entire contents of seafood pot. Bring gently to steam and simmer for 10 minutes. Now add a cup each of cut corn and green peas. With long handled fork stir contents to mix different layers of food. Simmer for 10 minutes more.

Serve in large platter with fried onions and almonds as garnish.

Khusbudar Pilaau (FRUIT AND ALMONDS)

2 cups rice (soak ½ hour in cold water)
rind of 1 orange
¼ cup oil
6 carrots
60 g sultanas and raisins
3 tbsp each of slivered almonds and pistachios
1½ tsp salt
2 tsps of slivered ginger/garlic
2 cups water
¼ tsp fine elachi
1 chicken (cut in small pieces)
Juice of 2 oranges
¼ cup ghee
1 onion (cut in thick wedges)
½ tsp black pepper (ground)
4 green chillies (pounded)
¼ tsp saffron (optional)
2 tbsp milk
1 stick cinnamon
few cloves and good pinch of jeera

Wash and cut chicken, wipe dry.

Make paste of salt, green chillies and elachi, smear this around chicken pieces.

Fry carrot strips in ghee/oil, remove carrots and keep aside.

Fry almond in this for a few seconds then remove.

Fry ginger/garlic slivers, tuj, onions, jeera in oil.

Add ½ of orange peel to chicken and when chicken begins to brown add drained rice and dried fruit and fry for 1 minute but keep on stirring contents of pot.

Now add orange juice and water, lower heat and steam rice with lid tightly closed. Meanwhile in a separate pot, put the other half of orange rind with ½ of cold water, bring to boil and drain off water. Soak saffron in hot milk. 10 minutes before serving pour this saffron liquid over contents of pot and stir with fork. the whole process should take about 1 to 1¼ hour. Serve rice dish in large platter arranging chicken and dried fruit neatly. Garnish with slivered nuts and the remaining orange peel. Serve with dahi and kachoomers.

Madumbi Kabaab Pilau

500 g madumbi (yams)
1 onion (grated)
1 tblsp chopped mint
½ tsp cummin (crushed)
1 tsp green chilli
½ tsp red chilli
2 tblsp grated coconut or dessicated
3 tblsp gram flour
1 tsp ginger/garlic
½ tsp turmeric
½ tsp gharum masala
½ tblsp chopped coriander leaves
1 tsp khus-khus (poppy seeds)
2 tblsp grated cheese

Wash and boil madumbis till soft. Scrape off skin and mash fine.

Grind fine the green chilli, fresh coriander and coconut and poppy seeds. Add this paste to the mashed madumbi together with all the other masalas. Add salt to taste.

Shape into balls and if mixture is too sticky, sprinkle with maizena (corn flour).

fill each ball with a little grated cheese.

Fry in hot oil, drain and keep aside.

THE RICE:
2 cups rice
1 tsp cummin
1/3 cup coconut milk (if not available use plain milk)
½ cup ghee/oil
2 green chillies
1/3 tsp fine elachi
2 cups tomatoes (blend and make puree)
2 onions
½ tsp chilli
1 tsp dhunia/jeero powder
1 tsp ginger/garlic
1/3 tsp fine cinnamon powder
pinch of fine cloves

Parboil rice in salted water and drain in colander while a hard kernel can still be felt.

Fry sliced onions in ghee/oil and remove half for garnishing. Crush the other half and add it to rice.

Fry spices in the oil in which the onions were fried for half a minute. In a pot put the oil, tomato puree, milk and ginger/garlic. Bring to boil and add the rice.

Toss lightly with a spatula then put kabaabs in the rice, tossing them around so that they are well covered.

Steam for 10 minutes. Garnish with left over fried onion and a handful of fried cashew nuts.

NOTE:
This is a lovely Biryani for vegetarians. One may substitute potatoes for the madumbis in which case add some frozen peas to the kabaabs.

Bukhari Pilaau

1 chicken (disjointed or cut to convenient size)
3 cups rice
1 dozen green chillies
2 tsp ginger/garlic
1 tsp crushed jeero (cummin)
¼ cup ghee/oil
1 large onion
3 grated carrots (medium size)
500g tomatoes (cut fine or grated)
2 pieces tuj (cinnamon)
2 tsp salt
A few cloves and whole peppers and elachi (cardomom)

Slice onion fine and braise in ghee/oil till light pink in colour.

Now add the meat previously marinated in the ginger/garlic, ground chillies and jeero, and salt.

Cook over medium heat and when moisture evaporates, add the grated tomatoes and cook again till dry.

Meanwhile, wash rice and allow to steep in hot water.

Grate the carrots and add them with the rice to the cooking pot of meat.

Add about a pint of water and leave to cook over medium heat, being careful to see that rice does not scorch. It may be necessary to add a cupful of water in order to allow proper cooking of rice.

Leave in 150°C oven for about half an hour. Just before serving, braise a little sliced onion, finely sliced ginger (optional) and a little jeero in 2 tablespoons of ghee and carefully spread over pot of rice.

Kabaab Pilaau

½ kg mince (not fatty)
2 tblsp saumnf (fennel)
1 tsp crushed jeero (cummin)
4 cloves garlic
2 tblsp dhunia leaves (coriander)
1 tblsp chopped mint
1 egg
2 green chillies (whole)
¼ tsp powdered tuj (ground cinnamon)
3 cloves
2 shelled elachi (cardomom)
1 grated onion (squeeze juice out)
2 cups rice
SAUCE TO PUT OVER KABAABS:
½ cup tomato puree
½ cup milk
1 tblsp lemon juice
good dash of chilli, salt and crushed pepper corns

Mix sauce ingredients together and pour over kabaabs.

Boil rice in salted water and when half cooked drain in colander.

Wash and drain mince in colander. (Squeeze out all moisture).

Pound together, dhunia leaves, elachi, chillies, garlic and cloves. Add crushed jeero to this with the other spices, onion, egg and chopped mint leaves.

Mix well with mince. Roll kabaabs in walnut sized balls. Braise in a little ghee/oil till dry. Leave aside.

In a pot, fry sliced onion (small sized onion finely sliced) in four tablespoons of oil.

When gold in colour, remove half onion. In pot to remaining onions add 1 tablespoon of ghee, a stick of cinnamon and 1 elachi and sprinkle half the rice in this.

Arrange kabaabs over this, then pour sauce over contents, and then add rice and allow to steam over medium heat till pot starts sizzling, then lower heat and steam slowly for forty minutes. Serve with spiced dahi, chutneys, achars and kachoomers.

Vhal-dhal Pilaau (Split Beans) or Mixed Dhal Pilaau

½ tsp salt
2 cups rice
1 tsp dhunia/jeero powder
½ tsp turmeric
3 tblsp ghee/oil
2 tblsp grated coconut (fresh)
A few whole cloves, peppercorns and stick cinnamon
1 tsp gharum masala
1 cup vaal-dhal (substitute 1½ cups of mixed dhals)
3 red chillies (dry)
1 lemon
¼ bunch dhunia (coriander)
1 tsp chilli powder

Soak vhal overnight. Wash off any loose skins.

Heat ghee/oil in pot and fry the whole cloves, cinnamon, peppercorns and whole red chillies. After a few minutes add salt, rice (previously soaked in water for half an hour) and the vaal-dhal. Fry for 1 minute, then add sufficient water for both to cook tender.

When half done, add all other spices and stir in lightly with a spoon.

Cook slowly till rice and beans are tender and fluffy. Before serving add juice of lemon and garnish with fresh coconut gratings and chopped dhunia.

Note:
Fresh grated coconut may be fried before adding.

Plain Yakhni Pilaau

½ kg mutton
1/3 cup oil
1 medium sized onion
6 small potatoes
1 large tomato
3 whole green chillies
1½ cups rice
¾ cup peas
1½ tsp salt
½ tsp turmeric
1 tsp ginger/garlic
1 tsp dhunia/jeero powder
½ tsp green pounded chillies
A few cloves and peppers
3 elachi (cardomom)
2 pieces stick cinnamon

Cube mutton in small pieces, wash and drain. Fry sliced onion in ghee/oil till pale golden brown, and add mutton with all the spices to it. Cook slowly till meat is tender, adding water if necessary. Add tomato and potatoes and steam slowly till potatoes half done.

Meanwhile, wash rice and cook in salted boiling water till half done. Drain well in colander. Add rice to stewing mutton, toss and mix lightly taking care not to break meat or getting the rice mushy. Add a little cold water if necessary and steam in oven or over slow heat for about half an hour. Brown a little onion in 2 or more tablespoons ghee and pour over rice just before serving.

Pakistani Yakhni Pilaau

1 tsp chillies
2 cups rice soaked in water for 2 hours
2 onions sliced
1 kg shoulder of lamb (cut in pieces)
A few cloves, cinnamon and whole pepper corns
3 elachi
1 cup yoghurt
3 cups water
3 tbsp of sultanas and seedless raisins
1 tsp slivered ginger
1 tsp slivered garlic
1 tsp crushed coriander seed
2 tbsp ghee
1 tbsp oil
½ tsp saffron soaked in 1 tbsp of hot milk
¼ cup almonds (blanched)

Marinate meat, onion, slivered ginger/garlic, salt, chillies, peppercorn and dhunia for a few hours. Heat oil and ghee with cinnamon, elachi and cloves then add meat mixture and cook slowly with lid tightly shut till meat begins to dry.

Add drained rice, cook slowly for 5 minutes, stirring constantly. Add yoghurt, water and saffron milk, almonds and sultanas. Mix well. Steam slowly till rice and meat done.

Moongh/Dhal Yakhni

1½ cups rice
1½ cups moong dhal (split moong)
750g leg mutton
2 green chillies
¼ tsp pepper
¾ tsp ginger/garlic
1 tsp green pounded chilli
2 tblsp oil
2 tblsp ghee
1 medium onion (sliced)
1 piece cinnamon
Few cardamoms and cloves
½ tsp jeero seeds (cummin)

Soak moong in cold water for a few hours. Do not wash off green skins completely for they add both to flavour and attractiveness. Wash rice. Cook rice and moong dhal in salted water to which has been added tuj etc., till nearly done. Drain off in colander.

Cut mutton in 4cm pieces and wash. Marinate in ginger/-garlic, salt, pepper, green pounded chilli and jeero seeds for an hour. Braise in oil over slow heat till the meat is dry. Add as much water as is needed to cook meat tender and when meat is nearly done and there is still a little moisture left, add the rice/dhal and cook all together till done. Fry onion and green chilli in ghee till onion is a gold colour. Pour over rice and serve with papads kachoomer and hot khuri.

ALTERNATE METHOD IN COCONUT SHELLS:
When meat/rice/dhal is nearly done, pile individual helpings in coconut shells. Pour a teaspoon of ghee from vagaar and a few slices of fried onion over each. Cover coconut with foil and keep in hot oven till required to serve. Each guest can spoon-in khuri directly into his shell and eat from the shell.

Afriki Yakhni Pilaau

(COLOUR PHOTO PAGE 160)

500g small chops or neatly cubed mutton (chicken may
  be used)
1¼ cups mixed vegetables (peas, toovar, sliced carrots,
  chana dhal)
1 medium onion
½ tsp ground chillies
¼ tsp ground pepper
¼ tsp turmeric (and good pinch saffron if possible)
2 cups rice
2 green chillies
½ cup dahi (yoghurt)
1 tsp jeero (cummin)
1 elachi (cardomom)
1 tsp ginger/garlic
A few cloves and whole peppers
¼ cup tomato
3 tblsp ghee/oil

The attractiveness lies in combination of colours, e.g.
carrot and peas. For really exotic flavour, add pinch of
saffron.

Fry onion, jeero and green chillies in ghee/oil, in pot.

Add meat with spices, tomato and dahi, and let simmer
slowly (adding water if necessary) till meat is nearly done.

Add carrots, peas, etc. Mix it well in pot with meat, let
simmer for 5 minutes, then add the 2 cups of uncooked
rice.

Add 2 cups of boiling water and simmer very slowly,
tossing and stirring gently a few times so that rice is evenly
distributed and mixed with other ingredients. Some types
of rice take longer to cook so more water should be added.

When done, fry a little onion in 2 tablespoons of ghee
and sprinkle over. Leave for 10 more minutes in the oven.
Serve with spiced dahi, kachoomer and papad.

Mattar Yakhni Pilaau

2 cups rice
6 potatoes
3 green chillies
1 small onion
1 cup peas (shelled)
1 tsp jeero (cummin)
1 small tomato
1 tsp ginger/garlic
4 tblsp ghee
1 tsp chilli powder
¼ tsp turmeric
½ kg chicken or mutton cut in convenient pieces
1 tsp salt

Boil rice in salted water till half done and then drain dry.

Fry onion in half of ghee, add meat and spices and braise
till meat is coated with masalas and fairly dry.

Now add tomato, and simmer till absorbed, and add
enough water to cook till meat is half done.

Add potatoes, and a little later the peas. Simmer for a
while then add the rice, carefully tossing it up and down till
evenly distributed amongst meat, etc.

Steam for half an hour (adding water if necessary). Just
before serving, fry few slices onion in rest of ghee and
sprinkle over rice.

Serve with fried papads, spiced dahi, kachoomers and
achars.

Khitchri (Kedgeree)

There is the classic joke about khitchris, that one serves it to house guests who have sort of overstayed their welcome, and that upon being served khitchri they should take the hint and start packing. However, in-so-far as we are concerned, it can be relegated to the file of classic jokes, for young and old all love khitchri and its inseparable accompaniment khuri, made of sour milk. Together with toasted papads, brinjal chutney and perhaps some sort of a fish dish, it can have pride of place in any home.

Khitchris are perhaps one of the most economical of rice dishes and can be made from rice with any combination of lentils, such as oil dhal, moong dhal or masoor dhal, but there can be no arguing the point that the classic khitchri is made of rice and oil dhal and that remains a firm favourite.

For buffets or formal entertaining, the hostess will welcome the idea of dressing up her khitchri by boiling a cupful of green peas and sprinkling it over her khitchri in the serving platter. The green and gold makes a colour picture which will fascinate, and guests will feel that they are still worth bothering about.

Khitchri
(YELLOW RICE) (Page 41)

½ tsp jeero (cummin)
2 cups rice
1 piece tuj (cinnamon)
¼ tsp turmeric
2 tblsp sliced onion
1 cup oil dhal (toovar dhal)
2 tsp coarse salt
2 elachi (cardomom)
2 tblsp oil
1 tblsp ghee

Wash dhal well, taking care to remove all outer skins. In 3 pints of boiling water (salted) add tuj, turmeric, elachi and throw in washed dhal and rice.

Boil rapidly and cook till done, but not mushy. Drain completely dry in colander. Put back in pot with a few spoons of cold water and allow to steam for 10-15 minutes over low heat.

Just before serving, fry onion in ghee/oil and carefully distribute over rice. With handle of spoon lightly stir inside to evenly coat khitchri with ghee. Serve with toasted papads, brinjal bharad and its essential accompaniment, Khuri (sour milk gravy)

Khuri
(SOUR MILK GRAVY) (Page 41)

500 ml yoghurt
1 dsspn pea flour (gram)
*1 small bunch dhunia leaves
*2 tsp dessicated coconut
*2 cloves of garlic
*2 green chillies
*A few slices onion
*1 tsp coarse salt
*1 tblsp shelled peas (optional)
1 tblsp ghee
Pinch of turmeric
½ tsp jeero

Pound all marked (*) ingredients together, and add to yoghurt; add pea flour and turmeric.

Whisk all well together then put on stove to boil, stirring constantly to prevent curdling.

Meanwhile, fry a little onion in ghee till golden brown, and add to boiling khuri.

In same frying pan in which onions were fried, add the jeero and braise it till it blackens; then add it to Khuri.

Boil till consistency of thin cream, garnish with mint or curry leaves.

Variations of Khuri

(1) To basic recipe add a tablespoon of mashed potato or a tablespoon of cooked brinjal or both.

(2) Instead of pea flour use ½ tablespoon of baghroo. This must be added after sour milk has come to boil; less salt must be added.

(3) Cut two bhinda in ¼ slices. Fry golden brown in a little ghee then add to sour milk before bringing it to boil.

Special Khuri
(SOUR MILK GRAVY) VARIATION (PHOTO Pg 45)

2 cups dhai (yoghurt)
¼ tsp whole mustard
¼ tsp ginger/garlic
1 sprig kuripulya (curry leaves)
¼ tsp whole cummin seed (jeero)
¼ onion (sliced)
Salt to taste
2 dry red chillies
½ tblsp chana flour (gram)

Mix salt,. ginger/garlic, chana flour and yoghurt and whisk well with egg beater.

Make vagaar of onions, mustard, curry leaves, red chillies and jeero in 1 tablespoon of ghee. Just as mustard seeds stop spluttering, add the yoghurt and stir continuously till it comes to boil and is consistency of cream. Serve with khitchri.

PAPER TABLECLOTHS

Harsh and rough were the times when our great-grandparents arrived from India. With prayerful hearts and sweating brows they tilled the soil or hawked the streets as vendors.

Long and lean were the years when our grandparents tried to strike new shoots around the parental trees. Of hardship there was no dearth but firm in their Faith they rather counted their blessings. When the home-spun cottons they had brought from India wore out and few had the money to buy new tablecloths, mothers substituted these with something for free.

Armed with a pair of scissors and dexterously folding old newspapers, beautiful repeat designs soon emerged. Shelves and tables were covered with these and it is in memory of those days that we present this menu on our newspaper cover with its pretty crepe paper flowers for decoration.

Wholesome and simple was the food of those days. The platter of rice, dhal or spiced yoghurt, curried potato slices, onion and tomato relish, quarters of oranges sprinkled with salt and roasted cummin seeds for dessert and a jug of iced water was sufficient for the most fastidious to exclaim Shukar Alhamdolillah (God be Praised for this Bounty).

A — Papads (285)
B — Khitchri (39)
C — Spiced cucumber (251)
D — Khuri (39)
E — Orange slices
F — Pumpkin Curry (134)
G — Fried Goovar (129)
H — Aaloo Fry (42)
I — Fried Bhinda (42)

Vagareli Khitchri

Use same ingredients as recipe on page 39, but soak dhal and rice separately for about 30 minutes in cold water. Fry onions, jeera, tuj and elachi in ghee/oil and just as onions turn gold in colour add 3 cups of water, salt and turmeric.

As soon as water starts boiling add washed rice and dhal and simmer very slowly till water is absorbed and khitchri is cooked.

If done too rapidly more water may have to be added but on no account must water be drained off!

Aaloo Fry
(SPICED POTATO CRISPS) PHOTO PAGE 41

4 large white potatoes
1 brinjal (optional)
¼ cup boiled peas (optional)
½ tsp chilli powder
½ tsp turmeric
Few slices of onion

Peel potatoes. Slice in thin wafers as for crisps. slice brinjal slightly thicker. Soak all in salted water. Drain dry before frying. Mix spices well with above. Heat oil well. Fry everything till pale gold in colour. Drain and decorate in platter with fried onion. Delicious with khitchri or bharkoo.

Aaloo Fry Curry

Use same ingredients as above. Heat oil, add marinating vegetables to oil, close lid tight and simmer till done.

CAUTION: Mix spices in vegetable before adding to heated oil for the contents must not be unduly stirred while cooking lest the vegetables get mashed.

VARIATIONS TO ABOVE:
1) Add wedges of tomato, thick rings of green peppers to above.
2) Dried lentil waris soaked in cold water for an hour can be added to basic aaloo fry.
3) Slices of quince and/or green mangoes make a lovely addition.

Some more accompaniments served with Khitchri, Dhal and Rice and Bhurkoo:-

Fried Bhinda (Okra) (PHOTO PAGE 41)

500 g Bhinda
2 tblsp dessicated coconut
½ tsp salt
1 tsp red chilli powder
2 tsp jeero (crushed fine)

Serve with rice dishes.
Select nice long bhindas. Wash and wipe clean, then slash through bottom to about ¾ way up. Stuff with above masala and fry in shallow oil, very slowly till crisp.

Fried Chillies
(LONG PEPPERS)

The same stuffing as above may be used for chillies. If thin chillies are used, omit chilli powder altogether as they are sharp enough. For capsicums add pinch of chilli powder. Fry as bhindas.

Brinjal Fritters
(PHOTO PAGE 41)

Cut brinjals into thick wafers (about 3 mm thick round or semi-circle wedges). Soak in salted water.

Meanwhile, prepare: Whisk 1 egg with ¼ teaspoon salt and ¼ teaspoon red chillies. Drain brinjals and dip in egg batter then coat with dry bread crumbs and fry slowly in oil till a lovely golden colour.

Drain and serve with khitchri or dhal and rice.

Potato Fritters

Instead of brinjals, slice potatoes in 3 mm thick slices and fry in batter as above.

Moong Dhal Khitchri
(CHINESE PEAS)

2 cups rice
3 tblsp ghee
Small piece ginger (slivered)
Salt to taste
2 cups moong dhal (split moong)
Small sliced onion
Tuj, elachi, cloves, etc. (cinnamon etc.)

Soak dhal for few hours till skins can be washed off. Wash off loose skins only and ignore those clinging to dhal for that lends it the proper characteristic and flavour.

Wash rice and add with dhal to pot of boiling, salted water and whole spices till done.

Drain in colander and when well drained and cool, return to pot and steam slowly, adding a little water if necessary. Meanwhile fry onion and slivered ginger in ghee and pour over rice.

Chicken Khuri
(SOUR MILK GRAVY WITH CHICKEN)

¼ chicken (cut in small pieces)
3 cups dahi (yoghurt)
2 tsp khus-khus (poppy seeds)
Good pinch turmeric
1 onion (medium)
1 tblsp fresh coconut
2 tblsp oil
4 whole almonds (optional)
6 pistachios (optional)
1 tsp dhunia jeero
Salt to taste
1 tblsp ghee
½ tsp ginger/garlic
1 tblsp khuri masala (see page 39)

Slice onion fine. Keep aside a few onion slices, and braise the remainder in the oil. Just as onions begin to change colour, add the meat, ginger/garlic, turmeric, and dhunia/jeero. Braise slowly till spices are blended and chicken nicely browned.

Pound the almonds, fresh coconut, khus-khus, and khuri masalas together till fine. Add the pounded ingredients to the sour milk and beat well with beater. Add to the braised chicken and bring to boil. Stir continuously to prevent yoghurt curdling. Simmer slowly and just before serving make a fresh vagaar as follows:

In the ghee braise the onions and a ¼ teaspoon each of methi seeds and whole jeero and when these are nearly black in colour, add to pot of khuri. Garnish with sprigs of fresh mint.

This khuri should be served with rotlas but may be served with moong dhal khitchri.

Murghi Khuri
(VARIATION) WITH COCONUT MILK
(PHOTO PAGE 171)

¼ chicken
¼ tsp red chillies
¼ tsp dhunia/jeero (coriander/cummin)
2 cups dahi (yoghurt)
Milk from 1 coconut
¼ bunch dhunia
2 cloves of garlic
¼ tsp ginger/garlic
1 tsp salt to taste
2 small onions (grated)
2 tblsp fresh coconut
3 green chillies
2 tsp chana flour (gram)
¼ tsp jeero (cummin)

Cut chicken in small pieces. Keep aside two teaspoons of onion and braise the remainder in 1 tablespoon of ghee till a delicate brown. Add chicken with the ginger/garlic, red chillies, salt and dhunia/jeero and the 2 tablespoons of fresh coconut grated or pounded as preferred. Braise slowly till masalas coat meat evenly and is delicately tanned.

Meanwhile to the dahi add a chutney made from the dhunia leaves, garlic, jeero, green chillies and last add the chana flour. Beat well with beater. Extract milk from rest of coconut and beat it into the dahi mixture. Add this liquid to the braising meat and bring to boil, stirring continuously. Reduce heat and allow to simmer slowly (with lid on) till chicken has cooked.

Finally make a vagaar with 1 teaspoon of ghee, a few onion slices, a good pinch jeero and 2 red chillies (dried ones). As soon as onion is a lovely gold, add to khuri and serve garnished with a few whole mint leaves.

This is to be served with khitchri made from moong dhal and rice or lentil dhal khitchri. (See above.)

A — Papads (285)
B — Brinjal gugra (127)
C — i Mango Raitha Achar (258)
    ii Lemon Achar (272)
    iii Peanut chutney
    iv Onion/tom kachumbar (281)
    v Onion/aamli kachumbar (281)
    vi Spiced cucumber (251)
    vii Carrot achar (269)
D — Pumpkin curry (134)
E — Special khuri (39)
F — Mixed (cholai) Bhaji (129)
G — Masala Fish (164)
H — i Brinjal fritters (42)
    ii Dodhi fritters (42)
    iii Fried mircha (42)
    iv aaloo crisps (42)
    v Fried Goovar (42)
I — Brinjal curry (126)
J — Khitchri (rice) (39)
K — Quince curry (125)

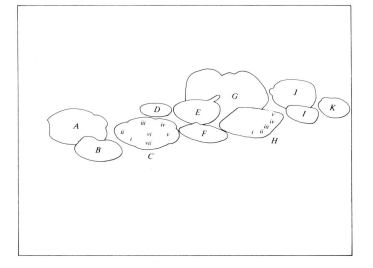

Bhoonji Khitchri
(TRADITIONAL)

2 cups rice
2 cups dhal (oil dhal also known as Toovar dhal)
2 pieces stick cinnamon
3 elachi (cardomom)
A few whole cloves and peppers.
½ tsp whole jeero (cummin)
1 small onion
2 tblsp ghee
2 tblsp oil
2 whole green chillies
A few thick slices of tomato

Boil rice in salted water and drain in colander.

Boil dhal separately in salted water. Care must be taken that dhal is only half done. Drain off but keep dhal water for gravy.

Fry onion in ghee/oil with the jeero and green chillies. Drain off half of ghee/oil and remove half of onions for later use.

Arrange the dhal (leaving aside about a ¼ cup for gravy) over the fried onion and chillies. Now arrange a few slices of tomato over dhal. Lastly arrange rice over this.

Sprinkle remaining ghee/oil and crisp onions over the rice. Pour ¼ cup cold water and steam for about 15 minutes. Serve with Khatoo. (Gravy, see below.)

Khatoo
(GRAVY FOR BHOONJI KHITCHRI)

¼ cup dhal (left over from dhal for Bhoonji Khitchri)
2 cloves of garlic
¼ bunch green dhunia leaves (coriander)
2 tblsp aamli juice (tamarind)
2 tblsp sugar
¼ tsp salt
1 tblsp fresh or dessicated coconut (fresh coconut must be pounded in chutney)
2-3 green chillies
¼ tsp jeero (cummin)
1 tblsp chana flour (gram)
1 tblsp ghee
Juice of 1 orange

Pound to fine paste, a chutney made from green chillies, garlic, dhunia leaves, and dhal. Add to this aamli, juice of orange, and the water left-over from dhal (about 2 cups), coconut and pea flour. Add salt.

Now brown a few slices of onion in ghee and when a delicate brown add the spiced dhal water to it. Let it boil to consistency of thin cream or soup. Add sugar to taste. Garnish with mint and serve hot with steaming khitchri.

Bhoonji Khitchri
(CONTEMPORARY)

2 cups rice
250 g raw mince
3 potatoes (halved/fried)
1 tomato
2 elachi (cardomom)
½ tsp jeero (cummin)
1½ cups toovar dhal (oil dhal)
3 hard-boiled eggs
1 onion
1 stick cinnamon
3 tblsp ghee
A few cloves and peppers

INGREDIENTS FOR MINCE

1 tsp ginger/garlic
3 whole green chillies
¼ tsp saffron (optional)
½ tsp salt
¼ tsp chilli powder

Braise mince in spices. When done add saffron or turmeric and mix well.

Boil rice in salted water and drain. Boil dhal in salted water and drain when only half done.

Fry onions an jeero in ghee till golden brown. Leave half of the onion in pot and remove the rest of the onions and set aside.

Spread dhal over onion and ghee, then put the braised mince over the dhal. Slice tomato in thick slices and set over mince. Arrange eggs and potatoes and, lastly, spread rice over all. Garnish with the remaining fried onion and sprinkle a tblsp of ghee.

Now sprinkle half a cup of cold water and bring to steam slowly over low heat for 20 minutes. Serve with khatoo.

VARIATIONS FOR KHATOO:

(1) Use juice of 3 oranges and decrease amount of dhal water.

(2) Use pineapple juice (freshly liquidized) instead of orange juice.

(3) When liquidising chutney and dhal add 1 green mango.

(4) When oranges are not available use frozen juice but adjust sugar content.

Bhurkoo and Khuri
(CRUSHED WHEAT PORRIDGE)
8-10 PERSONS

This is a great favourite at family gatherings when a simple and economical meal is called for. It is both very tasty and simple to prepare.

2 cups oil dhal
2 tsp coarse salt
1 medium onion
2 cups bharkoo (crushed wheat)
½ cup ghee (more if preferred)
¼ cup mealie meal or mealie rice

Soak dhal for 30 minutes and wash off all loose skins. Boil dhal, mince and crushed wheat in salted water and cook till soft and mushy.

Care must be taken that pot is stirred vigorously at this stage, since water will nearly have evaporated and there is danger of contents scorching. If mealie rice is used, it is added with the crushed wheat but if mealie meal is used, then this is the procedure.

Make a paste from mealie meal and a little cold water and add to pot when contents are mushy. Stir vigorously till content is consistency of thin porridge (allowing for the fact that this will be a lumpy cereal naturally).

Just before serving fry sliced onion in ghee and pour over. Stir well. serve with toasted papads, brinjal chutneys (bharads) and of course, Khuri, (See page 39) in generous quantities.

Sandwich Rice Dish
(COLOUR PHOTO 196)

2½ cups cooked rice
½ kg shrimps cooked in tomato/onion chutney
½ cup of dhunia chutney mixed with 2 tbsp dessicated coconut

Place a layer of rice in a greased baking mould. Spread a layer of dhunia/coconut chutney over this. Place a layer of rice over green layer.

Spread layer of shrimp and tomato chutney over rice. Finally cover with rest of rice. Sprinkle with (½ cup milk mixed with 2 tbsp ghee) and bake for ½ an hour in 300ºF (150ºC) oven.

Unmould on platter and serve with curry or yoghurt.

Bhoonjeli Khitchri

*2 Red dry chillies
2 cups rice
1 cup oil dhal
2 tblsp ghee
2 tblsp oil
1 onion sliced
*1 tsp whole jeera (cummin)
*2 sticks cinnamon, a few pods of elachi and a few cloves
*1 teaspoon peppercorns
*1 teaspoon slivered ginger
½ teaspoon turmeric
1 teaspoon methi seeds
2 sprigs curry leaves
2 tblspoons fresh coconut cut in thin wafers
2 tblspoons chopped dhunia
2 green chillies (slit)
Salt to taste

Wash rice and oil dhal separately then keep soaked in cold water.

In half of ghee and the oil fry the onions and spices marked with an *. When onions turn gold in colour, remove half of them and drain through strainer.

Add rice and dhal to the other half of onions in the pot with the ghee and fry for a minute. Now add salt, turmeric and about 4 or 5 cups of water. Bring to boil, then over low heat with lid closed, simmer until rice nearly done (20 minutes).

In remaining ghee make a vagaar with methi seeds, green chillie and curry leaves. Pour over rice and lightly stir with handle of spoon.

In pan in which vagaar was made put in the wafers of the coconut and just give them a good stir on the hot pan. When serving rice garnish with coconut wafers and chopped dhunia. Serve with spiced dahi, papads etc.

Lucknowi Khuri

After the decay of the Moghul Empire, the centre of literature, the arts and culture, shifted from Delhi to Lucknow — the newly formed Capital of the breakaway province of Oudh. Here the Moghul civilisation was to receive fresh impetus and to thrive for the next century. Not only music and poetry but even the culinary arts were transformed, for nowhere amongst the Moghlai dishes have we come across a khuri recipe that is so delicious and so rich as this one given to us by descendants of a family that at the beginning of this century had emigrated from Lucknow to South Africa.

Khuri as it is made in this recipe is no longer peasant--fare, but a meal fit for the Nawaabs of Oudh. (Photograph on Page 49 in brown casserole with ladle).

Lucknowi Khuri

SPECIAL GHARUM MASALA:

For this recipe pound some big elcha, cloves and black pepper and then use as specified.

THE KHURI:
3 cartons yoghurt (7 cups)
¾ cup chana flour (gram)
1 bunch dhunia (coriander)
1 onion (medium)
½ ball garlic (30 g)
Good pinch turmeric

Pound garlic, dhunia and onion to a fine paste. Mix chana flour in a little water till it is smooth and well blended. Add chana flour paste to pounded ingredients, and add the turmeric and salt to taste. Mix in well with sour milk.

Put on stove and bring to boil whilst stirring continuously. When khuri begins to boil and there is no longer any danger of it curdling, lower the heat and allow it to simmer for two hours. Meanwhile prepare the other items and keep on adding to the pot of khuri thus:

THE KOFTAS: (KABAABS)
½ kg mince (mutton)
½ tsp pounded garlic
1 tsp dhunia powder (coriander)
1 tsp special gharum masala
1 tsp salt
1 large onion
¼ tsp pounded ginger
1 tsp chilli powder
2 tblsp chana flour (gram)

Pound fine the onion, garlic and ginger. Keep aside a quarter of this paste and add the rest to the washed and well drained mince. Braise the chana flour in a little oil and when it begins to change colour add to the mince. Add rest of ingredients to mince and put through mincer once more to bind the mince well. Form into large sized kabaabs.

THE GRAVY:

To the left-over onion paste add a ¼ tsp each of dhunia powder, chilli powder, salt and turmeric. Heat 3 tblsp of oil in a pot and braise the above masalas in it till it is blended and dry. Add 2 cups of water and bring to boil. To this spiced water add the kabaabs and cook till they are done and the liquid has evaporated. Add the kabaabs to the pot of simmering khuri.

THE PHULKIS:
1 tsp finely crushed jeero (cummin)
1 cup chana flour (gram)
Salt to taste
Water
¼ tsp baking powder (optional)

Sift chana flour, jeero and salt. Add water and blend into a smooth paste which is the consistency of rich cream. "Phulkis", literally means baubles filled with air, so beat in as much air into batter as possible, with the help of a wire spoon or egg beater.

To test whether phulkis are ready for frying, drop small lumps of batter into a cup of cold water and when they float to the surface, the batter is ready.

Heat oil in pan and fry the phulkis like you would, bhajias. Remove and drain in colander when they are a light gold in colour. When cool add to pot of simmering khuri.

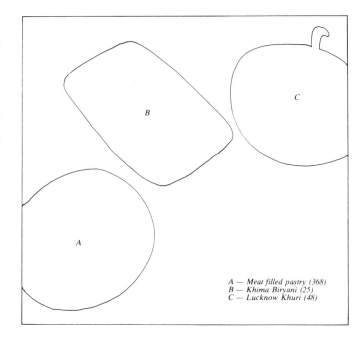

A — Meat filled pastry (368)
B — Khima Biryani (25)
C — Lucknow Khuri (48)

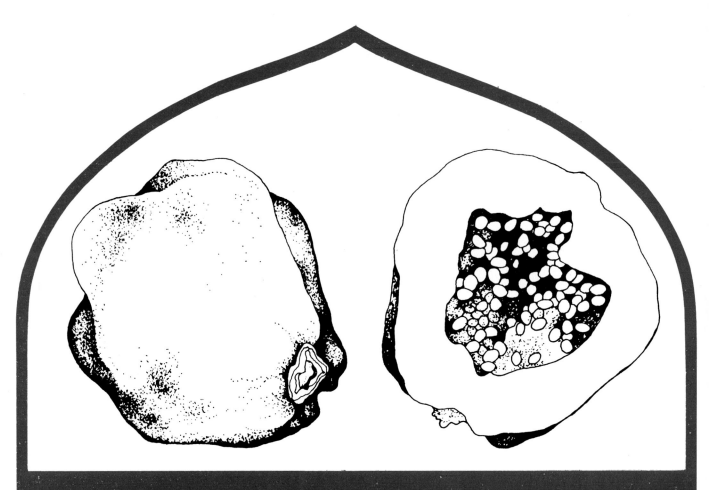

Pawpaw

Pawpaw is a wonderful tenderizer. A teaspoon or two of ground green pawpaw will be sufficient for 1 kg mutton. Mix in with masalas when marinating.

Pawpaw leaves washed clean can be used for tenderizing meat as well. Simply wrap the joints of masalad meat in the leaves for several hours unwrap and roast in usual manner.

Yoghurt Curdling in Curry

When yoghurt is added to a hot dish it often curdles and while this will not alter the taste it is unsightly, so always add yoghurt to cold ingredients but if recipe specifies addition during cooking then dilute yoghurt with a tablespoon or so of water before cooking.

Saffron

Place saffron strands in a pan and put over very low heat for a minute or two, till strings become crisp, but in no way change their colour.

Crush strands with back of spoon and steep in a tablespoon of boiling water till a flaming russet red colour results.

ALTERNATIVELY: Steep saffron strands in a tablespoon or two of hot boiling milk, then strain through sieve and use in recipes.

Jeera (Cummin)

Jeera powder is used for thickening and flavouring curries.

IF CURRY SPILLS ON DRESS, sprinkle talcum powder over it. The powder will absorb the stain and it will wash out later.

Oil stains on clothes can be removed by rubbing Sunlight soap over stain — allow to rest for an hour or so then rub and wash as usual. Stubborn oil stains can be washed out with hair shampoo.

SECTION 2

Curries or Tarkaris

THERE is a prevalent misconception amongst non-Indians that curry is an ingredient used in curries, whereas in fact the curry, or the more correct term, Tarkari, is the dish eaten with rotis or rice dishes. Curry powder as is sold in tins is never used by Indians, and instead, compounds of several spices mixed together, make the masala. Stew or bredie could classify as curry.

The basis of all good curries is the onion fried in ghee/oil and on this depends the attractiveness and palatability of the dish. The onions are usually sliced fine and fried in ghee/oil. Just as they change to a golden colour, the meat or vegetable and spices are added (except gharum masala, which is added with the garnishing just before serving). If the onion is fried too light there will be an oniony taste to the curry, if they be allowed to turn dark the colour of the curry will be ruined. Whilst the onions are being fried the meat and vegetables should be cut, cleaned washed and drained, and the spices added to them. Meat especially, should be allowed to marinate in the spices for some time. In meat curries or meat/vegetable curries the tendency now is to use oil only except in beef and chicken dishes where some margarine is to be preferred. In vegetable curries oil alone should be used. Any brand of cooking oil is suitable, especially sun flower seed or vegetable oils.

Tuj, elachi, cloves, etc., are optional, but they do enhance the exotic flavours which all good cooks aim at in Indian cooking. Tomatoes in curries have often been given in cup measurements since sizes vary so much. Half a cup of tomato means that much tomato finely cut up or grated or minced through a mincer.

We strongly advocate possessors of blenders to pulverise the tomatoes in the liquidizers to avoid loose skins which many people detest. Otherwise the tomatoes must be put through a mincer or grated, but that is a question of taste entirely. Where not specified use medium to large sized onions and tomatoes.

Meat will naturally be cut up to size preferred, but it must be remembered that when vegetables are added to meat as in stews, the meat must be cut up small.

Broad, flat-bottom casseroles are best for curries. Heavy stainless steel aluminium pots, or the heavy base enamelled ones, are excellent.

Naturally, some people will prefer to add more chillies than that specified in this book. We have been moderate with our chillies and spices, and find that children and people unused to Indian cooking, can tolerate the amounts used here. We have also used minimum amounts of ghee/oil and feel that the quantities specified are enough to ensure good cooking without any residue skimming on the top once the dish is cooked. That is both unsightly and uneconomical.

For details of ginger/garlic, turmeric, etc., look at the glossary at the beginning of the book.

Wherever possible, chillies in curries should be the fresh red ones pounded fine. If these are not available then dry red chillies can be substituted with equally good results. We find that some brands of red chilly powders are tinted artificially and this makes the curry unattractive, so, for those people who use chilli powder, we would like to add a note of caution, that they carefully select a brand that does not use artificial colouring.

The A B C of Curry Making

Do remember that onions and tomatoes control the texture, colour, and type of your curry. So when a recipe says:

SAUTÉ YOUR ONIONS: Put onion in oil or ghee and braise till they are soft and transparent, but have not changed their colour.

FRY YOUR ONIONS: Fry them in the oils till they are a golden colour — NOT BROWN OR BLACK.

Sliced onions are called for in most soups, meat curries etc. Chopped onions and tomatoes are called for in many vegetable curries, when the onion and tomato has to be visible even after cooking and not blended smooth.

Grated onion is best for creamy, saucy curries.

Pureed or liquidised tomato is essential for smooth creamy gravies.

Sunflower seed or vegetable oils can be safely used in all types of vegetable and meat curries and most Indian homes use them.

But chicken and beef tastes better with the addition of a little butter or ghee.

1 onion (sliced chopped or grated) = ¾ - cup full
1 tomato chopped or grated = ½ - cup full

The Basic Curry (A)

2 onions (sliced)
2 tomatoes (chopped, grated or liquidised)
1 tsp salt
1 tsp chilli
1 tsp dhunia/jeera powder
¾ tsp turmeric
¾ tsp ginger/garlic
2 tbsp oil

Sauté onion in oil and add tomato and spices when they are transparent. Toss and turn a few times.

Simmer gently with lid closed till spices mixed and tomato blended, but not smooth.

Basic Curry (B)

Use same ingredients as above but grate onions and liquidise or puree tomatoes before hand.

Fry onions and when gold in colour, add tomato and spices and simmer till smooth and creamy.

To above basic curries — add vegetables, lentils, cereals, meat etc., and you can turn out an infinite variety of dishes. For example Patta In Chutney.

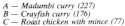

A — Madumbi curry (227)
B — Crayfish curry (176)
C — Roast chicken with mince (77)

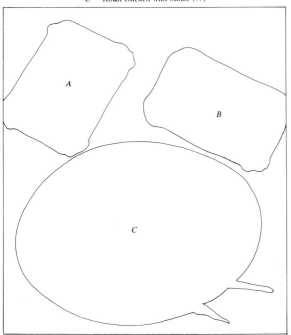

Gharum Masala
(PEPPING-UP SPICE)

NOTE: Gharum Masala is added to curries just a few minutes before serving, and is not to be added with spices after braising of onions.

15g elachi powder (optional)
500 g dhunia powder (coriander)
125 g jeero powder (cumin)
30 g cloves (fine))
60 g pepper (fine)
30 g tuj (fine) (cinnamon)

Mix all the powders well together and put in slow oven to brown and intensify in strength. When cool, pack away in tins or bottles and keep small bottlesful in front of pantry shelves, to use as required in curries about 10 minutes before serving.

NOTE: Good chefs buy the spices whole, roast them in the oven and then pound them fine.

SOUPS

In Indian cuisine some types of soup constitute the full meal. Haleem, Khichro, Harera are broths that come in this category. They can also be served as a first course in which event the additional dishes must be light to balance the menu.

Haleem
(NOURISHING BROTH)
(8 PERSONS)

750 g chicken or 500 g leg mutton
1½ cups wheat or mixture of: 1 cup wheat, ½ cup barley, 1 tblsp chana dhal gram (to be boiled in salted water till tender. Then grind through mincer.)
2 tsp ginger/garlic
1 fair sized onion
½ tsp arad (turmeric)
½ tsp red dry chillies
1 tsp whole jeero (cummin)
1 tsp gharum masala
¼ cup chopped shallot and dhunia leaves
A few elachi, pepper and cloves.
1 tsp salt
2 pieces tuj (cinnamon)
1 tsp green pounded chillies
1 tsp dhunia/jeero
2 whole green chillies
¼ cup oil
2 tblsp ghee

Boil wheat or combination of cereals till tender. Grind through mincer.

Braise jeero, green chillies and onion in oil till light golden colour. Add washed meat pieces and the masalas and braise till it is well coated on meat and add water to fill pot.

Cook meat till tender and add ground dhals. Cook till all well blended and haleem is consistency of broth (3 to 4 hours).

Make a vagaar of two tablespoons of ghee and a few rings of sliced onions with little jeero and the green chillies. Pour over haleem, add gharum masala and mix well. Just before serving add chopped greens.

Hareera
(COLOUR PHOTO 265)

* 250 g mutton or chicken for soup
1 cup chopped greens (mint, parsley, dhunia spring onions)
*1 tsp. black pepper corn
1 tsp black crushed pepper
3 red dry chillies
*2 tsp green pounded chilli
*2 tbsp oil
*2 tbsp ghee
¼ cup raw rice (soaked in cold water for an hour)
½ cup macaroni or noodles (broken up)
3 eggs (optional)
1 cup chana (chick peas)
*2 tsp salt
*2 tsp ginger/garlic
*1 cup sliced onions
*½ tsp ground cinnamon
*½ tsp cummin seed
1 tbsp chana flour (gram)

Soak chana overnight. Boil in salted water till soft and keep aside. Keep aside ¼ of onions but add rest to soup pot with all other ingredients marked with asterisk. Braise till contents are fairly dry. Now add 3 litres of water and cook till meat begins to flake off.

Add drained rice, boiled chana and macaroni and cook gently till all are done. There should be lots of liquid left so adjust water accordingly. Braise gram flour in ½ tbsp of ghee and when it begins to bubble add ½ cup of cold water and blend smoothly. Add to pot of Hareera taking care that no lumps are left. Finally beat eggs and while stirring soup, pour eggs thinly over hot simmering soup so that noodle like strings of egg is cooked in it.

Add half of chopped greens and pep-up with crushed black pepper. Serve in large casserole surrounded with small bowls of crisply fried onions, fried slivered garlic, chopped mint, juicy wedges of lemon, salt and chilli. Each person will dip deeply in casserole and fill their own soup bowls, sprinkling it with garnishes to suit individual tastes. A thick nourishing meal in itself. Ideal for family gatherings. Serves 12 persons.

Khichro
(MIXED CEREAL BROTH)

On the occasion of family gatherings, and especially to end off Bakri Eid festivities, Khichro is something to look forward to. It is both filling and nourishing, besides being delicious.

There are many variations of khichro as differences in tastes will prevail, and each housewife will want to use more of one cereal and less of another. That is, however, something best left to the individuality of the cook, but here is a basis recipe, the success of which is guaranteed.

500 g meaty soup bones (do not cut off the meat from bones as this is a broth and not a soup)
2 pieces tuj (cinnamon)
A few elachi, peppers and cloves
2 cups of mixed cereal (which we have made up in this way):
¾ cup wheat
¼ cup rice
2 tblsp oil dhal
2 tblsp barley
2 tblsp dhal (chana)
1 tsp salt
2 litres water
 onion
A few elachi, peppers and cloves
¼ cup chopped shallot and dhunia
2 tsp salt (coarse)
1 tsp arad (turmeric)
1 tsp chillies
1 tsp dhunia/jeero powder
2 tsp ginger/garlic
1 tsp whole jeero (cummin)
4 or 5 green chillies pounded up
1 tsp gharum masala

Boil the cereals in sufficient salted water till thoroughly cooked. Grind through mincer with the liquid. (Do not drain off any excess water.)

NOTE: Left-over rice or Khitchri is excellent, in which case use a little less of rice and dhal specified.

Slice onion and fry in ghee with jeero till golden brown. Add the bones with the masalas (except gharum masala) and the pounded green chillies, till bones are well coated with them. Fill the pot with water and cook over medium heat till meat on bones is tender. Grind the cereal and add to pot. Stir thoroughly and mix well. Let cook for at least forty minutes till broth is thick. Fry a few slices of onion in a little ghee and pour over broth. Stir in the gharum masala and garnish with the cut greens a little before serving.

Serve with chutneys and lemon.

Kabaab Khitchra
SERVES 12

2 tblsp oil
1 kg mutton (leg mutton, cut in large pieces — cut meat off bones)
1 cup rice
2 tblsp gram (chana flour)
1 tsp dhunia (coriander) seeds
½ tsp turmeric (arad)
2 tomatoes (chopped)
1 tsp ginger/garlic
1 cup fresh or frozen green peas
1 stick cinnamon (tuj)
2 tblsp ghee
½ cup chana (gram) dhal
2 eggs
1 tsp jeera (cummin seeds)
3 onions (sliced)
3 green chillies
1 tsp slivered ginger
2 whole elachi (cardamom)
2 tblsp chopped dhunia and mint
salt to taste

Put washed bones in large pot together with the oil, green chillies, tuj, elachi, slivered ginger, gram dhal, salt and the two sliced onions (but keep aside ½ cupful for garnishing later). Braise slowly till meat is dry.

Add 2 litres of water and simmer for two hours (may be pressure cooked). Meanwhile parboil rice in a little salted water.

Mince the meat that was cut off from the bones together with the third onion and green peas.

To mince, add the chopped greens, turmeric, ginger/garlic, eggs and gram flour. Add the parboiled rice.

Roast the jeera and dhunia seeds on a tava (or frying pan). Crush them coarsely and add to mince. Mix thoroughly and form into balls.

Bring pot of soup to boil, being careful to add sufficient water so that contents do not scorch.

Into the simmering soup lower the kabaabs gently.

When kabaabs harden somewhat and there is no danger of them breaking, lower the heat to simmering.

After 30 minutes the kabaabs will be cooked.

Make a vagaar of ghee/oil and the sliced onions. While onions are being fried, empty the khitchra into a deep serving bowl or soup tureen and when vagaar is a deep gold in colour gently pour over the khitchra in the tureen.

Do not disturb the contents but allow the onions to nestle lightly on top. Garnish with chopped greens and mint leaves. Serve hot with lemons.

ALTERNATIVELY:
Do not add parboiled rice to mince, but add rice to the pot of simmering soup before adding kabaabs. If rice absorbs too much liquid add more water.

Haressa/Dokra Soup
(DUMPLING SOUP)

250g-500g soup bones
3 green chillies
2 tsp coarse salt
2 sticks cinnamon
2 green tomatoes (chopped)
*1 tsp crushed jeera (cummin)
*1 tsp crushed coriander seeds (dhunia)
*½ tsp black peppercorns
2 tblsp ghee/1 tblsp oil
1½ tsp ginger/garlic
1 tsp slivered ginger
2 dry red chillies (whole)
few cloves and elachi
1 large onion (sliced)
3 large carrots
1 cup of either split peas or 2 cups fresh green peas

Roast in pan the ingredients marked with an asterisk (*) and pound fine.

Soak peas or soup mix (barley, wheat, lentils etc.) overnight. Boil cereal and carrots in water till tender — mash fine, or put through mincer.

Slice onion and sauté with ginger and garlic in ghee/oil and when they begin to change colour, add the soup bones and spices and braise till masalas are dry.

Add chopped tomato and braise till all well blended.

Add 2 litres water and simmer pot for 2-3 hours (or pressure cook).

Stir vigorously to flake meat off bone — now add mashed cereal and simmer for 30 minutes.

½ Hour before serving make Dokras of:

DUMPLING (1)

2 potatoes (mashed)
1 tblsp soft butter or ghee
salt, pepper and dash of chilli powder
2 tblsp flour
1 egg white, beaten
2 tblsp chopped mint

Combine all ingredients thoroughly. Divide into 14 balls. Chill. Drop gently into simmering pot of soup — close lid and do not stir pot. When serving, lift out dumplings carefully and return them gently on top of bowl of hot soup. To prevent Dokras from breaking, a thin paste of flour and water can be made and balls rolled in this before lowering into broth.

VARIATION WITH RICE DUMPLINGS
DUMPLING (2)

1 cup left over rice
1 egg white, beaten
¼ cup self-raising flour
¼ tsp each pepper, salt and pounded chilli

Mash rice till it is sticky. Add all other ingredients and form into soft dough.

Mould into balls and lower gently into simmering pot of soup. Close lid and steam for ½ an hour. Dumplings will absorb soup.

Now make a vagar of onion in a little ghee, pour over soup and serve hot. It will not be necessary to serve bread with this soup.

Russum
(SOUTH INDIAN CLEAR SOUP)

2 tblsp oil
1 dsp whole peppercorns
1 dsp whole mustard seeds
½ cup pulp of tamarind
Salt to taste
3 dry red chillies
1 ball garlic
1 tblsp cummin seeds (jeera)
1 litre water
1 small onion

Take garlic pods (with skins) and put in mortar (kundi) with the cummin, mustard and peppercorns. Crush just enough to bruise them.

Slice onion and fry in oil and when they begin to change colour add crushed garlic and spices and red chillies.

Braise for a minute or two, then add aamli pulp and water (mixed together previously) to pot. Allow to infuse two or three times then switch off. Serve piping hot with rolls.

NOTE: Russum may be sieved before serving in which event a very thin and clear consomme will result. However since it is a lovely soup for people recovering from colds, it is advised that the spices be retained when serving.

(VARIATION)
To above may be added ½ cup oil dhal (boiled separately in salted water) and mashed very fine before adding to rusum just before the aamli and water is added.

Trotters
(PAYA) VARIATION

2 onions
1 doz trotters
½ cup whole coriander seed
1 tblsp whole cummin (jeera)
3 tblsp saumf (fennel)
3 sticks cinnamon   **Put all spices in Muslin Bag**
6 cloves (whole)
4 black elachi
1 tsp whole black pepper

Put cleaned and washed trotters in pressure cooker with salt, bag of spices and 1 sliced onion. Cover with water and cook for 1-1½ hours till trotters are done. Remove trotters and keep liquid aside after sieving.

Slice one onion thinly and fry in 2 tablespoons of ghee. When they are gold in colour, add the following ingredients:

1 tsp ginger/garlic
2 tsp chilli powder (or less)
¼ cup yoghurt

Cook slowly till masalas are blended. Add trotters and liquid and cook for half an hour. Garnish with chopped dhunia and serve with lemon.

Carrot Soup

A handful of chicken pieces
6 carrots
1 onion
1 potato
2 cloves
¼ cup cream
2 sprigs mint or parsley
1 tsp salt
¼ tsp crushed pepper
½ tsp green pounded chillies
2 tblsp ghee
½ tsp slivered ginger
2 pieces tuj (cinnamon)
¼ tsp crushed jeera (cummin)

Peel, wash and grate carrots. Cube peeled potato. Slice onions.

Braise onions, slivered ginger and chicken bones in ghee till onions begin to change colour.

Now add carrots, potatoes and all the spices except the black crushed pepper. Braise till vegetables dry, then add 2 cups of water and cook till vegetables are done.

Mash chicken meat, carrots and potato fine then replace puree in pot. Adjust liquid if too thick.

Reheat soup, pour into serving casserole and pour cream on top. Do not stir in — garnish with mint.

(Paya) Trotters

Clean trotters very carefully by immersing in boiling water and scrubbing with salt and mealie-meal till absolutely no trace of skin or hair is visible. It is much more hygienic and easier to rip off outer skin from trotters.

2 tblsp oil
½ dozen trotters
½ cup chana dhal
2 tblsp barley (optional)
1 medium onion
1 tsp ginger/garlic
1 tsp salt
3 whole green chillies
1 tsp red chillies
½ tsp gharum masala
2 pieces tuj (cinnamon)
Few whole elachi, cloves and peppers.
Chopped dhunia and shallot.
2 tblsp ghee

Fry sliced onion in oil till a pale golden colour.

Add washed and cleaned trotters together with the masalas and dhal. Braise till masala well coated on trotters, then add water to fill the deep pot.

Continue to boil gently till soup is thick and trotters well cooked (a pressure cooker spares hours of time in cooking trotters).

When trotters reach the consistency of thick broth, make a vagaar with ghee and fry a few slices of onion with a teaspoon of Jeero in it. Pour over pot and close lid tightly. add gharum masala, and just before serving garnish with chopped greens.

Serve with slices of lemon, chutneys and rotis.

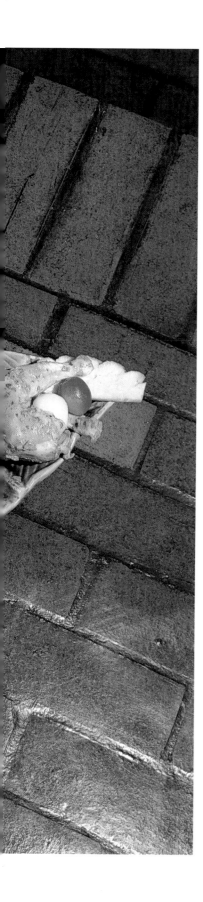

Cashew Nut Soup

(COLOUR PLATE OPPOSITE)

1 chicken (cut in small pieces)
2 bunches dhunia (coriander)
salt to taste
1 ball garlic (or less if preferred)
2 onions (chopped)
1 litre or more water
4 green chillies
1-1½ cups cashew nuts
2 tblsp ghee
2 tblsp oats
If available, also a handful of fresh garlic tops

Braise chicken and onions slowly in pot.

As you will not be using the fats just yet, you will have to keep on stirring to prevent the meat from catching.

When moisture from chicken and onions have evaporated, add the ghee and braise till the chicken begins to brown.

Add oats and salt and braise till ghee is absorbed.

Meanwhile blend fine the green chillies, garlic, nuts and dhunia.

Take out 3 tablespoons of this chutney and add the rest to the pot with the chicken.

Add water and cook till meat is tender.

Just before serving, add the remaining chutney to pot, infuse just once and serve immediately, garnishing with either the garlic tops or mint leaves. This is a very lovely green coloured soup.

Care must be taken in choosing fresh dhunia and seeing that at no stage do the contents turn brown for then the colour will be affected.

VARIATIONS:

1. Use half cashew and half peanuts.
2. After chicken is tender, take out chicken, flake off meat from bones and liquidise the meat with the nuts.

A Cashew nut soup (59)
B Kuri pulya achar (260)
C Cornish chickens or pigeon recipe (83)

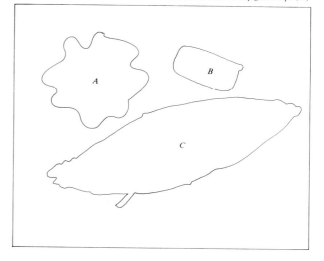

Malabari Soup

(VEGETARIAN)

1 cup cooked rice
1 tbsp slivered ginger/garlic
4 tsp methi seeds (fenugreek)
8 cups water
8 pepper corns
4 whole cloves
1 cup toovar dhal (oil dhal)
1 tbsp oil
½ coconut (extract milk, see pg 66)
4 red chillies
1 tsp jeera (cummin)
salt to taste
1 stick cinnamon
2 onions (sliced)
sprig curry leaves
1 tbsp ghee
1 lemon

Sauté onions in ghee/oil. Add washed dhal and fry till they are shiny. Add slivered ginger/garlic, curry leaves and all the other spices and braise for a minute longer.

Add water and cook till dhal is soft and mushy. Add coconut milk and juice of a lemon and the boiled rice. Infuse well.

Serve hot.

Almond Soup

250 g chicken (some bone & some meat pieces)
2 tbsp slivered ginger
2 oz butter or ghee
4 tbsp flour
1½ cups almonds (blanched and liquidised with milk or water
1 cup cream
salt
2 onions (chopped coarsely)
3 or 4 carrots
1 chopped tomato
black crushed pepper
2 green chillies (slit)

Put slit chillies, salt, ginger, chicken and vegetables in a large pot with cold water. Bring to boil and simmer for two hours. Strain through sieve and return strained liquid to pot. Slice off meat from bones and put in liquidiser with vegetable.

Return this puree to pot, but not the bones. Braise flour in butter and when it bubbles and an aroma arises add it to the pot taking care the flour paste is smooth and not lumpy. Allow pot to simmer gently. Just before serving-add pureed almonds and cream and stir into soup.
CAUTION: Do not allow soup to cook after almond and cream have been added. Add a grating of black crushed pepper and serve hot.

Chicken/Almond Soup

1 cup blanched almonds
1 cup milk
breast meat of one chicken
4 cups water
1 level tsp white pepper
1 onion (sliced)
1 tsp flour
1 tblsp ghee
1 tsp salt
pinch of elachi powder

Liquidise almonds in milk and keep aside. Wash and cut chicken breasts in large pieces. Braise meat with spices and onion in ghee. When onions sauted add water and cook till meat tender.

Cool soup, then blend chicken pieces with some of liquid till it is pureed. Return puree to pot and simmer. Braise flour in a teaspoon of ghee and when it begins to brown add sufficient water (few drops at a time to prevent lumping) to form a thin and smooth paste.

Add to pot of simmering soup. Just before serving add almond/milk mixture. Allow to come to boil and serve immediately with croutons, puris or toast.

OR

Cut rotis in small squares and in a tablespoon or two of ghee fry till crisp. Serve these with soup.

Onion Soup

2 large onions (sliced)
½ tsp jeera (cummin)
½ tsp pepper
4 cups water
¼ tsp slivered garlic
salt to taste
1 tblsp ghee

Put all ingredients in pot and simmer till liquid has been reduced by a third.

When cool, blend fine in liquidizer.

Heat again and serve piping hot with roti squares fried in ghee or bread croutons. (See above).

Nihari

(COLOUR PHOTO 189)

½ kg leg mutton (shin bone with meat)
2 onions (half grated, half sliced)
1 tsp ginger/garlic
1 tsp slivered ginger
1 tsp slivered garlic
1 tsp chilli
*2 tsp cummin seeds
*1 tsp coriander seeds
*5 each of whole cloves and peppers
1 slice stale bread
2 tbsp oil
2 tbsp ghee
3 tbsp chana flour (gram)
*3 dry red chillies
1½ tsp salt
*1 tsp saumph (fennel)
*2 sticks cinnamon
*4 elachi
½ tsp turmeric (optional)

Cut meat in big pieces — wash and to it add salt, ground ginger/garlic, chilli powder and turmeric.

Fry grated onion, 1 stick cinnamon and slivered ginger and garlic in oil and when onions are a lovely golden brown add marinating meat to it. Braise for a few minutes then add tomato and allow to puree before adding 2 litres of water. Keep pot simmering.

Braise sliced onions in the ghee and when they turn a light gold colour remove from oil and keep aside. Let ghee cool down then add the chana flour to it and braise slowly till it begins to change pinkish in colour. Add a little water and break down lumps then add this paste to Nihari pot, and stir well to mix in.

MAKE GHARUM MASALA THUS:

Roast over hot tava or in oven the ingredients marked with asterisk.

Remove red chillies as soon as they turn brown and add to pot of Nihari. Pound the other ingredients fine after they are roasted brown. Add half of this to pot and continue boiling till meat flakes off from bone.

Now add the bread cut in cubes and place inside pot. Just before serving add the rest of the gharum masala. Serve piping hot with naan, and little bowls containing chopped spring onions finely choped green chillies in vinegar, wedges of lemon and fried onion that was kept aside.

NIHARI is no soup. It is a tradition in Pakistan especially in the old city of Lahore. The mystique built around it is bound to arouse the curiosity of the uninitiated. Said to have been invented by the cooks in the kitchen of the Mughals to unblock their royal noses when suffering from colds, to this day professional male cooks are reluctant to part with recipes that have been handed down to them by their ancestors. So they claim!

For females to taste genuine Nihari is like a battle of wits, especially in Karachi. The five star hotels just do not have nihari chefs, for these have evolved their own restaurants around their secret Nihari formulas, and gourmets fight for the reputation of their favourite off-street, alley-way Nihari houses. Alas! These are restaurants for males only, since the types of jokes and tales that make Nihari eating a pleasant experience, are not meant for female ears.

Your friends who know your interest in food, vie to take you to the outskirts of the restaurant. In an adjacent alley-way at a discreet distance they will park the car with the female occupants. The males make off to the restaurant itself and will cajole the chef/proprietor to send out a khooncha for the ladies. Professing reluctance, a male bearer will make his appearance. On the bonnet of the car he will leave the tray with the huge tureen and the bowls of accompaniments and naan surrounding it.

When your male escorts reappear beaming with enjoyment, they will declare that the product outside could just not taste like the one within the restaurant. All the mystique surrounding Nihari no doubt adds to the reputation of the dish.

Nihari

This Nihari recipe was given by a Pakistani Hakim (traditional medicine doctor) two generations ago.

1 kg shin with bone (mutton)
1 tblsp chilli powder
1 tblsp dhania powder (coriander)
3 tblsp flour
6 elachi (cardomom)
6 cloves
1 tsp jeera (cummin)
1 tsp saumph (fennel)
1 tsp ginger/garlic
Salt to taste
2 large onions
8 whole black peppers
2 sticks cinnamon
¼ nutmeg
½ tsp mace

After cutting off meat from shin bone, crack it open lengthwise.

Wash meat and bones and put in soup pot with chilli, dhania powder, ginger/garlic and salt.

Make a paste with flour and water and blend into pot. Add about 3 litres of water and cook till meat nearly done.

Grate onions and fry in 3 tblsp of ghee and add to pot. Roast lightly the rest of spices in oven or over griddle and pound fine and add to pot.

Simmer for another hour. Soup should be like thick cream.

Serve with chopped raw onion, dhunia leaves and lemon slices.

Invalid Chicken Soup

1 small chicken
2 pieces cinnamon
4 cloves
4 whole peppers
2 elachi
1 tsp slivered ginger
salt to taste
1 tbsp ghee

Heat spices in ghee and when ginger changes colour, add chicken (cut in small pieces) and braise slowly till meat is well braised. Add 2 litres of water and cook till half of water evaporates. Serve hot with toast.

Barley/Dahi Soup

¼ chicken or 250 g mutton cut in pieces
2 onions (sliced)
1 tblsp fresh chopped mint
2 tblsp chopped parsley
1 large tomato (pulverised)
2 green chillies (chopped)
½ cup barley
2 tblsp ghee
1 cup dahi (yoghurt)
Salt and pepper
Piece tuj, a few cloves and elachi
1 tsp slivered ginger

Saute onions in ghee till soft and transparent. Add chicken and spices and braise till chicken is nicely browned.

Add 6 cups of water and allow to simmer till liquid is reduced to 4 cups. Braise barley in a little butter and add tomato to it. After braising for a few minutes add to pot of chicken stock and simmer for an hour.

Beat dahi well with egg beater and add to pot. Add mint and half of parsley, adjust salt and pepper. Keep on stove over low heat till required. Just before serving garnish with left over parsley.

Chicken/Vegetable Soup

Neck, back and few other small chicken pieces
1 tblsp barley
1 cup peas (shelled)
2 tomatoes (grated)
2 potatoes
2 tblsp ghee
6 whole black pepper corns
1 turnip
3 carrots
1 cup green beans
2 tblsp chana or pea flour
Salt to taste
¼ tsp ginger/garlic

Clean, scrape and wash vegetables. Put them through mincer. Braise in ghee the meat spiced with the pepper, ginger/garlic and salt.

Stir meat several times, in order to brown well on all sides.

Add minced vegetables, barley and sufficient water to fill soup pot. Bring to boil and simmer for two hours. Just before serving, braise the chana flour in a little ghee and mix into soup. Garnish with spring onions, and serve piping hot.

Chicken/Corn Soup

1 chicken (cut in small bite-size pieces)
bones of 2 chickens (in addition to above)
3 cups grated corn (green mealies)
whites of 2 eggs
½ cup maizena (corn flour)
1 tsp black crushed pepper
1 tsp chinese salt (monosodium glutamate)
1 tsp soya sauce
1 tsp mustard powder
1 tsp sugar
1 tbsp margarine or butter

Prepare stock from 3-4 litres of water, bones of 2 chickens, salt, pepper, thinly sliced onion.

Strain after 4 hours of gentle simmering. (2-3 litres of liquid).

Mix corn flour with a little cold water and mix into simmering soup. Add all spices to soup.

Braise chicken pieces in butter and when browned, add to soup pot.

Beat 2 egg whites lightly and while still runny, pour in thin streams to pot of soup, allowing egg whites to form noodle-like strings.

Serve in individual bowls and allow diners to spice it with condiments consisting of:
bowl of soya sauce, salt, chopped chillies pickled in vinegar, red sauce.

TO MAKE RED SAUCE:
2 tbsp tomato sauce
2 tsp red chilli powder
1 tbsp vinegar
½ tsp sugar
salt
Mix together and serve with soup.

VARIATION:
Instead of grated corn, substitute boiled noodles in soup.

Mealie Soup Variation
(ECONOMICAL)

Prepare as above right but omit tinned cream and milk. Instead mix 1 tblsp maizena to mustard powder and make into paste with a little water. Add to soup. Simmer for 5 minutes before adding vagaar.

Mealie Soup (Deluxe)

Put in a soup pot:
2 breasts of chicken
2 sticks of cinnamon
2 elachi (cardomom)
2 cloves
6 whole peppers
1 grated onion
1 grated tomato
1 tsp ginger/garlic

Braise all above ingredients slowly and stir at regular intervals to prevent scorching. When contents nearly dry sprinkle salt and pepper and 1 grated potato. Add 2 litres hot water and simmer till meat is cooked. strain through sieve. Remove whole spices and liquidise the pulp. Return pureed products to liquid. Now add:

1 tin cream style corn
1 tin nestles cream
1 tin ideal milk

Return to stove, bring allow to boil then add ½ tsp mustard powder. Just before serving fry together and pour over soup:

2 tbsp ghee
½ tbsp sliced onion
2 green chillies (slit)
2 cloves garlic (slivered)

Chicken Breast Soup

250g chicken breast
1 tsp slivered garlic
1 stick cinnamon
a few whole peppers and cloves
½ sliced onion
½ tbsp ghee
1 medium tomato (optional)
2 cups milk
½ tbsp butter

Braise chopped breasts with salt, spices and ghee.

When meat is dry, add 1½ litres water and cook till tender. Before serving add 2 cups milk.

Allow to infuse just once. Add butter and grinding of black pepper. Garnish with greens and serve hot.

Dhal Soup

½ coconut (extract milk)
1 cup dhal, (oil, masoor or urad)
500g of finely cubed vegetables (potato, dodhi, peas, carrots etc.)
1 onion (grated)
2 green mangoes or green apples (chopped or cubed like vegetables)
1 tblsp lemon juice or tamarind (aamli)
1 tblsp oil
1 tblsp ghee
½ tsp chilli
2 green chillies (slit)
1 sprig kurri leaves
1 tsp crushed cummin (jeera)
2 tsps crushed dhunia seeds (coriander)
1 stick cinnamon
3 elachi and a few whole peppercorns
Salt to taste

Soak dhal overnight, wash off skins and cook in salted water till mushy.

Fry cubed vegetables and fruit in oil for a minute then remove from pot. Add ghee to pot and fry curry leaves, cinnamon, elachi and whole peppercorns. Just as onion begins to change colour, add spices, mushy dhal and aamli, and braise for a few minutes. Now add water and allow pot to come to boil — add veg and fruit and simmer 15 to 20 minutes.

Add coconut milk and serve hot with rice or naan and papad.

Soup should be consistency of thin porridge.

Khowse

Khowse is a traditional Burmese dish which for many years has been incorporated into Indian cooking. It is served in the manner (as illustrated in photographs) with the large bowl of the actual soup in the middle of the tray, and surrounded by its accompaniments. The idea is that the guest takes as much of the soup as required on to her soup plate, and flavours, embellishes and garnishes it with the accompaniments as preferred. The result is fascinating.

Khowse Soup

(SERVES 10-12 PERSONS)

1 chicken (1 kg)
2 medium sized onions
1 small tomato (grated)
2 coconuts (fresh)
1 piece tuj (cinnamon)
2 tblsp oil
2 tblsp ghee or oil
3 cardamoms (elachi)
¼ tsp turmeric (haldi)
1 tsp dhunia/jeero
1 tsp red chilli (pounded)
1 tsp salt
1 tsp ginger/garlic

Braise onions in oil, till pink in colour. Add ginger/-garlic, braise for one minute and add chicken (washed and cut in convenient pieces) the tomato and rest of spices. Let is simmer over low heat till masala is well coated over meat. Meanwhile extract coconut milk (see page 66).

When meat is done add the coconut milk and as much more water as is required (each time pouring water over the coconut that was strained off, then using it) to make a thin soup.

Each guest will add to her bowl of soup, some green leaves, garlic, dash of lemon, pinch of chilli powder, 2 tablespoons of spaghetti, and finally, a liberal sprinkling of the delicious Pur. (See page 66).

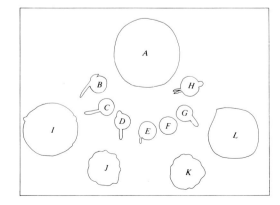

A — Khowse soup
B-H — Small bowls of spices, garlic, chillies etc.
I — Khowse pur
J — Crisp fried vermicelli
K — Boiled noodles

Khowse Accompaniments

In separate bowls surrounding soup serve:
    2 cups spaghetti (broken in pieces. Boil in salted water and serve hot)
    Khowse pur (see below).
    Little bowls of chopped dhunia and shallot.
    Little bowls of dry chilli powder.
    Little bowls of slivered garlic fried in oil to light pink colour.
    Slices of lemons.
    Little bowls of crisply fried onion.

Khowse Pur

2 cups flour
¼ tsp salt
2 dessertspoonful ghee
    Knead above ingredients into stiff dough with a little cold water. Roll out on floured board to very thin roti. Cut off 7cm strips (width of macaroni or noodles) and fry in oil over low heat to a pale golden colour. Drain off in colander and allow to cool. Serve separately with khowse and other accompaniments.

Vegetable Soup

1 tomato
1 medium onion
1 whole green chilli
2 teaspoons ghee/oil
1 teaspoon salt
1 teaspoon ginger/garlic
1 to 2 cups of diced vegetables
¼ tsp turmeric
¼ tsp pepper
1 stick cinnamon
A few cardomoms
Peppers and cloves
¼ tsp dry chilli powder
    Slice onions and braise in pot with ghee till light golden brown. Add spices and vegetables and cook for an hour or longer. When vegetables are cooked, strain liquid off. Put vegetables through wire sieve till it is well mashed and add again to the liquid. The soup will be creamy and rich. Just before serving garnish with dhunia or parsley.

    Serve with croutons, or bread, or toast.
    In last half-an-hour of cooking, add half a cup of noodles or vermicelli broken in small pieces. Children just adore the various shapes of noodles that are available on the market.

Coconut Cream

    All along the coasts of India in Malabar, Goa, Kokan etc., coconuts grow profusely.
    The inhabitants have discovered that the additon of coconut cream transforms a curry, elevating it from the ordinary into a highly exotic concoction. Like yoghurt and cream it also makes the curry more bland.
    When coconuts are cheap and plentiful, stock up on coconut cream and freeze it for future use.
    Although we give you a few basic recipes, try any of your masala fish, prawn, kalya and kurma recipes and add coconut cream to it. You will be amazed at the difference!

METHOD:
    Dehusk fresh coconuts and scrape off the dark filament from the white flesh. Wash and grate the coconut. Steep in water.
    Put into blender with just sufficient water to allow for liquidizing. When well pureed, push through sieve and squeeze out all the thick white liquid. This is the coconut cream.
    A second and third extraction can be made with the same coconut, but it will yield less, and thinner cream.
    Freeze in ice trays for future use. By steeping grated coconut in boiling water and liquidizing them when cool, yields more cream.
    If fresh coconut is not available use dessicated coconut.
    Freshly grated coconut keeps very well in the freezer.

Crispy Noodles

    Boil noodles in 2 cups water to which has been added a teaspoon each of chillie powder and salt for 15 minutes.
    Drain in colander under cold water.
    Taking small quantities at a time, fry noodles in hot oil till they are crisp.
    This is delicious with soup — allow guests to sprinkle noodles over their own bowl of soup.

Variation to Khowse

    When meat is done remove from pot and flake off some of the meat from the bones. Puree this meat in some of the coconut-milk liquid and return both meat and bones to pot. This makes a thicker soup.

Green Pea Soup

250 g of soup bones
2 cup dry split peas (soaked in cold water overnight)
1 medium sized onion
½ tsp ginger/garlic
2 tsp salt
6 small pickling onions
1 tsp dhunia/jeero powder
2 tblsp yoghurt (optional)
2 crushed green chillies (1 tsp)
¼ tsp ground pepper
1 stick cinnamon
2 cardamons (elachi)
1 tomato (green)
2 tblsp ghee/oil
1 tsp gharum masala
A few peppers and cloves

Slice onions and braise in ghee/oil till light brown. Add washed meat with spices and braise till masala nicely coated over bones; add the tomato. Braise till tomato is blended then add the dried split peas. Braise a few minutes, then fill pot with boiling water and cook slowly till peas are mushy. (Two to three hours). Add pickling onions. Add yoghurt, mixed with 2 tblsp of water or milk. Soup should be a consistency of cream soup. Just before serving braise a few pieces of onion in a little ghee and pour over. Garnish with green shallot and dhunia and add the gharum masala.

Chicken Soup

1 small chicken cut in small pieces
1 medium onion
1 piece fresh root ginger
2 cloves of garlic
1 stick tuj (cinnamon)
1 green chilly (optional)
¼ tsp fine pepper
A few whole elachi, peppers and cloves.
2 tblsp ghee/oil
¼ cup tomato (optional)

Slice onion fine, sliver ginger and garlic fine, braise all together in ghee/oil till a pale gold colour. Add chicken with all the spices and braise till masala is well coated over meat. Add tomato, simmer till absorbed and blended then fill pot with water and cook till meat is done and soup is the consistency of thin cream.

Garnish with greens. Serve with toast.

VARIATIONS:

(1) Add with spices one large potato or 2 carrots and allow to mash fine. Makes for a thicker soup.

(2) For thickening add ¼ cup of oatmeal.

(3) Half a cup of fresh green peas or other suitable vegetables mashed in.

(4) Half cup of either barley, or small spaghetti pieces. (Fancy varicties obtainable in stores are most attractive.)

(5) Half cup of cooked left over rice.

(6) Add ¼ cup of oats to thicken soup.

(7) Mash half a cup of fresh green peas or carrots or any cooked vegetable.

(8) Add ½ cup of half-cooked rice (left-over rice is excellent).

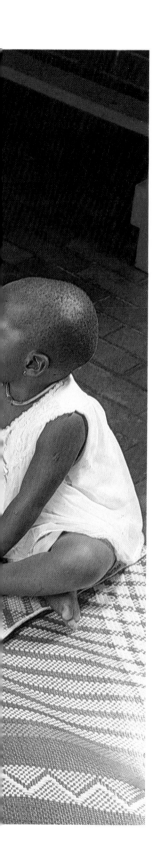

Etiquette

(COMMUNAL EATING)

Alas, communal eating platters are a thing of the past. With the family eating from one large round tray (khooncha) there was little washing up to do after the meal. But khooncha eating calls for great restraint and discipline in eating habits. Growing children, hard-working men, pregnant or ailing or breast-feeding mothers, these get the choice morsels. No one steps beyond his or her allocated position so when more food is required then one unobtrusively draws from the centre towards one's allocated position. Young children have to be coaxed into the art of eating and appreciating food and this task is best left to granny who has untold patience with children. Here she is initiating Faeeza and her young playmate Nandi, to savour the food and she tells lovely stories of *challa* and *challi* to retain their interest. Have you heard it?

Papa bird and Mama bird had a nest with birdlings. One day papa bird was late returning home and the little birdies started to cry from the pangs of hunger so mama bird went out in search of him. She had the rice and curry all ready, the papad was toasted and there was cool spring water in the halves of broken egg shells to quench their thirst. Before starting to eat, she went out to look for papa bird when just then a naughty uncle bird came by and when he saw the nest untended by adult birds, he swooped down on the food and gobbled it all up. "Quick now, quick now, let us start eating our food before uncle bird comes and gobbles down our food."

1. Gosht Dhal (70)
2. Brinjal Fry (42)
3. Rice
4. Potato Crisps (42)
5. Dodhi Fry (42)
6. Onion/tom Kachumbar (281)
7. Lemon Achar (271)
8. Carrot Achar (269)

Serva Curry (Gravy Curry)

To be eaten with Rotis or served with rice dishes.

500 g meat (chicken or mutton cut in convenient pieces)
2-3 onions
¼ cup oil
1 tsp turmeric
*2 elachi (cardomom)
*A few cloves and peppers
1 tsp red chillies (powder or fresh pounded)
*1 tsp ginger/garlic
*1 tsp salt
1 tsp dhunia/jeero
1 piece tuj (cinnamon)
2 tomatoes (chopped)
6 small potatoes (or large ones halved or quartered).
(For very thick gravy add 1 small brinjal peeled and cut fine and add it to curry with spices.)

Wash and drain meat. Slice onions finely and fry half of above quantity in oil, till pale golden colour. Add the meat to which has been added the spices marked with an asterisk and if desired the brinjal (but this is optional) and the rest of the raw onions. Add ½ cup water and simmer till masala is well coated over meat.

Add tomato and rest of spices and allow to simmer again till tomato is well absorbed and pureed in gravy; add potatoes and cook a few minutes. Now add 2 cups or more of water and cook till meat and potatoes are done. Just before serving, add half teaspoon gharum masala and 2 tablespoons of chopped dhunia leaves and if liked a little chopped shallot. Stir the masala in the gravy and serve hot with rotis or rice.

Note:
1 tsp dhunia/Jeero = ²/₃ tsp coriander power and ¹/₃ tsp cummin powder.

Gosht Dhal
(MEAT LENTILS) (PHOTO PAGE 69)

250 g mutton or chicken
1½ cup oil dhal
¼ cup masoor (black lentil)
1 tblsp chana dhal (gram)
1 tsp salt
1 tsp ginger and garlic
1 tsp dhunia and jeero
1 tsp arad (turmeric)
1 tsp red chillies
1 medium onion
½ cup tomato (one)
2 pieces tuj (cinnamon)
1/3 cup oil
2 elachi (cardomom)
¼ cup dhunia leaves and shallot (chopped)

Braise jeero and onions in ghee/oil till pale gold colour. Add masalas and meat and braise well. Then add tomato and allow to blend in. Then add washed dhals and braise a little longer. Fill pot with water and simmer slowly till meat and dhals done. With egg beater, whisk pot of dhal till it is of even consistency. But do not take off all the meat from the bones.

Now make vagaar thus:-

2 tblsp ghee
A few rings of onions
2 red whole chillies
1 tsp jeero (cummin)
½ tsp whole mustard seed
1 tsp slivered garlic

Braise the spices in ghee till onion is lovely gold colour. Add to pot of dhal and close lid tightly.

Add gharum masala. Just before serving, add chopped greens. Dhal is served with Chana Dhal Pilaau, Gosht Pilaau or Plain White Rice. Also eaten with roti or bread.

Chicken Dhal with Pumpkin

(PARSEE DHAN-SAAK)
(6-8 SERVINGS)

1 medium chicken
1 cup toovar dhal (oil)
1 potato
2 tomatoes
1 bunch methi bhaji (fenugreek)
1 piece cinnamon
½ tsp turmeric
½ tsp pepper
2 onions
8-10 mint leaves
1½ tsp salt
7-8 green chillies
1 bunch dhunia leaves
 5 cloves of garlic (pounded)
1 piece pumpkin
1 piece ginger (pounded)
1 tsp jeero (cummin)
1½ tsp dhunia/jeero
½ tsp chilli powder
1 tbls ghee
3 tblsp oil

Cut chicken into small pieces. Wash and drain. Grind together the ginger and garlic. Pound together dhunia leaves, chillies, jeero and cinnamon. Cut the pumpkin (peeled), potato, tomatoes and onions in medium sized pieces. Clean and wash the bhaji and mint and then chop up.

Wash dhal well and put in saucepan with 7 cups of water. Add the salt as well as chopped bhaji and mint. When dhal is nearly cooked add chicken with the ginger/garlic. When chicken is tender add the pounded masala as well as the remaining masalas, and the ghee and oil.

Let simmer over medium heat till the dhal is of required consistency. Remove chicken pieces and whisk dhal with an egg beater till it is smooth. Put back chicken and pour over the following vagaar:-

In 1½ tablespoon of ghee fry 2 cloves of garlic, 1 chopped green chilli and half teaspoon jeero. Serve with rice.

Vegetable/Lentil Dhal

2 tomatoes
2 carrots
2 limes
1 tblsp ghee
1 tsp methi seeds
1 small whole onion
1 tsp dhunia/jeero
1 tblsp rice
½ cup oil dhal (oil lentil)
1 coconut (extract milk)
1 sprig curry leaves
½ tsp ginger/garlic
1 sliced onion
¼ tsp turmeric
½ tsp saunmf (fennel)
1 tsp fresh powdered red chilli

Wash lentils and rice and put in pot with 1 litre of water and cook till mushy. Add chopped tomatoes, scraped carrots, whole onion, salt and rest of masalas excepting the saunmf. Simmer till vegetables are done. Pass through wire strainer.

Extract milk from coconut (see page 66) and add to pot of dhal. Add lemon juice and simmer slowly over low heat. Roast saunmf on hot tava and crush. Fry sliced onion in ghee and just as it begins to turn pink add the saunmf, braise for a second then pour over dhal. Do not stir the ghee and onions in the dhal but allow them to nestle on top. If you are serving the dhal in a heat-proof casserole then pour the vagaar directly into the serving dish. Serve with rice or with rotis.

Moong Dhal

(MOONG LENTIL)

1 cup moong dhal soaked in water for a few hours
3 green pounded chillies
2 onions (medium)
1 tsp salt
¼ tsp arad
½ tsp ginger/garlic
½ tsp dhunia/jeero
½ cup oil

Wash moong dhal till all loose skin is removed. Drain off water. Put dhal in pot with raw sliced onions, all the masalas and oil and cook very slowly till dhal is soft and nicely browned. Care must be taken that there is just enough water to cook dhal otherwise dhal will be soggy. Garnish with chopped spring onions.

VARIATION:
Ingredients as above.

¼ cup tomato (add to pot of dhal)

There are many ways of disguising left over foods and serving them again at the table. The enterprising hostess will discover many of the methods as she gains cooking experience. Meanwhile here is a traditional recipe of serving left over dhal in a delicious way.

Chikolyo
(MADE WITH LEFT OVER DHAL)

1 litre of left over dhal curry
Left over samoosa pur (fried)
2 tblsp of chopped greens
2 tblsp of ghee/oil
¼ sliced onion

Boil left over dhal after adding ½ cup of water and make a vagaar of a few slices of onion in ghee and pour over. Just before serving add slightly crushed samoosa pur over top with the chopped greens. Serve immediately in bowls with lemons, chutneys, etc. Any left over rice should be added to pot of Chikolyo. For samoosa pur see page 185.

Chikolian
(6-8 SERVINGS)

2 rotlas (or rotis which have been rolled and braised without ghee)
250 g mutton (optional)
1 tsp ginger/garlic
2 tomatoes (grated)
1 tsp dhunia/jeero
1 tsp red chilli powder
½ tsp turmeric
½ tsp jeero seeds (cummin)
1 cup toovar dhal (oil lentil)
3 lemons
A stick of cinnamon, few peppercorns, and cloves
2 onions (sliced)
½ bunch dhunia (coriander)
½ cup green peas
½ cup green beans (cut up)
4 green chillies
½ cup oil
Salt to taste
4 cloves of garlic (slivered)
3 medium potatoes (diced)

Marinate mutton in ginger/garlic, salt, chilli powder, dhunia/jeero and turmeric. Fry onions (keeping aside a handful) in oil and when they are a gold colour add the mutton and braise till masala and meat is browned. Add grated tomatoes and simmer pot with lid closed till the moisture has evaporated. Add 2 cups of water and keep pot simmering, till meat done.

Add vegetables to pot of meat. Boil dhal separately in water till soft and mushy. Mash fine and add to pot with meat and simmer till contents of pot is tender. Break rotis in small pieces and soak in water to which has been added the juice of a lemon and add to pot. Make a vagaar with a tablespoon of ghee, left-over onion, jeero seeds and slivered garlic and add to pot. Add gharum masala, and greens and serve hot with slices of lemon.

Vegetarian Dhal
(LENTILS)
(8 PERSONS)

2 cups oil dhal (or 1½ cups oil dhal, ½ cup masoor, 2 tblsp chana dhal)
1 onion
¼ tsp jeero (cummin)
¼ cup oil
1 tsp salt
1 tsp ginger/garlic
1 tsp dhunia/jeero
1 tsp arad (turmeric)
1 tsp chillies
½ cup tomatoes
2 pieces tuj (cinnamon)
2 whole elachi and a few cloves
¼ cup dhunia and shallot (chopped)
¾ tsp jeero (cummin)

Boil dhal in salted water till tender. Sieve through wire sieve or beat with egg beater. Meanwhile proceed thus:

Braise jeero and onions in ghee/oil till pale gold colour. Add tomato with all the other spices and simmer till even consistency. Add the strained dhal to this chutney. Simmer till it is of thickness required then add 1 teaspoon gharum masala.

Serve with rotis or rice.

Dhal with Vegetables

1 cup split masoor (pink lentils)
2 tsp coriander seeds (dhunia)
4 red dry chillies
2 tsp chana dhal (gram)
¼ fresh coconut (grated)
1 sprig curry leaves
¼ tsp turmeric powder (arad)
2 tbsp oil
1 litre water
1 tsp mustard seeds
1 tsp methi seeds (fenugreek)
1 tsp jeera seeds (cummin)
1 brinjal (cut in small cubes)
6 baby onions (peeled)
1 cup drumstick pieces (optional)
½ cup green beans (cut in small lengths)
salt to taste
2 tbsp tamarind pulp (aamli)

Roast coriander seeds, chillies and chana dhal on tava (thick pan) or in oven till they begin to brown.

Add coconut and allow to roast till it begins to tan in colour. Crush these ingredients together.

Boil lentils in salted water till soft and mushy. Fry mustard and methi in oil and when they stop spluttering, add the baby onions and washed, cut vegetables to it.

Fry vegetables for a minute and when they become shiny, add the tamarind pulp, the ground masalas and cook for a minute.

Now add this to pot of mushy dhal. Mix well. Simmer for 10 or 15 minutes.

Soup should be consistency of thick cream. Serve hot with rice and papads.

Urad Dhal
(LENTIL BROTH) VARIATION

1 cup urad dhal
¼ cup oil
½ tsp slivered ginger
2 sliced onions

Wash dhal. Boil in 3 cups water with salt and ginger. Cook till dhal is soft, but not mushy. Drain off excess water.

Fry onions in oil till gold in colour.

Put dhal in serving bowl and pour hot oil and onions over the surface of the dhal.

Sprinkle with chopped-up greens and serve with rotlas or parathas.

NOTE: In small bowls, chilli powder and crushed pepper may be served, in which case each diner will put a pinch of each into his or her bowl of dhal.

Urad Dhal
(SPLIT BLACK BEANS)

1 cup dhal (urad)
1 tsp salt
1 tsp dhunia/jeero
½ cup yoghurt
1 tblsp chana dhal
¼ tsp turmeric
½ tsp ground garlic
2 tblsp ghee

Soak dhal in water for few hours. Wash off skins. Boil with a little water till dhal is soft and mushy. Beat dhal with an egg beater till it is smooth. To dhal add the spices and the well beaten yoghurt, and keep over low heat on stove still required. Serve dhal piping hot in little bowls and with it serve the ghee which has been heated. Allow the diners to pour a teaspoon or two of ghee over the dhal in their bowls. Served with rotlas and Bombay duck this can be a real treat.

Moong Dhal Broth

1 cup moong dhal
1 onion
tsp red chilli powder
¾ tsp dhunia/jeero
2 tblsp oil
1 tsp salt
1 medium tomato
¼ tsp turmeric
1 tsp ginger/garlic (slivered)

Braise ginger and garlic in oil and just as they begin to change colour add dhal, coarsely chopped onion, tomato and spices. Cook till dhal is soft and mushy. Add sufficient water to bring dhal to consistency of kheer (milk pudding). Garnish with dhunia. Serve this dhal in individual soup bowls and serve a ghee vagaar with it thus: In 2 table-spoons of ghee make a vagaar with a few onion slices. Serve this in a separate bowl on the tray with the bowls of moong dhal and allow each diner to pour a teaspoon of the vagaar over his bowl of broth. Papads go well with this.

SECTION 2A

Kurmas & Kalyas

(EXOTIC DRY CURRIES)

NOTE:
We have inserted dry meat dishes, roasts, fried meats and grills in our curry section, as at the table these will be served immediately after the soup or entree. The other proper tarkaris follow these dishes, and therefore we have included them in that order.

A — Mutton in milk (86)
B — Chicken Tukras Lagan (80)
C — Mince Khowse Lagan (112)
D — Frikkadel (96)
E — Apricot/Almond Chutney (277)
F — Mash Potato

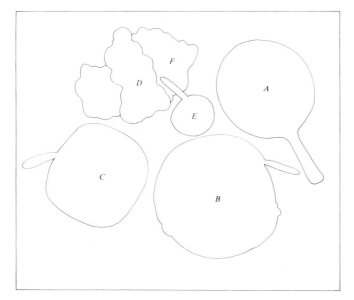

Kalya E Khaas
(TRADITIONAL KALYA)

1 chicken (1-1½ kg)
½ cup dahi (yoghurt)
2 medium onions (sliced very finely)
1 cup tomato (grated)
1 stick cinnamon
3 elachi (cardomom)
A few cloves and peppers
½ tsp whole jeero (cummin)
3-4 whole green chillies
¼ tsp saffron
¼ tsp turmeric (arad)
1 tsp chillies
1 tsp ginger/garlic
1 tsp salt
½ cup ghee/oil

Disjoint chicken. Wash and drain dry in colander. Add all the spices and salt. Mix well, now add the tomatoes, dahi and the whole green chillies. Let marinate, meanwhile:

Fry the onions in ghee/oil till they are a beautiful light brown; remove from oil and allow to cool. Crush the crisp onions with the back of a spoon and sprinkle over the marinating chicken.

Put the spiced meat in a pot with the oil in which the onions were fried, and cook slowly till juices evaporated and meat tender. A few whole prunes added at the last ten minutes of cooking, or a dozen whole blanched almonds, or both, if preferred, makes it really into an exotic Kalya.

If potatoes are to be cooked with the kalya, then they must be browned first in oil and added during the last half an hour of cooking. Garnish with some dhunia and mint leaves before serving.

Mutton may be used for above Kalya, but add another teaspoon of ginger/garlic and ½ cup of yoghurt.

Butter Chicken Breasts

1 kg breasts of chicken
juice of 1 lemon
2 tblsp butter
½ tsp crushed jeera (cummin)
1 tsp green pounded chilli
1 tsp salt
rind of lemon (1 tsp)
½ tsp freshly ground pepper
1 tsp crushed garlic

Mix salt, chilli, rind and cummin into juice and marinate for few hours. Thread skewer with meat alternating with baby onion, whole pepper, mushrooms (optional).

Grill over fire basting with butter or ghee.

Murghi Kalya
(VARIATION)

1 chicken (1-1½kg)
2 onions
1 tsp pounded green chillies
½ cup dahi (sour milk curds)
1 tsp red chilli powder
½ lemon (juice)
1 tsp salt
1 cup tomato or ½ cup puree
¼ tsp saffron powder (optional)
5 whole almonds (blanched and pounded)
2 square inch pieces of coconut
1 tsp ginger/garlic

Disjoint and wash chicken and drain in colander.

Grind or pound together the green chillies, fresh coconut and almonds. Add to this the rest of spices. Fry finely sliced onions in ½ cup of ghee/oil to a golden brown colour. Remove from ghee and cool. Crush these coarsely with back of spoon and add to spices. Now add the dahi, lemon juice and tomato pulp. Mix thoroughly together and marinate the chicken in this masala for at least 30 minutes. Cook slowly in ghee in which onions were fried till chicken is tender.

NOTE:
Instead of dahi, substitute 1 cup of coconut milk extracted from fresh coconut milk. (See page 66)

Pepper Kalya E Khaas

Omit red chilli from recipe — instead add ½ tsp ground pepper — thereafter proceed as above.

Roast Chicken No. 1

1 chicken (1-1½ kg weight)
4 potatoes (as many small sections of potatoes as required)
1 tblsp dhunia seeds (coriander)
Handful of whole blanched almonds
1 tsp red chillies, whole tuj, elachi, cloves and peppers
1 medium onion
¼ tsp fine saffron
2 green chillies (whole)
½ cup ghee/oil
½ tblsp whole jeero (cummin)
1½ tblsp ginger/garlic
1 tsp salt
½ cup bread crumbs (fresh)
3 tblsp of aamli juice ((see glossary)
¼ cup tomato juice

Fry onions in a little oil (extra amount and not included above) to a pale golden colour and drain and cool. Crush with back of spoon and set aside. Soak breadcrumbs in tomato. Crush dhunia and jeero fairly coarsely. Fry potatoes a golden colour.

To ginger/garlic, add saffron, crushed jeero and dhunia, salt and red chillies. To half of this add the soaked breadcrumbs, aamli, fried onion and cut up green chillies. Stuff this mixture together with the whole almonds and one or two potatoes inside well cleaned and washed chicken. Smear rest of masala on outside of chicken making gashes in the thicker meaty parts. In large flat pot, heat ghee with the remaining chilli, tuj, elachi, etc.; and place chicken carefully and brown it well on all sides. Add about ½ cup water and steam gently or bake in oven whichever is preferred. Fifteen minutes before chicken is done add potatoes and cook till all well done.

Roast Chicken No. 2

(WITH MINCE) (PHOTO PG 52)

1 chicken (1-1½ kg weight)
125 g chicken mince (taken from breasts of another chicken)
2 eggs (hard boiled)
3 small potatoes (halved)
1 tomato
3 prunes
1 piece tuj (cinnamon)
3 elachi (cardomom)
2 tblsp ghee
3 tblsp oil
4 tblsp sour milk (yoghurt)
1 onion
3 green chillies (whole)
¼ tsp powdered saffron (optional)
1 onion (finely chopped)
1 tsp fine red chillies
½ tsp turmeric (arad)
1 tsp salt
½ tsp dhunia/jeero powder
1½ tsp ginger/garlic

Fry potatoes in oil and when they begin to brown remove from oil.

Braise mince till dry. Add onion, braise for a few minutes, then add oil in which potatoes were fried. When mince darkens add grated tomato, salt and spices. Cook for a minute or two then add yoghurt and saffron (previously steeped in a tablespoon of boiling water).

Place shelled eggs, prunes and potatoes in Khima and stir/cook for a while. Stuff chicken with potatoes, prunes, eggs and half of mince.

To remaining mince add a tablespoon of flour and a little water. Mix well then smear this outside of chicken.

Put ghee in casserole and slowly braise chicken till it is nicely tanned, on all sides. Add ¼ cup of water, close lid and steam/fry till chicken is cooked.

Chicken Ashrafi

1 chicken (disjointed)
1 tbsp ghee
1½ tbsp lemon juice
½ tsp turmeric
¼ tsp pepper
1 tsp ginger/garlic
1 tsp green chilli
1 tsp crushed red chilly
1 tsp salt
¼ tsp elachi powder (cardomom)
* 2 tblsp tomato puree
* 2 tblsp ghee
* ¼ tsp chilli
* good pinch salt

Melt ghee in pot and add ginger/garlic and green chillies and braise. Remove from heat and add rest of ingredients.

Put chicken in this marinade and toss well to cover with masala. Leave for 2-3 hours. Place chicken and marinade in casserole.

Mix together 2 tbsp of tomato puree and 2 tbsp of yoghurt. Sprinkle a little salt and chilly in it. Mix into marinating chicken.

Dot with a little ghee. Put over high heat for 2 minutes, then switch down and finish cooking over low heat. Potatoes, prunes or pineapples may be added.

Chicken Piyazi
(ONION — CHICKEN)

2 tbsp ghee
1 chicken (disjointed)
1 medium onion (boil soft and liquidise)
*1½ tsp green pounded chilli;
*1 tsp. ginger/garlic
A few whole peppers, cloves and a piece of cinnamon stick.
½ tsp pepper
¼ tsp powdered saffron
¼ tsp powdered elachi
3/8 cup yoghurt
braise together in ½ tbsp of ghee the ingredients marked with asterisk

Wash and pat dry the chicken pieces. Add pureed onion and braised ingredients to it. Marinate for 2 hours.

Steep saffron in 1 tbsp of boiling water for a minute. Mix into yoghurt and pour this over marinating chicken, with rest of spices and mix well together.

Heat 2 tbsp of ghee in casserole — add chicken marinade to it and simmer till done or bake in oven.

NOTE: Lamb may be cooked in above manner.

Irani Chicken

1 chicken (1½ - 2kg)
1 dsp poppy seeds (khus-khus)
1 cup dahi (yoghurt)
1½ tsp cummin seeds
*3 cloves, 1 stick cinnamon
*4 peppercorns
2 tsp crushed garlic
salt to taste
8 baby onions
10 prunes
1 cup mixed nuts (almonds, pistachios, cashew & peanuts)
2 onions (sliced)
2 tsp red chillies
1½ tsp coriander seeds
2 tblsp dessicated coconut (preferably freshly grated)
1/8 tsp saffron
1 tblsp ghee or margarine
1 tblsp oil

Disjoint chicken, wash and drain dry. Blanch almonds and pistachios and grind to paste with other nuts as well as the spices (excluding saffron) and coconut.

Blend in salt and yoghurt. Apply masala well to chicken pieces and marinate for an hour. Fry onions and spices marked with asterisk in pot and when they turn a pinkish/gold colour, arrange all chicken pieces in pot, taking care to scrape out all masala from marinating bowl to pot.

Close lid and simmer till nearly done.

Add peeled baby onions and prunes, cook about 10 minutes then finally just 5 minutes before serving, add saffron. (strands put over very low heat, crushed fine and blended into a tablespoon of milk).

This is a very rich curry, may be served with rice, vegetables or roti.

Chicken Satay
(SOSATIES)

1 kg chicken breast cut in cubes
2 tsp crushed garlic
½ tsp ground cummin (jeera)
½ tsp ground black pepper
1 tsp red pounded chilli
1 tblsp shelled peanuts
1 cube fresh coconut (5cm sq.)
juice of ½ lemon
1 small onion (grated)
2 tblsp oil

Pound coconut and peanuts fine — add all other ingredients (except chicken) and mix well.

Marinate chicken in the marinade for a few hours. Put on small skewers and braai (grill) over charcoal till meat is done. Serve with chutneys and lemon slices.

Badam/Kopra Murghi
(COCONUT CHICKEN)

1 chicken (1 kg)
2 tsp ginger/garlic
½ tsp jeero (cummin)
1 tsp khus-khus (poppy)
½ cup ghee/oil
60 g almonds (2 tblsp)
1 tsp salt
Juice of 1 lemon
½ cup fresh coconut
1 tblsp cream
2 tblsp pistachios (optional)
2 onions
1 piece tuj, a few whole cloves and elachi (pounded together)
3 green chillies (pounded)

Grind to fine paste the coconut, cloves, elachi, tuj, khus-khus, jeero and chillies. Add saffron, ginger-garlic and cream, mix well. Now add slivered almonds and pistachios.

Fry onions in ghee/oil to golden colour.

Cool and crush with back of spoon. Add rest of masala.

Marinate chicken pieces in masala for half an hour then put on stove and cook slowly till tender, or bake in oven.

A truly exotic dish.

Dried Apricot Chicken

1 chicken (1 kg)
1 large tomato (chopped)
1 tsp jeero (cummin)
2 green chillies
1½ tsp pounded garlic
1 dozen dried apricots (chopped)
2 large onions
1 tsp fresh pounded red chilly
1 tsp salt
3 tblsp oil/ghee
1 tblsp cream

Disjoint, wash and drain chicken. Fry sliced onions in oil till they are crisp. Add chicken previously smeared with a masala made of the garlic, salt, red chillies, and jeero. When nicely browned, blend apricot, cream and tomatoes together and simmer slowly till chicken tender. Garnish with strips of green chillies and sprigs of parsley.

Variation Almond/Murghi
(ALMOND CHICKEN)

1 chicken (disjointed)
1 tblsp ground almonds
2 tblsp dahi (yoghurt)
2 tblsp cream skimmed off from top of milk bottle
1 onion (medium)
8 small potatoes
1 tsp ginger/garlic
1 tsp green pounded chilli
2 grated tomatoes
3 tblsp ghee/oil
Salt to taste

Wash and drain chicken. Add spices and cream to chicken and marinate for an hour.

Braise sliced onions in ghee/oil till crisp and gold. Drain off oil. Cool onions and crush fine with back of spoon.

Fry potatoes in the oil in which onions were fried. When the potatoes are a pale gold colour, remove them from the oil.

Pour the oil over the marinating chicken. Add tomatoes and crushed onions. Mix well and arrange in casserole and bake till chicken cooked.

NOTE: The potatoes must be added when chicken is half done.

Chicken Chargas in Tomato Puree

Dissect chicken. Use legs, thighs and breasts only. Alternatively divide chicken in quarters. Wash and drain well. Prick well with fork or sharp skewer. Toss chicken well in one teaspoon of ginger/garlic and ¾ teaspoon of salt. Fry slowly in a small quantity of oil till browned.

Sauce:
1 kg tomatoes
½ tsp black crushed pepper
2 whole green chillies (slit)
2 small sticks cinnamon
2 elachi (bruised open)
1 tsp salt or more
2 tblsp lemon juice
1 tsp red chilly powder
½ tsp whole jeero
3 whole cloves

Skin tomatoes by plunging in boiling water and then immediately thereafter in cold water. Cool and mash. Add spices to tomato pulp and mix well. Place chicken in greased casserole and pour puree, carefully covering chicken pieces. Pour 2 tablespoons of oil over puree. Half submerge a dozen pickling onions in puree and bake in 180°c oven for 40 minutes.

Chicken Tukras Lagan
(CASSEROLE OF CHICKEN) (COLOUR PAGE 75)

1 chicken (1½ kg)
1½ tsp salt
2 tsp red chilli powder
1 tsp pounded garlic
1 tblsp oil
1 tblsp ghee
6 pieces potato
2 tblsp lemon juice
*1 dsp coarsely crushed coriander seeds
*1 tsp cummin seeds
*1 piece ginger (1 cm x 2 cm) cleaned, washed and
  slivered)

Disjoint chicken, wash and drain dry. Add all masalas except those marked with asterisk and toss around chicken portions till spices cover them evenly.

Heat oil in pot, fry potatoes in it till they begin to turn gold in colour.

Remove potatoes from oil and add spiced chicken to it. Fry chicken pieces, stirring and tossing them for a few minutes till they begin to brown.

Add ½ cup water, close lid and cook slowly until chicken is nearly done. Roast cummin and coriander seeds in thick frying pan.

Crush seeds when a lovely aroma arises. Add these and the slivered ginger to pot. Mix in well, taking care to toss over chicken carefully.

Now lift each chicken portion out of pot and arrange neatly in a glass or ovenproof dish, with the fried potatoes tucked in between meat pieces.

Decorate with 1 large tomato (50g) cut into wedges, a few green chillies slit lengthwise and wedges of a boiled egg.

Cover with foil and place in hot oven for 12-20 minutes. Serve immediately.

Easy Butter Chicken

1 chicken cut in pieces
½ tsp pepper
juice of ½ lemon
1½ tsp salt
2 tsp red chillies
¼ cup Butter

Melt butter and add all spices, and the lemon juice. Marinate chicken in this. Cook slowly on stove, or put in casserole and bake in oven till chicken is a lovely red colour.

Tanduri Chicken
(GRILLED CHICKEN FOR ROAST)

1 tender spring chicken (1 kg)
6 wedges of pineapple
Juice of 1 lemon
½ tsp pepper (fine)
2 tblsp oil
2 tblsp ghee
1¼ tsp green pounded chillies
1½ tsp ginger/garlic
¾ tsp fine salt
1 tsp coarsely crushed jeero (cummin)
1 tsp coriander seeds
2 tblsp cream

Split chicken in two equal halves (from neck down through centre between legs). Wash and drain dry. Mix ghee and oil together.

Make paste of spices mixed with cream, lemon juice and add about a tablespoon of oil to make it sticky. Smear chicken and let this marinate a few hours, then, place in deep pan and with lid closed bake in oven for half an hour. Remove lid, place pan directly under griller and pour a tablespoon of ghee/oil at 5 minute intervals over chicken and grill till moisture evaporated and chicken done.

Place wedges of pineapple amongst chicken and braise under griller for a few more minutes, and remove before pineapples lose colour. Serve immediately as there is a tendency for chicken to become too dry. Serve on large platter with sections of tomatoes and a few fried almonds.

Bhaigora's Chops

500g chops (trimmed) or disjointed chicken

MARINADE:
1 tsp ginger/garlic
½ tsp salt
½ tsp red pounded chillies
1 tsp dhunia/jeero
½ tsp turmeric (arad)
2 tblsp yoghurt
1/8 tsp saffron (optional)
½ cup oil

Wash and drain chops. Marinate in masala for 3 or 4 hours. Sprinkle with bread crumbs, dip in slightly beaten egg and fry over low heat. Put in oven with any left over masalas, cover with lid and steam for ½ hour.

NOTE:
If using mutton chops, select small lamb chops.

Chicken Chops

1 chicken (disjointed)
1 tsp dhunia/jeero
1½ tsp chilli powder
½ tsp ginger and garlic
¼ tsp arad (turmeric)
salt

Marinate chicken pieces in spices for few hours.

2-3 tblsp bread crumbs
1 tblsp chana flour
2 eggs
1 tblsp cake flour
1 tsp baking powder

Beat eggs well, with baking powder and flours. Dip chicken in batter, roll in crumbs and fry in hot oil, turning down to low. If chicken is not done, you can steam it by covering with foil and baking in moderate oven for 30 mins.

Chargha or Chicken Tikka

(FOR BRAAI)

2 chicken
1 tblsp chilli powder
2 tsp ginger garlic
1 tblsp pulverised green pawpaw
1 tblsp lemon juice
2 tblsp yoghurt
Salt to taste

Cut each chicken into four portions, and make cuts in meat portions. Wash and drain well. Smear well with chilli powder, ginger garlic and salt.

Two hours before braai add yoghurt, green pawpaw and lemon juice. Braai (grill) over charcoal.

NOTE:
Split chicken can also be made like above. The same recipe can be used for smaller pieces of chicken breasts.

Chicken Pakoras (Fried)

1 chicken
2 eggs (well beaten)
Juice of 1 lemon
1 cup oil
1 tsp ginger/garlic
1 tsp red chillies (freshly ground)
1 tsp salt
½ tsp black ground pepper corns

Disjoint chicken. Wash and drain dry. Prick well with a skewer or fork. Marinate in above spices, either overnight, or for at least a few hours. Beat two eggs well. Dip chicken pieces in egg and fry slowly in oil till gold in colour.

Tomato Puree Chicken Roast

1 chicken disjointed
1 egg
Salt to taste
2 tblsp lemon juice
1 tblsp dried mint
1 cup tomato puree
1 tsp ginger/garlic
¼ tsp chilly powder
Dry bread crumbs
1 tsp crushed cummin (jeera)
¼ tsp fine elachi

Wash chicken and drain off moisture. (Use leg, breast and thigh portions only. Leave bones for a soup). Add tomato puree, lemon and spices to chicken and mix well together. Whisk egg and add to marinating chicken.

Coat well with masala then roll each piece in bread crumbs.

Place in greased casserole, in fridge for a few hours. Pour two tablespoons of oil over top.

Seal with foil and bake in oven for about an hour at 400ºF (200ºC) till meat is tender. Remove foil and grill for 10 mintues. Serve hot with salads.

Butter Chicken

(MAKHAN MURGHI)

2 chickens (split in halves)
½ cup yoghurt
2 tsp ginger/garlic
1 tsp crushed black pepper
1 tbsp oil
¼ cup butter
¼ cup cream
1 tsp white pepper
2 tbsp lemon juice
¼ tsp powdered tuj (cinnamon)
¼ tsp powdered elachi (cardomom)
¼ tsp cloves (powdered)
1 can tomato puree (1 cup)
1 tsp salt
1½ tsp freshly pounded red chillies

Mix yoghurt, oil, ginger/garlic, ½ of lemon juice and spices together.

Smear over chicken halves and allow to marinate for a few hours. Grill over live coals or rotisserie till browned, or lightly fry and cook them.

SAUCE:
To tomato sauce, add rest of lemon and butter. Any left over marinade from chicken should be added to sauce. Blend over warm heat. Just before serving add cream to sauce.

Put chicken in platter, spread sauce over. Serve hot. Garnish with mint springs.

Chicken Tikka
(GRILLED CHICKEN)
(COLOUR PHOTO 189)

1kg chicken meat (breasts, thighs, drum sticks with
  bones removed)
1 tsp ginger/garlic
2 tsp chilli powder
2 tblsp oil
1 tblsp green pounded pawpaw
1 tsp salt
1 tblsp yoghurt
1 tblsp lemon juice
1 tsp jeera (cummin)

Cut chicken in small sized cubes and pound slightly to
tenderise. Pound together the garlic, chillies and jeera.

Add salt, lemon juice and oil and mix this paste over
chicken. Marinate a few hours. Just before grilling mix in 1
tsp pounded green pawpaw.

Skewer meat on pins and grill or braai over coal. (While
grilling, the left over marinade must be poured over meat).

ALTERNATELY:

Chicken must be disjointed, the paste spread over and
then marinated. Preheat oven to 400°F (200°C).
Dot with a little butter and place pan of chicken in oven to
roast till done. Serve with Aamli kachoomer and chutney.
(See page 281).

Fried Chicken Sections

3 breasts of chicken (or 6 thighs, legs, etc.)
½ tblsp dried mint (or fresh 2 tsp)
2 tblsp cream (or malaai)
1 egg
1 tsp salt
1 tsp freshly ground red chilli
½ tsp crushed cummin
1 tsp ground garlic
juice of 1 lemon
3 tblsp ghee
½ tsp black crushed pepper
1 grated onion

Wash breasts after deboning and splitting open. Divide
in halves and shape like chops.

Mix garlic, grated onion, cummin, salt, pepper, chilli,
lemon and 1 tblsp of ghee.

Spread halved breasts with this and put in well buttered
dish. Cover with foil and bake in oven for half an hour at
180°C. When cool take out breasts.

Keep on wire rack and when all liquid has drained off
dip each breast in flour, then coat well with breadcrumbs
seasoned with dried mint. Chill these chops in fridge till
required.

When serving, beat egg, dip breasts in it and fry in
shallow oil.

At the end of the harvesting season, the farmers in
India stage a braai on the fields. Drums are beaten and
friends from adjoining farms bring their contributions.
Meat, vegetable and pulses are all thrown pell mell in
clay pots and the whole lot buried in the ground under
live coals. This is a basic recipe for a Ubaryo.

Peasant Braai

2 kg of freshly plucked papdi (Indian type flat broad
  bean)
1 nice plump fowl
Vegetables for stuffing (cauliflower, baby carrots,
  wedges of tomatoes)

Wash chicken and wipe dry. Rub insides with a mixture
of salt, chilli powder and black crushed pepper.

Clean, wash and cut vegetables for stuffing.

Sprinkle a little salt and ajwain over them and stuff inside bird. Make a paste of a little ground ginger, salt, chilli
powder and pepper and smear outside of chicken.

Wrap chicken in washed banana leaves and seal well.
Clean papdi, wash and drain.

Mix a tablespoon of ajmo and a teaspoon of salt in a
tablespoon of water. Place half of papdi on the bottom of a
clay casserole, and sprinkle with half of ajmo water.

Place banana-leaf wrapped chicken on it and cover with
rest of papdi.

Again sprinkle with left over ajmo water. Close lid
tightly.

In a deep hole place some coals and get them to smoul-
der well. When they stop smoking, place the casserole over
them. Take some of the charcoal and place on lid of pot.

Cover pot with an old tin or some stones and bricks and
cover with earth taking care that the soil does not fall inside pot.

Leave for an hour or two by which time the chicken and
contents of pot will be done. Serve with green mangoes
plucked from the orchard, or wedges of lemon. Naan
baked over live coals are the usual accompaniment.

Tittar (COLOUR PHOTO PAGE 58)

DUCK, PARTRIDGE OR CHICKEN IN POMEGRANATE SAUCE

1½ kg meat (split small birds in halves and dissect
    large ones.) Wash and pat dry.
2 grated onions
½ cup ground walnuts (or almonds)
½ cup walnuts (quarter or chopped)
2 tsp freshly pounded red chilly
1½ tsp salt
½ tsp black crushed pepper
¼ tsp elachi powder
2 tbsp ghee
2 tbsp oil
3 tbsp cream
2 tsp ginger/garlic
Juice of 1 lemon
3 tbsp pomegranate juice (optional)

Fry onions in ghee/oil and just as they turn a lovely pink
add ground nuts, spices, (but not the pepper) cream, and
lemon juice.

Simmer a few minutes to blend masala, then add cream,
pomegranate juice and ground pepper. Stir and put meat
into this masala. Spread over pieces till they are well covered. Simmer slowly till meat is done.

Orange Duckling

1 duckling (1½ kg)
1½ tsp salt
2 tsp fresh pounded red chillies
1½ tsp ginger/garlic
½ tsp blacked crushed pepper
1 tsp crushed cummin (jeera)
½ cup walnuts or almonds
juice of 2 oranges
grated rind of 1 orange
1 tblsp flour
1 tblsp honey
2 tblsp oil
2 tblsp ghee
1 doz baby potatoes (fried in oil)

Wash duckling and pat dry inside and out. Mix all spices
together and rub inside and outside of duck with this. Stuff
half of walnuts and potatoes inside duck. Fry duckling in
pot till it is evenly browned on all sides. Remove — put in
roasting pan.

Mix honey, flour, rind and juice of orange together,
pour carefully over duckling. Place in oven and cook till
done. Put the rest of the nuts and potatoes in the gravy.

Serve on platter with thickened gravy ladled over duckling. Arrange walnuts and potatoes around duck. Garnish
with thin long strips of orange rind and sprigs of mint or
parsley.

NOTE:

Any of our roast chicken, tithar or duckling recipes
can be adopted for roast turkey.

Ghee

We recommend that you use ghee only when roasting beef, wild game or chicken.

For curries — both vegetable or meat, only oil or a
blending of ghee and oil may be used. Remember that
khitchri (yellow rice) is quite tasty if oil is used in the
vagaar (for tempering), but that Biryanis will require
some proportion of ghee, so use your discretion and
keep an eye on costs!

Curried Pigeon or Partridge

(GREEN MASALA)

2 pigeons (washed, wiped and split in halves)
½ ball garlic
1 tsp black crushed pepper
1/3 tsp saffron
½ cup melted ghee
½ cup dhunia and mint leaves
2 tsp salt
Juice of 1 lemon

Pound leaves and garlic and add to rest of ingredients.
Make a paste of masala with lemon juice and a spoon of
oil. Spread masala well into and over pigeons.

With a thick food syringe inject half of melted butter
into meaty portions of pigeons. Or make deep gashes into
bird and push ghee into them. Heat rest of ghee and braise
pigeon in them till they are evenly browned.

Add a little water, close lid of pot tightly and simmer
over low heat till pigeons done.

SAUCE FOR PIGEONS

Grate 1 onion and fry in 2 tablespoons of oil till they are
gold in colour. Add ½ cup tomato puree and 2 tablespoons of cream (previously mixed together).

Flavour with salt, chilly and spoon over pigeons when
blended. Arrange pigeons attractively.

Put boiled eggs in between and with lid closed allow to
cook. Garnish with parsley.

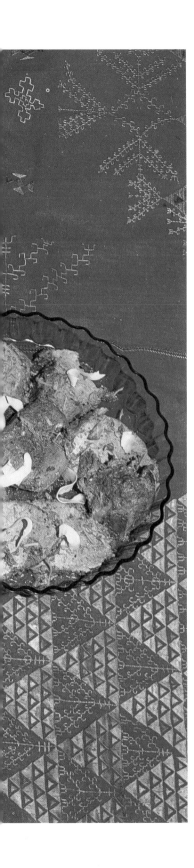

Malayan Beef
(POTROAST)(OPPOSITE)

1 cup dried apricots
1 kg topside beef
1½ tsp salt or to taste
1 tsp black crushed pepper
1 doz baby onions
1 doz baby potatoes
2 tsp green chillies (pounded)
2 tsp garlic (crushed)
1 tsp grated rind of lemon
2 tblsp margarine (or ghee)
1 tblsp oil
1 tsp cummin (crushed jeera)

Soak apricots in 1 cup water overnight. Wash chunk of beef and pat it dry.

Make deep cuts in beef and cover with paste made of salt, pepper, garlic, chilli and cummin.

Brown the beef in the ghee/oil over medium heat, carefully turning and lifting to brown it evenly.

Puree apricots and add it to pot of beef. Add lemon rind and close pot tightly.

Simmer very slowly (1½-2 hours) till meat done.

Remove beef from pot and keep it on warm platter. Put potatoes and onions in pot and cook till done.

Arrange around beef, spreading the gravy over vegetables and meat and serve hot.

1. *Malayan Beef (85)*
2. *Coconut Cream Lamb (94)*
3. *Coconut Patetli (321)*
4. *Spicy Potato Salad*
5. *Chicken/Bhinda Curry (136)*

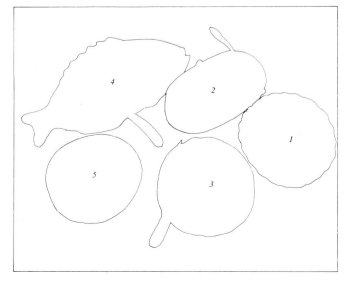

Roast Mutton

1 small shoulder lamb
1 tsp crushed jeero
Juice of 1 lemon
½ tsp turmeric powder (arad)
2 tsp freshly pounded red or green chillies
5 tblsp oil/ghee
1 tsp salt
2 tsp crushed coriander seeds (whole dhunia)
1 tblsp ginger/garlic

Pound chillies and add to crushed dhunia seeds and jeero, add all other spices and make into paste with 1 tblsp of oil and lemon juice. Wash shoulder and make deep cuts all over. Stuff as much masala into the cuts and smear the balance over the shoulder.

Put ¼ cup of ghee/oil in roasting pan, place shoulder in it and bake it covered for about 1½ hours. Uncover pan and allow to bake and brown.

It will be necessary to baste the meat by pouring a little ghee or oil from time to time. Meat is done when tender and a lovely golden brown. During the last 15 minutes of baking, arrange chunks of fresh peeled pineapple on roasting pan. (The pineapple is optional, but those that have tasted it say that it makes a world of difference to the flavour of especially chicken and mutton).

Serve on large platter with chunks of pineapple, some oven baked potatoes and onions or vegetables of choice.

Meat Curry with Milk
(COLOUR PAGE 75)

1 kg lamb (cut in small cubes)
2 onions (sliced)
3 potatoes (peeled and cut in quarters)
½ cup water
1 cup milk
1 tsp crushed jeera (cummin)
2 tsp ginger/garlic
2 tsp green pounded chillies
1 tsp salt (or more)
2 tbsp oil
1 tblsp ghee
1 stick cinnamon

Marinate lamb in ginger/garlic, chillies, jeera, cinnamon and salt.

Fry potatoes in fats till they are a golden brown. Remove from fat. In same oils, fry onions till they are a gold colour — remove onions, allow to cool.

Fry marinated meat in same oil over very low heat and when it begins to dry, add the milk and water.

Close lid of pot and simmer till meat nearly done.

Add potatoes and half of onions and cook till meat and potatoes are tender. Serve in platter, garnishing with rest of onions and chopped mint leaves.

Roast Shoulder with Garlic

A small leg or shoulder of mutton
8 cloves
Juice of 1 lemon
2 tsp ginger/garlic
1 tsp crushed cummin
8 cloves of garlic (small)
1 tsp salt
1½ tsp green or red pounded fresh chillies
½ tsp pepper
2 tsp crushed coriander seeds

Clean and wash mutton well. Make deep gashes in meat and fill these alternately with garlic and cloves.

Mix salt and other spices with lemon juice and add a tablespoon of oil to this.

Rub this paste well over whole joint and allow to marinate a few hours.

Pour ½ cup of oil over joint and bake at 200°C in tray covered with foil for ½ an hour. Reduce heat to 150°C and bake for another 1½ to 2 hours. Remove foil and allow to brown rapidly basting with oil or butter to brown evenly.

Gravy: Remove joint from oven when browned but masalas not yet burnt. Scrape this masala from oven dish and stir in 2 tablespoons of maizena mixed with a little water. Stir continuously over low heat till sauce blended and creamy. Add good pinch of sugar and a little more lemon juice. Pour over joint before serving or serve sauce separately in a sauce boat.

Aden Gosht
(ADEN MEAT)

1 kg mutton (cut up in chop sized pieces. Chops are excellent too)
1 ball garlic
1 tsp salt
2 pieces tuj, a few elachi and cloves
6 whole red chillies
½ tsp arad (turmeric)
½ cup oil

Clean garlic; wash, sliver fine, braise in oil to a light pink colour, then immediately add cut up chillies and braise a little longer. Now add mutton with rest of ingredients and add sufficient water to cook meat tender. Curry must be cooked slowly and the result should be a lovely gold shade.

Serve with potato crisps which must be sprinkled over meat platter just before serving. Garnish with parsley or mint.

Stuffed Rolled Lamb or Fillet

1 kg boneless ribs of lamb (or fillet)
2 tblsp butter
1 tblsp flour
1 tblsp chopped dhunia
1½ tsp ginger/garlic
1 tsp mustard powder
½ tsp ground black pepper
¼ cup chopped liver (chicken or sheep)
2 thick slices bread
¼ cup milk
2 eggs
1 tblsp chopped mint
¼ cup chopped nuts
1 tsp salt
1 tsp ground green chillies
1 tblsp lemon juice

Soak milk in bread and when soft squeeze out milk. Put bread in pan with butter and slowly simmer till mixture resembles thick, cooked pudding. Allow to cool then beat in eggs. Add nuts, greens, chopped meat, flour and half of spices. Smear inside and outside roll with the rest of the spices (mixed in paste with lemon juice) and put the stuffing in the middle. Roll and close and tie with cotton at distances of two inches. Put roll in greased baking pan, cover with foil and bake in 180ºC oven for two hours. Remove foil, pour two tablespoons of oil over surface and allow to brown well. Serve with vegetables of choice.

Ladup
(VARIATION)

750g mutton
1 tsp dhunia/jeero
Salt to taste
1 medium onion
500g tomatoes
2 whole elachi (cardamom)
2 fresh green chillies
1 tsp ginger/garlic
½ tsp turmeric (arad)
1 tsp ground chillies
6 small potatoes
1 stick cinnamon
3 whole cloves pepper
½ cup ghee/oil

Marinate chunks of meat in above spices. Fry onions and remove from oil. Leave aside to cool. Fry potatoes till golden in colour. Remove and keep aside. Fry marinating meat slowly in pot with oil/ghee till lovely brown. Add water and steam slowly till nearly done. Meanwhile, boil tomatoes and blanche off skin. Mash fine. Add crushed onions and potatoes to tomato puree. Add this sauce to the pot of meat. Continue cooking till excess moisture has evaporated and oil floats to top and sides.

Soji Fillet
(FILLET WITH CREAM OF WHEAT)

500 g fillet (4 cm wide by 6 mm thick strips)
1½ tsp ginger/garlic
½ tsp turmeric (arad)
1 tblsp cream of wheat
2 tblsp oil
1 tsp fresh pounded chilly
1 tsp dhunia/jeero
½ tsp baking powder
1 tblsp ghee

Wash and wipe fillet. Mix spices in a tablespoon of ghee. Smear fillet with masala. In each piece of fillet, enclose either, a small onion, a small potato, a stoned prune, or half a boiled egg. Roll fillet over and tie with a piece of thick cotton. Marinate for a few hours. Heat oil in a baking dish or casserole. Place rolled fillet in casserole and cover with foil. Bake in 180ºC oven for two hours. Remove foil and brown. Delicious with chutneys.

Easy Pot Roast
(KURMA) (3-4 PERSONS)

500g mutton or chicken (chops, disjointed chicken, etc.)
1 onion
3 cloves of garlic
2 green chillies
1 piece tuj (cinnamon)
3 tblsp ghee/oil
1 small piece ginger
Salt to taste
¼ tsp pepper
2 elachi, a few whole peppers

Wash and drain meat. Place in pot with ghee. Slice onion, sliver ginger and garlic and add to pot. Add other spices. Bring to steam and allow to simmer slowly, adding water if necessary till meat is done. This is easy and a delicious variation from usual curries and meat dishes.

Meat Curry with Milk

(COLOUR PHOTO 75)

750g lamb (cut in small pieces)
2 potatoes (cut in 1/8's)
1½ cups milk
2 tsp ginger and garlic
3 tbsp oil
6 pickling onions
2 cups water
2 tsp ground green chillies
1½ tsp salt

Fry onions and potatoes lightly in oil and remove and set aside. Fry meat in same oil, but before it browns add milk and water. Simmer slowly over low heat till meat is nearly done. Add onions and potatoes and simmer till done. Serve garnished with diced green and red peppers.

VARIATION:

The two recipes with milk can also be made with coconut milk instead of ordinary milk. The result is quite different.

Lamb Chops

(CHAAP MUSALLAM)
(COLOUR PHOTO153)

500g lamb chops
3 large tomatoes
3 large potatoes (par-boiled)
3 eggs (boiled)
3 large onions
250g peas
¼ cup vinegar
½ tsp gharum masala
¼ cup water
3 tbsp ghee/oil
1 tsp ground ginger
½ tsp ground garlic
1 tbsp ground dhunia seeds
1 tsp red chillies
½ tsp pounded green chillies
1 tsp salt

Mix all spices together and smear this masala over the chops. Leave to marinate for a few hours.

In a large flat casserole put in ½ of ghee/oil and over it arrange the chops. Cut the tomatoes and boiled potatoes and onions in thick round slices (see colour plate).

Over each chop place a slice of onion, potato and tomato and finally a slice of egg. Sprinkle peas all around chops (if using frozen variety this must be added in last stages of cooking).

Mix vinegar and water and any left over marinade and sprinkle this over the contents. Dot with rest of ghee/oil.

Sprinkle a mixture of ¼ tsp salt and ¼ tsp freshly ground pepper over pot. Cook over low heat till meat is tender. Keep in warm oven.

Kerhaay Gosht

Kerhaay is a Chinese type pan (wok) widely used in India and known as Kerhaay. If not available, a heavy cast iron pot could be substituted.

1 kg chicken or mutton
1½ tsp salt
2 tomatoes (chopped coarsely)
1 tsp black ground pepper
2 tsp ginger/garlic
1½ tsp red chillies
1 tblsp green chopped chillies
1 cup oil

Cut meat in convenient pieces. Wash and drain dry. To it add the salt, ginger/garlic and chilli.

Heat oil in kerhaay and fry. Stir meat gently in it till all moisture evaporates.

Add tomatoes and green chillies and cook till tomato is cooked, but not blended in.

Sprinkle pepper and some chopped dhunia leaves over meat just before serving with hot rotis or parathas.

Bhuna Gosht

(ROAST LAMB) SERVES 8 PERSONS

1 kg lamb
4 tbsp oil
½ cup yoghurt
2 tsp red chilli
1 tbsp coriander seeds (crushed)
1 tbsp ginger/garlic
½ tsp turmeric
½ tsp elachi powder
½ bunch dhunia (coriander)
4 large tomatoes (cut small)
2 onions (sliced)
1½ tsp salt
1 tsp crushed jeera (cummin)
¼ tsp powdered cloves
¼ tsp powdered cinnamon

Cut mutton in small pieces. Heat oil and fry onions till pale brown. Add tomatoes, all spices and fry slowly for a minute. Add meat and yoghurt and cook very slowly with lid of pot covered.

¼ cup of water may be added if meat is not tender. Serve on platter with chopped dhunia. Raw onion rings and slices of lemon as garnish.

Pasinda

(BEEF MAY BE USED)
3-4 PERSONS

¼ cup ghee/oil
500 g mutton (free from bones and sliced 1 cm. thick in fairly long pieces)
1 full tsp of either red pounded chillies or chilli powder
1 tblsp fresh grated coconut or dessicated coconut
1 tblsp khus-khus (poppy seeds)
½ tblsp ginger/garlic
½ cup fresh cream or malaai
1 tsp salt
½ tsp turmeric powder (arad)

Pound chillies, khus-khus and coconut together and add to ginger/garlic, and other spices. Lastly add cream and smear meat slices with it and allow to marinate for at least one hour, but preferably over night.

Heat ¼ cup of ghee/oil in a pot, and add the meat. Lower heat immediately and allow to steam till meat is tender and a lovely brown colour. It may be necessary to add a little water to ensure proper cooking of meat.

Kashmiri Pasinda

500g chops or shoulder mutton
1 tsp ginger/garlic
3 elachi
1 tsp chilli
½ tsp pepper
1 stick cinnamon
1 cup milk
1 tblsp saumf (fennel)
½ tsp cummin seeds (jeera)
salt to taste
oil for frying

Cut mutton in thin chop-sized pieces. Wash and apply all the spices to it. Put in milk and cook slowly till meat is tender and milk evaporated.

Now Make a Paste Thus:
½ cup yoghurt
salt and pepper
2 tblsp corn flour

Dip meat in paste and keep turning till they are coated well. Heat oil in pan and fry meat. Serve hot.

Pasinda Chops

Using same ingredients as above, but try chops instead of other cuts. In addition, add 2 tbsp of tomato puree and juice of ½ lemon. Marinate chops for an hour in marinade, then cook slowly till done. Can be baked in oven with equally good results.

Beef Pasinda

(FILLET OF BEEF)
(3 PERSONS)

2 tblsp ghee (or margarine)
500 g fillet or rump steak
3 green chillies
1 cm piece ginger
Salt to taste
2 tblsp freshly ground coconut
4 cloves of garlic
1 tsp jeero seeds (cummin)
¼ cup oil

Pound fine the coconut, garlic, ginger, green chillies and jeero. Add salt and mix well. Coat fillet, with masala and marinate for an hour or two. Heat oil and lower beef in pot. Close lid and reduce heat. Cook slowly till fillet is tender and brown. Delicious served with khitchri and khuri

Pasinda-e-Khaas

1 kg mutton (leg or shoulder)
½ cup oil
1 dozen blanched almonds
1 tsp green pounded chillies
1 tsp ginger/garlic
½ tsp red chilli powder
1 piece tuj, 3 each cloves and peppers
2 onions
2 tblsp dessicated coconut
1 tblsp khus-khus (poppy seeds)
1 tsp salt
¼ tsp turmeric (arad)
1 cup yoghurt
¼ cup malaai or cream

Cut mutton in convenient pieces. Wash and drain well.

Pound the coconut, almonds, khus-khus, ginger/garlic, chillies and turmeric.

Slice onions fine and fry in oil with the stick cinnamon, cloves and black peppercorns.

Remove onions when a lovely gold in colour. When cool, crush with the back of a spoon.

To ground spices add salt and crushed onions. Smear this paste well over meat.

Finally add the yoghurt and cream and toss well. Put meat in pot with the oil in which onions were fried. Cook over low heat.

Alternately: Put in a casserole, cover with foil and roast in (180°C) 350°F oven for an hour. Remove foil, reduce heat to 150°C and allow meat to brown slightly.

Pasinda Dil Khusha

(ROLLED MUTTON) 3 PERSONS

500g mutton, cut in thin broad strips and well-pounded
    with mallet
MARINADE:
1 tsp salt
½ tsp turmeric
¼ tsp pepper
1 tsp red pounded chillies
½ tsp crushed jeero (cummin)
2 tblsp sour milk

Mix spices in sour milk and marinate mutton in this for
two hours.

FILLING:
1 mashed hard boiled egg
1 tsp green pounded chillies
2 tblsp of freshly pounded coconut
1 tblsp cream or top milk, or malaai
1 tblsp ghee/oil
1 tsp ginger/garlic
1 grated onion
1 tblsp chopped mint

Fry onion in a little oil. Remove when a lovely gold
colour. In same oil fry separately the garlic and coconut.
Add fried ingredients to cream. Add the other ingredients.
Remove marinating mutton from the marinade and in each
place some of the stuffing. Roll up and tie with thread.

In roasting pan or casserole heat the ghee and place each
roll of mutton nestling alongside the other. Pour left over
marinade over it. Cover pan with foil and bake in moderate oven till mutton is tender and moisture has evaporated.
Remove foil and allow to fry till brown. Serve with tomato
chutney or vegetable dishes.

Malayan Steak

750g flank steak cut into 4cm chunks
1 tin (190ml) pineapple chunks (drained)
3 tblsp ghee
1 tsp garlic
2 tsp brown sugar
1 tsp ginger
1½ tsp salt
250g baby tomatoes or (1½ cups chopped)
1½ tsp green chillies (ground)
12 baby onions
2 tblsp aamli juice (tamarind)

Place beef chunks with juice, aamli, garlic, sugar,
ginger, salt and marinate overnight.

Place in greased pan, cover and roast in oven and when
nearly done, add onions, tomatoes, pineapple chunks and
scoop juice from pan over them.

Allow tomatoes and onions to cook. Serve hot with
vegetables and rice or bread.

Pasinda Dilruba

(COLOUR PHOTO PAGE 121)

750 g of silverside beef or mutton, (shoulder or leg)
2 tsp ginger/garlic
1 tsp salt
1½ tsp jeera seeds (cummin)
1½ tsp dhunia seeds (coriander)
½ tsp elachi seeds
Good pinch of fine cloves and cinnamon
1 medium onion, peeled and cut in small pieces
3 green chillies
1 tblspoon ghee
½ cup of ghee/oil

Slice meat thin, and cut in long narrow strips.

Put onions, peppercorns, jeera and dhunia seeds on
tava. Braise, then crush fine. Put these spices in blender
together with the green chillies, salt, and other spices.
When blended, mix into a paste with a tablespoon of ghee.

Wash mutton and pound with a meat mallet. Smear
masala on both sides and marinate for a few hours. Roll
meat pieces and tie lightly with a piece of cotton. Put in
pan with ghee/oil (oil only for mutton) and fry gently till
browned on all sides. Cover pan and simmer in its own
juices till meat is tender.

Crumbed Fillet

Juice of 1 lemon
2 tsp garlic
Salt to taste
1 egg (egg white beaten stiff then yolk added-in)
1 kg fillet
1 tsp fresh pounded chilly
½ tsp crushed black pepper

Wash the fillet and then slice off in ¼ inch or thicker
slices. Marinate in above masalas for few hours. Dredge
each piece of fillet with flour, dip in beaten egg, coat with
bread crumbs and fry in little oil over medium heat. Place
fried fillet in casserole and leave in warm oven for 40
minutes. Serve with boiled vegetables, mashed potatoes or
khitchri.

Haran Roast (Venison)

Note: Buck-meat, whether Springbok, Gemsbok or other wild game is more bloody and rare than domesticated animals and therefore calls for special treatment before and during cooking. You may use your favourite recipes but remember to use butter or ghee only. Cream and yoghurt will help to balance the dryness and the serving of a separate sauce also helps. Try this favourite of ours.

2 kg of buckmeat
2 tsp salt
3 tsp ginger/garlic
3 tsp of freshly pounded red or green chillie
*2 small sticks of cinnamon
½ cup ghee
125 ml fresh or sour cream
*2 tsp dhunia seeds (coriander)
*1 tsp jeera seeds (cummin)
*½ tsp peppercorns
1/3 tsp elachi powder
*A few whole cloves
½ tsp turmeric
1 cup vinegar

Make deep cuts in the venison and wash it thoroughly so that all clots of blood are washed out. Place the meat in a bowl of water to which has been added the cup of vinegar. Soak overnight. Rinse out in morning and pat dry.

Roast ingredients marked with an * in a heavy pan or tava. When aroma arises, crush them coarsely and add to salt and other spices.

Beat together half of the ghee and the cream. To it add the spices and smear this marinade well into cuts and all over meat. Marinate for a few hours.

Place meat in greased pan with the marinade and dot remaining ghee over meat. Cover pan with foil and bake in 350 (180° oven) until meat is tender. This will depend on the toughness of the meat.

When meat is done scoop out some of the marinade from the pan and add it to:

½ cup of fried, crushed onion
2 tablespoons of tomato puree
2 tablespoons of either yoghurt or ½ of lemon juice
2 tablespoons of cream

Add sufficient water to this to make it the consistency of thin cream. Infuse once over high heat and serve hot with meat. Garnish with whole mint leaves.

Also see Zafran/Malaai Sauce

Zafraan Malaai Sauce

3 tblsp milk
125 ml cream
½ tsp saffron strands
1 tblspoon lemon juice
½ tsp black crushed pepper
2 green chillies (slit)
1 tbsp ghee
2 tblspoons freshly ground almonds or pistachios
Salt, chilly and elachi to taste

Steep saffron in a little boiling milk then strain through into cream. Fry green chillie and ground almonds in ghee and as soon as almonds appear to change colour add saffron milk and spices to pan. Infuse just once and serve hot as a sauce with roasts.

Gil-Dum

(WILD GAME COOKED IN EARTH)

To cook wild game when on shikar (hunt) the hunters of India swear by this method. The food is left cooking unattended leaving the hunter free to go for more game, and yet protecting it from marauding animals.

Clean and wash venison, guinea fowl or what have you. Make a paste of chilli, turmeric, garlic, very little salt, (some hunters refuse to add salt, saying that it makes the meat tough) fat or ghee, and cover the joints of bird with this paste. Wrap in banana or other large palm leaves (foil will do) and tie meat up so that it is protected from loose soil.

Dig a hole in the ground at least knee deep. Put in a few stones and lay the meat over this. Cover the hole well with soil. Stamping down the loose sand.

Place glowing embers over hole, adding more wood as they die down, (2 to 3 hours).

Serve with chutney or lemon.

Alternatively the hole must be well dampened. The soil on the sides and bottom patted into a clay and then the meat lowered into it.

Dum Ka Gosht

(SMOKED MEAT)(COLOUR PHOTO PAGE 141).

1 kg leg of mutton (cut in pieces)
1 tblsp pounded green pawpaw (8 g)
1 tsp gharum masala
2 tsp dhunia powder (coriander)
2 tsp chilli powder
2 onions sliced
2 lemons (juice)
6 almonds (ground)
1 tsp poppy seeds (khus-khus)
1 tsp sesame seeds (tal)
1 cup yoghurt
1½ tblsp dessicated coconut
1 tblsp ginger/garlic
½ tsp turmeric
1 tsp whole cummin (jeera)
2 tblsp chopped dhunia (green)
2 tblsp chopped mint
2 tblsp spring onions
1/3 tsp ground nutmeg
½ cup oil

Mix pawpaw and spices in yoghurt and smear all over meat. Marinate for 4 hours.

Fry onions in oil till they are a gold colour, add meat to the onions and stirring frequently cook till soft. Meat will flake off slightly.

When oil floats to top of meat, make a space in the centre of the pot and place a small pot therein.

In that pot put 2 tablespoons of oil from the curry and in it place a red hot charcoal.

Close lid quickly and seal off with damp cloth. Keep lid sealed for about half an hour till meat is infused with smell of smoke. Serve hot with rotlas and lemon slices. Garnish with greens.

Photo opposite shows how to smoke meat.

Namaqua Steak

½ kg fillet
1 large egg
salt and pepper
flour
bread crumbs (seasoned)

Marinate thinly sliced steak in salt and pepper for two hours or longer.

Beat egg well. Now roll pieces of steak in cake flour, then dip them in the egg and finally coat well with the seasoned breadcrumbs.

Heat oil and fry on each side to a nice golden brown.

Mustard Steak (Rump)

1 onion (grated)
2 tsp mustard
2 tsp vinegar
2 tsp ginger/garlic
powdered red chillies
salt
1 kg steak (rump)
3 pieces garlic
3 red dry chillies
1 cup tomato puree
2 tblsp solid ghee

Marinate steak for 1 hour in first 6 ingredients.

Braise sliced garlic and dry red chillies in ghee. Add marinated steak, simmer till steak is cooked.

Now add tomato puree and simmer till gravy is thick.

Rump Steak

½ kg steak
1 onion (thickly sliced)
ginger/garlic
3 tbsp ghee
2 tsp worcester sauce
3 green chillies (chopped)
salt and pepper

Marinate steak in ginger/garlic, salt and pepper. Braise well in hot ghee on all sides. Remove from pan.

In same ghee braise onions and green chillies. Add the Worcester sauce and the braised steak. Close lid tightly and let simmer till steak is tender, adding a little water if necessary.

Oven Baked Potatoes and Onions

Select small sized potatoes and onions. (The latter as for pickling).

Peel onions and potatoes, soak them in cold salted water for half an hour. Either bake in same roasting pan as with meat, or in separate one, in which case it will be necessary to add a little salt and pepper, and a tablespoon of ghee. Remove onions before they go soft and out of shape. Potatoes should be tested in order to see that they are well done.

Delicious with grilled meats and roasts.

Kopra Malaai Lamb

(COCONUT CREAM LAMB) (COLOUR PAGE 84) (SERVES 8)

1 kg mutton (leg or shoulder cut in cubes)
6 pods garlic
1 onion (grated)
3 tblsp oil
4 dry red chillies
1 stick cinnamon
1 doz prunes or dried apricots
1 tblsp lemon juice (or 1 grated green mango)
1 tsp slivered ginger
1 tsp pepper-corns
½ fresh coconut (extract cream — see Page 66)
1 tsp salt
½ tsp cummin seeds
2 pods elachi (cardamom)
1 tblsp honey (optional)

Fry grated onions in oil and remove when gold in colour. Fry fruit in oil for a minute and remove when shiny.

Put cinnamon, elachi, peppercorns, whole chillies, slivered ginger and garlic pods in oil.

As soon as garlic begins to change colour, add the meat cubes with the salt and braise.

Shake pot and stir meat continuously till meat is evenly browned. Return onions to pot.

Finally add coconut cream, lemon juice, honey and cummin seeds to pot.

Mix all well and simmer slowly with lid tightly covered till meat is done.

Add dried fruits a few minutes before serving.

Malabari Gosht

1 tsp chilli
500g boneless mutton — cut in cubes
juice of ½ lemon
½ doz baby onions
½ fresh coconut
1 piece cinnamon
a few cloves
2 tblsp oil
1 tsp crushed garlic
1 doz baby potatoes (or large ones cut)
salt and pepper to taste
2 whole green chillies — slit

Extract coconut milk, but keep 1st extract aside. Pour hot water over grated coconut again and keep the 2nd extract separately.

To mutton add lemon juice, spices and 2 cups water. Boil till tender. Strain and keep mutton and stock separately.

Heat oil and fry potatoes till lightly browned. Add mutton and the 2nd coconut extract and stock to pot. When potatoes nearly done, add onions and simmer for few minutes.

Now add first thick extract of coconut milk. Bring to boil and serve immediately, garnish with greens.

To extract coconut cream
See Page 66

Badam/Kopra Kurma

(SERVES 8)

1 kg lamb chops or leg mutton
2 tblsp oil
1 tsp freshly pounded red chilli (or more)
2 green chillies (slit)
¾ tsp arad (turmeric)
½ tsp crushed jeera (cummin)
good pinch elachi, cinnamon and cloves (ground) or 1
    tsp gharum masala
1/3 fresh coconut (extract cream)
4 tblsp tomato puree
2 onions (grated)
1 tsp ginger/garlic
1 tsp salt
1½ tblsp ground almonds (fresh)
1 tsp crushed dhunia seeds
1/3 tsp black ground pepper
1 tblsp lemon juice

Boil chops in ½ cup water, salt and a stick of cinnamon.

When water has evaporated and chops are half done prepare marinade as follows:

Fry grated onions in oil till they are a gold colour. Add tomato puree, lemon juice and all the spices to onions. Lower heat and allow to simmer.

Blanch almonds and grind them. Add coconut cream and almonds to pot and stir till all ingredients are well mixed. Add half-done chops and with lid shut tightly, simmer till meat is done.

Alternately, cook chops in water till done. Make curry separately and pour over chops. Leave in oven for 15 minutes then serve hot.

Kurma

1kg mutton (leg or breast or chop) cut in thickish
    pieces
2 medium grated onions
1 tsp fresh pounded chillies (red or green)
Juice of lemon
3 tblsp oil
½ tsp ground cinnamon
1½ tsp ginger/garlic
Salt to taste
¼ tsp pepper

Wash mutton. Add spices to it and allow to marinate for a few hours. Heat ghee in a pot and add marinating meat to it. Cook mutton very slowly adding water only if necessary. Allow to brown well just before serving. Serve in large platter with vegetables of choice.

May be roasted in oven.

Boiled/Fried Chops

1 cup water
500g chops or disjointed chicken
Salt to taste
¼ tsp pepper
1 tsp ground chillies
1 tsp ginger/garlic

Boil meat in water with masalas above till tender.

Whisk white of egg till it stands in peak, add egg yolk (beaten).

Dip meat in breadcrumbs then in whisked egg, and fry in shallow oil till gold in colour. Drain off.

VARIATION:

First dip in egg, then sprinkle with coarsely crushed Post Toasties and fry.

Malayan Satay
(SOSATIE)

½ cup dried apricots
1 cup vinegar
4 onions
½ tsp turmeric
3 tsp freshly ground red chillies
1 tsp crushed cummin (jeera)
½ tsp crushed black pepper
1½ tsp salt
1½ kg mutton (from leg)
3 cloves
6 peppercorns
1 stick cinnamon
6 lemon leaves
2 tblsp sugar
4 tblsp oil
2 tblsp ground roasted peanuts

Soak apricots in vinegar for an hour. Add sugar and simmer over low heat till soft and pulpy. Puree through sieve.

Grate onion and fry in oil till a pale gold in colour. Drain off oil and add onions to puree.

Add spices and simmer for ten minutes. Cut meat in cubes (3-4 cms) and marinate in the sauce for 2 days. Turn every few hours.

Put meat on skewers and grill over coal or electric griller. Remaining sauce can be used as a dip.

Corned Beef

4 kg silverside beef
1-2 tblsp saltpetre
500g salt
A dozen each of whole cloves and peppercorns

Mix salt in sufficient water to cover meat. Mix well till salt dissolves. Mix in saltpetre and spices and keep meat in this brine for 4 or 5 days. A wooden barrel or an earthenware vessel should be used.

Remove meat from brine and rinse off slightly. In additional cold water, add a tablespoon each of crushed coriander and cummin seeds, and 2 tablespoons of red crushed chillies. Boil meat in this till it is done.

Remove from water and drain dry. Keep covered in fridge and use for sandwiches etc. as required.

Indian Biltong
(SOOKHA GOSHT)

2 kg leg mutton, rump steak, silverside or other beef
  cuts

Cut meat in two finger-wide and thick strips. Boil washed meat in salted water (½ cup coarse salt in 2 litres of water) till done.

Roast cummin and dhunia seeds on a tava (thick pan) crush them and mix with a little turmeric, chilli and pepper.

Rub the mixture well into meat strips. String them on a line and hang in cool place till well dried out.

Cover with net or muslin to keep off flies.

Home Made Sausages

2½ kg fatty leg mutton
1 tblsp coriander seeds
½ tblsp black pepper corns
½ tblsp crushed garlic
2 cups dried bread crumbs
2 tblsp lemon juice or vinegar
4-5 tsp salt
1 tblsp cummin seeds
1½ tblsp green pounded chilli
1½ tsp red chilli powder
1 tblsp dried crushed mint

Wash and grind mutton twice. More fat from sheeps tail may have to be added if meat is too lean. Squeeze out all moisture.

Roast cummin, peppercorn and coriander on tawa and when strong smell arises, crush them fine and add to mince.

Add all other ingredients and mix well. Fill in sausage casings.

Twin-Frikkadels
(JORYA-KABAABS)

500 g mince (mutton)
1 tomato (medium) (or ¼ cup puree)
1 tsp chilly powder
½ tsp white pepper
4 green chillies (pounded)
½ tsp mustard powder
salt to taste
1 onion (medium)
½ tsp turmeric
1 egg
½ tsp dhunia/jeeroo powder
1/3 cup chopped mint, spring onion and dhunia

Wash and drain mince. Grate onion and tomato and add to mince. Add rest of ingredients and mix well. Divide mince in two lots and shape each into a large flattish round. Brush with beaten egg and pour a tablespoon of oil over each.

Place in greased baking dish and bake at 150ºC oven for 30 minutes till nicely browned basting with a little more oil if necessary.

Decorate with a few slices of raw onion rings, arrange a few slices of tomato alongside and add a few sprigs of mint. Serve on a bed of lettuce. Surround with lemon slices, wedges of tomato and other colourful salad greens.

Giant (Variation) Kabaabs

Using same ingredients as above form into one giant kabaab with a rounded dome. Place in a deep frying pan with 3 tblsp of oil and fry till kabaab hardens — while frying spoon oil and gravy from sides of pan over top.

When underside is browned, either turn over or place kabaab in oven and allow top to get brown. Remove pan from oven and spread over with a can of spaghetti in tomato — grate ½ cup cheese over and replace in oven till cheese melts. Garnish with pepper strips and parsley. Serve hot.

Frikkadels
(CAPE MALAY KABAABS)
(COLOUR PHOTO 75)

1 kg mince
3 tsp pounded green chillies
4 tsp baking powder
4 egg yolks
6 slices white bread (5mm thick)
1 bunch dhunia (coriander leaves)
2 tsp white pepper (level)
½ tsp fine nutmeg
2 tsp salt
1 large onion (grated)
1 bunch spring onions
Quantity: 2-2½ doz large sized kabaabs (2cm thick and 6cm diameter).
Squeeze out all moisture from washed mince. Add green chillies, baking powder, salt, egg yolks, spices and chopped greens.
Soak bread in water, squeeze out water and add to above. Squeeze out water from grated onions and add.
Shape mince into balls flatten slightly then dip into whisked egg white and fry in deep oil till a light brown in colour.
ALTERNATIVELY: (oven method)
Dip frikkadels in egg white then place on greased tray. Pour a teaspoon of oil over each and bake at 180ºC for 45 minutes. Serve with mashed potatoes, boiled peas and rice.

Beef and Dahi Kabaabs
(BEEF AND YOGHURT)

500 g minced steak
1 grated onion
2 slices bread
*2 tblsp tomato puree
½ tsp black crushed peppers
½ tsp crushed garlic
1 tblsp ghee (margarine or butter)
1 tblsp chopped spring onions and mint
*1/3 cup yoghurt
*1 tblsp red chutney
1 tsp red pounded chilly
½ tsp crushed jeera (cummin)
Add all ingredients (except those marked with asterisk) together and mix well. Form into 6 large kabaabs, place in greased pan and bake for 30 minutes in 180ºC oven under foil.

Remove foil and allow kabaabs to brown but any excess moisture must be tipped out into a bowl. To this add the tomato puree, yoghurt and chutney. Mix these together then pour over kabaabs.

Serve surrounded with halves of boiled eggs, baby potatoes and carrots but spoon some of tomato gravy over vegetable taking care not to douse them completely with the sauce. The kabaabs must be swimming in the sauce.

Methi Seeds with Khima

½ cup methi seeds or 1 cup methi sprouts
500g chicken mince
2 tblsp oil
1 tblsp ghee
1 tsp red chilli
1 tsp dhunia/jeera
1 large tomato
1 tsp salt
2 onion (chopped)
1 tsp ginger/garlic
½ tsp turmeric
¾ cup frozen peas

If using methi seeds, soak overnight in cold water. Wash in several rinsings of water then boil till soft.

Braise seeds in oil, then add mince and spices and cook till water evaporated and no lumps left in khima.

Add onion and braise slowly. Then add tomato and cook till tomato blended.

Finally add ¾ cup frozen peas. Garnish with greens.

If using sprouts then braise khima and spices and cook till khima is fine like breadcrumbs. Add onion and cook till water from onion is evaporated, then add tomato and sprouts, and cook till tomato blended. Add peas, serve garnished with greens.

Kabaab Curry
(MEAT BALL CURRY)

500g mince meat
1 large onion (grated)
1 tblsp dhunia leaves (coriander)
1 tblsp of either shallot or mint or both
1 tsp jeero (cummin)
3 cloves of garlic
4 green chillies (pounded)
½ tsp turmeric (arad)
1 tsp salt
½ tsp red chillies (fine)
1 cup tomatoes (grated or juiced)
¼ tsp ground cinnamon (tuj)
3 tblsp oil

Wash mince and drain well. Pound green chillies, garlic and jeero and add to the mince. Add rest of dry spices to mince.

Add half grated onion to mince. Fry the rest in oil to a crisp golden brown and when cool add to the mince. Lastly add chopped greens to mince and pound all together well till it is stiff. If preferred it can be put through mincer again. Mould mince into walnut sized round balls and place these gently in oil in which onions were fried. Gently simmer to a brown colour and when moisture from meat has been evaporated add the tomato and let simmer till kabaabs are cooked and gravy is thick.

Chicken Meat with Double Beans

250g chicken meat (cut in small pieces)
500g shelled and peeled double beans
1 tsp ginger/garlic
½ tsp turmeric (haldi)
1 tsp salt
1 tsp red chilli
¼ cup oil
2 fresh chillies (red or green)
1 onion
2 tomatoes
¾ tsp dhunia/jeera powder
1 tblsp chopped dhunia

Shell beans, soak in cold water and take off filament. Slice onion. Slit fresh chillies.

Braise onion in oil and before they change colour, add chicken pieces and spices and cook slowly till moisture evaporated.

Add tomato and cook till blended in meat. Add peeled double beans, and allow to cook very gently in moisture of tomatoes. It is not necessary to add water but a tblsp or two may be added.

5 Minutes before serving, add slit chillies. Serve garnished with green dhunia.

NOTE: To cook double beans for vegetarian omit meat. Onions must only be sauteed and spices decreased slightly.

Methi Bhaaji
(FENUGREEK)

1 doz bunches of small leaved bhaaji, or ½ doz big
   leaved variety
250 g raw chicken or mutton mince
2 medium sized onions
1 small potato
3 tblsp oil
2 tblsp fresh green peas
1 tsp ginger/garlic
1 tsp turmeric (arad)
1 tsp dhunia/jeero
1 tsp ground chillies
1 tsp coarse salt

Braise half of sliced onions in oil till gold in colour. Add mince with a ¼ of remaining onion and all the spices. Braise till dry. Add tomato and vegetables and cook till it is well mixed in mince. When no moisture is left, add the rest of the onions with well washed and well drained bhaji. (On no account must moisture be added after addition of bhaaji as this will render it bitter).

Let cook slowly till moisture from bhaji has evaporated, stirring a few times during process of cooking.

Egg, Noodle and Kofta Curry
(PAGE 99)

Boil 1 cup of thin noodles and drain
Boil 4 eggs. Cool and shell
GRAVY:
2 grated onions
1 tin tomato puree (410g)
3 tblsp oil
½ tsp ground garlic
½ tsp chilli powder
½ tsp dhunia/jeero
Juice of ½ lemon
½ tsp salt

Fry grated onions in hot oil and when they begin to turn pink, add all above ingredients. Blend well by stirring a few times. Reduce heat and simmer slowly till chutney is done.

The Koftas (KABAABS)
500g mutton mince
1 tsp green pounded chillies
¼ bunch chopped dhunia
1 medium onion (grated)
¼ tsp ground black pepper
1 tsp salt
¼ tsp crushed jeero (cummin)
1 tsp crushed garlic

Add all ingredients to mince and put through mincer again. Cut boiled eggs in halves and enclose each half well with the mince. Place each egg-covered Kofta in a well greased baking dish, and bake them in 200°C oven until nicely browned. Shake and turn koftas thrice during baking period.

FINALLY: In a large platter arrange noodles in round rings. Place koftas strategically inside noodle circles. Pour tomato gravy in such a way that it practically covers both koftas and noodles, yet leaves the whole sufficiently uncovered as to reveal both kabaabs and noodle design. Serve with vegetables or rice.

Kabaabs in Tomato
(VARIATION)

For those who prefer a tomato soup base for kabaabs, use Kofta recipe but use more tomatoes as stated here under.

Take 7 or 8 fair sized ripe tomatoes and steam them in ¼ cup water to blanch. When cool, peel off skins, mash the pulp.

Now fry 1 grated onion in 3 tblsp oil to a golden colour. Add 2 elachi, a piece of tuj and a few cloves to pot. Now place kabaab balls as in above recipe and braise till brown. Then add the tomato pulp to which has been added a pinch of salt and red chillies and let simmer till tomato fairly thick like sauce. Garnish with sprigs of mint leaves. Delicious with boiled spaghetti or with rice dishes.

NOTE: Kofta and Kabaab both mean meatballs.

1 Sutherfeni (359)
2 Prawn Biryani (26)
3 Mutton Kurma with Potato dumplings (110)
4 Varkhi Samoosas (191)
5 Green Mango with Methi Masala (253)
6 Grilled Prawns (173)
7 Qumquat Pickles (267)
8 Pasinda with Stuffed Dodhi (89)
9 Badam Halwa (357)
10 Dahi Kabaabs (209)
11 Egg Noodle & Kofta Curry (98)

SECTION 2b

Dokras, Moothias, Wari
and Bhatakias

As an introduction to this titillating chapter of Indian cookery, here is a folk tale which is known all over India in some variation or other, the moral being that the young housewife is too lazy to make this type of curry.

The new son-in-law went on some errand to the little village, from where he had so recently brought a bride. Naturally, he paid the courtesy call to his in-laws. As he arrived thus unexpectedly, the poor mother-in-law went into a dither. In an age when refrigeration was unknown, and when each meal was prepared as the need arose, she fell back on her precious store of preserves. She espied the bottle of Wari, and in no time added some to the pot of bhaji, freshly gathered from her garden. Son-in-law greatly enjoyed this appetising peasant fare, which was served with piping hot chapatis, papads, and achars, and he virtually licked his fingers as he savoured the waris. Shy as he was, he asked when taking leave: "What were the little cakes you served in the curry Ma-ji?"

Proudly replied the old lady: "I taught your wife how to make them. Just ask her for wari." Thanking her, the son-in-law took leave, and on his return to the city he kept on repeating Wari, Wari . . .

Soon he came to a little ditch filled with stagnant water and he wondered whether he should jump or wade through! He decided to jump, and as the Indian word for jump is kudu, after his little leap he began to say kudu, kudu . . .

Poor little bride, she knew not what the husband was talking of when he demanded that she make kudu. To her protests he shouted: "You lazy girl, your own mother said you could make them".

Before the breach occured, the bright girl asked him to describe the dish, and soon guessed what was required. "Surely you mean wari?" she said. "Yes, yes, that is it. Wari."

And all's well that ends well, so here is your classic wari recipe.

Platter of Beans/Moothia Curry on opposite page.

GIVEN the right spices, any housewife can turn out a pot of curry, but there are those grannies and aunties who have justly earned a reputation as outstanding cooks by virtue of their technique of dokra and wari making.

Basically, the above exotic names simply mean dumpling, fritters or roti, made from any or a combination of pea, cake or maize flours, which are delicately spiced with onions, herbs, and what-have-you. These dumplings are then moulded and gently lowered into a pan of half-done meat or vegetable or meat/vegetable curry and allowed to simmer therein till done. In this way, the dumpling lends some of its own distinctiveness to the basic curry or stew and borrows and absorbs into its own little form some of the aroma and flavour from the basic dish.

There are several procedures for making these dumplings, and the variety of curries that they may be added to, are infinite. For this section, we have selected some of the classic ones, but urge the housewife to experiment on her own, for, if there is anything that transforms the indifferent pot of curry into a tempting offering, it is the moothia or dokra in any one of its enchanting forms.

The secret of identification of the various types lie in their shapes, for example:

DOKRA

Moothias. Meaning fist-shaped — that is, the lump of dough is placed in the palm of one's hand, the fingers closing over it and with gentle natural pressure the dough is allowed to form into a sausage shape. (See illustration).

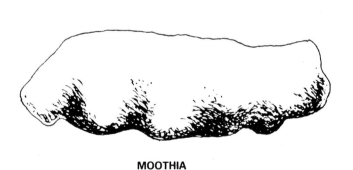

MOOTHIA

Bhatakia. The dough is rolled into a thick rotla or scone, which is dried and then cut in pieces and added to stews, or in case of scones, they are simply placed over curry.

Wari. These are made from lentils, beans and rice, which have been soaked in water till soft, then ground, spiced and put in little lumps to dry in the sun. The bhatakias and waris can be packed in airtight containers and stored for future use, whereas the others are for immediate use.

Rice Wari

1 cup cooked rice (preferably left-over cooked rice)
2 tsp green ground chillies
1 tblsp oil
½ tsp crushed jeero
Salt to taste

After cooked rice is at least a day old, put through mincer with other ingredients. Form into small balls or lumps. Arrange these on a clean cloth spread in the sun and dry slowly till dry and hard. Pack in airtight tin or bottle and use in curries.

ALTERNATE RECIPE:
Combine left-over rice to key wari ingredients and grind. Mix well and form into waris.

Basic Wari Stew

1 large onion
2 green chillies (whole)
½ tsp turmeric (arad)
¾ tsp dhunia/jeero powder
3 tblsp oil
1 medium tomato
Salt to taste
½ tsp chilli powder
½ tsp ginger/garlic
¼ bunch chopped dhunia

Chop onion coarsely. Braise in oil till soft and transparent. Add masalas, braise a minute then add chopped tomato. Stir well then add a dozen or so of wari and allow to simmer for 10 minutes. Add half a cup of water and allow to cook till wari is done. Garnish with dhunia and serve hot with freshly made rotlas (see bread section).

Wari
(LENTIL DRY CAKES)

1 kg moong
1½ doz methi bhaji (large leaf)
1 bunch shallot
125 g garlic
2 tsp turmeric (arad)
1 tblsp dhunia/jeero powder
500 g chori (Indian types of beans)
3 bunches dhunia
2 tblsp oil
250 g green chillies
Salt to taste
½ tblsp gharum masala

Soak lentils overnight. Put through mincer in morning. Cut up greens after cleaning and washing and draining. Add to the minced lentils. Add oil and spices and mix well. Put dessertspoonsful quantities shaping in a rough peak with hands on to a tray (slightly greased) and dry in sun till dry and hard. Pack in airtight tins or bottles and use in stews when required.

VARIATIONS TO ABOVE:

(1) To above curry a bunch of garden bhaji or any available type may be added.

(2) A cupful of fresh peas or cubes of potatoes may be added.

(3) Left over meat as from roasts, etc., may be chopped up and added to a pot of wari.

(4) Instead of wari, put in left over moong dhal bhajias.

The Moothias
(DUMPLINGS)

3 bundles large leaf bhaji or if small leaf variety use 6
    bundles bhaji (chopped fine)
1 onion (chopped)
1 tsp green pounded chillies
1 level teaspoon salt
¼ tsp turmeric (arad)
3 tblsp ghee
½ tsp dhunia/jeero
½ tsp baking powder
1 tsp oil for binding
¾ cup mealie meal
½ cup chana flour (gram)
½ tsp crushed cummin

Sift pea flour, mealie meal and spices. Mix well. Add
rest of ingredients.

CAUTION:
The cleaned, chopped and washed bhaji must be well
drained before adding to flour/spice. After addition of
bhaji, the mixture must be handled lightly so as not to
bruise the leaves further, for it must be remembered that
the juice from bhaji is bitter and unnecessary handling
must be avoided. Lightly mix bhaji, so that flours and
spices coat it evenly. Form into moothias (a tablespoon of
mixture formed into a sausage shape. (See page 102). these
moothias must be placed over stewing meat or vegetable
curries.

Papdi-Moothia Curry
(INDIAN TYPE FLAT BEAN CURRY) (COLOUR PLATE 100)

500g chicken diced small as for stews
500g papdi or green beans or chori beans
2 tblsp shelled peas or papri beans
2 onions (sliced)
2 tomatoes
½ cup ghee/oil
½ tsp ajmo (optional) (Celery or Tymol seeds)
1 tsp salt
1 tsp turmeric (arad)
1 tsp dhunia/jeero
1 tsp red chillies
1 piece tuj
1 tsp ginger/garlic
2 tblsp dahi (yoghurt)
A few whole cloves and peppers

Braise onions in ghee/oil till pale golden colour. Then
add chicken pieces to which has been added the spices and
simmer till meat is well coated with spices and moisture
evaporated. Add yoghurt and tomatoes and allow to blend
in well.

Add vegetables (papri, cleaned but left whole; beans
must be halved) and simmer till meat and vegetables are
nearly done.

Then add prepared moothias (see Moothia recipes) and
place on top of curry. Sprinkle four tablespoons water and
steam very slow for 30 minutes.

Ten minutes before serving pour 2 tablespoons oil over
top and brown moothias. Garnish with chopped dhunia
and serve.

Dokra Curry
(TOOVAR DHAL DOKRA) (COLOUR PHOTO PAGE 107)

1½ cup fresh toovar (shelled Indian peas)
1 onion
¼ tsp salt
¼ tsp ginger/garlic
¼ tsp turmeric (arad)
1 small tomato (chopped or grated)
¼ tsp dhunia/jeero powder
½ tsp chillies
3 green chillies (whole)
2 tblsp oil

Slice onion and fry half in oil. Meanwhile to the other
raw sliced onions add the tomato and the spices and add
this to the fried onion when it is a light brown colour.
Braise for a minute or two then add the shelled toovar peas
and when these are well coated with masala add about 1½
cups of water. Take off heat and meanwhile prepare the
dumplings thus:-

Dokras

1/3 cup cake flour
1½ tsp green chillies
2 dessert spoon ghee
Pinch turmeric (arad)
½ tsp black ground pepper
1 cup mealie meal
¼ tsp ginger/garlic
½ tsp salt
¼ bunch chopped dhunia leaves

Mix all ingredients into the flour and form into a stiff
dough. Mould into moothias or flatten little pieces of
dough into tiny discs. (2 cm in diameter and 6 mm thick).
Place discs gently over curry (Dokra curry). Close lid and
steam curry slowly for at least half an hour. Gravy of curry
should be consistency of soup. When dokras are cooked
add a little fried onion over top, garnish with green dhunia
and serve with lemons.

Dhal Dokra Curry

1 cup moong or chana dhal
2 tomatoes
½ tsp jeero (cummin)
½ tsp green pounded chilli
1 tsp red chilli powder
1 tsp salt
3 medium potatoes (peeled & cubed)
2 onions
½ tsp ginger/garlic
¼ tsp turmeric (arad)
1 tsp dhunia/jeero
¼ cup oil

Soak dhal overnight. In the morning wash off skins. Drain and put in processor with one onion (cut in pieces). Blend fine till dhal is frothy. (Alternativley put through mincer twice).

To dhal, add ginger/garlic, jeero, salt and green chilli. Heat one tablespoon of oil in pot and add dhal mixture to it. Allow to simmer slowly till all moisture has evaporated. Pack mixture in greased pan and allow to cool. Cut in 3 cm squares.

Heat remaining oil and fry cubed potatoes till they are a light brown. Remove potatoes from pan. Add cubes of dokra to pan and fry till golden brown. Remove dokras. Finally in same oil fry the sliced onion to a lovely gold colour. Add masalas and the tomatoes cut in quarters and cook slowly till tomatoes are mashed. Add potatoes and cook for 5 minutes. Now add dokra cubes and allow to simmer till curry is done, adding water if necessary. Garnish with chopped spring onions and pep-up with a little gharum masala.

NOTE: Left over moong bhajias may be used instead of dokras.

Spicy Potato Salad
(COLOUR PHOTO 84) (PAKISTANI CHUT PATI)

3 boiled potatoes cut into cubes
2 tblsp jeero braised slowly and pounded slightly
4 fried green chillies (cut small)
salt to taste
green cut dhunia (coriander)
samoosa pur (see page 185)
3 cloves fried lasan (garlic slivered)
¼-½ cup amli sauce (tamarind)

Place cubed potatoes in Pyrex dish.

Sprinkle the jeero, fried chillies and garlic, salt and amli sauce.

Garnish with greens and just before serving, fry pur and arrange on top.

Cabbage Packets in Mutton Curry
(COLOUR PAGE 107)

500 g minced mutton
½ cup top milk (thin cream)
2 cloves of garlic
1 tblsp slivered almonds
1 slice white bread
3 green chillies
½ tsp black pounded pepper
½ tsp salt

Soak bread in milk taken from top of bottles; otherwise use thin cream. When bread is soft, add mince and spices and mix well. Put through mincer again or pound well.

Divide into 15-18 kabaabs and flatten each slightly. Fry slightly in little oil to harden but don't cook kabaabs.

Meanwhile boil outer leaves of cabbage in water (one leaf per kabaab) for a few minutes, then drain off in colander. When cool, place a kabaab in centre of each leaf, wrap over well and tie with cotton, or paste down with white of egg. Spinach leaves may also be used.

The Curry
(FOR CABBAGE PACKETS)

1 onion
1 tsp ginger/garlic
1 tsp dhunia/jeero
Salt to taste
500 g lamb chops
½ tsp chillies
¼ tsp turmeric (arad)
4 tomatoes (medium sized)

Wash and trim chops. Add spices and marinate for 15 minutes. Meanwhile slice onions and fry in two tablespoons of oil in pot. When onions are a light golden brown, add marinating chops and simmer slowly with lid closed, till water has evaporated. Add chopped or pulverized tomatoes and stir well. Simmer slowly till chops are nearly done, adding more water if necessary.

Place cabbage packets over chop curry. Add ¼ cup water, close lid tightly and gently steam for about half an hour. Garnish with a few slit green chillies and sprigs of parsley or thyme.

This makes an attractive dish and when done in an oven in one of the new see-through type of casseroles it can be served straight from oven to table.

Although in our photograph we have put the pumpkin scones over a beans curry it can be used as a covering for a wide range of meat, mince or vegetable dishes. It is especially delicious with kabaabs in tomato sauce, so try it with our recipe on page 97 . Just remember that the curry underneath must have lots of thick saucy gravy for in the oven it will dry out and the scones too will absorb some of the juices of the curry.

Gadra Beans with Pumpkin Bhaturas (Scones)
PHOTO PAGE 107

500 g freshly shelled french beans or papdi beans
2 tomatoes (liquidised)
1 large onion (sliced)
¼ tsp ajmo (tymol seeds)
1 tsp salt
2 tbsp aamli or 4 tbsp of yoghurt
2 tbsp oil
1 tsp red chilli
½ tsp arad (turmeric)
1 tsp dhunia/jeero
1 tsp ginger/garlic

Saute onions in oil and when they are transparent add pureed tomatoes, beans and spices and cook till beans are done, water will have to be added according to the maturity of the beans.

Now add the aamli juice or yoghurt and mix gently into curry. There should be a thick gravy in the curry before you cover with scones. (See page 108)

Continued on Page 108

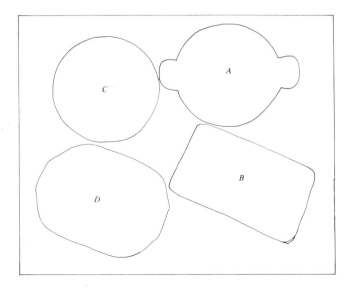

A Mutton/Kopra Moothias (110)
B Beans/Bhatura (107)
  (Pumpkin Scones)
C Cabbage Packet Curry (105)
D Toovar Dhal Dokra Curry (104)

Pumpkin Bhaturas (Scones)
(COLOUR PAGE 107)

Pumpkin Scones are delicious eaten on their own, but cooked over a saucy curry such as kabaabs in tomato, or fish curry etc., they are doubly delicious. Try them out with kabaab curry on Page 97.

1 cup cooked pumpkin (or potato or dodhi)
1 egg (beaten)
1/3 cup milk
3 tbsp margarine
1½ cups flour
½ cup mealie meal
1 tsp green chilli
¼ tsp black crushed pepper
¼ tsp nutmeg (crushed)
½ tsp salt
3 tsp baking powder

After kabaabs have been simmering in gravy for about 5 minutes, empty contents in an oven casserole. Keep aside.

Sift flour with dry ingredients. Rub in butter till fine like breadcrumbs.

To cooked dry pumpkin, add green chilli, milk, egg and beat smooth. Mix flour with pumpkin and make soft dough.

Roll out dough on floured board to two finger thickness. Cut out in rounds and place carefully over the kabaabs and gravy, putting them close together to form a cover.

Bake in medium oven for 30 minutes.

Scones should be done, but there should be lots of tomato gravy in casserole.

Alternatively, scones can be put on kabaabs in a pot and cooked with lid of pot tightly closed.

Alternative for Vegetarians
(EGGLESS)

1 cup cooked mashed pumpkin
3 tbsp margarine
2 cups self raising flour
¼ cup milk
¼ cup water
2 tbsp cream (optional)
¼ tsp black crushed pepper
¼ tsp salt
¼ tsp crushed jeera (cummin)

Sift flour and spices together, rub in margarine, cream and pumpkin. Using just sufficient milk/water make soft scone dough. Finish as above.

REMEMBER try different fillings for this scrumptious dish.

Cabbage Rolls with Prawn Stuffing
(SERVES 6)

3 onions
6 greenchillies
1 bunch dhunia leaves (coriander)
500 g prawns or shrimps
1 medium cabbage
Salt to taste
1 tsp dhunia/jeero
1 egg
1 cup tomato
½ tsp chilli powder
1 tsp turmeric
½ tsp ginger/garlic
1 cup ghee/oil
Breadcrumbs

Shell prawns, clean and wash and braise in one tablespoon oil till pink, then chop in small pieces.

Remove about one dozen outer cabbage leaves, clean, wash and parboil in salted water. Drain in colander. (If leaves are large divide in two.) Take half of inside cabbage and shred very finely. Heat ghee and fry sliced onion to golden colour. Add green chillies and dhunia leaves (pounded beforehand) also add ginger/garlic and shredded cabbage and simmer till cooked. Now add tomatoes with rest of spices and prawns and cook slowly for five minutes.

Spread cabbage rolls with this curried prawn mixture in centres. Fold sides and roll up. Beat whites of eggs to stiff froth. Smear each cabbage roll with white of egg, sprinkle dry bread crumbs and fry in deep oil till crisp golden colour.

Toovar or Chana Dhal Dokras

1 cup chana dhal (gram)
1 tsp garlic
1 heaped tsp greenchillies
¼ tsp pounded pepper corns
Juice of ½ lemon
½ bunch dhunia leaves (coriander)
1 onion (grated)
¼ tsp crushed jeero (cummin)
1 tsp salt
CURRY:
2 onions
1 tsp chilli powder
¼ tsp turmeric (arad)
1 tsp methi seeds (fenugreek)
3 tblsp oil
2 tomatoes (pulverized)
1 tsp dhunia/jeero
1 tsp ginger/garlic
¼ cup tamarind juice
Salt to taste, 1 clove of garlic (slivered)

Soak dhal overnight. Grind it through mincer or pound till fine. Add spices and chopped dhunia. Add grated onion and lemon juice; mix well. Grease a baking tin, pack dhal mixture in this and put over a wire rack. Place this in large pan with water and steam till dhal is cooked. If necessary cover dhal mixture with foil or cloth whilst cooking. Whilst still hot cut up dhal cake in diamond shapes or 2,5 cm squares and keep aside. Meanwhile prepare curry like this:

Heat oil in pan add methi and slivered garlic and allow to turn pink. (A sprig of curry leaves added at this stage lends a delightful aroma). Add onions and fry till gold in colour. Add rest of spices, tamarind juice, tomatoes and 3 cups of water. Allow to come to boil and cook slowly. Place squares of dhal dokras to curry. (One may fry these in a little oil before adding to curry but is not necessary).

Close lid tightly and simmer very slowly till dokras well cooked and half of juice absorbed. This is a thick juicy curry. Garnish with half an onion finely sliced and fried crisp and pour over dokras, and some chopped greens. Serve hot with rotis.

Bhatakyas in Vegetables

BHATAKYAS:
1 cup mealie meal
1 tblsp oil
1 cup flour
½ tsp salt
½ tblsp ghee

Method: Sift mealie meal with salt. Rub in ghee. Add just sufficient boiling water to dampen mealie meal. Allow to cool then add flour and knead in dough.

Roll dough on greased paper to ¼ inch thickness, then turn paper upside down over a hot greased tava. Braise on both sides till bhatakyas are nicely freckled and cooked. When cold cut in 5 cm squares.
NOTE: Left over mealie meal or bajra flour rotlas serve excellently as bhatakyas.

THE STEW:
1 kg of vegetables (cabbage wedges, pieces of mealies, pickling onions, baby potatoes, green beans, peas, broad beans, small brinjals) in fact any vegetable in season may be used
1 large onion
¼ cup oil
1 tsp salt
1 tsp fresh red ground chillies
¼ cup sour milk or aamli juice
½ cup grated tomato
¾ tsp ginger/garlic
½ tsp turmeric (arad)
1 tsp dhunia/jeero powder

Fry onion in oil till gold in colour. Add all spices, vegetables and the sour milk or aamli. Simmer slowly till vegetables are nearly done. Add bhatakya squares, half immersing them in the stew and carefully pouring juices from curry over them at frequent intervals. Serve hot, garnished with chopped dhunia and ½ tsp of gharum masala.

NOTE: Bhatakayas maybe added to any vegetable or meat/vegetable stewed curry.

Chicken/Macaroni Lagan
(CASSEROLE) (PHOTO PAGE 115)

500-750g chopped and cooked chicken breasts
1 onion (grated)
1 tbsp margarine
2 tsp red chilli
salt and pepper
2 cups mixed diced vegetables (boiled)
Freshly fried chips from 2 potatoes
2 green peppers (sliced)
½ cup grated cheese
½ pkt macaroni (boiled)
2 tomatoes (sliced)

Grease a glass casserole and arrange half of cooked chicken in it. Put a layer each of chips, then macaroni and mixed vegetables over it. Again put a layer of meat, chips, macaroni and vegetables.

Season each layer with salt and pepper. Lastly cover with alternating slices of green peppers and tomatoes.

Sprinkle and cover casserole with grated cheese. Dot with margarine and bake in 350°F (180°C) oven till done.

Snoek/Vegetable Dokra Stew

(SERVES 8) (COLOUR PAGE 206)

500 g snoek (soak overnight after cutting in 5 cm sized
  pieces)
1 bunch drum sticks (sekta singh. Scrape and divide
  each in three pieces)
1 cup gadra beans (shelled, fresh Canadian wonder or
  dry beans soaked overnight)
250 g green beans (clean and divide in three pieces)
½ cup peas
2 brinjals (halved or quartered)
4 small potatoes
 large onion (sliced)
4 green chillies (slit)
½ ball garlic (or more)
1 cup oil
3 tsp dhunia/jeero powder)
1 tsp whole methi seeds
Salt to taste
½ cup double beans
4 small carrots
1 large tomato
250 g small pickling onions
½ bunch dhunia leaves
250 g tamarind (extract maximum juice)
2 tsp chilly powder
1 tsp turmeric (arad)
1 tsp whole jeero seeds (cummin)

Pound garlic. Add chilli powder, dhunia/jeero and
turmeric powder. Add salt and mix into smooth paste.
Coat snoek slices in this masala. Brown onions in oil. Add
fish and braise till nicely browned. Remove fish pieces and
leave on plate. Meanwhile to pot of onions, add cleaned,
washed vegetables and braise slowly till vegetables are
nicely coated with masala. Add sufficient water to cook
vegetables. Meanwhile make Moothias thus:

Moothias

½ cup mealie meal
1½ tsp salt
2 tblsp oil
1½ cup bajra flour (millet or sorghum)
1½ tsp chilli powder

Sift flours and spices together. Rub in oil. Add sufficient
boiling water to make stiff dough. Form into moothias.

When vegetables are tender, carefully arrange moothias
over them. Place fish pieces over moothias. Finally pour
aamli juice carefully over contents in pot. Seal lid tightly
and simmer over low heat till moothias are done. Garnish
with chopped dhunia.

NOTE: This is a large family casserole. The moothias take
the place of rotis, so it can be served without rotis.

Mutton Kurma with Kopra Moothias

(COLOUR PAGE 107)

1 tblsp ghee
1 kg leg and breast mutton (cubed in small pieces)
1 tsp red chillies (preferably freshly pounded)
1 tsp green freshly pounded chillies
2 onions (grated)
½ bunch chopped up dhunia leaves (coriander)
1 tsp crushed dry coriander seeds
½ cup oil
1 tsp crushed jeero (cummin)
3 whole green chillies
½ cup rice flour
½ tsp turmeric
1 tsp ginger/garlic
Salt to taste
1 fresh coconut
¼ tsp ground cloves
½ tsp ground cinnamon

Extract milk from ¾ of coconut (see Page 66). Grind
the rest. Rub 1 tblsp ghee in the rice flour. Pour hot water
over rice flour and work into stiff dough. Keep aside.
Meanwhile in oil, fry the red chillies, turmeric,
cloves, cinnamon, coriander, ginger/garlic, whole green
chillies and half of the grated onions. Fry till lovely aroma
arises and an even textured gravy results. Add mutton and
salt and cook very slowly till mutton nearly done.

Add ground coconut, jeero (cummin) and rest of grated
onion to the rice flour. Work in well. Add half of chopped
dhunia. Mix and form into small moothias. Add carefully
to pot of kurma and allow to simmer, taking care that they
do no break. Pour coconut milk over moothias and mutton
and simmer slowly till gravy is thick. Serve with rotis.

Mash Potato Coated Chops

(SERVES 4)

½ kg mutton chops
¼ tsp ground cinnamon
¼ tsp ground pepper
2 tblsp poppy seeds (khus khus) for dusting
1 tblsp mild tomato/chilli chutney
1 tsp ginger/garlic
¾ tsp salt
2 tblsp oil
½ tsp ground chillies

Prepare 1½ cups mashed potato. Mix-in 1 teaspoon lemon juice and 3 tablespoons maizena.
Wash and drain chops.
Mix spices together and rub over chops. Marinate for a few hours.
Put in pot with marinade and steam gently till chops are done.
When chops are tender and dry, smear dhunia or any other chutney lightly over them. Coat with mashed potato.
Dust with poppy seeds and fry till a pale gold colour.

Salt and Pepper Stews

Small pieces of mutton or chicken are best for stews. Naturally the housewife will use whatever meat is on hand, but, cutting it to small cubes.

250g meat
3 small potatoes (halved if bigger ones are used)
1 tsp ginger/garlic
3 carrots (halved lengthwise)
2 or 3 wedges of cabbage
A handful of each of green beans (cut in 5cm pieces); peas; double beans or whatever is available
1 brinjal (quartered)
1 large onion (sliced)
¼ cup oil
1 piece tuj (cinnamon)
A few whole peppers and cloves
2 elachi (cardomom)
1 tsp salt
½ tsp fine pepper
2 whole green or red chillies
½ cup yoghurt
½ cup tomato juice or grated tomatoes

Cut and wash meat, drain. Prepare vegetables, wash and drain them. Put vegetables and meat in deep dish. Add to it all the masalas, the sour milk and tomatoes. Fry the onions in ghee/oil till a lovely golden brown. Remove from ghee and add to bowl of meat and vegetables. Mix all well together and put back in pot with ghee. Simmer slowly, stirring at intervals carefully, in order not to break vegetables. When stew is done, garnish with parsley and serve

Chana Dhal Curry

NOTE: Other cuts of mutton or chicken can be used with equally good results.

350g breast or rib mutton
1 tsp ginger/garlic
1 tsp turmeric (arad)
1 tsp dhunia/jeero powder
1 tsp salt
1 tsp red chillies
2 whole green chillies
1 stick cinnamon
1½ cups chana dhal (gram lentils)
¼ cup ghee/oil
2 medium onion
½ cup chopped tomato

Soak dhal in cold water after cleaning it. Meanwhile prepare curry as follows:

Braise the sliced onions with green chillies in ghee/oil till light brown. Add meat cut in inch sized cubes together with masalas and braise till they are well blended. Add tomato and cook slowly till soft. Add a cup or more of water and cook slowly till meat is half done. Now add the chana dhal; braise a little then add water and cook slowly till all is well done. The curry when cooked is moist but not watery like gravy curries. Garnish with green dhunia before serving. Many people prefer to pour a tablespoon of fried onion over it before serving, but this is optional.

Mash Potato Casserole
(AALOO LAGAN)

2 cups mashed potato
½ cup flour
2 tblsp butter
3 tblsp grated cheddar cheese
1/3 tsp baking powder
good dash pepper and red chilli

Mash potatoes with a little butter, milk and salt.

When potatoes have cooled down add flour, red chilli and pepper and form into a soft dough.

Line half of dough over a greased tart plate. Cover the dough with half of grated cheese, then cover with filling of choice. Master mince, or flaked meat for pie fillings, or moong dhal or vegetable filling are all suitable for this pastry.

Cover the filling with rest of dough, patting neatly to cover entire surface. Sprinkle with rest of grated cheese.

Brush over with egg, dot with butter, and bake in 200°C oven for 15 minutes. Switch down to 180°C and continue baking for another 20 or more minutes. By this time the pie should be a lovely gold colour.

Dodhi/Kabaab Curry
(COLOUR PAGE 182)

1 cup grated dodhi (Indian marrow or gourd)
½ bunch dhunia leaves (chopped)
½ tsp pounded garlic
½ cup chana flour (gram or pea flour)
1 tsp crushed cummin seeds (jeera)
1 tsp crushed dhunia seeds (coriander)
1 onion (grated)
1-1½ tsp green pounded chillies
1 tbsp mealie meal
½ tsp B/powder
1/3 tsp black crushed pepper

Squeeze out excess moisture from dodhi and onions but keep this moisture aside. Add all ingredients together and fry ping-pong sized balls of dodhi bhajias in hot oil. Drain on kitchen paper. Meanwhile make curry as follows.

Grate 2 onions and sauté in 2 tbsp of oil and just as they begin to change colour, add a cup of chopped tomato, the left-over juices from onion and dodhi, ½ tsp of salt, chilli powder, gharum masala and a dash of turmeric powder.

When gravy is blended add the dodhi kabaabs and allow to simmer for a few minutes. Garnish with greens and serve hot with rotis.

NOTE: Any left over chanadhal or moongdhal, bhajias may be put in curries like above to give you another novel dish at the table.

Macaroni Steak

½ kg fillet (dice small)
1 onion
3 pieces garlic
salt and pepper
2 green chillies
3-4 tomatoes
½ tin tomato puree
parsley
¼ cup grated cheese

Braise onions and garlic.

Add diced pieces of steak with salt, pepper, green chillies and parsley.

When braised, add grated tomatoes and tomato puree. Simmer till a nice thick gravy is formed.

Boil macaroni in salted water. Add to steak and mix well. Arrange in a casserole.

Grate cheese over and leave in oven just long enough for cheese to melt slightly.

Mince Khowse
(COLOUR PAGE 75)

4 tomatoes (750g)
2 cups noodles or macaroni
½ tsp ginger/garlic
1 tsp red chillies
¾ tsp turmeric (arad)
3 tblsp oil
¼ cup vinegar (or lemon juice)
500g mince (chicken)
1 tsp salt
1 tsp dhunia/jeero
1 large onion
½ tsp gharum masala

Put washed tomatoes in pot with the vinegar, ½ tsp of red chillies and salt to taste, and bring to boil. Thereafter allow to simmer slowly till tomatoes are mashed. Put through sieve or liquidiser and keep aside as a sauce.

Boil noodles or macaroni in salted water and a teaspoon of oil to prevent macaroni from sticking and when done, drain in colander.

Put mince in frying pan with the salt, ginger/garlic, turmeric, dhunia/jeero, and chillies and braise well. When nearly done, add sliced onions and oil, and allow onions to cook soft, and mince to brown.

Grease a casserole. Spread with half of boiled noodles; cover with half of mince and pour half of the sauce over this. Repeat process once more.

Bake in 180°C oven till done but taking care that the sauce does not completely dry out. Serve hot, garnished with dhunia leaves.

Macaroni-Gosht Casserole
(MACARONI AND MEAT) (COLOUR PAGE 115)

1 chicken (cut in small pieces as for stews)
½ pkt macaroni (broken in 5cm pieces, boiled and drained)
2 cups tomato (juiced or grated)
2 medium onions (sliced)
½ cup fresh grated coconut, optional
1 cup left over samoosa pur (fried and when cool crush coarsely)
1 tsp salt
2 tsp chillies
½ tsp turmeric (arad)
4 whole green chillies
½ cup ghee/oil
1 tsp ginger/garlic
1 tsp dhunia/jeero

Brown onions a golden colour in ghee/oil. Add chicken with spices and grated coconut and when moisture is absorbed add the tomato.

Cook till tomato is absorbed, then add about a cup or as much water as is necessary to cook chicken. The consistency of curry should be like thick chutney.

Transfer chicken in heat-proof casserole, arrange nicely and cover it with the drained macaroni. Toss some of sauce over macaroni.

Cover casserole and cook for ten minutes. Just before serving add fried Samoosa pur over this.

Garnish with a little dhunia leaves. Serve hot.

P.S. — Post-Toasties may be substituted for the samoosa pur.

Khima Gosht Lagan
(LEFT OVER MEAT CASSEROLE)

½ lb left over mince or shredded meat from roast, etc.
1 tblsp dhunia chutney
1 cup boiled rice
½ cup milk
½ cup grated cheese
1 tblsp butter
2 eggs
½ cup tomato puree
1 onion finely chopped
coconut (optional)

Mix all ingredients well together (except cheese and butter). Add salt, pepper and if necessary a dash of red chillies. Place in greased heat-proof casserole. Cover with grated cheese and dot with butter and sprinkle liberally with post-toasties. Bake in moderate oven for ½ hour. Serve with chutneys and lemons.

Patta Curry (MADUMBI LEAVES CURRY)
(COLOUR PLATE 160)

Select 1 dozen small patta leaves. Spread with patta batter (as for individual pattas — (see page *225*) and roll up tightly. Fry in little oil till nicely browned but do not steam.

Make a chicken or mutton curry as follows:-

500 g chicken or mutton (cut in small pieces as for stew)
1 tomato (grated or juiced or finely cut-up)
1 stick cinnamon
2 elachi (cardomom)
A few cloves and peppers
1 tsp salt
1 large finely sliced onion
½ cup oil
1 tsp turmeric (arad)
1 full tsp chillies
1 tsp ginger/garlic
¼ up sour milk curds
1 tsp dhunia/jeero

Fry onions in oil till pale golden colour. Add meat (washed and cut) to which has been added all the spices, the sour milk, tomatoes and allow to cook slowly till juices are absorbed. When meat is nearly done, arrange the pattas over it, add 3 tablespoons of water and allow to steam for 20 minutes longer.

Karela Lagan
(BITTER GOURD)(COLOUR PAGE 217)

500 g karela
4 medium onions (grated)
¼ tsp turmeric
¼ tsp crushed coriander
1 tsp salt
2 tblsp ghee
2 tblsp oil
¼ tsp pepper
¼ tsp crushed cummin (jeero)
4 eggs
2 tblsp chopped coriander leaves (dhunia)
1 tsp green chillies (ground)

Scrape karela and boil in salted water. Split in middle and remove seeds.

Fry karela in 1 tablespoon of ghee till they are a light brown in colour. Fry the grated onion in oil and the remaining ghee but do not allow to change colour.

Remove from stove and allow to cool. Beat 4 eggs and add the cold onions to them. Now add chopped dhunia, fried karela and all the spices to it.

Mix well and pour into a greased glass casserole. Bake at 180°C till a light gold in colour. Serve hot with meat dishes.

Quick and Easy Baked Beans/Cheese Casserole

(PHOTO OPPOSITE)

1 tin baked beans in tomato sauce
¼ cup grated cheese
1 tsp dhunia/jeera powder
½ tsp turmeric powder
1 tsp chilli powder
2 green chillies (slit)
½ tsp salt
1 onion finely sliced
1 tomato (sliced)
2 green peppers (cut in rings)
1½ cup macaroni
2 tbsp oil

Put macaroni in boiling water with salt and cook till done (20 mins). Five minutes before macaroni is done, add 1 tsp of oil in pot. Drain and rinse in cold water, keep in colander. Fry onions in oil and when they become soft add pepper rings and fry till onions begin to change colour.

Add tomato and spices and cook gently till tomato blended. Then add baked beans and toss well. Arange half of macaroni in casserole over this arrange ½ of beans curry, rest of macaroni and the rest of the beans curry. Bake in 350°F (180°C) oven for 10 minutes. Remove from oven sprinkle with grated cheese and bake till cheese melted.

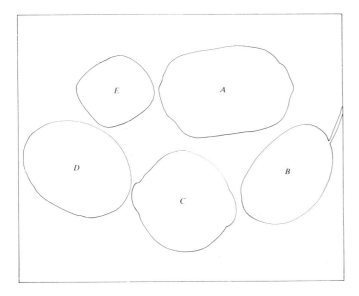

A Macaroni Chicken Lagan (113)
B Torai Sev Curry (131)
C Quick Easy Bean Casserole (114)
D Sev Curry (131)
E Same as A

Chicken Lagan Marhaba

500 g breasts of chicken
*1 tsp ginger/garlic
*2 tblsp frshly ground almonds
*2 tblsp ghee
*1½ tsp green chillies (freshly pounded)
*¼ tsp pepper
*½ tsp crushed jeera (cummin)
*1 tsp salt
1½ cups milk
3 slices bread
½ bunch dhunia leaves (coriander) chopped
½ tsp green pounded chillies
5 eggs
1 tsp baking powder

Wash and cut chicken breasts into small 3 cm squares. To them add the ingredients marked with asterisk. Mix well then put in pan and braise fairly rapidly till nearly dry but not browned.

Meanwhile blend milk, coriander, bread, chilli and eggs in processor. Pour this mixture over cooled chicken and mix all well together. Grease a casserole and pour mixture in it.

Bake in 350°F (180°C) oven for one hour. When casserole is half done sprinkle nuts and poppy seeds over top then finish baking.

NOTE: Into above just before putting chicken in casserole add 1½ cups of frozen vegetable such as peas, carrots, cut corn, cauliflower etc., and bake them with the chicken. It will save you from cooking vegetables separately.

Khowse Gosht (Kaswa)

500g mutton
½ cup yoghurt
1 tsp turmeric (arad)
2 lemons (juice)
1 tsp chilli powder
1 tsp ginger/garlic
4 tsp khus-khus (poppy seeds)
Few sprigs coriander
1 cup macaroni
4 green chillies (slit)
½ cup oil
3 onions (medium)
1 tsp jeero (cummin)
Few cloves and elachi (cardomom)
Few pepper corns
Salt to taste

Cut mutton in 2cm cubes and marinate in salt and ginger/garlic for 15 minutes.

Grind khus-khus, jeero, cloves, elachi and pepper corns to a fine paste. Add the other spices and the yoghurt to this. Mix well and add to mutton.

Slice onions and fry till gold in colour. Add marinated mutton and fry slowly till nicely browned. Add chillies, fresh coriander and sufficient water to tenderise meat. Now add macaroni broken in 6cm pieces. Fry for few minutes. Add more water to cook macaroni tender. Squeeze lemon juice just before serving.

Dhodhi Lagan
(VARIATION)(PHOTO PAGE 217)

1½ cups grated dhodhi
1 grated onion
4 tblsp oil
1 egg (beaten)
1 tblsp chopped dhunia
½ cup milk
2 level tsp baking powder
¼ cup chana flour (gram)
¼ cup mealie meal
½ cup cake flour
1 tsp salt
1 tsp pounded red chillies
1 tsp crushed jeero (cummin)
½ tsp garlic

Mix together all the above ingredients. Grease pan and bake in 350°F (180°C) oven for 30 minutes. Five minutes before removing from oven, brush with egg and sprinkle with tal or khus khus/poppy seeds.

VARIATIONS FOR DODHI LAGAN:

Instead of dodhi use any of following:

1. 1½ cups chopped green and red peppers.

2. Sliced torai (ridge gourd) or karela

3. Grated green mealies.

4. Potato and green peas.

Pancakes in curry sauce

GHAWLA CURRY (PHOTO PAGE 27)

Either make small pancakes from any of our recipes or make tortillas as hereunder:

1 cup flour
¼ tsp salt
1 cup cold water
1 tblsp milk
good pinch bicarbonate
½ cup mealie meal
1 egg
1 tblsp ghee or soft butter
2 tblsp yoghurt

Sift flours and salt and rub in ghee. Beat egg, yoghurt, bicarb, milk and water together. Make soft batter.

Beat with rotary beater to make it smooth.

Heat griddle and make small sized pancakes. Keep warm under cloth.

FILLINGS:

1. Using any of our kabaab mixtures, shape mince like tiny vienna sausages. Place sausages in a frying pan with a little water and gently steam till sausage is set and does not disintegrate — alternatively fry them.

2. To master mince recipe add some cottage cheese and mould gently like sausages.

3. Try any dhal or vegetable filling such as mashed potatoes and peas etc., but add to this a few tablespoons of grated cheddar cheese.

In each pancake or tortilla place filling of choice and roll up. Paste down with white of egg.

Put tortillas in baking dish and pour sauce (recipe hereunder) over.

SAUCE:

2 tblsp grated onion
1 cup tomato puree
1 tsp chilli powder
1 tblsp oil
2 tblsp grated cheese
1 tblsp flour
¼ tsp crushed garlic
1 tsp salt
½ cup milk (½ yoghurt and ½ milk)

Brown onion in oil, stir in flour, spices and puree. Cook till creamy. Beat in yoghurt when slightly cooled. Pour over tortillas. Sprinkle cheese over the lot. Bake in 180° (350°F) oven for 20 minutes.

Ghawla Lagan

(PANCAKE CASSEROLE) (COLOUR PHOTO 27)

1 cup flour
1 cup milk
½ tsp salt
3 eggs
4 tblsp water

Sift salt and flour together. Make well in middle of flour and pour in eggs, milk and water.

Beat with rotary beater till batter is thick and creamy. Leave in fridge for an hour.

Batter should be of pourable consistency. If too thick, add a few teaspoons of water. Beat again with beater before making small pancakes.

Keep under damp cloth when pancakes are made. Fill with filling of choice and roll up and place in greased fire proof casserole. (For fillings see alongside).

NOW MAKE A SAUCE OF:
Juice of 1 lemon
1 cup tomato puree
2 tblsp yoghurt
2 tblsp oil
¼ cup cream
4 tblsp grated onion

Fry onion in oil, as soon as they begin to turn gold, add puree, cream and yoghurt.

Season with salt, chilli powder and grinding of black crushed pepper. Pour this sauce over the filled pancakes. Cover with foil.

Bake in 180° oven for 20 minutes. Garnish with onion rings and sprigs of mint.

FILLINGS: Kabaabs or chicken filling etc.

Bhurta

(MASHED SPICED POTATOES)

2 tblsp oil
4 large potatoes
1 bunch chopped dhunia (coriander)
6 green chillies (chopped)
2-3 tblsp aamli juice
1½ tsp crushed jeero (cummin)
1 large onion
Salt to taste

Wash potatoes, boil till done. Peel and mash, adding salt, jeero and dhunia. Fry onions in 2 tblsp of oil and when they are soft, add green chillies and cook for a few minutes. Now add spiced, mashed potatoes. Pour tamarind (aamli) juice over just before serving. Serve hot, as side dish with rotis or khitchri.

Basic Souffle
(COLOUR PHOTO FRONT COVER)

3 tblsp butter
flour (½ cup)
1½ cup grated dodhi (marrow)
1½ cup milk
3 eggs (separated)
1 tblsp chopped greens
1 tblsp chopped pickles (optional)
½ tsp cummin (crushed) (jeera)
1½ tsp salt
1 tsp chillie
½ tsp crushed dhunia seeds

Melt butter, add flour and cook for 1 minute.

Remove from heat and add milk drop by drop — beating all the time till sauce is creamy and smooth.

Replace pot on heat and allow to thicken. Cool slightly then beat in egg yolks. Add dodhi and spices and mix in.

Finally beat egg whites till stiff and fold into mixture. Pour souffle in greased pan and bake 40-45 minutes 190ºC. Serve immediately.

The above basic souffle can be converted into very delicious savouries. While the housewife is encouraged to experiment with left-overs or her own choice fillings, here are a few suggestions: To the basic souffle, before you fold in the white of egg, add and mix in only 50 g of cheese and 150 g of:

Any of the following:

(1) Fried karela on page 134.
(2) Chana dhal/Bhaji — recipe on page 129.
(3) Methi seeds with khima — recipe on page 97.
(4) Moong dhal or moong sprouts curry — page 137.
(5) Any bhaji curry.
(6) Flaked fish or chicken.
(7) Left-overs chopped fine or flaked.
(8) Left-overs kabaabs, cutlets etc. broken down and added.

Caution: Oils from curries must be drained out before adding ingredients to souffle.

This is a modern version of rotlas. Try it, it is superb!

Mealie Meal Casserole
(ROTLA LAGAN) (CASSEROLE PHOTO 217)

PASTRY:
1 cup water
1 tblsp butter
½ tsp salt
¼ cup grated cheese (optional)
1 cup mealie meal
1 cup milk
1 egg

FILLING:
Bhinda curry, chana dhal and bhaji, or any dry mince, moong dhal curry, harga etc.

Bring water and salt to boil. Make paste of mealie meal and milk and add to water (lower heat) and stir till mixture is smooth. Cover pot with lid and allow to cook gently for 10 mins. Add butter and allow to blend in.

Now beat egg and add a few tblsp of warm mealie meal to egg, and beat quickly so that egg does not cook.

Now add egg/mealie meal mixture to pot and beat in well.

If cheese is to be added, mixture will have to simmer for 5 more minutes on stove. Grease oven dish with oil or butter.

Pat half of dough on bottom of pan. Add filling and pat rest of dough over filling.

You may have to grease lunch paper, pat dough on this and then invert paper over filling. Remove paper and smooth edges etc. to cover well.

Dot top with a little butter and bake at 180ºC for 40 minutes.

Baked Macaroni

1 large onion (sliced)
½ tsp crushed garlic
2 tbsp ghee
250 g mince
2 tsp chilli
¼ tsp pepper
1 tsp salt
1 tbsp tomato sauce
2 cups marcaroni

Boil macaroni in salted water and drain dry when tender but still firm. Heat ghee and sauté onions. Add mince and spices and cook till done. Avoid lumps in mince. When dry and done, switch off heat and add tomato sauce and mix in. Mix mince and macaroni together. Make sauce as follows:

2 oz butter
1 cup flour
2 cups milk
1 egg
Salt, pepper, and crushed jeera

Melt butter in pan and stir in flour and cook over low heat. Add milk and stir vigorously and allow sauce to thicken. Add seasoning, beat in egg and add a little of sauce to it, and beat well. Then mix in rest of sauce to egg.

Add ¼ of sauce of cooked mince/macaroni and mix in. Pour mixture in greased casserole and pour rest of sauce evenly over it. Bake in moderate oven for 30-40 minutes. Remove from oven while still moist and not too dried up. Serve with chutneys.

VARIATION:
With cheese. When sauce is made mix in 1 cup of grated cheddar to it. Bake and serve as above.

NOTE:
Chop up any left over roast or meat add to vegetables, macaroni etc. Make a sauce like above and pour over veg/meat and bake.

Mango/Banana/Egg Casserole

6 bananas or half ripened mangoes
6 eggs
2 onions
2 tblsp ghee
salt
¼ tsp turmeric
½ tsp dhunia/jeeroo
2 tomatoes (pulverized)
2 green chillies
1 tblsp dhunia (fresh)
¾ tsp red chilli
¼ tsp black crushed pepper
½ tsp crushed garlic

Fry finely sliced onion in ghee. When they are soft and transparent, add tomato and spices and simmer for 1 minute.

When tomatoes are blended in, add bananas (peeled and sliced lengthwise) or if using mangoes, peel and cut in halves. Cook gently, turn bananas carefully so that masalas coat fruit.

*Make hollows in curry and break eggs inside. Slit chillies and arrange in between. Cook till eggs are set.

From this stage * banana curry can be arranged in a fireproof casserole, the eggs added and allowed to cook in 180°C oven for 10 to 20 minutes. Decorate with a little chopped mint or dhunia.

SECTION 2C

VEGETARIANISM

The concept of vegetarianism was first conceived of in India as early as 550 B.C. in the minds of two spiritual giants who were born in the Royal Palaces of States near the foothills of the Himalayas.

Mahavira the founder of Jainism and Gautama the Buddha were contemporaries. They recoiled on the one hand from the carnage and wastage of a society whose palates demanded such exotic fare as pheasant livers and peacock tongues, and on the other at the utter poverty and misery of the masses. Both renounced their Royal station and chose to tread the path of mendicants, searching for the Truth.

After years of contemplation, Buddha attained enlightenment and he mapped out a rigid discipline for his followers based on the Law of Compassion which advocates the sanctity of all sentient and animant beings.

After many ups and downs, and although never enjoying overwhelming popularity, the Buddhist teachings were bound to influence India. Both in the kitchens of the elite and the masses therefore, experiments in cooking with vegetables have been carrying on for over two thousand five hundred years. It is not to be wondered at then, that Indian vegetarian cookery is so rich and varied and that it is satisfying to both those that eat in order to exist and those that exist in order to eat.

In this edition, dishes have been stamped as vegetarian even when appearing in other sections.

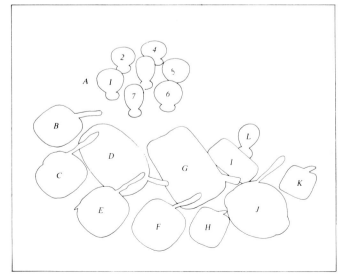

A 1 Dodhi Falooda (314)
   2 Mango Juice (311)
   3 Sherbet Milk (313)
   4 Punch (310)
   5 Orange/apricot/mango (310)
   6 Dodheli (313)
   7 Pomegranate Juice (311)

B Masoor Sprout Curry (137)
C Bhinda/Peppers Curry (136)
D Karela Lagan (113)
E Goovar Sing Curry (131)
F Methi Sprout Curry (137)
G Pasinda Dilruba (90)
H Brains Curry (147)
I Brinjal/Khima Rawayya (127)
J Hyderabadi Brinjal (127)
K Onion/tomato Kachumbar (281)
L Watermelon/Orange/Lemon Drink (310)

Vegetables

We remember an aunt in Johannesburg. To watch her cook was sheer delight.

Her bhajis must be nipped off with the fingers from the stems or just above the roots and never cut for that would make the bitter juices flow more easily.

Karelas should be rubbed with salt and turmeric and then sun-dried rather than the current tendency of frying them before addition to curries.

Bhindis should conform to the size of ladies fingers and larger ones thrown into the stew-pot the following day.

No vegetable dish was complete without its wari, neatly rolled patta, dokra or bhatakya and should this not be possible then at least freshly grilled mealiemeal rotlas.

Though deceased for more than three decades, she is remembered by the guests that were priviledged to eat at her table.

In Indian cookery, vegetables are seldom boiled.

Instead they are steamed, braised, fried or curried in their own juices or aided with the addition of coconut milk, curds, or tomato and lemon juice.

The good cook ensures that the distinctive flavours of each vegetable is retained and judicious use is made of spices with the aim to enhance their flavours rather than smother the vegetable.

Onions, whether grated, sliced or chopped, are used raw or just sautéed and rarely fried brown.

Light vegetable oil rather than ghee is to be preferred and in order to retain shape and colour, vegetables should be left slightly underdone.

Jackfruit Kabaab Curry

500 g jackfruit segments (green)
½ tsp ginger/garlic
pinch of elachi (fine)
salt to taste
1 tsp green pounded chilli
⅓ tsp powdered cloves

Wash and dry the jackfruit. Grease fingers to peel of thin skin from segment. Cut in pieces and put into a pot with the spices.

Add a cup of water and simmer for 30 minutes. Drain off water and mince the fruit.

NOW ADD:
⅓ cup gram flour (chana flour)
½ onion grated
1 tblsp oil
⅓ tsp chilly powder
¼ cup peanuts (crushed without red skin)
⅓ tsp salt

Mix the ingredients together and shape into balls with the help of a little flour if necessary.

The kabaabs can be fried and served as a savoury or used in a gravy as follows:

THE CURRY:

Fry one slivered onion in 2 tablespoons of oil and when a pale gold in colour, add 2 chopped tomatoes with a little chilli and salt and simmer till well blended in curry.

Add a cup or two of water to make a thin gravy. Carefully drop in one kabaab at a time (fried beforehand).

Shake the pot gently from side to side so that the gravy covers the kabaabs. Serve immediately, garnished with sprigs of mint.

Pumpkin
Ridge gourd
Green peppers
Sekta Singh (Drumstick)
Karela
Bhindi (okra)
Snake gourd
Dodhi (Indian calabash)
Coconut
Chibra (Gherkins — in middle of photo)

Sekta Sing
(DRUMSTICK CURRY) VEGETARIAN
(PHOTO ON COVER)

This is a variation from the usual drumstick curry which is cooked in meat.

1 cup toovar dhal
1 bunch drum sticks
1 tsp chillies
1 tsp jeero (cummin)
1 tsp dhunia/jeero
1 tsp ginger/garlic
1 tsp turmeric
¼ of a fresh coconut
1 tsp mustard seed
1 onion (sliced)
1 tsp salt
2 tblsp oil

Clean and wash dhal. Boil in 4 cups of water till tender. Parboil the cleaned drumsticks (cut in pieces) separately. Pound coconut fine.

Fry mustard seeds till they stop spluttering; add onions and fry till they begin to change colour. Now add pounded coconut and all the remaining spices and braise a while. Add this to cooked dhal. Lastly, add the parboiled drumsticks to pot of dhal and cook for 10 minutes. Garnish with greens and add a pinch of gharum masala. Serve with rice.

Jackfruit Fritters (with eggs)

10 or 15 segments of Jackfruit (half-ripe)
2 tsp flour
½ tsp chilli powder
1 tsp oil
salt to taste
pinch of bicarb
1/3 tsp pepper

Separate segments.

If fruit is not sufficiently mature then steam for a few minutes or boil in salted water.

Mix flour, egg yolk and oil and beat well. Leave for 10 minutes. Remove seeds from jackfruit.

Beat egg whites till stiff and fold into yolk batter. Add bicarb. and spices. Dip segments into batter and deep fry in hot oil.

Drain well on paper and serve hot.

Mango Curry

6 medium sized green or half-ripe mangoes
¼ tsp mustard seeds
½ onion (sliced)
1 sprig curry leaves
¾ cup sugar (depending on ripeness of mangoes —this has to be adjusted)
1 tblsp oil
2 green chillies
¼ tsp turmeric
Salt to taste
1 tomato (optional)

Peel mangoes, wash and cut in quarters and keep in water till required. Fry mustard seeds in oil and when they stop spluttering add the slit chillies and onions. Just as onions begin to change to a light gold colour, add the mangoes, tomato, turmeric, curry leaves and about 2 cups of water. Add salt and close lid of pot. Allow to simmer till mangoes are half done. Add sugar and simmer gently till a thick shiny puree results.

Mango Curry
(ALTERNATIVE METHOD)

Proceed as above and just as onions begin to change colour add piece of fresh ginger (finely chopped in cubes). Braise till an aroma arises and then add the rest of ingredients as above. Also add a teaspoon of dhunia powder and juice from a ping pong sized lump of tamarind. Allow the mangoes to cook till nearly done. Add the sugar and simmer till puree is thick and shiny.

Mango Curry
(COLOUR PHOTO 45)

6 green mangoes
2 onions chopped coarsely
4 pods garlic (slivered)
4 green mircha (chillies)
1 large tomato
1 tsp red chilli
salt to taste
3 tblsp oil

Peel mangoes, wash and cut in halves or quarters as desired.

Put oil, mangoes, slit chillies and spices in waterless cooking pot and allow to simmer till done. (If using other pots, add water)

Just before serving make a vagaar of 1 tablespoon of oil and ½ teaspoon of whole mustard. Pour over contents of pot.

Mango Curry

½ kg green mangoes (wash, peel and cut into quarters)
½ cup sugar
8 cloves garlic (slivered)
3 red dry chillies
½ tsp turmeric
1 level tsp salt (adjust to taste)
2 tblsp oil
½ tblsp jeera (cummin seeds)
½ tblsp methi seeds (fenugreek)
1 tsp mustard seeds
1 tsp freshly pounded green or red chilli
3 medium tomatoes grated

Heat oil, add methi, cummin, garlic and chillies. Fry till garlic begins to change colour. Add grated tomatoes, mango pieces, rest of spices and the sugar. Allow to simmer slowly till sugar and spices are well blended with mangoes and tomatoes.

ALTERNATIVE METHOD:

Instead of grating tomatoes cut them in quarters or select small gem tomatoes and halve them.

Simmer curry slowly, open lid at frequent intervals and spoon the sugar and spices over the mangoes and tomatoes, taking care that the latter do not get mashed-up. When serving arrange the tomato halves in between the mango pieces.

Vegetarian Karela

250g karela (5 or 6)
juice of 1 lemon
2 onions (sliced)
1 tsp freshly pounded red chilli
½ tsp black crushed pepper
1 tsp ginger/garlic
1/3 cup yoghurt
1 tsp dhunia/jeero powder
2 tblsp oil
1/3 tsp nutmeg
salt to taste

Scrape karelas and cut into half lengthwise.

Remove seeds. Rub salt all over and leave for about 20 minutes. Squeeze out water and rub karelas well with the yoghurt.

Put karelas in a piece of cloth, spread it over a pan of hot water and cover with a lid. Steam for 10 minutes. Mix spices together.

Heat oil and fry half the onions to a light gold colour, then put in the karelas and sauté them slowly. Remove the karelas from the pot then add the spices and the remaining onions and fry for a minute.

Return karelas to pot and add lemon juice and cook soft. Garnish with chopped greens and serve with rotis.

Quince

Quince is a much neglected fruit. Apart from quince jelly or jam it has been neglected and left to rot in the gardens. There are some novel ways of using it at your table. Give them a chance and get your family raving.

Please note that all recipes in this book in magenta coloured ink, are vegetarian recipes. Some do contain eggs.

Quince Curry
(PHOTO PAGE 133)

2 quince (scrub off fluff and wash well)
1 onion (sliced)
1 tomato (coarsely chopped)
½ tsp methi seeds (fenugreek)
2 tbsp oil
1 tsp sugar (optional)
1 tsp chilli
1 tsp salt
3 green chillies (cut each in 3 pieces)
¼ tsp turmeric (arad)
1 tsp each of slivered garlic and ginger (optional)

Cut quince in pieces (like potatoes for curries). Put all ingredients in pot and steam very slowly till quince are tender. If done over low heat addition of water will not be necessary.

VARIATION:

To above add green or red peppers (quartered).
Add quince pieces to any curry in which you would ordinarily add potatoes and taste the difference.

Quinces in stews are delicious.

Put quinces on trays and leave in hot oven till they are thoroughly cooked. Skin will be dark brown and crackling crisp but fruit inside tender. Just serve piping hot for dessert.

Cold baked quince and fresh cream are also delicious.

1. Grated quince mixed with left over methi achar masalas — just try them.

2. Add slices of quince to vegetable/carrot achar

3. Sprinkle slices of quince with methi masala.

Recipes using Coconut Cream In Vegetables

3 cups vegetables (small pieces carrots, beans, papdi, peas, potatoes, double beans in various combinations)
2 tsp green pounded chillies
1 tsp pounded garlic
½ cup cream of fresh coconut (see page 66)
2 tblsp oil
1 tsp salt
1 tsp ajmo or jeera (tymol or cummin seeds)
1 onion

Sauté sliced onion in oil and when it becomes transparent, add vegetables and spices. Add coconut cream.
Close lid tightly and cook till done.

Gugra Brinjal
(BRINJAL BELLS) (PHOTO PAGE 141)

A large brinjal lends itself very well to this recipe. Otherwise a few smaller ones can be used.

1 large or 4 small sized brinjals
½ tblsp lemon juice
1 tsp dhunia/jeero powder
1 tsp red chillies
1 tblsp dessicated or freshly pounded coconut
½ tsp pounded garlic
2 tblsp sour milk (dahi)
1 tsp crushed jeera (cummin)
1 tsp salt
1 tblsp oil
½ tsp turmeric powder
1 sprig curry leaves (kuripulya)

Destem and wash brinjals. Make slits from bottom towards stem-end so that you have an open flower. Mix masala in dahi, lemon and oil and smear inside and outside of gugra with this paste.

Now put into a baking dish. Dot brinjal with butter or margarine.

Cover dish with foil and bake in 180°F oven for 40 minutes or till brinjal is done.

Uncover and place curry leaves on top and then brown. This is a tasty dish served with rice or rotis or you may prefer to serve it with other vegetables in which case cook separately, a pot of mixed vegetables.

Serve vegetables on large platter with the brinjal gugra as centre pieces in the middle of the vegetables.

Baby Brinjal Curry

(COLOUR PAGE 45)

500 g baby brinjals
1 medium onion
1 tblsp sesame (tal) seeds
½ cup peanut (fried and red skin removed)
1 tsp chilli powder
½ tsp coriander (dhunia) seeds
½ tsp poppy (khus khus) seeds
good pinch cinnamon powder
½ cup dessicated coconut
1 tsp ginger/garlic
2 green chillies
salt to taste
2 tblsp oil
3 whole black peppers
1/3 tsp cummin (jeera) seeds
coriander leaves for garnishing

Slit brinjals in halves, keeping intact at stem end. Leave in salted water. Fry sliced onion in oil and remove from oil when a pale gold in colour. Allow to cool then crush fine.

Toast coconut, jeera, and dhunia seeds on a griddle. Crush fine with the peppercorns and khus-khus. Add this to the other spices. Fry masala for a minute in the same oil in which the onions were fried.

Add peanuts, crushed onions, masala and the brinjals to pot together with the green slit chillies and salt, and keep on turning brinjals till they are well coated with the masalas.

Add just sufficient cold water to cook brinjals. Close lid of pot tightly and simmer till done. Serve with rice as a side dish or with rotis. Waterless type of cooking pots will not require additional water. Serves **6**.

Aaloo Saag

(VARIATION — POTATO CURRY)

Salt to taste
500 g potatoes (quartered or cut in convenient pieces)
2 tsp dhunia/jeero (crushed)
1 tsp mustard seeds
1 tblsp aamli juice (tamarind)
½ bunch chopped dhunia (coriander)
Pinch of turmeric
½ tsp chilli powder
2 tblsp oil
½ cup grated coconut
1 green chilli

Fry mustard seeds in oil till they stop spluttering. Add potatoes, salt, and spices and fry till potatoes begin to turn pink. Add water and cook till potatoes are nearly done. Add tamarind juice, coconut, green chillies and chopped dhunia and cook slowly till gravy is thick and spices are well blended. Serve hot with roti or rice dishes.

Bhagare Bhegan

(STUFFED BRINJALS)
(COLOUR PAGE 141)

6 medium sized tender brinjals
1 ball garlic (pounded)
6 whole dry red chillies
1 tsp cummin seeds (jeera)
1 tsp poppy seeds (khus-khus)
salt to taste
2 onions (slice 1, chop 1)
1 tblsp coriander seed
1 tblsp dessicated coconut
1 tsp sesame seeds (tal)
2 tblsp tamarind juice (aamli)

Heat tava and roast each of above spices separately. Then roast the coarsely chopped onion and then the chopped garlic. Now grind all these together into a paste, adding as much salt as is necessary.

Cut each brinjal into gugras (making a slit first from top to bottom and then across to form a bell, but keep intact at stem edge).

Smear masala into slits and over each brinjal surface. Keep aside the left over masala.

Slice one onion and fry this in a pot together with a teaspoon of mustard seeds in 3 tablespoons of oil

When onions begin to brown, add left over masala paste to it together with the aamli juice.

When juice is blended into paste, lower the brinjals carefully into pot, spooning the gravy over them and turning them when necessary.

With lid of pot closed tightly allow to simmer till brinjals done. Garnish with dhunia leaves and serve with rice or rotis.

Aaloo/Piaz Saag

(POTATO/ONION CURRY)

500 g potatoes (baby potatoes or large ones cut into pieces)
250 g onions (pickle onions or large onions cut to size of potatoes)
1 large tomato
2 green chillies
2 tblsp oil
1 stick cinnamon
Salt, pepper and chilli powder
2 tsp of slivered ginger/garlic

Peel and cut potatoes and onions. Heat oil and fry slivered garlic and ginger in it. Add cinnamon stick and quartered chillies. Add onions, potatoes, and spices. Braise for a few minutes then add as much water as is needed to cook vegetables. Cut tomato in thick wedges and place in pot and allow to cook till soft but not mashed. Garnish with chopped dhunia and serve hot.

Hyderabadi Brinjal

(STUFFED BRINJALS) (PHOTO PAGE 121)

250g brinjals (fist sized or larger)
2 medium onions (chopped coarsely)
1 tsp ginger/garlic
1 tsp chilli
1 tsp dhunia/jeera
1/3 cup oil
1 tblsp tamarind pulp (aamli)
1 tsp salt
1 level tsp turmeric
VAGAAR: (Tempering)
½ tsp white cummin (safed jeera)
2 dry red chillies
2 pods slivered garlic
1 tblsp oil

Split brinjals in quarters but leave intact at stem end.

Mix the spices with a little of the oil and smear ¾ of this paste inside and over the brinjals before they start getting black.

Fry onion in oil till soft, then add the left-over masalas to them. Place brinjals inside pot, turn them slowly on all sides then cover lid and simmer for 10 minutes.

Add tamarind (if not available add lemon juice or better still, 2 tablespoons of green grated mango).

Turn brinjals over so that the gravy coats them all over. Cover lid and simmer till done.

Fry the vagaar spices in the tablespoon of oil and pour it carefully over the brinjals.

Serve on platter garnishing with chopped spring onions. Serve with meat or rice dishes.

Brinjal in Green Chutney

1 kg brinjal (cut in finger-thick round slices)
LIQUIDISE TOGETHER:
1 tblsp dessicated or fresh coconut
1 clove garlic
1 tsp salt
2 tblsp lemon juice or vinegar
¼ cup chopped dhunia leaves
1 tsp jeera (cummin)
4 green chillies

Keep brinjal in salted water for a few minutes, then drain.

Place drained brinjal slices in pot or casserole, pour masalas over them. Mix well so that slices are well coated with spices.

Add 3 tablespoons of oil, cover tightly and bake at 180°C (350°F) oven for 30 minutes.

If it is very liquidy, remove cover and allow to dry out slightly.

Garnish with a sprig of curry leaves.

Delicious with khitchri, rice dishes or rotlas.

Brinjal Kurma

(PHOTO PAGE 141)

6 small tender brinjals
½ cup yoghurt
½ tsp jeero (cummin)
1 tsp salt
¼ cup oil
2 red chillies (cut in ¼ inch pieces)
3 green peppers
½ tsp mustard seeds
¼ tsp methi seeds (fenugreek)
1 tsp sugar
¼ tsp red chilly powder
1 small green mango (optional)

On a tava, roast the mustard and jeero seeds. Crush coarsely. Cut brinjals lengthwise. Cut peppers in half. Heat oil and fry methi seeds and the cut chillies. When braised, add mango and brinjals and fry slowly till shiny. Add peppers and braise a minute.

Mix yoghurt with ¼ cup water. Add all left over spices into it. Pour spiced sour milk over brinjals, reduce heat, close lid tightly and simmer slowly till vegetables are done and gravy is thick.

Brinjal Rawayya

(SERVES 6) (PHOTO PAGE 141)

2 large brinjal
4 tomatoes (cut thinly)
2 onions (finely sliced)
1 tsp chilli powder
½ tsp black crushed pepper
½ tsp salt
½ tsp crushed cummin
¼ tsp turmeric
1½ tsp coarse salt
125g cheddar cheese (slice very thinly)
juice of ½ lemon
1 tblsp oil
1 tblsp crushed dry mint
1 green pepper (cut in rings, then cut each ring in half)

Slice aubergines 5 or 6 times lengthwise from tip to stem but do not cut through.

Sprinkle with coase salt and stand for 20 minutes. Drain off liquid.

Between each slit arrange tomato wedges, onion rings, cheese and green pepper. Mix spices together in lemon and oil and brush this liberally over brinjal and fillings.

Place in ovenproof dish, pour 2 tablespoons oil over each and cover with foil or lid.

Bake at 175°C for 30 minutes.

Bhaji

(SPINACH)

Thanks to the early Indian immigrants, South Africa has been much enriched by the varieties of vegetables obtainable. Many of these early immigrants brought with them, or later imported precious seeds and roots carefully tied up in homespun white calico 'kerchiefs', and entrusted them to the foreign soil. Some strains did not take, others grew vigorously and so with love and tender nursing, there evolved South African types. As a result, the stalls at the Indian Market today are a riot of colours and shapes, with fruits and vegetables not indigenous to South Africa. Too numerous to enumerate, a few such as mangoes, tamarind, jambalas, betel leaves, madumbi, fenugreek, drumstick, bitter gourds, Indian squashes and toovar beans may be mentioned.

The various types of bhaji must be included in daily diets for they are an excellent source of roughage, vitamins and minerals. Besides being health promoting, these vegetables are delicious, having distinctive flavours, so welcome to sensitive taste buds. One often sees recent European immigrants to this country, bending down at the Indian Market and selecting tops of such root vegetables as carrots or beets, which have been discarded by other housewives, who have not realised their nutritive value. The old Indian housewife has long appreciated the vitamin content of vegetable tops and made delicious curries from them.

The thing to remember about leafy vegetable is:

(1) Wash well several times in cold water, to remove all the sand and dirt. Do not keep them soaking in water however, for that makes them soggy.

(2) Prepare and eat as soon as possible, for they lose both flavour and nutrient value when stored.

(3) Spice delicately in order to retain their own special flavour.

(4) Do not overcook or over-stir.

Aaloo Saag (POTATO CURRY)

500 g baby potatoes (small new ones)
Good pinch jeero seeds (cummin)
2 tblsp oil
½ tsp methi seeds (fenugreek)
½ tsp mustard seeds
2 red chillies
Salt and pepper and chilli powder

Wash and scrub potatoes but do not peel. Heat oil and fry the mustard, methi and jeero seeds till they stop spluttering. Add potatoes with salt and rest of spices. Braise for a few minutes, then add a little water till potatoes cooked and nicely tanned.

Methi Bhaji with Potatoes

1 doz baby potatoes or large potatoes cut into small pieces
1 doz methi bhaji
1 tsp chilly powder
1 tsp dhunia/jeera powder
2 tsp slivered ginger
3 tbsp oil
2 medium onions (sliced)
1 tsp salt
2 tbsp dessicated coconut
½ tsp turmeric

Wash methi bhaji and drain well. Scrub baby potatoes and peel. In pot saute onions, methi seeds, slivered ginger and potatoes till onions are soft and transparent. Add all other ingredients, close lid of pot tightly and simmer over very low heat till done.

Boujou Bhaji (BOUYOO)

1 bunch watercress
2 sliced green chillies
1 sliced onion
¼ cup tomato
3 cups rice water
2 cups fresh water
1 tblsp oil
Salt to taste
Pinch turmeric (arad)
¼ tsp methi seed (fenugreek)
1 tsp ginger/garlic

Clean watercress. Break off in little stalks. Wash thoroughly and drain well.

Heat oil, add methi seed, onion, green chillies, ginger/garlic, arad and salt. Let it cook till onion is soft but not brown, then add rice water (water drained off from rice after cooking) diluted with fresh water and bring to boil. Add watercress and tomato and boil till bhaji cooked and well blended with ingredients. The boujou should be consistency of thick soup.

Cholai Bhaji
BACK-YARD SPINACH

3 bunches red bhaji
1/3 tsp cummin
2 cloves of garlic
1 tblsp oil
1 onion (chopped)
2 tblsp dessicated coconut
1/3 tsp methi
2 red (dry) chillies
salt to taste

Clean, wash and dry bhaji.

Sauté onion, methi, slivered garlic and chopped chilli in oil for a minute.

Add bhaji with rest of ingredients, cover pot, and simmer till done.

Chana Dhal/Bhaji

1 cup chana dhal (gram lentils)
1 tsp salt
¼ tsp ginger/garlic
¼ cup oil
¼ tsp turmeric
½ dozen bhaji bunches
6 green chillies
½ tsp dhunia/jeero
2 large onions

Soak dhal overnight. Clean and pick bhaji clean. Wash and drain dry in colander. Slice onions thickly and braise in oil till they are soft and transparent. Add spices and braise for a minute, then add dhal.

Simmer slowly till nearly done. Add bhaji and simmer slowly till done. Garnish with chopped dhunia and strips of green chilli.

Variation with Tomato

Prepare as above but cut up a medium sized tomato and add with bhaji allowing both to simmer slowly. Stir lightly a few times during cooking, so that masalas blend in evenly.

Soowa Bhaji with Moong Dhal
(DILL HERBS)

1 cup moong dhal
2 green chillies (chopped up)
½ tsp turmeric (arad)
¼ cup oil
½ tsp dhunia/jeero
1 onion (chopped)
1 bunch soowa bhaji (fresh dill leaves)
Salt to taste

Soak moong dhal overnight. Wash off skin. Clean bhaji using leaves only. Wash and drain. Chop onion coarsely. Put all the ingredients into pot and simmer slowly till dhal is done. Stir once or twice during cooking.

Serve with Rotlas (see page 290).

Bhaji Variation
(PHOTO PAGE 45)

Any one type of bhaji or mixed herbs (6 bunches)
1 tblsp fresh grated coconut
½ tsp pounded garlic
2 tblsp oil
Salt to taste
1 large onion (chopped coarsely)
½ tsp jeero seeds (cummin)
½ tsp methi seeds (fenugreek)
2 dry red chillies
¼ tsp red chilli powder
Pinch of arad (turmeric)
Small piece of ginger (slivered)

Wash and drain bhajis or spinach. Fry methi seeds, chopped chillies, slivered ginger and grated coconut in oil for a minute. Now add chopped onion and bhajis with rest of spices. (If preferred bhajis may be chopped coarsely). Close lid and simmer slowly, stirring occasionally.

NOTE: Any type of bhaji can be cooked as mentioned above. Bhaji and mealie meal rotlas are a combination relished by peasants as well as aristocrats. The secret is that both must be piping hot. Lemon pickle goes well with it.

Fried Goovar (PHOTO PAGE 40)

500 g goovar
Juice of lemon
1 tsp gharum masala
3 tbsp oil
1 tsp salt
2 tbsp dessicated coconut
1 tsp chilli powder
¼ tsp turmeric
1 tsp crushed jeera (cummin)

Soak goovar after cleaning in salted water for ½ an hour. Drain dry and mix in with other ingredients.

Heat oil in pot — add spiced goovar and close lid of pot. Simmer slowly for 10 minutes. Open lid of pot and cook till goovar is fried crisp.

BANANAS

Like every other produce that grows in India, maximum use is made of the banana. Reputed to be the most ancient fruit in the history of mankind, legend has it that it was the banana and not an apple, with which Eve tempted Adam. Also that for the posteriors of those days, the fig leaf was too small and only a banana leaf would have been large enough to do the job well.

Indian mothers swear that a running tummy can be put right with a banana diet and there are others who swear that it clothes the bones of their anaemic children with adequate flesh. In India, the banana is not just a fruit, it is food as well. Mashed in milk it is the porridge and if cream and sugar is used then it is a lovely dessert. Most delicious puddings can be made from it. For the poor it is the friend in need, for economical curries and chutneys can be made from the fruit. The skin blanched in water is another source for a rich curry. Dried bananas are ground and the flour used as a gruel for a nourishing soup or cereal or biscuits and breads. Above all it can grow in the bottom of one's garden next to the garbage can. Have you forgotten what gorgeous place mats and picnic plates the banana leaf makes?

Banana Curry in Tamarind Sauce

3 to 4 bananas (half-ripe)
½ doz prunes or dried apricots
1 tsp cumin (jeero) seeds
salt and red chilli to taste
few dried mint leaves
½ tblsp oil
3 tblsp tomato puree
½ tsp crushed garlic
3 tblsp thick aamli juice (tamarind)
3 tblsp crushed jaggery (ghor)
black crushed pepper

To thick tamarind puree, add tomato puree and about 2½ cups water. Roast jeera seeds on tawa, crush and add to sauce.

Add all other spices, oil, ghor and mint leaves to sauce.

Put sauce on stove to boil and remove when consistency of cream, and add dried fruit.

When sauce is cool, peel banana, cut into slanted rings and float in sauce. Serve with rice or purees.

* Brown sugar may be substituted for jaggery.
* Instead of bananas use green apples, green mangoes or quince.

Banana Kabaabs in Gravy
(PHOTO PAGE 141)

THE KABAABS:
3 green bananas
salt and black crushed pepper
1 tsp green crushed chilly
½ tblsp gram flour
1 tblsp flour
1 tsp crushed garlic
1 tsp toasted cummin seeds
good pinch bicarb. of soda

THE GRAVY:
2 large tomatoes (or ½ cup tomato puree)
2 green chillies
1 cup fresh green peas
1 tsp sugar
2 tblsp oil
½ tsp ginger/garlic
¼ cup fresh dhunia leaves
1 tsp gharum masala
¼ tsp turmeric powder
salt

Boil unpeeled bananas in salted water till tender. Peel and mash. Add flour and spices and form into small balls. Roll in flour. Fry in oil. Drain and keep aside.

Heat oil. Add tomato puree, salt and spices and put on stove. When mixture is blended — add peas and simmer slowly till nearly done. Add kabaabs and simmer till done. Garnish with greens and serve with rice or roti.

Sekta Sing (Drumstick)
(PHOTO ON FRONT COVER)

1 bunch drumsticks
1 onion grated coarsely
1 tsp crushed cummin (jeera)
2/3 tblsp oil
salt to taste
½ tsp turmeric (arad)
*6 green chillies
*2 tblsp dessicated coconut
*2 cloves garlic
*½ cup dhunia leaves (coriander)

Pound ingredients marked with asterisk. Scrape drumsticks, cut in pieces and wash.

Sauté onions in oil and when they begin to change colour, add ground spices, turmeric and salt. Braise for a minute then add drumsticks and braise a while.

Add 2 cups of water, cover pot and simmer till sekta done and thick gravy results.

Garnish with diced pepper or tomatoes (optional) and some chopped dhunia.

Sev

Buy from sweetmeat confectioners or make your own from the recipe below.

500g chana flour (gram flour)
Salt to taste (1½ teaspoons)
¼ teaspoon bicarb. of soda

Sieve flour, salt and soda in mixing bowl. Gradually add warm water, kneading as you go and making a stiff dough. Knead for a few minutes. Heat oil in pot or kerai. Hold sevia machine (vermicelli shredder with finest gauze disc) over hot oil and push through, so that the sev falls directly into the oil. Fry till crisp, remove and drain in colander. Repeat till all dough is used up. (For picture of machine see page 243).

Sev in Chutney (SEE ABOVE)
(PHOTO PAGE 115)

1 cup sev (savoury as purchased from mithai shops)
1 medium onion (sliced)
1 large tomato (grated or pureed)
1 green chilli
little chopped dhunia
¼ cup oil
½ tsp salt
½ tsp red chilli powder
¼ tsp turmeric powder
¼ tsp crushed garlic

Sauté onion in oil till soft, add spices, tomato and green chillie.

Remove from stove and add sev, and dhunia just before serving.

Torai and Sev (SEE ABOVE)
(RIDGE GOURDS) (PHOTO PAGE 115)

½ kg Torai
1 medium onion (sliced)
2 tomatoes (grated or pureed)
juice of ½ lemon
½ cup oil
1 tsp salt
1/3 tsp turmeric
1 level tsp crushed jeero (cummin)
½ tsp garlic
1 cup sev (spiced fried savoury noodles)

Fry onion in oil till soft. Add torai which have been peeled and cut in convenient pieces and lower heat. Let cook for about 10 minutes, add all the spices, tomato and lemon. Simmer till cooked and just before serving fold in 1 cup of sev.

VARIATIONS:
Instead of torai use diced boiled potato and peas.

Jackfruit with Methi Seeds

1 tsp methi seeds (fenugreek)
4 red chillies
¼ tsp turmeric
500 g jackfruit segments
6 cloves garlic
1 tblsp oil
Salt to taste
1 tblsp fresh grated coconut

Wash and boil jackfruit in salted water till tender. Pound garlic and chillies. Add coconut, salt and turmeric to this and toss the jackfruit in this. Fry methi seeds in the oil and when browned add the jackfruit and braise till masalas have blended in and jackfruit is done.

Goovar Phalli
(NARROW INDIAN BEANS) (PHOTO PAGE 121)

500 g goovar
2 onions (sliced)
¼ cup oil
1 tsp salt
1 tsp dhunia/jeero
1 tsp red chillies
½ cup peas
2 medium tomatoes (chopped)
½ tsp ajmo (tymol seeds)
1 tsp ginger/garlic
¾ tsp turmeric

It is usual just to nip off stem and tail ends of goovar beans but to really enjoy a super dish we would suggest that in addition you carefully cut off (lengthwise) stringy sides of each bean. This takes a lot of time but the result is well worth it.

After cleaning and pruning goovar as suggested, wash well. Saute onions in oil and just as they begin to soften add beans, tomatoes and spices. Turn and toss spooning spices and oil over tomatoes and beans to mix well. Add 2 tbsp of water and with lid tightly closed simmer very slowly till beans nearly done.

Add peas and finish cooking. Cooked in a waterless type of cooking pot there will be no need to add the water.

The Pumpkin Story

The old mother had a premonition that her daughter who had so recently married a forester, was ill. Although none of her sons could be spared during harvesting season, the urge to go and visit her daughter was so strong that the old lady undertook the long and arduous journey on her own.

Excepting for the hut of the forester, this forest had no other human habitation. When the old mother was half-way through it, she saw a fox that seemed to be trailing her. Soon the fox was joined by a jackal, then a wolf, and so the animal entourage increased until she was surrounded by a legion, whose only desire was to devour her.

'You have fairly cornered me,' said the old lady, 'and have every right to lunch on me, but pray have some patience. I am visiting my daughter, who will feed me honey and cream and when I return in a fortnight you will have nice juicy joints to crunch on, instead of this bag of bones that now stands before you.'

The pact was agreed upon and the old mother was allowed to reach her daughters' home unmolested. The daughter upon seeing her mother soon regained her spirits and set about the task of feting the old lady with all sorts of appetising fare.

On the day of departure the old mother looked utterly depressed and to the persistent queries of her son-in-law, revealed to him the reason for her dejection. The son-in-law was duty bound not to leave the area of the forest under his care, unless there was a suitable replacement so he devised a scheme which would ensure the old mother's safe return. He made her sit inside a huge hollowed-out calabash, then he carefully replaced the top and gave it a gentle push that set it rolling merrily down the forest trails towards her village.

A wolf was the first to see this strange sight and he called out: 'Pumpkin, pumpkin did you not see an old lady coming this way?'

In a falsetto voice the old mother replied:
'What old lady, what did you say?
No I have not seen anyone today;
Many things there are awaiting me,
Come dear pumpkin away, away.'

Thus she replied to each subsequent query from the tiger, the fox, the cheetah and the lion, but she could not dupe the jackal. That crafty fellow winked at a baboon sitting high on a coconut palm and gestured to it to throw a coconut at this queer vehicle. No sooner said, then down came a hail of coconuts that broke the shell of the calabash and out tumbled old mother.

"Aah, hah," said the animals gathering around her. "Nice juicy chops as promised." The old lady started thinking fast for remember she had been fed on nuts, honey and cream, and all these being good for the intellect her plans were soon set.

"Your meal has been well earned. Pray let me be seated on this huge mound of sand and you all gather around me, and when I say one, two three! You all pounce on me and may the lucky fellows get the nice plumpy joints."

The old mother seated herself on the mound of sand and waited till all the animals had gathered around. She said, "One, two . . ." and instead of giving the third call she quickly twirled around and with her hands and legs threw as much sand as she could in the eyes of her tormentors. Whilst they rubbed at their burning eyes the old mother ran as fast as her legs could carry her, till she came upon her sons who were waiting to escort her home.

The moral is that if you want to improve your mental capacity, eat honey, almonds and cream.

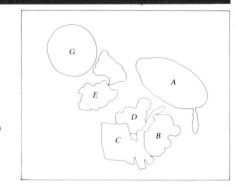

A Prawn Brinjal Rawaya (173)
B Dodhi Bhaja (229)
C Bobotie (202)
D Mealie/Mince Kabaab (211)
E Pumpkin Curry (134)
F Quince Curry (125)
G Pumpkin/Veg STew (134)

Pumpkin Curry (PHOTO PAGE 133)

¼ pumpkin
1 tblsp dessicated coconut
1 tblsp chopped dhunia (coriander)
2 tblsp sugar
2 tblsp oil
4 green chillies
 medium onion
¼ tsp methi seeds (fenugreek)
Salt to taste
1 cup water

Pound chillies and coconut and add to pumpkin with remaining spices. Braise onion (sliced) and methi seeds in oil, till onion is soft and transparent, but not changed in colour. Add pumpkin and spices to pot and allow to simmer slowly.

Stir several times to baste pumpkin well. Add water and simmer till pumpkin is tender. Add sugar and allow curry to absorb sugar and blend-in evenly. Garnish with a dry red chilli and chopped dhunia and serve with khitchri.
NOTE: Pumpkin must be tender but not mashed.

Stews or Bredies

Stews, bredies or turkaris whatever you may wish to call them are best made from cheaper cuts of meat.

Breast, ribs or tail of sheep or ox are ideal for this.

Remember to use much less oil than you would normally do for the mutton is fatty and when simmered slowly, will ooze out its fattiness.

When the finished product looks very oily it is best to blot up the excess by gently lowering kitchen paper towel or clean brown paper over the stew and allow the paper to absorb the extra fat.

Pumpkin Stew (PHOTO PAGE 133)

250g sheep ribs etc., cut up in small pieces
3 tblsp oil
500g pumpkin
1 tblsp sugar
dash of grated nutmeg and cinnamon
salt
2 onions chopped up or sliced coarsely
2 red chillies (cut up)
1/3 tsp black crushed pepper
½ inch fresh ginger (slivered)

Wash the meat. Add the spices and allow to marinate for 15 minutes. Braise onion till it begins to change colour. Remove onion from oil.

In same oil braise meat till it is browned. Return onion to pot, close lid and allow to simmer till meat is done.

More water may be added if necessary.

When meat is done, add pumpkin which has been peeled and cut in blocks, together with the sugar.

Allow to simmer slowly with lid closed, turning at intervals but taking care not to mash up pumpkin.

Garnish with a sprig of curry leaves.

Serve with rotis, rotlas or khitchri (Indian unleavened bread, mealie meal bread or yellow lentil rice).
NOTE:
Any vegetable may be substituted for pumpkin, but omit sugar. Cooking time will have to be adjusted depending on choice of vegetable.

Kokani Vegetable Stew

2 potatoes (cut in thick chips)
½ cup green beans (small pieces)
½ cup double beans
2 green peppers
2 brinjals (sliced in round discs)
½ cup drum sticks
3 small green mangoes (halved)
1 sprig curry leaves
½ tsp chilli
Salt to taste
½ cup carrots
3 gem tomatoes (halved)
2 tblsp coconut
3 tblsp yoghurt
2 green chillies (pounded)
1 tsp saunmf (fennel)

Peel, cut and wash vegetables. Steam-cook the vegetables (except the peppers and tomatoes) in a pot with as little water as possible.

When vegetables are half-cooked, add the tomatoes and peppers, and simmer till everything is cooked but not soft and mushy. Now pound together 2 tblsp fresh coconut, 2 green chillies and 1 tsp saunmf (fennel).

Mix into a paste with 3 tblsp yoghurt. Place the cooked vegetables in a oven-proof casserole and pour the yoghurt mixture over it. Carefully toss and turn the vegetables so that the paste is distributed fairly evenly.

Temper ½ tsp each of mustard and methi seeds and also 1 tsp of slivered garlic in 2 tblsp of oil and pour over vegetables. Place in moderate oven for 5 to 10 minutes. Serve with rotis.

Fried Karela (BITTER GOURDS)

500 g Karelas
¼ whole fresh coconut
3 tblsp oil
4 green chillies
Salt to taste

Scrape and wash gourds. Cut in thin rounds. Add coarse salt. Rub in palm of hand to remove seeds and wash and drain dry. Slit green chillies. Cut coconut in thin slivers. Cook karela, chillies and coconut in 3 tablespoons of salted water. When done, heat oil and fry till crisp.

Dodhi/Chana Dhal

¼ tsp cummin seeds
1 cup chana dhal (gram)
Few slivers of fresh ginger
2 onions
½ tsp turmeric (arad)
3 green chillies
2 tomatoes
¼ cup oil
Juice of ½ lemon
½ dodhi (Indian gourd)
1 tsp chilli powder
1 tsp dhunia/jeero
1 tsp ginger/garlic
1 tsp gharum masala
Few sprigs dhunia (coriander)
Salt to taste

Soak dhal overnight or for a few hours. Heat oil and fry onions to light golden colour. Add all spices except gharum masala and braise for a few seconds. Add finely chopped tomatoes. Slit the green chillies and saute for 2 minutes. Add dhal that has been soaked in cold water for some time and braise slowly. Add 1 cup of water. Close lid and allow to simmer. Peel and cut dodhi in cubes and add to dhal when nearly done. Add more water if necessary. Before serving make a vagaar by heating one tablespoon of oil, braise gharum masala in this, then add one whole red chilly, few slivers of ginger, and ¼ teaspoon cummin seeds. Braise for a minute, and pour over curry. Garnish with chopped dhunia. Serve hot with Rotis.

Chana Dhal with Green Peppers

Follow recipe of dodhi/chana dhal as on top of page but substitute pepper for dodhi.

Methi Seeds Curry

½ cup methi seeds (fenugreek)
3 tblsp oil
1 tsp chilli powder
½ tsp dhunia/jeero
1 tomato (chopped)
1 onion (chopped coarsely)
Salt
¼ tsp turmeric (arad)
½ tsp ginger/garlic
Chopped dhunia (coriander)

Soak methi seeds overnight. Rinse off several times then boil in little salted water till soft. Braise in a tblsp of oil for 2 minutes.

In curry pot braise onions in oil till soft and transparent. Add tomato and spices and simmer till tomato blended. Add methi seeds, and simmer till curry done. Garnish with dhunia and serve with rotlas.

Green Pepper Curry

250g long green peppers (mild type)
* 2 tblsp tal (sesame)
* 1 tblsp whole dhunia (coriander)
* 2 tblsp khus-khus (poppy seeds)
* 1 tblsp jeera (cummin)
* 1 tblsp peanuts
* 2 tblsp dessicated coconut
2 tsp crushed garlic
1 medium onion, grated
2 tblsp tamarind (red amli)

Roast ingredients marked with asterisk (*) lightly on tava or in oven (do not brown) crush coarsely.

Fry onions, add garlic and roasted masala, then put in peppers, tossing to coat with the masala. Pour tamarind paste over peppers and cook for just 5 to 10 minutes.

Special Leela Mircha Curry

(SWEET/SOUR)
(PHOTO PAGE 156)

6 large green mirchas (green capsicums)
2 large potatoes
¼ cup roasted ground peanuts
2 tblsp chana dhal (boiled)
½ tsp mustard seed
1 tblsp methi masala (See page 253)
1½ tsp red chillies
1½ tblsp tal seeds (sesame)
1½ tblsp grated coconut (fresh or dessicated)
2 tblsp tamarind juice
2 tblsp oil
Salt to taste
1 tblsp brown sugar

Cut each green mircha (capsicums) into eight pieces. Peel potatoes and cube into pieces. Crush peeled peanuts coarsely.

Into a pot put the oil and slowly fry the green mircha and potatoes in it till they just begin to change colour. Remove peppers and keep aside. Add the crushed peanuts, tamarind juice, sugar and salt to taste. Add 1 cup water and cook very slowly till potatoes are done. Return peppers to pot.

Meanwhile pound the boiled chana dhal and add the mustard seed, tal, and coconut and pound a little longer. Add the methi masala (Grandma's methi masala, Page 253) and the red fine chillies and add to the pot of mircha and potatoes. Stir in well and cook for just 5 minutes longer. Serve hot with puris or rotis.

NOTE: Any vegetable such as karela, bhinda, green mango, etc., can be used instead of peppers and potatoes.

Bhinda Curry

(OKRA) (PHOTO PAGE 121 & 84)

500 g bhinda
2 onions
¾ tsp salt
1 tsp chillie powder
1 tsp dhunia/jeero
¼ cup oil
¾ cup tomato juice (or finely cut tomato)
2 tblsp yoghurt
½ tsp ginger/garlic
1 tsp turmeric

Wash bhinda. Dry well on cloth. Cut them in convenient pieces (5 cm pieces). Fry in two tablespoons of oil till a light brown. (This frying before cooking prevents stickiness in curry). Remove bhinda from oil.

Add left-over oil and fry the sliced onions in it till a pale golden brown.

Add tomato with the spices. Cook for a few minutes till soft, then add fried bhinda, braise a while and pour over sour milk curds. Steam gently.

Add ½ tsp of gharum masala just before serving (Bhinda, fried as above, could be added to a dry meat curry).

Chana Dhal and Onion Kachoomer

1 onion (grated)
1 med tomato
2 tblsp oil
1 cup chana dhal (boil in salted water till soft, but not mushy)
1 onion (sliced fine as for kachoomers)
½ tsp salt
½ tsp chilli powder
¼ tsp dhunia/jeeroo powder
¼ tsp turmeric (arad)

Braise first three items together till ingredients are blended. Add spices to this.

Place hot puree in glass casserole. Spread hot chana dhal on it.

Slice onion fine and squeeze out water.

Blend together 1 tablespoon of vinegar, 1 finely sliced green chilli and a little chopped dhunia or mint leaves.

Mix onion in this spiced vinegar and toss well. Garnish chana dhal with kachoomer and serve immediately with hot rotis.

Green Mealie Curry

Cut off mealies from cob and boil in salted water till done, or boil cobs, then cut off 2cm chunks
2 cups mealie kernels
1 tsp jeera (cummin seeds)
1 tsp tal (sesame)
1 tsp ginger
2 tbsp ghee or oil
3 tbsp poppy seeds (khus-khus)
1 tbsp peanuts
1 tsp dhunia seeds (coriander)
½ fresh coconut
4 green chillies

Grate 1/3 of fresh coconut.

Extract milk from the rest to make 3 cups (see page 66) Pound together all ingredients except the mealie kernels. Fry pounded masalas slowly in ghee for a few minutes.

Add boiled kernels and coconut milk and allow to simmer slowly for 10 mins, till gravy is thick.

Serve hot, garnished with green pepper rings and thin strips of tomato.

Beans

(RED CANADIAN WONDER OR ANY OTHER DRY BEANS)

1 cup beans (soak overnight)
1 litre water
1 large onion
2 medium tomatoes (chopped)
3 green whole chillies
1 tsp chilli powder
½ tsp turmeric (arad)
½ tsp dhunia/jeero
1½ tsp salt
½ tsp ginger/garlic
¼ cup ghee/oil

Boil the beans till absolutely soft and mushy. Beans must be boiled very slowly to ensure thick mushy gravy. Add more water if required. When beans are ready, in a frying pan put whole chillies, the onions and cook slowly in ghee/oil till soft and pinkish, then add tomatoes and cook till all the moisture has evaporated.

Add all the spices and about 1½ tblsp of water and cook till the masalas have blended thoroughly with pureed tomatoes. Add to simmering beans and cook slowly till the gravy is thick and onions cannot be seen in the gravy. If desired, add chopped dhunia leaves before serving. Serve piping hot.

Excellent for Bunny Chow (see note page 297)

VARIATION:
When curry is done, add ¼ cup aamli (tamarind) puree.

Moong Curry

1½ cup moong (chinese peas)
1 onion (sliced)
1 tomato (chopped)
2 green chillies (slit)
2 tbsp yoghurt
chopped dhunia for garnishing
¾ tsp ginger/garlic
1 tsp salt
1 tsp dhunia/jera
¾ tsp turmeric
1 tsp chilli
1½ tbsp oil
1 tbsp ghee

Wash and soak moong overnight or for a few hours. Boil in 2 cups water till moong is soft and mushy.

In ghee/oil fry the onions and green chilli and when browned add tomato and spices and cook gently till tomato is blended. Add chutney to pot of moong and mix well.

Garnish with dhunia and serve hot with rotis or rotlas.

TO SPROUT MOONG METHI ETC.

Soak 1 cup moong in cold water. After a day or two the skins will begin to burst. Place moong in a colander and place colander in deep plastic container and put on the lid of the container.

Moong will have to be sprinkled with ½ a cup of water each morning and evening. By second or third day very lovely tender shoots will have emerged. In summer the process is much faster.

OR:

Alternatively cover colander with a plastic bag. Place colander in basin and leave in dark corner — sprinkle with water.

OR:

Soak moong in water (cold in summer and warm in winter) overnight. Next day drain off excess moisture, leave in muslin-thin cotton cloth in a dish. Sprinkle water to dampen and keep in shady place till sprouts appear (about 2 days).

TO COOK: Wash sprouts in several rinsings of water to remove all loose skins but retaining sprouts.

Brinjal/Moong Sprouts Delight

3-4 brinjals
½ tsp ground garlic
1 tsp red chilli
2 tomatoes (chopped
½ cup grated cheddar cheese
2 tblsp oil
1 cup moong sprouts
1 tsp salt
½ tsp crushed jeera (cummin)
½ tsp crushed dhunia (coriander)
1 onion chopped
¼ tsp black crushed pepper

Cook brinjal in water for 10 minutes. Halve brinjals. Scoop out flesh and leave firm wall and base.

Sauté onions in oil and as soon as they are transparent add well washed sprouted moong, spices, tomatoes and scooped out flesh of brinjal.

Cover pot and simmer till sprouts nearly done. Pile mixture into brinjal halves, dot with grated cheese and butter. Bake at 180°C (350°F) oven for 15 to 20 minutes.

VARIATIONS:
1. Moong dhal or chana dhal curry.
2. Any left over khima curry, vegetable curries etc.
3. Instead of cheese, top with a beaten egg and sprinkle liberally with corn flakes or rice crispies.

Sprouted Moong
HARGA (COLOUR PAGE 121)

2 cups sprouted moong
2 onions (chopped)
1 tbsp slivered ginger and garlic
3 tbsp oil
1 tsp red chilli (or more)
3 green chillies chopped
salt to taste
1 tsp crushed jeera

Heat oil and fry slivered ginger and garlic, and chopped green chillies.

When chillies begin to change colour, add onion and other spices and fry for 2 minutes.

Add moong, adding just a sprinkling of water and allow to steam cook. Take care not to over-cook — 10 minutes ought to be sufficient.

SECTION 2d

The Art of Stuffing Vegetables

THE artistry of the home-maker is pleasantly stimulated when she eyes the wide array of stuffable vegetables obtainable in those parts of South Africa, where Indian, Portuguese and Chinese market gardeners offer their delectable wares.

In Durban, at the Indian markets, it is pleasant to watch the glint in the eyes of the Italian, Portuguese and Indian housewives, as they load their baskets with tender gourds, squashes, brinjals, peppers, marrows and okra. One can visualise the women measuring up to the challenge thrown forth by these attractively shaped vegetables.

Undoubtedly, the ancient food gatherer, when he stumbled across a pumpkin or marrow, must have been attracted by its shape, size and colour. In India commonly known as gourds, they play an important role in Indian cookery and many are the fables that have been interwoven around them. Used as a basic ingredient in curries, desserts and savouries these healthy vegetables should continue to play an important role in man's diet.

The Hakims and Vaids of India attribute high medicinal properties to gourds. Even South African Indians will vouch that Karelas (bitter gourds) have high therapeutic value for diabetics.

The secret of stuffing vegetables lies in choosing firm, tender and small-sized vegetables, and then stuffing them with appropriate fillings in such a way that colour, shape and taste of the original vegetable is retained. The recipes selected for the adventurous housewife range from basic stuffings to quite exotic fare. Though numerous examples are given, this is in no way the complete encyclopaedia for stuffed vegetables, and we hope that housewives will exert themselves to devise their own stuffings from left-overs in the fridge, or from the stores on their pantry shelves.

Stuffed Vegetables On Tray
Ridge guord
Patta (individually rolled)
Butternut squash
Cabbage packets with shrimps

On Round Platter
Long green peppers
Bhinda (okra)

Stuffed Dodhi

(MARROW) — SEE COLOUR PLATE 265 & 99

Left-over roast meats or left-over khima and rice is excellent for stuffing dodhi, brinjal, capsicums and tomatoes. If, however, there is no left-over meat or mince, prepare some as follows: 125g mince or diced meat. Braise this with masalas as in Master Mince Recipe. Add 1 onion after braising and cook till onion is soft and well blended in mince. When cool, add 2 tablespoons tomato juice and 2 tablespoons of chopped dhunia leaves.

To ¾ of this mince mixture, add 1 raw egg. Peel dodhi, core inside, remove pips. But add the pulp that was removed from dodhi to mince. Now stuff dodhi well with mince mixture. Smear remaining mince on outside of dodhi. Place in deep casserole to which has been added 2 tablespoons of oil and bake in 200ºC oven for half an hour with lid on. (A little water may have to be added to cook dodhi tender.) Glaze dodhi with a little beaten egg (saved from egg which was added above) and a little oil. Decorate with mint or parsley sprigs. Serve with roasts.

NOTE: Left-over rice (a few tablespoonsful) may be added to above stuffing. Baking times will have to be adjusted according to vegetables chosen.

Butter Nut Squash

(STUFFED) (PAGE 138)

3 medium sized butter nut squashes
1 onion (grated)
½ cup butter
¼ cup sour milk (yoghurt)
Seeds of 1 elachi (cardomom)
½ tsp freshly ground black pepper
1 cup cream or top milk
1/3 cup ground almonds
2 tsp lemon juice
1½ tsp crushed dhunia
½ tsp salt

Split squashes in two, from stem end downwards. Scoop out flesh leaving a half inch wall on all sides. Slightly boil squash shells in salted water (5 minutes)

Meanwhile saute in half of butter, the grated onion and scooped out pulp. When blended (after 5 minutes), add cream, lemon, salt and ground almonds. (Peanuts may be substituted). Simmer for another 5 minutes, then pile mixture in squash shells. Dot with remaining butter, sprinkle with crushed pepper and dhunia. Bake in 180°C oven for 20 to 30 minutes. Delicious with meat dishes.

Stuffed Cabbage

1 small cabbage head
2 onions
250 g mutton (diced small), chicken breast or mince
1 tsp red chilli powder
½ tsp turmeric
1 tsp salt
1 stick cinnamon and 2 cloves
2 tomatoes
½ cup yoghurt (dahi)
1 tsp dhunia/jeero
1 tsp ginger/garlic
3 tblsp oil

Remove outer leaves of cabbage. Cut off an inch from stem end so that cabbage can stand flat. Wash well between leaves, then steam in water to which has been added salt, tuj and cloves.

Meanwhile braise onions in oil and when they begin to turn pink add the meat and spices and brown well. Add tomato and dahi and cook till tomato is soft and well blended in curry.

Remove cabbage from stove and allow to cool. Core out some cabbage from centre, shred fine and add to chutney. Make space between leaves of cabbage and stuff in these spaces, as much meat/chutney as possible. Pour the left-over chutney over outside of cabbage and return cabbage to pot and finish cooking. Serve on large platter.

Green Peppers stuffed with Sweet Corn

(PHOTO PAGE 156)

4 green peppers
½ tsp pounded garlic
Salt to taste
cups frozen cut corn
½ tsp pounded chillies
2 tblsp butter or oil

Add 2 tblsp of butter to the mealies. Add other ingredients and braise till mealies are coated with spices. Parboil peppers. Then cut in halves — lengthwise. Stuff with above mixture. If preferred sprinkle each with a little grated cheese. Place a dab of butter over each and bake in 150ºC oven till peppers begin to change colour.

Alternatively, do not parboil peppers but stuff after washing. Place in greased casserole, dotting with butter and cover with foil for 20 minutes. Thereafter remove foil and gently bake in oven till peppers done.

Rawayya

(STUFFED VEGETARIAN BRINJAL CURRY)
(SEE COLOUR PAGE 45)

500 g baby brinjals
2 tomatoes (medium sized)
1 tblsp lemon juice
1 tblsp crushed tal (sesame seeds)
¼ cup oil
½ tsp each of methi, mustard and jeero seeds
  (fenugreek, cummin)
1 level tsp ground garlic
1 tsp chilli powder
¼ tsp turmeric
1 tsp jeero powder (cummin)
Salt to taste
3 green chillies

Wash brinjals. Cut in four quarters from bottom end but leave stem-end intact (like gugras). To lemon juice add tal, salt, turmeric, chilli powder, jeero powder and garlic. Mix into smooth paste and stuff into brinjals.

Cut chillies in quarters. Heat oil in pot and add cut chillies, the whole mustard, methi and jeero, and when they stop spluttering, lower the stuffed brinjals into pot. Braise brinjals for a while and when shiny add grated tomato. Reduce heat and simmer slowly with lid closed tightly, till brinjals are soft but not mushy.

Caution: When turning brinjals take care not to bruise or break them. Garnish with freshly cut dhunia leaves, and serve with rotlas or khitchri.

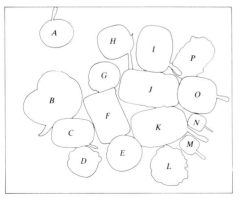

A Rasgulla (356)
B Parathas (292)
C Cauliflower
D Mealie Moothia (210)
E Mush Ki Dhal (149)
F Bhagare Began (126)
G Bhaji Paneer
H Veg/Potato Pie
I Papdi Gosht with Patta (113)
J Dum ka Gosht (93)
K Chabli Kabaab (149)
L Pandella (193)
M Red Mircha/Peanut Chutney (276)
N Mint Chutney (274)
O Banana Kabaab Curry (130)
P Savoury Pancakes (219)

Green Peppers with Methi

(COLOUR PAGE 255)

½ kg green peppers (quartered)
1/3 cup methi seeds (fenugreek)
¼ cup oil
¼ tsp turmeric powder (arad)
¾ cup yoghurt
juice of 2 lemons
1 tsp salt
½ tsp crushed garlic

Soak methi overnight. Rinse several times to render it less bitter.

Heat oil and when hot, put in the methi and the green peppers. Let cook for about 5 minutes on medium heat.

Add spices, lemon juice, and yoghurt and let cook till moisture is evaporated. Delicious as a side dish.

Masala Stuffed Mircha

(LONG THICK PEPPERS)

6 mircha (capsicums)
1 tblsp khus-khus (poppy seeds)
2 tblsp of frozen sweet corn
½ cup oil
Salt to taste
1 tblsp coriander seeds
1 tblsp freshly grated coconut
3 red chillies
1 dozen cashew nuts

Wash and slit mirchas down to stem. Keep in water till required. Heat one tablespoon of oil in pot and fry coriander seeds and red chillies (dry or fresh) together. Remove chillies and seeds and in same oil fry cut corn and coconut. Lastly roast khus-khus in little oil. Put fried ingredients in mortar, together with nuts and pound up coarsely. Stuff each mircha with this masala and gently fry in left over oil till golden brown, taking care that masalas do not fall out. Serve hot with rice or meat dishes.

Stuffed Green Peppers

¼ cup crushed cummin (jeera)
1 grated onion
salt to taste
2 tblsp coconut (fresh or dessicated)
1 tblsp sesame seeds (tal)
gram flour (chana) for binding

Pound tal and jeera together. Add rest of ingredients and stuff the washed, and halved green peppers. (May be left whole and only slit for stuffing). Fry in shallow oil over low heat till peppers are done. Delicious as side course with rice or meat dishes.

Stuffed Karelas

(BITTER GOURD)

6 large karelas
500 g mince
1 tsp ginger/garlic
½ cup tomato
1 tsp red chillies
½ cup yoghurt
½ tsp gharum masala
2 medium onions
½ cup ghee/oil
1 tsp salt
1 tsp arad (turmeric)
½ tsp dhunia/jeero

Scrape outer roughness off karelas. Slit and boil in salted water to which has been added a good pinch of arad. Remove seeds, when half done and cooled. Meanwhile, prepare a curry thus: Fry onions in ghee/oil till they begin to change colour. Add mince with spices and braise till moisture has evaporated. Add tomatoes and allow to blend in well. Now stuff each karela with little of mince and fry in little oil (separate from above quantity) till nicely browned all over. Replace karelas in curry, add yoghurt and simmer slowly till curry done. Add gharum masala. Just before serving, garnish with chopped dhunia leaves. Serves 6.

VARIATION:

If preferred, one raw egg may be added to mince which is used for stuffing karelas. This will bind mince firmly inside.

Green Peppers

3 tblsp oil
1 slice (6 mm thick) bread
¾ tsp salt
2 tsp crushed jeero (cummin)
6 green peppers
¼ tsp black crushed pepper
¼ tsp red chilli powder

Soak bread in water. Drain off moisture and add spices to bread. Mix well. Slit bottom of peppers and stuff bread mixture in cavity. Fry slowly in shallow oil till a crisp golden brown. Thick long peppers can be used in this way too.

VARIATION:

Omit bread and use dessicated coconut instead.

Section 2 E

A GOURMET'S DELIGHT

The Sultan was taking a walk around the Royal gardens and being in an observant mood, stopped every now and then to watch the men at work. One old fellow with striking features, looked most dejected and seemed to work without much interest. The Sultan went up to him and asked him the cause of his sadness.

"Aah Sir. I, too, am noble born but have now fallen on bad days and you see me trying to work for a living."

"Hmm." Said the Sultan, "If you are of noble birth tell me what are the best portions to serve of a poultry, a fish and an ox."

"Your Majesty," replied the man with a glint in his eye. "The crackling skin of poultry, the tail of a fish and the tongue of an ox, these are the good things of this earth."

"Excellent! Excellent!" said the Sultan and he asked his vizier to reward the fellow with a hundred gold sovereigns.

A fellow labourer who had watched and listened to this episode with keenness, abided his time and when next the Sultan came to the garden, he too pulled a long sorrowful face and started to shed crocodile tears. The Sultan much surprised at this sight asked: "Why, what ails you my man?"

"Oh sir," said the crafty fellow. "I am of noble birth but fortune having dealt me this cruel blow, I now have to do work for which I am ill equipped."

"Hmm" said the Sultan. "Perhaps you can tell me what are the best parts to eat of a fish, a bird and an ox."

The imposter excitedly gave his well rehearsed answers. "The best portion of a fish is its tongue, of a bird its tail, and of an ox its good crackling skin."

With utter disgust the Sultan strode off, telling his vizier to reward the fellow appropriately with a hundred lashes.

Tripe (Ojri)

After buying a well cleaned tripe from a butcher it still entails a lot of work in rendering it absolutely clean and edible. Cut a tripe in four pieces and immerse in boiling water. Wash each piece by lifting it with a pair of tongs or a fork and scrape well with a knife. This procedure will bleach the tripe and it will resemble a clean turkish towel. Wash in several rinsings of cold water till no trace of uncleanliness is left.

Now boil tripe in water for two to three hours and about half an hour before it appears done, add a little salt and turmeric in the water.

Meanwhile prepare a chutney thus: Slice 1 large onion and fry it in ½ cup of oil till it begins to change colour. Add to this:

1 cup tomato
1 tsp ginger/g arlic
1 tsp turmeric (arad)
1 tsp salt
1 tsp dhunia/jeero
1 tsp red chillies
2 whole green chillies (slit through)

Let it simmer for a minute or two then add tripe cut in 2cm squares. Add 2 tablespoons water and braise for about 5 minutes or till excess moisture evaporated. Garnish with chopped dhunia and shallot and sprinkle ½ teaspoon gharum masala. Serve with rotis.

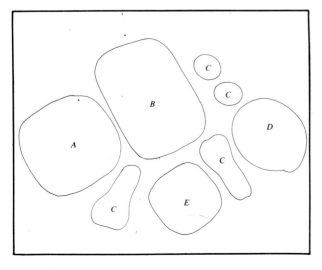

A Tripe (ojri) delights (144)
B Fish Almond (170)
C/E Mealies in Dahi (154)
D Brain Curry (147)
E Brinjal Pickle (264)

Ojri Delights

(TRIPE CURRY)
(PHOTO PAGE 145)

500 g tripe (scrubbed clean in salted water like a towel
    and cut in bite sized pieces)
3 tblsp chopped mint
1 tsp freshly ground red chilli
1 large red or green pepper (cut in small pieces)
6 black peppercorns
salt
1 ball garlic (slivered)
8 cups water
2 tsp crushed jeera (cummin)
½ cup oil

Fry half of slivered garlic in oil and as soon as it turns colour add tripe and all other ingredients except the pepper and cook gently for 2 hours.

Tripe should be nearly cooked by now and the water sufficiently evaporated to leave a pot full of mushy contents. Now add 3 tomatoes (sliced) and peppers cook till tomato blended.

Serve hot with garnishing of mint leaves.

VARIATION:

Prepare as above but use only half quantity of oil for frying garlic. When tripe nearly done fry one sliced onion in the other ¼ cup oil and when they begin to turn pink in colour add quarters of green and red peppers.

Fry for a minute then add the pot of tripe and as well juice of one lemon. Sprinkle ½ tsp of gharum masala over contents and serve before peppers loose colour.

Brain Cutlets

6 brains
1 tsp dhunia/jeero
½ tsp chilli powder
¼ tsp turmeric
Pinch of salt
¼ cup ghee
¼ cup oil
Breadcrumbs
2 eggs

Boil brains as in Brain Curry. Drain dry, cool. Divide each brain in 4 portions (flat). Now mix all the spices and salt with a little water (not a thick paste). Smear slices of brain with paste then roll in bread crumbs.

Heat ghee and oil in frying pan, dip in well-beaten egg fry in medium heat till golden brown. Drain on wire rack. Serve with chutneys.

Tripe Kabaabs

500 g cleaned boiled tripe
1 medium sized onion
½ bunch dhunia leaves (coriander)
½ bunch spring onion (chopped)
¼ cup chana flour (gram or pea)
1½ tsp salt
½ cup dahi (yoghurt)
1 tsp ginger/garlic
½ tsp turmeric (arad)
1 tsp ground green chilli
½ cup mealie meal
¼ cup cake flour
1 egg
¼ tsp black crushed pepper

NOTE: Being rubbery it may be difficult to mince the tripe. Therefore freeze slightly then put through mincer.

Mince or chop fine the boiled tripe: To it add above ingredients and mix well. Adjust salt and chilli. Mould into kabaabs the size of a large walnut and fry in fairly hot oil, till kabaabs are a golden colour. Drain in colander and serve hot.

OR ALTERNATIVELY

Mould into kabaabs but flatten them slightly. Place in greased tray and grill in oven till done. A few tablespoons of oil may be poured over kabaabs if they look too dry.

Brain Cutlets

6 portions sheep's brains
1 tblsp milk
breadcrumbs
¼ tsp crushed jeera (cummin)
½ tsp dried mint
1 tsp salt
2 tsp vinegar
1 tblsp rind of lemon
½ tsp chilli powder
¼ tsp black crushed pepper
1 egg

Soak brains in cold water for 2 hours to loosen blood-clots. Rinse and place in pot with cold water to which has been added salt and vinegar. Bring to boil and keep simmering for 10 minutes. Drain and soak again in cold water. Brains will now be firm. Pluck off any bloody spots that may still remain. Rinse separately and pat dry.

Mix bread crumbs with salt, chilli, pepper, lemon rind, jeera and dried mint. Beat egg and milk together.

Dip brains in egg and roll in spiced crumbs.

Fry gently in warm oil till they are a golden colour. Drain on kitchen paper.

Sheep's Tongue (Roast or Fried)

3 tongues
1 stick cinnamon
Few cloves and peppers
2 tblsp oil
2 cups water
½ tsp chilli (freshly pounded)
1 tsp ginger/garlic
1 tsp salt
¼ tsp turmeric (arad)
½ tsp crushed jeero (cummin)
½ tsp crushed coriander (dhunia)
¼ tsp black crushed pepper

Pour boiling water over tongues and allow to steep for 10 minutes. Put tongues on a board and with back of knife scrape well. Slit tongues in half and wash.

Put tongues in a pot with the water, cinnamon stick, cloves and peppers and simmer for 2 to 3 hours. By this time the water will have evaporated. Remove tongues from pot and allow to cool.

Meanwhile make a paste with the chilli, ginger/garlic, crushed coriander, jeero, pepper and salt. Smear the tongues well with this masala, and return to pot with the oil and brown slowly till masalas are well braised.

Alternatively put masala smeared tongues in a casserole and brown in oven.

Tongue Curry

Proceed as above but smear tongue slightly with only half of the masala paste. Slice two medium sized onions and braise in the oil. When they begin to turn pink add 2 grated tomatoes and the left over masala paste. Allow to simmer for a while and then add to it the slightly braised tongues. Close lid of pot and allow to cook for 15 minutes. Serve garnished with mint sprigs.

Boomla
(BOMBAY DUCK)

This is a great delicacy with people with gourmet tendencies. Braise small pieces of bombay duck (washed) in oil till light brown. Serve with bharkoo, porridge khitchris, etc. It can also be added in papdi curry or a special chutney curry made as follows:-

Fry one onion to very pale colour, and add chopped tomato to which has been added the usual masalas. Add braised bombay duck. Garnish with chopped greens.

Sheep Tail Curry

Cut sheep tail through discs.
 Wash and drain (500 g)
1 tsp ginger/garlic
1 tsp salt
1 tsp dhunia/jeero
2 tblsp oil
1 large onion
¼ cup yoghurt
1 tsp chilli powder
½ tsp turmeric
½ cup pulverized tomato

Braise onion in oil till they are a lovely golden colour. Drain off oil and leave onion on plate to cool. Crush with back of spoon. To sheep's tail, add above spices, the yoghurt and tomato. Lastly add the crushed onion and return to pot in which the onions were fried. Cook slowly over low heat till meat is done and the oil in the curry starts to float to the top.

Masalaad Brains
(BHEJO) (PHOTO PAGE 145)

2 medium onions
3 green chillies
½ tsp dhunia/jeero
1 tsp ginger/garlic
1 brain (sheep's)
½ tsp fine salt
¼ tsp red chillies
¼ tsp arad (turmeric)

Boil washed and cleaned brain in water till hard. Braise onions and green chillies (cut into small pieces) till soft but not brown. Add brain with the masalas. (Use fine salt in brain only). Add a few tablespoons of water to allow masala to seep in well. Serves four.

Livers

The Hakims (doctors of traditional medicine) often prescribe livers in the diet of weak and ill patients. They are a rich source in iron and vitamins, but it often happens that the patients are put off by the same type of liver dish being presented to them. A handful of livers can make a nice dish of food for even the most fastidious so why not try these tempting dishes.

Remove from oven just as it begins to brown. Serve with mashed potatoes, vegetables or as a savoury on puris.

ALTERNATELY:

After steaming allow to cool. Slice thinly and serve on rounds of toast or puri or use in salads.

Kaleji/Vegetable (Liver)

250g liver (chicken or lamb)
250g brinjal
2 tomatoes
2 tblsp aamli extract (tamarind)
½ doz baby onions
1 tsp cummin seed (jeera)
1 tsp ginger/garlic
250g potatoes (baby preferably)
2 mangoes (green)
½ freshly grated coconut
1 tsp turmeric
2 tsp chilli
2 tsp crushed coriander seeds
1 sprig curry leaves
extract milk from coconut

If sheeps liver, cut into small cubes.

Cut potatoes, brinjals and mangoes in small pieces — sprinkle salt and keep for about 10 minutes then fry in a little oil, and remove vegetables.

Crush coriander and cummin after roasting in dry pan. Add to ginger/garlic and other spices and make into a paste.

Mix masalas and chopped tomatoes with liver. Heat oil in pan in which vegetables were fried and fry onions and liver in this.

When masalas are blended with tomato, add the tamarind, coconut milk and fried vegetables and cook till done. Serve hot with rotis or rice.

Baked Liver

250g chicken liver
2 eggs
1 cup milk
1 clove garlic crushed
1 red pepper (diced small)
salt to taste
1 tblsp butter or ghee
½ cup flour
2 tblsp sour cream or malaai
2 egg yolks
1 tsp pounded chillies (red)
1/3 tsp black crushed pepper
dash of elachi or fine cinnamon

Clean and cut livers in small pieces. Wash and drain. Add spices and braise in butter till browned.

Beat eggs till frothy. Add flour, cream and milk and beat again.

Now add the liver and the diced pepper and pour in greased baking dish.

Cover dish, then put it in a baking pan, half filled with water.

Bake in oven at 150°C for 40-50 minutes.

ALTERNATELY:

You may puree the livers and then add it with the flour to the eggs and milk. Serve on rice or bed of salad with tomato chutney.

Or — add a cup of mashed carrots to the pureed livers and proceed as above.

Pureed Chicken Livers

(KALEJI KABAAB)

1 kg livers
1 tsp red crushed chillies
2 tblsp chopped mustard achar
3 tblsp oil
salt to taste
½ tblsp lemon juice
2 onions (grated)
1 tsp crushed garlic
3 tblsp ghee (butter or margarine)
½ tblsp lemon rind (grated)

Heat oil in pan. To this add washed liver, grated onions, garlic, chilli, a dash of salt and braise till onions are transparent and livers half cooked.

Cool and puree, together with the rest of the ingredients. Form into a roll and cover completely with foil.

Steam in oven for 20 minutes (180°C). Remove foil and brush melted ghee all around roll.

Sheesh Kaleji
(VARIATION)

1 grated onion (optional)
Salt to taste
½ tsp crushed cummin
Juice of a lemon
2 tblsp oil (or ghee)
1 tsp fresh pounded chillies
1 tsp ginger/garlic
½ tsp crushed black pepper
1 sheep liver (cut in 3mm thick and 5cm square piece)

Cut liver in pieces and wash and drain. Marinate for few hours in above spices. Put through skewers and alternate with boiled, diced potato and pieces of thick tomato wedges. Grill over open fire or in oven. If grilled in oven, you may need to pour a tablespoon or two of oil over livers.

Beef with Chana
(CHICK PEAS)

500g rump steak (cut in cubes)
2 tblsp oil
1 tblsp ghee
1 lemon (wash and cut in rings — remove seeds)
salt and black crushed pepper to taste
2 onions (grated)
1 tblsp slivered ginger
2 cloves garlic (crushed)
1 tsp each of chopped mint, coriander and spring
    onions
½ cup boiled chana (chick peas)
½ cup tomato puree or 1 cup tomato pulp
½ cup sour cream (or add 1 tblsp yoghurt to fresh
    cream)
1 tsp crushed jeeroo (cummin)
1 tsp chilli powder
2 tblsp flour

Mix salt and dry spices in flour. Roll meat cubes in this, then fry in ghee/oil till meat is evenly browned. Remove meat from pot.

In oil braise onions till they are soft and transparent. Add garlic and after a few minutes add tomatoes and cook till they blend in. Add meat cubes and simmer slowly with lid of pot tightly closed till meat is nearly done.

Add chana and soured cream and simmer slowly till meat and peas are cooked. If necessary, a little water may be added.

Just before serving place lemon rings within casserole.

Braise slivered ginger and a tablespoon of sliced onions in a little ghee and pour over casserole.

Garnish with chopped green and ½ teaspoon of gharum masala.

Chapli Kebaabs
(COLOUR PAGE 141)

1 kg steak mince
½ cup spring onions (chopped)
3 tblsp chopped dhunia
1 tsp or more crushed chillies
2 tblsp chopped mint
2 tblsp pomegranate seeds (optional)
2 tblsp dhunia seeds (coriander)
1 tblsp cummin seeds (jeera)
1 tblsp sour milk (yoghurt)
1½ tsp salt
2 tsp ground green chillies
½ cup mealie meal
1 egg

Roast whole dhunia and jeera on griddle or tava. Crush them coarsely. To beef mince, add all spices, onions and mealie meal. Mix well and knead mince mixture at half-hourly intervals.

After two hours add one egg, the chopped greens, pounded pomegranate seeds and yoghurt.

Make into huge hamburger-sized kabaabs (forefinger thick). Put on greased tava or very thick pan and grill them over slow heat, pouring a bit of oil when necessary and pressing down the kabaabs in the middle so that there is even contact with the griddle.

Serve warm with onion kachoomers, lemons, and chutneys.

Mixed Dhal Curry to serve with Chapli Kebaabs (Mush Dhal)
(COLOUR PAGE 141)

½ cup chinese peas (moong dhal)
½ cup chana dhal (gram)
1 tsp dhunia powder (coriander)
1/3 tsp turmeric
½ cup urad dhal
½ tsp baking powder (optional)
½ tsp chillies
salt to taste

Wash dhals and put in pot with 2 cups of water.

Sprinkle salt, spices and baking powder and cook till soft and mushy. By this time water must have evaporated.

Fry a teaspoon of slivered garlic and 2 whole red dry chillies in 2 tablespoons of ghee or oil and pour over dhal.

Garnish with chopped greens and a good sprinkling of gharum masala.

See photograph plate (page 141).

Section 2 F

Unexpected Guests

Guests are staying over for meals and there is nothing in the house? Well don't panic for here are some suggestions that will tide you over the embarrassment.

Calmly take stock of your provision cupboard, the bread tin and the left-overs in the fridge. Make a basic curry with a couple of onions and tomatoes and add to it a tin of baked beans, or fish, or some potatoes and peas, or left-over kabaabs, or moothias, or bhajias, or roast, and you have a delicious curry to serve. On their own the few bhajias, kabaabs or bits of meat will look pretty inadequate but in their new environment, nestling on the curry bed, they will not only look delicious but go a long way.

The following recipes will suggest ways of improvising more methods of using left-overs.

'Tos' Khima

(MINCE TOAST)

Slices of toast
Chopped onion
Left over mince, roast meat or fish
Chopped achar
Mashed potatoes to cover toast

Cover bread slices with leftover meat or what have you. Garnish with chopped onion, diced achar or chutney and cover with mashed potato. Dot with a little butter, place on greased baking sheet and bake in hot oven till mash is set.

Bread Curry

4 thick slices of bread
2 large onions
½ tsp turmeric (arad)
¾ tsp salt
1 tsp mustard seeds
¼ bunch dhunia leaves (chopped)
1 large tomato
½ tsp ginger/garlic
1 tsp dhunia/jeero (coriander/cummin)
1 tsp chillies
1 tblsp oil
1 whole green chilli

Fry mustard seeds in oil till they stop spluttering. Add finely sliced onions and braise till they are transparent. Add masalas and braise for a minute or two. Now add chopped tomato and cook till soft and blended in curry. Meanwhile cut bread in cubes and toast and add to curry, gently allowing it to soak-up masalas but taking care that they do not mash up. Garnish with green slit chilli, chopped dhunia and a dash of gharum masala. Serve with other left-overs or fried eggs.

VARIATION:

Put curry in casserole, cover with slices of bread. Brush tops with butter and bake in oven (180°C) till bread toasted.

Stuffed Rotis

(LEFT OVER ROTIS TO USE UP)

3 left over rotis
1 small tin baked beans *or* left over Moong sprout
 curry *or* dry dhal curry
2 medium onions
1 tsp green pounded chillies
½ tsp salt
2 tblsp oil
1 cup tomato (puree or fresh)
1 tsp ginger/garlic
1 bunch coriander leaves (chopped)
¼ tsp gharum masala
½ cup grated cheese

Braise chopped onion in ghee/oil. When light pink add ginger/garlic and chillies. Braise a minute then add baked beans. Stir and allow to simmer till thick. Add gharum masala and chopped coriander. Remove from stove. Spread equal amounts of baked bean mixture over rotis and roll up placing them in a greased casserole. Pour tomato puree over the lot and sprinkle with grated cheese. Dot with a little butter and bake in moderate oven for 25 minutes. Garnish with thin strips of chillies and some fresh dhunia leaves.

Beda Puras
(OMELETTES)

We give here a basic recipe with 2 different methods of making an omelette. Thereafter we give several variations of the recipe and the good cook will improvise reflecting her own individuality.

BASIC RECIPE:
  3 eggs
  Salt to taste
  1 medium onion (grated or chopped)
  ½ tsp chilli powder or green pounded chillies
  3 tblsp milk
  1 tblsp chopped dhunia
  3 tblsp ghee

FIRST METHOD:
Separate egg whites and beat till stiff, beat-in yolks. Add chopped onion, dhunia, milk and spices and fold-in. Heat ghee in heavy frying pan or skillet and pour egg mixture into it. Lower heat and slowly cook egg till it sets. Turn whole omelette over and fry in same way on second side.

SECOND METHOD:
Beat whole eggs till stiff and lemon coloured. Add milk, chillies and salt. Beat well. Heat ghee in skillet, pour in egg mixture and lower heat. Slowly cook till egg sets on underside. Now carefully distribute onion and dhunia over top of egg and fold over. Cook little while longer.

VARIATIONS:

(1) Add chopped tomato, boiled diced potatoes or boiled peas.

(2) Add flaked left-over fish or meat.

(3) Add chopped pieces of carrot or mango achar.

Whole Masala Beda
(WHOLE EGGS) (SEE PAGE 265)

Use same ingredients as above but add two whole green chillies. Fry chillies and onions in ghee. Remove half of chillies and onions and in rest stir in tomato and masala. Carefully break eggs in pot, leaving little space between each. Allow to set gently and try and scoop little of gravy over each egg. When eggs are set, arrange in serving platter and garnish with a little cut-up dhunia and the fried onions and chillies.

Methi Beda Bhaaji
(INDIAN SPINACH WITH EGGS)

  ½ doz bunches of bhaaji
  1 large onion
  1 small tomato
  ½ tsp fine salt
  ¼ tsp turmeric
  ½ tsp chillies
  1 tsp dhunia/jeero
  ½ tsp ginger/garlic
  3 tblsp ghee/oil (melted)
  3 eggs

Braise onions in ghee/oil till soft but not brown. Add tomato (cut up) and masalas and cook for one minute till well mixed. Add the carefully washed and drained bhaaji and cook very slowly till moisture evaporates. Add eggs and cook slowly till eggs slightly set. Stir a few times whilst cooking so that egg coats bhaji well. Serve immediately.

VARIATION:
Instead of scrambling eggs make spaces in between bhaji and allow whole eggs to set. See colour plate (265).

Bhaji Pura
(EGG OMELETTE)
(SEE COLOUR PHOTO 189)

  2 eggs
  2 bunches large leaved methi bhaji
  1 bunch dhunia (coriander)
  Good pinch turmeric
  2 tblsp chopped shallot
  1 tblsp chana flour (gram)
  1 tblsp mealie meal
  1 medium sized onion
  ½ tsp dhunia/jeero
  ½ tsp baking powder
  1 tsp pounded green chillies
  Salt to taste
  1 tblsp cake flour

Wash bhaji and greens and drain-off moisture in colander. When well drained put on board and chop-up coarsely. Chop onion fine. Pound green chillies. Mix all flours and dry spices together. Add chopped greens, onion and green chillies and mix well. Beat eggs well (preferably beat whites of egg till stiff then add beaten egg yolks) and add bhaji mixture to them. Put little oil or ghee in heavy skillet or pan and fry like omelettes.

Page 151

Poached Masala Eggs

6 eggs
1 large onion (sliced)
2 tblsp ghee
1 tblsp chopped dhunia
2 medium tomatoes
1 tsp chilli powder
¼ tsp crushed black pepper
Salt to taste

Fry onions in ghee. When they become soft and transparent add the tomatoes and spices. Stir well. Place a tablespoon of this chutney in individual earthern-ware pudding dishes and carefully break an egg in each. Put a pinch of gharum masala a few dhunia leaves and a teaspoon more of chutney over each, and gently poach eggs by lowering the pudding dishes in a baking tin half filled with water so that three-quarters of pudding bowls are immersed in water. Cook for a little while then cover with a baking sheet and allow to set in hot oven.

VARIATION:

Proceed as above, but instead of individual dishes put the tomato chutney in a heat proof glass casserole. Make little spaces in between chutney and gently break in eggs. Sprinkle with chopped dhunia and teaspoon of gharum masala. Cover and cook gently in hot oven till eggs set. (See colour plate 265).

Boiled Eggs in Chutney

Prepare chutney as above. Cut boiled, shelled eggs in halves or thirds and place in chutney. Simmer these for a few minutes and serve decorated with dhunia leaves and thin long strips of green peppers.

Masala Eggs

(SCRAMBLED MASALA EGGS)

6 eggs
¼ tsp turmeric
½ tsp dhunia/jeero
½ tsp chilli powder
½ tsp gharum masala
1 onion
¼ cup ghee
Salt to taste
Dhunia leaves

Fry onions in ghee till soft but not brown. Add spices to eggs, beat slightly, and add to onions. Close lid of pan for one minute, then stir to scramble eggs and close lid again and allow eggs to set over very low heat. Garnish with cut-up dhunia leaves and serve hot.

Mushroom Omelette

Salt to taste
50g button mushrooms
½ tsp chillies
salt and black crushed pepper
½ chopped pepper
1 tblsp ghee
4 tblsp cream
1 tblsp grated onion
1 tblsp chopped dhunia (coriander leaves)

Heat ghee and fry washed and sliced mushroom and onion in it. When nicely fried, add rest of ingredients and cook over low heat till dry. Set aside.

THE OMELETTE: (2 OMELETTES OR 1 LARGE ONE)

Beat yolks of 4 eggs blending in 3 tblsp of hot water in between beating till mixture is lemon coloured. Add salt and black crushed pepper.

Beat egg whites until stiff and fold them into yolks.

Heat some ghee in a heavy pan, spread egg mixture all over bottom and cook slowly until it is fluffy and begins to set.

Spoon mushroom mixture over it. Carefully turn over in half. Cook both sides till beginning to brown. Serve immediately.

A Tithar Biryani (Pigeon) (28)
B Chicken/Beans/Moothia Curry (104)
C Chaamp Musallam (88)

The Mealie Story

THE mealie and its by-products was the staple diet of our African, and till quite recently, to some extent of our Afrikaner population in South Africa. From ancient times Indians have included maize in their diet in some form or other. Though never an essential item of food, as rice is, it has nevertheless been a stand-by.

In India the coarser type of bread known as rotlas, have always been made from home-milled millet, or maize.

All the cooking lore of the early Indian immigrants found ready expression in preparing dishes using fresh green mealies and its stamped, riced and floured by-products. For economic reasons it also became a main item of food of the indentured labourers.

Our small selection of mealie recipes will undoubtedly suggest many more ways of preparation to the ingenious housewife. Appropriately, we open our chapter on mealies with good old mealie-pap and khuri, (a sour-milk gravy) to serve with it.

Putu
(CRUMBLY MEALIE PORRIDGE)

Traditionally, putu must be made in a three-legged cast iron pot over burning coal or wood for best results. However, this seems no longer possible and one may have to make do with ordinary thick based pots and electric ranges.

1½ cups water
2 cups mealie meal
1 tsp (or more) salt

Bring water and salt to boil. Pour mealie meal in middle of pot, to slowly form a heap. Close lid tightly, lower heat and simmer gently until water is partially absorbed and a skin forms around the putu. Crumble putu by stirring with a long handled fork. Close lid once more and simmer for another 10 minutes, by which time putu should be dry and crumbly.

World Favourite Green Mealies

BOIL green mealies in water for 20 minutes adding salt during last few minutes. A few green mealie leaves left in boiling water improves flavour. Serve straight or with butter.

ROAST green mealies over open fire. Alternatively roast under grill of electric stove.

Mealie Pap
(PORRIDGE)

4 cups water
Few slices onion
1 tsp ghee or oil
1 cup mealie meal
½ tsp salt

Bring to boil, three cups of water and salt in a thick pot. Meanwhile mix the mealie meal with other cup of water into a smooth paste. Slowly stir in the mealie paste in the water which has come to boil and continue to stir in order to avoid lumps. Simmer for about 20 minutes till pap is fairly thick. Fry onion in a little ghee or oil and pour over porridge. Do not stir but allow the fried onion to nestle decoratively on top.

Mealies with Dahi (Sour Milk)
(PHOTO PAGE 145)

3 cups frozen cut-corn
½ tsp salt
½ tsp pounded green chillies
1 small onion grated or finely chopped
60 g butter
1/3 cup chopped green pepper
2 tblsp flour
½ cup sour milk (dahi)

Fry onion and green peppers in little butter until soft and just beginning to change colour. Add mealie and other ingredients. Mix in flour and dahi gradually. Stir till thick.

VARIATION:

Beat 2 eggs till thick, combine well with above mixture, then bake in 180°C oven for 15 minutes.

Mealie Rice

2 cups mealie rice
1 tblsp ghee or oil
4 cups of water
1 tsp salt
Few slices of onions

Wash and soak mealie rice overnight or for at least a few hours. Drain. Bring salted water to boil and add mealie rice stirring occasionally to avoid lumping. Allow to simmer slowly till water has practically evaporated and mealie rice is cooked but not mushy. Fry onion rings in ghee and pour over mealie rice. Serve with dhal or sour milk gravy (khuri). See page 39.

Curried Mealie Rice

Cook mealie rice or samp as above (naturally samp will need more water and will take longer to cook) but to the salted water, add a pinch of turmeric and a teaspoon of either chilly powder or green pounded chillies. When frying onion rings in ghee or oil add a little grated fresh coconut as well and pour over the pot of cereal.

Mealie Rice Biryani

½ cup yoghurt
500 g mutton or other meat
1 tsp salt
2 whole green chillies
1 tsp dhunia/jeero powder
1 tsp ginger/garlic
1 onion
¼ cup ghee or oil
2 cups mealie rice (parboiled)
1 tsp red chilli powder
½ cup tomato (finely cut)
¼ tsp turmeric
1 cup fresh peas or green mealie kernels
A stick of cinnamon, two each of cloves and
    peppercorns.

Fry onions in half of ghee and remove when golden brown. In same oil, braise meat with the spices and when nicely browned, add tomato and sour milk. Simmer slowly till meat is nearly cooked, adding water if necessary. Boil peas or green mealies separately. Arrange half of fried onions over cooked mutton then put a layer of the peas or mealies, and over this spread the mealie rice sprinkle ¼ cup water over mealie rice. Lastly add the left over onions and left over oil. Close lid and simmer till done. Garnish with fried onion rings and strips of pepper.

Savoury Green Mealie Pudding

1½ cups fresh grated mealies (corn)
2 green peppers
¼ cup flour
Salt and pepper to taste
1 cup grated cheese
¼ cup butter
½ cup milk
2 large onions
1 tsp baking powder
1 tsp green pounded chillies
3 eggs slightly beaten

Chop onions and peppers and saute in butter till peppers are tender. Remove from heat and cool. Sift flour and seasonings and mix with milk into the peppers, blending well and avoiding any lumps. Return to stove and cook over low heat, stirring in cheese till well blended. Cool again. beat eggs slightly and add small quantities of cooked batter to it, thus making sure that eggs do not cook if batter is still hot. Grease casserole and pour batter into it. Bake in 180º C oven for 30 to 40 minutes. Dot a little butter over it and garnish with pepper strips and dhunia.

See also Lagan and Savoury Sections for other recipes containing fresh mealies.

Mealie/Peanut Bread

1 dozen green mealies (corn)
6 green chillies
¼ tsp turmeric (optional)
1 cup peeled peanuts
Salt to taste
1 tblsp oil

Cut mealies off cob. Put mealies, peanuts and chillies twice through mincer. Add salt and bind with oil.

Over a wire rack spread a clean white cloth or aluminium foil and put mealie/nut mixture in middle in a thick slab. (About 2 cm thick). Tie or seal all ends. Place mealie cobs in large pot and add water reaching half way up cobs. Lower wire rack with mealie bread onto cobs. Bring to boil and simmer for an hour. Cut in thick squares and serve hot with chutneys.

Alternately the slices may be fried lightly in a little oil and then served. The slices may also be dipped in egg before frying.

Tinned Salmon

(OR ANY TINNED FISH)

1 tin salmon (300 g)
½ cup tomato
2 green chillies
½ tsp turmeric (arad)
1 tsp dhunia/jeero
1 tsp chilli powder
½ tsp ginger/garlic
1 large onion
½ tsp gharum masala
1 tsp salt
¼ cup ghee/oil
Chopped dhunia leaves

Slice onions and fry in oil to a light colour. Add tomato and spices and simmer till well pureed. Add contents of tin removing bones, and mix with masala. When moisture of fish is evaporated, the salmon is done. Sprinkle gharum masala and garnish with cut-up dhunia

Ways with Tinned Foods

Any variety of tinned foods will lend itself to the making of a delicious curry by using the method and ingredients as above. Tinned beans, asparagus, sprouts, etc.

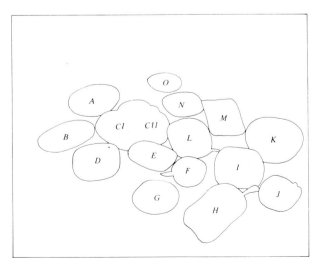

A Patta in chutney (226)
B Brinjal/Prawn Curry (173)
Ci White Flour Roti (259)
Cii Brown Flour Roti (289)
D Prawn/Pepper Curry (173)
E Dry Bean curry (136)
F Khuri (39)
G Carrot Pickle Traditional (269)
H Bhurkoo (47)
I Methi Sprout Curry (137)
J Chana Dhal/Pepper (142)
K Varkhi Samoosa (cheese/veg filling) (191)
L Masala Fish (164)
M Bhinda Curry (136)
N Leela Mircha Curry (135)
O Baath (Laapsi) (326)

Stuffed Vegetables

(VEGETARIAN)

500g of either karela, bhindi, pepper or baby marrow
½ tsp each of mustard and jeero seeds (cummin)
*6 cloves garlic
*1 onion
*1 bunch dhunia leaves (¾ cup)
*3 or 4 green chillies
*2 tblsp fresh coconut
*juice of 1 lemon
2 tblsp ghee
2 tsp sugar
Salt to taste
2 tblsp chana flour
3 tblsp oil

Wash Bhindi, wipe dry, cut off head end and split through middle. Karelas must be scraped, boiled in salted water, then split and seeds taken out. Baby marrow must be scraped lightly, washed and split.

Blend into chutney the items marked with an asterisk (*). Braise chana flour and jeero seeds in the ghee, then remove pan from stove and work chutney into the braised flour.

When paste is cold, stuff it into the vegetable of choice.

Fry the stuffed vegetables slowly in the oil, browning them well on all sides. Close lid of pot and adding water (if necessary) to steam cook vegetables. When oil starts floating, the vegetables will be done and cooked.

Dry Bean Curry

2 cups chrome beans (or any other of your choice) washed and soaked in cold water overnight.
2 onions (sliced)
1 tsp of dhunia chutney (see page 274)
½ tsp Jeero (cummin)
½ tsp mustard seed
3 cloves garlic (quartered or sliced)
2 whole red chillies
1 tblsp ghee
2 tblsp oil
1 tsp chilli powder
2 chopped tomatoes
1 sprig curry leaves (kurripulya)

Braise garlic, jeero and mustard seeds and the red chillies in the ghee and when the mustard seeds start spluttering, add the green chutney and beans, and add 2 cups of water and cook beans till they are soft and water nearly evaporated. Add tomatoes and continue simmering over low heat.

In separate pan, sauté the onion and curry leaves in the oil and when onions are transparent, pour contents of pan over beans.

Garnish with spring onion and dhunia.

Aunty Salligram's Fruit Curry

500g of half-ripe fruit such as mangoes, loquats, quince, pear, peach, apricot, bananas and orange segments
*½ cup dhunia leaves
*6 green chillies
*6 cloves garlic
*2 tblsp freshly grated coconut
*Juice of 1 lemon
2 tblsp gram flour (chana)
Salt to taste
2-4 tsp brown sugar
½ tsp jeero seeds (cummin)
½ tsp mustard seeds
2 tblsp ghee or oil
1 onion coarsely chopped

NOTE: Waterless type of cooking pot is best for this curry. If using any other, then a little water may have to be added.

Blend first five items in liquidiser and make a chutney.

Peel mangoes, peaches and bananas — rub off fluff from quinces or loquats. Apples etc must retain skin but deseed and remove pips. Cut fruit in orange segment sized chunks. Sprinkle salt and half of sugar over it.

Braise mustard, jeero and chana flour in oil slowly. Add fruit, onions and dhunia chutney, toss fruit well in this, then seal pot and cook very slowly for 5 minutes. Taste and adjust sugar. Finish cooking.

Serve as a side dish — brown rotis are excellent with this.

NOTE — Pomegranate seeds, hard fresh graps are also exellent in above curry.

Remedy for Ants and Cockroaches

Mix equal quantities of sugar, alum and borax and sprinkle around corners and railings.

To Freshen Sour Cream

Add a pinch of bicarbonate of soda — beat well, then add a little sugar and a few drops of vanilla essence. Beat again.

The End of the Story of Curries

The story of Indian curries can never have an end, since it is entirely dependent on economic circumstances, taste and availability of products. A curry can be made of any vegetable and meat or seafood available. People make curries from herbs that have sprouted up in their backyards after a rain, or with vegetation growing in the veld. They also make curries from carefully tended and cultivated vegetables that are so expensive and rare as to render them in the class of gourmet fare. As I have stated before, this is dependent on circumstances.

From the wide range of curries compiled here, the intelligent housewife will be able to improvise a curry from any vegetable or lentil or meat which we have not included in our repertoire. The reason for not including these is that it would become repetitious, since the ways of preparing curries are, when you really get down to brass tacks, basic.

We wish you many happy experimentations in your curry making and we are confident that, by referring to this book, you will not go wrong.

SECTION 3

FREEZER DELIGHT

NOTE: Excepting for fresh fruit and vegetables all the dishes in the photograph were packed away in the freezer and thawed at room temperature. Normally it would be heated and then served, but in order to illustrate how well food keeps in the freezer, we show them in the containers in which they were frozen.

MICROWAVE OVENS

The signs are there that, they will be increasingly used in the future. For the working mother, this means a more relaxed period with her family once she is at home from work, for she can take pre-planned dishes from the freezer, pop them in the oven, lay the table and call to the family that dinner is ready. Naturally each owner will experiment with her own model using her favourite recipes.

B Various Mithais (352, 353)
C Various Biscuits
D Bhaji Curry (128)
E Pattas (225)
F Afriki Yakhini Pilaau (38)
G Kashmiri Pasinda (89)
H Halwa-E-Muzaffar (336)
I Ginger Halwa in Milk (341)
J Lemon Achar (272)
K Coringee Achar (263)
L Cutlets (212)
M Brinjal Bharad (274)
N Aamli Achar (258)
O Tomato/Aamli Chutney (276)
P Rotis (289)
Q Mithi Roti (342)

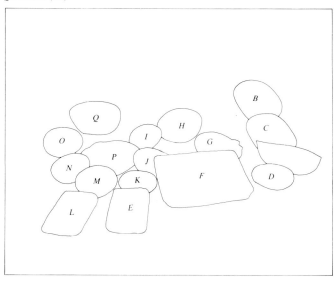

The Deep Freeze

Nothing can ever compare with the pot of curry freshly prepared, garnished with onion vagaar and dhunia, pepped-up with gharum masala and served with piping hot rotis just off the griddle. however, that is a way of life fast disappearing from the scene, and most of us have now to devise short cuts which will earn us some leisure for relaxed entertaining. This is where the deep freeze can be of invaluable help.

There are many advantages in having a freezer. To list the obvious such as buying in bulk in the season of plenty, when the products can be obtained cheaply. However our reason for promoting the freezer is to assist the housewife in utilising the precious space in her freezer in such a way that it will earn her some valuable free hours.

It is common knowledge that it takes more or less the same time to prepare a double quantity of batter as it does a single amount. Therefore with articles such as bread rolls, rotis, moothias, pattas, cutlets,etc; may we suggest that you do just that. Make a double amount of whatever you are preparing (time and budget permitting) use the one lot for the day's meal and store the other away for future use. A full freezer with semi-cooked foods means a relaxed confident mother and hostess who can cope with any emergency that may arise.

SAMOOSAS: Prepare and fill samoosas as usual. Put neatly in plastic bags as many samoosas as will be needed for any one serving in the future. Put the bags of samoosas in a large plastic box and put in freezer. Do not crush samoosas closely. Allow space between bags.

When required for use, put oil on stove and heat oil to 180°C and fry for 2 minutes, but lower heat and fry slowly till an even beige in colour. Do not thaw before hand.

BREAD ROLLS: Bake all your bread rolls or naan. When cold, pack the ones for storing in the freezer in a thick plastic bag. Knot the mouth of the bag tightly and put on freezer shelf. For serving, thaw at room temperature or enclose in foil and place in hot oven for 10-15 minutes and serve hot.

VARKHI TYPE OF SAMOOSAS: Varkhi type samoosas with either meat, fish or sweet fillings can be prepared and filled and left in freezer after baking. Put the samoosas in foil and place them inside a plastic box. If a second layer has to be put over the first, then put another layer of foil over the first batch of samoosas and lightly put in the second lot. Put a layer of foil over these and close lid of box, but take care that samoosas are not squashed.

When required for use, the samoosa must be popped in a hot oven to thaw and get crisp.

PASTRY AND PIES: Fill pies with meat, mince, fish, vegetables or coconut. Cover with foil and place in plastic box and close lid of box. Butter pastry must not be thawed. Heat oven to required degree, place pastry on sheets, make cuts on top, brush with egg yolk, and bake as usual. Baked pastry also keeps very well in freezer.

ROTIS: These preserve excellently in freezer. The rotis must be put in batches of twos or threes (or separated with plastic sheets), carefully wrapped in foil and then put in a large enough plastic box wherein they can be stored flat, without any rolling or folding. When required, they should be put into a warm oven for a few minutes and they will be remarkably fresh.

CUTLETS: Prepare mince cutlets and put in a hot oven for a while so that they dry out slightly. When cold sprinkle with breadcrumbs and pack cutlets between sheets of foil and place in a plastic box and freeze. When required, remove from freezer, separate whilst still frozen and dip in batter and fry as usual.

MASALAD FISH: Only fresh line fish must be used for this. Smear fish with your favourite masala and keep in plastic containers and seal well. When required, thaw the fish for at least half and hour, then bake in a hot oven on a greased tray and pour a little oil over each slice of fish. Baste once or twice with oil whilst baking.

These are just a few suggestions. The housewife will soon gain experience and find out which types of food products freeze well. If done properly her dishes will taste no different from those that have been freshly prepared.

NOTE: See also notes at bottom of recipes.

To keep Chillies in Freezer

Fresh red or green chillies can be put through mincer. To each 500 grams of chillies add ½ teaspoon salt and 1 tablespoon of oil. They will last indefinitely without loosing colour or going off. When dealing with large quantities, after they have been minced, pack in ice cube trays and freeze. Remove from tray and store in Tupperware containers or plastic bags and keep in deep freeze. In this case one simply takes out as many blocks as are necessary when needed. Lemon juice, green dhunia chutney etc. can be stored in the same manner.

The Harvest of the Seas

Although man early in his development discovered the gifts contained in the rivers and oceans, and though he hunted therein for his food as vigorously as he did on land, the fisherman has somehow never been looked upon as a devourer and despoiler of life. On the contrary, fishing either as a sport or as a means of earning one's livelihood has been associated with a genteelness that was never to be accorded to the hunter.

In ancient times the aphrodisiac value of shell fish was accepted as gospel. Priests and women were in some societies barred from partaking of it and to this day our Zulu women in the rural areas do not eat fish.

Some Hindu tribes, though strictly vegetarian in other aspects, have no compunction about eating fish. this is expecially so in the densely populated Bengal area where the masses virtually subsist on seafoods. Many Indians will not eat fish when they are plagued with any skin disease or troubled with sores and boils. Some Muslims will not have milk and fish at the same meal though there is nothing in the scriptures to prevent this.

Fish, so rich in vitamin, oil and protein, has always played a prominent role in the Indian diet. It has been eaten raw, dried, powdered, baked, steamed, fried curried and kabaabed. The South African Coloured and Indian seine netters have long braved the storms to bring this cheap source of nourishing food to the tables of the Public. For the lower income groups a fish head can still be turned into a delicious curry for the family.

Of recent years, the rich beds of prawns which have been discovered on the Natal coast promises a richer harvest of more exotic fare in the future.

NOTE: Sprinkle coarse salt and lemon juice (if available) over washed fresh fish — allow to marinate for at least one hour. Wipe off salt then smear with masala as indicated in recipes. This procedure will ensure that fish does not go soft and break up when cooked.

Hot Tamil Sauce
for Fish Curry

3 tblsp oil
3 large tomatoes
1 tsp mustard seeds
1 tblsp crushed garlic
3 tsp chillies
1½ tsp dhunia/jeeroo powder
2 springs kurripulya (curry leaves)
1 large onion
1 tsp methi seeds (fenugreek)
1 tsp jeera (cummin seeds)
salt to taste
½ cup tamarind juice
1 level tsp turmeric

NOTE: This is just for the gravy. The fish must be smeared with its own masala, for which use your favourite recipe.

Braise onions, methi, mustard, garlic and jeera in oil and when onions soften and become transparent add the tomatoes, (chopped or pulverised). Lower heat and allow tomatoes to blend in smoothly.

Now add chillies, turmeric, salt and dhunia/jeeroo, and curry leaves. Braise for a minute then add the tamarind and a cup or two of water. Simmer slowly, allowing the spices to saturate curry, then lower the masala smeared fish slices into the gravy and simmer slowly till fish is cooked.

Serve with hot rice.

Fried Fish (No. 1)
(PAGE 45)

1 kg fish (cleaned, sliced, washed and drained dry)
1 tblsp dry coriander seeds (whole dhunia)
6 or 7 cloves of garlic
6 red chillies (or green if preferred)
1 tblsp jeero (cummin)
Juice of 1 lemon
1 tsp turmeric
1½ tsp salt
1 tblsp oil
1 tblsp grated coconut (optional)

Pound chillies, garlic, jeero, coconut and coriander. Add dry spices and mix into paste with oil, and lemon juice. Smear fish slices and let them marinate for at least one hour. Or keep in fridge and fry when required. Masala smeared fish freezes very well. When required thaw at room temperature.

Fry in hot oil (medium depth) on both sides till it is golden brown. Any masala that is shaken off in process of frying must be rescued by straining oil when frying is done. This masala is sprinkled over platter with fish. Decorate with strips of green chillies or arrange on bed of lettuce, and slices of lemon.

Fish Curry

Prepare ingredients as for Masala Fish above. Smear fish slices with masala but leaving aside about a tablespoon of it. Grate one onion and fry it in a little oil. When a golden colour add two cups of fresh tomato (pureed or grated) in the pot of oil and onions. Add 1 sprig of curry leaves or thyme. Now put masalad slices of fish in this pot or casserole and cook slowly over low heat. For best results, bake in hot oven till fish is done and gravy thick.

Kokani Fish Curry

1 kg fish
2 tsp crushed garlic
1 tsp salt
2 tbsp oil
4 large tomatoes
6 red dry chillies
½ tsp turmeric
1 cup water

Clean, wash and slice fish. Soak chillies in water to soften. Put all the spices, tomatoes, chillies and water in blender and blend fine.

Put blended ingredients in pot and bring to boil. Lay fish slices in pot and simmer till fish is done.

Half an hour before serving, put some lemon or curry leaves in pot of fish. Serve hot with rice.

White Fish

(PHOTO PAGE 166)

1½ to 2 kg fresh line fish
Marinate fish in 1½ tsp salt, ¼ cup lemon juice for 1½ hours. Wipe off salty moisture.

MAKE A PASTE OF:
2 tsp ground garlic
1 tsp salt
½ tsp white pepper
1½ tsp ground green chillies
3 tblsp olive oil (or salad oil)

Smear paste well over fish and into cuts. Before baking dot fish with ¼ lb (125 g) of margarine and slivered garlic and onion rings. Bake in 180°C oven for approx. 40 minutes.

Masala Fish

(PHOTO PAGE 166)

1½ to 2kg fish
Marinate fish in 1 tblsp salt, ¼ cup lemon juice and leave for 1½ hours. Wipe off salty moisture then smear with paste made as follows:

4 green chillies
1 bunch dhunia
1 tsp salt
1 tsp red chilli powder
1 tsp whole jeera
1 tblsp dessicated coconut
3 sprigs of curry leaves
1 tblsp whole dhunia
1½ tsp dhunia/jeera

Liquidise the above ingredients in ¼ cup lemon juice. Smear fish thoroughly with paste, pour oil over it and bake in 180° oven.
When fish is half baked, garnish with onion, and tomato slices and finish baking.

Masala Fish Curry

(LADUP) (PHOTO PAGE 157)

1-1½ kg fish (fresh line fish cleaned and sliced)
½ ball garlic
4-5 fresh chillies (green or red)
3 pods elachi (cardomom)
1/3 tsp peppercorns
1 sprig curry leaves
½ cup water
Juice of 1 lemon
1 small grated onion
4 ripe tomatoes (blanched and pureed)
½ tsp whole jeera (cummin)
1 tsp dhunia/jeera powder
4 tblsp oil
1½ tsp salt (or to taste)

Pound together garlic and green chillies. Mix well with grated onions and pureed tomatoes.
Take an additional medium onion, slice it fine and fry it in the oil. When they turn a beautiful golden colour, add elachi, cloves, salt, peppercorns, jeera and the tomato/onion mixture to it.
Add dhunia/jeera powder and braise all these ingredients for a minute to blend together.
Now add lemon juice and water and the raw slices of fish. Mix well, carefully spooning the gravy over the fish.
Cover lid of pot and simmer slowly till gravy is thick and fish cooked. Five minutes before serving place a sprig of curry leaves over fish in pot.

Green Masala Fish

500g fish (either whole or sliced)
1 tsp salt
½ lemon juice (1 tablespoon)
1 tblsp dessicated coconut
2 tblsp oil
1 tsp crushed jeera (cummin)
1 tsp crushed garlic
1½ tsp crushed green chillies
½ bunch dhunia (coriander leaves) chopped

Wash and drain fish dry. Mix all spices into oil and lemon juice. Smear fish with masala paste. Wash and oil banana leaves.
Put fish in middle and parcel it neatly by bringing sides of leaves to cover entire fish.
Turn parcel upside down so that the unfolded side comes on top. Place fish packet on a baking pan and bake in oven. (40-50 minutes in 180°C oven.)
Ideal method would be to put fish over low embers and allow it to grill slowly till done.

Sardines

When winter sets in, the Natal coast is dotted with sardine watchers. These little silvery fish provide fun and food. here are some recipes for the next sardine run:

1 doz sardines
2 tblsp lemon juice
Salt, pepper and red chilli powder to taste
6 cloves of garlic slivered
2 tblsp butter

Scale, gut and wash sardines. Damp dry, then marinate in spices and lemon juice. Put in oven tray with butter and bake crisp

OR:

Fry, but add 2 tblsp oil to butter.

Fish Batter

1 egg
2 tblsp flour
1 dessertspoon oil
1 tsp lemon juice
Pinch salt
3-4 tblsp water

Put flour and salt in bowl. Make well in centre and drop in egg yolk, oil, lemon juice and water. Beat with wire whisk until flour is worked in. Continue beating for a few minutes. Allow to stand for one hour. Just before using, fold stiffly beaten egg white with metal spoon. If too thick you may use more water to thin down the batter.

This is a lovely batter for fish and if instructions are followed, no oil will seep through leaving ugly dark blotches on surface.

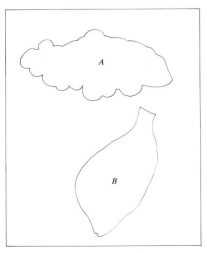

A Masala Fish (Rokayya) (165)
B White Fish (165)

Mango/Fish Curry from Malabar

2 tsp freshly pounded red chillies
1/3 tsp turmeric powder
salt to taste
1 kg fish (fresh line)
2 tblsp oil
1 ball garlic
1 tsp dhunia (coriander) powder
1/3 tsp crushed jeera (cummin)
4 green mangoes
½ tsp jeero powder

Pound garlic and chillies fine. To this add all the other spices and mix into paste with half the oil.

Place the other tablespoon of oil in a pot and lower the masala smeared slices of fish into it.

Peel and cut mangoes into halves. Place pieces in between fish slices.

Add a cup of water to pot and simmer fish in this till it is done.

Coconut cream from a 1/3 fresh coconut is a delicious addition to this casserole.

Serve with dhal and rice, or with rotis. If mangoes are not available then a tablespoon of aamli juice (tamarind) may be added to pot.

Kokani Fish Curry
(VARIATION)

1 kg fresh line fish
2 tbsp aamli pulp (tamarind)
1 tsp turmeric
2 tsp garlic (pounded)
½ cup freshly grated coconut
Salt to taste
2 tsp red chillies (freshly pounded)
2 tsp coriander seeds
2 tsp jeera seeds (cummin)
2 onions
1 green mango (medium)
2 green chillies (slit)

Cut fish in slices — wash and damp dry.

Pound chilly, garlic and fresh coconut to a fine paste. Coarsely pound cummin and coriander and add to paste with salt and turmeric. Peel and slice green raw mango. Sprinkle with a little salt and keep aside.

Put sliced onion, green chilli and the paste into a pot. Add tamarind pulp and 3 to 4 cups water and bring pot to boil.

When curry is blended with spices, add mango slices and fish pieces and simmer for 20 minutes.

When fish is cooked and gravy thickened, garnish with curry leaves. Serve with rice.

Banana Leaves versus Foil

THE ancient Indian technique of wrapping fish or meat in banana leaves for stewing, steaming or baking, is rapidly being replaced by the use of tin foil. The contemporary housewife can no longer bother hunting for the banana leaf, even though it may be growing in her back yard.

With intelligent usage, tin foil need not be an expensive item, for it is easily wiped clean with a damp cloth and can be used over and over again. Since rapid dehydration is prevented when foodstuff is covered with foil, it is excellent for the odd casserole that has no lid, for left-over chutneys, whites of egg, for fresh and cooked products that have to be stored in the freezer, for oven cooking, and especially for steaming such items as pattas, meat-rolls, roasts and puddings.

Many of the dishes in this book can be prepared well in advance, packed in casserole covered with foil and refrigerated, and put in the oven just an hour or so before serving.

Fish in Banana Leaf or Foil
(SEE COLOUR PAGE 265)

1 kg fresh line fish
2 tsp coriander seeds
½ tsp turmeric
2 tsp red fresh ground chillies (or green)
1 medium onion (grated)
1 tblsp tamarind or lemon juice
2 tsp ground garlic
2 tsp whole jeero (cummin)
1 tsp salt
1 tblsp oil
½ bunch dhunia (coriander)
1 tblsp fresh coconut (optional)

Pound coconut and spices fine. Add grated onion and chopped dhunia to masala. Add lemon or aamli juice and bind into a paste with oil. Wash and drain fish well. Make deep incisions on top half of fish. Smear inside and outside of fish with masala paste, and marinate for a few hours.

Heat oven to 200°C. If using banana leaves grease them and then wrap fish in them. Put on tray and bake for an hour. If using foil, grease a pan and lower fish in this. Pour two tablespoons of oil over fish, cover with foil and bake for 40 minutes. Remove foil and allow to brown.

VARIATION:
Onion may be baked in oven first and then pounded with the masalas. This gives it a different flavour.

Fish with Green Garlic Tops
(SEE COLOUR PLATE)

500g fish (sliced)
¼ cup oil for baking
2 tblsp oil
1 tblsp crushed dhunia seeds (coriander)
1 tsp crushed jeero (cummin)
½ tsp crushed black pepper
1 tblsp chopped green garlic tops
½ tsp salt or to taste
1 tsp green chillies
1 tsp garlic
½ bunch dhunia

Mix dry spices in oil. Pound garlic, green chillies and dhunia leaves and add to spices. Lastly add chopped garlic tops. Smear this masala over fish slices. In baking tray or pot, heat 2 tablespoons of oil and place masala smeared fish pieces in it. Cover pot and allow to cook gently till fish is done.

To make Sauce for above

The above is very tasty. If, however, a more saucy dish is required then thicken a cup of water with 2 teaspoons of cake flour. When fish is half done, make place between fish slices and pour in water. Shake pot gently, so that liquid is distributed evenly in base of pot. Garnish with more chopped, green garlic tops.

Fish in Banana Leaves

2 small fish (fresh line fish)
1 bunch dhunia (coriander)
1 tbsp cummin (jeera)
½ ball garlic
½ cup mint leaves
3 tbsp oil
Banana leaves or foil for wrapping
1 tsp sugar
1 tbsp pomegranate seeds (optional)
2 tbsp lemon juice
4-6 green chillies
1-1½ tsp salt

Wash the cleaned fish well. Mark top but do not cut through.

Pound all spices together (including the fresh mint and dhunia and chillies). Mix into paste with oil and lemon juice.

Oil the banana leaves, wrap fish in them (if using foil, oil is not necessary).

Cook in 350°F oven (180°C) for 30 to 40 mins.

Serve with lemon, onion and tomato wedges.

Fish Kofta Curry

500 g fish
2 dessertspoons butter
½ egg for binding (optional)
½ tsp pounded garlic
½ tsp ground nutmeg
Bread pulp from 1 slice of soaked bread
1 medium grated onion
2 tblsp of chopped greens (mint, parsley, shallot or
   dhunia)
1 tsp salt
1 tsp green pounded chillies
½ tsp ground black pepper

Boil or steam fish till cooked. Flake of all meat, carefully removing skin and bones. Add all other ingredients to this and form into koftas (flattened fish balls). Fry in oil. Prepare curry as follows:

In a dry pan, roast the following: **½ teaspoon each of dhunia and jeero seeds; small piece of tuj; seeds from 2 elachi; 4 red dry chillies; 4 whole almonds.**

Pound all these together. Remove koftas after they are fried and in same pot add the pounded masalas and braise for three minutes. Now replace the koftas and add two large grated tomatoes. If liked a strand of saffron may be added. Simmer all together till tomato is well blended in. Garnish with fresh greens and serve with rotis or rice.

NOTE: Left-over fish may be used for above kabaabs. Do not add spices when moulding kabaabs.

Tinned Salmon Lagan

1 tin tuna or salmon (fresh fish may be used)
¼ fresh coconut (grated)
1 chopped onion
salt and pepper
2 eggs
1½ tsp pounded chilli
1 tomato chopped fine
1 tblsp oil
1 tblsp chopped mint

(If fresh fish is used, steam fish in salted water or milk and when done flake with fork, removing skin and bones.)

Flake fish with fork. Add all other ingredients except the eggs and mix well. Beat egg yolks and mix into above. Beat egg whites very stiff and fold into fish.

Grease a casserole, pour mixture into it.

Sprinkle a little grated cheese and bake in oven till browned. Serve hot.

Fish Roe

Wash fish roes and put to boil in salted water.

To Braise: Sprinkle well with chilli powder, salt and pepper and braise in a little oil till nicely browned.

To Fry: Cut boiled fish roes in convenient sized slices. Sprinkle with a mixture of chilli, salt and pepper, dip in beaten egg and fry till browned.

To Curry: Make a basic curry with onions, tomatoes and spices. Put pieces of boiled fish roe and simmer till done.

To Pickle: Cut boiled fish roes in slices and fry in a little oil till done. Cool. Meanwhile prepare a pickle marinade as follows:

500g roe
1 tblsp mustard powder
1 tblsp ghor (jaggery)
1 tblsp chilli powder
½ bottle vinegar
½ cup oil
1 tsp turmeric

Beat mustard in a little of oil and vinegar till it is thick like mayonnaise. Add to this the turmeric, chilli powder, vinegar and oil. Add ghor, adjust salt, and mix well. Keep the marinade for half an hour before adding the fish roes to it. Pack in jar and stir slightly every two days to mix ghor in well. Should be ready for eating after a week.

Chilli Sauce for Prawns

(PHOTO PAGE 171)

½ cup butter
1½ tsp salt
½ tsp black crushed pepper
1 cup lemon juice
1½ tsp chilli powder
3 cloves garlic (cut in slivers)

Cook above ingredients over heat till thick and creamy. Marinate a kg of prawns in a little lemon juice to which has been added salt, pepper and chillies, for an hour.

Remove from marinade and braise quickly over heat. Put hot prawns in a tray and cover with prawn sauce and put in moderate oven for 10 to 15 minutes. Serve hot. Alternatively use chilli sauce like a hot dip for prawns.

Almond Fish

(PHOTO OPPOSITE)

1-1½ kg fish (fresh line)
1 small onion (grated)
1 tblsp aamli or lemon juice
2 tsp pounded garlic
2 tsp crushed coriander
2 tsp fresh pounded coconut
2 cups tomato puree (fresh)
½ cup almonds
1 large onion (sliced)
1 tsp salt
2 tsp crushed jeero (cummin)
1½ tsp fresh red chilli (pounded)
½ cup oil
1 tsp turmeric (arad)

Clean, wash and slice fish in pieces. Drain well. Roast unblanched split almonds on tava till browned. Leave half. Pound well the other half and mix with other pounded spices, salt, aamli juice and bind with a teaspoon of oil. Keep aside a quarter of the masala and smear the rest well over fish slices. Put in greased baking tin and pour half of the oil over. Bake for 40 minutes.

Meanwhile fry onions in the remaining oil. When they begin to change colour add tomato puree and the remaining masala. Lower heat and simmer for a few minutes till curry is nicely blended. Pour this puree over fish in oven, garnish with left-over whole almonds and bake till fish is done. Decorate with parsley sprigs.

A Mix Dhal Pilaau (36)
B Almond Fish (170)
C Murghi Khuri (43)
D Grilled Prawns
*   with chilli sauce (169)*

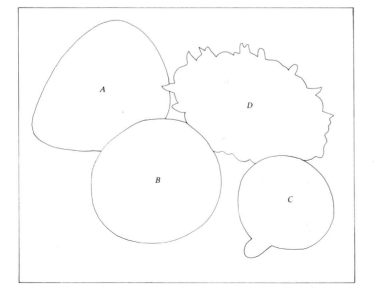

Some Things are Free

Every rice or curry recipe calls for a piece of cinnamon stick, some cloves and elachi and often saffron. These items are not at all essential to a good and tasty dish, so instead of these costly items, why not make your own flavourings?

(1) When mint is in season: Gather fresh leaves in the early morning or in the evening. Wash and shake dry. Then put on layers of paper and leave in sun for a few days. These crisp leaves can be crushed and stored in airtight bottles. Delicious in stews or final pep up for soups and dhals.

(2) Kurripulya leaves can be dried and stored whole in airtight bottles.

(3) Do not discard orange, lemon and naartjie peels. Wash and cut in thin strips and dry in the sun and pack in airtight jars. Fry a few strips with vagaar in curries and soups and add to rice water. We assure you that you will not miss the elachi or tuj.

(4) Grate the rinds of squeezed out oranges, lemons, limes and naartjies. These will dry very quickly. Again pack in bottles or leave in plastic containers in fridge. Add to biscuit and cake dough or beat in with milk puddings or garnish top of desserts and you can even spare on slivered almonds and pistachios. Delicious in milk shakes as well.

> **NOTE:**
> For this recipe only fish heads plus a handful of shell fish and/or a few slices of fish may be used. In fact, any odd raw pieces of fish will turn out this lovely soupy dish to be eaten with rotis or rice.

Fish Bouyou
(BOUILLEBAISSE)

500g fish
3 green chillies (chopped)
1 tsp garlic
¾ tsp salt
Lemon juice
1 onion (sliced)
500g tomatoes (pureed)
½ cup oil
½ tsp mustard seed
2 sprigs curry leaves or thyme
½ tsp red chilli

Wash, slice and dry fish. Sprinkle with a little salt and red chilli.

Fry the slices in ½ the oil. Remove fish and prepare curry.

Fry mustard seeds in the remaining oil and when they stop spluttering, add green chilli and onion.

When onion begins to change colour, add tomatoes and garlic and cook till tomato blends in.

Add fish slices, adding lemon juice and curry leaves, a little water and simmer till curry is thick.

VARIATION:
Add to above:
2 tblsp tamarind and omit lemon juice.

> **NOTE:**
> In any recipe calling for freshly pounded red chilli, dry chilli powder may be substituted.
> In savoury recipes where green pounded chilli is called for, effort must be made to obtain them, but should you fail, then the red dry one may be used instead.

Fish Head Soup
(BOUILLEBAISSE)

1 large or 3 smaller heads of fresh fish (500g)
250g fleshy fish pieces (deboned) (optional)
1 large onion
2 tomatoes (chopped or pureed)
1 level tsp garlic (crushed)
1 tsp salt
1 tsp chilli
¼ tsp pepper
1½ sprigs curry leaves
2 cloves garlic (slivered)
Juice of 1 lemon
2 tblsp aamli (tamarind) — optional
1 tsp dhunia/jeero
½ tsp salt
2 tblsp oil
1 green chilli (slit)
2 tsp saumph (fennel seeds)

Wash and clean fish heads and pieces well, taking care that no small or loose bones adhere to it.

Make a paste of crushed garlic, salt, chilli, turmeric, dhunia/jeero and lemon — smear this over fish.

Braise onion in oil and when it is pink in colour, put in fish slices, slivered garlic, green chillies and curry leaves and braise slowly for 3 to 4 minutes, turning fish so that it fries on all sides.

Now add fennel, aamli and tomatoes and simmer gently till tomato well pureed and begins to dry.

Add 1 litre of boiling water and simmer for about an hour. Serve hot with rice or bread rolls.

VARIATION:
Instead of 1 litre of water add coconut milk (see page 66) from 1 fresh coconut, but omit tamarind and adjust salt.
NOTE:
Fish heads can be used in stews or cooked in a pot of vhal dhal.

Jinga Curry
(SHRIMPS OR PRAWNS)

500 g prawns
¼ cup oil
½ cup tomato
4 tblsp yoghurt
2 green chillies
1 large onion
¾ tsp arad (turmeric)
2 tsp grated coconut (fresh if possible)
1 tsp garlic
¾ tsp salt
1 tsp chillies (red)
1 tsp dhunia/jeero

Shell prawns. Wash after cleaning well and drain in colander. Braise in little oil (separate from above quantity) till they change to light pink colour. In another pot, fry sliced onions to pale gold colour (just as they begin to deepen in colour) add tomato with all the other ingredients. Braise for a few minutes and add prawns, adding a little water to cook them well. When curry is nice and thickly pureed, add ¼ tsp gharum masala and garnish with a sprig of curry leaves.

Malabari/Jinga Grilled Prawns
(COLOUR PHOTO PLATE 99)

500 g deveined large prawns
¼ cup butter
4 cloves garlic (crushed)
½ tblsp chopped fresh mint
1 level tsp chilli powder
Juice of 1 lemon
½ tsp salt
¼ tsp crushed black pepper corns

Try and retain shells of prawns. Marinate prawns in above spices and lemon juice for few hours. Pour in basting pan and grill for about 10 minutes. Turn a few times during grilling and serve whilst still juicy and piping hot. When turning baste with butter.

VARIATION:
Instead of chilli use ½ tsp of peri peri.

Shrimp/Brinjal Rawayya
(STUFFED EGG PLANT) (PHOTO PAGE 133)

Proceed as for Malabar Prawns above, but omit oil, add 2 Tbsp of tomato puree and marinate prawns in this. Meanwhile take 2 large brinjals, wash and make cuts from above at fingerwide distances, but leave bottoms intact. Stuff prawns into cuts and pour left over marinade over brinjals. Allow to marinate for 20 minutes. Put oil in pot, lower brinjals carefully in it and cook gently till done, or put in casserole, cover with foil and bake slowly till done.

Pepper and Prawn Curry
(PHOTO PAGE 157)

500 g headless prawns
6 green and 6 red peppers (small variety with scalloped-edges otherwise 3 each of larger peppers)
1 large onion (grated)
6 pickling onions
1½ tsp red chillies (freshly pounded if available)
1 tsp salt (or more)
2 tbsp lemon juice
¼ tsp black crushed pepper
½ tsp turmeric
2 tsp slivered garlic
½ cup thick coconutcream or
2 tbsp fresh cream
4 tbsp oil
3 tbsp tomato puree
1 tbsp ground almond
½ tsp crushed cummin (jeera)

Shell and devein prawns. Wash and drain dry. Braise in 1 tbsp of oil for just 1 minute then remove prawns to bowl. Fry pickling onions in 1 tblsp of oil till they begin to shine. Empty onions and oil into bowl with prawns.

Add lemon juice, puree, and all spices except slivered garlic to prawn. Fry grated onion in pot and just when they turn a light gold in colour add garlic, prawns, ground almond and marinade to pot, and mix well.

Slit peppers, spoon a little of marinade and a prawn inside each pepper and put into pot.

Pour coconut cream or fresh cream over peppers. Toss gently so that all ingredients are well mixed in marinade.

Cook very gently over low heat till peppers are done. Serve hot.

NOTE: Small pieces chicken or mutton may be substitutes for prawns.

Prawns or Shell Fish Cocktail

1 head crisp lettuce (leaves broken in pieces)
250 g shelled deveined prawns or shell fish
Salad vegetables in season
Few bottled gherkins or cucumber
French salad dressing (see page 281)

Braise, cleaned prawns in a tablespoon of oil till pink. Toss lettuce, salad vegetables, gherkins, and prawns in a bowl. Arrange daintily in tall cocktail glasses or in side plates. Top generously with French dressing. (Page 281).

Kerala Prawns

500g prawns (shell, de-vein and wash)

Pat dry then sprinkle over them ½ tsp of salt. Braise in 1 tblsp of oil till they are flushed pink.

2 onions (grated)
1 tsp garlic
½ tsp salt
3 tblsp oil
1½ tsp red chillies (freshly pounded)
½ tsp crushed jeera
¾ cup coconut cream (from ½ coconut)
2 tblsp yoghurt
POUND TOGETHER:
1 small piece cinnamon
1 clove
3 elachi (cardamom)
1 tsp jeera

Roast the spices for pounding on a tava and then pound fine.

Mix together the grated onion, garlic, red chillies, jeera and salt.

Fry this onion paste in the oil and when onions are fried, add prawns and curds and simmer slowly for a few minutes.

Add coconut milk and pounded spices. Allow to infuse just once, then lower heat and simmer for 5 minutes by which time the prawns will be done.

Serve hot with rotis or rice.

Japanese Tempura
(PRAWN AND VEGETABLES)

1 doz. Tiger prawns (shell but leave tails on). Slit on underside and spread out two halves and it will give you an attractive fan shape. Marinate prawns in lemon juice, chilli, salt and pepper for 1 hour. Pieces of cauliflower, green peppers, slices of brinjals etc.

THE BATTER:
1 egg
½ cup water
¾ cup flour
salt

Beat eggs lightly. Gradually add water and continue to beat. Gradually add flour and salt with wire whip. Set aside for half an hour before frying. Serve hot.

Prawns in Egg White Batter

500g prawns (de-vein, shell and wash)
Marinate them for a few hours in:
1 tsp salt
1/3 tsp crushed black pepper
¼ tsp crushed jeera (cummin)
1 tsp crushed garlic
1 tsp red chilli
1 tblsp lemon juice
BATTER:
2 egg whites
¼ tsp salt
2 tblsp maizena

Beat egg whites with salt till they are stiff. Blend in the maizena. Dip each prawn into batter and fry in deep oil till they are crisp. Do not crowd pan but fry few prawns at a time. Serve hot.

Sweet Sour Prawns

500g prawns (wash, shell and de-vein)
1 tsp garlic
½ tsp salt
1 egg
1 tblsp cornflour
½ tsp chilli
½ tsp soya sauce

Dry prawns by patting with kitchen paper. Make a paste of the other ingredients and rub it into the prawns. Leave for half an hour then beat the egg, mix the prawns into it and deep-fry in oil till they are gold in colour.

SAUCE (to serve with prawns):
2 tblsp sugar
¾ cup water
2 tblsp tomato sauce
2 peppers cut into thin strips
½ tsp slivered garlic
2 tblsp oil
3 tblsp vinegar
½ cup tomato puree
1 tsp soya sauce
1½ tblsp maizena
1/3 tsp ginger

Mix tomato sauce, vinegar, sugar, ginger, puree and soya sauce in bowl.

Mix maizena with 2 tblsp of water and add with rest of water to bowl. Mix well.

Heat oil and fry garlic and pepper strips for a minute then add the sauce but continue to stir, adding prawns and cooking them over low heat till they are glazed. Serve immediately, for the longer you cook the prawns, the more tough the meat becomes.

Jinga (Prawns) Burtha

500 g fresh prawns
1 tsp pounded garlic
1 tsp dhunia/jeero powder
1 large tomato
2 tblsp thick extract of coconut milk
Chopped dhunia for garnishing
1 large onion
2 pods garlic slivered
1 tsp fresh red ground chillies
3 tblsp oil
Salt to taste

Pulverize tomato. Slice onion finely and fry in oil. As soon as onions start to change colour, add slivered garlic, ground chillies and dhunia/jeero. Braise till dry. Shell and devein prawns and braise in little oil till shell pink in colour. Add to curry together with the salt, pounded garlic and tomatoes. Allow to simmer slowly and when it begins to get dry add the thick extract of coconut (see Page 66). Serve piping hot with rotis or khitchri.

Karela/Jinga

6 large karelas (bitter gourds)
2 large onions
2 tblsp tamarind juice
1 tsp dhunia/jeero powder
Salt to taste
¼ tsp arad (turmeric)
250 g jinga (shelled and braised in little oil)
½ bunch dhunia leaves
1 tsp fresh red chillies
¾ tsp pounded garlic
4 tblsp oil

Wash and scrape karelas. Boil in salted water. When done drain in colander and cool. Make three inch gash in middle of karela and remove seeds. Now prepare curry thus:

Heat oil in pan and fry sliced onions till a pale pink.

Add the pounded garlic, chillies and the rest of the spices and braise for a minute.

Now add the shrimps and cook till done. (If prawns are used then they may have to be chopped in smaller sized portions). Take tablespoonful of prawn/curry mixture and stuff into split karelas.

Fry each karela in a little oil. This must be done very slowly and the gourds must be browned well on all sides.

Now place karelas back in curry pot and pour the tamarind juice over it. Garnish with dhunia leaves. Serve with rotis.

Chaza
(COCONUT MILK PRAWNS)

500 g prawns
1 medium onion
coconut milk (1 cup) (see page 66)
1 tsp ginger/garlic
1 tsp chilli powder
1 tsp salt
GARNISH:
1 small fried onion
1 tblsp dried shrimps (powdered and roasted on tava)
½ ball garlic (slivered and fried)
Chinese noodles (transparent Chinese)

Cream and de-vein prawns. Wash and dry on cloth.

In about 2 tablespoons of oil fry the onions and just as they become transparent add spices, prawns and braise over heat till all moisture is evaporated. Keep aside.

Boil noodles in salted water and keep warm, till serving.

TO SERVE: Add coconut cream to pot and bring to boil and instantly add the pre-boiled noodles and switch off heat.

Put prawns in a large serving platter. Garnish with the fried onions, fried garlic and the powdered and roasted dried shrimps, taking care to sprinkle them evenly over the platter. Garnish with chopped spring onions.

Kopra/Jinga
(COCONUT PRAWNS WITH PEPPER AND BRINJALS)
(PHOTO PAGE 156)

500 g prawns
4 small brinjals
½ tsp gharum masala
2 onions
1 tsp crushed garlic
¼ tsp turmeric (arad)
¼ coconut milk (see Page 66)
3 green peppers
½ cup oil
1 tsp green pounded chilli
1 tsp dhunia/jeero powder
Few sprigs dhunia leaves

Shell and devein prawns. Braise in one tablespoon of oil. Heat rest of oil and fry the thinly sliced onions, till they are a lovely golden colour. Add spices and salt to taste. Fry masalas for a minute, now add prawns and simmer till oil starts floating to top. Cut brinjals and peppers in halves and add to pot of prawns, lastly add the coconut milk. Allow to simmer slowly till thick gravy results. Pep-up with gharum masala and garnish with parsley or curry leaves. Serve with khitchri or rotis.

Rawayya
(PRAWN STUFFED BRINJALS)

½ cup corn flakes
3 large brinjals
1 onion
1 tsp salt
¼ tsp turmeric
½ tsp crushed dhunia
½ cup oil
Juice of a lemon
3 cloves of garlic (slivered)
2 tomatoes (medium)
250 g or more prawns or shrimps
1 tsp red chilli
¼ tsp crushed jeero (cummin)
1 egg
¼ tsp crushed garlic

Parboil brinjals. Cut in half, lengthwise and scoop out centres leaving ½ inch thick wall. Fry slivered garlic in one tablespoon of oil. In same oil braise the shelled, deveined prawns till shell pink in colour.

In rest of oil, fry onions till crisp and gold in colour. Drain and cool. Crush with back of spoon.

To the oil in which onions were fried, add crushed onions, slivered garlic, lemon juice, spices, grated tomato and scooped out flesh of brinjals. Simmer on stove for 5 minutes, add prawns and allow curry to thicken slightly.

Pile prawn curry in brinjals. Beat egg and lightly mix in a cup of corn flakes. Pile this all over brinjals. Dot brinjals with little butter and bake in hot oven till nicely browned.

VARIATIONS:

(1) Instead of prawns use mince.
(2) Substitute diced mutton or chicken and prepare as above.
(3) Any type of flaked fish or tinned red salmon may be used in place of prawns.
(4) Peas and diced potatoes may be used in place of meat or fish.
(5) Using yoghurt instead of lemon juice gives a lovely variation.

Dried Snoek or Dried Jingas
(PRAWNS)

All dried varieties of fish may be either braised like boomlas or added in chutney curry. They are served with bharkoos, khitchris or rotlas.

Crayfish Curry

500g crayfish (meat and tails)
3 tblsp oil
2 tsp slivered garlic
1 tsp pounded garlic
1 cup coconut cream
½ cup tomato puree
1 tblsp khus khus (poppy seeds)
1 tsp crushed dhunia (coriander seeds)
1 tsp crushed jeera (cummin seeds)
1 bunch curry leaves
1½ tsp red pounded chilli (or powdered)
1 tsp salt

Soak poppy seeds in a tablespoon of water and liquidise. Fry slivered garlic, onion and curry leaves in oil and when onion begins to change colour, add crayfish, khus khus and spices and cook uncovered over low heat till curry becomes dry.

Add tomato and coconut cream, close lid and cook slowly till sauce thickens and crayfish done.

Garnish with mint or parsley and serve with rotis or rice.

Crayfish Curry
(VARIATIONS)

1. Instead of coconut cream, increase tomato puree to 1 cup. Also add juice of 1 lemon and 1 tablespoon crushed cashew nuts.
2. Instead of lemon juice in variation one, add 1 grated green mango and add to curry with masalas.
NOTE: Crab meat and claws may be used instead of crayfish.

Crayfish Curry
(VARIATION) (PHOTO PAGE 52)

500g crayfish (meat and tails)
11g onion
4 tblsp oil
1 tsp methi seeds (soak in hot water)
1 tsp whole mustard
1 tsp pounded garlic
1 tsp chilli
½ tsp turmeric
1 tsp dhunia/jeera
1 tblsp lemon juice (or tamarind puree)
1 tsp salt
2 tomatoes (liquidized)

Braise onion and methi seeds in oil and when they begin to change colour add all spices, braise for two minutes. Add tomato and crayfish, braise for a few minutes and finally add lemon juice.

SECTION 5

Dekchi (Cauldron) Cooking

Traditionally some occasions call for the feasting of the clans. Near and far flung friends and acquaintances and the entire neighbourhood whatever its colour, creed, class or social habits, are invited. None are forgotten. None dare be forgotten, for when the guest list runs into hundreds then such over-looking is akin to an insult.

On such days the huge deks (cauldrons) are scoured with sand, ashes, homegrown and dried loofah or coconut hair or steel wool. Heavy with their 50kg of food, they steam steadily over split-wood embers under the professional eye of the male cooks who have built up great reputations in the community over the years. Some of these great giants are still remembered nostalgically even though deceased like Mullah Chacha; Manjra Mota who learnt the art at the feet of this great master is now retired but his sons whom he taught, carry on this service for the community. For it is not just a money earning job, rather it is a service to the Community especially on the occasion of Milad Un Nabee (commemorating the birth of the Prophet) or Ijtimas when Muslims from throughout the republic gather for a week-end of religious discourses and communal prayers. With the males tending the pots, the women are left free to attend to the chutneys, pickles, papads, salads, fruit drinks, table laying and the myriads of chores mass feeding entails. That does not mean that capable and efficient women do not abound to do Dek cooking. In every extended family these super male and female cooks carry on the good traditions.

Gajar Halwa for 100

12 litres milk
3 kg carrots grated (12 cups)
1 kg Klim powder
3 tins condensed milk
3 tins cream (3 x 310g)
750g freshly ground almonds
250g chopped blanched almonds
125g slivered pista and almonds
30g fine elachi
375g cream of wheat
2 kg ghee
1¼ kg sugar (please adjust to taste)
½ fresh coconut

Over the years I have had request from many parts of the Republic for recipes for mass cooking. I am indebted to Manjira Mota (photo below) and my two aunties Mrs. Essop E. G. Paruk and Mrs. Ebrahim Mayat for amounts and tips with regards to cooking these huge quantities.

Jardo for 100 persons

2 litres water
4 kg sugar
¼ tola saffron (optional) 2,5g
Egg yellow colouring
10 whole cloves
1 tblsp elachi seeds
Few sticks cinnamon
4 kg rice
2 kg ghee
250g sultanas
500 g slivered almonds and pistachios

Boil rice with a level dessertspoon of turmeric till well done. Drain in colander.

Dissolve sugar in water — add saffron (since this is an expensive item, it can be dispensed with altogether and only egg yellow colouring used to tint syrup), cloves, elachi and bring to boil.

When sugar is dissolved and syrup thickens (but not sticky) add rice to pot of boiling syrup — keep simmering briskly allowing the syrup to steep well into the rice grains.

Heat ghee, add sultanas, braise a minute then add nuts and pour all the ghee over the jardo.

Keep on very low heat till serving time.

VARIATION WITH PINEAPPLE (SOHLO)
Increase sugar in syrup by another kilo.
Grate 6 pineapples — to it add juice of 6 or 8 lemons.
Add above to syrup just before pouring over sohlo.

NOTE: Syrup for sohlo should be slightly thinner than for jardo.

Biryani for 100 People

30 g elachi (cardomom)
25 kg chicken or mutton
7 kg rice
750g ginger
250g garlic
2 kg ghee
5 bottles oil
5 kg masoor (black lentils)
50 g whole cinnamon
3 tsp cinnamon powder
2 kg tomatoes (pureed)
3 kg onions
10g saffron (1 level tablespoon of strands)
125 g whole green chillies
125 g red chilli powder
125 g red crushed chillies (fresh or dry)
28 g turmeric (optional)
56 g (shah jeera) cummin
14 g cummin powder
6 x 500ml plain yoghurt
2 doz eggs
4 kg potatoes
salt approx. 600 grams
2 cups lemon juice or white vinegar

NOTE:
For chicken biryani, use only 4 boxes of yoghurt.
Marinate meat with spices and fried onion.
At bottom of deks put only oil over which layer your meat, masoor, eggs etc., finally the rice.
Just put lumps of all the ghee called for in recipe over top of rice.
Seal deks with double layer of foil before closing lid.
This is easier and more economical than the old fashioned flour and cloth seal.

NOTE:
As chillies vary in sharpness, more or less than specified quantity must be used. Salt too must be adjusted to taste.

Gajar Halwa for 800

60 litres milk
18 kg carrots
5 kg Klim powder
15 tins condensed milk
12 tins cream (12 x 310g)
2½ kg ground almonds
1 kg blanched chopped almonds
500g slivered pista and almonds
100g fine elachi
2 kg cream of wheat
10-12 kg ghee
6 kg sugar
2 fresh coconut

Dhal for 200

10 kg leg mutton or chickens
2 kg onions
650g ginger/garlic
90g turmeric (or more)
1½ kg tomatoes
375g chilli powder (adjust to taste)
Salt to taste
375g dhunia/jeero powder
3 bottles oil
30g cinnamon
30g elachi
30g whole cloves and peppers
60g gharum masala
6 kg oil dhal
500g chana dhal
2 kg masoor

FOR VAGAAR:
2 kg ghee
125g green chillies
60g slivered garlic
30g jeero
1 kg onions
20g mustard seeds

Haleem for 200

6 kg mutton with bones (or chicken)
2 kg onions
500g ginger/garlic
30g turmeric
125g chilli powder
250g green chillies (reserve ¼ for Vagaar)
60g gharum masala
125g dhunia/jeero
30g whole jeero
Salt to taste
2 bottles oil
½ kg ghee
30g tuj
30g elachi
30g cloves and peppers (whole)
3 kg wheat
1 kg barley
500g chana dhal

FOR VAGAAR:
30g jeero
1½ kg ghee
½ kg onions
Left over green chillies

MASS COOKING

Soji Halwa for Mass Cooking
(FOR 300 PERSONS)

30g cinnamon sticks
7 x 500g (cream of wheat) soji
7 x 310g tinned cream
2 x 397g condensed milk
7 x 397g evaporated tinned milk (ideal)
1 bottle egg yellow colouring (use just enough to
   obtain desired colour)
3 fresh coconuts (grated)
1½ kg almonds (blanched and ground)
2 tblsp elachi powder
2 tblsp crushed elachi
1 tblsp elachi seeds
2½ litres milk
3 litres water
4 kg ghee
200g sultanas
Sugar to sweeten
Slivered almonds and pistachios for garnishing

To all tinned products add milk, water, grated coconut, ground almonds, powdered and crushed elachi and sufficient sugar to sweeten. Tint with colouring to pale yellow colour.

In large heavy based pot, braise in ghee the soji, elachi seeds, tuj and sultanas, when soji turns a pale pink colour, add the milk products.

Taste for sugar and adjust to taste. Also adjust colour with colouring for more may have to be added. Stir frequently over low heat till ghee floats on top. This is an indication that Halwa is done.

Decorate with slivered almonds and pistachios.

Biryani for 800 people

4 kg ginger
2 kg garlic
200 kg mutton (cut 6 pieces from each 500g of meat)
50 kg rice
32 kg masoor
80g saffron (8 tolas)
2 kg chilli powder (red)
2 kg crushed chillies (red)
500g whole green chillies
360g elachi
250g turmeric (use sparingly of this quantity and use
   egg yellow to obtain richer colour)
500g jeera
250g shah-jeera
250g tuj
20 kg ghee (use sparingly. If mutton is fatty, less with
   be needed)
20 litres oil
1½ litres lemon juice (or vinegar or ½ vinegar and ½
   lemon)
40 x 500ml yoghurt
12-16 doz eggs
25 kg potatoes
20 kg onions
1 kg fine salt (use only as much as is required)
6 kg coarse salt (for rice and meat)

Carrot Achar for about 500 people

Soak Mebos in 1 bottle vinegar — puree and add to masala.

*1 cup turmeric
500 g pawpaw (green) or cauliflower
5 kg beans
500 g mustard powder
10 cups crushed chillies (either fresh or dry)
4 bottles vinegar
500g mebos or dried apricots
salt to taste
10 kg carrots
1 kg cabbage
6 cups dry chilli powder
8 litres oil
500 g dried prunes

METHOD: Follow instructions for making veg/carrot achar.

SECTION 6

SAVOURIES AND SNACKS

YOUNG, old, whatever, one's taste in food, all love savouries, and amongst Indians in formal entertaining they play a leading role, serving more or less as a gateway to the rest of the meal to come. The tin of snacks or the plate of savouries in the fridge is indication of a loving mother.

There is no dearth in savouries as far as Indian cookery is concerned. They are made from the large variety of lentils available, from flours made out of various cereals from post toasties and other allied cereals, as well as meat and vegetables. There are occasions which call for certain savouries such as Sookh Mookh at weddings or after meals, chevda at tea parties, or chana chut-pati when something more filling is required in the way of a savoury. Often Indian wedding festivities stretch over a week and on one of these nights when a musical concert has been arranged for the entertainment of guests, chana chut-pati is served. It is a very welcome break, as all guests will assure you.

Samoosas have been a must at all formal dinners and parties for as long as we can remember and it is a hors d'oeuvre that never fails to satisfy.

Amongst the many types of savouries we must make mention of a few which have been established as classics. Bhajias, which non-Indians know as chilly bites, the cutlets made from raw mince, its allied twin the kabaab, or seekh kabaab, the many savouries with cooked mince fillings and pattas made from large palm-like leaves in a way fairly similar to the dolmas of the Greek people.

With our collection of savouries for you, we leave you to give to your main courses those accessories that make or mar the dress. We are confident that it will distinguish your table in a way long remembered by your guests.

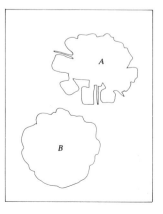

A Chicken Popsicles (203)
B Dodhi Kabaab Curry (112)

Samoosas

Beginners and non-Indians are often put off attempting samoosas as they have heard that it is a laborious and complicated procedure. Admittedly, it is time consuming, but shown the know-how properly, it need not be complicated at all. Again Samoosas are the tastiest of savouries, made from the most economical dough ever devised by the ingenuity of cooks. Therefore, the art of samoosa making should be a must for whosoever wishes to learn Indian cookery.

Provided the beginner and novice has each stage of samoosa making just right, and pays due attention to our photographs, illustrations and explanations, we feel confident that even amateurs will get the knack of it and no difficulty should be encountered.

However, like good pastry making, samoosas tend to get better and better with each subsequent attempt, and perfect specimens may only be turned out after considerable experience. We wish you every success in your first venture in the field of samoosas.

See following three pages for illustrations and notes.

Samoosas

See following three pages for illustrations and notes.

Key recipe for Khima

(MASTER MINCE RECIPE)

In savouries which call for a mince filling, we give you master recipes. These are used in most khima filled savouries.

Master Mince No.1

500 g mutton or chicken mince (or half of each)
2 medium sized onions (chopped very fine)
2 tsp pounded green chillies
1 tsp salt
½ tsp ginger/garlic
½ tsp gharum masala
½ tsp crushed cummin (jeera)
1 tblsp ghee
*1 small bunch dhunia leaves (washed and chopped)
*2 tblsp green shallot (washed and chopped)
*2 tblsp green mint (washed and chopped)
¼ tsp black crushed pepper
¼ tsp turmeric (arad)

Wash and drain mince. Braise in frying pan and when it begins to get dry add salt, ginger/garlic, green chillies, pepper and arad. When dry add onions and braise just enough till moisture is evaporated. Add ghee. Khima should now be fine and dry like breadcrumbs. Cool khima and add the chopped greens (well washed and drained dry) and gharum masala. Use in savouries as specified.

CAUTION: Keep stirring the khima to avoid lumping of meat.

Master Mince No.2

Use same ingredients as above.
Squeeze out all moisture from chopped onions by placing them in muslin cloth and wringing them dry.
After mince has been braised with spices, allow mince to cool, then add onions, chopped greens and gharum masala.

THE FILLING:
Prepare 500 g of mince as Master Mince Khima (2) recipe. Cool before filling samoosas.

CAUTION: On no account must mince be soggy.

THE DOUGH:
3 cups flour
Cold water
Good pinch of salt

Sift flour and salt. Make into fairly stiff dough with cold water. Inexperienced cooks will be well advised to add one teaspoon of vinegar or lemon juice to the cold water as it will give more resiliency to the finished pur. The pastry ready for filling is known as pur.

This amount is for two pur rotis (quantity of samoosas 4 dozen).

The Making of the Pur

From this stage it is essential that frequent references be made to photographs on Pages 185 to 188.

Illustration A — Divide dough into 12 portions and roll each between palms to size of smooth ping-pong balls. Use 6 portions for each pur. Roll out 6 portions on floured board with Indian type roller into 6-8 cm diameter discs.

Illustration C — Now roll out the pile of 6 discs into one large roti (12 inches in diameter) with swift smooth strokes. Trim off sides to form a square.

Illustration B — Pile the 6 discs one on top of the other after carefully brushing both sides of each round disc well with a teaspoon of melted ghee, and sprinkling flour between them. Only underside of bottom disc and topside of top disc must be left ungreased.

Illustration D — Put roti on hot ungreased griddle iron plate. Toss and turn lightly several times on both sides in order to separate layers. Deftness in turning will ensure that the pur is not freckled like rotis. As soon as layers appear loose, take off from tava (griddle) and set aside. Prepare a second roti with remaining 6 discs.

NOTE: Experienced cooks handle as much as 20 discs at a time.

Illustration E — Rolled out pur put in hot oven to separate layers (see note below).

E — Pur being separated in the oven.

Illustration F — When slightly cool, trim and cut pur into two-inch wide and ten or more inches long strips. An easy way of cutting strips is to roll the pur up like a swiss roll and after trimming off sides cut through in four equal distances.

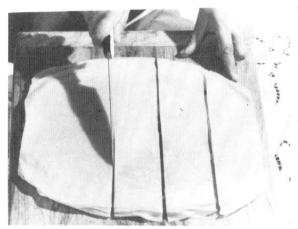

The pur cut into strips

Rolled out discs being piled on top of each other. Large pur has just come out of oven, showing how easily the layers separate.

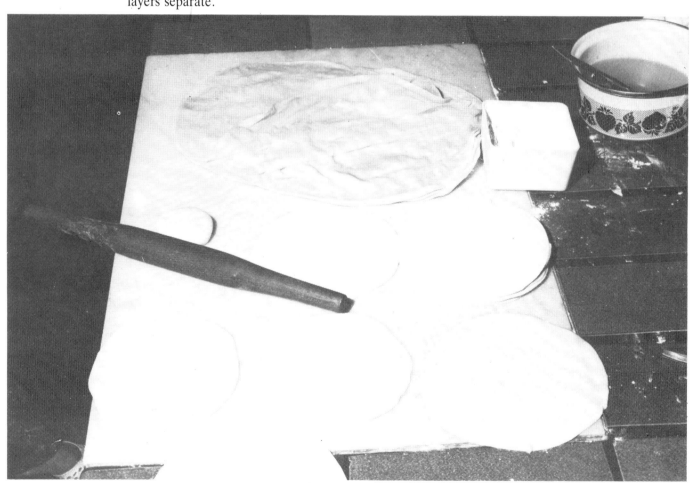

Pur can very successfully be separated in an oven. Place rolled out pur on a baking sheet, cover with foil and keep in hot oven 225°C over for 7-10 minutes. (Illust. E).

Illustration G — Separate layers and fill samoosas. In our illustration our model, Ayesha, has a few filled samoosas on the board, one that is filled but not rolled, and another in her hands in the process of being filled, with khima.

TO FRY:
In deep oil over medium heat, (180°C), fry samoosas, turning them over a few times so that they are evenly browned. Remove from pan when a lovely buff cream shade. Drain in colander. Serve with lemons and chutneys.

Illustration H — Samoosa Strip — Firstly fold CD, then CE along EF, so that D falls on F. Now hold strip of pur between thumb (Point B) and fore finger of left hand and fill pocket with 2 teaspoons of mince. Now fold EF over pocket so that G falls at Point C. Then fold FG over pocket so that H falls on E; then HG again over pocket and so on till strip is used up. Paste final length down.

We suggest you practice on a strip of paper first, to get the knack of folding samoosas neatly. The dotted lines on the illustration will indicate how to use the strip up for folding. Fold a corner of the strip of pur, fold it over to resemble a three-cornered cone, put in two teaspoons of prepared khima filling, then fold it over and over according to dotted lines, till the strip of pur is used up. The end of the strip is pasted down with a paste made from flour and water.

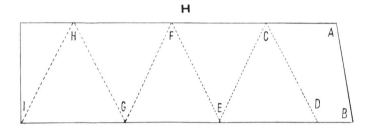

Samoosas put in a plastic box between layers of lunch paper can be stored most successfully in the freezer. Do not thaw when required for use. Put the oil (deep frying) on to heat and when it reaches medium heat, put the frozen samoosas in the oil. After 2 minutes, lower heat and deep fry very slowly, carefully turning samoosas till they are crisp and deepened to a rich biscuit colour. Drain on kitchen paper over a wire rack or colander.

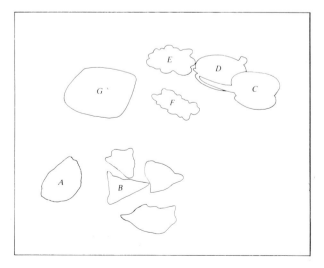

A Dough with Khima (fried egg is
  still to be included) (194)
B Fried Egg/Khima Samoosa
C Egg/Khima Samoosa being fried
D Bhaji Omelette (151)
E Savoury Choux Pastry (379)
F Chicken Tikka (82)
G Nihari (61)

Farmaas Puri (PHOTO PAGE 239)

7 samoosa pur (whole)
350g of master mince no 1. (see page 185)
¼ cup cream
2 eggs

Beat eggs and cream together.

Put one pur flat on table. Brush all over with egg/cream paste. Cover this with another pur and smooth out all air bubbles.

Brush paste over second pur and sprinkle liberally with about ½ cup of khima.

Cover with another pur, spread paste and then the khima. Proceed like this till all the pur have been used up and the khima has been sprinkled over it.

Now starting at one end, proceed to roll over tightly like a swiss roll. Enclose in foil and refrigerate for a few hours.

Cut finger-wide slices off the swiss roll and place each flat in a plastic container. Separate each layer of farmaas puris with lunch or plastic paper. Freeze.

When required, do not thaw, but fry farmaas puri while it is still frozen.

Beat 2 eggs — dip each puri in egg and fry in shallow oil over moderate heat till puris are a lovely pale gold colour on both sides. Drain on kitchen paper and serve hot with chutneys.

To Freeze

After swiss rolling the fermaas, cover roll tightly with foil or lunch paper and leave in fridge for a few hours. Then remove paper, place roll on board and cut firmly but neatly in fore-finger width slices. Carefully pick up each slice as you cut it and place them flat in a tupperware container. Put plastic between layers.

DO NOT THAW when required, but dip in batter in frozen state and fry in medium oil. Drain on wire rack. When frying is complete, the vermaas will have thawed.

Varkhi Samoosas or Indian Pastry

Indian pastry is basically made of flour with very little shortening. It is then divided into equal portions and each portion rolled out to paper thin rotis. Each of these thin rotis is then brushed over with melted ghee, sprinkled with flour and piled one on top of the other, leaving only underside of bottom roti and top side of the top roti ungreased (somewhat on the principle of samoosas but instead of little discs the rotis are rolled out paper thin and large). If large amounts of dough are handled at a time then as many rotis are rolled out as the recipe calls for, but the average housewife who works with as little as 1 or 2 cups of flour at a time, will welcome this short cut method introduced here.

Divide (assuming 1 cup of flour is handled) the dough into 4 sections. Roll each out to paper thinness. Brush each roti well with melted ghee and sprinkle flour (many people prefer to use maizena, or to braise a little flour in ghee and brush that over and do not sprinkle flour separately. That is entirely a matter of preference and no method is to be recommended over the other). Pile rotis on top of one another. Cut this pile of roti and divide into four equal quarters. Brush each quarter again with ghee and pile one on top of the other so as to get all angles matching.

If dough had been divided into 6 portions then rotis must be divided into half only and then piled on the other half. The idea is to have at least 12 layers of paper-thin rotis put together which, when baked or fried will separate out, giving a beautiful crusty and attractive pastry. The piled-on rotis are then further cut out into 2 inch squares and each square rolled out till it is 3 mm thick. This is then filled with the appropriate savoury or sweet filling and fried or baked as the recipe calls for.

For recipes in this pastry see: Mince Pies, Meat Pies, Banana Puri, Khaja, Mitha Samoosas.

DOUGH (FOR VARKHI TYPE SAVOURY SAMOOSAS)

COLD WATER RECIPE:

1 cup flour
½ tsp baking powder
2 tsp ghee
1/8 tsp salt
A few drops of lemon juice
cold iced water

Rub ghee in dry ingredients. Make into fairly stiff dough with lemon juice and cold water. Roll out into 4 portions and prepare as for varkhi type samoosa.

HOT WATER RECIPE (very easy and successful):

maizena for sprinkling
1 tblsp ghee
Flour to form dough
½ tsp salt
1 tsp baking powder
½ cup milk and ½ cup water

Bring to boil the milk and water. Remove from stove and pour into mixing bowl over the salt and baking powder and ghee. Add as much flour as is needed to form dough. Divide into 4 portions and prepare as for varkhi type samoosas. (This will assure 16 layers).

For Mitha Samoosas and Khajas, which are made in varkhi type pastry, see Section in Sweets and Desserts.

Varkhi Samoosa Easy Hot Water Recipe (COLOUR PHOTO PAGE 99)

½ cup milk
½ cup water
½ tsp salt
1 tsp baking powder
2 tsp ghee
sufficient flour to form stiff dough

Bring water and milk to boil — into mixing bowl put ghee, baking powder and salt and pour boiling liquid over it.

Sift cake flour over liquid to form a stiff dough. Divide dough in 16 portions and use 8 portions for each roti.

Roll out each disc as for samoosa pur and spread evenly with melted ghee and sprinkle with maizena. Pile smeared sides of disc one on top of the other till only bottom disc and top of topmost disc remains unsmeared.

Allow ghee to congeal. Then roll out like samoosa par.

Cut out into 10 cm squares, fill with a tblsp of filling (see next page), seal edges with white of egg.

Place samoosas on greased tray, brush with egg yolk and pour a tsp of oil over each and bake at 190°C till samoosas are done.

SAVOURY FILLINGS FOR VARKHI TYPE SAMOOSAS

Mince Pies

Use Master Mince No. 1 Khima recipe for filling. Roll out each square of dough, fill two or more teaspoons of khima and fold over like a jam tart, pasting edges down with white of egg. Put samoosas in greased baking tray. brush over with yolk of egg. Pour 2 teaspoons of oil over each samoosa and bake in hot oven 180°C till crisp and a deep buff cream colour. Cool on wire rack till excess grease has drained off.

Meat Pies

Instead of mince, fill in with:

1 cup diced breasts of chicken or mutton
1 medium onion
½ tsp salt
½ tsp green pounded chillies
¼ tsp pepper
½ tsp ginger/garlic

Cook diced meat with spices till tender. Flake meat slightly then add onion and cook till well absorbed and fairly dry. Cool and add 4 tablespoons of chopped shallot and dhunia. Roll out dough, fill in with meat filling, paste down and bake as for mince pies.

Meat/Cheese filling

To above meat or mince, mix in 1 carton of cottage cheese and use for filling varkhi samoosas.

Cheese filling for vegetarians

1 carton cottage cheese, 2 tblsp chopped achar.

Different variations of dough and fillings have been given. Choose any one and make lovely varkhi samoosas.

If you have any difficulty in following these instructions, then please refer to more elaborate details in dessert section (Page 346).

Pin Wheel Pastry (PHOTO PAGE 347)

2 cups flour
½ tsp baking powder
½ lb (1 cup soft butter)
½ cup milk
¼ cup fridge water

Sieve together the flour and baking powder.

Take about 2 tablespoons of butter and rub into flour till it is fine like breadcrumbs.

Mix water and milk and make into a pliable dough. Divide dough into 8 portions. Roll each out to size of a dinner plate.

Use up remainder of butter except 1 tbsp. for smearing it over the rotis evenly.

Pile each of the circles one on top of the other and reverse the last roti so that the butter-smeared side is on the underside.

Roll the pile to size of a dinner plate and smear the top with the leftover butter.

Roll over like a Swiss roll. Leave in fridge for an hour. Remove from fridge and divide roll into six equal portions. Roll each out to fit a 10 inch (25cm) round pan. Grease pan very slightly and put roti inside. Spread thickly with khima or filling of choice. Cover with another roti. Brush with beaten egg, dot top with butter, and bake in 400°F (200°C) oven till pastry is done.

Parethas
(VERY SIMPLE)

2 cups flour
1 tblsp ghee
½ tsp baking powder
Pinch of salt
2/3 cup milk/water
500 g prepared Master Mince No. 1 Recipe

Sift dry ingredients together, rub in ghee and make a soft dough with the milk/water mixture. (Caution: Use just enough of the liquid as is required to make the dough).

Divide dough into two. Roll each out to 3 mm thick rectangles. Brush with ghee, smear a little beaten egg then spread liberally with prepared khima. Fold one-third of roti over and brush the top again with ghee, brush with beaten egg and spread some more khima. Lastly, fold over the other third of roti over the first leaving you with a long oblong khima filled dough. Slightly fold over both sides so that khima does not fall out. Fry this whole paretha in medium oil so that it is slightly brown and crisp. Drain and cool on wire rack. Leave in fridge and use when needed as follows: Cut in 6 mm thick slices, dip in beaten egg and fry very slowly in oil till a beautiful golden colour. Serve with chutneys and lemons.

Araby Lagan
(ARABIAN MINCE TART)

500g of master mince No. 1 (page 184)
DOUGH:
2 cups flour
60g butter
¼ tsp salt
1 tsp baking powder
¾ cup milk/water

Sift dry ingredients — rub in butter then make stiff dough with liquid.

PASTE: Mix ¼ cup oil and ½ cup flour into smooth paste.

Divide dough into 6 portions and roll each out into a large roti that will fit into your casserole (30cm diameter). Grease casserole and lay one roti in it.

Brush top of roti with paste and again brush over paste with little beaten egg. Spread 1/8 of khima over roti.

Brush beaten egg over another roti and invert egg smeared side over khima.

Brush top of roti firstly with paste then the beaten egg. Pile all rotis on top of each other, over top of last roti brush with beaten egg only.

Sprinkle with nuts and khuskhus (poppy seeds). Pour 2 tblsp of oil over roti and bake in 200°C oven for 30-35 minutes. When cold cut into squares and serve.

Khima in Scone
(SAVOURY SCONES)

500 g Master Mince No 1 (Page 184)
2 cups flour
3 tsp baking powder
½ tsp salt
A little pepper
2 eggs
125 g soft butter
*1 egg
*1 cup milk

Sift together in bowl the flour, baking powder, salt and dash of pepper.

Add the butter and lightly mix with fork. Then add to it the egg whisked in the milk and form a soft dough with minimum handling.

Beat 2 eggs, keeping aside just about a quarter of it, add the rest to the Master Mince No. 1 recipe.

Mix eggs thoroughly with mince. In a pan which is well greased, spread half the scone dough, patting it with a wet hand. Spread mince evenly over it then spread rest of scone dough.

Brush left-over egg carefully over adding a few blobs of butter on top. Sprinkle with sesame seeds (tal). Bake for 30 minutes in 180°C oven, remove and cool slightly before cutting it in 5 cm squares. Serve warm as savoury with tea.

Steak Bhajias (Rump)

(EGG DIPPED STEAK)
(COLOUR PAGE 206)

½ kg steak (cut in small cubes)
2 tsp chilli
salt to taste
1 tsp ginger/garlic
2 egg whites
1 green chilli (cut in thin strips)

Mix spices with steak and add sufficient water and simmer till steak is tender.

When cool, beat egg whites with a pinch of salt and fold in green chilli. Dip steak cubes in egg white and fry a pale gold colour.

Drain on kitchen paper.

Serve on bed of salad greens and tomato and lemon slices.

Pandella

(FLAT VEGETABLE PATTIES)
(PHOTO PAGE 141)

3 cups grated vegetable (pumpkin or pawpaw, or cucumber)
1 cup cake flour
1 cup chana flour (gram or pea)
1 cup mealie meal
1 tsp sugar
1 large grated onion
1½ tsp salt to taste
1½ tsp garlic
3 tsp green pounded chillies
1 tsp soomph (fennel)
½ tsp crushed cummin (jeera)
½ tsp crushed coriander

NOTE: The grated green paw paw or pumpkin must be allowed to steep in boiling water for 10 minutes. Then drain dry in colander. Cucumber is used raw. Sift all dry ingredients together.

Mix the grated vegetables, green chillie, garlic, onion and 2 tablespoons of chopped fresh spring onion.

This will be like thick bhajia (chillie bite) batter.
Take tablespoonsful at a time and drop into hot oil.
Fry gold on both sides and drain on kitchen paper.

Pandellas can also be grilled over a tava — in this case pour oil on each side and braise till browned. But take care to press each spoonful flat with the back of the spoon.

Note: This makes a large quantity of pandellas.

Dahi-Baras

1 cup split moong or urad dhal
2 tsp green pounded chilli
1 tsp pounded garlic
1 tsp salt
1 small onion (grated)
¼ tsp bicarb
1 carton yoghurt

Soak dhal overnight. Wash and drain dry in morning.
Either put through mincer or in food processor. The consistency of the dhal must be slightly gritty so don't process it too fine.

Add the other ingredients to the dhal and beat well to incorporate as much air as possible.

Take 1½ to 2 tablespoons of batter at a time and mould into balls.

Flatten each ball as you lower them in hot oil to fry till crisp. Drain off on kitchen paper.

Put 2 cups of water and ½ tsp of salt in a flat bowl. Into this place the bhajias and steep for 5 to 6 minutes.

Squeeze moisture out of bhajias by pressing each gently between palm of hands.

Place bhajias in serving bowl and pour over it 1 carton of yoghurt mixed with 1½ tsp chillies and ½ tsp salt. Garnish with pep-up gharum masala made thus:

½ tsp jeera seeds
1/3 tsp whole coriander
small stick cinnamon
1 whole clove
½ tsp whole peppers

Roast these ingredients in hot oven or over a tava and pound them fine.

Sprinkle them over the bowl of yoghurt and bhajias. Decorate with some chopped mint.

NOTE:
This is a delicious savoury served as an appetiser in hot weather. A teaspoon of sugar may be added to the dahi for that distinctive sweet/sour flavour.

Mince/Egg Samoosas(COLOUR PHOTO PAGE 189)·

2 cups flour
2 tsp ghee
½ tsp baking powder
8 eggs (for frying to enclose within pastry)
1/8 tsp salt
2/3 cup milk/water
500g prepared master mince No. 1 (Page 184)

PASTE:
3 tblsp rice flour
3 tblsp ghee

Melt ghee and mix in the rice flour as it starts melting — form into a smooth paste. Do not allow paste to darken.

A. As you commence to roll out long and fairly thin, wind the rolled portion around a spare roller after spreading with rice flour paste.

B. Cut across over whole length of roller to free roller from dough. (See next page).

On floured board commence to roll dough into a strip slightly narrower than your roller (vehlan) and as long and thin as you can roll it (thickness of very thin puris).

Starting from one end, brush paste over small area of rolled out length. Place vehlan across and start rolling up.

Continue to smear paste over entire surface of dough and roll up till all the dough has been rolled up.

With a knife cut right across top of roll over entire length of vehlan. This will free the roller and you will have a long narrow but many layered piece of dough.

Divide into 8 pieces. Roll each piece out to a longish triangle puri. Fill thickly with khima (master mince No. 1). See colour photo Page 189.

Over khima in centre of each puri, arrange a whole poached or fried egg. Smear edges with egg white and fold into a three cornered samoosa.

Heat oil in deep pan to 180°C and slowly fry till layer opens out and they are crisp. Drain well on wire rack.

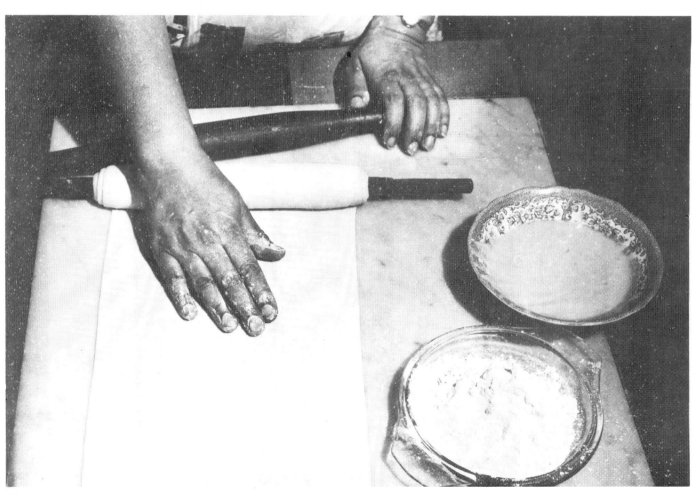

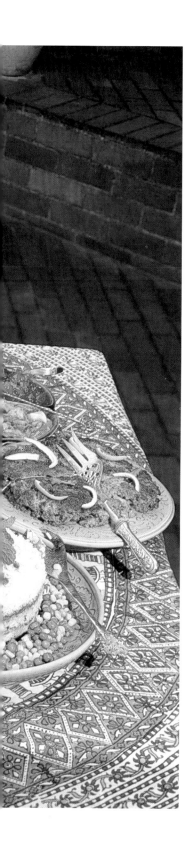

Giant Pastry Pie
(COLOUR PHOTO ON OPPOSITE PAGE)

Pastry dough made from 500g of butter or margarine. Large pot of kokani stew (page 134); 1 pot of kabaab curry. (Page 98)

(a) Roll out 1/3 of pastry into as large a circle or rectangle as your oven will accommodate. This must be rolled out fairly thin (as for bottom of pies). Make a few slashes on this pastry after putting it on baking sheet. Keep in fridge.

(b) Roll out rest of pastry into 1½ times the size of bottom circle and leave it slightly thicker as for jam tarts etc. Keep in fridge separately.

(c) Make a cushion of brown paper slightly smaller than bottom pastry as follows: Take a double sheet of brown paper and plump it into shape like a round cushion. Make a few slashes on top and fill the interior with strips of paper like you would stuff a pillow. This cushion must be fairly rigid to enable it to withstand weight of top pastry. Place cushion paper on smaller circle of pastry.

(d) Carefully spread larger pastry over paper pillow. Brush edges of pastry and press down on bottom circle with a fork. Score top of pastry in diamond shapes with a sharp knife. With knife cut a circle 4 inches away from edge of top pastry. This will make it easier for removing paper afterwards.

(e) Brush pastry top with egg yolk mixed with a little water. Bake blind as for pastry but allow more time for its size, and also allow it to harden and dry out before removing it from oven.

(f) When pastry is cold — very carefully remove top circle. Carefully remove paper pillow — if any danger of pastry collapsing, then put hand through top slashes of paper and remove paper strips from within. This collapsed pillow will come out easily.

JUST BEFORE SERVING:
(g) Heat pot of vegetables and kabaabs and fill huge pastry cavity with it. Cover carefully with pastry lid — pop in hot oven and serve hot.

A Coconut/Jalebi Lagan (321)
B Pastry Twists (200)
C Giant Pastry Pie — (Above)
D Vadde (231)
E Various Pickles
F Mince/Mealie Lagan (218)
G Rice Ring (47)
H Mawa Gulaab Jamun (355)
I Chicken/Prawn Paella (34)

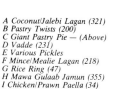
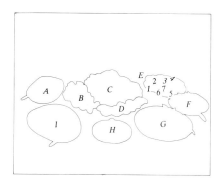

Pastry

USE YOUR FAVOURITE PASTRY RECIPE
OR TRY OURS

500g margarine
500g flour (minus ¼ cup)
½ tsp salt
1 tsp cream of tartar
1 egg yolk
1 tblsp lemon juice
1 cup iced water

FOR SPRINKLING:
¼ cup maizena
1 tsp cream of tartar

Sift this together and divide into 4 parts

Divide margarine in 5 equal portions.
Sift flour and cream of tartar twice.
Beat egg yolk, add lemon juice then mix with iced water.

Rub one portion of butter into flour and mix till fine like breadcrumbs. Make soft pastry dough with liquid, and knead dough slightly. Roll dough out into a rectangle, fold and roll out again. After you have rolled it out the second time, grate the one portion of butter over it but keep 2cm of edges butter-free. Over butter sprinkle liberally with the maizena mixture.

Fold the edges inwards. Now bring the four corners towards the centre to form an envelope shape.

Roll out three more times, dotting with butter and layering maizena over the butter.

Roll out two more times — without butter (since it has all been used up) and fold. Rest dough overnight before rolling out and adding fillings or keep in deep freeze till required.

TO BAKE:

Roll out and fill pastry. Brush with egg yolk. Bake in 200°C oven till pastry is well puffed out (7 to 10 minutes) then switch down to 180°C and finish baking.

Hot Water Pastry
(VERY QUICK AND EASY)

2 to 3 cups flour
1 tsp salt
250g margarine
1 cup boiling water

Sift flour and salt twice. Melt margarine in boiling water and make a dough.

Roll and fold three times — there is no smearing of additional butter involved in this recipe.

If a more flaky pastry is required, then you may roll out seven times.

Fill with filling of choice and bake at 180°C.

NOTE: Measure flour and water in same sized cups.

Quickie Pastry for Savoury or Sweet Pies

· **1½ cups self-raising flour**
2 tblsp castor sugar
pinch of salt
¼ cup cooking oil (75ml)
¼ cup water (75ml)

Put flour, sugar, salt, oil in a bowl — sprinkle contents with the water.

Cover bowl with tight fitting lid for half a minute. Shake contents in bowl from side to side for a minute. Then uncover and gather dough together with hands. Roll out and put on base of pie dish.

Put in filling of choice over it and bake immediately in oven for 30 minutes at 200°C.

Cream Cheese Pastry
(VEGETARIANS WILL WELCOME THIS QUICK AND EASY PASTRY)

½ cup butter
½ tsp salt
½ cup creamed cottage cheese
2 cups self-raising flour

Beat butter and cheese and salt till light and creamy. Add flour and mix roughly with hands.

Put dough inside plastic bag, chill for 1 hour, and roll to thickness required.

Use for savoury pies etc., or cut in fancy shapes with dainty cutters.

Brush top with egg yolk and bake in 400°F (200°C) oven for 10 minutes.

Savoury Fillings for Pastries

Fish and Potato Filling:

1 large potato (boiled and diced)
500g hake or stock fish
1 tsp green pounded chillies
½ tsp nutmeg
½ bunch chopped dhunia
2 tblsp chopped mint
2 tblsp chopped pickles (optional)
1 medium grated onion
2 cloves of garlic pounded
½ tsp pepper
1 tsp salt

Flake steamed fish, carefully removing bones. To this add spices, chopped greens and grated onion. Mix well with fork. Sprinkle fish mixture over rolled out pastry dough. Next sprinkle diced potato and pickles strewing them fairly evenly over the lot. Now roll over like swiss roll and press down slightly the end, to ensure that it does not open up during baking. Put sealed edge down on baking tin and follow instructions for baking, (make cuts at finger wide distances on top).

Mince

Sprinkle mince prepared as in master mince recipe. In addition sprinkle carrot pickle which has been diced fine and from which excess masala is removed. Roll and bake as in above.

Meat/Vegetable

500g chicken breasts or mutton

Chop up small and cook as follows. To any of above add 1 tsp salt, ¼ tsp pepper, 1 tsp green pounded chillies, ½ tsp ginger/garlic, and 2 tsps oil. Simmer slowly till done and all moisture absorbed, adding water if necessary. Boil 1½ cups of diced vegetables. (Potatoes, carrots sweetcorn and peas). Cut up ¼ cup of carrot/bean pickles (optional). Roll up like swiss roll and bake according to instructions.

Flaked Meat Filling for Pies etc

500g chicken breasts (or mutton etc)
1 tsp salt
¼ tsp pepper
½ tsp crushed jeero (cummin)
½ tblsp ghee
2 tblsp chopped greens
½ tsp ginger/garlic
1½ tsp crushed green chilli
Sufficient water to cook meat soft
1 sliced onion

Cook meat soft with spices. Flake meat, then add onion and ghee, braise slowly till onion cooked.
Cool and add chopped greens.

Steak for Fillings (Rump)

500 g steak (washed and cut small)
1 onion (grated)
1 tsp salt
½ tsp crushed jeera (cummin)
1 tomato
1/3 tsp black pepper
1 tsp chilli
1 tsp ginger/garlic

Add spices to steak and cover with sufficient water to cook soft. When soft add onions and cook for five minutes more.

Flake meat with fork. Add chopped dhunia. This filling can be used in any of our pie or savoury tarts. Mutton or chicken may be substituted.

Vegetable Filling
(COLOUR PHOTO PAGE 239)

1 cup mashed potato
1½ cups diced boiled vegetables (carrots, peas, sweet
    corn)

Toss and mix in above: Salt, chillies, cut-up dhunia, pepper, 2 green chillies cut up fine and a tablespoon of chopped vegetable achar. Smear or sprinkle mashed potato over. Now sprinkle vegetables. Roll and bake as above.

NOTE: Any of above fillings can be used for individual tarts.

Pastry Kabaab Twists

(SERVES 4)   (PHOTO PAGE 196)

200g of pastry dough
250g mince
1 tsp pounded fresh green chillies
1/3 tsp crushed cummin (jeera)
1 grated onion (medium)
½ tsp ginger/garlic
½ tsp salt
1/3 tsp black crushed pepper
1 tbsp chopped dhunia (coriander leaves)

Wash and drain mince completely dry.

Squeeze out water from onion and add it to mince with all the spices.

Pound and mix mince well so that kabaabs mould easily. Now mould into small forefinger length sausages.

Put sausages in a frying pan with just 2 tbsp of oil and grill them on top of stove, just long enough for liquid to evaporate.

Sausages must still be wet and juicy. (10 or 12 sausages).

Roll out about 200g of pastry fairly thin.

Cut pastry into long strips (forefinger wide).

Take each long strip and wind it around each sausage-shaped kabaab, leaving a little space between each winding. (See photograph on Page 196).

When you have covered all the kabaabs, leave them on a baking sheet in the freezer while oven is getting hot.

Before baking brush with egg yolk and bake in 230° hot oven for 10 mins. Serve hot with chutneys.

Chicken "Toffee Apples"

6 legs of chicken
½ tsp ginger/garlic
½ tsp salt
1 tbsp lemon juice
1 tsp fresh green pounded chillies
1/3 tsp crushed cummin (jeera)
1/3 tsp black crushed pepper

Cut meat loose from tendon at bottom of leg. Make a small slit and draw it slowly over top of bone. The meat should have been turned completely inside out, but take care not to detach it from top end of bone, for what you want is a toffee apple shaped lump of meat at the top of the bone.

Marinate these toffee apples in the above marinade for several hours. Beat 2 egg whites stiff till they begin to form peaks.

Beat egg yolks till they are thick and creamy, then fold them into egg whites.

Roll each leg in fine crumbs, dip in egg and slow fry in frying pan till they are a beautiful golden colour.

Place wire tray over a metal tray. Place meat chops on wire tray and keep in 350°F oven for 30 minutes. Serve hot with salads.

Pastry Drummies

Prepare chicken legs as for "toffee apples". Add masalas and steam in pot with a little water till meat is done.

Roll out pastry and cut into strips as for pastry kabaab twists and wind around meat. (See Page 196).

Bake in hot oven till pastry is done.

Dress up the bone with frills made from doyleys or foil

Rolled Fillet Pie

(COLOUR PHOTO 204)

1 kg fillet of beef
2 tsp pounded garlic
2 tbsp butter
2 tsp green pounded chilli
½ tsp crushed cummin
1 tsp black crushed pepper
2 tsp dry mustard powder
2 tbsp flour
Salt to taste
Juice of lemon

Place fillet on table and slice through thickness but leaving it intact at one end. Then cut through again both halves of fillet and again leaving only one side intact. This will give you a broad flat rectangle piece of fillet. Spread with masala made of above spices, lemon juice, flour and butter.

Taking care that all meat areas are covered. Pat back fillet into original shape, cover with foil. Place in casserole and steam gently in oven for an hour (180°C). Remove foil and put fillet on wire sieve and allow excess moisture to drain off. This can be used for gravy later. Cover roll with a pastry dough when cold.

Make designs on pastry and cut through at a few places to allow steam to escape. Bake in hot oven for 10 minutes. Lower heat and leave in oven for 10 more minutes. Cook on rack. Serve with chutneys.

NOTE:

The rolled fillet is in itself delicious. The pastry cover is for special occasions.

Pastry Roll with Mince

250 g pastry dough (Page 198)
250 g prepared Master Khima Recipe (Mince) (Page 184)

Roll out pastry to thickness as for jam tarts. Spread with yolk of egg and sprinkle with mince fairly generously. Moisten edges of pastry with white of egg and roll over like swiss roll. Glaze the roll with milk. Place on ungreased tray and bake for 20 to 30 minutes.

VARIATION:

The above pastry roll is equally delicious with a vegetable or chopped meat filling.

Mayonnaise/Mash Potato Pastry

A very tasty and easy pastry and a great favourite with those newly introduced to it.

2 cups flour
1/3 tsp salt
75g instant mash potato flakes
2 tblsp butter
7/8th cup milk
2 tblsp grated cheddar cheese
1 tsp bicarb
½ cup mayonnaise
1 tsp cream of tartar
2 tblsp sugar
2 tsp green pounded chilli

Sift flour with salt, bicarb and cream of tartar. Rub the butter in lightly and add sugar and green chillies. Mix together with a fork. Now add the milk, potato flakes (keep aside a handful) and mayonnaise and form into a soft dough.

Wrap in plastic and keep in fridge for half an hour. Roll out on floured board and line a tart plate with half of dough.

Now cover with filling of choice (fish, meat, mince or vegetable). Dot here and there with a little chutney or chopped pickles.

Grate remaining dough with coarse side of grater over the filling. Take care that entire surface is covered.

Sprinkle rest of grated cheese over dough as well as a handful of mash potato flakes.

Dot with a little butter and bake in 200°C (400°F) oven for 15 minutes. Switch down to 180°C and bake another 15 minutes.

NOTE: Instead of grating dough push through a sevia or gaanthia disc.

Lebanon Lagan

MINCE COVERING:
250 g minced meat
1 cup laapsi (crushed wheat)
¼ tsp cummin powder
1 large onion
1 tsp green pounded chilli
Salt and pepper
STUFFING:
½ cup oil
½ cup chopped peanuts
½ tsp chilli powder
1 medium chopped onion
250 g minced meat
¼ tsp cinnamon powder
Salt and pepper

Wash and soak laapsi in cold water and leave overnight. In the morning drain off excess moisture. Add mince, onion and spices and grind two more times through mincer. Knead with hands to form into a stiff meat-covering for mince stuffing.

THE STUFFING:
Saute onions in half of oil till soft and transparent. Add mince, chopped peanuts and spices and braise till fine like bread-crumbs.

In greased casserole pat in less than half of meat covering.

Spread mince stuffing over this and finally cover with leftover meat covering. Brush over with rest of oil, sprinkle with khus-khus and bake in 200°C oven for 20 to 40 minutes. With sharp knife cut into diamond shapes and serve hot with chutney and lemon.

Garlic Chicken

6 breasts of chicken (500 g)
1½ tsp freshly pounded red chillies
3 tsp freshly pounded garlic
Juice of ½ lemon
2 tbsp tomato puree
2 tbsp ghee or margarine
1 tsp salt

Wash and pat dry chicken portions. Make deep slits in meat. Mix spices together and add to ghee or margarine.

Smear masala into slits and all over meat. Marinate for few hours. Place on greased oven tray — cover with foil and bake in 350⁰F (180⁰C) oven for 40 minutes.

Remove foil, dot each breast with butter and bake in oven for 10 minutes, in hot oven.

ALTERNATIVELY: After removing foil place slices of thin cheese over breasts and put under grill till cheese melts.

Rolled Chicken Breasts with Lemon/Butter (COLOUR PAGE 265)

500g chicken breasts
2 cloves garlic (1 teaspoon)
juice of ½ lemon
½ tsp crushed cummin seeds (jeera)
125g butter (leave to harden in fridge)
6 green chillies
1 level tsp salt
1 tblsp chopped dhunia (coriander leaves)

Wash and pat breasts of chicken dry. Place on board and pound each till it is flattened. Cut in rectangles.

You should have between 12 and 14 rectangular pieces of chicken from the 500g. Mix all the other ingredients (excepting the butter) together in a bowl.

Roll the chicken breasts well into it so that the spices and moisture cling to both sides of the chicken.

Place pieces of chicken on a board strewn with dry bread crumbs. Place a pencil thickness of butter across each strip and roll them individually to resemble small thin sausages. Keep in fridge till required. (May be frozen and later thawed when required).

Beat egg white lightly, and incorporate into the beating another tablespoon of chopped dhunia. Dip each rolled breast in egg white and fry in shallow oil over medium heat till rolls are a beautiful gold colour.

Best served hot with sauces and chutneys.

Malay Bobotie (BOBOTIE LAGAN)

500g steak mince
1 tblsp butter/margarine
½ tsp black crushed pepper
2 tsp green crushed chilli
2 tsp salt
2 tblsp chopped coriander leaves
½ cup dried apricots
1 tblsp lemon juice
2 slices bread
1¼ cup milk
2 eggs
1 large onion chopped
1 tsp crushed cummin
½ tsp crushed coriander seed

Soak dried apricots in cold water overnight. Chop fruit next morning and reserve water. Wash mince and drain dry completely. Soak bread in ¼ cup milk — when soft squeeze out milk and crumble bread into bowl of mince.

Melt butter in pan and cook chopped onion till transparent. Add chopped fruit, water and all the spices and simmer (stirring constantly) till juice is thick and pulpy.

Add sauce to mince — when cool add chopped dhunia (coriander), blend well. Place in greased oven dish. Beat eggs with milk and pour over mince lagan.

Add a sprig of mint or kuripulya leaves and press onto lagan. Bake at 325°F (165°C) until golden brown. Serve with vegetables, rice, chutney, etc.

Turkey or Chicken Meat Botie Lagan

(BOBOTIE)
(COLOUR PAGE 133)

2 med onions (grated)
1½ tsp crushed garlic
1 tsp crushed jeera (cummin)
2 tsp red pounded chillies
2 green apples (grated with skins) OR
2 green mangos (peeled and grated)
1 slice bread soaked in ½ cup milk
1 tbsp tomato sauce
2 eggs (beaten)
lemon leaves
½ cup milk
500g minced chicken or turkey
2 tbsp ghee or oil
½ tsp turmeric
2 tbsp aamli (tamarind sauce) optional
1 tsp salt (or more)
2 small eggs (beaten)
1 tbsp mircha chutney (hot)

Sauté onions in oil and when they are soft add spices.

Braise for a minute then remove from stove. Mix the soaked bread and milk into the beaten eggs and add to onions. Add grated apples, (or mango) sauces and chutneys and tamarind pulp to eggs.

Finally add mince and mix all ingredients well together. Grease a baking tin or deep casserole and pat mixture into it.

Scald the other milk, remove from stove and quickly mix in the other two beaten eggs.

Pour this over the bobotie. Press in the lemon leaves into the lagan (if not available dhunia or mint leaves will suffice).

Bake at 350°F (180°C) for 30-40 minutes. Serve hot with vegetables.

Bobotie in Pastry

(COLOUR PAGE 204)

After bobotie is baked (but not dried out) remove from pan and allow to cool. Cover entire bobotie with flaky pastry dough. Score designs over dough and bake as for pastry. Looks very dramatic on a table as you slice off helpings for guests.

Rolled Breasts in Pastry

(PHOTO PAGE 204)

After the breast-roll has been steamed, allow breast-roll to cool down.

Meanwhile roll out pastry, place roll inside and seal with egg white.

Place sealed side down on baking sheet. Make cuts on top of pastry at finger wide distances. Brush with egg yolk and bake in hot oven till pastry done.

VARIATION:

Omit pickle, prunes and apricots and substitute 2 slices bread (soaked in little milk to soften) and 2 tblsp of green dhunia chutney. Mix well with other ingredients and spread this over breasts, and roll as indicated.

Chicken/Khima Loaf

500g chicken breasts
* 1 tsp ginger/garlic
* 1 tsp salt
* 1 tsp green chilli
* juice of ½ lemon

STUFFING:
250g minced meat (mutton)
1 medium onion
1 egg
1 slice of bread
1 tsp salt
1 tsp green chilli
1 tsp ginger/garlic
½ tsp black crushed pepper

Slice chicken breasts in large thin slices. Wash and wipe dry.

Place foil on wooden board and place chicken breasts on it, laying the pieces to fit the piece of foil. Pound well to tenderize. Smear masalas marked with asterisk (*) well over the breasts and leave on board while preparing mince.

Put ingredients for stuffing in food processor (or mince through mincer). The egg will bind the ingredients together.

Spread this stuffing over the meat on the board, add a few blobs of butter over it at even distances, carefully roll over like a swiss roll.

It will be easy to pick up roll with foil.

Place roll with foil in a loaf pan. Brush margarine all over and bake in 180°C oven for about an hour. Serve with vegetables.

If roll dries out, more margarine will have to be smeared over top.

Steak Popsicles

(PHOTO PAGE 182)

8-10 Servings
1 kg steak
1 tblsp lemon juice
1 tblsp crushed jeera (cummin)
½ tblsp oil
1 tsp (or more) salt
2 tblsp ghee plus 1 tblsp oil
5 green chillies
3 cloves garlic
¼ cup dhunia (chopped)
white of egg
1 tblsp ghee

Wash steak and cut in 12 to 16 rectangular pieces each the thickness and length of a ladies' forefinger. Wipe dry and pound each piece well.

Crush chillies and garlic and add to lemon juice and ½ tablespoon ghee. To that add one tablespoon salt, cummin and chopped chopped dhunia leaves, and mix into a paste. Smear beef slices on both sides with this masala. Now Spread each one out and fold 1/3 over from right edge. Smear the other edge with white of egg and bring over to lap over the rest.

You will be left with a small ice cream shaped rectangle. Insert a wooden ice cream stick through meat to hold layers together. Place neatly in pan and slow fry in oil/ghee till meat done. Serve with salads.

See page 182 where chicken breasts were used instead of steak for popsicles.

Boiled Mince Roll

500 g mince
3 cloves of garlic
7 black peppers
1 onion (grated)
3 eggs
6 green chillies
1 tsp jeero (cummin)
1 tsp whole coriander
¼ tsp cinnamon (ground)
Salt to taste

Pound green chillies, garlic, jeero, peppers and whole coriander in mortar. Wash mince and drain off all moisture. Grate onion and drain off all extra moisture. Fry half of onion in little ghee, and add to mince. Also add raw onion and all pounded masalas and salt. Put through mincer again.

Shape into swiss roll with whole boiled eggs enclosed inside. Wrap foil around this and seal off both ends. Place on wire rack and steam over shallow water for ½ hour. Cut in slices and serve with vegetables. Or use in sandwiches.

VARIATION:
Enclose mashed potatoes, peas, carrots, inside.

Rolled Breasts of Chicken

500g chicken breasts
1 tsp crushed garlic
1/3 tsp black crushed pepper
1 tblsp juice of lemon
1 doz chopped prunes or apricots
1 tblsp ground almonds or other nuts
1½ tsp pounded chilli (red or green)
½ tsp crushed cummin
1 tsp salt
2 tblsp butter
2 tblsp fresh cream
2 tblsp vegetable pickle

De-bone breasts. Place flat on board and slit each breast carefully through the middle but leaving the end intact.

This will leave you with large flat pieces of breasts. With a blunt chopper, pound meat all over to tenderise it.

Mix cream, butter, lemon, ground almonds and spices together. Spread this marinade on both sides of breasts.

Put meat on a piece of foil, piling them up in a way that you will be able to have a nice long and thick roll of meat.

From the side where you will begin to roll the meat like a swiss roll, arrange the cut-up dried prunes and apricots and dot with pieces of mustard pickle all along the dried fruit.

Now roll-up like a swiss roll. Close well with foil.
Place this roll in a bowl that can be sealed.
Place this bowl inside another pot with water and steam for about 45 min.

Unroll meat loaf, brush all over with butter and beaten egg and brown lightly in the oven.

Cut a few slices of meat, but leave rest of roll intact and it can be cut at table as needed.
Serve with lots of salads and vegetables.

VARIATION:

Omit pickle, prunes and apricots and substitute 2 slices bread (soaked in little milk to soften) and 2 tblsp of green dhunia chutney. Mix well with other ingredients and spread this over breasts, and roll as indicated.

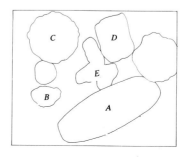

A Rolled Chicken in Pastry (203)
B Mitha Beda
C Sev (244)
D Bobotie in Pastry (204)
E Chicken roll (sliced)

Shami Kabaabs from Steak

*1 kg steak, cut into fat free cubes
*½ cup chana dhal (gram dhal)
*1 large onion sliced
*3 tsp ginger/garlic
*1 tsp whole pepper
*2 sticks cinnamon
*3 cloves
*2 black elachi
1 large potato peeled and cubed
Salt to taste
1 egg

Chutney for Kabaabs

¼ cup chopped dhunia and mint
6 green chillies
1 onion
Salt
A little lemon juice

Pound and keep aside for filling inside the patties.

In a large pot add 1 cup water and the first 8 ingredients. Cook slowly and when half done add cubed potato and salt. When contents is dry and meat is cooked remove peppers, cinnamon sticks, cloves and elachi from it.

Put the mixture through a mincer, allow to cool and then beat egg and add to the above mixture. Now make the patties (like hamburgers) but remove a little from the centre, fill in the dhunia/green chilli chutney, close up the centre.

Fry in deep hot oil slowly or in shallow oil. Serve with chutneys and kachoomer.

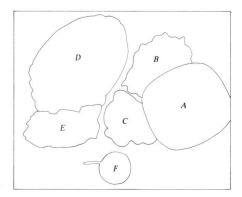

A Snoek Stew/Dokra (110)
B Steak Bhajias (193)
C Beef Burgers (96)
D Shaami Kabaabs (above)
E Corn Lagan (230)
F Mayonnaise Chutney (278)

Seekh Kabaabs
(BRAAI KABAABS)
  500 g mutton (fatty)
  1 tsp ginger/garlic
  1 tsp green pounded chillies
  ½ tsp pepper
  1 tsp salt
  ½ tsp crushed jeero (cummin)
  1 grated onion
  ½ tsp red chilli

Wash mutton and put twice through mincer. Add to it the green pounded chillies and garlic. Then the salt and pepper and grated onion, but squeeze out juice of onion. Mix the spices well in the mince and form in ping-pong sized balls of kabaabs. Push skewers through kabaabs — pat and mould till mince clings around skewers. Grill over charcoal or place in greased roasting pan and bake uncovered in 200⁰ oven till kabaabs are dry and brown. Instead of kabaabs, one can form the mince in cutlet shapes. Meats grilled in the oven have a delicious braaivleis taste.

NOTE: A teaspoon or two of pounded green pawpaw added to mince just before grilling renders them more digestible.

Instead of moulding into balls, shape mince like sausages and mould around skewers.

Egg Kabaabs
(NARGISI KOFTA)

  500 g mince
  1 tsp pounded garlic
  ¼ tsp ground cinnamon (tuj)
  ¼ tsp ground pepper
  2 tblsp chopped dhunia leaves
  6 boiled eggs
  1 tsp pounded green chillies
  1 grated onion
  1 tsp salt

Wash and drain mince completely dry by squeezing through muslin cloth. Except for eggs add all other ingredients and pound the mince or put through mincer again. Wrap mince around each shelled boiled egg. Dip in dry crumbs and fry in deep oil over medium heat or place in greased casserole and brown in oven, turning over a few times.

Lucknowi Kabaabs

  1 tsp pounded green chilli
  500 g beef mince
  1 medium sized onion
  *6 whole pepper corns
  *3 cardamoms
  *¼ whole nutmeg
  *1½ tsp dhunia/jeero seeds
  1 tblsp chana flour (gram flour or pea flour)
  1 tblsp sour milk
  ½ cup green grated pawpaw
  3 cloves garlic (crushed)
  *6 whole cloves
  *2 small pieces of cinnamon
  1 tsp red chilli powder
  Salt to taste

Roast ingredients with asterisk in hot oven. Then pound fine. Squeeze out all moisture from washed mince, using a muslin cloth for the purpose. Put in bowl with the pounded spices. Pound pawpaw and garlic in mortar and add to mince. Grate onions and add to mince. Braise chana flour in a tablespoon of oil and remove from heat when light pink. Allow to cool and add sour milk to it. Add to mince. Put mince through mincer again, mixing all the masalas well in it. The mixture will be sticky so dampen hands and mould in small kabaabs. Heat a little oil in tava (griddle) and grill the kabaabs in this.

Khus-Khus Tunduri Kabaabs
(POPPY SEED MEAT BALLS)

  500 g mince meat (mutton)
  2 tblsp khus-khus (poppy seed)
  1 tblsp chana flour (gram)
  1 tblsp chopped dhunia leaves
  1 egg
  3 tblsp oil
  ½ tsp garlic
  1 tsp green chillies (pounded)
  ½ tsp black ground pepper
  ½ tsp crushed jeero
  1 tsp salt
  ½ tsp red chilli

Pound a teaspoon of khus-khus, jeero, peppercorns, garlic and green chillies in kundi (mortar). Add this to washed and well drained mince. Put through mincer again or pound it well. Braise chana flour in oil till a delicate pink in colour. Add to mince. Lastly add chopped dhunia and egg to mince and mix well. Form into small ping pong sized balls and roll each lightly in left over khus-khus. Put meat balls in greased baking tin. Swirl balls around till they are covered in oil. Brown in moderate oven, turning over once or twice during the roasting period. When nicely browned remove from oven. Serve hot with lemons and chutneys.

Meat Kabaabs

(PARSEE)

500 g minced meat
1 tsp ginger/garlic
1 onion
1 bunch dhunia
½ tsp chilli powder
1 egg
5-6 green chillies (pounded)
5-6 mint leaves
1 small potato
1 tsp turmeric
½ tsp dhunia/jeero
1 tsp salt
3 tblsp ghee

Boil the potato and mash. Wash mince and drain in colander. Add chillies, chopped ginger/garlic, chopped dhunia and mint leaves to the mince. Also add the chopped onion, salt, turmeric, dhunia, jeero, chilli powder and mashed potato. Cover in a basin and keep for an hour. Beat the egg and add to the mixture. Shape into 8 large meat balls. Heat the ghee in a large frying pan and fry the kabaabs until brown. Serve with rice and kachoomer.

Dahi Kabaabs

(SOUR MILK) (COLOUR PHOTO PAGE 99)

500 g raw minced meat
1 tsp dhunia/jeero
1 tsp arad (turmeric)
½ tblsp ground almonds
1 tsp gharum masala
2 tsp green pounded chillies
1 tsp ginger/garlic
1 tblsp pea flour
1 tblsp freshly pounded coconut (or dessicated)
1 onion (sliced fine)
½ cup dahi (yoghurt)
1 tblsp chopped mint leaves
Salt and pepper to taste

Put meat through mincer twice. Mix all ingredients well together. Mould into walnut sized kabaabs and place on greased tray. Put tray in 180°C oven and brown kabaabs well. Serve with lemons and chutneys. May also be fried in oil.

Kabaabs with Bajra Flour

(MEAT BALLS WITH MILLET FLOUR)

500 g mince (mutton)
1 bunch spring onions
1 bunch dhunia (coriander)
1 tsp red chilli powder
1½ tsp salt
1 cup bajra flour (millet)
1 tsp ground ginger/garlic
1 medium chopped onion
1 tsp green pounded chillies
2 tsp dhunia/jeero powder

To washed and drained mince add all spice and the (chopped) greens. Now add as much of bajra flour as the mince will absorb. The consistency of the mince after addition of flour should be that of kabaabs (meat balls). Heat oil. Make small bhajia sized lumps of mince (like a largish marble) and fry in hot deep oil. Serve hot with lemons and chutneys.

Bajra Kabaabs

250g minced mutton or chicken
250g finely chopped mutton or chicken
500g bajra flour (millet or sorghum)
1 tsp or more salt
1 tsp crushed dhunia seeds (coriander)
2 tblsp yoghurt (dahi)
½ cup chopped dhunia (coriander leaves)
½ cup chopped mint
1 tomato (chopped)
1 tsp garlic (crushed)
2 tsp green pounded chilli
1 onion (chopped)

Mix all ingredients well together. Mould into ball like lumps and fry in deep oil over medium heat. Serve with lemons.

White Meat Bhajias

500g Chicken breast cut into small bite-size squares. Marinate for a few hours in the following ingredients:

Salt to taste
2 tbsp semolina
2 tbsp chana flour
6 green chillies (pounded)
1 tsp jeero OR
1 tsp dhunia
1 grated onion
½ bunch dhunia (chopped)
¼ bunch mint leaves (chopped

Just before frying beat 2 eggs slightly and mix in. Then add 1 tsp baking powder. Fry in deep oil. Serve hot with chutneys.

Mealie Bhajias

2 tsp coarsely crushed dhunia (dry coriander seeds)
¼ cup mealie meal
1 tblsp chana flour
1 medium sized onion (grated or chopped fine)
1 cup ground fresh green mealies
Oil for frying
3 green chillies pounded fine
1 tsp fine salt
¾ tsp baking powder
1 bunch chopped dhunia leaves (coriander)
2 tblsp chopped shallot

Sieve dry ingredients into a large bowl. Add remaining ingredients to it and mix to the consistency of a thick pancake batter. Heat oil in pan.

Take dessertspoonsful of batter at a time and spread gently in pan, taking care not to overcrowd the frying pan and leaving sufficient space in between bhajias to allow for turning. The oil must be pre-heated fairly well. Turn bhajias over when golden brown and when reverse side is a similar colour remove and drain in colander. Serve while hot.

Mealie Moothias
(PHOTO PAGE 140)

Same as above, except that batter must be very dry, like moothia dough. Shape into moothias and fry slowly in shallow oil, until crisp and golden.

Makay Squares or Green Mealie Squares

6 green mealies (Grate kernel off cobs, or put through mincer)
1½ tsp pounded green chillies
¼ tsp pepper
2 tblsp fresh coriander or parsley chopped fine
1 tblsp butter
1 tsp baking powder
1½ tsp salt
1 egg (beaten)

Mix all above ingredients well together. Pack in greased tray and bake in hot oven till set. Serve hot with lemons, and chutneys.

VARIATION:

Cut lagan in 2 cm cubes. Dip in beaten egg and fry in oil till pale gold in colour.

For other mealie savouries, see mealie section.

Mealie Rotlas
(MEALIE BREAD)

6 mealies (Kernels put through mincer or grated off from cobs)
1½ tsp ground green chillies
1 tblsp sugar
2 tsp baking powder
¼ cup milk
1 tblsp butter
Salt to taste

Mix all above ingredients together and mould in shapes resembling miniature sized mealies. Put each on well-washed mealie leaves. Roll and cover-up and tie ends with string. In a deep pot place mealie cobs (from which kernels were grated off) and cover with water. Put extra mealie leaves over these. Finally, place the moulded mealie breads over them and allow to steam for an hour till the rotlas have swollen and cooked, or oil the inside of an empty baking powder tin, fill with mixture then close lid and steam untill done.

Serve hot with butter mixed with a little green chutney. Left-over mealie bread can be re-fried in butter and then served.

Mealie Cake

60g butter
6 bunches of large leaved bhaji
½ cup oil
1¼ cups freshly grated mealies or sweetcorn
¼ cup mealie meal
1 grated onion
1½ tsp green pounded chillies
½ tsp dhunia/jeero
2 eggs
¼ cup chana flour
¼ cup cake flour
1 cup milk
2 tsp baking powder
1 tsp salt
¼ tsp turmeric

Wash bhaji. Drain well and chop. Grate onion. Sift flours, rub in butter, and add to grated mealies. Add bhaji. blend in all spices with fork. Beat eggs and mix in with mixture. Mix milk and oil, add to powder and combine well with mealie batter. Grease casserole and pour batter into it. Bake in moderate oven for 30 to 40 minutes. Just 5 minutes before it is done, lightly brush with egg. Decorate with dhunia and tal and leave in oven for a few minutes. Serve hot with chutneys.

Mince/Mealie Kabaabs

(KHIMA/MAKAY KABAAB) (COLOUR PAGE 133)

500g minced mutton (or chicken)
1 onion (grated)
1½ tsp fine salt
1 tsp crushed cummin seeds
½ tsp crushed coriander seeds
3 tblsp chopped greens (coriander, mint or spring
   onions)
1 tsp pounded garlic
1 tblsp margarine
3 or 4 green mealies (grated)
2 tsp pounded green chillies
½ tsp crushed black peppers
½ tsp turmeric powder
1½ tsp baking powder
1 egg (optional)

Wash and drain mince off all excessive moisture.

Squeeze out water from onions and green grated mealies
(but do not throw it away for it can be used in soups and
curries.)

Wash and chop greens, then add all ingredients together
and mix well.

Form into golf-ball sized balls and fry lightly in oil over
medium heat.

Serve hot with slices of lemons and chutneys.

Oven Shami Kabaabs

1 cup chana dhal (gram)
1 large onion
½ tsp ground garlic
½ tsp crushed jeero (cummin)
Rind of ½ lemon (grated)
1 tsp salt
500 g mutton
2 tsp green pounded chillies
¼ tsp crushed black pepper
Good pinch ground cinnamon
1 egg
½ bunch dhunia leaves

Soak dhal overnight and wash well in morning. Cut
mutton in small pieces and wash well. Boil till soft. Grind
mutton and dhal together. Grate onion and add to mince.
Add spices, chopped dhunia and rind of lime. Mix well together. Add egg and mix again. Form mince mixture in
ping pong sized balls. Flatten slightly and place in well
greased baking tray and bake in hot oven for an hour and
allow to brown well. Serve hot with lemon and chutney
(preferably mint chutney).

Fish Cutlets

500 g steamed fish (baracuda, hake, salmon etc. or
   whichever is available)
2 tblsp of either mint, dhunia, shallot or parsley (cut
   fine)
1 egg (optional, but it has a binding effect)
1 tsp salt
1 tsp ground green chillies
2 medium slices of bread soaked in water or 1 large
   mashed potato
2 dessertspoonsful butter
½ tsp ground garlic
½ tsp grated nutmeg

Flake fish finely and remove all bones. Add above
ingredients and mix well in fish. Take golf ball sizes of fish
and pat roundly and firmly in palm of hand to 1 cm thickness. It should be about 6 cm in diameter. Sprinkle each
side with dry bread crumbs or crushed post toasties. Dip in
well-whisked eggs and fry in medium hot oil in pan on both
sides till it is a beautiful golden brown. Drain in colander
and serve warm with chutneys.

Fish Cutlets

(VARIATION)

Omit egg, and instead add juice of a lemon. Add ½
teaspoon black crushed pepper corns.

Fish Kabaabs

(VARIATIONS)

The ingredients for fish kabaabs remain the same as
above. The difference is that the kabaabs are left fairly
thick and rounded, like balls. The kabaabs are fried without dipping them in egg and crumbs.

Seekh Gosht

½ tsp red chili powder
500 g mutton
½ tsp salt
1 tsp ginger/garlic
½ tsp crushed jeero
1 tsp pounded green chillies
1 tblsp lemon juice or vinegar
2 tsp pounded green pawpaw (or grated)

Cube meat in 2 cm thick by 5cm squares. Marinate in
this masala for a few hours. Skewer meat in irons and grill
over open fire.

Seekh Kabaabs

(MEAT BALLS)

500 g mutton (fatty)
1 tsp garlic
2 tsp green pounded chillies
1 tblsp ghee
½ tsp pepper
1 tsp salt
½ tsp crushed jeero
½ grated onion
¼ tsp chilli powder

. Wash mutton and mince twice through mincer. Add to it the green pounded chillies and garlic. Then the salt and pepper, and the grated onion, but squeeze out juice. Mix the spices well in the mince, and form in ping-pong sized balls of kabaabs. Remember to pound mince stiff. Put kabaabs on skewer and braai over charcoal.

Boti Kebaabs

1 kg boneless lamb
½ tsp elachi (cardomom)
¼ tsp powdered cloves
1 tbsp khus-khus (poppy seeds)
2 tbsp oil
salt to taste
1 tbsp ginger/garlic
½ tsp black crushed pepper
¼ tsp powdered cinnamon
1 tbsp ground cashew nuts
2 tsp fresh ground chillies (red)

Wash and cube meat in squares (40 pieces).

Wet sesame seeds with little water, then pound till seeds are milky. To this add all other ingredients and marinate meat in them for 10 hours.

Arrange on skewers and grill over red hot coals or rotisserie. May also be roasted.

Serve hot with lemon and chutney.

Dum Ke Kabaab (PHOTO PAGE 92)

500g mince
1 tsp ginger (pounded
10 cloves garlic (crushed)
1 tsp pounded green pawpaw
*1 tsp saumph (fennel)
*1 tsp shah jeera
*1 tsp whole dhunia (coriander)
*10 black peppers
*4 cloves
*4 big elachi (cardomom)
1 onion grated
2 tblsp dhunia leaves
2 green chillies pounded
1 tsp chilli powder
1 tblsp yoghurt
salt to taste
1 egg

Wash and drain mince. Add ginger, onion, garlic, salt, dhunia, chillies and yoghurt. Lightly roast the spices marked with asterisk, pound fine and add to mince.

Mix well and keep aside for 2 or 3 hours. Add egg and green pawpaw and mix. Mould into moothia shapes and fry in shallow oil.

Place kebaabs in pot make space in centre for a small pot in which place a tablespoon of oil and a piece of burning charcoal. Close lid for 5 minutes. Serve hot. (See black and white photograph on Page 92).

Cutlets

500 g mince
4 cloves of garlic
5 or 6 green chillies
½ tsp jeero (crushed cummin)
1 tsp salt
¼ tsp ground pepper
2 tblsp green dhunia (coriander)
2 slices bread (1 cm thick)
Instead of bread, ½ cup of Jungle Oats OR
1 cup of mashed potatoes

Wash mince and drain thoroughly, pound green chillies and garlic and jeero and add to mince. Add salt and pepper. Soak bread slices in water for five minutes. Squeeze out all water and add bread crumbs to mince. Put all through mincer again or pound it stiff in mortar. Add chopped dhunia leaves. Pat into cutlet shapes and dry out in 180°C oven for about 5 minutes. When cool dip in beaten eggs and fry as for cutlets.

For best results in frying cutlets, beat white of eggs first till they stand in peaks. Then whisk yolks of eggs and fold into the whites. This ensures beautiful cutlets. If you have a lot of egg whites left over then use them up in cutlets without the yellow.

Singhora

(Potato Savoury)

THE DOUGH:
1 cup flour
1 tablespoon ghee
½ teaspoon salt

Sift flour and salt. Rub in ghee and make dough with water, the consistency of puri dough.

THE FILLING:
250g boiled potatoes
½ teaspoon chilli powder
½ teaspoon salt

Dice the boiled potatoes. Toss with salt and chillies. Make a vagaar of 1 tablespoon of oil and a teaspoon of whole mustard and pour over potatoes, tossing them lightly.

TO ROLL AND FILL: Divide dough into small ping pong sized balls.

Roll each out into an oval shaped puri (See diagram) approximately 15 x 5 cm wide.

Cut in half to give two puris from each round of dough.

Place a lump of potato mixture in centre.

Brush edges with egg white or flour paste.

Bring oval sides together in centre, holding them between thumb and forefinger and bringthe whole down towards the straight cut side.

This should not give you a little horned pyramid, which is what the term singhora means.

TO FRY: In deep oil over medium to high heat fry the singhoras. Drain in colander and serve hot, with lemon and chutneys.

Chana Puri

(CONTEMPORARY VERSION)

Many people find it awkward to make chana puris in the traditional way, so we suggest to you this version which does not compromise with taste in any way. They will be a success at your table, we assure you.

2 green pounded chillies
250g Master Khima recipe (mince) (Pg 184)
½ cup boiled chana dhal
1 egg
2 cups flour
1 tblsp ghee
1 mashed potato
½ tsp jeero
Pinch of salt

To prepared mince, add ½ cup chana and leave aside on a plate. Mix ghee in flour and salt. Add jeero and chillies and with mashed potato make into dough, using a little of the dhal water if necessary. Divide dough into two portions and roll out like rotis. On one roti place the meat balls at equal distances and cover with the other roti. With small scone cutter, carefully cut out balls covered with dough. Roll out left-over dough and use up similarly. Flute edges of dough and dip each chana puri in beaten egg and fry in medium oil till lovely golden colour.

Khima Puri
(MINCE STUFFED PURIS)

1 small tin cream (155g)
2 cups flour
1 tsp ghee
¼ tsp salt

Mix ghee and salt into cream and incorporate just sufficient flour to make a soft puri dough.

Divide into 8 balls and roll each out into a round circle. Fill 4 circles with mince or filling of choice, brush edges with egg white and press other rotis over this.

Grill over tava, brushing with ghee to freckle it gold.

Drain on wire rack and serve hot with tea.

NOTE: Vegetable filling made of diced potato etc., may be used.

Chana Puri
(TRADITIONAL RECIPE)
(SEE PHOTO OPPOSITE)

For the nimble-fingered, Chana Puri is a delightful savoury to prepare. The art in covering the meat ball completely with the dumpling paste comes only with plenty of experience. We hope you succeed in your first attempt.

250g Master Khima Recipe (Mince) (Pg 184)
½ cup chana dhal (boil in salted water with one peeled potato)

Boil dhal with peeled potato and when done, drain off water.

In a clean receptacle, mix the dhal well with the prepared mince.

Gently form into balls the size of a large walnut. Keep the balls aside in a plate and meanwhile prepare the paste as follows:

The drained-off dhal water and the mashed potato
½ tsp salt
1 cup flour
1 tsp ghee
1 tsp baking powder

Mix together the dry ingredients, add ghee and mix with as much of the dhal water and mashed potato as is needed to form a thick gluey paste. Keeep for about 2 hours.

Heat oil in deep pan and over medium heat fry the balls as follows:

Grease palm of left hand with a little ghee, put a tablespoonful of paste in it, then place a ball of mince inside and quickly spread the paste to cover the ball completely.

Any clumsiness will result in broken mince balls which are both unsightly and unappetising. Drain in colander.

Chana Puri
(VARIATION) (SEE PHOTO OPPOSITE)

500g mince (mutton or chicken)
1 tsp salt
½ tsp gharum masala
2 tblsp chopped dhunia leaves
1 large onion
1½ tsp green pounded chillies
1 tsp ginger/garlic
½ cup chana dhal (gram lentil)

Boil dhal till soft but not mushy. Wash and drain mince. braise in frying pan with spices, stirring and breaking any lumpy mince. When dry and fine like breadcrumbs, add finely sliced onions and a tablespoon of oil, and braise till onions are well mixed in mince. When cold add gharum masala, chopped dhunia and boiled dhal. Gently mould in palms and form in small ping pong sized balls. Leave these on a plate in fridge till required.

BATTER:
2 cups flour
2 tsp baking powder
2 tblsp ghee (solid) or oil
¼ tsp salt
2 tblsp yoghurt

Rub ghee and yoghurt in flour till it resembles mealie meal. Add half of baking powder and the salt. Add sufficient water to make a batter (gluey paste), and leave for few hours in sunny position. Just before frying, add rest of baking powder and mix well. Heat oil in deep pan. Take a tablespoonful of batter and spread it on wet palm of left hand. Place a mince ball on batter. Now dip fingers of right hand in water and carefully close mince ball while extending batter. This needs a little practice, for rough handling will result in broken meat balls. When kabaab is well enclosed in batter, lower into oil. Continue this way till pan full but not crowded, and fry till chana puris are a lovely golden colour. Serve hot with chutneys.

The Ramadaan Story

The month of Ramadaan has special significance for Muslims. Being the month in which the first verses of the Holy Quran were revealed; Muslims all over the world commemorate this Great Happening with fasts and prayers.

All day for the entire month — between the hours of sunrise and sunset, no food or drink not even a sip of water may be taken. While normal working hours must be adhered to, all leisure time is devoted for charitable works and prayers.

When evening draws near, children are to be seen carrying trays of food to and from neighours. Mothers vie with each other in preparing dainty snacks, nourishing drinks and soups for their families. When at last the light in the mosque minaret is lit to announce the time for the breaking of the day-long fast, the children scamper home singing little ditties.

The Light it shines, the light it shines
Break your fast — Its time to dine.

Our drinks and savoury section introduces a wide variety of new dishes which will be a great boon during Ramadaan. Try them and hear the praise of your family!

A Bhaji Lagan
B Karela Lagan (113)
C Mealie Meal Lagan with Bhinda Filling (118)

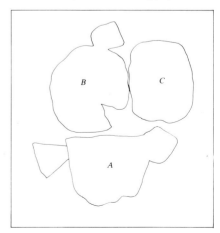

Lagans

Do not be confused if you see lagan recipes in the curry, savoury and the dessert section. Lagan means a casserole. The Indian thali or lagan was used to set out meals or to cook in the oven and in current usage any oven cooked meal qualifies to be termed a lagan.

Again at lunches and dinners the lagans (such as chicken lagan, bhaji lagan etc.) are served as one of the curries of the day, but the same lagan when served at a tea party or buffet, it is accepted as being one of the savouries.

We have, after much thought, split our lagans for the curry and the savoury sections. It will pay you to look at both sections if you wish to serve something original in the way of vegetable or meat dishes.

Vegetarians should also take a look at the curry and savoury recipes in the non-vegetarian sections, many are both meatless and eggless, but since these are classical favourites we have added them to the general sections. Again many dishes can easily be converted for vegetarian needs and tips have been given wherever it was possible to do so.

Mince Loaf

500 g mince
Dried breadcrumbs from 2 slices of 2 cm thick bread
1 tsp crushed cummin (jeera)
1 tsp arad (turmeric)
1 green chopped chilli
1 large onion (grated)
3 tblsp sauce
1 tsp chilli powder
Salt to taste
SAUCE:
6 tomatoes (boiled and pureed)
3 green chillies
4 cloves of garlic
¼ cup oil

THE SAUCE:

Braise chopped chillies and slivered garlic in oil. When well blended add boiled pureed tomatoes and simmer till consistency of sauce. Add 3 tablespoonsful of this to mince. Leave rest to serve with loaf.

Mix sauce in mince ingredients and put in deep greased pan loaf. Pat in with hands and bake in oven till nicely browned. Slice and serve with sauce and lemon.

Lagan
(WITH LEFT-OVER MINCE)

250 g prepared mince or any left-over quantity
2 beaten eggs (reserve about ½ egg for dipping later)
2 tsp dhunia chutney

Mix all together. Spread in greased tin. Bake in 180° oven for 10 minutes or till egg is set. Cut in 5 mm squares. When cool, dip in left-over egg and fry in hot oil.

Mince/Mealie Loaf
(KHIMA/MAKAI LAGAN) (PHOTO PAGE 197)
SUFFICIENT FOR 10-12 SERVINGS

2 tomatoes cut in thin slices
1 kilo mince
3 eggs beaten (reserve 1 white)
¾ cup tomato puree
½ cup (125g) frozen cut corn (or frozen peas)
2 slices white bread
2 tblsp chopped coriander
2 tsp green pounded chillies
1 large grated onion
1 tsp crushed garlic
½ cup grated cheddar (125g)
1 tsp black crushed pepper
2½ tsp salt
1 tsp red chilli powder
1 tsp crushed coriander
2 tblsp tamarind juice (see glossary)
or alternatively
1 tblsp lemon juice
TOPPING
1 egg white
2 tsp sesame seeds

Soak bread in tomato puree. Wash and drain mince in colander, squeezing out all excess water. Put mince in basin and add beaten eggs, tomato puree and bread, chopped coriander, onion and spices and salt.

Grease 4cm deep baking dish and pat in half of burger mixture.

Spread thinly sliced tomatoes which have been sprinkled with a little salt and pepper and the cheese. Lay cut corn or peas over this.

Now add rest of mixture over it and sprinkle 3 tablespoons oil evenly over the contents.

Bake in 200°C (350°F) oven for 30 minutes or till all moisture has evaporated and mixture has browned a little .

Beat white of egg till stiff and spread carefully over mixture. Sprinkle with sesame seeds and bake again till egg turns dark. Cut in squares and serve with lemon slices.

Ways with Pancakes

Using any of our pancake recipes, use your imagination and make spectacular dishes like this:

1. Serve in old fashioned way by spreading sweet or savoury filling between individual pancakes.

2. Serve like dosais by putting in a tablespoon of filling at edge. Roll over and seal sides and end with either white of egg or flour paste.

3. Make giant pancakes the size of your griddle. Put a pancake in a large round oven type casserole, spread filling (see next page) thinly all over. Stack rest of pancakes over it, strewing filling carefully over each. Finally brush top-most pancake with a little beaten egg, sprinkle khus-khus (poppy seeds) over top and put in warm oven for 10 minutes.

4. Make curry sauce (see page 220). Put pancakes in casserole, pour gravy or sauce over them and bake in oven for 15 minutes.

5. Make giant pancakes. Roll each up with a filling then cut in small pieces to resemble swiss rolls. Serve as savouries with chutneys.

See illustrations for ideas. (Page 333).

See also Dosais Page 221.
(COLOUR PHOTOS PAGE 27, 141).

Fillings

Use your ingenuity when filling pancakes. The ideal is to use up leftovers, dress them with a little chutney, chopped onion and pepper. However when larger quantities are wanted, one will obviously have to prepare the fillings. Any of our khima or pie fillings are ideal. The thing to remember is that the fillings must be creamy so that they do not fall out. The addition of grated cheese, cottage cheese, a little sour cream etc., not only makes the filling easier to handle but vastly improves the taste.

Happiness is unto him who imparts happiness. The dish cooked with joy is eaten with joy.

Basic Pancake Batter

1 egg
½ tsp bicarb
1 tsp baking powder
2 tblsp melted butter or ghee
1½ cups buttermilk (half milk and half yoghurt)
1¼ cups flour
½ tsp salt

Mix bicarb into buttermilk. Beat egg and add to buttermilk. Add rest of ingredients to mixture and beat well till batter is smooth, and consistency of cream or thin custard.

When a few drops of water are sprinkled on the tava and they start skidding around the tava (griddle) it is ready for use. Greasing of griddle will not be necessary but should this be so then wipe with an oiled cloth.

Pour batter from lipped jug to form pools on the tava. When small ones are required then several pancakes can be made at the same time. As soon as top of pancake bubbles, turn it over and allow other side to brown delicately.

Hot pancakes are delicious served with jam, cream or honey. Basic batter can be used to give interesting variations.
1) Fold-in a cup of rice crispies into batter before making.
2) Fold in chopped nuts.
3) Omit sugar, add more salt. Spice with jeera (cummin) and ground green chillies. Add this to batter together with a grated onion and chopped bhaji. This is delicious for breakfast or tea snacks.

Crepes
(LIGHT PANCAKES)

2 cups flour
2 eggs
½ cup milk
1 tblsp oil
½ tsp salt
2 tblsp soft butter
½ cup water

Sift flour and salt together. Beat egg and very soft butter well together.

Mix water and milk together then add to egg alternately with flour. Beat till you have a smooth pourable creamy mixture.

Keep in cool place for two hours. Lightly grease a pancake pan or griddle with oil. Pour two tablespoons of batter at a time and make small pancakes. Use these for savoury and sweet fillings.

Variation II

1 cup flour
2 eggs
1 tblsp oil
½ tsp salt
1¼ cups milk
2 tblsp melted butter (or ghee)

Sift flour and salt. Make a well in middle and break one egg within.

With wire whip work flour into egg. Add half of milk and beat well till light and bubbly.

Add rest of milk, and oil and beat.

Chinese Spring Rolls

(QUANTITY 1 DOZ ROLLS)

1 cup flour
3 tbsp corn flour (maizena)
1 egg
1 tsp mustard powder
½ tsp salt
2 tsp soya sauce

Sift dry ingredients together. Make well in centre, and add egg and just sufficient water to make thin pancake batter.

Grill tissue-thin pancakes over slightly greased griddle.

FILLING:

500g shelled prawns or shrimps
½ ball garlic
6 red chillies
1 small tomato
2 tbsp chopped onion
1 cup slivered mushroom
3 tbsp corn flour (maizena)

Liquidise tomato, chilli and garlic.

Cut prawns up in small pieces and add to above. Cook till done.

Add chopped onion, mushroom and cook for 5 minutes over high heat.

Mix cornflour with cold water and pour over pot of prawns. Toss and turn till prawns are glazed. Cool.

When cold, garnish with spring onions.

Spread each spring roll with a tbsp of mixture and roll over, closing sides. Paste down with white of egg or flour paste.

Fry spring rolls in hot oil and serve piping hot with soup or as a savoury.

NOTE:

This filling is excellent for pancakes as well.

Shrimps or Prawns

500g prawns
1½ tsp crushed red chillies
½ tsp black crushed pepper
2 tblsp oil
1 tsp crushed garlic
½ tsp crushed cummin (jeera)
1 tblsp lemon juice

Clean and devein prawns. Braise in oil and remove from fire as soon as they begin to turn pink. When cold, add above ingredients and marinate for 2 hours. (If prawns are big, chop up. Use for fillings in crepes etc.)

Sea Food Filling For Crepes

Tin of Tuna or pink Salmon
1 tblsp of dhunia chutney
1 tblsp of mixed vegetable achar (mustard pickles)

Flake fish. Chop pickles fine and add to fish with the chutney. Toss around and use as fillings for pancakes, pies etc.

Liver Pancakes

500g liver
2 cloves garlic
2 tblsp ghee
1 onion (grated)
3 green chillies
1 tblsp chopped mint
salt to taste
1/3 tsp black crushed pepper
½ tsp crushed jeera (cummin)

Wash and chop liver fine. Braise onions, liver and spices in ghee but remove from fire before livers are dry.

When cool, mix in 2 tablespoons of cottage cheese and the chopped mint. Make pancakes or crepes.

Place a tablespoon of liver filling in each and roll over. Dip in lightly beaten egg and fry in shallow oil and serve as savouries.

ALTERNATELY: (Curry Sauce)

Place pancakes in baking dish. To a cup of tomato puree add 2 tablespoons of cream and 2 tablespoons of yoghurt.

Spice with red chillies, salt and pour over pancakes. Pour over a tablespoon of oil and bake in 150°F oven for 15 minutes.

Serve hot with vegetables or rice.

PIES

Liver can be used in pies — they are delicious.

Dosais

Known in Gujerat and North India as Kani Roti (roti with punched holes), the dosai is really South Indian in origin, where it is made with all types of flour and has been perfected to a fine art. Like the pancake, it lends itself to an infinite variety of sweet and savoury variations. It can be made from either rice, wheat or maize flours, or from brown unsifted meal, cream of wheat or ground rice. It can be made plain or spiced or with a filling of your choice. The dosai is a wonderful way of using up left-overs.

A flat heavy based tava (griddle) is ideal but a heavy skillet or frying pan will do the trick. In any event, since the dosai calls for very light greasing, wiping the surface of the heated tava with a cut onion is recommended, for that prevents it from sticking.

The recipes given here include all types of dosais and the housewife will have much fun experimenting and enriching her own repertoire once she masters the art.

Rice Dosai

1 cup rice (or coarsely ground rice meal)
1/8 tsp bicarb
1 level tsp salt
1/4 cup urad dhal or moong dhal
1 tsp sour milk

Soak rice and dhal overnight. In the morning grind rice through mincer. Pound dhal in kundi to fluffy smoothness. Mix together in mixing bowl; add salt and bicarb to the sour milk. Add sufficient water to form a creamy pancake-like batter. Leave aside in warm part of kitchen for several hours. Heat griddle and wipe with a cut onion. Grease lightly with a teaspoon or so of oil and pour two tablespoons of batter at a time to form a 8 cm in diameter roti. Cook for a minute, turn it over and cook reverse side, adding sufficient oil to cook and brown dosai.

Spiced Dosai

To above ingredients add a teaspoon of freshly ground green chillies (or red chilli powder) and 1 teaspoon of sugar. Make dosais as above.

Note: If mixture is too thick add little water just before making. If mixture is too thin add a little cake flour to thicken.

FILLINGS:
(1) Any left over bhaji or dry mince or vhal dhal or bean curry may be used as a filling.

(2) Left over meat from roasts etc. can be used by flaking and adding to a little braised onion, chopped tomato, etc.

Chinese Proverb

When you prepare a dish, you must keep three things in mind. It must be pleasing to the eye; the aroma must whet the appetite; and it must be appetising.

Aaloo Dosai
(POTATO FILLED)

DOSAIS:
250g cream of wheat
1½ cups water
Pinch of salt
2 tsp sour milk
½ tsp bicarb. of soda

FILLING:
4 potatoes
2 green chillies
1 tblsp chopped dhunia
Salt to taste
3 onions
¼ tsp turmeric
½ tsp mustard seeds
¼ tsp ginger/garlic

Dosais: Soak the cream of wheat in the water. Add curd, bicarb and pinch of salt. Blend well together with egg beater, till an even creamy mixture results. Leave overnight in mixing bowl.

Next morning heat a tava (pancake pan) and pour a little ghee on it and use two to three tablespoonsful of batter at a time, spreading it into a circle as for pancakes. Cover with a lid for the mixture to cook. Remove lid and place a spoonful of potato mixture in centre of dosai. Fold over like an omelette, adding small amounts of ghee to brown and prevent dosai from sticking. Serve with coconut chutneys.

Filling: Boil potatoes till done. Dice coarsely. Heat a tablespoon of oil in a pot and add mustard seeds and when they stop spluttering add finely sliced or chopped onions and fry till golden brown. Add other spices, fry a few seconds longer, then add diced potatoes. Blend well and use in dosais as required.

Quick Pizza Pastries

(COLOUR PHOTO OPPOSITE)

1 cup flour
2 tsp baking powder
2 tblsp butter
4 tblsp cold water
¼ tsp salt
½ tsp green pounded chilli
1 egg

Sift the dry ingredients. Rub in butter and green chillies. Beat egg with water and add to the flour.

Mix lightly with knife or hands into a soft dough. Roll out on a floured board to size of a round pan.

Grease pan lightly and fit in the rolled out dough. Bake at 220°C (425°F) for 7 minutes. Remove from oven. Put in fillings of choice and bake another 10 to 15 minutes.

Quick Bake Pizza

2 cups flour
½ tsp salt
½ cup butter or margarine
2 eggs slightly beaten

Sift salt and flour. Rub in margarine till fine like breadcrumbs. Lastly add eggs and form into soft dough, adding a tablespoon or two of cold water to knead it.

Roll out to thickness of forefinger and spread in greased pan (round or square) fluting edges by pinching with thumb and forefinger.

Then put in filling of choice and bake another 10 minutes.

A Cheese/Tomato
B Methi Bhaji
C Asparagus/with cream/mayonnaise
D Mushroom
E Pineapple
F Sausages
G Sardines in Chutney

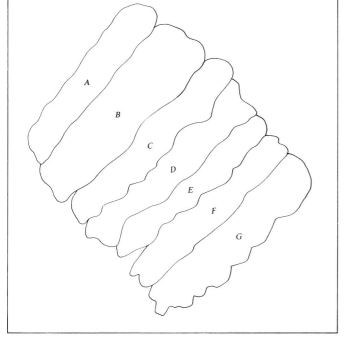

Pizza

Use any basic pizza dough or any of the pastry dough for making your pizza. This giant one will give you ideas how to use fillings to give interest to your pizzas. Remember that cheese and tomato must either be the base or the covering for your filling. The methi bhaji beaten into eggs did not require cheese and tomato for the egg prevented the bhaji from drying out.

Kachori

1 cup moong dhal (chinese peas)
½ teaspoon ginger/garlic
1 tablespoon oil
1 teaspoon salt
¼ teaspoon turmeric (optional)

Soak dhal in cold water and leave overnight. Drain off moisture and put in pot with above ingredients. Stir well and allow to cook over slow heat till moisture has evaporated and dhal is nearly done. Care must be taken when stirring that dhal is not mashed up. Tilt out dhal on a tray and allow to cool. Now add following spices:

1 teaspoon green pounded chilly
2 tablespoons desiccated coconut
¼ bunch chopped dhunia (coriander)
1 teaspoon lemon juice
¼ cup, fresh, parboiled peas
½ teaspoon red chilly
1 teaspoon sugar
½ teaspoon gharum masala

Toss dhal lightly with above ingredients till nicely mixed. Form into ping pong sized balls and keep on a platter till required.

THE COVERING
1¾ cup cake flour
¼ teaspoon salt
½ cup oil
½ cup water

Put water and oil on stove and bring to boil. Quickly remove from stove and add to flour and salt in mixing bowl.

When slightly cool knead well till smooth and velvety.

Divide dough into balls the size of the filling.

Take a ball of dough and stretch it in palms of hand (that has been greased with a little oil) to size of a small puri.

Place a ball of dhal in the middle and carefully enclose with extended dough, smoothing over to form a ball.

In hot deep oil fry the kachoris when they have been filled. Serve with lemon and chutney.

VARIATIONS: Note — Frozen peas may be used straight from packet. They swell beautifully when used in kachoris.

Kachori Fillings

(1) Any filling may be used for kachoris. See chana puri and prepare mince as stated but instead of chana batter enclose in kachori dough and fry as above.

(2) Instead of moong dhal alone use half of master-mince filling and half moong dhal. Mix well. Make in balls and fry as stated. The housewife is strongly recommended to experiment with different types of dhals, vegetables, chopped meat, flaked fish, etc. and use it for fillings for kachori.

Pattas
(MADUMBI LEAVES)

BASIC RECIPE
1 dozen Madumbi leaves
1 cup pea or gram flour
1 tablespoon mealie meal
2 tablespoons flour
3 tablespoons sour milk (yoghurt)
1 tablespoon whole coriander
3 green chillies
1 onion (grated)
2 oz. tamarind
1 tomato (grated)
1 teaspoon salt
1 teaspoon jeero (cummin)
4 cloves garlic (small)

Scrape veins from leaves, wash and dry.

Grate onion and tomato and add to tamarind juice and sour milk.

Pound the jeero and dhunia seeds and the garlic and chillies and add to above.

Then add rest of dry ingredients and mix into thickish paste.

The tomato, onion and other liquids should be sufficient to make the paste, but should it still be too thick, vinegar may be added to make it thinner.

Spread batter over each leaf (about a dessertspoonful to a leaf) lay them one on top of the other, then neatly fold in at the two longer sides (about 1 cm) and roll tightly over like a swiss roll.

Put several left-over patta leaves at the bottom of a pot and place the rolls of pattas on top of them. Add about two cups of water and steam slowly for about one hour. Remove from pot, cool on wire rack and use when needed as follows:

TO FRY: Cut in 3 mm thick slices and fry in hot shallow oil on both sides to a golden colour. Drain on wire rack and serve with puris and appropriate chutneys, such as grated mango chutney or any of the mint and dhunia variations.

INDIVIDUAL PATTAS: Spread the above patta batter on each individual leaf and fold it up separately like small sausages. Fry these in small quantities of oil to which half a cup of water has been added and allow to steam slowly till water is evaporated. Allow to turn a beautiful golden brown and drain in colander. Serve on rotis or in side plates with vegetable salads on the side.

NOTE: The experienced cook gives her own individuality to her pattas as to her other dishes. The addition of a green grated mango, a mashed banana, a tablespoon of methi masala, vinegar, lemon, gharum masala, a dash of ground cinnamon or cloves and so on, gives that distinction to her pattas which the good cook always aims at.

Patta Deluxe
(VARIATION)

1 dozen madumbi leaves
¾ cup chana flour (pea or gram flour)
¼ cup mealie meal
2 tablespoons cake flour
5 tablespoons dahi (sour milk)
1 tablespoon crushed coriander
1½ teaspoons green pounded chillies
1 tablespoon freshly pounded or desiccated coconut
1 tablespoon of thick sauce from lemon achar
1 large onion (grated)
1 tablespoon chopped dhunia (coriander)
1 tomato (grated)
1 teaspoon salt
1 teaspoon pounded garlic
2 tablespoons oil
1 grated green mango

Note: Patta batter can be used to spread over spinach, lettuce or cabbage leaves.

Patta
(MADUMBI LEAVES)

VARIATION
2 cups chana flour (gram)
½ cup mealie meal
½ cup cake flour
3 teaspoons green chillies
1 bunch coriander
½ bunch green onion
3 tomatoes (medium)
1½ teaspoons salt
3 large onions
½ cup sour milk
250g aamli (tamarind)
1 teaspoon whole dhunia seeds
8 black peppers
6 cloves garlic

Grind green onions, chillies, tomatoes, garlic, etc., in mincer. Add spices and aamli juice. Now add all this to the flours and then mix with sour milk (adding more if necessary to make batter like bhajias). Spread over leaves and roll as in key recipe. Steam in colander — wrapping in foil for 30 minutes.

Patta
(NEW STYLE)

Use either patta leaves (edible madumbi leaves) or spinach leaves. Wash and dry leaves. Pile up on board and cut up in narrow finger length strips, (as you would cut lettuce or spinach for bhajia). Make patta batter (see also page 225) and mix leaves in this batter. Grease a 5cm deep baking tray and pour batter in this.

Cover with foil and bake in 180°C oven for 30 minutes. When cool, cut finger length strips (2 fingers wide) or squares.

Fry in hot oil or rebake in hot oven (180°C) for 20 minutes.

Before baking, pour about ½ teaspoon of oil over each square or strip. (20 minutes in 180°C oven).

Patta in Chutney (PHOTO PAGE 157)

Steam a roll of patta (madumbi leaves) as in basic recipes and when cold, cut in slices. Make basic curry A or B (see page 53) depending on texture you prefer.

Arrange a little of curry in a casserole and arrange most of sliced pattas attractively over it. Spread remaining chutney over patta and the remaining pattas on top. cover with foil and cook gently in 180° oven for 15 minutes.

Puris (PHOTO PAGE 287)

2 cups flour
½ tsp baking powder
Pinch of salt
1½ tblsp ghee
Enough milk to make a smooth dough
Optional: ¼ cup yoghurt (then add less milk to mix dough)
Ghee or oil for deep frying

Sift all ingredients. Add ghee mix with milk (or sour milk) into a soft smooth dough. Roll out into 3mm thickness, cut in rounds. Fry in hot ghee or oil till a pale gold colour.

Steamed Pattas in Oven (PHOTO PAGE 160)

Figure conscious housewives will welcome this patta which needs no frying. When making patta rolls put them in a pan with two tablespoons of oil, and a cup of milk and water. Cover with foil and steam for 20 minutes. Remove foil and allow to brown.

The amadumba or madumbi is a tasty and nourishing vegetable. Care must however be taken that they don't become gluey and sticky from wrong cooking methods.

After a thorough scrubbing, boil them in salted water with their skins till they are tender. Scrape off skins, sprinkle with salt, black crushed pepper and chilli powder. Eat while hot.

Fried Madumbi

After removing skins, slice madumbi thickly. Sprinkle with salt, chilli, crushed cummin (jeera) and black pepper. Fry lightly in oil and serve hot.

Madumbi Bhajia
(CHILLI BITE)

The sliced spiced madumbis can be dipped in bhajia batter or a batter made from a tablespoon of flour, two tablespoons of chana flour and to this add salt, chilli, jeera and pepper. Dip madumbis in this and fry in hot oil.

Madumbi Kabaabs

500 g madumbis
1 tblsp chopped mint
1/3 tsp turmeric
1/3 tsp jeera (cummin)
1½ tsp pounded green chilli
1/3 chilli powder
1 tsp khus khus (poppy seeds)
3 tblsp chana flour (gram)
1 tsp garlic (ground)
1/3 tsp gharum masala
1 grated onion
1 tblsp chopped dhunia
2 tblsp grated coconut
adjust salt

Boil madumbis in salted water and scrape off skins when tender. Grind fine the coconut, khus-khus, green chilli and dhunia leaves. Mash madumbi fine and add to above with the rest of spices.

Adjust salt and shape into kabaabs by rolling on maizena sprinkled board. Fry in hot oil and serve hot with chutneys.

Poy Leaf Moothias

The thin leaf poy is best for this but you may use spinach leaves with equally good results.

3 cups of chopped poy leaves
6 green chillies (pounded)
2 cloves garlic (pounded)
¾ cup chana flour (gram)
1 large onion (chopped)
juice of 1 lemon
2 tblsp chopped dhunia leaves
1 tsp crushed jeera (cummin)
1 tsp crushed dhunia (coriander)
1 tsp salt (or more)
2 tblsp yoghurt (dahi)
2 tblsp oil
1 tsp ajmo (thymol)
white of one egg

Mix flours and spices in bowl. Add oil, lemon juice, yoghurt, chopped onion and slightly beaten white of egg and mix well. Finally add chopped greens and mix lightly to form a very soft dough.

Mould into moothia shapes and place in frying pan greased with just a few tablespoons of oil. Fry till moothias change colour and hold shape.

Place over pot of half cooked vegetables such as bean or papdi curry or meat/vegetables stew. Close lid of pot tightly and steam till vegetables done and moothias cooked.

NOTE: When these moothias are fried crisply they are delicious as a snack.

Bhajias (PHOTO PAGE 238)

(CHILLI BITES)
BASIC RECIPE

1 cup pea or chana flour (gram)
1 tblsp cake flour
1 medium sized onion (grated or chopped fine)
1 medium potato (grated coarsely)
1 tsp coarsely crushed jeero (cummin)
2 tsp coarsely crushed dhunia (dry coriander seeds)
3 green chillies pounded fine
1 tsp fine salt
1 tsp baking powder (optional)
1 bunch chopped dhunia leaves (coriander)
2 tblsp chopped shallot

Sieve dry ingredients into a large bowl.

Add the rest of ingredients to it and mix with sufficient water until it is the consistency of a thick pancake batter.

Take dessertspoonful at a time, batter and spread it gently in pan, taking care not to overcrowd the frying pan and leave sufficient space in between bhajias to allow for turning.

The oil must be pre-heated fairly well. Turn over when bhajias are a golden brown and when second side is a similar colour, remove and drain in colander. Serve while hot.

VARIATIONS OF BHAJIAS (Chilli-Bites)

(1) Add cupful of shredded lettuce, or spinach or watercress or poy leaves to basic recipe.

(2) Add 1 thinly sliced potato in which case omit the grated potato. In frying these, cover both sides of potato with batter and then fry.

(3) Thinly sliced brinjals covered and fried as potatoes. If brinjals are cut beforehand, they must be kept in salted cold water lest they turn black.

(4) Banana or shredded dodhi (marrow) or cut lettuce leaves or onion rings may be covered with batter and then fried.

Khima Bhajias

(VARIATION)

500g mince (mutton)
½ tsp pepper
½ bunch chopped dhunia (coriander)
2 tblsp chana flour (pea or gram)
2 eggs
1 onion (grated)
½ tsp ground garlic
1 tsp salt
1 tsp chilli

Wash and drain mince well. Add chopped greens, flour, onion and spices. Mix well. Add eggs and mix well till evenly mixed. Mould into ping pong sized kabaabs. Fry in hot deep oil. Serve warm with chutneys and lemon slices.

Khima/Chana Dhal Kabaab

500g mutton mince
2 eggs
4 cloves garlic
1¼ tsp salt
1 medium grated onion
¼ cup chana dhal (gram lentil)
6 green chillies (pounded)
1 doz black pepper corns
½ bunch chopped dhunia

Wash and drain mince. Put in pan and cook dry, breaking all lumps whilst cooking.

When mince has cooked dry and fine like breadcrumbs add chana dhal (previously boiled) and rest of ingredients excepting eggs.

Put through mincer again. Mix in eggs and form into ping pong sized balls. Pat each ball itno a flat cutlet shape and fry in oil over medium heat.

VARIATION:

Slice 1 onion fine. Squeeze out water. To this add 1 finely chopped green chilli and a tablespoon of chopped mint. Into each chana/mince kabaab put a teaspoon of the onion kachoomer. Then flatter into a cutlet. Fry as above.

Jinga Bhajias

(PRAWN CHILLI BITES)

1 cup diced shrimps
1 tsp green pounded chillies
¼ tsp crushed jeero (cummin)
¼ tsp crushed garlic
1 medium onion (chopped)
1 tablespoon cake flour
1 cup chana flour (gram)
¼ tsp red chilli powder
½ bunch chopped dhunia (coriander)
1 tsp salt
Good pinch pepper
½ tsp crushed dhunia

Braise diced shrimps in little oil, until shell pink. Drain and cool. Sift chana flour and cake flour with dry spices. Add pounded chillies, grated onion and chopped dhunia. Finally add prawns and mix into stiff bhajia batter. Fry in hot deep oil as for bhajias.

Moong Dhal Bhajias

(CHINESE PEAS)

1 cup moong dhal soaked overnight
1 medium onion (chopped)
1 teaspoon baking powder
1 teaspoon salt
1 teaspoon crushed coriander seeds
1 teaspoon pounded green chillies
¼ teaspoon fine chillies (powder)
1 tablespoon fine chopped coriander leaves
1 tablespoon fine chopped shallot
1 egg

Wash dhal well, removing all outer skin. Drain well. Grind it twice through a mincer. Add spices, onion, egg, greens and chillies. Mix well until frothy, adding a tablespoon of flour if mixture is too watery. Mould with hands like bhajias and fry in deep hot oil till deep brown. Drain in colander. Serve with chutneys.

VARIATION: Cut slices of tomato, coat well with batter and then fry as above.

Moongh Bhajia

(VARIATIONS)

1. Spices and method (as above) but omit egg and add 1 tablespoon of fresh grated or desiccated coconut.

2. When mincing dhal, mince also 1 raw potato.

3. To ingredients add 125 g of raw mince.

Split Pea Bhajias

1 cup split peas (soaked overnight)
1 large onion (grated)
1 level teaspoon baking powder
1 tablespoon fine chopped spring onions
1 teaspoon crushed coriander seeds
1 tablespoon chopped dhunia leaves
1 teaspoon green pounded chillies
¼ teaspoon red chilli powder
1 teaspoon salt

Soak split peas overnight. Wash off all loose skin. Drain and mince twice through mincer. Add spices, onion, greens. Mix well. Beat egg till frothy and add to ground pea mixture. Whip well with spoon till whole mixture is frothy. If mixture is too watery, the addition of a tablespoon of pea flour may be necessary. Form into round bhajia balls and deep fry in hot oil until a golden brown. Drain in colander. Serve hot with chutneys.

Flour and Mince Bhajias

500g mince
1 medium sized onion
½ bunch dhunia leaves (coriander)
½ bunch shallot (springs onions)
½ cup sour milk or yoghurt
1 egg
1½ tsp salt
1 tsp ginger/garlic
½ tsp turmeric
1 full tsp ground green chillies
1 cup mealiemeal
½ cup bread flour
½ cup chana flour (gram)

Wash mince and drain well. Meanwhile chop onion finely, cut shallot and dhunia finely and add it all to the mince, together with the spices, sour milk and egg. Lastly, add all the flours and mix thoroughly. Shape walnut-sized lumps of mince into balls and fry in deep oil (fairly hot) till dark golden brown.

Dodhi Bhajias

1 dodhi (2 cups grated)
1 bunch dhunia leaves
1 teaspoon garlic
1 teaspoon crushed dhunia
1½ teaspoons salt
2 tablespoons oil
2 teaspoons baking powder
1 large onion
6 green chillies (ground)
1 teaspoon crushed jeero
½ teaspoon ground black pepper
½ cup fine mealie meal
1 cup gram flour (chana)

Peel and grate dodhi. Grate onion and add to dodhi. Add oil, chopped dhunia and spices. Mix all together.

In separate bowl, sift flour, mealie meal and baking powder. Divide dodhi mixture into four. Take each quarter and mix in with a quarter of the flour in a small bowl. Form into bhajias and fry in shallow oil. Use the rest of dodhi and flour mixture similarly. This is a slightly tedious method but the idea is that the dodhi and flour must be freshly mixed. The result is worth the extra bother. If however you wish to avoid this extra labour then by all means mix dodhi and flour together, form into bhajias or moothias and fry in shallow oil as usual.

VARIATION: Instead of dodhi use grated fresh green mealies.

Cabbage Moothias

1 small cabbage head
2 cups mealie meal (fine)
1½ teaspoons green pounded chillies
1 teaspoon salt or to taste
1 tablespoon oil
¾ cup chana flour (gram)
1½ teaspoon dhunia/jeero
dhunia seeds
½ teaspoon ginger/garlic
1 chopped onion (medium)
3 dessertspoons sugar

Shred cabbage very finely. Wash and drain well.

Add grated onion, pounded chillies and rest of ingredients.

Mix well with spoon, then rub between palms of hands so that liquid from cabbage, partially absorbs the spices.

Add just enough water to make a soft pliable moothia dough.

Put a cake wire rack in a pot to which has been added 1 litre of boiling water and a tablespoon of oil.

Over the rack spread outer leaves of cabbage or a cloth.

Mould moothias and carefully place on rack. Close lid of pot and steam for 45 minutes. Serve moothias piping hot with chutneys.

Left Over Moothia Relish

If you have left over cabbage moothias serve them in this way. Break moothias in pot with a fork. Add dessertspoon of desiccated coconut for every ten moothias. Add a little chopped dhunia. Make a vagaar with a tablespoon of oil and a teaspoon of mustard seeds and pour over pot. Mix lightly with fork and serve in little bowls with a teaspoon. **Note:** A dash of salt and chilli powder may be required, to counter balance the coconut.

Mealie Corn Lagan

1 tin sweetcorn
3/8 cup butter (soft)
2 cups self-raising flour
3 eggs
2 green chillies (pounded)
1 tsp salt
½ bunch dhunia
¼ tsp turmeric powder
¼ tsp white pepper
¼ tsp dhunia/jeera

Mix all above ingredients together. Pour mixture into a greased pan. Bake in 180ºC till set (25-30 minutes)

Dodhi Moothias (PHOTO PAGE 239)

1 small dodhi (2 cups grated)
1 cup fine mealie meal
½ cup chana flour (or pea)
2 tablespoons oil
1 medium sized onion
1 teaspoon salt
1 teaspoon ground green chillies
¼ teaspoon turmeric

Grate peeled dodhi and onion. Sift dry ingredients in bowl, add green chillies and the grated dodhi and onion. Add oil and form into moothia-like dough. Form into moothias (see page 101) and fry in shallow oil over medium heat, turning when underside is done. Brown on all sides and drain on lunch paper or colander. Serve hot. **Caution:** Fry slowly in little oil.

Green Paw-Paw Moothias

1½ cups grated paw-paw (green)
1½ teaspoons baking powder
1 medium sized onion (chopped)
1 tablespoon cake flour
1 teaspoon salt
1 cup pea flour
¹⁄ cup mealie meal
1 teaspoon jeero (cummin)
1 teaspoon fresh pounded chillies
2 cloves of garlic (pounded)

Mealie Loaf

1 cup flour
2 tsp baking powder
1 tsp salt
60 g butter
2 cups grated mealie
2 well beaten eggs
¼ cup milk

Sift flour, baking powder and salt together. Rub in butter and add the grated mealie, well beaten eggs and milk. Mix ingredients well and bake in greased loaf tin at 180ºC.

Chana Dhal Pakoras

½ cup chana dhal
1 tsp green pounded chillies
1 tblsp cake flour
1 tblsp chana flour
2 cups milk
1 egg yolk
1 tsp salt
¼ cup rice
¼ cup grated cheddar cheese
1 tblsp ghee
Small grated onion
½ bunch chopped dhunia

Wash and soak gram dhal for an hour. Drain off water. In fresh salted water boil dhal till tender. Drain well and put through wire strainer whilst dhal is still hot and mash fine. Boil rice in salted water and drain when done. To dhal-mash add cold rice and grated cheese. Melt ghee in pan and stir in flour and green chillies. Blend smoothly then add milk and dhal-mash and cook till thick like a sauce. Remove from fire and stir in the grated onion, dhunia, jeero and egg yolk. Mix well and spread in thali to cool.

With floured hands, shape mixture into small sized buns. Dredge each in seasoned flour, dip in beaten egg and finally roll in breadcrumbs. Fry in hot oil till crisp and gold in colour. Serve hot with chutneys.

Vadde (PHOTO PAGE 196)
(A SOUTH INDIAN CHILLI-BITE)

500g soaked split peas or white long dhal (vhal dhal)
½ bunch spring onion
1 onion (finely sliced)
1 tablespoon dhunia
2 inch piece ginger (ground)
1 tablespoon saumf (fennel)
1 ripe banana
1 teaspoon baking powder
1½ teaspoon salt
6 green chillies
Oil

Grind all the ingredients (not too fine). Mix well together. On the palm of hand or a piece of banana leaf, pat about 1 tablespoon of mixture to the size of bhajia and make a hole in centre. Fry in moderate deep oil till golden colour.

VARIATION: Omit banana and ginger. Substitute 2 tsp cummin for saunmf.

Sprouted Moong and Cheese Cutlets
(VARIATION)

1 cup sprouted moong
50g grated cheese (2 tblsp)
½ tsp ginger/garlic
½ tsp chillie
1 tsp salt
dash ofturmeric
1 tblsp gram flour (chana)
1 medium onion (grated)
2 tblsp chopped dhunia
2 green chillies pounded
1 tsp gharum masala
⅛ tsp bicarb

Bananas in Batter

3 green bananas
2 egg whites
salt and pepper
2 tblsp milk
2 tblsp chana flour
1 egg yolk
chilli and crushed jeeroo

Boil bananas in salted water. Peel when cold. Cut into rings.

Beat egg yolk, flour, milk and spices together. Beat egg whites stiff and fold into batter.

Dip banana rings into batter, and fry a few at a time in deep hot oil. Drain on paper. Serve with lemon and chutneys.

Potato Chops (Vegetarian)

2 cups mashed potatoes   1 small onion (grated)
1½ tblsp chopped mint or coriander leaves
2 green chillies (pounded fine)
oil for frying
¾ tsp salt (or to taste)
½ tsp fine pepper
½ tsp crushed cummin (jeera)
1 egg (yolk and white separated)
½ cup frozen green peas
Amount: 12 to 15 chops

Wash peas and wipe of all moisture. Flatten slightly by pressing down on them. Fry grated onion in a cup of oil and remove when a lovely gold in colour. Drain off in a wire sieve to cool and get crisp.

When cold add to the mashed potatoes with all the other ingredients except the white of egg. Mix well with a wire whip. Take lumps of potato and pat into shape and size of mutton chops.

Heat a pan of oil well (200°C) then dip each chop into the slightly whipped white of egg and fry till they are a pale gold in colour. Drain off on kitchen paper. Serve with chutneys or side dishes.

ALTERNATIVE METHOD FOR FRYING:

Pat chops on paper which has been sprinkled with either bread crumbs or maize flour (maizena).

Sprinkle top with same then fry as above. This prevents chops from sticking on paper.

Vegetable Kabaabs

(EASY AND TASTY)

¼ cup chana dhal (soaked overnight)
1 large potato (boiled and chopped small)
1 cup mixed frozen vegetables (peas, beans, cauliflower etc.)
1 medium onion (grated)
1-1½ tsp salt
2 tsp crushed coriander seeds
2 tblsp chopped dhunia (coriander leaves)
1/3 tsp black crushed pepper
1 carrot (grated)
1 egg (optional)
2 tsp green pounded chilli
1 tsp crushed jeera (cummin)
1/3 tsp pounded cinnamon
1 tblsp chopped spring onions

Put soaked gram dhal in food processor (or through mincer) till it is fine like breadcrumbs.

Add frozen vegetables, grated carrots and onions, chopped greens and spices. Mix well. If mixture has too much moisture and does not form into balls, then add a tablespoon or two of chana (gram flour) or maizena.

Form into ping pong sized balls and fry in hot oil. Drain on kitchen paper.

Serve hot with lemon slices and chutneys.

Vegetable Cutlets

1 cup fresh peas
¼ lb green beans
2 medium potatoes
1 carrot
½ bunch coriander
1 large onion
1 beetroot (optional)
1 cup bread crumbs
1 lemon (juice)
½ teaspoon ginger
1 teaspoon sugar
1½ teaspoons (or to taste) salt
1 teaspoon red chilly powder
1 teaspoon gharum masala
4 green chillies (pounded)
3 tablespoons desiccated coconut
1 tablespoon maizena

Peel, scrape and wash vegetables. Boil potatoes separately and mash. Dice rest of vegetables finely and boil. Add to mashed potatoes. Grate onions and add spices and breadcrumbs and mix well together. Pat flat on maizena sprinkled board and cut in shapes with a biscuit cutter, or cut in squares or rings as desired. Pat bread crumbs on either side and fry in hot oil.

Alternative Method: Mash hot potatoes adding salt and pepper to taste. Prepare rest of vegetables as above and use for filling. Pat a layer of mashed potato on board sprinkled with maizena. Put in layer of filling and pat another layer of potato on top. Cut in shapes and fry as above.

Tava method: Prepare as in method 1. Instead of frying put a tablespoon of oil in tava (griddle) and brown well on both sides.

WITH EGGS FOR NON-VEGETARIANS:

Prepare as in 1. Cut in shapes, dip in beaten egg then sprinkle with breadcrumbs and fry. Serve with Lemons and Chutneys.

Banana Cutlets

2 or 3 green bananas
2 tblsp chana flour (gram)
salt and black crushed pepper
1 tblsp corn flour (maizena)
½ tsp gharum masala
1 large potato
1 medium onion (finely chopped)
1 tsp chilli powder
1 green pounded chilli

Boil bananas in salted water — when tender peel and mash. Boil potatoes and mash while hot. To above add all spices and chana flour. Mix and form cutlets.

Mixture will be sticky so dust with corn flour. Fry in shallow oil and drain on kitchen paper. Serve with chutneys.

Dephlas

2 cups flour (cake or unsifted brown meal)
½ tsp red chillies
¼ tsp green pounded chillies
1 tsp salt or more to taste
½ tsp turmeric
A pinch of hing (optional)
1 tblsp ghee
2 tblsp chana flour (gram)
2 tblsp oil
¼ bunch bhaji (large leaves)
¼ tsp crushed jeero
¼ tsp crushed pepper

Sift flours and dry spices together. Rub in ghee and oil till like fine breadcrumbs. Add green chillies and the chopped methi leaves.

(Caution: Methi leaves must be washed and well drained in colander and then chopped).

Form into dough adding small quantities of warm water till it is consistency of roti dough. Grease a square of lunch paper with oil.

Divide dough into six portions. Take each portion and roll in palm of hands till smooth. Place on oiled paper and pat flat into round smooth roti. Lift paper and turn over in tava so that roti drops inside. Baste like rotis, adding alternately ghee and oil till nicely freckled and done.

Masala Sakar Pada

1 cup moong dhal (soaked overnight, skins washed off
  and drained)
2 cups cake flour
¼ cup brown flour (unsifted)
½ bunch dhunia leaves
1 tablespoon ghee
3 tablespoons oil
2 teaspoons salt or to taste
1 teaspoon turmeric
1 teaspoon red chillies
2 teaspoons green ground chillies
1 tablespoon lemon juice
2 teaspoons sugar

Grind moong dhal twice through mincer. Add spices, oil, lemon juice, chopped greens and sugar and mix well. Now add the chana flour and brown flour and as much of cake flour to form a rollable dough-like puri (depending on water content of soaked dhal flour needs adjusting). Roll out on board or even easier on lunch paper greased with a little oil. Cut in diamond shapes and fry in oil. Serve hot.

Kandwi

1 cup chana flour (gram)
½ tsp ginger/garlic
2 tsps fresh coconut (ground)
½ tsp mustard seeds
1 cup dahi
3 green chillies
½ bunch dhunia leaves
¼ cup oil
1 cup water

Beat curds well. Add water and continue beating till smooth.

Add chana flour and mix well till no lumps remain.

Pound chillies, dhunia and coconut fine. Add to batter with salt and ginger/garlic.

Stir well and put onto slow fire till flour has cooked.

Remove from fire and pour on greased sandwich tin, in a thin layer.

When cool, roll tightly like swiss roll and cut in 3mm wide strips. Place rolled kandwi on serving platter. Heat oil and fry mustard seeds and when they stop spluttering, pour over kandwi.

Garnish with chopped coriander and freshly grated coconut.

Khaman or Pea Flour Savoury

3 cups chana flour (gram)
2 cups warm water
1 cup sour milk (yoghurt)
1 tablespoon mustard seeds
1 cup oil
2 teaspoons baking powder
1 teaspoon ginger/garlic
2 teaspoons green pounded chillies
2 teaspoons salt (or to taste)
2 tablespoons oil

Beat sour milk and water well with beater and add to chana flour. Mix well and take care that no lumps remain. Leave overnight. In morning add ginger/garlic, chillies, and salt and leave aside. Now put two or three inches of water in a large steaming pan or pot. When water starts boiling, mix the baking powder with the two tablespoons of oil and add to the chana flour mixture. Pour this in a greased thali (casserole) and seal well with aluminium foil. Place this thali over wire rack in the boiling water and steam gently for at least half an hour.

Fry mustard seeds in the cup of oil and as soon as seeds stop spluttering pour over the thali which has now been removed from the pan with water. Decorate with long shredded desiccated coconut and coarsely chopped dhunia. Cool slightly and cut in two inch squares.

This must be eaten hot and is delicious with afternoon tea.

Dhal Roti
(STUFFED PARATHAS)

500g chana dhal (soaked overnight)

Boil with salt and a teaspoon of sugar till dhal is soft. Drain very well.
Put drained dhal on table and puree fine with a roller.
To the pureed dhal add:

2 tbsp chopped dhunia
3 tsp Jeero (roasted and crushed)

DOUGH:
2 cups flour
2 heaped tblsp ghee
Salt
¼ tsp ginger/garlic

Rub ingredients into flour till it resembles fine bread-crumbs. Make into a soft dough with boiling water.
Divide dhal and dough into 12 ping-pong sized balls. Roll out dough (as for mithi rotis) put a ball of dhal in centre, pat down, then enclose it with the dough.
Roll out and grill over tava, liberally brushing with ghee on both sides.

> **Photograph opposite shows how to stuff the rotis.**

Chana Rotlas
(GRAM FLOUR ROTIS)

1½ cup chana flour (gram flour)
1 grated onion
¼ tsp black pepper
½ tsp ground garlic
1 tsp green chillies (ground)
1 tblsp oil
3 tblsp ground peanuts
6 bunches methi bhaji (fenugreek leaves)
¼ tsp crushed jeera

Clean and wash bhaji and drain dry in colander. Chop on board. Add to chana flour with all other ingredients — moisture from onions, bhaji and oil should be sufficient to make a dough, but should it not be pliable, then add just enough water to make it soft and rollable.
Grease a sheet of wax paper and roll out each roti on this (4 or 5). Invert paper over griddle (tava) or thick frying pan and braise like roti.
Melt together ¼ cup ghee and ¼ cup oil in a pot and use 2 teaspoons of ghee/oil on either side of roti and remove from heat when freckled evenly.
Serve hot with soup or tea.

Bhaji Rotlas
(FENUGREEK LEAVES SAVOURY BREAD)

¾ cup mealie meal
½ cup chana flour
1 tsp pounded green chillies
Salt to taste (1 level tsp)
¼ tsp turmeric
1 medium sized onion (grated)
2 doz bunches (small) bhaji

Chop bhaji up fine. Grate onion, squeeze out juice and add to bhaji. Mix dry ingredients together and with a fork lightly mix all together to form dough. Roll out into little rotis on well-floured board and roast over griddle till lightly freckled. Add about 2 teaspoons of oil over each side and brown well.

Chana Roti

1 cup gram dhal (chana dhal)
1½ tsp fresh ground chillies
½ tblsp crushed jeero (cummin)
½ bunch of dhunia (coriander) leaves
1 tsp salt
1 tsp pounded garlic
1 tblsp oil

Boil dhal till soft. Drain off water which must be saved for making dough. Add spices to dhal and pound well or put through fine wire sieve. Add oil and take ping-pong sized balls of dhal and flatten slightly. Keep aside on floured board.

THE DOUGH:
2 cups flour
¼ tsp crushed black pepper
1 tblsp oil
2 tblsp ghee

Sieve flour and pepper. Rub in fats. Make dough with warm dhal water to consistency of soft biscuit dough. Take ping-pong sized lumps of dough and roll out in 8 cm diameter circles. Place ball of dhal inside and enclose carefully. Roll out like mithi roti and fry on tava in same manner. Serve as savoury with tea.

Mince Filled Parathas

(ROTI)

Make soft Dough with:
2 cups flour
2 tblsp ghee
2 tsp baking powder
½ tsp salt
cold milk

Divide dough into 8 or 10 portions. Roll each out into a small roti. Smear top of rotis with oil, pile them on top of each other, roll out slightly then roll into a swiss roll.

Slice swiss roll and roll each slice out like a roti. Smear inside of rotis with a little beaten egg, fill with khima and cover with another roti, pressing down sides.

Grill over tava with very little oil or ghee till paratha freckles to a pinkish brown colour.

NOTE: The parathas must be small like the size of a saucer or a side plate.

Bhakar Wadi

500g potatoes
2 cloves of garlic
½ bunch dhunia
1 tblsp maizena
1 lemon (juice)
2 or 3 tblsp dessicated coconut
1½ tsp salt or to taste
1 tsp red chillies
1 tsp sugar
1 tsp green ground chillies
¼ tsp ground ginger
1 tsp gharum masala

Mash potatoes whilst hot. Add above spices and mix well.

DOUGH:
2 cups flour
½ cup cream of wheat
½ tsp salt
3 tsp ghee
3 tsp oil

Sift flour, salt and cream of wheat. Rub in ghee and oil. Make dough with warm water to consistency of puri dough. Roll out to size of large roti. Spread mashed potato mixture. Roll over like swiss roll. Cut in finger wide slices and fry in hot oil.

Khaman Dokras

2 cups chori beans
¼ cup rice
¼ cup chana dhal (gram lentil)
1 small bunch dhunia
¾ teaspoon turmeric
3 teaspoons green chillies
2 teaspoons baking powder
1 cup split peas
1 cup moong dhal
2 tablespoons crushed coriander (dhunia)
1 teaspoon ginger/garlic
2 tablespoons oil
1 teaspoon dhunia/jeero

Soak dhal, beans, peas and rice overnight. Grind twice through mincer in the morning and then pound in kundi (mortar) till the beans etc. are frothy. Put in mixing bowl and add to it the chopped dhunia and rest of ingredients, mix well and pack in greased baking dish covered with foil. This must now be lowered into a larger receptacle containing a wire rack and cover with a lid and steam for two hours. By this time the Khaman Dokras will have swollen and if pricked with a skewer the latter will come out clean.

Whilst still hot make vagaar of:
2 tablespoons of oil
2 chopped up chillies (green)
2 teaspoons mustard seed

Pour vagaar over Khaman Dokra, decorate further with chopped dhunia. Serve fresh with lemons and chutneys.

Brinjal Chops

500g brinjals — slice across in thin slices like bread and keep in salted water till required.

POUND TOGETHER INTO A PASTE:
1 bunch dhunia (fresh coriander)
2 green chillies
1 tblsp tamarind (aamli) juice
4 tblsp dessicated or fresh coconut
2 cloves garlic
½ tsp salt

Make a batter of 3 tablespoons flour, dash of salt and chilli, and sufficient water to make thin batter. Wipe brinjal slices on cloth and smear coconut paste on both sides.

Press two slices together. Dip in batter and fry in shallow oil till done. Drain on kitchen paper and serve as side dish.

Bher-Puris

You have heard of cheese and wine parties and cheese dips, where the purpose is light snacks, minimum of bother and plenty of talk and fun. May we suggest that you have a "chaat party".

Chaat literally means lick — not an elegant term at all when used in the context of dining, we agree, but that does not mean that a chaat party is a rowdy, riotous affair. It only means an escape from the usual stiff and formal entertaining, a party with a difference, one that will be remembered and enjoyed by both hostess and guests.

Those of you who have been to India and "snacked" at the chaat stalls which in recent years have cropped up like mushrooms, will recall the initial embarrassment and the ensuing fun of eating panipuris, gol-gappas and bher-puris. It is unbelievable how one can go on and on, eating those delicious little puris.

The idea of a chaat party is to have a relaxed hostess. Make a huge tinful of the puris well in advance. When serving, put these in the middle of a large khooncha, surrounded with bowls of bhers, sev, chutneys and sauces. Allow guests to concoct their own combinations as they proceed from bowl to bowl; to dip in this, to take a spoonful of that, extra spice from another, dousing the whole with the pani, and all this onto the most inadequate of little puri! The fun however only begins when they attempt to pop it in their mouths, and try to prevent it slopping down their lips and over their clothes.

Try a chaat party by all means. Great fun for teenagers and adults!

Suji Paani Puri

1 cup cream of wheat
¼ teaspoon salt
¼ cup water

Soak cream of wheat in water till grains swell. It will be seen that it practically binds itself into a dough but should too much water have been used, then it can be remedied by adding a tablespoon of cake flour. Add salt and knead into stiff dough. Use marble sized dough lumps and press with roller into a small puri. Alternately roll out with as little flour sprinkled on board as possible, and cut out in small round discs and fry as soon as rolled in hot oil till they balloon out to lovely golden orbs. Cool on wire rack.

> This puri can be rolled very flat to prevent ballooning and these flat puris when cold, are crushed up coarsely and added to the bhers.

Flour Puris

2 cups cake flour
¼ teaspoon salt

Sieve flour in bowl and add just sufficient water to make a stiff dough. Knead smooth and finally rub a little ghee or oil in palms of hands and go over dough to make it even textured. Roll out to thickness of puri on lightly floured board. Cut out with tiny round cutter into small round discs (1 or 1½ inch in diameter) and fry in hot, deep oil till they rise and puff out like balloons. Remove when an even golden colour. Drain on wire rack. Pack in airtight tins when cold.

Gol Gappas or Paani Puris

SAUCE

¼ lb tamarind
½ teaspoon roasted cummin
½ teaspoon crushed black pepper
2 pints water
Small bunch dhunia
Sugar to taste
Salt to taste
1 teaspoon red chilly powder

Boil aamli in water till soft. Sieve through strainer. Add ground spices, salt, sugar and chopped dhunia. Keep with chutneys so that guests can spoon some of this over their puris stuffed with various chats, or allow them to use it as a dip.

Variations to Paani

(1) Use good pinch of hing.
(2) Use good pinch of ajmo.
(3) Pound some mint and dhunia and green chilly in kundi and add to paani.

Masala Puris

(SPICED PURIS)

1½ cups cake flour
½ tsp salt
½ cup chana or pea flour
1 tblsp oil
1 tblsp ghee
Pound together a few dhunia leaves
4 green chillies
4 cloves garlic

Sift dry ingredients together. Add ghee, oil and pounded spices. Mix with sufficient water to make dough consistency of puris. Roll out to an eighth of an inch thickness (like puris) and cut in rounds and fry in deep hot oil till light golden brown colour.

Bher

1 cup mumuras or rice crispies
1 small (chopped) onion
6 flour puris (crushed)
2 tablespoons finely chopped dhunia
Hot chutney
1 cup sev.
2 medium boiled potatoes.
1 chopped raw mango
Sweet chutney

In large bowl mix mumuras, sev and crushed puris. Add finely chopped onions, diced potatoes and raw mango. Just before serving, add chutneys and garnish with dhunia.

(See Page 240 for chutney recipes)

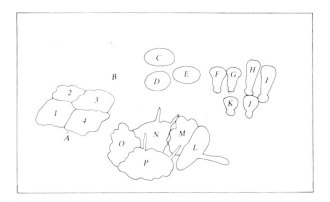

A 1 Masala Gaanthia (246)
  2 Chevda (244)
  3 Gaanthia (246)
  4 Sev (244)
B Lassi (313)
C, D, E Naan Puri (291)
F-I Juices and Milk Drinks (310 & 313)
L Pastry Roll (199)
M Pasty/Vegetable Slices (199)
N Dodhi Moothias (230)
O Farmaas Puri (190)
P Bhajias (228)

Sweet Chutney

¼ lb aamli
½ bunch dhunia
Salt to taste
Ghor or brown sugar to taste
1 teaspoon coriander seeds
1 teaspoon chilly powder
1 teaspoon aniseed
1 teaspoon jeero seeds

Soak tamarind in water and strain out all pulp through wire sieve. Grind ghor and other ingredients together. Brown sugar must be put with equal amount of water on stove and boiled to thin syrup. Mix all together. Water must be added to bring chutney to pourable consistency. Decorate with dhunia leaves.

Chaat Masala
(TASTY SEASONING)

1 tablespoon salt
1 teaspoon white pepper
1 tablespoon roasted jeero
1 teaspoon black pepper
½ teaspoon red chilly powder
½ teaspoon powdered mint

Crush dried mint leaves fine. Roast cummin seeds on tava and when crisp crush coarsely. Coarsely crush peppers and mix all spices and salt together. Keep in bottle and use as required.

Date Chutney

1 packet dates
1 teaspoon red chillies
¼ bunch dhunia
1 teaspoon jeero seeds
1 tablespoon tamarind
1 teaspoon dhunia/jeero
1 teaspoon dhunia seeds
Salt to taste

Wash dates. Soak in hot water then extract maximum juice by sieving through wire sieve. Add aamli juice. Roast dhunia and jeero seeds in pan, then crush in kundi. Chop dhunia, and mix all ingredients together adding salt to taste.

Garlic Chutney

½ ball garlic
1 teaspoon salt or more
2 teaspoons lemon juice
2 tablespoons fresh red chillies
1 teaspoon sugar

Pound garlic and chillies very fine. If not using a liquidiser add a little water in kundi and keep on pounding till absolutely smooth. Add all other ingredients and sufficient water to bring it to pourable consistency. Adjust salt to personal taste.

Aamli Sauce
(TAMARIND SAUCE)

Half cup aamli. Soak in hot water and extract enough juice to make about ¾ cup of juice, the consistency of thin cream. Add ¼ tsp salt and ¼ tsp red chilli powder. Pour over chana served in individual bowls.

Also a kachoomer made from finely sliced onion, green chillies and mint added to the sauce makes a delicious variation.

Other Chutney

The above are just suggestions. Any of our chutneys from the chutney section may be used, but for gol gappas it must be of pourable consistency. So please adjust salt, sugar and water accordingly.

Khooncha Parties
(LARGE ROUND INDIAN TRAY)

For those large gathering when space is limited, and guests many, go traditional and have an 'On the Floor Party'.

Ideal occasions for such parties are Quawali or musical evenings, Mushairas, Mehndhi ceremonies or any of those traditional get togethers, where the emphasis is more on culture and not so much on food.

Arrange the seating of your guests on rugs and scatter cushions around the walls of the room with the artists placed so that everyone can well observe them and participate in the entertainment.

Large khoonchas or platters should be attratively laid out with a variety of snacks and guests can then help themselves. The hostess will be left with only the task of serving the Kahwa, coffee or sherbet.

Chut Pati Puris

A delightful idea at parties is to serve chana chut pati on individual puris. Puris must be made more crisp than normally and they must not be allowed to puff up, but kept flat.

Ingredients for stiff puris. Make a stiff dough from:

2 cups flour
Salt (pinch)
1 tsp ghee
Oil for frying

Fry puris in hot oil till crisp and deep cream in colour. Make a hole in each puri and stuff with 1 tablespoon of chana chut pati (see above). Pass chutneys and tamarind juice for each guest to pour on according to individual preferences.

VARIATIONS:

(1) On individual puris, place a little sev, garnish with grated mango chutney, a little of aamli chutney and a few cut-up dhunia leaves.

(2) Crush up some puris coarsely in a bowl. Add some sev, chevda or mumras. Grate in a raw mango, sprinkle a tablespoon of methi masala, garnish with cut up dhunia leaves and serve in individual bowls with lemons.

Chana Chut-Pati
(DELICIOUS SAVOURY FOR PARTIES)

1 cup chana (chick peas)
¼ cup vaal or small white beans (or 1 tin baked beans)
Soak overnight. Boil in salted water to which has been added: ¼ tsp turmeric and cook till soft. Drain off water. Meanwhile prepare:

1 large onion (sliced)
¼ cup ghee/oil
2 green chillies
1 tsp turmeric (arad)
1 tsp dhunia/jeero
1 large tomato (cut up or grated)
1 tsp ginger/garlic
½ tsp red chillies (fine)
1 tblsp dessicated coconut or fresh grated coconut (optional)

Fry onion in ghee/oil till soft and just about to change colour. Add tomato with all the spices and the whole green chillies. Braise for 2 minutes then add the drained chana and beans and cook till chanas are well coated with the masala. Serve hot with lemons, chutneys and the special tamarind sauce that is an essential accompaniment of chut-pati.

Pakistani Chut Pati
(PHOTO PAGE 84) (MASH POTATO RELISH)

4 potatoes
½ ball garlic (slivered)
1 small onion (sliced thin)
6 green chillies (chopped)
½ bunch dhunia leaves
2 tblsp jeero (cummin)
60 g tamarind (½ cup juice)
1 cup left-over samoosa pur (pastry)
½ cup oil
1 tsp red ground chillies
½ tsp pepper
2 tblsp fine salt

Boil potatoes and dice in bean sized pieces. Sprinkle ground chilli, salt and pepper over potato. Toss well then arrange in bowl or platter.

Roast jeero on griddle and crush fine. Sprinkle over potatoes. Fry slivered garlic and green chillies in a tablespoon of oil and sprinkle over potatoes.

Now sprinkle ½ of chopped dhunia and onions over potatoes, and then the tamarind juice and remaining dhunia. Finally fry samoosa pur in left over oil — drain dry then crush them coarsely and cover the surface of potato dish.

Farsee Puris

2 cups cake flour
½ teaspoon pepper
½ teaspoon crushed pepper corns
2 level teaspoons salt
3 tablespoons cold milk
½ tablespoon crushed jeero

Sift flour with spices. Pour in milk and add sufficient cold water to make very stiff dough. Knead very well or even better, put through mincer. Roll out flat and prick all over with a fork. Fry in deep oil over medium heat and remove just as they start to change colour. Drain dry in colander. When cold pack in tins with tightly fitting lids.

Variation
(CHAT PATI PURIS)

1 dozen crushed flat puris
1 chopped green mango
3 boiled potatoes
Sweet chutney
1 cup sev.
1 chopped onion
Hot chutney
2 tablespoons chopped dhunia

In large bowl have ready the crushed puris, sev, finely chopped onion, mango and the diced potatoes. Just before serving toss around with sweet and hot chutney and garnish with dhunia.

Aaloo Chaat Salad
Tasty Potato Salad

6 medium potatoes
1 teaspoon sugar
½ teaspoon chilly powder
½ teaspoon gharum masala
1 green chilly (chopped fine)
Salt to taste
2 tablespoons lemon or aamli juice
1 teaspoon roasted cummin seeds

Boil potatoes soft. Cool and cut in ¼ inch thick rounds. Roast jeero in tava then crush slightly. Add all spices and toss potatoes well. This is a spicy cold salad.

Moong Sprout Chaat Special

1 cup moong sprouts
3 large boiled potatoes
Salt and chillies to taste
Dhunia for garnishing
¼ cup dahi (yoghurt)
½ teaspoon jeero (roasted and crushed) cummin
Sweet and hot chutney

Spice dahi with a little green chutney and salt. Braise moong sprouts in a tablespoon of oil and just sufficient water to cook tender. Toss well with salt and red chillies. Garnish with little chopped dhunia. Cube potatoes and toss with salt, chillies and roasted cummin, that has been crushed fine. Garnish with chopped dhunia. In large khooncha (tray) put plate of puris in centre. Surround with bowl of moong sprouts and potato. Have little bowls containing sweet and hot chutneys. Allow guests to punch holes in own puris, stuff them with potato and moong and spoon-in the chutneys, spiced dahi, and pani.

Sev
(Home-made Noodle Savoury gadget for making sev opposite)

500 g chana flour (or rice flour)
Salt to taste
1 tablespoon ghee
¼ teaspoon bicarbonate of soda

Sieve the dry ingredients together rub in ghee and make a stiff dough by gradually adding warm water. Knead well till smooth dough results. Heat cooking oil in a deep pan and push dough through sev-making gadget into the pan directly and fry till gold and crisp. Repeat till all dough is used up. Cool in colander.

Aaloo/Mumra

3 large potatoes
2 tblsp soji (cream of wheat)
¼ tsp chilli powder
2 eggs
2 tblsp grated cheese
Salt to taste

Boil and mash potatoes well. Add grated cheese and spices. Add soji. Mix well. Beat eggs and beat in mashed potato and mix to consistency of pancake batter. Push through sev machine or force through colander with a spoon into hot deep oil and fry till rich golden orange colour. Drain on lunch paper and serve as savoury with tea.

Sev Variation
(PHOTO PAGE 243)

1½ cups chana flour
½ cup cake flour
3½ teaspoons salt
5 teaspoons oil
½ teaspoon red chillies

Sift dry ingredients together. Add oil and mix with water to a thickish paste, the consistency of cake batter. Push through colander or noodle machine and fry in deep oil over medium heat, till crisp and mustardy yellow in colour. Drain well in colander.

Special Chevda

1 cup pawha (cracked rice puffs)
1 cup chana dhal (split gram)
1 cup peanuts
½ cup cashew nuts
1 tablespoon saunmf (fennel)
1 tablespoon tal (sesame)
Salt to taste
3 large potatoes
½ cup sliced fresh coconut (slivered)
5 green chillies
½ tablespoon red chillies
½ tablespoon whole mustard (optional)
1 tablespoon khus khus (poppy seeds)

Soak chana dhal overnight in cold water to which has been added 1 teaspoon of bicarbonate of soda. Before frying, drain in colander and wipe off excess moisture on dry cloth.

Peel potatoes. Grate from coarse side of grater into bowl of cold water. Before frying drain well and squeeze out all moisture.

Heat oil in deep pot. Lower a large sieve in pot and fry peanuts, dhal, pawha, potatoes and coconut separately. Tip out fried items onto lunch paper as soon as they are a golden colour. Remember that potatoes and dhal must be fried till hard and crisp (but not brown).

In small frying pan in just 3 tablespoons of oil fry the mustard seeds and when they stop spluttering add the green chillies (slit) saunmf, tal, ajmo and khus-khus till tal turns a delicate pink. Pour over chevda and toss well with slotted wire spoon.

Allow paper to absorb excess oil. When chevda is cold, sprinkle chilly powder and salt and toss and turn ingredients well so that chillies etc; coat the chevda evenly. Pack in airtight tins.

Photo opposite shows Gaanthia dough being pushed through perforated pan into hot oil.

Chevda
(A must at tea parties)

1 cup rice flakes or post toasties
1 cup rice crispies
½ cup chana chal (soaked overnight)
½ cup split peas (soaked overnight)
1 cup peanuts
1 small onion (sliced fine)
4 green chillies (cut up small)
2 tablespoons of fresh coconut (sliced in thin ½ inch flakes)
1 tablespoon of saunmf (fennel)
¼ cup cashew nuts (optional)
1½ teaspoons red chilly powder (more if liked hot)
1 bottle of oil
Salt to taste

METHOD 1 — (Contemporary): Instead of laboriously frying each ingredient, we suggest a short-cut which method needs much less oil. Toast in hot oven the crispies, flakes, saunmf and coconut. Fry the other ingredients as in Method No 2. Mix all well.

METHOD 2 — (Classic): Heat oil in deep utensil and place a sieve (large size) in it for deep frying each of above ingredients separately. All must be fried to pale golden colour and tipped out onto greaseproof paper for draining. The chana dhal and split peas will require to be wiped dry on a clean cloth, otherwise it will splutter. The dhals must be fried till they are hard and crisp and must not be browned. Lastly, fry onions and green chillies till golden brown and sprinkle over draining ingredients. Let cool and drain properly. Then add salt and chilly powder, mix well and store in a tight tin or fruit jar.

Gaanthias
(PHOTO OPPOSITE SHOWS GAANTHIA GRATER)

500g chana flour (gram flour)
1½ cups oil
3 tsp Ajmo (Tymol seeds)
1 cup water
1 tblsp hanchoro (block ammonia)
2 tsp salt
1 tsp fine white pepper or black pepper
Oil for deep frying

Sieve flours and spices together. Rub in oil with hands till flour resembles coarse meal. Heat hanchoro very slowly in pan till aroma arises. This can take up to 5 minutes. Add water slowly and keep boiling till only about ¾ cup of liquid is left. Remove from stove and allow to cool completely. Then use water to make stiff, thick, smooth batter. Adding little at a time and beating it in with hands, to get it the right consistency. Push through gaanthia grater — some people prefer to use bottom of an enamel mug to do so, as this will prevent palms getting sore. Add water till batter is the required consistency. Press through machine and fry in deep hot oil.

Potato/Mince Pie

FILLING:
500g mince
6 cloves garlic
6 green chillies
1 slice bread (5 mm thick)
1 tsp baking powder
1 tsp crushed jeero (cummin)
½ tsp khus-khus (poppy seeds)
¼ tsp black crushed pepper
1 heaped tsp salt
1 egg

TOPPING:
4 large potatoes
½ egg
½ tblsp butter
Salt and pepper to taste

Pound chillies and garlic fine. Add khus-khus and pound further. Now add this to mince and other ingredients. Pat or mould into greased baking casserole (heatproof glass or earthenware dish). Boil potatoes and mash whilst hot with butter. Add salt, pepper and cover mince with potato topping. Brush with egg. Bake in 180°C for about one hour. Serve hot with lemon and chutney.

VARIATIONS:

To mince, add boiled diced carrots, boiled egg slices, boiled peas, etc.

Vegetable Kabaabs

250g green beans (optional)
250g green peas
500g potatoes
½ tblsp maizena
1 tsp lemon juice
½ tsp gharum masala
1½ tsp salt
¼ bunch dhunia
1 tsp green chillies
½ tsp ginger
½ tsp red chillies

Boil beans (diced small to size of peas) and peas together till done. Drain in colander. Put a tablespoon of oil in pan and braise peas and beans till dry. When cold add spices. Form into balls. Boil potatoes in skin. When tender peel and mash whilst hot, adding sufficient salt and the maizena flour. Pat mashed potato into a flat puri and place a ball of pea mixture into each, now carefully enclose the pea ball with the mashed potato. Smooth over with wet hands. Roll these in maizena and fry in hot oil.

Plain Ganthias (PHOTO PAGE 239)

500g chana flour (gram)
1 teaspoon black crushed pepper
1 level tablespoon hanchora (block ammonia)
1 cup water
2 teaspoon ajmo (tymol)
¾ cup oil
2 level teaspoons salt

Sift chana flour with ajmo and pepper. Rub in oil with palm of hands till flour resembles coarse mealie meal. Heat ammonia in pot very slowly for about 6 minutes and when aroma arises add water and boil till only ¾ cup of water remains. Leave water in fridge for 2 hours then use it to make a batter with the chana flour. Push through machine and fry in hot oil. Consistency of batter can be adjusted with a little oil and water mixed together.

Masala Ganthias

500g chana flour
1 teaspoon hing (asoefactida)
3 tablespoons hot oil
1 tablespoon red chilly powder
3 teaspoons salt
1 cup cold water

Sift flour and spices together. Rub in oil with palm of hands. Make dough with cold water. Fry in hot oil by pushing batter through into hot oil and fry.

A 1 Khima Stuffed Dodhi (139)
*   2 Fried Potatoes*
*   3 Kurma (94)*
B Sutherfeni (359)
C Mookoos (248)
D Tomato Pickle (269)
E Mince Lagan with Sweetcorn
F Varkhi Samoosas with Mince and Vegetable Filling (190)
G Sweet/Sour Qum Quat Achar (267)
H Grilled Prawns (173)
I Mango with Methi Masala

Murku (Moorkhoo)
(PHOTO OPPOSITE)

4 cups murku flour
½ tsp bicarb
1 tbsp ghee
1 tbsp jeera (crushed)
1½ tsp salt

Sift dry ingredients, rub in ghee and make dough with boiling water. Dough should be soft enough to push through a murku machine. With murku machine make one or two dozen murkus on clean table top.

Heat the oil and deep fry carefully pick up the murkus and lower gently into oil.

Some people find it convenient to form the murkus on to large slotted spoons. The spoons are simply lowered into oil and murku allowed to drift off into oil, and the empty spoon then used for more murku again.

Murku (COLOUR PHOTO PAGE 247)
(VARIATION)

2 cups boiling water
salt to taste
1 tsp jeero (cummin)
1 tsp sugar
pinch of bicarb
2 cups corn flour (extra fine mealie meal)
½ cup chana flour (gram flour)
1 tsp ajmo (tymol seeds)
1 tsp tal (sesame)

Boil salt, fine jeero, ajmo, tal and sugar in water. Add to flour with bicarb and knead into a biscuit-like dough.

Press through murku nozzle of a sev machine on to a tray, or on to grease proof paper. Remove from tray and fry in hot oil till done.

Moorkhoos (Murku)
(VARIATION)

500g extra fine mealie meal
1 teaspoon salt
2 teaspoons baking powder
½ teaspoon crushed jeero
½ teaspoon ajmo (crushed)

Sift above together. Make batter with boiling water. The batter will be consistency of biscuit dough. Shape Moorkhoos through machine and fry in hot oil. Drain in colander. **P.S.** — "Machine" means special contraption for making moorkhoos.

Moorkhoos with Rice Flour

500g rice flour
½ tablespoon crushed jeero (cummin)
½ tablespoon tal (sesame seeds)
2 tablespoons oil or butter
2 teaspoons salt
2 teaspoons red chilly powder
2 teaspoons green pounded chillies
1 tablespoon lemon juice

Sift flour with above spices. Rub in oil and green chillies and make into dough with sour milk to consistency of sev, etc, so that it can be pushed through moorkhoo machine. Fry in hot oil.

Photo opposite shows murku (moorkhoos) being pushed through gadget on to smooth surface and some being fried.

End of Story of Savouries

Sookh Mookh
(AFTER DINNER SAVOURY)

500g kernel of coriander (tandra)
60g saunmf (fennel)
3 coconuts (fresh)
60g tal (optional)
500g almonds
If liked, pawha, etc., may be added

Pick all ingredients clean. Slice each almond (retaining skins) in about four pieces. Dehusk coconut, remove pulp and cut in 2 mm thick wafers. Or cut in matchstick sized pieces, or any way that the individual prefers.

In separate trays, put tandra saunmf and tal after damping them in salted water (just a tablespoon of water with enough salt to make it tasty), and bake in slow oven till beautifully crisp but still retaining colours. In separate trays bake the almonds and coconuts also, after salting them. When all is deliciously crisp, allow to cool in trays and pack tightly in tins and bottles.

Serve after meals or at weddings and parties. As this is an exotic savoury, teaspoonfuls at a time are taken.

NOTE: Coconut will not need salting.

SECTION 7

Pickles
ACHARS, CHUTNEYS AND KACHOOMERS
(PICKLES, CHUTNEYS, SALADS
AND RELISHES)

The world of kachoomers, chutneys and achars is rich and varied and one can — like jewellery dressing up the plainest of dresses — disguise a plain meal with the right type of relishes and salads. No meal is complete without them and no Indian will want to omit it entirely from his diet.

There are dieticians who insist that these highly spiced additions are injurious to health, and others who maintain that the piquancy of chutneys titillates appetites and should therefore be encouraged, but the gourmets just smack their lips and say: "But you have not lived if you do not partake of these".

Whilst we will allow differences of opinion, we will not tolerate any intereference in our rendering of the piquant, tantalising, appetising recipes that we have collected. Naturally, to our wide store of classic recipes, we have added many others typically South African Indian and the results are just too delicious.

In dedication of the various races of South Africa we humbly submit this achar in which you add the vegetables and fruit of your choice, and allow the spices to bind it into an interesting and harmonious whole. (Page 268)

Hints on Pickling

Bottles. Wash bottles and lids in hot soapy water and rinse several times in cold water. Leave to dry in the sun. This not only makes them sterile but also crystal clear.

Ingredients. Choose only the best available. When choosing mangoes, vegetables or citrus for pickling, select those that are fresh, unmarked and firm of flesh. Spices must be picked clean of all impurities, and sun-dried if possible.

Mangoes. Although large, mature green mangoes preserve better, my own prejudice against the pithy fibres that accompany these aged mangoes, makes me always choose firm tender ones which can easily be cut without encountering the hardened pith. Another reason for encouraging others to use more tender mangoes, is that the housewife of today no longer makes achars to last a season or two. The tendency is to make small batches of achars at more frequent intervals.

Mustard. This might be confusing to amateurs for it is used in several forms. **Whole mustard seeds** are braised in oil and added to the bowl of achar after the seeds have stopped spluttering. **Crushed mustard** is not to be confused with mustard powder. The addition of coarsely crushed mustard seeds gives a coarser texture to pickles. **Mustard powder** has to be whisked in vinegar and oil till it is thick like mayonnaise. As a shortcut method, the mustard powder may be added straight to the mixing bowl and allowed to mix-in with the rest of spices, but for more successful ventures, the classic method of beating till thick is highly recommended. In many recipes, items are braised in hot oil and then added to the mixing bowl. In this event, any addition of mustard powder is done after the oil has had time to cool down.

Oil. Reading through an old cookery book from India, I could not help but laugh at the quantities of oil required for achars. One recipe of 2 kg. of vegetables, asks for 4 litres of mustard oil. Why! One could take an oil bath in that amount! It will be noticed that all our recipes call for minimum quanitities of oil, even when compared with recipes of just a few years ago. The reason is that with vegetables and mangoes available practically throughout the year, there is no longer the need to make massive amounts to last several seasons. Again, economy, health and figure-conscious housewives have drastically scaled down the use of oil in diet.

Aamli and Vinegar. When boiling aamli or vinegar it must be done in unchipped enamel pots, for these corrode and eat into brassy vessels. Furthermore aamli acquires a bitter flavour when boiled in an aluminium pot.

Utensils. Mixing bowls and spoons for pickles should be enamel, porcelain or stainless steel.

Crushed Ingredients. If crushed jeero, dhunia, methi, etc. is kept tightly bottled there is no need to crush it each time when recipes call for them.

Methi Masala

(VARIATION) (COLOUR PHOTO PAGE 99)

500 g crushed methi (fenugreek)
10 g asafoetida (½ tblsp ground hing)
½ cup arad (turmeric) or more
few sprigs kurrypulya leaves
¾ bottle oil
1¾ cup coarse salt (500g)
½ cup coarsely crushed dhunia (coriander)
500 g crushed red chillies

Dry salt in oven and pound before adding to methi masala.

Heat oil in pan and when it begins to smoke, switch down to low heat and stir in the methi, till it is a gold colour. Add salt and stir well.

Add rest of ingredients (except the hing) and braise till masala is a deep ruby colour. Add hing to methi masala. Switch off and remove from plate.

NOTE: For keeping methi masala omit crushed dhunia.

Ways with Methi Masala

Instant Relish: Grate a few mangoes (1 cupful). Sprinkle a tablespoon of methi masala over it. Make a vagaar of ¼ teaspoon mustard seeds and a tablespoon of oil and pour over mango. Mix well and serve.

Instant Achar: Peel and divide mangoes in sections. Toss sufficient methi masala to lightly coat mango pieces. Serve.

Variation to Instant Achar: To above add a tablespoon of oil, vagaar of mustard seed and a tablespoon of aamli juice. Mix and serve.

Pineapple, Cucumber or Apple Relish: To chunks of any one of above fruit or vegetable, sprinkle sufficient methi masala to coat lightly. Serve with meat and rice dishes. The above fruit and vegetables may be combined and then used with methi masala.

To Madumbi Leaf Pattas: When making pattas add 2 tablespoons of methi masala to the batter and then spread on leaves. It makes a delightful variation.

In Your Achar Recipes: When recipes call for crushed methi, chilly, salt, etc. use a proportionate amount of methi masala and thus avoid the bother of adding each item by itself.

Garlic and Ginger. This is used whole, slivered or pounded. Again it may be used in its raw state or after braising in oil. A few whole cloves of garlic does add distinction to a bottle of achar.

Fresh Chillies. When fresh red or green chillies have to be used in achar that are meant for keeping for a long period of time, it is advisable to blanch them for a few seconds in hot boiling water to which a good pinch of bicarb has been added. This preserves colour and prevents rapid deterioration. Again whole chillies look most attractive in any bottle of achar.

Methi Masala. Many recipes call for so much of crushed dhunia, jeero, methi, etc, in achars. Since these are the basic components of which methi masala is made, it is easier to use it instead of the separate items.

Methi Masala Master Recipe

500g methi (crushed coarsely)
1¾ cups coarse salt (500g)
30g turmeric
500g red crushed chillies
100g hing (asoefaetida)
1 bottle oil
5 whole red chillies

Crush coarse salt, then put in heated oven to dry out slightly.

Heat oil in deep pan, till oil begins to exude a bluish smoke. Add whole red chillies, lower heat and add crushed methi — stir for about 2 minutes. Add salt, stir a minute, then add all other ingredients except the hing and stir continuously (for about 15-20 minutes over low heat).

The masala should be a lovely deep ruby colour.

Remove from stove and add ground hing. Cool and pack in bottles.

VARIATION WITH CORIANDER:

To above add 125g of crushed coriander and add with chillies etc., to pot on stove.

VARIATION WITH CASTOR OIL:

To master recipe add about 60 mls of castor oil.

Left over Methi Masala

It often happens that when the bottle of achar is finished there is still some masala left even if the mangoes have been eaten. Rescue the masala and stuff some green peppers with them. If too strong some bread crumbs (fresh bread) may be added first to the masala before use as stuffing for the peppers.

Pickled Delights

In this deluxe edition we have omitted many of the variations of the classic achars given in earlier impressions.

The reason is that novices in achar making found it difficult to choose between the variations.

Instead we give a master recipe of each of the classic achars, and bring you a much wider range of other types.

With these key recipes the housewife can experiment with wide variety of fruit and vegetables and improvise her own variations.

With our easy to follow methods, we have ripped the mystique of achar making and instead of relying on granny, the newly married home-maker can successfully make her own chutneys and pickles.

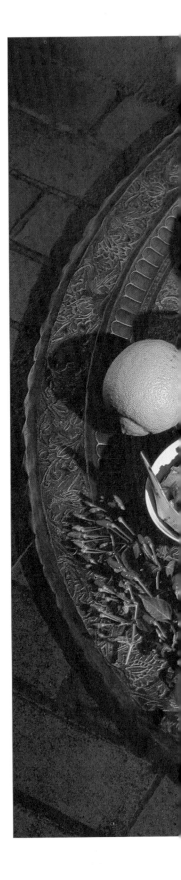

A Tamarind Sugar Achar (260)
B Methi/Pepper Relish (142)
C Marmaria Raai Sarka (261)
D Maizena Vegetable Pickle (270)
E Dahi Achar (263)
F Lemon Pickle (272)
G Mitha Gorya (266)
H Dajela Achar (261)
I Instant Mango (259)
J Qum Quat Pickle (267)
K Mango/Onion Seed (260)

L Mango Murabba (258)
M Red Mircha Chutney (276)
N Grated green Mango (263)
O Mayonnaise Chutney (278)
P Cottage Cheese Chutney (278)
Q Mango Choondo (273)
R Lemon/Sauce Achar (271)
S Curry Leaves
T Pitipin Chillies
U Red Chillies

MANGOES

The cultivation of mangoes is deeply embedded in Indian history. Mention has been made of it in early Sanskrit literature. Alexander the Great spotted a mango orchard when he came with his army into India in 326 BC but it was the Chinese traveller Hsuan-Tang who really brought it to the notice of the outside world when he spoke eloquently about it in his writings in 632 A.D.

The Paisley pattern, long, the bone of contention between the Persians and Indians has been claimed by the Indians as their very own national pattern inspired by the mango leaf.

The raw green fruit is pickled, chutneyed, and curried. Delicious cool drinks can also be made from it. The ripe fruit is the dessert of the epicures and many a legend has grown around the mango which was the fruit coveted by noblemen. Indeed the Moghuls who encouraged the cultivation of good trees have many a strain named after them, Himayyudin, Jehangiri and Imam Pasha varieties are but some of these. Talk of Alphonsos, Bomabaya, Langra, Dasheri, Malguba and you can see mouths watering.

Every part of the mango is used. The dry twigs can be burnt at sacrificial fires for religious ceremonies in the Hindu religion. Leaves festoon the ceremonial pandals, oils are extracted from the leaves, mango gum mixed with lime juice is good for skin ailments; smoke of burning mango leaves are a cure for hiccups and sore throats; kernels are dried and given in medicines as a cure for asthma and diarrohea; sugared pulp of green mangoes is used in nursing plague and cholera patients back to health.

In the lean years after the ripe fruit is eaten, the piths are dried and then powdered for gruel, biscuits or sweets. After all that we share with you a classical joke.

The great Indian poet Mirza Ghalib was a lover of mangoes. His friend once drew his attention to some donkeys sniffing at a basket of mangoes saying: "See Mirza even asses don't eat mangoes."

"How right you are my friend," said the poet. "They are asses who don't eat mangoes."

Note on Methi Achar Gugras

In pickles, when fruit or vegetable is left whole, with only cross incisions made, then it is known as gugra (bell) or gugri (small bell). Here we detail the procedure for making mango gugras.

Choose tender mangoes in which the seed has not yet hardened into a fibrous pith. Wash and wipe clean on cloth.

Make first cut from bottom end of mango to about three-quarters way up towards stem. Make next cut crossing former (which in effect gives four equal quarters) to same depth towards stem as first. Carefully remove seed from inside, without injuring the stem end, which must be left intact.

The ready prepared masala must now be stuffed into the cavity. Carefully place mangoes in jar in layers, and liberally sprinkle masala over every layer until all mangoes and masala have been used up.

Pour oil over, to cover mangoes at least 4 cm above last layer. Shake jar gently, to ease out air bubbles and close tightly.

Any of our traditional methi achar recipes may be used for making either gugras or sliced pickles.

Traditional Methi Achar

Note: In the old days when bulk lot achars were made to keep for a year or two, special attention was paid to preservation of colour, and for retaining firmness of fruit. In this recipe the addition of castor oil aims to do just that. If it is your intention to make pickles to last a few seasons, you may want to try this old recipe.

60ml castor oil
2½ kg mangoes
½ kg master methi masala (Page 253)
oil for bottling

Mix methi masala and castor oil. Wash mangoes and dry. Cut as for gugras. (See note above). Stuff mangoes with methi, masala and sprinkle remaining masalas over each layer in jar. Leave mangoes in jar until next day. Then pour oil in jar to cover mangoes, till they are completely submerged and oil is 4 cm above last layer. Tightly close lid.

Mango-Kopra Achar
(GREEN IN COLOUR AND VERY SPECIAL)

2 kg mangoes — peel and cut in smallish pieces
*2 tblsp mustard powder
*2 tblsp crushed methi
*5 tblsp green ground chillies
*Salt to taste
½ cup sugar (or more)
½ cup cake flour
½ tblsp maizena (corn flour)
¾ bottle vinegar
½ cup oil + ½ cup
3 tblsp sunflower seeds
3 tblsp sesame seeds
1 cup curry leaves
½ cup coconut slivers (fresh and dried)

Wash and drain mangoes dry.

Sprinkle items with asterisk (*) over bowl and toss. Put sugar, flours, vinegar and ½ cup oil to boil and when it is like thin porridge, pour over mangoes. Toss and mix.

Fry last 4 items in the other oil and just as the coconut begins to change colour pour over mangoes. Mix well, adjust salt. Bottle when cold.

Mango Maizena Achar

1½ kg mangoes
5 tsp salt
4 tblsp chilli
2 tblsp whole jeera
1 tblsp crushed coriander (dhunia)
3 tblsp methi masala
1½ cups sugar
2 cups vinegar
½ cup maizena

FOR VAGAAR:
1½ cups oil
8 green chillies (slit)
10 cloves garlic
2 tblsp whole mustard
2 bunches curry leaves

Peel, wash and drain mangoes dry. Sprinkle first 5 ingredients over. Boil sugar, maizena and vinegar — stir continuously and when it thickens pour over bowl of mangoes.

Fry vagaar ingredients in oil and pour over mangoes. Mix and toss well. Bottle when cold.

Grandma's Mustard Pickles

(MANGO RAITHA) (PHOTO PAGE 44)

2 kg mangoes
45g coarse ground mustard
125g mustard (1 cup) powder
125g ground chillies (1 cup)
125g salt (little less than ½ cup)
1 tblsp turmeric
½ bottle vinegar (350ml)
125g garlic (ground or cut thickly)
1½ bottles oil
1 tblsp cloves (whole)
30g cinnamon (stick)
1 tblsp whole pepper (optional)
1 tblsp mangrel (also known as kalonji or onion seeds)

Cut mangoes in convenient pieces. Marinate them in salt and 1 tblsp of turmeric.

Place in tightly screwed jar for three days. Drain off all excess moisture after rinsing them and allow to dry in sun for two hours.

In ½ bottle of oil and a little of the vinegar whisk to frothiness the mustard powder and add to mangoes. Add ground or chopped garlic. Add coarse mustard and rest of dry ingredients.

Add vinegar and rest of oil to mangoes. Bottle in a cool place.

Mango Achar in Brine

(OILLESS)

2 tblsp methi seeds
1 kg mangoes
2 tblsp turmeric powder
¼ cup crushed chillies
½ cup salt
¾ cup mustard powder
½ cup saumph (fennel)

Wash unpeeled mangoes and dry well. Cut in convenient sized pieces. Mix mangoes with salt and turmeric powder and keep for 24 hours. On a griddle or heavy pan with heavy base, roast the fennel and methi seeds. Grind coarsely.

Drain mangoes but keep the brine in a jar. Mix all other ingredients together and toss well with cut mangoes till they are well coated. Press into a sterilised jar and pour the brine over them so that mangoes are well covered.

Close lid tightly. Keep in sunny position for a week before storing on pantry shelf.

Aamli Achar

(TAMARIND/MANGO PICKLE)
(PHOTO PAGE 265)

1 kg mango (peeled and cut in cubes — about 5 from each mango)
125g tamarind (aamli)
60g slivered garlic
30g ground ginger (fresh)
1 tblsp crushed coriander seeds
1 tblsp crushed mustard seeds
1 tblsp whole mustard seeds
1 tblsp crushed jeera
1 tblsp mustard powder
4 tblsp red chillies
½ bottle oil
¼ bottle vinegar (1 cup)
Salt to taste
2 sprigs curry leaves
6 green chillies (slit)

Soak tamarind in vinegar — steep well then extract maximum pulp.

Wash, peel and cut mangoes to convenient size. Put in mixing bowl.

Add pounded ginger, salt and all dry ingredients, except the garlic, mustard seeds and curry leaves. Mix well.

Fry green chillies, garlic and curry leaves in ¼ cup oil and pour over bowl.

Fry mustard seeds separately and when they stop spluttering, add to mangoes. Add tamarind.

Add remaining oil. Mix well. Bottle when cool.

Murabba

(MANGO JAM) (PHOTO PAGE 255)

1 kg raw mangoes
2 cups sugar
1 tsp salt
1 tsp kalonji (onion seeds)
1 tsp chilli
1 ball crushed garlic
1 cup vinegar

Mix altogether. Steep for 5 hours, and cook till syrup forms.

Mango Pickle with White Flour

25 green mangoes (2 kg)
*3 tblsp mustard powder
*3 tblsp methi masala
*½ to 1 teaspoon turmeric (depending on colour
   required)
*salt to taste
*8 green chillies (wash, dry and slit in middle)
*3 tblsp red chillies
½ cup sugar
½ cup cake flour
⅝ bottle vinegar
½ cup oil
2 tblsp whole mustard
2 tblsp whole jeera (cummin) (or less, to taste)
2 tblsp oil
2 sprigs curry leaves

Peel and cut mangoes in convenient pieces (size of marshmallows). Sprinkle over mangoes the spices marked with asterisks. Then in an enamel pot mix together the vinegar, flour, oil, sugar and bring to boil.

Stir all the time to prevent scorching. When contents is like thin porridge, remove from stove and cool slightly. Pour over mangoes while still warm and mix well so that each mango piece is well covered with masalas. (Marinade).

Finally in the 2 tablespoon of oil fry the mustard and cummin (jeera) seeds and the curry leaves. Remove from stove when mustard seeds stop spluttering and pour over mangoes. Mix well bottle when cold.

Whole Mango Achar

2 kg mangoes (24) large sized ones with developed piths

Soak overnight in salt then wash and wipe dry in morning and leave in sun for a while.

Mix together and add to mangoes:

3 tbsp mustard powder
3 tbsp crushed mustard
3 tbsp methi masala
½ cup red chilly
1 tbsp arad (turmeric)
few sprigs of curry leaves
2 tbsp coarse salt
½ cup white vinegar
½ cup green chillies chopped in rings
1 cup oil
1 tbsp garlic (ground)

Pack in bottles.

City of Durban Achar
(PHOTO PAGE 265)

1 kg green mangoes
125 g tal (sesame)
500 g peanuts
60 g garlic
60 g ginger
500 g green chillies
2 tblsp methi (fenugreek) coarsely crushed
3 tblsp red ground chillies
2 tblsp turmeric
1 kg white sugar
250 g tamarind
1 bottle vinegar
1 bottle oil
125 g fine mustard

Cut mangoes in pieces (6 pieces from each mango) and marinate in a handful of salt overnight. Next morning drain off all excess moisture. Put mangoes in a large dish and add turmeric, red ground chillies and the coarsely ground methi to it.

Whip the mustard powder in a little oil and vinegar till frothy and pour over mangoes. Then fry each of the following separately in small quantities of oil and add whilst still hot to the mangoes:-

First the green chillies cut finely beforehand; then the finely slivered garlic; then the finely slivered ginger. And lastly the coarsely broken peanuts.

Put to boil the pitted and cleaned tamarind with the vinegar and sugar and when thick and syrupy add to the mangoes.

Mix all well together. Add rest of oil (and more if necessary, but heat it first) and bottle tightly when cool.

Instant Mango Achar
(PHOTO PAGE 255)

1 doz green mangoes (1 kg) (peeled and cut in thumb
   sized pieces)
1 doz whole peppers
1 tblsp mustard powder
salt to taste
1 cup oil
½ ball garlic (cut in slivers)
6 green chillies pounded
6 green chillies cut in thin rounds
¾ cup vinegar

Put mangoes in bowl, add all other ingredients and mix well. Toss and turn once or twice a day for the next 3 days. Ready for eating immediately.

Tamarind/Sugar Achar

(PHOTO PAGE 255)

2 tsp arad (turmeric) or less
25 mangoes (2 kg)
4 tblsp methi masala
2 tblsp mustard powder
2 tblsp sesame seed (tal)
125 g amli (tamarind)
2 cups vinegar
2 cups sugar
1 cup oil

Peel and cut mangoes in convenient pieces. Wash and pat dry. Put sugar, vinegar and tamarind in enamel pot — stir well and bring to boil. Remove from stove when tamarind soft and sugar is dissolved.

Strain and pour syrup over mangoes. While syrup is boiling, mix mangoes with mustard and methi masala and add to bowl, adjust colour with turmeric. Fry sesame seeds in oil and add to mangoes. Bottle when cool — this pickle keeps well.

Mango Pickle with Onion Seeds

(PHOTO PAGE 255)

1 kg green mangoes
1½ tblsp methi seeds
½ tblsp turmeric powder
1 tsp onion seeds (kalonji)
50g fennel (2 tblsp) (saunf)
1/3 cup salt
3 tblsp crushed chillies
2 cups oil

Clean methi and saunf, dry them in sun or roast in oven then crush coarsely. Clean onion seeds and add to methi, with the salt, chillies, turmeric.

Wash mangoes and cut in convenient pieces, and dry well on cloth. Mix sufficient oil in the masalas to make it wet. Mix mango in masala then arrange in jar. Close lid tightly and leave in sunny spot for a few days.

Open jar and pour remaining oil over top. Mangoes should be well covered with oil, close lid tightly.

Mango in (Water) Brine

2 kg mangoes
½ cup salt

Wash whole, unpeeled mangoes and pack well in bottles. Mix salt in water and fill to top covering mangoes completely. Smear castor oil on inside of lid then screw tightly.

These mangoes can keep for a year. Best stored in earthenware jars.

Kurri Pulya Tukri Achar

(VARIATION) (COLOUR PAGE 255)

2 kg mangoes
½ cup ground chillies (red or green)
½ cup curry leaves
1 cup oil
2 tblsp lemon juice (or vinegar)
4 tblsp salt
1 tblsp mustard seeds
1 tblsp crushed methi
1 tblsp mustard powder

Wash and dry curry leaves. Wash, peel and cut mangoes in small cubes. Put in bowl and add all ingredients together. Mix and toss well.

Heat oil and pour over bowl of mangoes. Mix well together. Cool and bottle.

Choti's Kurripulya Achar

(VERY QUICK)

2 kg mangoes
3 tblsp mustard powder
3 tblsp crushed methi
3 tblsp crushed mustard seeds
1 cup oil
½ cup green ground chillies
½ cup curry leaves
1/3 cup coarse salt (please adjust to taste)
2 cups white vinegar

Peel, wash and cut mangoes in small cubes. Put in mixing bowl. Wash curry leaves and put in blender with vinegar but do not blend too fine for bits of leaves must be visible — alternatively pound leaves fine.

To bowl of mangoes add all the ingredients and mix well. Bottle and keep in cool place for immediate use.

Jeera Achar

(CUMMIN SEED PICKLE) (COLOUR PHOTO 45)

salt to taste
4 tblsp crushed jeera (cummin)
2 tblsp crushed red chillies
¾ tblsp crushed mustard powder
1 dozen green mangoes (1 kg)
½ cup white vinegar
½ tsp turmeric (arad)
½ cup or more oil

Wash, peel and cut mangoes in pieces. Pat dry. Mix all ingredients in vinegar and add to mangoes. Toss till masalas coat mangoes evenly. This achar must be kept in fridge, and is for quick consumption.

Mustard/Sugar Mango Pickles

(PHOTO PAGE 265)

1 kg green mangoes
Salt to taste
2 tblsp powdered chilli
125 g mustard powder
1 ball garlic
1 cup sugar
1 cup oil
2 tsp turmeric
½ cup water
1 bottle white vinegar

Peel mangoes and cut off from pith in flattish pieces. Marinate in salt and turmeric for a day. Wash well and drain off all moisture. Dry on cloth.

Boil sugar and vinegar till sugar blended in. Cool. Meanwhile whisk mustard in water. To mustard add chilli, salt, turmeric, and oil and add to mangoes.

Keep a few of garlic cloves whole, and sliver the remainder in rounds and add both to mangoes.

Lastly add vinegar syrup. Mix well together. Pack in jars.

Leave on pantry shelves for a week or two. Thereafter store in fridge and serve when required.

Dajela Achar

(SCORCHED ACHAR) (PHOTO PAGE 255)

2 kg mangoes
¼ cup salt (coarse)
1 cup oil
1 tblsp maizena
½ cup water
½ cup vinegar
***1 tblsp crushed cummin (jeera)**
***1 tblsp crushed dhunia (coriander)**
***1 tblsp crushed methi (fenugreek)**
***1 tblsp ground garlic**
***1 tblsp ground ginger**
***½ cup ground chillies**

Wash, peel and slice mangoes. Put in bowl. Fry ingredients marked with asterisk in the oil till they are dark brown. Mix maizena in water and vinegar and put on stove till it thickens (like thin porridge).

Pour over mangoes. Mix well, bottle when cool.

Marmaria Raai/Sarka Achar

(PHOTO PAGE 255)

25 mangoes (1 kg)
1 bottle vinegar
6 green chillies
60 g red crushed chillies
1 tblsp red chilly powder
1 tblsp tal (sesame)
1 tblsp crushed dhunia (coriander)
1 cup peanuts
125 g ginger
125 g garlic
125 g green pounded chillies
2 tblsp mustard
1½ tblsp crushed mustard
1 tblsp white mustard seeds
1 tblsp black mustard seeds
1 cup fresh green grapes (fresh but not ripened)

Wash peel and cut mangoes in convenient sized pieces. Marinate mangoes in a cup of coarse salt and a tablespoon of turmeric for 3 days. Wash and dry on cloth.

Grind ginger and garlic and add to vinegar. Add all other ingredients to vinegar. Mix well. Pour vinegar over mangoes. Finally add ½ bottle oil (or more) to give a shiny finish.

Sil's Achar

2 kg green mangoes (25). Peel, cut and marinate in salt and turmeric overnight.
125 g garlic (slivered)
125 g ginger (slivered)
125 g green chillies (make slits in half and cut rest in thin rings).

Marinate garlic, ginger and chillies overnight in a little salt in a separate bowl. In the morning squeeze out excess water. Wash the mangoes in the morning and dry in the sun for few hours.

1 cup peanuts — roast and slightly crush
1/3 bottle vinegar
¼ bottle oil
2 tbsp crushed mustard seeds
salt to taste
1 tbsp turmeric
2 tbsp red chillies
2 tbsp mustard powder

Whisk mustard in small quantity of oil and vinegar. To bowl of mangoes add chilly/ginger mixture. Add all spices and rest of oil and vinegar. Mix well.

Vagarya Achar

(WHITE PICKLES) (PHOTO PAGE 265)

1 kg mangoes (peeled and cut into long sections)
90 g finely chopped green chillies
30 g pounded garlic
30 g pounded ginger
1 tblsp coarsely ground dry coriander
1 tblsp coarsely ground methi (fenugreek)
1 tblsp coarsely ground mustard
1 tblsp coarsely ground jeero (cummin)
1 tblsp whole mustard)
½ tblsp fine mustard
1 cup vinegar (white)
¼ bottle oil (1 cup)
4 whole green chillies (slit)

Wash, cut and peel mangoes. Add four whole green chillies, and salt to taste.

Add vinegar. Fry garlic and ginger in oil till it changes a very delicate pink in colour then add rest of ingredients after taking pan off from stove and, when whole mustard starts spluttering, add it over mangoes.

When cool, mix mustard powder in a little water and mix to paste, then add it to mangoes. Bottle tightly.

Kuripulya Pickles

(CURRY LEAF)

1 kg mangoes
*6 green chillies (slit)
1 tblsp crushed mustard
1 tblsp mustard powder
*1 tblsp crushed jeero (cummin)
*1 tblsp tal (sesame)
*1 tblsp crushed methi
1 tblsp whole methi (fenugreek)
½ bottle vinegar
¾ bottle oil
1 tblsp slivered ginger
2 tblsp garlic (slivered)
*125 g green ground chillies
1 tsp white mustard seeds
*Salt to taste
1 bunch karipulya
*1 tblsp crushed dhunia (coriander)
1 tblsp black mustard seeds

Wash, peel and cut mangoes in small chunky pieces. Put in bowl. Add all ingredients marked with *. Fry ginger and garlic in a little of the oil and pour over mangoes. Fry curry leaves, mustard and methi seeds in more of the oil, and pour over mangoes. Beat mustard in oil and vinegar till thick and add to mangoes. Add rest of oil and vinegar, adjust salt; mix well and bottle when cool.

Mango Vegetable Pickle

(PHOTO PAGE 255)

1 kg green mangoes
1 kg carrots
250 g green chillies
125 g mustard seeds
125 g methi seed (fenugreek)
125 g dry coriander seeds (coarsely crushed)
2 tsp whole black peppers
2 tblsp turmeric powder
4 tblsp chilli powder
6 tblsp salt
4 tblsp ginger (finely slivered after cleaning and scraping)
1 doz. cloves
1 doz. cloves of garlic

Wash and scrape carrots, cut in thick lengthwise slices as for achar. Place in bowl and add one tablespoon of salt and leave to marinate overnight. Drain moisture off in morning and leave in sun till dry.

Meanwhile peel and cut each mango in 4 to 6 pieces, remove pits and wash. Dry on clean cloth.

Wash green chillies, wipe dry and slit through middle. Put mangoes, chillies and slivered ginger in bowl, and add 2 tablespoons of salt and 1 tablespoon of turmeric powder and leave overnight to marinate.

Next morning drain off excess moisture in another dish and keep it for further use. Allow mangoes, chillies and ginger to drain in colander till required.

Clean mustard and methi seeds and moisten them with a little of the mango water and allow to soak for 4 hours.

Now put methi and mustard seed in a large bowl, add all other spices to it. Add carrots and mangoes to this and mix thoroughly. Fill in clean earthenware jars or bottles (glass). After three days fill jars to rim with cooking oil.

Mango Achar

(VARIATION)

3 doz green mangoes (1½ kg)
5 tsp salt (adjust to taste)
4 tblsp chillies, red
2 tblsp whole jeero
1 tblsp crushed dhunia
3 tblsp methi masala
VAGAAR:
1½ cups oil
8 green chillies (sliced)
10 cloves garlic
2 tblsp mustard (whole)
curry leaves

Peel, wash and dry mangoes and add salt and spices. Mix well, then fry vagaar ingredients in oil and pour over mangoes. Mix, cool and bottle.

Grated Green Mango Achar

(PHOTO PAGE 255)

1 kg green mangoes
2 tblsp slivered garlic
1 dozen green chillies (chopped)
1½ tblsp red pounded chillies
1 tblsp crushed mustard (or fine if preferred)
2 tsp whole mustard seeds
1 tsp turmeric
Salt to taste
½ cup vinegar
¼ cup oil (or more)

Peel mangoes, wash and dry. Grate coarsely or sliver in large flakes. To mangoes in bowl, add salt, red pounded chilli, turmeric and the crushed mustard.

(If fine mustard is used then it must be whipped thick with a little of oil and vinegar before adding).

Fry green chillies and garlic till latter turns pink; remove pan from stove and add mustard seeds and when they stop spluttering pour contents of pan over mangoes. Add vinegar, mix well — bottle when cold.

Simple Mango Achar

1 kg mangoes
125 g garlic (keep a dozen cloves whole. Sliver the rest)
2 tblsp fine mustard
6 tblsp red chillies
Salt to taste
2 tblsp crushed mustard seeds
½ bottle vinegar
½ bottle oil

Wash and peel and cut mangoes. Drain dry on cloth. Put in bowl and add crushed mustard and chillies. Add salt to taste and whole garlic pods.

Braise the slivered garlic in a little oil. Pour over bowl.

Finally add the mustard powder either straight or whisked with a little vinegar and oil as in the classic recipes.

Mix all ingredients well with spoon. Add rest of vinegar and oil and mix well so that masalas cling to the mangoes. Bottle tightly.

Curdy Mustard Pickles

(DAHI ACHAR) (PHOTO PAGE 255)

1 kg mangoes peeled and cut in small pieces
4 tblsp mustard powder
4 tblsp green pounded chillies
1 tblsp whole mustard
½ bottle vinegar
½ bottle oil
Salt to taste

Beat mustard in a little vinegar and oil till frothy like mayonnaise, and add to mangoes. Add pounded green chillies. Heat whole mustard in a little oil till they stop spluttering and pour over mangoes. Lastly, add rest of vinegar and oil. The consistency will be curdy and these are pickles that cannot be kept for lengthy periods, so make small quantities at a time.

Coringee Achar

(COLOUR PAGE 160)

1 kg mangoes (peeled and cut in convenient pieces)
2 tblsp salt (coarse)
60 g mustard powder
1½ tblsp red ground chillies
1 tblsp crushed peppercorns
¼ bottle oil
½ bottle vinegar
Few sprigs curry leaves
30 g ground garlic
2 tblsp ground green chillies
30 g slivered garlic
1 tblsp whole mustard
2 tblsp coarsely ground coriander (dhunia seeds)
1 doz. whole green chillies

Marinate mangoes in salt overnight. In the morning drain off all excess moisture. In separate dish marinate overnight garlic and whole chillies in one tablespoon of salt.

Wash mangoes in morning and drain off and dry for about two hours. Whisk mustard in oil and a little vinegar till frothy.

Add rest of vinegar and all dry ingredients to the marinating chillies and garlic. Lastly, add dry mangoes and salt if necessary. Fry curry leaves in oil and add to bowl. Mix well and bottle tightly.

After a few days, stir the mixture in the bottle with a long spoon, shake bottle well, and add more oil if necessary to cover mangoes.

Brinjal Pickles

(PHOTO PAGE 145)

1 tblsp pounded garlic
1 kg brinjals
1 tblsp slivered garlic
1 tblsp slivered ginger
½ tblsp pounded ginger
2 tblsp sugar
¾ bottle vinegar (500 ml)
1 sprig curry leaves (kuripulya)
1 tsp methi seeds (fenugreek)
1 tsp jeero seeds (cummin)
1 tsp mustard seeds
4 tsp chilli powder
1 tsp turmeric powder
4 tsp salt
1 cup oil
6 green chillies

If small, divide brinjals in quarters, otherwise divide in convenient sized sections. Leave in cold water till required. Slit green chillies from bottom towards stem. Mix pounded ginger/garlic in one tablespoon vinegar. To this add chilli and turmeric powders. Mix into smooth paste.

Heat oil in heavy enamel pot. Add methi, mustard, jeero, slivered ginger and garlic, and the curry leaves. When mustard seeds stop spluttering, add the spices mixed in vinegar and braise for a minute or two. Add brinjals, green chillies, remaining vinegar, sugar and salt. (Adjust salt to taste).

Simmer till vegetables tender but not mushy, and oil starts floating to top of pot. Cool and bottle tightly.

VARIATION:
Add to above 3 tablespoonsful of aamli (tamarind) pulp.

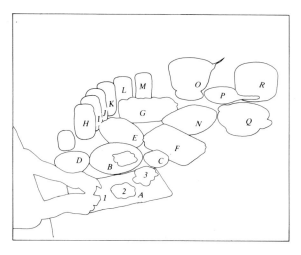

A 1 Chicken breast being rolled (202)
  2 Chicken breast with stick of butter (202)
  3 Chicken marinating (202)
B Fried chicken breasts (202)
C Apricot/Almond Chutney (277)
D White of egg with Dhunia
E Dodhi stuffed with Chana Dhal (139)
F Chicken breast rolls for freezing
G Fish in Banana leaves (168)
H Sugar/Mustard Achar (261)
I Vagaarya Achar (262)
J Lemon Achar (272)
K Aamli Achar (258)
L City of Durban Achar (259)
M Methi Achar (257)
N Eggs in Bhaji (153)
O Harera Broth (54)
P Chicken breasts being fried
Q Peppers stuffed with Moongh Dhal
R Masala Dish (spice container)

Mitha Gorya Achar

1 tblsp tal (sesame seeds)
1 tblsp crushed mustard seeds
1 kg mangoes about to ripen
3 cups sugar
1 tblsp vinegar
1 cup water
2 pieces tuj
3 elachi
3 cloves

Peel mangoes and put into pot onto stove with remaining ingredients. Simmer till syrup blended.

Take off stove, add 1 tblsp crushed mustard and 1 tblsp tal.

Bottle when cool.

Gorya Mango Relish

1 kg mangoes
1 tsp mustard seeds
2 tsp chilly powder
1 tsp coarsely crushed dhunia seeds
1 tblsp salt
1 cup sugar
¾ cup ghor

Wash mangoes. Peel and chop in pea sized pieces. Marinate in salt overnight. Pour off excess liquid in morning and spread mangoes on clean cloth and dry in sunny position for half a day. Heat mustard seeds in warm oven, then crush coarsely in mortar. Put dried mango pieces in bowl. Crush ghor over them. Add all other ingredients. Taste for salt for it may be necessary to add another teaspoonful. Mix all well together and fill in jar. Stir every alternate day for next two weeks, until ghor begins to form into a syrup. Ready to be served after a month.

Mitha Gorya

2 kg mangoes
1 kg sugar
2 cups vinegar
1 cup water
1 tsp chilli powder
1 tblsp sesame seeds (tal)
2 tblsp salt
2 pieces tuj
2 or 3 cloves

Peel and cut mangoes in large slices. Put all ingredients in an enamel pot and mix till sugar is dissolved. Put over high heat for 5 minutes. Sugar should be dissolved and become syrupy.

NOTE: The syrup must be thin and liquidy.

Remove from stove — add 1 tablespoon of crushed mustard seeds. Mix well and bottle when cool.

Mitha Gorya or Syrup Pickles

(PHOTO PAGE 255)

2 kg green mangoes
500 g white sugar
½ tblsp mustard powder
½ tblsp tal (sesame)
500 g gor (molasses)
250 g brown sugar
1 tblsp fine red chillies

Marinate mangoes overnight, after peeling and pitting them, in a handful of salt. Rinse in the morning and drain in colander, or on gauzy cotton material.

Boil sugar and molasses with one cup of water, and when syrup is thick add the mangoes and allow to boil for 5 to 10 minutes.

Cool. Meanwhile, make a paste of mustard with one tablespoon of water and add to mangoes with the chillies and tal.

Mitha Gorya

(VARIATION)

Substitute 500 g of dried fruit from the quantity of mangoes and add to gorya. Dried peaches, prunes, aloe bokhara, etc., may be used.

Dried Fruit Achar

(SOUR FIGS, BOR, PRUNES, APRICOTS, etc.)

NOTE: Instead of ghor, substitute ¾ cup golden syrup decrease sugar by ½ cup
Bor (dried wild berry obtainable from Indian grocers).

1 kg dried fruit
1½ tblsp mustard
2 tsp vinegar
1½ dessertspoons oil
1½ cup sugar
1 1/8 cup ghor (jaggery)

Clean fruit and put in mixing bowl. In smaller bowl blend the mustard in oil and vinegar. To mustard, add sugar and crumbled ghor and mix well. Add spices to bowl of dried fruit and toss and turn till spices coat the fruit evenly. Pack loosely in jar. Every alternate day, for the next two weeks, stir the pickled fruit with a long handled spoon. By this time the ghor will have begun to form into a syrup. Keep on shelf for about two months, before serving.

Fresh green root ginger may be added to above. If this is desired then select young ginger, scrape, wash and dry well on cloth before adding to bowl of fruit.

Sour Figs Pickle

STEP 1:
500g sour figs
1 bottle vinegar
1½ cups sugar
500g red tamarind

Clean sour figs and soak overnight in cold water.

Soak tamarind separately in cold water — strain through wire sieve in the morning.

Nip off stems after draining off water. Put above ingredients in an enamel pot and boil till sugar melted and a thin syrup forms.

STEP 2:

Add the following ingredients to pot and infuse for just 3 minutes:

2 tbsp crushed methi
2 tbsp crushed mustard
2 tbsp mustard powder
2 tbsp mustard seed
1½ tbsp crushed red chillies
2 tsp chilli powder

STEP 3:

In a separate pan make vagaar of:-

½ cup oil
1 tbsp tal (sesame seeds)
1 pod garlic (slivered)
2 sprigs curry leaves
4 green chillies chopped in rings

Add vagaar to pot, bring to boil then remove immediately. Bottle when cold.

NOTE:
Consistency of pickle must be like thin treacle.

Qumquat Pickles

(PHOTO PAGE 255)

2 dozen qumquats (Seville orange)
1 tblsp ground chillies
Juice of 6 lemons
1 tblsp coarse salt

Slit each qumquat half way through. Put them in a basin and sprinkle chilli and salt mixture over them. Toss lightly and pack in a clean jar. Pour lemon juice to cover qumquats. Bottle tightly. Use after two weeks.

Qumquat Pickles (Sweet)

(MITHA) (PHOTO PAGE 247)
1 kg qumquats
3 cups sugar
1 bottle vinegar
2 tbsp red chillies
1 tsp turmeric
6 elachi (cardomom pods)
1 doz whole cloves
few strands saffron (optional)
1 tbsp mustard powder
3 cinnamon sticks

Cut down fruit from top to bottom dividing each into halves.

Soak in a handful of salt and a tbsp of turmeric for three days. rinse well.

Dissolve sugar in vinegar. Place in enamel pot and allow to boil.

Add cinnamon, cloves, elachi and saffron strands. Boil mixture till syrup begins to form but remove before it thickens.

Add chilli, turmeric and mustard powder but whisk mustard in a tbsp of water before adding to qumquat.

Mix qumquat into syrup and bottle when cool.

NOTE:
Syrup must cover fruit completely.

Dried Fruit Pickle

125 g dried apricot
125 g dried figs
3 cups vinegar
3 tsp chilli powder
2 tsp salt
125 g kharek (dried dates — may substitute with dried peaches or prunes)
125 g seedless raisins
350 g jaggery (ghor)

Soak apricot and kharek in ½ cup vinegar overnight. In the morning drain off vinegar and remove seeds from kharek. Chop fruit in halves or quarters. Grate ghor. If using prunes do not soak beforehand.

Pour ghor, vinegar, salt and chilli powder in large enamel pot, bring to boil then allow to continue boiling for 5 minutes. Add fruit, boil for another 5 minutes then lower flame and cook till mixture thickens.

Stir continuously to prevent scorching. Remove from fire and cool before bottling.

South African Delight Achar

In submitting this recipe we give thanks to God for endowing our country so richly with the great variety of fruit and vegetable.

NOTE:

Any fruit and vegetable in season can be used to make this very colourful pickle. Unpeeled quinces, hard cling peaches, pomegranate seeds, cherries, hard grapes, green pears and apples, seville orange or large oranges cut in small pieces, green paw paw, pickling onions, unpeeled cucumbers, peppers all or any of these lend interest and colour.

Step No. 1

4 tblsp full mustard powder
8 tblsp red chillies any type (powdered or fresh)
2 tblsp arad (turmeric) optional
¼ bottle vinegar

Beat all above ingredients together very well.

Step No. 2

1 bottle vinegar
1 cup sugar

Boil together until sugar blended and slightly sticky.

Step No. 3

1 cup cake flour
1 bottle vinegar
1 bottle water
1 tblsp maizena

Mix well and bring to boil, allow to thicken slightly.

Step No. 4

3 kg fruit and vegetables

Fluff from quince must be rubbed off, peaches must be peeled, then the fruit washed and dried for cutting.

In a big dish slice fruit and vegetables of choice into small pieces.

Take care that fruit is hard.

Pour mixture No. 1, 2 and 3 over bowl, then add:

Step No. 5

2 tblsp whole jeera (cummin)
2 tblsp whole dhunia (coriander)
2 tblsp whole rye (mustard seeds)
2 tblsp whole peanuts (braise for few seconds in little oil after peeling off red skin)
2 tblsp tal (sesame)
2 tblsp khus khus (poppy seeds)
2 tblsp sultanas

FINALLY: Heat about 1-1½ cups oil and pour over all ingredients. Add salt and mix well.

Dil Pickles

(PHOTO PAGE 196)

1 dozen cucumbers or 3 dozen pickling gherkins

Wash cucumbers and soak overnight in a brine made of ½ cup of coarse salt and 3 litres of water. In morning pack cucumbers into jars (but wipe them dry first) and between each layer of cucumbers sprinkle thin layers of dill stalks and seeds. The fresh dill (Suwa bhaji) can be dried at home and then used. Also add a few grape leaves, a few pepper corns and a ½ inch cube of alum to the bottle.

LIQUID:

Make a liquid by boiling together: 1 cup vinegar, 5 cups water and 2 tsp of salt. Cool mixture and stand overnight. In morning pour over jars containing gherkins and close jar lids loosely. After two or three weeks fermenting will have stopped. Seal tightly and store in cool place.

Traditional Carrot/Vegetable Achar

(PHOTO 196 & 157)

1 kilo carrots
½ kg green beans
1 small cabbage (250-300g)
1 doz green chillies
1 tblsp turmeric (adjust colour)
1½-2 bottles oil
¾-1 bottle vinegar
½ cup shelled peas
1 small cauliflower (250g)
1 small green pawpaw (400g)
6 tblsp mustard
salt to taste
4 tblsp red chillies
prunes, sour figs (optional)

Scrape, wash and cut carrots lengthwise in forefinger thick pieces, leave overnight to marinate in salt. In the morning, wipe off moisture and leave to dry in the shade. String and cut beans in forefinger length pieces. Divide cauliflower head in small flowerettes. Peel pawpaw and cut in small but thick wafers. Remove outer leaves of cabbage and cut in wedges (2cm thick) and wash and dry. Wash and slit chillies from bottom towards stem.

Put beans, cauliflower, cabbage and peas in pot. Pour boiling water over and allow to reach boiling point on stove, drain off immediately in colander and dry in shade.

Beat mustard (or put in blender) alternately adding small amounts of vinegar and oil till about ½ bottle vinegar and half of oil has been used up. Mustard mixture will be thick like mayonnaise. Put all vegetables in large bowl, add mustard mixture over it.

Add rest of spices, salt, vinegar and as much of the other bottle of oil to give a nice shiny finish to achar.

Bottle tightly.

NOTE: Green loquats, green mangoes, dried fruit etc., may be added to achar.

VARIATION: To above add: 60g of mebos or dried apricots. Soak these overnight in 1 cup of the vinegar, blend fine in morning and add to bowl of achar.

Add rest of spices, salt, vinegar and as much of the other bottle of oil to give a nice shiny finish to achar.

Bottle tightly.

NOTE: Green loquats, green mangoes, dried fruit etc., may be added to achar.

Pickled Gherkins, Cucumbers

(COLOUR PHOTO 194)

1 kg cucumber (or gherkins)
2 cup water
1 cup vinegar
1 tblsp salt
2 tsp sugar
5 pepper corns
1 tsp dill (soowa)
3 tsp mustard seeds
1 sprig curry leaves

Wash cucumbers and pack compactly in earthernware dish or jar. Sprinkle dill over them. Boil water and vinegar in an enamel pot with rest of ingredients and pour it boiling over the cucumbers.

Tie mouth of jar with greaseproof paper and place a saucer over it. Leave for 24 hours. Drain off liquid into enamel pot and boil once more.

Pour it again over the cucumbers in the jar. Close lids of jar tightly and when cool leave in fridge and use as required.

Papdi Achar

1 kg papdi (young tender papdi)
1 cup papdi beans (or toovar beans)
*¼ cup coriander seeds
*1/8 cup jeera seeds (cummin)
*2 tblsp whole mustard
*1½ tblsp whole methi (fenugreek)
1 tsp turmeric
oil for bottling
1 ball garlic (chopped or slivered)
handful of fresh green garlic leaves (if available)
2 tblsp crushed red chillies
1 doz red piti pin mircha (tiny sharp one)
2 tblsp mustard oil
1 cup vinegar

Clean and break large papdi in halves. Wash papdi and the fresh shelled beans — drain dry. Then marinate in a handful of coarse salt and spread out in sun for a few hours.

Wipe off all moisture from papdi and beans with a clean cloth — put in mixing bowl. Roast ingredients marked with asterisk in moderate oven till a strong aroma arises.

Crush coarsely and sprinkle over papdi. Add turmeric, garlic, chillies, vinegar, mustard oil and mix well — adjust salt to taste. Pack in bottles and top with cooking oil.

Green Tomato Pickle (or Red)

Same as Papdi Achar but cut tomato in quarters or eighths and marinate in sun so that they dry out well. TOMATOES MUST NOT BE BLANCHED.

Vegetable Carrot Pickle Variation Special

2-2½ kg mixed vegetables (carrots, beans, green paw paw etc)
2-3 tblsp freshly ground green chillies
2 tblsp freshly ground red chillies
½ cup sultanas
2 tblsp mustard powder (50g)
¼ cup sesame (tal)
½ fresh coconut (or dessicated)
½ bottle oil
3 cups vinegar
1½ cups water
¼ cup maizena

Mix mustard powder with a small quantity of water and mix into a paste.

TEMPERING:

1 tblsp cummin (jeeroo)
1 tblsp sesame (tal)
1 tblsp mustard seeds

Scrape, clean and cut vegetables in attractive shapes. Wash and drain dry.

Grind together the chillies, sultanas, sesame and coconut. In half the quantity oil, braise the above ingredients till a lovely aroma arises and they begin to change colour. Switch off heat.

Fry the sesame, cummin and mustard seeds in a little oil and add to ground mixture. Allow to cool.

When cold, add salt to taste and adjust colour with a teaspoon or so of turmeric.

While above is cooling, mix the vinegar/maizena mixture. Put it on the stove and bring to boil.

Allow to cook gently, but keep on stirring till it is like thin porridge. Care should be taken that it does not curdle or lump-up.

Allow maizena mixture to cool before adding the mustard paste and the ground ingredients to it. Add vegetable and mix into mixture.

Finally fry a few sprigs of curry leaves in rest of oil and pour over pickle.

NOTE:

Should the sauce have become too thick, then it can be diluted with extra vinegar.

Maizena Vegetable Pickle

(PHOTO PAGE 255)

8 to 10 cups of vegetables (beans, peppers, cauliflower, carrots, green pawpaw, cabbage, small onions etc. — all cut in small attractive pieces).
2 tblsp oil (extra
½ cup flour
1 tblsp maizena
1 bottle vinegar
1 cup water
1 cup oil
2 tsp mustard seeds
1 tblsp mustard powder
2 tsp green chillies pounded (or more)
½ doz green chillies (chopped)
2 tsp methi masala (optional)
2 tsp sugar (or more)

Prepare vegetables wash and drain dry. Mix sugar, mustard and flour into paste with a little of the water, then mix in with rest of water, oil and vinegar and put on stove till it thickens (like thin porridge).

While mixture is still hot pour over bowl of vegetables. Sprinkle methi masala and pounded green chilli and chopped chilli over bowl of vegetable.

Fry mustard seeds in 2 tblsp of oil and when they stop spluttering pour over vegetables.

Chilli Pickle

(VARIATION)

500 g chillies (long, mild type)
2 tblsp crushed methi
2 tblsp crushed dhunia
2 tblsp crushed jeero
125 g aamli (tamarind)
3 tblsp salt
1 ball garlic (slivered)
1 tsp mustard seeds
2 cups vinegar

Braise crushed masalas in little oil and add to bowl of slit chillies. Braise whole mustard in little oil and add to bowl of slit chillies.

Braise slivered garlic in oil and add to bowl of slit chillies. Boil vinegar and aamli together till thick and mushy. Strain through sieve and add to chillies.
Add salt. Bottle tightly.

Sweet/Sour Lime Pickles

1 kg lemons or limes
2 tblsp red chilli powder
2 tsp coarsely crushed methi (fenugreek)
2 tblsp oil
2¼ tblsp coarse salt
1 cup sugar
½ cup ghor (jaggery)
1 tsp turmeric

Wash and dry limes. Make deep cross cuts, as for gugris (see note page 257). Crush ghor. Mix all dry ingredients in oil and add to ghor. Fill lime with the prepared masala and pack in jars rather loosely. For next three days stir with long handled spoon into jar, and turn limes at this stage.

It is advisable to keep jar in slightly sunny position in kitchen, as this aids the ghor in melting rapidly and giving that syrupy texture which is being aimed at. Remove bottle and place on pantry shelf for at least two or three months before attempting to serve.

Lemon Achar (Pickle) Sauce
(PHOTO PAGE 255)

Boil 6 lemons until tender. Cool and when cold cut up into tiny pieces. Put pieces into bowl.

ADD:
2 tblsp red ground chillies
2 tblsp crushed coriander seeds (dhunia)
½ tblsp turmeric
½ cup light brown sugar
6 green chillies (cut up)
1 tblsp mustard powder
1 tblsp salt (or more)
1 cup lemon juice

Roast 1 tablespoon cummin seeds (jeera) in a thick pan till black.

Now add ½ cup oil and 2 sprigs of curry leaves (kurripulya) and when leaves begin to turn colour, pour over lemons in bowl.

Mix well and bottle.

NOTE:
If the juice is not sufficient to cover the lemons then add more.

Mogris

Wash mogris and serve on a small plate with savouries, khitchri porridge, bhurkoo, etc. They have a piquant taste, and are not as sharp as green chillies.

Lemon/Pepper Achar Special
(COLOUR PHOTO 196)

2 doz lemons or 4 doz limes (cut in pieces)
1 cup coarse salt
2 tbsp turmeric
4 tbsp crushed coriander seeds (dhunia)
¾ cup chilli powder
1 bottle vinegar

Cut lemons mix above ingredients well into them and leave in earthenware container or enamel pot for 2 days.

THEN ADD TO POT:

¼ cup methi masala
2 tbsp crushed jeera (cummin)
2 doz green peppers (preferably the small crinkled type resembling bells)

Mix with ingredients in pot and leave for 2 hours. Make a vagaar by frying:

2 tbsp oil
¼ cup curry leaves
2 tsp slivered ginger
1 tsp mustard seeds
4 green chillies (slit)

Pour vagaar over contents. Mix and bottle when cool.

Lemon Chutney
(PHOTO PAGE 255)

Juice of 12 lemons
salt to taste
½ cup sugar
1 tblsp mustard
½ cup methi masala
1/3 cup red chilli (whole, dry)

Soak ingredients together for a few hours.

When softened, put in liquidiser and blend fine. Keep in fridge.

Lemon Achar

(LEMON PICKLES) (PHOTO PAGE 265)

1 doz. limes (soaked in warm water for a few hours)
¼ cup Pitipin chillies (small sharp ones)
2 tblsp of fresh red chillies (pounded)
3 tblsp of coarse salt
1¼ cup lemon juice (or more)

Dry lemons on cloth. Cut down and across in old fashion way. Or cut lemon in 5 mm thick round slices.

Put lemon slices in a bowl. Add pounded chillies and salt. Toss around till mixed then pack in fruit jar or pickling bottle and fill jar to top with lemon juice. Screw tightly and keep a few weeks before using. Boiling the lemon juice before topping pickle adds to long life of pickle.

VARIATIONS:

(1) Use above recipe but omit pitipin chillies. Add 1 tablespoon or more of pounded red chillies. Finish as in above recipe.

(2) Instead of red chillies use green chillies.

(3) Lemons may be substituted for limes.

(4) Instead of lemon juice use white vinegar.

(5) Add 2 tablespoonsful of ajwain (Celery seeds) to above.

Lemon and Green Ginger Pickle

(PHOTO PAGE 44)

To any lemon pickle add small bits of scraped green ginger (very tender roots) or fresh root turmeric (haldi roots).

Preserved Lemon Peel for garnishes

After squeezing out juice from lemons, fill the rinds with coarse salt and keep in a sealed stoneware jar or casserole in a dry place. After 4 or 6 weeks they will turn a leathery colour. They are now ready for use.

When needed soak a rind in cold water, for a few hours to remove excess salt and add to pot of stew, meat or soups. A lovely garnish for fowl or fish.

Lemon Achar (Spanish)

(MASS QUANTITY) (PHOTO PAGE 160)

½ pocket fresh lemons
1 bottle oil
½ cup red chilli powder
1 tblsp crushed coriander seeds
1 tblsp crushed jeera (cummin)
2 cups methi masala
1 1/3 cups sugar
1½ tblsp mustard powder
Salt to taste
4 bottles vinegar

Wash and dry lemons. Cut each in 6 or 8 pieces. Soak them in the vinegar into which 1½ cups of salt has been dissolved for two days.

Stir several times a day so that the top layers have a chance to nestle at the bottom. On third day, add all the other ingredients and mix well. bottle and seal.

CAUTION: Please use either an enamel or earthenware basin to soak lemons in vinegar brine.

Lemon and Orange Peel Achar

Do not throw away the peels of oranges or Spanish lemons from which you extract juice. Instead, make extra pickles like this:

Remove all pith from rind of a dozen squeezed out lemons. Wash and dry on cloth.

Cut the rind in 5mm x 6cm strips (length and width of ladies small finger). Over rind add 3 tablespoons of freshly ground green chillies and 3 tablespoons of coarse salt.

Mix well and pack into a litre jar.

Keep for 3 days, then add 2 cups of lemon juice and pour over contents of jar, or add 2 cups vinegar. Place a few red chillies within jar.

When cool, close lid tightly. Ready to serve after a month.

To lemon rind you may also add rind of 1 orange or two naartjies.

Peeled Lemon Achar

Peel a dozen Spanish lemons. Put the segments in a bowl. Wash and dry the peel of 2 lemons and cut in long narrow strips and add to segments.

Add 4 tablespoons of salt and one tablespoons of either red or green pounded chillies (The green pounded chillies make an attractive picture with the pale lemon and rind.) and juice of a dozen lemons. Toss lightly. Bottle.

Methi Masala Chutney

(PHOTO 42)

1 cup aamli (tamarind) (250 g)
2 tblsp methi masala (dry)
4 green chillies (slit)
1 tsp mustard seeds
1 tsp sugar
2 sprigs curry leaves
1 small ball garlic
2 tblsp oil

Steep aamli in water till soft. Extract juice by straining through wire sieve. Put in pot with sugar, and bring to boil. Remove from stove. When cool add methi. Meanwhile in half of oil fry the slivered garlic, curry leaves, slit chillies and add to pot of aamli juice. In rest of oil fry the mustards seeds, and add to aamli juice. Cool, then bottle and keep in fridge.

Sweet Sour Mango Chutney

500 g green mangoes
2 tblsp sugar
6 cloves garlic (pounded)
6 dates (pitted)
2 tsp salt
½ bottle vinegar
2 tsp mustard seeds
6 tsp red chillies (fresh pounded)

Peel washed mangoes. Grate coarsely. Sprinkle salt to prevent discolouration. Bring vinegar to boil and add sugar, dates and mangoes and cook over low heat till mango is soft (about 10 minutes).

Add all other spices except mustard seeds. Fry mustard seeds in a tablespoon of oil before adding to pot on stove. Simmer slowly till well pureed. Cool and pack in small chutney jars.

Umlaas Chutney

1 kg green mangoes
2 doz. green chillies
1 whole garlic
1 tblsp salt
1 doz. whole peppercorns
¾ cup oil
2 tblsp sesame (tal)

Peel and grate mangoes coarsely. Pound chillies and garlic fine. Heat oil in frying pan, add ground chillies, garlic, whole peppercorns, tal and salt to grated mangoes and cook in hot oil for about five minutes. When cool place in bottle or, for better preservation, store in fridge and use as required.

Choondo

1 kg mangoes
2 tblsp slivered garlic
½ cup kuripulyi leaves
2 tblsp mustard powdered
2 tblsp crushed mustard
1 tblsp whole mustard
¼ cup vinegar or ½ cup aamli juice
1 tblsp methi masala
6 green chillies (ground)
1 cup oil
2 tblsp salt, adjust to taste

Peel and grate mangoes. To bowl of grated mangoes, add mustard powder, methi masala, aamli or vinegar.

Fry curry leaves in ¼ cup oil, crush, then add to mangoes. In rest of oil fry ground green chillies, slivered garlic and whole mustard and pour over bowl of mangoes. Adjust salt.

Mix and bottle when cool.

Red Choondo Achar

(RED PICKLE/CHUTNEY)
(COLOUR PHOTO PAGE 255)

20-25 mangoes (2 kg)
125 g red chillies
2 tblsp crushed mustard
2 tblsp mustard powder
¼ bottle vinegar
2 balls garlic (or less)
1 cup oil
salt to taste

Peel half the mangoes, cut in pieces and marinate overnight in salt and a little turmeric powder. Drain off moisture in morning and pat dry. Peel and grate the remaining mangoes. Puree the garlic and red chillies with the vinegar and add to the grated mango.

Whisk powdered and crushed mustard in the oil — add all ingredients together. Keep bottled in fridge and use immediately for this is for quick consumption.

Tahini

(MASHED CHANA)

2 cups whole chana (Gram). Boil in salted water till soft. Puree in blender. Also add to blender half chopped onion, ½ bunch chopped spring onions, 6 green chillies, a handful of mint leaves and sufficient lemon juice. Puree to a thick paste. Serve with meat dishes.

NOTE: The same chutney can be made by using crushed sesame seeds (tal) instead of chana.

Dhunia Chutney

(KEY RECIPE)

2 only whole peppercorns
1 bunch dhunia leaves (coriander)
2 green chillies
2 cloves garlic
¼ tsp jeero (cummin)
¼ tsp salt
Juice of 1 lemon

Pound peppers, chillies, and garlic, dhunia and jeero finely, add salt and lemon juice. A liquidiser blends a very smooth chutney.

VARIATIONS TO ABOVE CHUTNEYS

(1) Add boiled and skinned tomato to above. Delicious with rice dishes.
(2) Add 2 tablespoons of mint leaves to above. Excellent with mutton roasts and dry meat dishes.
(3) Add 1 bunch of Kuripulya leaves to above. (Just the thing with khitchris).
(4) Add 1 mashed banana to key recipe.
(5) Add 1 green apple to key recipe.
(6) Add 2 inch square of 5 cm coconut (fresh) or 1 tablespoon of dessicated coconut.
(7) Add 1 tablespoon of aamli sauce. More tangy flavour is assured.
(8) In 1 pint of dahi whisk up 1 tablespoon of key dhunia chutney. This is the dahi to serve with biryanis and is also a healthy drink for those who like sour milk. However omit lemon juice as yoghurt is sour enough.
(9) Add a handful of pounded peanuts or cashew nuts to basic chutney.
(10) Add two tablespoons of peanut butter to basic recipe.
(11) Add a grated tomato and a tablespoon of tamarind juice to basic chutney.
(12) Add 2 mashed potatoes, but increase vinegar or lemon proportionately.

Brinjal Bharad

(BHURTA)

Wash 1 large brinjals. Smear oil over outside. Put into oven to bake. When baked soft, skin brinjal and remove pulp. To pulp add salt, a tablespoon of green dhunia chutney, a tablespoon of yoghurt and a tablespoon of grated onion. Mix well and serve with khitchris or rotlas.

Curry Leaf Chutney

COLOUR PHOTO PAGE 160)

Juice of 2 lemons or vinegar
1 bunch dhunia leaves (coriander)
½ ball garlic
1 tsp jeera (cummin seeds)
1 cup curry leaves
4 green chillies
salt to taste

Pound all ingredients fine or add juice of one lemon and liquidise fine. Fry one teaspoon mustard seeds in one tablespoon of oil and when seeds stop crackling pour over chutney.

Close lid of chutney pot for fragrance to penetrate. More lemon juice may be added to thin down chutney if too thick. Bottle when cool.

Mint Yoghurt

(DAHI CHUTNEY OR DAHI RAITA)

1 tblsp each of very finely chopped mint and onion
½ tsp of finely pulverised green chilli
salt to taste
dash of crushed cummin seeds
1 box yoghurt

Add all ingredients together and serve cold.

Coriander Chutney Yoghurt

(DAHI/DHUNIA CHUTNEY) (TO SERVE WITH BIRYANI)

2 tsp of green coriander chutney (dhunia)
salt
1 box yoghurt

Brinjal Bharad

(PHOTO 160)

2 brinjals (boiled)
½ chopped onion
1 bunch dhunia leaves
2 green chillies
2 cloves of garlic
Sour with either sour milk, vinegar or tamarind or combination of any two of these.

Remove pulp from boiled brinjals. Pound chillies, dhunia and garlic fine in kundi (mortar). Add chopped onion and brinjal and pound little longer. Remove from kundi and sour with any of the above ingredients. Salt to taste. Delicious with khitchris, bharkoo, etc.

Tomato Chutney

4 tomatoes
1 tsp jeera (cummin)
4 cloves garlic
1 sprig curry leaves
2 tblsp oil
1 tblsp coconut
4 red chillies
1/3 tsp peppercorns
1 tblsp methi masala (optional)
4 tblsp lemon juice

Blanch tomatoes and peel off skin. Add jeera, coconut, chillies, garlic and peppercorns and blend fine.

Add lemon juice and boil all together. Add methi masala. Fry curry leaves in oil, and pour over chutney.

Bottle when cool.

Tomato Puree Chutney

125g aamli sauce (soak tamarind in water and extract pulp)
125ml vinegar
1 medium ball garlic
4 tblsp methi masala
1 tsp salt (or more)
1 tsp mustard seeds
1 large onion
410g can of tomato puree
1 tsp red chilli powder
3 tblsp oil
3 sprigs curry leaves

Mix vinegar with 60mls water and put on stove to boil. The moment it boils, remove the pot from stove and keep aside.

Grate onion. Pound garlic and add both ingredients to pot of vinegar.

Also add the tomato puree, methi masala, chilli, aamli sauce, and salt. Heat the oil and add mustard seeds to them.

When the seeds stop spluttering, add the curry leaves and fry for a few seconds.

Add oil, seeds etc. to pot and mix all well together. Bottle when cold.

Tomato/Date Chutney

6 large ripe tomatoes
1 cup vinegar
2 tblsp chilli powder
1 tsp jeera (cummin)
2 cups tomato sauce
2 tblsp methi masala
250g dates
4 tblsp aamli pulp (tamarind)
1 ball garlic
salt to taste
2 tblsp sugar

Blanch tomatoes and rub off skins.
Dates must be soaked in vinegar overnight.
Blend tomatoes, date/vinegar, aamli pulp, chilli, garlic and jeera till fine.
Fry a teaspoon of mustard seeds and a handful of curry leaves in 2 tablespoons of oil and when seeds stop spluttering, add it to chutney. Now add tomato sauce, sugar and methi masala and put on stove to boil.
As soon as it starts boiling, mix well and remove from stove. Cool and bottle.

Tomato Sauce/Chilli Chutney

20 dry red chillies
½ cup white vinegar
1 tsp mustard seeds
½ ball garlic
500g tomato sauce
salt to taste
2 sprigs curry leaves

Soak chillies in hot water and leave for an hour.
When soft, drain off moisture and put in blender with the garlic, tomato sauce, vinegar and salt.
Blend fine. Fry curry leaves and mustard seeds in 2-tablespoons of oil and when seeds stop spluttering add to chutney.
Bottle when cold.

Tomato Sauce Chutney

2 cups tomato sauce (ready made from shops)
1 cup aamli juice (tamarind)
1/3 cup vinegar
Handful of curry leaves
1 cup methi masala
2 tsp mustard seeds
1/3 cup oil

Blend ingredients (sauce, aamli, methi masala and vinegar together). Temper mustard seeds and curry leaves in oil and add to chutney when seeds stop spluttering. Taste for salt.

Red Mircha and Peanut Chutney

(PHOTO PAGE 141)

1 cup peanuts
2 tblsp tal (sesame seeds)
1 tblsp jeero (cummin seeds)
4 lemons
½ cup dessicated coconut
6 red fresh chillies
8 cloves of garlic
Salt to taste

Fry peanuts. Fry separately in small quantities of oil, the tal, jeero, coconut, whole chillies and garlic. Pound or liquidize. Mix well with juice of lemons adding salt to taste. Bottle tightly and use as required. Keeps indefinitely in fridge.

Boiled Mircha (Chilli) Chutney

500 g dry red chillies (split open and remove seeds)
Soak overnight in water. Pour off water. Re-boil in fresh water and pour off water again. Soak ½ cup tamarind in water overnight in a separate bowl.

Sieve through wire strainer and extract maximum juice from this. Put in blender with chillies and blend into smooth paste. Fry 2 teaspoons of whole mustard seeds in 2 tablespoons of oil. Pour over chutney and bottle when cool.

Red Pepper Chutney

3 red peppers (green ones may be used in which case a
   different colour will result)
3 green tart apples
1 tblsp maizena
2 tblsp methi masala
2 tsp sugar
½ cup lemon juice
½ cup vinegar
1 tsp red chillies

Mix maizena in small quantity of lemon juice.

Soak vinegar, methi masala, red chillies and sugar for 15 minutes.

Put all ingredients in enamel pot and boil till thick. Add salt to taste.

Fry 2 teaspoons of mustard seeds in 2 tablespoons of oil and pour over chutney.

Cool and bottle.

Tomato Puree Chutney

(PHOTO PAGE 255)

425 g tin of tomato puree
1 tsp salt
2 tsp fine red chillies
1½ tblsp finely slivered garlic
2 green chillies cut fine
¼ cup oil
Juice of ½ lemon

Fry garlic and chillies in oil till light brown. Add tomato puree, lemon juice and cook over medium heat with lid on till it is thick like a tomato sauce.

Aamli Lal Mircha Chutney

(TAMARIND SAUCE) (PHOTO PAGE 160)

6 cloves garlic
6 red chillies
1 tsp whole mustard
1 tblsp oil
¼ cup vinegar
¼ cup tamarind juice
Salt to taste

Pound garlic and chillies very fine till no seeds are left whole. For those who use a liquidiser master, liquidise the garlic and chillies with the vinegar until a very smooth sauce results. When chutney is fine add vinegar, tamarind and salt. Fry mustard seeds in oil and when they stop spluttering add to it the chutney. Cool and bottle tightly, serving it with dry meat and savouries.
NOTE: If dry red chilli is used, they will require to be heated in the oven before pounding.

Baked Tomato/Aamli Chutney

60 g aamli (½ cup tamarind)
1 bunch dhunia
6 green chillies
2 large tomatoes
2 tblsp mint leaves
3 cloves of garlic

Soak aamli in water and when soft mash and put through strainer. Bake tomatoes in oven and when done put in liquidiser with mint, dhunia, garlic and chillies and blend fine.

In a tablespoon of oil fry a few slices of onion, 2 chopped green chillies, and a teaspoon each of methi and mustard seeds. Pour vagaar over aamli and return to stove and boil. When it starts thickening add chutney and simmer till chutney is the consistency of tomato sauce. Add a teaspoon of sugar and salt to taste. When cold, bottle and use as required.

Date Chutney

½ cup dates
1 tblsp tal (sesame seeds)
Salt to taste
4 cloves of garlic (slivered)
½ cup vinegar
2 tsp green chillies

Fry garlic in oil. Then add tal, mircha, dates (cut up in halves) and the sugar. Keep stirring over low heat till soft. Add vinegar and simmer till chutney is well pureed. Add salt to taste. Bottle tightly and serve as required. Keeps indefinitely in fridge.

Soowa Chutney

1 bunch soowa bhaji (dil leaves)
2 cloves garlic
2 green chillies
Salt

Pound the cleaned, and washed ingredients well together. Add salt, and thin well with lemon juice.
Good for constipation. Take 2 teaspoons with food.

Dried Apricot/Almond Chutney
(COLOUR PHOTO PAGE 75)

½ bottle vinegar
250 g dry apricots
½ cup lemon or tamarind (aamli) juice (see glossary)
½ cup blanched almonds, cashew or peanuts
2 tblsp tomato sauce
½ cup oil
1 cup whole dry red chillies
¼ pkt dates (125 g)
1 tblsp sesame seeds (tal) Salt to taste

Soak all ingredients (except oil and tomato sauce) in vinegar and allow to steep overnight. In morning add tomato sauce and oil and blend smooth to a fine chutney. Bottle in small containers. Keeps indefinitely in freezer.

Tropical Delights Chutney
(COLOUR PHOTO PAGE 277)

500g peeled pieces pumpkin
1 tsp chilli powder
1 tblsp sugar
½ cup vinegar
3 tblsp methi masala

Soak methi masala in vinegar. Boil pumpkin pieces in salted water till soft.
Put all ingredients in blender and blend smooth. Tilt out in enamel pot and cook till thick like chutney.
Fry 2 teaspoons of mustard seeds in ½ cup oil and pour over chutney. Add salt to taste. Bottle when cold.

Pineapple Chutney

Grate 1 pineapple. Sprinkle a teaspoon of salt over it and keep for about an hour.
Liquidise in blender and puree the following:-

2 cups vinegar
½ tsp ginger
3 green chillies
½ cup brown sugar
3 dry red chillies
1 tsp garlic
1½ cups seedless raisins

Heat ¼ cup oil in an enamel pot. Add pineapple and the pureed mixture.
Boil till thick like chutney. Add salt to taste.
Bottle when cool.

Green Mango Chutney
(PHOTO PAGE 255)

4 large green or half ripe mangoes (peel and cut in small cubes)
1 onion (cut in pieces)
3 cloves of garlic
1 tblsp sugar
3 red chillies (fresh or dry ones)
2 tsp jeera (cummin seeds)
salt to taste

Pound or blend jeera, salt, garlic and red chillies till fine.
Add onions and mangoes and blend or pound till almost fine, (like choonda consistency). Add sugar and mix well.

Date Chutney

1 pkt dates (250g)
½ cup vinegar
½ ball garlic
2 tsp jeera (cummin)
¼ cup lemon juice
2 bunch fresh dhunia (coriander)
8 green chillies
Salt to taste

Make a fine chutney by pounding together the dhunia, chillies, garlic and jeera. (If using blender add the lemon juice for the liquid).
Boil the dates in the vinegar till they are soft.
Add chutney and mix all well together. Bottle when cold.

Green Pepper Chutney

6 green peppers
¼ cup sugar
1 tsp mustard seeds
125g tamarind soaked in white vinegar
½ cup methi masala
2 tblsp mustard powder
2 tblsp oil
handful of curry leaves

Strain the soaked tamarind through sieve and to the pulp add all other ingredients except the mustard seed and the curry leaves.

Put in blender and puree fine.

Fry the curry leaves and mustard seeds in the oil and when seeds stop spluttering, add to the chutney. Bottle when cool. Best kept in fridge.

Sweet Chutney
(PARSEE MANGO CHUTNEY)

8 green mangoes (without pips)
3 cups sugar
3 tblsp fresh grated ginger
1 tblsp chilli powder
12 cloves
6 cloves garlic
2 cups white vinegar
Salt

Peel and grate the mangoes, add salt, and strain any excess juice and dry. Add all the other ingredients, mix and pour in the vinegar. Simmer over medium heat until soft and cooked. Serve with rice and curries.

Green Mayonnaise Chutney
(PHOTO PAGE 255)

½ cup mayonnaise
4 tblsp creamed cottage cheese (optional)
6 green chillies
salt and pepper to taste
2 cloves of garlic
2 tblsp lemon juice
1 red pepper chopped very fine
1 tblsp chopped parsley or mint

Grind chilli and garlic fine. Blend ingredients in liquidiser (except red pepper and parsley) till you have a smooth chutney.

Now fold in parsley (or mint if you prefer) and the red chopped pepper. Delicious with mashed potatoes and savouries.

Mayonnaise Chutney
(VARIATION)

12 tblsp mayonnaise
4 tblsp lemon juice
4 tblsp vinegar
¼ tsp pepper (whole)
½ tsp salt
1 tsp red chillies
6 pickled onions
6 pickled gherkins
1 tsp green ground chillies

Blend all ingredients (except mayonnaise) in liquidiser. Mix them into mayonnaise and add a few drops of green colouring till chutney is a pale green colour.

Green Chutney (or Red)
(COTTAGE CHEESE) (PHOTO PAGE 255)

4 tblsp freshly grated coconut
½ bunch dhunia (coriander)
4 tblsp creamed cottage cheese
6 green chillies (or red)
4 cloves garlic
salt to taste

Grind coconut, dhunia, chillies and garlic to smooth paste. Blend in cream cheese and salt.

This paste is lovely as a spread but should it be required as chutney or dip then blend in addition to above 2 tablespoons yoghurt.

Dahi
(YOGHURT)

Yoghurt is no food-fad in India.

It is a staple stand-by for babies, adults and convalescents and can be consumed throughout the day with all meals.

Accompanied with rice dishes it is a delicious sauce or gravy. With snacks and teas it becomes the cool and refreshing drink and and when added to curries it mellows the spices.

In earlier years, all milk left-over at the end of the day, used to be utilised for making a fresh batch of curds for the next day and the little earthen-ware pots were never empty.

To Make Milk Curds at Home

½ litre milk
¼ tsp yoghurt (for starter)

Boil the milk, cool till lukewarm then pour in porcelaine or earthenware pot. Mix in curd starter, cover and allow to set overnight.

NOTE:
In cold weather use a teaspoon of starter and increase setting time.

Cheese from Yoghurt (Paneer)

To make Paneer strain yoghurt or milk curds through muslin.

Allow muslin bag with curds to hang for an hour or two and finally press on the muslin bag to remove all excess moisture.

You will be left with a massy lump.

Place this under some weight and leave overnight.

The hardened paneer must then be left in the fridge till required.

To use in vegetable curries, simply cut blocks and lightly fry in oil.

Yoghurt Drink
(LASSI)

1/3 cup seedless raisins or dry apricots
1 cucumber
2 hardboiled eggs (chopped fine)
1 tblsp chopped mint
2 green chillies
1 litre yoghurt
1 bunch spring onions
1 cup milk
black crushed pepper
2 cloves garlic

Soak raisins or apricots in water for an hour.

Drain off water and blend fine with garlic and chillies (or you may chop it up coarsely) but chillies and garlic must be ground.

Put yoghurt in bowl. Wash spring onions and chop up finely.

Peel cucumber and chop fine.

Now add all ingredients to bowl and beat slightly with milk as required. Serve ice-cold.

Brinjal Yoghurt
(BENGAN RAITA)

Wash and wipe dry 2 brinjals. Smear a little oil over them. Make deep splits in each and put in pan and bake in hot oven for about half an hour (or wrap in foil and then bake). When brinjals are soft, remove from oven and allow to cool, then peel and mash.

To this add a grated onion (medium), 2 teaspoons of oil, salt, dash of black pepper, crushed cummin and ½ teaspoon of either green pounded chilli or red chilli powder, 2 tablespoons of finely chopped green coriander.

Add all these to a box of yoghurt. Adjust salt.

Banana Yoghurt
(RAITA)

1 firm banana sliced in rings
1 box yoghurt
salt
1 tblsp oil
2 tsp dhunia chutney
2 tblsp grated fresh coconut
½ tsp mustard seed

Splutter mustard seed in oil and add coconut. Fry for a few seconds.

Remove from heat and pour over ¼ of yoghurt. Then add salt, dhunia, chutney and banana rings and finally rest of yoghurt. Mix well.

Chilli Bite Yoghurt Delicacy

(BOONDI RAITA) (COLOUR PHOTO PAGE 27)

½ tsp baking powder
½ cup gram flour
½ tsp salt
sufficient water to make stiff batter (about 3 tblsps)
½ tsp black crushed pepper

To sifted ingredients add water to make stiff batter. Beat with wire whip till batter feels light.

Fry small globules of batter in deep hot oil till they are browned like chilli bites (bhajias).

They should be the size of large broad beans. Remove from oil and drain on kitchen paper to cool.

To box of yoghurt add salt, ½ teaspoon of crushed roasted cummin, ¼ teaspoon of either chilli powder or green pounded chilli and mix well. Add bhoondis (chilli bites) to yoghurt just before serving.

VARIATION:

Combine bhoondis with potato/yoghurt salad.

Radish, Cucumber Yoghurt

(MOORA, KAKDI RAITA)

1 box yoghurt
2 tsp coriander chutney (dhunia chutney see page 274)
salt
½ cup of finely sliced radish
1 cucumber peeled, cut in quarters lengthwise, then slice fairly thin

To bowl of yoghurt, add chutney and salt. Mix well then fold-in vegetables lightly.

Potato Yoghurt Salad

(AALLOO RAITA)

Boil three large unpeeled potatoes. (Scrub well beforehand). When nearly done, cool, peel and dice in half inch cubes.

In 1 tablespoon of oil fry ¾ teaspoon mustard seed and ½ teaspoon of cummin seeds.

When seeds crackle, pour over potato cubes. Then add to potatoes 2 teaspoons of dhunia chutney and salt.

Toss around till spices coat potatoes well.
Finally add box of yoghurt. Mix well.
Serve decorated with mint leaves.

Dahi with Red Chillies

(RAITHA)

1 red dry chilli
1/3 tsp jeera (cummin)
1 tblsp oil
salt to taste
2 cloves garlic
½ cup yoghurt

Liquidise or pound the dry ingredients and mix into yoghurt.

Heat the oil and pour over bowl of yoghurt. Serve cold.

Dahi Salad Dressing

1 cup yoghurt
1 tblsp finely chopped radish
1 tblsp chopped mustard achar
salt and pepper

Using vegetables of choice for the salad which must be arranged attractively in bowl or platter, pour over the dressing, prepared thus:

Stir radish and finely chopped achar into yoghurt. Add salt, but take care, for there is already salt in your achar.

If too thick, you may add a tablespoon of milk or buttermilk. Pour over salad and toss a few minutes before serving.

Sikhand — Banana Yoghurt (sweet)

1 carton yoghurt or freshly made curds
2 ripe bananas
¼ tsp crushed elachi
1 tblsp castor sugar

Beat sugar into thick creamy yoghurt — pour into shallow bowl. Peel and cut bananas in thin rings and submerge these partially in yoghurt.

Sprinkle grated elachi and nutmeg — chill and serve cold.

French Dressing

1¼ cup oil
2 tblsp sugar
2 cloves of garlic
½ cup white vinegar
1 small onion
2 tsp mustard powder
2 tsp salt
1 tsp red chilli
½ tsp pepper

Pound together garlic and onion. Add all other ingredients and in mixing bowl beat with rotary beater till well blended together. Alternatively, put all ingredients in liquidiser and pulverize till smooth. Keep in bottle in fridge and use over salads as required.

Tartare Sauce

1 cup mayonnaise
1 tsp prepared mustard
1 tblsp chopped olives
2 tblsp chopped gherkins
1 tblsp finely chopped red or green peppers

Pineapple — Cabbage Salad

Salt to taste
1 grated pineapple
1 grated apple (red variety)
½ small cabbage (shredded very fine)
1 tblsp vinegar
2 tblsp mayonnaise
2 tblsp fine shredded radish
½ cup boiled peas
¼ tsp red chilli

Soak shredded cabbage in salted water. Drain very dry. Add grated pineapple and other ingredients, toss well so as to combine everything. Serve with meat dishes. A lovely and attractive salad.

Kachoomers (or Sambals)
(A MUST WITH RICE DISHES) (PHOTO PAGE 44)

To ½ cup of any one of the undermentioned salad greens, add 1 tblsp of Key DHUNIA CHUTNEY (Page 274) together with a little more salt and lemon.

(1) Finely chopped cucumber,
or Finely chopped cucumber, radish and onion,
or Finely chopped cucumber, and onion,
or Finely chopped onion and radish,
or Finely sliced onion, carrot, lettuce, tomato and radish.

(2) To any of the above combinations, add a few tablespoonsful of sour milk curds or vinegar.

Onion/Tomato Kachoomer

2 onions
1 tbsp chopped mint
1 green chilli (cut in very thin rings)
salt
1 red tomato medium
1 green tomato small (beginning to ripen)
2 tbsp vinegar

Slice onions thinly then put on board and chop across. Squeeze out water and put in bowl. Chop both green and red tomatoes very small and add to onions together with any escaping juices.

Just before serving add mint, salt, chilli and vinegar and toss.

Onion/Aamli Kachoomer
(ONION/TAMARIND RELISH)

¼ tsp red chilli
125 g aamli (pulp from aamli)
1 tsp salt
12 green chillies (slice fine)
1 onion (1 cupful finely sliced)

Add salt to chillies and aamli sauce. Mix together. Slice onion fine. Remove excess water by squeezing through muslin cloth.

Arrange onions in small salad bowl and mix in half of above chutney. Garnish with chopped green chilli and a little chopped mint. Serve with broths or rice dishes.

SECTION 8

Gone are the Days

GONE are the days when the grannies and aunties gathered to make the pickles for the clan. For days before the event, granny's home was a flurry of activity. The spices were picked clean, spread on trays and put out in the open to absorb some of the richness of the sun. Each variety was then divided into heaps that had to be coarsely ground, finely pounded or kept intact. Stocks of oil, ginger, garlic and chillies arrived daily, and these too had to be sorted and kept for the great day.

Messages were sent out to relatives and neighbours informing them of the great event. They too would offer silent prayers that the morrow would turn out bright and sunny, that being, a pre-requisite for successful achar and papad-making as well as for calm tempers.

On D Day, granny would personally supervise the cooking of a large cauldron of dhal and rice to feed the clan. Gradually the aunties would filter in bringing biscuits, bhajia batter, a dessert, or chutney to augment the menu for the day. If it was a papad-making session, they would come equipped with a rolling pin and thali, but for achar sessions they would bring sharp knives and mixing bowls.

Some of the aunties came equipped with the latest versions of classic jokes, stories, and folk songs to entertain the women immersed in their task. Actually these stories and folk songs served also as an inducement to the young girls in the family who became work-shy in the face of such collective know-how. Whilst they sat and listened, they were also shown how to manipulate the dough, dry the papads or whisk the mustard.

Those days are no more — everyone prefers to work at a table but agreed to sit on the floor for the photograph. The young lady in the middle is cutting the dough with a piece of string clenched between her teeth.

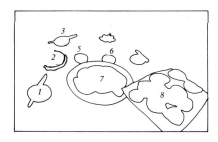

1 Small disc being rolled
2 Papad Dough minced and pounded
3 Rolling out thinly
4 Cutting of discs in equal sizes
5 & 6 Bowls of oil
7 The dried product
8 Papad still drying

Papad
(PAPADUMS)

PAPAD-MAKING is not for the timid person. It is also not for the one who likes to work on her own. It calls for the gathering together of the clan, or the co-operation of a few friends.

Essential for papad-making is a bright sunny day. Many people insist on preparing the dough the night before, but there is always an element of uncertainty in this, for one never knows whether the skies will be clear and blue or overcast the next day. May we therefore suggest the following:

(1) Warn your friends or family to be ready at a moment's notice. Their help with rolling and drying is essential.

(2) Have all ingredients cleaned in advance.

(3) Wake at dawn on the morning of the eventful day, and if it promises to be clear and sunny, start well before breakfast.

(4) Prepare the dough and allow it to rest for an hour or two, whilst you quickly clean the house and prepare a quick lunch for those who will be helping you.

(5) Have ready large sheets of brown paper, clean white sheets, extra rolling pins and thalis for those friends who forget to bring their own.

(6) Invite a granny or an elderly aunt from the neighbourhood, who is renowned for her stock of jokes, folktales and folk-songs. Your aides will love this diversion.

(7) Start pounding your dough. By the time the first helpers arrive you should already have started. This way there will be no delay and everyone will know that you intend finishing the task in hand.

Urad Papads
(PAPADAMS)

2 kg urad flour (lentil)
125 g hinchora (block ammonia)
125 g fine salt
2 tsp hing (asoefaetida))
500 g gram flour (chana)
500 g green chillies (pounded)
2 tsp crushed jeero (cummin)
2 tsp ground pepper

Boil one cup of water and add hinchora. Allow it to infuse two or three times, then remove from stove and allow to cool. Grind chillies fine and add salt to them. Mix well.

Sift all dry ingredients together. Add green chillies and hinchora water to it. Mix by rubbing through palm of hands till chillies and liquid are evenly distributed in flours. Keep adding small quantities of cold water (up to three cups) and knead and pound till a stiff, smooth and shiny dough results.

Put dough through mincer three times. If dough sticks to inside of mincer, rub a tablespoon of oil around dough and then put it through. Keep dough covered with a damp cloth and let it rest for an hour.

Break off small amounts of dough and manipulate in palms till soft and pliable. This is now ready for rolling. Take ping-pong sized lumps of dough and roll on greased thali to required thinness.

Over thick brown paper, spread clean white cloth. Spread papads smoothly over cloth, taking care that they do not crease or rumple in handling.

A few hours in strong sunlight is sufficient to dry out papads. When thoroughly dried pack in airtight tins and use when required.

To Fry: Heat oil well in frying pan. Lower papad in pan and quickly turn over. Fry reverse side as rapidly. This ensures a light mustard colour and a crisp papad. (Drain in colander).

To Toast: Toast under griller of electric range. Or toast over a wire rack placed over a coal stove. As soon as papads are crisp and mustard in colour they are done.

Serve with: Porridge for breakfast. Khitchri and khuri, or bhurkoo, or mealie rice dishes.

To Fry Rice Papads

Heat oil till hot. Lower papad in oil, but with help fo two spoons, stretch across width of papad so that they spread to nearly 1½ times its size. Turn over for a few seconds and remove. Drain in colander.

CAUTION: Frying must be done at great speed.

Rice Papads

500 g rice flour
1 tsp pounded jeero (cummin)
1 tsp (4 g) salt (just rounded)
1 tblsp green pounded chillies
1 tsp Hinchora (4 g)

(1) Carefully measure hinchora and salt separately. Each item to just roundly fill a teaspoon.

(2) 500 g of rice flour is approximately two cups depending on the size of the cup used. so carefully measure the flour in a cup, and use the same cup to measure off an equal amount of water (e.g. if the flour measured 2¼ cups then the same amount of water must be used).

(3) Put water to boil. Add hinchora, salt and green chillies.

(4) Sift flour and add to water on stove.

(5) Immediately remove from heat and stir very briskly till the flour is well absorbed in water and a rubbery dough results.

(6) Place dough in a muslin bag. Put this in a colander or large sieve and suspend over boiling water taking care that water does not touch or seep up, whilst boiling. Dough will require to be steamed for at least half an hour.

(7) To test if dough is done pierce a knife into it and when it comes out clean without any dough sticking to it, it is done. Cool slightly and put through mincer once.

(8) Roll and dry as for arad papads, keeping in mind that these will be thicker.

Papads

(VARIATION KANKI)

1 kg rice flour (cake flour may be substituted)
1 level tblsp red pounded chillies (dry ones)
½ packet bicarbonate of soda
½ level tsp of coarse salt

Sift flour. Put to boil as many cupsful of water as there is flour. Add chillies, bicarbonate of soda and salt to boiling water. Pour boiling water over the flour, but take care to stir very vigorously in order to avoid lumps. When well mixed and dough is formed, wrap it in muslin bag and put in top of double boiler and cook for one hour. To test if dough is done, pierce a knife into it, and when it comes away clean and without any dough sticking to it, it is done. Cool slightly and put through mincer once and roll and dry as for arad papads.

Urad Papads (Thick)

If a thickish papad is required then a combination of the following types of flour should be used:

1 kg moong flour
30 g jeero powder (cummin)
150 g bicarb
500 g green chillies (or 125 g chilli powder)
90 g coarse salt
15 g hing (asoefaetida)

Method as on page 284.

SECTION 9

Roti Bread and Naan

Traditionally the thing to serve with turkaris, is either roti or rotla instead of bread and it would be true to say that most homes still make their daily batch of fresh rotis.

Roti is unleavened bread made of either white flour or unsifted meal with a little shortening but instead of being baked they are toasted over a griddle till they are freckled gold. To see a freshly stacked pile of rotis is a sight that will tempt any age group and many a child has snatched one whilst mother is not looking.

Rotla is a more economical version of roti and is the fare of peasants in India. They are made of mealie meal or corn flour and are delicious with burkhoo, porridges and fish dishes.

With curries containing lots of gravy, naans — which are the equivalent of the western breads are served. Bread and breadrolls too are every day fare with all Indians. So we have collected recipes of all these types of breads and can vouch safe their excellence.

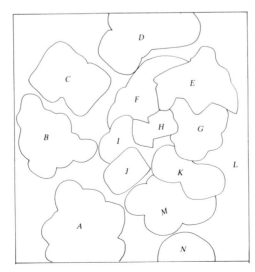

A Yeast rolls (295)
B Rolls with oil (298)
C Featherlite Bread (295)
D Bread (296)
E Puri (226)
F Rotla (290)
G Cream Scones (292)
H Wholewheat Bread (296)
I Rolls with buttermilk (297)
J Wholewheat Bread (296)
K Croissants (370)
L Roti with Pumpkin (342)
M Wholewheat Rolls (296)
N Naan (294)

How a Lady serves her Prince Charming

There were these venerable old neighbours of ours. He was huge, tall and stout, while she petite and frail. With his flowing white beard and hooked nose he looked stern and ominous, while she was graciously feminine with her soft muslin scarves.

Seldom were the two seen conversing with each other, for his staccato commands she would execute before they had echoed around the home. When they sat on their verandah enjoying the afternoon cup of tea, he would merely gesture for another cup, and she would silently offer him betel leaf which she folded intricately with her delicate fingers. It was as if they were relishing the silences that were only punctuated by the cooing of the doves in the dovecote.

Each day, as soon as they had performed their evening prayers, he would commence to stroll around the block, giving her the time to lay out his dinner on the brass tray.

Leisurely stroll over, he would arrive to enjoy his two hot curries, jug of iced water, pickles and a solitary piping hot roti on the side plate. On the other half of the table she was busy rolling out another roti, meanwhile checking and turning the one that was half done on the grilling plate. This way she replenished his roti plate with as many hot rotis as his massive appetite required.

She and the children only ate after he had been fully appeased. Theirs was a tranquil home, with little stress and no upheavals. He lived to a ripe old age but she preceded him a year earlier. A fragile body had laid itself down to eternal rest after a lifetime of faithful service. Her Prince Charming never had cause to complain.

This little sketch illustrates but too well, a family scene of days gone by, when husbands lived to ripe old ages, grunting through life contentedly, and wives agilely and lovingly scampering around to get the work done in time for their lord and masters.

Pour boiling water and milk over mealie meal. Let cool slightly. Add ghee and salt and mix well. Add flour and knead to soft dough. Cover with a clean cloth and keep for at least an hour before rolling. Roll as follows:

Divide dough into 4 sections. Roll each out to 22 cm diameter. Brush with melted ghee or baghroo. Fold over in half. Brush top of fold with ghee sprinkle flour and fold over again. Roll out again to one eighth of an inch thick circle (about 22 cm diameter). Put on hot griddle and turn over several times till lightly freckled. Brush over with melted ghee (about 2 teaspoons on each side) and brown well on both sides.

P.S. — The well turned out roti is the one with a light background with golden brown freckles dotting it evenly. Note that baghroo is residue of strained ghee. Do not discard it but use it in rotis.

Electric Frying Pans are ideal for making rotis.

Brown Flour Roti

1 cup flour
1 cup unsifted flour
1 tblsp ghee
¾ cup water
¼ cup milk
Pinch of salt

Mix flour with ghee and salt; heat milk and water together till fairly warm, and add to flour kneading to a soft dough. Prepare like White roti.

NOTE: The malaai (cream forming on boiled milk is excellent for rotis).

White Roti

2 cups flour
¼ cup mealie meal
1 tblsp ghee
1 cup boiling water (less 2 tablespoonsful)
2 tblsp milk or skimmed cream from boiled milk (malaai)
Pinch of salt

Rotlas (PHOTO PAGE 287)

1 cup mealie meal
1 cup flour
½ tsp salt
1 tblsp ghee

Moisten mealie meal with boiling water, stirring well to avoid lumps (just sufficient water to really coat meal well). When slightly cool add ghee and salt. Mix well then add the flour and knead to a fairly stiff dough. (If necessary add a little cold water but normally the moisture from wet mealie meal takes care of the additional flour). Divide into two portions and roll each between palm of hands till no fine cracks are visible. Roll out to 6 mm thickness and put on hot griddle. Turn over when underside is light brown, then brown on other side. Pour about a tablespoon of ghee on either side and freckle slightly more (optional).

See also mealie meal casserole where rotla dough is placed over curry and then baked in oven. (Page 118).

Choprela Rotlas
(SMEARED)

1 cup fine mealie meal
½ cup flour
½ tsp salt
2 tsp oil

Sieve mealie meal with salt. Rub in oil. Add just sufficient boiling water to make mealie meal slightly soggy. Allow to cool slightly, then add flour and knead into soft rotla dough. Roll out like roti and smear with ghee. Fold as for roti and roll out again to a thinnish rotla.

Grill on tava like a roti smearing with ghee when nearly done or alternatively grill in oven and when rotla puffs out, turn and grill the second side.

Kapari Rotlas

Prepare bajra rotlas on greased paper. Put on tava to grill and when underside is done, criss cross (into diamond shapes) the top with a sharp knife. Turn over and grill second side. When rotla is done put on plate and smear with a little ghee and sprinkle powdered ghor inside the cuts. Eat hot. Especially loved by children.

Khameer Rotlas

4 cups flour
½ cube yeast
1 tbsp ghee
½ egg
1 tbsp sugar
¼ cup milk
½ tsp salt
1 tblsp oil

Mix sugar into yeast. Sift dry ingredients together.

Add beaten eggs, oil, ghee and milk to yeast mixture and form into dough, using as much of lukewarm water as is necessary. Allow to rise double in size.

Roll out into small discs (like fat rotis) allow to rise again.

Grill over hot griddle (tava) like roti. When nicely browned, brush over with oil and serve hot with curries, soups etc.

Bajra Rotla
(MILLET FLOUR BREAD)

1 cup bajra meal
¼ tsp salt
1 tsp ghee

Rub ghee in flour sifted with salt. Make a dough with cold water. As bajra dough is sticky pat it into rotlas with palms or grease a piece of lunch paper and pat the dough on it to an 20 cm diameter disc which is a 6 mm thick.

Invert the paper on to a tava and remove paper. Grill like rotlas.

To serve as a breakfast porridge:

¼ cup chopped green garlic shoots
2 tblsp ghee
¼ tsp salt

Fry the green garlic (which has been chopped like spring onions) in ghee. Break the bajra rotlas in individual porridge bowls and add hot milk to fill bowl. Sprinkle with little salt and some of the fried garlic. Drink hot. Most nourishing drink on wintry mornings. Served with toasted papads and brinjal bharad (bhurta), it makes a delicious meal.

Arabian Mince Rotlas

2 cups whole wheat flour
½ tsp salt
1 tsp sugar
10 g cake yeast
2 tsp ghee
125 g mutton mince

Crumble yeast in ghee and a little cold water. Add salt and sugar and mix this into the flour adding more water if necessary. Knead for 15 to 20 minutes. Cover dough with damp cloth and leave to rise for few hours. Wash mince and put in pan with a little salt and chilli powder and braise till all lumps are broken and fairly dry. After dough has risen knead in the mince. Divide dough into four parts and pat into thick buns on palms of hands. On a greased oven sheet pat each bun into a thick rotla like disc. Bake in 200ºC oven till rotlas baked (about 10-15 minutes). Serve hot.

Bhatooras

2 cups flour
½ tblsp melted ghee
½ cup milk
1/8 tsp bicarb
1/8 tsp salt
Oil for frying

Sift flour with salt and soda. Rub in ghee and knead into puri dough with the milk. Dampen a piece of muslin and cover the dough in it. Lower the dough into a deep mixing bowl, cover bowl with blanket or thick cloth and leave in warm place for several hours. The batter will rise and form a sponge in the centre. Heat oil. Break down dough slightly. Break off small lumps and roll out lightly into puris. Fry as for puris. Serve hot as these do not keep.

Jeero Puri
(PURI WITH CUMIN SEEDS)

2 cups cake flour
½ tsp salt
1 tsp whole black peppers coarsely crushed (optional)
1½ tblsp ghee
1 tsp jeero

Mix dry ingredients together, add ghee and enough water to make stiff puri-like dough. Roll out thin as puris and cut either in rounds or in delicate finger shapes and fry in deep hot oil to a deep golden colour. Drain dry in colander. Delicious with breakfast or light teas.

Alternate: Roll dough out very thin. Cut into very narrow strips (in finger length) and fry.

Pitta Bread (Arabian)

8 cups flour
2 tsp active dry yeast
2-2½ cups water (lukewarm)
1½ tsp salt
3 tblsp ghee or oil
½ cup fine mealie meal (corn meal)

Add yeast to 3 tblsp lukewarm water — after 5 minutes, stir in and rest for 5 more minutes.

Sift flour and salt and rub in ghee — make well in middle and pour in yeast mixture. Make into dough by adding ½ cup of water till dough forms. Push and knead for 20 minutes till dough is elastic.

Shape into bowl and place in lightly greased bowl. Cover and leave in warm place for 40-50 minutes.

Pound down and form into 8 round balls. Place those under towel for half an hour.

Heat oven to 225ºC. Roll ball out (on mealie-meal strewn surface) to thickness of ladies' small fingers. Place on baking sheet. Sprinkle with mealie meal. After ½ an hour, place in oven on lowest shelf for 5 minutes, then put on middle shelf and finish baking.

Keep warm wrapped in foil.

Soji Puri
(CREAM OF WHEAT PURI)

2 cup flour (minus 3 tblsp)
2 tsp oil
½ cup milk/water
3 tblsp soji (cream of wheat)
½ tsp salt

Boil milk/water. Sift flour, soji and salt. Rub in ghee and make dough with hot milk/water. Roll out and fry like puris.

Naan Puri
(VARIATION OF KHAMEERA ROTLA)
(COLOUR PAGE 239)

Sesame (tal) seeds for sprinkling
2 cups flour
1 tblsp solid ghee or if melted 2 tblsp
4 tsp baking powder
1 tsp sugar
½ tsp salt
1 egg (keep a little for brushing puris on top)
Make dough with half water and milk

Roll out as thick as roti and with a 7 cm cutter, cut out into rounds, and brush with egg, and sprinkle with sesame or poppy seeds. Then in deep oil fry slowly, pouring oil on top till the puri has risen to double its size. Then turn over and fry till a pale golden colour.

Cream Scone

(MALAAI) COLOUR PHOTO 287

2 cups malaai (cream skimmed off milk that was boiled)
½ cup butter (125g)
*3½ tsp baking powder (see method first)
Flour to form dough (self-raising flour)
1½ tblsp sugar
¼ tsp salt

Mix butter and cream, add other ingredients and mix well. Finally add just sufficient self raising flour to form very soft dough. (In event of using plain cake flour add Baking Powder).

Roll out 2cm thick, cut out in rounds. Place on baking tray, brush with beaten egg and bake in hot oven.

Tal/Jeero Tukras

2 cups flour
1 tsp baking powder
Cold water for dough
1 tblsp jeero (cummin)
1 tblsp tal (sesame)
1 tblsp melted ghee

Sift flour and baking powder. Add tal and jeero then rub in ghee. Knead into soft dough with cold water. Pound well then roll out thinly on floured board. Cut in diamond shapes or in 7 cm x 1,5 cm wide strips. Fry in hot oil. Drain on wire rack and when cold, store in air tight tins. Ideal for breakfast or teas.

Parathas

(COLOUR PHOTO 141)

Central and North Pakistan is famous for this fried bread known as parathas. The Pathans make them long and huge and when served with their kerhaay meat, roasts or shami kebaabs it is food to feast a hungry army. (For rolling procedure see opposite).

1 tblsp ghee (optional)
3 cups flour
cold water
1 tsp salt

Sift flour and salt. Rub in ghee. Add just enough water to make a puri-like firm dough. Keep under damp cloth for 3 hours.

Knead on floured board (by wetting hands if necessary) for 15 minutes till dough is soft and elastic.

Divide into 6 balls. Roll each out to size of a plate. Spread thickly with a dessertspoon of ghee.

With a knife, make a slit into each roti from centre to edge (see diagram).

Now roll the cut portion around till you have a cone shape. Hold cone with base at bottom of board and the narrow side on top and press down narrow side to the centre of the broad side.

The dough will now resemble a bun (Granny's hair bun). Keep these buns aside for half an hour, before finally rolling out like rotis.

Grill over hot tava and freckle a golden colour by putting a dessertspoon of ghee on either side.

Serve hot.

Thel Naan

Poppy seeds for sprinkling
5 cups flour
½ cup sugar
1½ tsp salt
3 cups milk
2 eggs
¼ cup butter
20 g yeast
Saunmf (Fennel)

Mix all dry ingredients with butter. In another bowl mix well beaten eggs, yeast and milk and add to like flour mixture. Knead thoroughly and cover with clean thick cloth and leave to rise. When dough has risen to double its size, knead and leave to rise again. Knead again when it has risen a second time and weigh into 250 g quantities. Shape to 20 cm diameter by 2 cm thick rounds. When handling dough use oil as dough is very soft and difficult to handle. Put into suitable naan pans (well greased) and leave to rise, till double its size. Coat with well beaten egg. Sprinkle with poppy seeds. Bake for 25 to 30 minutes in 180°C oven.

Naan

(PHOTO PAGE 287)

3 tblsp oil
7 full cups flour
*1 cake yeast (20 g)
*½ tblsp salt
*1 tblsp sugar
*1 cup luke warm water
6 tblsp sugar
4 tblsp ghee
2 eggs
1 tblsp saunmf (fennel)
1¼ cups water
1½ cups milk (room temperature)
Quantity: 6 naans

Mix ingredients with asterisk together. Cream together oil, sugar and ghee. Add eggs, beat in well then add saunmf. Now add the yeast mixture and the water and milk. Mix well and carefully add the sifted flour and make into dough. Cover with cloth and leave to rise double in size. Knead and divide dough into 6 portions, moulding each to 18 cm in diameter and about 2,5 cm high. Leave to rise double again. Bake in 180°C oven for 20-25 minutes.

Moong or Methi Sprouts Bread

1 cup digestive bran
2 cups cake flour
1 cup oats
1 cup sunflower seeds
1 tsp salt
1 tsp green pounded chilli
half green chopped pepper
2 tblsp soft butter
3 cups whole-wheat meal
1 cup moong or methi sprouts
½ cup chopped pecan nuts
1 carton maas (yoghurt)
1 tsp bicarb
1 tsp saunmf (fennel seeds)
1 tblsp honey

If methi sprouts are used, please use 2 tablespoons of honey. The honey, butter and yoghurt must be mixed well together in bowl.

Add rest of ingredients to bowl and mix well by hand. Grease baking pan and bake for 1 hour at 180°C (350°F).

When done, remove from pan. Serve with butter.

Khameera Naan

12 cups flour
1 litre water (warm)
1 tin condensed milk (397 g)
¾ cup butter
2 eggs
2 tsp salt
Saunmf (fennel)
1 cake compressed yeast (20 g)

Mix flour, saunmf, salt and rub in butter till a breadcrumb-like mixture results. Mix in a bowl: warm water, condensed milk, the well beaten eggs and softened yeast (this is done by mixing 1 teaspoon sugar with the yeast in a cup). Make dough with this yeast mixture and flour and knead well. Cover. Leave to rise to double in size. Knead dough again. Weigh into 250 g quantities, shape in 2 cm thick by 15 cm in diameter rounds and leave to rise on a clean cloth on a table.

Let it rise to double its size, fry in deep pan in ghee/oil moderate heat till golden brown. Remove on to wire rack, to cool.

Khameera Naan

(VARIATION)

Poppy seeds for sprinkling
1 egg
½ tsp salt
2½ tsp baking powder
1 tsp saunmf (fennel)
1 tblsp ghee or butter
1 tblsp sugar
¾ cup milk
Flour

Mix egg, ghee and sugar and beat well together. Add remaining ingredients and mix. Add as much flour as is needed to make a soft spongy dough. Cover and leave to rise for 1½ hours. Divide dough in 6 portions, and roll each out to 10 mm thick rotla. Smear top with beaten egg, sprinkle with khus-khus and tal.

Fry each naan in deep oil over moderate heat till golden brown.

Caution: Do not turn naan over. Ladle hot oil from sides of pan, over top of naan till it puffs, hardens and browns.

Feather-lite Bread

(PHOTO PAGE 287)

½ yeast (10g)
1 tsp salt
8 cups flour
2 eggs
3 dssp sugar
4 tblsp oil
2 cups milk — lukewarm
1½ cups water — lukewarm

Mix yeast and 1 dessertspoon sugar and leave aside till bubbly. Mix all liquids together, add eggs and beat with a whisk. To this add rest of sugar and yeast mixture.

Add salt to flour and knead a dough with the liquid mixture. Cover the dough and leave to rise until double in size. Knead the dough and form into desired shapes for rolls, or form into loaves.

Let the dough rise for about an hour or until double in size. Bake in 180°C oven for 15 to 20 minutes or until done. Brush with butter.

Alternatively:
Before baking smear egg yolk over tops of rolls. Sprinkle poppy seeds (khus khus) over it.

Bread Rolls

4 cups flour
1 cube yeast
1 tblsp sugar
1/3 cup oil
1 tsp salt
1/3 cup milk
¼ cup water

Dissolve yeast in sugar and when it dissolves add a quarter cup of the water and a 1/3 cup milk to it.

Sift flour and salt and rub-in oil so that it is well distributed in flour.

With yeast liquid make a dough and knead for a few minutes.

This dough does not require much kneading so be careful not to overhandle.

Cover and leave in warm place till it rises double in size (about 2 hours).

Knead again and shape into balls or fancy shapes as desired. Place on greased baking trays and allow to rise again (approx. ½ an hour).

Brush tops of rolls with beaten egg and sprinkle khus khus (poppyseeds) or tal (sesame seeds).

Bake in 400°F (200°C) oven for 15 to 20 minutes.

BASIC RULES FOR MAKING BREAD AND BREAD ROLLS

1. We give you a variety of recipes which should satisfy the most discriminating of eaters. The thing to remember is that yeast must be fresh. After liquids have been added to the flour and the initial mixing done, tip out dough onto floured board and knead, punch, fold and slap till the dough is really elastic and smooth. It should also no longer have the tendency to stick to the board.

2. The first rising will take longer, so allow it to rise to double its bulk before commencing to shape and mould your bread and rolls.

3. Punch down the risen dough and knead and press with heels of hands till all air has been pressed out. Now mould into required loaves and shapes.

4. Place the sealed edge of rolls and bread down on the greased trays. Allow to rise again.

5. If a highly glazed crust is required then brush with egg yolk to which a little water has been added.

6. For a crisp crust, do not grease loaves with butter, and allow to cool uncovered.

7. For a soft crust brush with melted butter after taking out rolls from oven, then cover with a kitchen towel for a few minutes.

8. Bread and rolls should be taken out of pans as soon as they are done and allowed to cool on wire rack.

Bread Rolls

4 cups flour
½ cup sugar
1 rounded tsp salt
20g yeast
1 tblsp marge or butter
*1 cup water
*1 cup milk
  mix together

Blend yeast and sugar and when it is bubbly, mix into milk/water mixture and dissolve rest of sugar in it.

Sift flour with salt, rub in butter. Make a soft dough, using just enough of liquid as is necessary.

Let rise double in size. Pound and knead well then mould to fit into 3 small loaf pans.

Grease pan and put dough inside — let rise again.

Brush top with beaten egg — sprinkle poppy seeds on top and bake in 180°C oven for 30 minutes.

Bread

(PHOTO PAGE 287)

1 kg flour (8 cups)
1 tblsp salt
1 tblsp ghee
20 g yeast
2½ cups warm water

Mix salt and flour with ghee, mix liquid and yeast and add to flour. Knead to a soft dough. Cover and leave to rise double. Knead. Cover and leave to rise a second time.

Knead and divide dough into half or into 4 equal portions. Grease 2 bread tins well, shape into 1 full loaf or into 2 half loaves and put into pan, to rise again to slightly above the bread pans. Coat with egg and bake in 180°C oven for 1 hour or slightly longer till golden brown on top.

Smear with a little butter or ghee while still warm to give a lovely gloss and also to keep top of bread soft.

Bread with Holsum

3 cups flour
2 tsp salt
1¼ cups luke warm water
1 tblsp of holsum (margarine)
10 g cake yeast

Rub marge in flour till flour resembles fine bread crumbs. Crumble yeast, add salt and mix smooth with a little water. Add rest of water and make a dough, kneading well. Rub a little butter over top of dough. Cover with a damp cloth and let rise till dough is twice its present size. Knead well and divide in two halves. Grease a loaf pan and put dough in this. Allow to rise again (about 40 minutes). Bake in 200°C oven for ½ an hour. Reduce heat to 150°C and bake another 30 minutes. A few minutes before removing bread from oven, brush surface with a little melted oil.

Yeast Rolls

1 kg flour (8 cups)
¾ cup butter
2 level tsp salt
6 tsp sugar
20 g cake yeast
1 cup water (warm)
1 cup milk (warm)

Mix all dry ingredients with butter till a breadcrumb like mixture results. Mix in bowl the water, milk and yeast (yeast should be previously mixed with 1 teaspoon of sugar in a cup. Add to flour. Knead well. Dough should be fairly soft, the softer the dough the lighter the rolls, so if more liquid is required add more milk. Cover with thick clean cloth and leave to rise to double its size. Knead and leave to rise a second time. Knead again, and weigh into 45 g quantities. Roll and shape as desired and put on well greased pans a few spaces apart (leaving enough room for it to rise to double its size). Cover pans and leave to rise to double the size, coat with well beaten egg and bake in 180°C oven for 25 to 30 minutes.

Wholewheat Bread

(PHOTO PAGE 287)

5 cups unsifted tru-wheat flour
2 tsp salt
1 yeast (20g)
1½ cups low fat milk (skim milk)
3 tblsp sugar
2 tbsp margarine
1 cup warm water
1 egg

Add sugar, salt and margarine to the flour and mix. Dissolve yeast in the warm water. Beat the egg and milk and add this to the above, and make a soft dough.

Let is rise for a few hours, till it doubles in bulk. Shape as desired and let it rise for another ½ hour.

Brush with skimmed milk, sprinkle with bran and bake at 220°C until pink.

Switch off oven and leave in oven for another 20 minutes.

Bunny Chow

Bunny Chow is a word that is now firmly entrenched in the South African vocabulary. It has been included in Professor Jean Branfords dictionary of South African English.

Derived from the original Indian term Bania (referring to Hindus belonging to the mercantile class, who in the majority are vegetarians, this slang term arose in the Indian restaurants which served hunks of bread filled with a saucy bean curry. Bania chow was destined to become Bunny Chow.

This very economical and nourishing food has become so popular in Natal that diners used to it can just not revert to sandwiches again. Its a working man's meal supreme!

Using any of our recipes for bread rolls make your own Bunny-chow with our dry bean curry on Page 136. Teenagers especially welcome this at their get togethers.

Rolls with Buttermilk

(PHOTO PAGE 287)

This recipe does not require double rising, so for quick rolls try them.

1 cup buttermilk (or half milk and half yoghurt)
1/3 tsp bicarb.
3 tblsp butter (soft)
1 tsp salt
10 g yeast
2½ cups flour

Mix buttermilk, bicarb, sugar and salt together. Add crumbled yeast and dissolve into above. Now add soft butter. Sift flour into liquids and form into dough. This dough is very soft and is slightly difficult to handle.

If dough is too soft and difficult to handle, a little extra flour may be added. Knead well and mould into desired shapes. When rolls are double in size bake in a 400°F (200°C) oven for 15 to 20 minutes.

Quantity: 1½ dozen.

Easy Rolls

3 cups white flour
1 tsp salt
¾ cup scalded milk
½ cup hot water
1 tsp dried yeast
1 tblsp sugar
2 tblsp butter

Melt sugar in hot water, add dried yeast and leave to activate for 15 minutes.

Melt butter and scalded milk. Sift flour and salt, make a well in centre and pour in butter/milk mixture.

Stir well, now add yeast/water liquid to flour, mix into dough and knead well.

Form into rolls or bread. Place in greased container to rise. Brush with egg and bake in 180°C oven for 15-20 minutes for rolls and 30-35 minutes for loaves.

Mutton Filled Bread Rolls

THE FILLING:

1 kg mutton (or chicken or steak)
1 tsp salt
¼ tsp crushed jeero
1 tsp ginger/garlic
1½ tsp green chilli
¼ tsp pepper

Cut mutton in 1 cm cubes. Wash and drain. Put in pot with the spices and mix well. Add a tablespoon of oil and braise slowly till dry. Now add sufficient water to cook mutton tender.

THE ROLLS:

4 cups flour
90g butter
¼ cup oil
1½ cup warm milk
½ cake compressed yeast (10g)
2 tblsp sugar
1½ tsp salt

Crumble yeast and blend into paste with a little of the warm water. To this add the sugar and salt and finally the rest of the liquids. Sift flour into large bowl and make a dough with the liquid yeast mixture. Knead and allow to rise double in bulk. Break down dough and take golf ball sized lumps and stretch this in palm of hand and put a tablespoon of the mutton in the middle. Close over, taking care to wrap mutton well and place on baking sheet with the enclosed side at bottom. Allow to rise again. Brush top with beaten egg, sprinkle with poppy seeds and bake in 200°C oven for 5 minutes, reduce heat to 175°C and bake for another 20 minutes.

NOTE:

Large fancy loaves may be made with this dough and the meat filled therein.

Cheese and Pepper Bread

2 tblsp soft butter
1 tblsp sugar
1 1/3 cups milk
1 green pepper finely chopped
1 cake yeast
3 tblsp flour
2 tsp salt
1/3 cup grated cheese
¼ cup water
3 to 3½ cups flour

Put butter, 3 tblsp flour, sugar and salt in a saucepan and stir till mixed. Add milk and keep stirring till mixture is thickened.

Add cheese and chopped peppers and stir till cheese is melted. Allow mixture to cool.

Meanwhile mix together the yeast and water and when cheese mixture is luke warm, add the yeast mixture to it.

Mix in 3 to 3½ cups flour.

Knead well and allow to rise double in size. Shape into a loaf and put in bread pan that has been slightly greased.

Allow to rise again (allowing 30 minutes for it).

Bake in 375°F (185°C) oven for 45 to 50 minutes.

This is delicious served with butter.

Rusks

12 cups self-raising flour
4 cups cake flour
4 tsp baking powder
375g butter (1½ cups)
2 cartons buttermilk (1 000ml)
2 eggs
1½ dsp salt
1½ dsp aniseed (saumf)
1½ cups sugar

Rub butter into sifted flour and baking powder. Beat together the buttermilk, eggs, salt, aniseed and sugar. Keeping aside about 3 tablespoons of this mixture, pour the rest into the dry ingredients, to make a nice pliable dough, (like bread dough).

Dough should not be sticky.

Roll into fat sausage shapes and flatten one end so that they can stand on greased bread pan next to each other.

Brush top with left over buttermilk mixture.

Bake in 350°F (180°C) oven for about an hour until done.

When baked, separate rusks from one another.

Put back loosely in pans. Dry overnight in oven at 100°C (200°F).

Rolls with Oil

5 cups flour (sifted)
¾ cup oil
1 tsp salt
2 eggs
2 tblsp sugar
2 cups milk
2 x 20 grams cake yeast

Beat last six ingredients together and add to flour. Mix into a sticky dough. Shape rolls. Let dough raise once double in size.

Dough is very sticky and difficult to handle so oil fingers when shaping and put into greased pan.

Bake in 200°C oven for 5 minutes, lower to 180°C and bake till done (25 to 30 minutes).

Baigles
(JEWISH ROLLS)

4 cups flour
1 tsp salt
2 tbsp oil
¼ cup water (lukewarm)
½ yolk of egg
1 block yeast (20g)
1½ tbsp sugar
1 tbsp ghee
¼ cup milk (lukewarm)
Poppy and sesame seeds (khuskus and tal)

Mix yeast with ½ tbsp of sugar and 2 tbsp of warm water.

Blend and keep in warm place for about 10 minutes by which time the yeast mixture will have become bubbly.

Sift flour, salt and rest of sugar in a bowl. Mix together milk, water, oil, ½ egg yolk and yeast mixture to this and knead into a dough (as for rolls) more water may be necessary.

Knead dough well on flour strewn surface. Place in lightly oiled bowl and keep in warm place till it has risen double in size. This should take about an hour or two.

Punch dough back, knead then form into 10 portions.

Roll each portion into size and thickness of a sausage. Form into a circle by moistening the end overlapping them slightly and pressing down on them. Place rings on a lightly oiled tray for about 10 minutes to rise again.

Boil water in a large pot and lower 3 or 4 baigels at a time (they should not touch each other) and allow to soak for a minute. Turn them over, cook for another minute. Then lift out with perforated spoon and replace on oiled tray.

Brush top of baigels with an egg yolk which was beaten with 2 tsp of water. Sprinkle well with sesame and poppy seeds (tal and khuskhus) and bake in 375°F oven (190°C) till they are gold in colour, about 15-20 minutes.

SECTION 10

Convalescence &
Remedial Foods

The hakims of India make a great play of nature cures and with the medicines prescribe also diets, often giving recipes of palatable herbs which help towards the recovery and well being of patients. Some of these formulae are heirlooms of the past and as such have a prized position in the cooking repertoires of the Indian grannies. The making of these foods is a dying art, as the modern trend is to imbibe medicines and vitamins in the form of a sugar coated pill rather than a laboriously processed food.

We record some of the more popular formulae in this book for its cultural value and also as a token to the wisdom of the past. We neither belittle nor advocate revival of these paaks or phakis but feel that intelligent usage should in no way be decried.

Modesty in women is a virtue much cherished in the East. The Indian bride was traditionally required to be shy and at the dinner table this was expressed in the lack of appetite she displayed. Often it must have happened, that when she returned to her parental home for her first confinement, the expectant mother was extremely emaciated and it then rested on her aunts and mother to feed her back to a physical fitness for the impending delivery. No doubt this is the reason why custom dictates that Indian women have their first baby in the home of her parents. After delivery it is not only expected that her maternal fighting spirit will be aroused, but it is generally insisted upon that the feeding mother eat vigorously in order to maintain the milk supply.

Before confinement, foods rich in prophylactic, gestation and foetus maturation values, are prepared and it is strongly believed that the mother's well being will be inherited by the child. After delivery her diet is strictly circumscribed. She is to eat foods that will ward off colds, and prevent backaches; she is to avoid foods which will distress the breast-fed child; her diet must ensure regular bowel movement and certain foods taken by her will aid her baby in burping out wind.

The folk lore of these foods could fill a book by itself and one is reluctant to tread on grounds one is not conversant with.

Kaahyo

(MEDICINAL PUDDING)

250 g singhora flour (1 cup)
*500 ghor (1½ cup)
60 g saalum moosli (3 tblsp)
60 g punjabi moosli (3 tblsp)
60 g asaryo (3 tblsp)
60 g gokhroo (3 tblsp)
*3 whole nutmeg
1 tsp ganthora
375 g ghee (1½ cup)
90 g goondar (4 tblsp)
1 tsp pepper
30 g powdered elachi (1 tblsp)
125 g khus-khus (¾ cup)
250 g coconut (1½ cup)
*250 g almonds (1½ cup)
125 g char magaj (½ cup)
*250 g charoli (1 cup)
*125 g pista (½ cup)

1. Fry flour in ¼ of ghee. Put aside.
2. Fry goondar in 2 tablespoons of ghee till it melts and bubbles. Cool and it will become crisp. Pound fine in imam dasta (brass mortar).
3. Pound rest of dry ingredients excepting those marked with asterisk. Mix together.
4. Grate nutmeg fine and add to dry ingredients.
5. Grind the blanched almonds, pistachios and charoli.

In pot, put rest of ghee with the ghor and slowly allow to melt. Add all the flours, goondar, dry ingredients, almonds, etc. to ghee/ghor and simmer for 5 to 10 minutes. Continue cooking till ghee floats on top and sides. Pack in slightly greased thali. When cool cut in diamond shapes. Sprinkle top with slivered almonds and charoli.

Soova

This is a savoury that confining mothers partake after each meal. It is believed to regulate bowel movements, and aid baby in burping after being breast fed. Almonds are supposed to be good brain food and are added in most paaks and halwas.

60 g tandra (kernel of coriander)
250 g soova (1 cup)
125 g khus-khus (½ cup)
250 g coconut (preferably fresh)
250 g almonds
Black salt to taste (hancher)

Pick all ingredients clean. Scrape coconut and cut in wafers as for sookh mookh. Cut up almonds with their skins. Dampen each lot of ingredients in salted water (just enough to coat the salt on) and put in separate trays in slow oven till crisp. Do not darken in colour. Pack in bottle when cool and serve 2 teaspoons at a time, after meals.

Diabetes

Though no population group is immune from sugar diabetes, research has established that there is some link between rich fatty foods and incidence of diabetes. Two important causes seem to be heredity and obesity and there is a tendency for the diesease to develop during middle age. Those with a high standard of living, and lack of exercise seem to be especially prone to the disease and for this reason care taken with food intake will help greatly in preventing the disease.

Sweet and starchy foods help in getting you those ugly rolls of fat so food intake should concentrate on low-kilojoule (low calorie) and sugar-free foods. Good wholesome food, simply cooked and discipline in so far as overeating is concerned is the ideal. Sweets and cakes can be replaced by fresh fruit; fatty curries replaced by vegetables and fat-free meat grilled or cooked with minimum of fat and oil and high-protein foods must be included in every meal.

Karyatoo

People with diabetes drink a lot of bitter fluids made from ingredients such as bitter gourds (karelas), and methi seeds. Here we give you two recipes:

60 g karyata sticks
30 g under jav (1½ tblsp)
30 g kari jiri (1½ tblsp)
30 g ajmo (1½ tblsp)
30 g jeero (1½ tblsp)
4 only small array

After washing and cleaning ingredients, place in enamel saucepan and boil together with 2 litres of boiling water. Boil 5 to 10 minutes.

Remove from stove. Strain off ¼ glassful every morning and drink straight before breakfast.

Phaaki

60 g soova (3 tblsp)
60 g ajmo
60 g methi
60 g jeero
30 g hancher (black salt)
30 g senna leaves
30 g hing (asoefitaeda)
30 g array (harde)
60 g under jav.
1 small piece soonth (dry ginger)

Heat ingredients in slow oven till crisp. Pound coarsely and pack in bottle. Take 1 teaspoon at a time whenever necessary.

Methi Paak

125 g methi flour (½ cup)
250 g singhora flour (1 cup)
250 g coarsely ground almonds (1 cup)
125 g goondar
125 g dessicated coconut
4 tblsp aheryo (aseryo)
125 g sultanas (¾ cup)
500 g ghee (2 cups)
1 tsp javatri
1 tsp nutmeg
1 tsp salaum moosli
1 tsp gunthora
1 tsp pipper (not pepper)
2 tblsp gokharo
4 tblsp khus-khus
500 g ghor (1½ cups)

Braise singhora flour in little of ghee till light pink. Remove from heat.

Fry goondar in little ghee till they puff like rice crispies, drain off ghee, pound when cool.

In remaining ghee add ghor and soften till melting stage. Add methi, braised singhora, powdered Goondar, other flours and spices taking care to stir vigorously to prevent lumps. When well braised and mixed, remove from stove and cool.

Spread in shallow thali (pans) and allow to cool and set. Sprinkle liberally with slivered almonds and charoli, and cut in diamond shapes.

Note:
Methi Paak is a definite preventive against backache, so the old people say.

Ginger Paak

Made just before onset of winter. Prevention against colds.

250 g ginger
375 g ghor (1 1/8 cup)
60 g coarsely ground almonds (½ cup)
125 g dessicated coconut (2/3 cup)
60 g khus-khus (3 tblsp)
125 g blanched slivered almonds (6 tblsp)
60 g Charoli (3 tblsp)
250 g ghee (1 cup)

Scrape, wash and grind ginger through mincer. If a course texture is required then grate instead of mincing it.

Heat ghee and ghor and when ghor melts, add ginger, braise slowly till it is evenly browned and dry.

Add coconut, ground almonds, khus-khus and cook slowly for 15 minutes over low heat.

Cool and mould in golf ball-sized balls, rolling it well in charoli and slivered almonds.

Eat one ball with breakfast tea or coffee.

Poppy Seeds Halwa for Head Ache/Insomnia

250 g poppy seeds
3 litres milk
250 g misri (sugar candy)
250 ghee
150 g almonds
125 g pistachio nuts
60 g Elachi

Clean poppy seeds, wash and dry in sun. Pound them in mortar.

Pound separately the misri almond and pistachio.

Place milk, add to poppy seeds on stove and boil until thick. Add ghee and misri.

When dry, add ghee and misri.

Stir until completely dry.

Add almond, pistachio nuts, elachi and remove from heat.

One tblsp should be taken every morning (breakfast).

Goondar Paak

NOTE: If menstruating too frequently or unable to fall pregnant

125 g goondar
250 g misri
60 g white moosli
60 g almonds
60 g pista
30 g white pepper
30 g elachi
30 g gokhroo
½ cup dry coconut
2 cups ghee

Pound the above ingredients fine. Beat in ghee until frothy.

Grease lagan (round pan), pour mixture into it and place lagan in a pot of boiling water and steam for 2 hours.

Remove and cut into squares or diamond shapes.

Take 1 piece with a glass of milk for breakfast.

Soowa Methi

Mix a ¼ cup of soowa and a ¼ cup of methi. Leave in a warm oven for a few hours. Take a teaspon of this and infuse in a ¼ cup of boiling water. Strain through sieve and drink whilst still warm.

Ghor Papdi

3 cups unsifted brown flour
¾ cup cream of wheat
500 g ghor (1½ cups)
500 g ghee (2 cups)
1 tsp elachi powder
500 g almonds (ground with skins)
¼ cup milk

Braise flour in half of ghee till pale brown.

Braise cream of wheat in little of ghee till pale brown.

In remaining ghee melt ghor. Add above ingredients, stir vigorously and add almonds.

Braise over low heat, add milk and let it dry out. Set in shallow thali (pan) and cut in diamond shapes after sprinkling liberally with slivered almonds and charoli.

NOTE: Kuvaar paak is made at onset of winter as the labas are just well matured then. They are believed to prevent colds, strengthen joints as well as tone up muscle and health.

Kuvaar Paak (Aloes Halwa)

4,5 litre milk
500 g kharak
500 g almonds (ground)
60 g nutmeg (ground — 3 tblsp)
30 g elachi (fine — 1 tblsp)
125 g char magaj (ground)
Icing sugar to sweeten to taste
500 g labas (edible cacti)
250 g khus-khus (6 tblsp)
375 g singhora flour (1½ cup)
30 g javatri (ground — 1½ tblsp)
2 kg ghee (10 cups)

Soak Kharak in water overnight. Drain off water and mince.

Into milk add the washed, cleaned and sliced labas, the khus-khus and the kharak. Allow to come to boiling point, then simmer slowly and allow to thicken, stirring very often to prevent scorching. The mixture should be the consistency of thin cream.

Mix singhora flour in a cup of additional milk and stir in vigorously into pot of kuvaar seeing to it that it does not form lumps.

Add rest of ingredients and stir constantly and mix in.

Add ghee, stirring constantly till thick brown halwa results and ghee begins to float free. This is a sign that no moisture is retained which will cause halwa to deteriorate.

Kuvaar Paak with Mawa

4,5 litres milk
30 g elachi (1 tblsp)
500 g laaba (edible aloes — see glossary)
125 g sugar candy (saaker)
375 g singhora (1½ cup)
30 g saalum musli (1½ tblsp)
1 tsp array (or Harde)
1 kg ghee (5 cups)
½ dodhi
500 g kharak
500 g almonds (3 cups)
250 g gokhuroo
60 g khus-khus (3 tblsp)
Sugar to taste

Slowly boil 1 litre of milk and make mawa (see glossary). Soak kharak in water and when soft mince. Grate dodhi. Wash laabas and cut in pieces.

Put the remaining milk in a cauldron and slowly boil with the laabas, dodhi, khus-khus and kharak. Allow to simmer slowly and stir frequently in order to prevent scorching.

When the ingredients are well blended and the milk is like thin cream, add mashed mawa, singora flour and the remaining ingredients, excepting the ghee and the sweetenings. Stir vigorously till mixture thickens, and is smoothly blended.

Add well pounded sugar candy and enough sugar to taste. Stir till sweetenings have melted and blended in. Finally add ghee.

When paak is toffee brown in colour and the ghee starts to float to the surface of the pot, it is done.

Pomegranate Syrup
(FOR PILES)

1½ glass of water
1 pomegranate (seeds of)

Liquidise pomegranate and water, add sugar. Drink 3 times a day.
(The quantity is for 3 drinks).
The two parts can be left in the fridge until needed.
This should be done for seven days.

Heera Bor

Pound sufficient bor to fill 10 empty capsules (obtainable from chemists). Give a capsule each night before retiring. This is reported to be excellent for backaches.

The ancient method was to mix a pea-sized lump of bor into a teaspoon of honey in order to disguise the bitter taste.

Honey: wherein is Healing for Mankind

Even before he had domesticated animals and started agriculture, man had learnt to help himself from the hives of bees. This liquid gold is mentioned in all the Scriptures of mankind and the Quran has a whole chapter named after the bee. One of the verses read:

"And thy Lord inspired the bee, saying:
Choose thou habitation in the hills
and in the trees and in that which they hatch;
then eat of all fruits,
and follow the ways of thy Lord, made smooth (for thee).
There comes forth from their bellies a drink of diverse hues,
wherein is healing for mankind."

Unlike other food products, honey does not lose the potency of its vitamins. It keeps indefinitely. Honey found in tombs in Egypt though 3 300 years old was perfectly edible. The Greeks regarded it as a youth elixir. Pythagoras who loved honey developed a drink made of honey and milk which came to be known as ambrosia and he supplemented this with fruit, nuts and vegetables. He lived until he was ninety. Hippocrates ate honey every day and he prescribed it for those who wished to enjoy a healthy life. The Arabs who developed Greek (unani) medicine, used honey profusely in their elixirs.

Before the days of glucose, Muslims gave the new born babes a drop of honey in water and the loved one on the death bed would be speeded on his or her way with a last sip of honeyed water. For those that make their beauty packs at home, honey is indispensible.

A natural laxative, honey is assimilated in the blood stream within 20 minutes. It generates tremendous energy without shocking the system. Its therapeutic purposes are many and varied. High in mineral content, it is also a powerful germicide and it is capable of killing off any bacteria that may settle on it. Rich in vitamin C it acts as a sedative. For sore throats and for coughs it is a soothing medicine.

Taking its flavour from its environmental flora, honey comes in many colours, fragrances and flavours. Whether you like the delicate fragrance of orange blossoms, or the heady smell of the khakhi bush, may you use more and more honey in your culinary preparations. It's good healthy food.

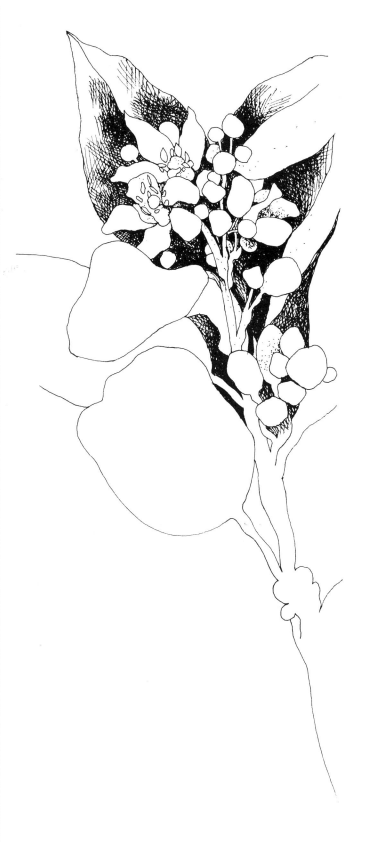

Laai
(ALMOND DRINK)

During convalescence and to help students through periods of intense studies, special foods are served. The almond has traditionally been considered to top the list of nutritious foods.

There is the amusing story of the elderly aunt in the family who was much concerned that the young bride of her favourite nephew was unable to conceive. Taking the matter in her capable hands, aunty began to send a jugful of delicious almond brew to the young couple's boudoir each evening.

The pale pallor of the bride soon gave way to a rosy hue and after some months the family doctor confirmed that the bride was pregnant.

Aunty asked the doctor to check her as well for she was undergoing some strange symptoms.

This the doctor did and pronounced aunty pregnant as well!

You see, before sending off the jug, aunty used to take a tumblerful for herself and uncle, and so she too had fallen prey to her own concoction!

Laai
(MILK DRINK FOR CONFINING MOTHERS)

½ tblsp ghee
1 tsp char magaj (ground)
1 tsp fresh coconut
A few pistachios and charoli
1 tblsp singhora flour
6 blanched almonds
1 tsp ghor
1 tsp aseryo

Braise singhora flour in ghee and just as it begins to change colour add ground nuts, coconut and ground char magaj.

Add a cup of water and simmer till slightly thickened.

Add ghor, a teaspoon of aheryo and enough milk to bring it to a thin porridge consistency.

Serve hot in soup bowl. Excellent for lactation and for soothing mother's nerves.

Brew for Confining Mothers

4 tblsp dry ginger powder
2 tblsp sugar candy
1 tblsp poppy seeds (ground)
1 tblsp ground almonds
1 tblsp aheryo (ground)
1 tsp salam musli punjabi
1 tsp salam musli (white)
2 tblsp singhora flour
2 tblsp slivered almonds
1 tblsp charoli
2 tblsp dessicated coconut

Mix all ingredients and pack in airtight bottles.

TO USE: Take one tblsp of ghee and one of ghor and slowly heat in pan till they melt and bubble, then mix in 3 tblsp of above mixture of powders. Take a tblsp of this mixture with breakfast every morning.

Soova Water

1 tsp soova
1 tsp methi
Boil in water. Strain and leave in covered container. Drink when required.

Methi Waters

Wash and clean 1 tablespoon methi seeds and immerse in a bowl of boiling water overnight. The next morning sieve water through strainer and drink it before breakfast.

Bruises and Sprains

Braise equal amounts of arad and brown sugar in a thick bottomed pan. Add a tablespoon of alum in this. Remove from fire and cool. Mix in beaten egg white. Paste over sprains or bruises. Cover with cotton wool and bandage.

HEALTH PARLOUR

Dhuwa
(STEAM/SMOKE DISINFECTANT)

In an age when the steam-bath, the hot poultice and the home compounded medicine played a major role, the dhuwa must have had its psychological and therapeutic value. We are in no way advocating a revival of this primitive method of administering a disinfectant, which has completely gone out of use. It is recorded here merely to amuse the reader.

In special type coal burner, sprinkle a tablespoon each of ajmo and lobaan over the hot coals. Place the burner under a chair from which the seat has been removed. Seat the patient on the frame of the chair and drape a blanket around her (for remember she has just had her daily bath and is unclothed). The fragrance and fumes will penetrate deeply and allow free running of menses. After 5 or 10 minutes give a good rub down, quickly clothe her warmly and tuck her into bed.

This particular dhuwa used to be given daily to all confining mothers, in order to speedily exorcise all menstrual impurities.

Naah
(INHALENTS)

For steaming out nasal and head colds, the old grannies swore that there was nothing better than a naah.

Plug the spout of a kettle or jug with thick wad of cotton wool wrapped in cloth. Add a lump of any mentholated balm (such as vicks vaporub, etc.) and pour sufficient boiling water to half fill the kettle. Close lid quickly and put the kettle on a table and cover it with a blanket.

Seat the patient on a chair and cover his head with edge of blanket. At frequent intervals patient is to open lid of kettle and inhale deeply of the medicated fumes. After 5 to 10 minutes of this put the patient to bed, keeping the head wrapped in a towel.

Eucalyptus Bath

Strip the leaves from a branch of the eucalyptus tree to fill a fair sized basin. Rinse the leaves and put them in the bath. Run in boiling water and fill the bath to two-thirds its capacity. Patient accompanied by an aide must strip in bathroom and when water has cooled down sufficiently he or she must sit in it. Hold a large towel or blanket over head of patient so that steam penetrates well. As soon as patient complains he must be taken out, given a quick and thorough rub down and put to bed with a warm drink.

Champi

Massaging is an art which the old aunties knew but too well. Unlike in Japan where this was always done by young maidens, the Indian masseurs were older. They knew how to loosen each digit of one's joints and remove all the aches. Even the imaginery ones! Many of them, whilst massaging could relate stories that the patients would remember ever afterwards.

The professional champi-wallahs would in their barefeet tread the backs of tired people and get them in a fighting mood in no time.

SECTION 11

Let us Talk of Health and Diet

Even though obesity may not be a problem, everyone is or should be concerned with keeping a trim figure. It not only looks well but feels good to cut a neat and trim figure.

Owing to daily stress, diseases such as hypertension and coronaries are raising their ugly heads in the Indian community just as they have amongst all urban societies. Added to this is the hereditary factor of diabetes amongst Indians which can be alarmingly aggravated with the wrong types of food.

This is in no way intended to be a guide for those affected with the above diseases but our contention is, that one can retain a slim and healthy figure on a strictly Indian diet, provided of course that common sense is allowed to prevail and certain factors given due concern.

Fats, Oil and Ghee: That Indians are not fond of fatty meats, is a blessing and it is a pity that this should be nullified by a larger intake of ghee and oil.

In recent years, most Indians in South Africa have cut down their ghee intake by 75% or more. Some families have cut it out altogether, preferring the use of sunflower oil. I would seriously suggest that they further cut down the amount of oil used in daily cooking and this can so easily be done without affecting the taste or attractiveness of their dishes.

(a) Measure out the oil used in any cooking carefully, with a spoon instead of measuring with the eye or instinct as is the habit of all experienced cooks. You will be surprised to discover just how much extra you have been using.

(b) Depend more and more on your oven to do your cooking. For some years now, I have done all my kabaab dishes, potroasts (kurma, pasinda, kalya, etc.) fried chicken, chops and fish in the oven. You will agree that frying fish in a pan on top of the stove can be a messy task and that it calls for a fair amount of oil to fry the fish in. It is the same with kabaabs. So instead of frying, place masalaad fish or kabaabs in a deep, slightly greased oven tray,

cover with foil and bake, removing the foil just five minutes or so before serving time. Pour a tablespoon of oil over the contents and allow to brown well on all sides. You not only have attractive and tasty kabaabs and fish but have in the process saved well over a cup of oil.

(c) Supplement your diet with heaps of salad, fresh fruit, drinks and desserts assembled from fresh fruit and vegetables. Your family will look forward to your salads if they resemble those in the colour picture on page 308.

(d) Be constantly on the alert when handling oils. Try and economise in every dish so that soon the family will accustom itself to a less fatty diet.

While the above hints may not assure one the figure of a model, nor perhaps the muscular physique of an athlete, they will be an aid towards curbing alarming tendencies. Although it is considerably influenced by hereditary characteristics, let us face it — obesity is the product of overeating. Here it is important to make a distinction between overweight and muscular development. Whereas the former is a result of over-indulgence, the latter depends upon regular exercise.

How then does one reduce weight? Unfortunately there is no magic pill that will melt away unwanted fat and the only safe method is by strict dieting and selective eating. Heat energy is released when food is digested and this is expressed in units of CALORIES/KILOJOULES. A person doing sedentary work requires about 2 000 calories a day. On a thousand calories, such a person will lose as much as a pound a day, during the first week of dieting and thereafter half a pound a day. After a month of dieting, the calory intake must be brought back to normal, and provided that the rules of selection and preparation of foods are observed, it will be seen that the weight will stabilise itself. One important factor to remember is that the caloric value of fat is 9, whereas that of starch (carbohydrates) is 4. The list at the end, will give some conception of the dangerously high caloric value of some foods.

CALORIES TABLE

Name	Qty	Calories	Kilojoules
Milk	1 cup	160	670
Milk skimmed	1 cup	80	330
Butter milk	1 cup	80	330
Yoghurt plain	1 cup	90	375
Cottage cheese	1½ tblsp	30	125

Eggs

Name	Qty	Calories	Kilojoules
Fried	1	135	565
Omelette	1	110	460
Poached or boiled	1	75	335

Juice and Drinks

Name	Qty	Calories	Kilojoules
Cold drink (bottled)	1 glass	100	450
Milk shakes	1 glass	180	680
Lemon juice (fresh)	1 glass	20	90
Orange juice (fresh)	1 glass	320	
Fresh juice punch	1 glass	75	320

Fats

Name	Qty	Calories	Kilojoules
Ghee	1 tblsp	140	585
Veg oil	1 tblsp	120	440
Butter	1 tblsp	110	420

Fresh Fruits

Name	Qty	Calories	Kilojoules
Apple	1	40	165
Apricot	1	20	
Grapes	1 small bunch	100	250
Cherry plum etc	½ cup	40	
Litchis	1	10	40
Peaches	1	50	210
Orange	1	40	165
Mangoes	1 medium	100	420
Melons	1 slice	50	

Vegetables

Name	Qty	Raw	Cooked Cal
Spinach, methi	1 cup	25	50
Beetroot	2 large	55	
Bhindha	1 cup	35	60
Brinjal	1 med	15	25
Beans	1 cup	80	90
Potato	1 cup	90	110
Pumpkin	½ cup	40	50
Karela	½ cup	25	35
Peas	½ cup	40	
Tomato	1 medium	20	
Lettuce	1 cup	12	

Meat & Fish

Meat & Fish	Boiled cal.	kiloj	Curried or Fried cal.	kiloj.
1 portion fish (120g)	110	460	240	1000
Mutton chop (100g)	450	1760		
Chicken 1 leg & 1 thigh	220	900	350	1470
Prawns or sea foods (3 large)	100	430	230	900
Beef grilled steak (100g)	300	1255		
Rice boiled (100g)	120	500		

Indian Snacks

Indian Snacks	Qty	Cal.	Kiloj.
Bhajiahs or chilli bites	1 cup	250	1000
Bhajias Moong Dhal or Wadde	6 med	250	1000
Kachori	40g	250	1000
Puri	1 med	150	630
Dokras or Moothias	4 (40g)	250	1000
Cutlets (mince)	2	300	1260
Sheesh Kabaab	2	300	1260
Kabaabs in curry	2	350	1470
Samoosas	2 large	150	630
Rotis with ghee	1 med	150	630

Sweets

Sweets	Qty	Cal.	Kiloj.
1 Laddoo	40 g	250	1000
Masoor	40 g	220	920
Ras Malaai	40 g	250	1000
Halwa Badam	40 g	250	1000
Halwa carrot or dodhi	1 cup	300	1260
Dodhi or coconut lagans	1/3 cup	250	1000
Burfee with klim	30 g	200	900
Burfee with fresh milk mawa	30 g	250	1000
Jalebi	40 g	200	900
Gulab jambun	40 g	250	1000
Potato or veg chops	60 g	150	630
Kheer	½ cup	300	1260
Sev soji etc	½ cup	300	1260
Ice cream	½ cup (1 por.)	180	680
Shrikhand	1 cup	240	985
Bread pudding	1/3 cup	100	420

NOTE: A healthy diet consists of between 4 200-5 000 kilojoules.

SECTION 11A

Ice Cream Fruit Juices and Punches

In South Africa, with its semi-tropical climate and the many varieties of fruit obtainable throughout the year, it is a pity that more use is not made of the fruit for refreshing drinks. We give you a few basic recipes but hope that you will experiment with different fruits and obtain heady flavours each time.

Fruit should always be pulverised in a liquidiser or juices extracted in a juice extractor. Either gives wonderful results. Clean and cut fruits to convenient size and put into liquidiser with sufficient water to make a fine textured juice.

The best results are obtained when oranges or pineapples are used as a base. At least one (but preferably more) lemon should be used to bind the flavours. Salt acts as a preservative and should always be included. Sugar is the best sweetening agent.

Decree of Shah Tahmass
(16TH CENTURY)

Upon the arrival of the royal guest, let him drink fine sherbets of lemon and rosewater, cooled with snow; then serve him preserves of apple, watermelon, grapes and apricots, with white bread. Prepare each drink with sweet attars and ambergis, and for each day of his stay prepare a banquet of 500 rare and appetising dishes. O my son, on the day of the Royal guest's arrival, give a feast tremendous, of meats and sweetmeats, milk and fruits to the count of 2 000 trays.

Bounty of the Land

Blessed indeed is the Republic in that such a variety of fruit is available throughout the year. Though there is little indigenous to it, with the exception of some types of wildberries, its history of fruit introduction and cultivation could fill many books.

From the early days when the Cape was founded as a half-way house to the East, fresh vegetables were grown to supply the ships. The French Huguenots brought their knowledge of viticulture, and with the contribution of the Dutch and English Settlers, the slopes and valleys of the Cape mountains were soon transformed into orchards laden with the fruit of the Cool Temperate and Mediterranean climates of Europe.

To this was added the knowlege of the Malay and Batavian slaves of tropical fruit, and different techniques of preserving fruit, resulting in such exotic fare as Mebos and cooking in vine leaves.

On the East Coast, with the arrival of the Indians from India, the care of the sugar plantations, the orchards of banana and litchi, the fields of pineapple, the mango and tamarind groves, were tended to with a zest and love that assured the permanent stay of these hard-working people.

As a result of the sweat and love of so many diverse peoples there is available today an abundance of fruit of many varieties. Apricot, peach, pear, orange, fig, grape, cantaloupe, melon, litchi, mango, cherry — the choice is great.

There are several reasons why we advocate that instead of rich and costly desserts, the South African housewife must introduce more fruit to her table. Whole, sectioned, attractively arranged in salads, accompanied by fresh cream and ice cream, with a little planning the home-maker can serve a different fruit dessert each week of the year.

A Salad as a meal

An attractive plate of salad is most welcome on hot days. From the platters arranged here, the homemaker will be able to serve an endless variety of salads to appease her family. It will be seen that practically anything can be incorporated into a salad. All types of salad greens, chunks, balls and wedges of melons, citrus sections, pickled vegetables, onions and olives, seafoods and meat left over from last night's repast, slices of cold meat, cutlets or polony, chunks of cheese, or boiled eggs — all these blend beautifully into a colourful salad. To lend further distinction one can utilise pastry and choux cases, rings of fried bread or scooped-out halves of pineapples, melons and baby cantaloupes.

Fruit Juice (PHOTO 239)

6 oranges
2 lemons
1 pineapple
1 tsp salt
4 tblsp sugar (more or less as desired)

Squeeze out juice from citrus. Pulverize pineapple with 2 cups of water. Mix altogether after straining citrus. (It will hardly be necessary to strain juice from liquidiser since it pulverises so smoothly). Add salt and sugar and enough water to make a juice the consistency of soft drinks.

NOTE:
Do not throw away pineapple skins — but wash them and soak in a litre of water overnight. Strain them. Use this water in your juice.

CAUTION:
Fresh fruit drinks must be made daily. They will not keep unless you bottle them with a benzoic acid or other preserving agents.

Serve ice cold in tall glasses garnished with sprigs of mint, thin slices of orange or with floating pieces of pineapple, strawberries or any type of fruit used.

VARIATIONS OF FRUIT JUICES AND PUNCHES:

(1) To the basic recipe add ¼ waterlemon, pulverizing it fine. This makes a lovely rose colour. Always add more lemons when using extra fruit.

(2) Use half of sweet or musk melon to basic recipe.
(3) Half cup of slightly crushed strawberries or cut in eighths.

(4) Add ½ dozen grenadillas to basic recipe then sieve through strainer and add pulp to juice, or use pulp straight without straining.

(5) Skinned grapes, pears, peaches, apricots, mangoes or any suitable fruit can be added to basic recipe. Remember to add more lemons, salt and sugar for extra fruits used. Some types of fruit, like pears, lack tanginess and will require more lemons and salt. Apples, especially the green types are delicious.

Fruit Punches

(1) To basic fruit juice recipe add a bottle or two of soda water. This makes a softer drink. Soda water or other minerals used must be added just before serving.

(2) Add a bottle or two of ginger ale, and there will be more punch and kick in the flavour. Combinations of both soda water and ginger ale will give another variation.

(3) Old tea well strained (without milk of course) may be added.

Spiced Orange Drink

2 cups orange juice
5 whole cloves
1 tsp orange rind
2 tblsp honey
1 small stick cinnamon
additional sugar if necessary

Put ingredients in enamel pot and bring to boil. Simmer for 5 minutes, with pot covered. Sieve through gauze or a fine sieve.

Cut an orange in thin rings and push the cooked cloves through each ring after twisting it into an attractive shape. Garnish each glass with a twist of orange.

Serve either hot or cold.

Lemon Sherbet

½ cup fresh lemon juice
¾ cup sugar (adjust to taste)
1½ cups water
1 egg white

Boil sugar and water till sugar dissolves and water slightly syrupy. Cool and add lemon juice. Freeze till mixture is mushy. Beat egg white till stiff and fold in mushy lemon syrup. (Serve in crystal goblets).

Lime Juice

3 limes (unpeeled)
Sugar to taste
1 litre water (iced)
½ tsp salt

Wash lemons, cut in pieces, remove pits and put in liquidiser with all other ingredients. When blended fine, sieve. Adjust sugar and serve ice cold.

Grape Juice Punch

2 kg purple grapes (2 kgs)
½ litre water
Juice of 3 lemons
1 bottle gingerale
250 g sugar (1 cup)

Wash and de-stalk grapes. Put in liquidiser for just a minute till the grapes are broken. Sieve through a wire sieve, to remove seeds and return pulp to liquidiser. Blend smooth. Make syrup with sugar and water. Cool and add lemon and grape juice. Just before serving add gingerale. Taste for sweetness.

Pomegranate Juice

6 pomegranates
Cut in halves, remove filaments and extract seeds. Put seeds in liquidiser with just sufficient water to cover. Switch on for just a few seconds so that seeds do not get pulverized. Sieve through fine mesh. Add juice of 2 lemons.

Sufficient sugar to sweeten
1 tsp of salt
Mix well and chill thoroughly. Serve over crushed ice. Serve in crystal glasses with a grinding of black crushed pepper.

Fresh Lemonade
(6 GLASSES)

3 lemons or limes
750ml water
110g castor sugar
Scrub fruit clean. Cut in halves and express juice. Keep halves in a clean bowl and sprinkle sugar over them.

Boil water and pour over halves. Stir till sugar well dissolved.

When cold, strain through sieve and add juice to water. Chill thoroughly.

Mango Juice

Peel 6 ripe mangoes, slice off pulp and put in liquidiser. Add ¼ cup milk and sufficient condensed milk to sweeten. Pulverise smooth and strain through a sieve. Thin down juice with more milk to consistency of thin cream. Delicious with boiled vermicelli or served iced in tall glasses.

ALTERNATIVE:
Instead of milk, add ½ cup orange juice and sweeten with sugar.

Quince Sherbet

3 Quinces
1 litre water
2½ to 3 cups sugar
¼ cup lemon juice
1 tsp salt
Peel quinces, remove pith and seeds.
With half of water put into liquidiser and blend fine. Sieve through and discard pulp. Put rest of water and sugar on stove and boil till sugar dissolved. Add quince liquid, lemon juice and salt to pot and simmer for 5 minutes. Bottle when cool. Serve ice cold diluted with water if too tangy.

Kokum Sherbet

The sour fruit known as kokum can also be used for flavourings. Take a cup of kokum and cut into small pieces. Add ¾ cup sugar, mix well and keep in air-tight bottle for about 15 days before it starts to become syrupy. Can be used as spread on bread or as chutney.

P.S. Dried apricots can be used instead of kokum.

Saumnf Tea

2 tsp saunmf (fennel)
Sugar to taste
2 cups strong black tea
Milk (optional)
Boil fennel seeds in a cupful of water. Make strong black tea and strain saunmf liquid into it. Add sugar to taste and milk if liked. May be served hot or ice cold.

Masala for Tea

125 g Ganthora
60 g dry ginger
30 g cinnamon
30 g cloves
15 g elachi
30 g black elcha (optional)
Roast all ingredients in oven till strong aroma arises. Grind into very fine powder. Cool and pack in air tight bottle.

The Rose in Eastern Folk-Lore

Tradition reports that the Prophet Muhammad's favourite flower was the rose, and that his favourite attar was extracted from roses; His friend and disciple Salman, who was a convert from Zoroastrianism, cultivated many strains of roses in his garden at Medina.

On joyous occasions such as the celebrating of engagements, or at religious festivals, the serving of sherbet milk is a must. Introduced into India by Persians and Arabs it is much loved by the Indians. Of all the classic sherbets, the one made from Gulaab (which is the Indian term for the rose) is the one best loved. In fact, sherbet is more or less a synonymous term for a drink in which rose water or rose essence has been added.

At banquets, Indians often welcome guests by sprinkling over their hands water perfumed with attar of roses. After the repast such water is again poured over the guest's hands.

Rose petals are profusely used to decorate sweets and desserts, and rose petals are also candied; Again fresh rose petals are often inserted in between pages of the Quran or other religious literature in order to keep the pages delicately perfumed.

Gulaab Syrup
(SYRUP OF ROSES)

Petals of 20 full blown roses (dark red or dark pink)
3 lemons
1 litre water
Rose colouring
1 kg sugar
1 tblsp milk

Wash rose petals in running water. Put in deep glass bowl and pour juice of 2 lemons over them. Steep overnight. In morning crush petals and put through wire strainer, and extract maximum liquid. Alternately put in liquidizer and strain through muslin. Put aside.

Put sugar and water on stove and stir till sugar has dissolved. Add juice of one lemon and milk to absorb scum. When syrup begins to spin thread, add the essence of roses and boil once to infuse properly. Remove from fire, add colouring and cool. Bottle tightly. A tablespoon of this in a glass of milk makes a delicious rose milk shake.

Syrup For Ramadaan

10 cups sugar
1 tblsp lemon juice
1 bottle rose water (30ml)
2½ litres water
1 pinch citric acid
1/3 bottle jelly red colouring

Add sugar to water and dissolve by stirring well. Put on stove to boil. Just as it comes to boil, add the juice of lemon in middle of pot. Allow to boil but do not stir at all. Scum will be seen rising to the surface of the water, which must be carefully skimmed off. Add citric acid and allow to boil till syrupy but not thick. Cool. Add colouring and rose water and fill in bottles.

Ramadaan Sherbet
(VARIATION)

5 cups sugar
1 litre water
1 bottle jelly red colouring (30 ml)
1 bottle rose water (30 ml)
1 tsp elachi powder (cardomom)

Soak sugar overnight in water. In morning boil over high heat and keep simmering fairly rapidly for ½ an hour. Add colouring and rose essence. Bottle when cool.

NOTE: All the sherbet recipes can be used for green coloured or orange coloured sherbets.

For green add green colouring till desired shade is acquired and flavour with peppermint essence.

For orange coloured sherbet tint with egg yellow and a drop of jelly red colouring for the required shade. Flavour with vanilla essence and elachi.

Gulkhand
(ROSE SYRUP)

Collect rose petals in early morning or late evening.

Place in air-tight container and when an inch deep sprinkle with sugar and a dash of salt.

Continue this way till at least three or four layers have been formed.

On no account must the petals be stirred.

Moisture will collect and gulkhand (rose-sugar) will form, after 10 days.

This very aromatic flavouring will be ready for use in tea, puddings, etc. Use only ½ teaspoon in a litre of milk.

Bottled Syrup

(VARIATION)

For use with milk drinks, falooda etc.

6 cups sugar
1 litre (5 cups) water
Red colouring (1/3 bottle)
1 lemon (optional)
1 ½ tsp fine elachi
1 tsp rose water

Cut lemon in halves, and add to pot with sugar and water. Mix well together and leave overnight. Put to boil in the morning and boil for just 5 minutes. Cool, add flavourings and tint a lovely sherbet colour with red colouring. Pack in bottles for use as required.

Falooda Crush

1 litre milk
2 pints milk (1 litre)
¼ cup slivered almonds
1 cup ice cream
2 tblsp falooda (prepared)
1 tbls slivered pistachios
Rose syrup

To prepare Falooda: Dissolve 2 tblsp of corn flour in ¼ cup water. Blend till smooth. Put a cup of water on stove to boil and slowly heat to avoid lumping and cook till thick. When mixture begins to take on translucent appearance it is done. Remove from stove and force through sevia machine which has been placed over a basin of cold water. Thin vermicelli-like strings will result. Leave in cold water and use when required.

In tall glasses put a tablespoon of ice cream, add helping of falooda, fill ¾ of glass with sweetened milk, top with ice cream and nuts and pour a little rose syrup so that it trickles down the sides. If desired a few falooda seeds may be added over falooda.

Falooda Milk Shake

Boil 1 tablespoon of agar agar powder in 1 cup of water till thick. Strain and allow to set till firm like jelly. If preferred this may be tinted to a light pink colour before setting but the white transparent ghaas or jelly, does look attractive enough.

Meanwhile soak 2 teaspoons of tookmaria seeds (falooda seeds) in a little water. Strain. For each glass of milk shake required, add 2 teaspoons of finely grated falooda jelly and a little of seeds. Sweeten with sugar, add rose water and add a dash of light pink colour.

CAUTION:

Use tint and colouring very sparingly since light ice cream shades are not only attractive but also look cool.

Dodhi Milk

1 litre milk
1 tblsp custard powder
¾ cup grated dodhi
Elachi and sugar to taste

Liquidise milk and dodhi. Boil milk and dodhi slowly and keep simmering for 20 mins. Add sugar to taste. Meanwhile whisk custard powder in a tablespoon of cold milk. Add to dodhi/milk and boil for a minute. Stir well in order to avoid lumps.

When cool, add vanilla or elachi and keep in fridge (consistency of milk shake). This is a delicious and refreshing drink. Tint a pale green in colour.

Carrot Milk

Using the same method as above but substituting carrot for dodhi, will give a delicious variation. Tint pale pink in colour.

Eid Milk Drink

As served on Eid Mornings. Delicious for invalids.

1 litre milk
Sugar to taste
4 kharak
1½ tblsp vermicelli (extra fine)
2 tsp coconut
2 tblsp nuts (slivered almonds, pistachios and charoli)
Elachi for flavouring

Sliver kharak fine. Break vermicelli in small pieces. Put milk to boil, and add sev and kharak and simmer over low heat till vermicelli is cooked. Add coconut, nuts, sugar and flavouring and serve in porridge bowls.

Honey/Milk

1½ cups milk
Dash of grated nutmeg or elachi
1 tblsp honey

Bring milk to boil. Remove from fire and stir in honey. Chill. Serve in glasses with a little grated flavouring of nutmeg or elachi on top. Both refreshing and nutritious.

Lassi (PHOTO PAGE 239)

1 cup curds (sour milk curds)
½ tsp jeero
Dash of pepper (black crushed)
Salt to taste

Roast jeero and crush fine. Whip up curds until mixture is smooth and add crushed ice and water to consistency preferred. Add pepper and salt and serve cold in glasses.

Kahwa

4 litres milk
½ cup rice
1 tin condensed milk (397g)
2 tins Nestles cream (if preferred use 1 tin cream only.
   Each tin to weigh 155g)
1 tsp elachi
90g almonds
1/3 cup sugar

Soak rice for 3 hours in cold water. Put milk to boil slowly. Lower rice which has been tied in a muslin bag into the milk and cook slowly, till milk is consistency of very thin cream (3 hours). Bag must be loosely tied to allow for swelling of rice grains.

Meanwhile, blanch almonds and grind or liquidize find. Add almonds to milk an hour before serving. Add tinned milk, sugar and flavourings at same time. Serve hot.

Fruity Falooda (PHOTO PAGE 239)

2 cups of fresh fruit juice such as apricot nectar,
   orange etc.
1 litre milk
2 tblsp honey
2 egg yolks
additional sugar to taste

Fruit of choice such as a banana, strawberries, canned peaches, apricots, pears etc; in event of canned fruit being used, then the syryp must be used and the honey and sugar omitted. Pulverize and blend all ingredients at high speed in blender. Serve cold. This is an excellent and nourishing drink in summer.

Strawberry Ice-Cream Mush

4 cups sliced strawberries (or mangoes, crushed pineapple or other fruit of choice, suitably sweetened)
2 tblsp castor sugar
3 egg whites
1 small carton cream (125ml)
1 litre ice cream (vanilla)

Wash fruit. Slice and drain if too watery. Sprinkle castor sugar using just enough to sweeten fruit.

Chill in fridge. Thaw ice cream slightly (just enough to soften but not to melt). Meanwhile beat cream till thick. Beat egg whites stiff.

Mix ice cream and cream and fold in egg whites.

Lastly fold in the strawberries and pour mixture in oiled moulds or containers.

Seal with plastic wrap or foil and freeze if required for later, in which instance it will have to be thawed before-hand.

If needed immediately, place in freezer for about 20 minutes. Serve after decorating top with a few whole strawberries.

Laai
(ALMOND DRINK)

½ litre milk (2½ cups)
3 tsp ground almonds
Sugar
Elachi

Boil almonds in milk till it is blended in. Add sugar and elachi. Drink as a hot milk beverage.

Ice-Cream
(KULFI)

Originally a Chinese discovery. The Arabs and Persians introduced it into the Middle East and Marco Polo to the Italians.

Not for us the plain vanilla ice creams. In India the ice creams are sometimes even dressed up in gold or silver paper, rendered edible, but we here in South Africa, unable to afford such luxuries, have to be satisfied with more modified forms.

Ice cream made in the old fashioned hand cranked tubs has a flavour all its own. Whilst every housewife will have her own prized recipe, here are some of ours.

Quantities given are to be made in 4 litre tubs.
CAUTION:
Hand cranked tubs require that the ice be well packed with salt which increases freezing capacity of ice. The bottom of outer circle of tub must be well packed with salt, then the ice packed with a layer or two of salt in between and the top again covered with salt. (Coarse salt naturally).

Ice Cream
(SERVES 20 PERSONS)

4 litres milk
2 tblsp custard powder
1 tsp elachi (powdered cardomom)
2 small cans of cream or 500ml fresh cream
3 egg yolks
1 tsp vanilla essence
2 tins condensed milk

Bring milk to boil. Beat egg yolks and custard powder in a little cold milk. Flavour with elachi and vanilla and make a custard just as milk comes to boil.

Switch off heat and as soon as mixture is consistency of fresh cream, add the condensed milk.

If mixture is not sweet enough, use extra sugar. Strain milk mixture into ice cream tub when cold to remove any lumps.

Finally add cream and beat with egg beater to distribute it evenly. Pack into tub and crank as usual.

Variation Ice Cream

2 litres milk
½ cup sev (extra fine vermicelli)

Simmer sev slowly in milk for ½ an hour. Then liquidise very fine. Add flavourings such as elachi and vanilla. Sweeten with condensed milk. Crank in tub.

Vanilla/Almond Ice Cream

2 LITRE QUANTITY

2 Litres fresh milk
1 tin cream
Enough condensed milk to sweeten
1 tsp vanilla essence
1 tblsp custard powder
1 tblsp maizena
¼ lb ground almonds (optional)

Heat milk to boiling point then immediately remove from stove. Add the custard and maizena previously mixed into a paste with a little cold milk, to the hot milk and stir vigorously (but do not cook) in order to avoid lumps.

To hot custard add condensed milk. Cool custard, then add cream and vanilla. Pour into ice cream tub. Pack outer circle well with salt then crank till ice cream is firm. Leave in the tub fifteen minutes longer before serving.

VARIATIONS:

NOTE: Read variation 4 first before adding any fresh fruit.

(1) One tablespoon coffee essence. Mix with custard into paste. Then add to rest of ingredients.

(2) One tablespoon granadilla. (Strain pulp of granadilla till no pits remain). ½ tsp lemon juice. Add to rest of ingredients.

(3) Two trays strawberries. Mash with little sugar. Then add to milk.

(4) Any fresh fruit which will not curdle milk may be pureed and added to ice cream milk to give distinguished flavours. After addition of fruits, taste the milk and if more sugar is required then sweeten with condensed milk.

(5) Make a kheer from 2 tablespoons rice boiled in 1 cup of milk till it is thick. Puree the rice through strainer and add to other ingredients.

(6) Half cup of any fresh or canned fruit. Fruit must be pureed fine before adding.

(7) Quarter cup of crushed cashew nuts (roasted first).

(8) Quarter cup of any such nuts, as walnuts or pecan nuts.

(9) 1 Cup finely blended avocado pulp.

Kulfi (Ice Cream)

2 litres milk
1½ tblsp corn flour
½ tin condensed milk
½ cup almonds
½ cup pistachios
1 tsp ground elachi (cardomom)
sugar to taste

Blanch almonds and pistachios separately.

Liquidise almonds very fine in ½ a cup of milk. Grind Pistachios coarsely.

Meanwhile boil milk gently on stove till it thickens (like thin cream).

Mix corn flour in a little cold milk and add to pot of boiling milk. Stir vigorously until a thin custard forms.

Now add nuts and flavourings and simmer for a few minutes — remove from heat, cover pot and allow to cool.

Pour in kulfi tins and freeze. Unmould when required.

Note: This mixture can be used in ice cream tubs as well.

Section 12

Sweets and Desserts

(HALWAS, MITHAI, LAGAN AND OTHERS)

The piece de resistance to any meal in any part of the world is the dessert and here the housewife spares no effort and energy in the preparation of it. Traditionally Indians serve a sweet at the beginning of a meal as a gesture of goodwill. Nowadays this custom is not prevalent, and the sweet dish is served at the end of the meal as the Indian hostess endeavours to lull the most voracious of appetites into quiet appreciation, and to placate the sweet toothed ones by making them rember the classic adage "May its sweet taste linger in your back teeth and memory for a long time to come."

There are a great variety of Indian sweets and desserts, and the profuse use of rice, vermicelli, crushed and ground wheat, milk, and a host of other ingredients ensures a wide range. Western sweet dishes are great favourites at Indian tables.

Halwas and lagans can be called the equivalent of western puddings. The ingredients used, decide whether it is palatable fare for every day use, or a creation fit to be served to royalty.

The Mithais may be compared to fudge but strictly speaking there can be no comparison as there is a great difference between mithai and fudge. For many years the professional mithai makers remained the doyen of this art in South Africa, but nowadays housewives make varieties at home, and some supplement the family income by making and selling mithai. The results are out of this world and here we give you a few prized recipes. If they do entail a lot of work, it will soon be forgotten when you see your family drooling when the results appear on the table.

Kheer
(THICK RICE PUDDING)

1½ litres milk (8 cups)
1/3 cup rice
2 tblsp coconut
1 tblsp slivered blanched almonds
1 tblsp charoli
1 tsp fine elachi
1 tsp rose water (optional)
Sugar to taste

Soak rice in cold water for about 30 min.

Bring milk to boiling point and add rice. Lower heat and simmer very slowly till rice is cooked and milk is consistency of thin porridge. Add coconut, nuts and flavourings and sweeten to taste.

CAUTION:

After addition of sugar, care must be taken that kheer does not scorch. Serve hot in bowls.

Kheer in Spanspek
(MUSKMELON AND RICE PUDDING)

2 baby spanspek (orange colour melons with rough skin)
1 litre milk
2 tblsp sultanas
¼ tsp elachi (cardomom powder)
½ cup water
1½ tblsp thick variety rice
2 tblsp slivered almonds
3 tblsp sugar or condensed milk to sweeten

Serves 8.

Soak rice in cold water for a few hours. Drain off water and crush rice coarsely in mortar. Cook this broken rice gently in half a cup of water and the milk. When soft, add sugar and allow to simmer slowly till the mixture is mushy.

During last stages there will have to be frequent stirring of pot to avoid scorching. Add sultanas and flavouring and just a drop of jelly red colouring to tint the kheer to the colour of the spanspek.

Cut spanspek into halves or quarters (depending on size of individual serving). Remove seeds and chill in fridge till required. Allow the kheer to cool. Into each portion of melon scoop a generous amount of kheer, sprinkle with slivered almonds and serve.

NOTE: Often spanspeks are not sweet enough and the family refuse to eat them. Served with kheer they will be most popular.

If using sweet melons (small green variety) instead of spanspek then tint the kheer with a drop of green colouring. Decorate with slivered pistachios instead.

Gajrella
(CARROT/RICE PUDDING)

1½ litre milk
½ kg grated carrot
1 tin nestles cream
pista and almonds
½ cup rice (soak in water for an hour)
elachi
rose water
sugar or condensed milk for sweetening

Boil milk, add washed rice and simmer for ½ an hour. Now add finely grated carrot and cook slowly till thick and mushy (2 hrs.). Add cream and flavourings and sweeten with condensed milk or sugar. Decorate with slivered pista and almonds.

Dodhi Falooda (DODHELI)
(MARROW MILK PUDDING)

1/8 tsp fine cardomom (elachi)
1 litre milk
1 cup of grated dodhi (Indian marrow)
1 level tsp falooda powder
a drop of green colouring
1 tblsp custard powder

For fine consistency the dodhi should be pulverised in a blender but take care that it is still visible. Put milk on stove and add dodhi just as it comes to boil. simmer very slowly till dodhi is cooked, meanwhile.

Mix the falooda (China Grass) powder in a tablespoon of cold milk and add to the pot and continue simmering till milk is like cream. Mix custard powder in 2 tblsp of cold milk and add to simmering falooda. Sweeten with condensed milk. Add elachi and cool.

Tint with green colouring to a pale green colour. Pour gently in individual dessert bowls (or large one for family) and refrigerate till set. Decorate with slivered pistachios.

VARIATIONS:

Instead of dodhi use finely grated carrots. In this case tint with a drop of egg yellow and a drop of jelly red colouring, to give the desired carroty colour. Decorate with blanched almonds.

Strawberry Falooda

Boil milk till creamy. Add falooda powder and custard and when milk is like thin cream remove from heat and allow to cool. Beat the milk till frothy then add a cup of washed, cut and crushed strawberries. Use a few drops of strawberry essence and pile strawberry/milk into bowl to set.

NOTE: Any fresh fruit like mangoes, apples, peaches, etc. can be used instead of strawberries. It gives the falooda a more piquant taste. But remember that fruit pulp must be added after custard has cooled down.

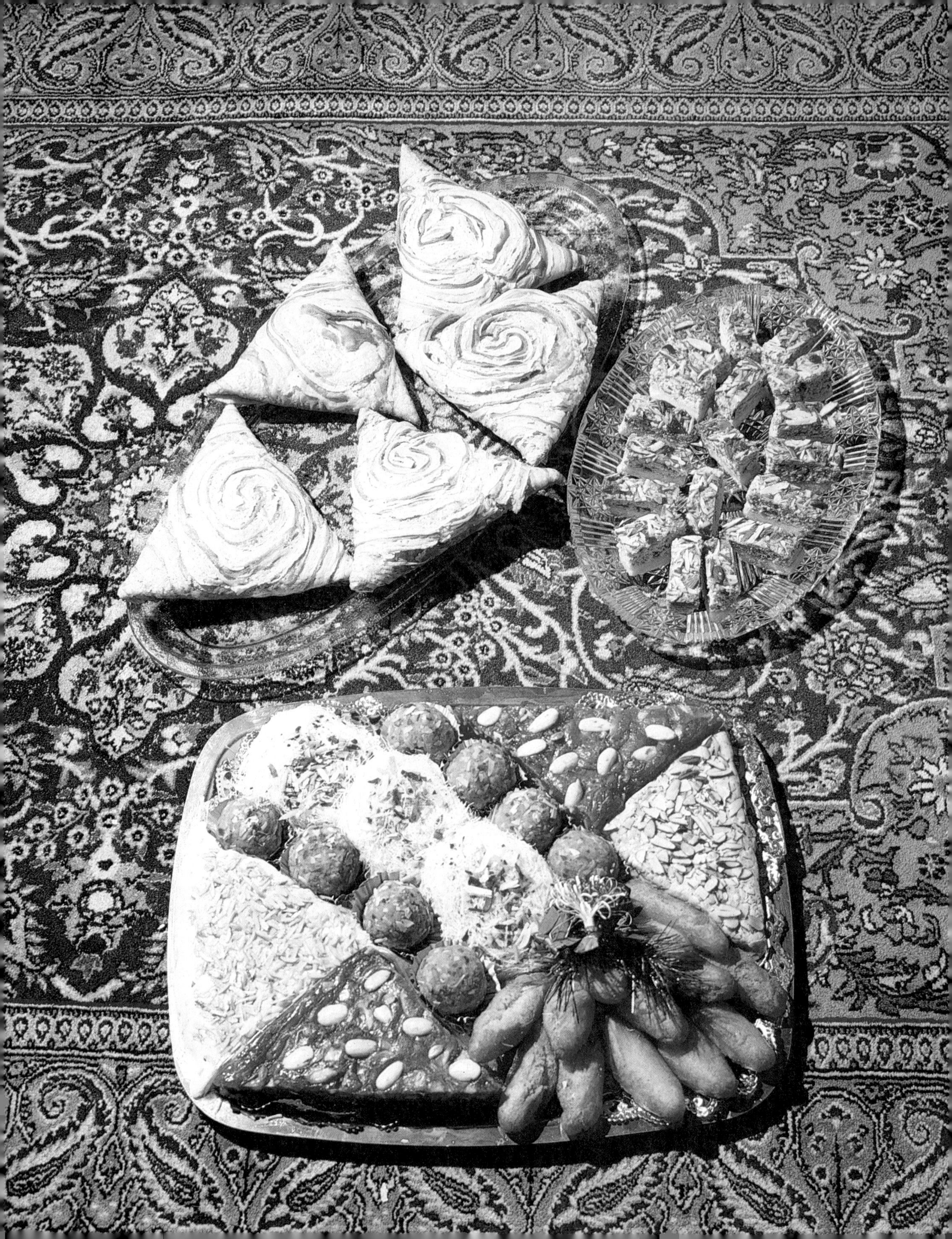

Falooda
(SIMPLE)

1 litre milk
1½ tsp falooda powder
1 tin cream (small)
½ tin condensed milk (adjust to sweeten)
1 tblsp sugar
½ tsp vanilla essence
½ tsp elachi powder

To milk add all the above ingredients and beat, then put on stove and bring to boil. Cool, beat again and then set.

NOTE: The above mixture must only be allowed to boil once.

A Mitha Samoosa (346)
B Coconut Toffee Bars (372)
C Sutherfeni (359)
D Laarwa (358)
E Badam Halwa (357)
F Magaj (353)
G Gulaab Jamun (355)
H Burfee (352)

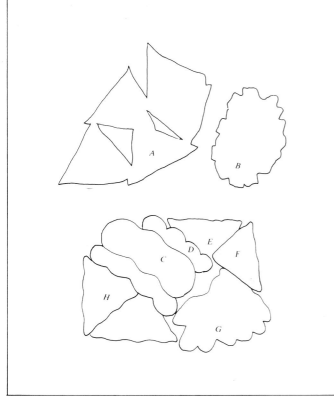

Falooda
(FROTHY)
(MILK JELLY)

2 tblsp ground almonds (optional)
1 small tin cream
1 litre milk
½ tsp elachi powder
4 tblsp condensed milk
2 tblsp sugar
1½ tsp agar agar powder or
¼ cup of china grass strands

Boil milk and agar agar and simmer till milk slightly evaporated.
If using almonds, add to milk while it is simmering.
Remove from stove and add elachi, sugar and condensed milk and tint a light pink in colour. Cool slightly then add cream.
Beat with rotary beater till light and frothy.
Spoon gently in tall glasses or bowls and allow to set in fridge.
Decorate with almonds etc.

Fresh Coconut Falooda

1 fresh coconut
Sugar to taste
2 tsp agar agar
1½ cups boiling water

Grate fresh coconut and soak in boiling water for about ½ an hour.
Pour into blender and liquidise till coconut is blended thick and milky.
Strain through sieve to make ½ litre of thick coconut cream. Leave this in fridge.
Boil an additional ½ litre of water and add agar agar and sugar till well blended.
Put cold coconut milk in a heat proof casserole and pour the hot agar agar mixture over it.
Do not mix or stir, but give casserole a good shake.
Leave for an hour till the dessert sets.
Garnish with silver edible paper and a few slivered pistachios etc.

Variation with Gor
(JAGGERY)

Instead of sugar, sweeten with ghor.
This will give a lovely beige/brown colour to the falooda.

Fresh Coconut Pudding (PHIRNI)

½ cup fresh coconut (grated)
½ tin condensed milk
1 litre milk
Sweeten with more sugar
1 tblsp cream of wheat (soji)
1 tblsp ghee
1 tblsp fine vermicelli
1 tin cream (155g)

Braise vermicelli and cream of wheat in ghee till pale pink in colour. Add milk and boil over low heat for 20 minutes. Add coconut and condensed milk. Stir vigorously and boil until thick. Cool slightly, then add cream.

Pour in pudding dish to set, decorate with slivered almonds.

Phirni (DELUXE)

1 litre milk
2 tblsp rice flour (or 2 tbls custard powder)
¼ cup ground almond
1 tsp powdered elachi
½ tsp rose essence (or 2 tsp rose water)
½ cup water
½ tsp falooda powder
2 tblsp fine vermicilli
1 tin cream
Condensed milk to sweeten

Mix falooda powder in ¼ cup boiling water.
Crush vermicelli and boil in 1 cup milk till it is cooked. Blend rice flour in 2 tblsp of water.

Put milk on stove and stir in the blended rice flour and falooda powder and cook till it begins to thicken, stir in ground almonds, cooked vermicelli and flavouring and cook till thick (like kheer).

Cool slightly and beat in cream and sweeten with condensed milk. Pour into individual bowls, grate a little nutmeg over each and sprinkle with slivered almonds.

Phirni may be tinted a pale pink or green in colour.

Phirni (MILK PUDDING)

1 litre milk
2 tblsp taystee wheat (soji)
2 tblsp sugar (or enough to taste)
1 tblsp ghee
Nutmeg, slivered almonds, etc.
1 tblsp sultanas

Braise taystee wheat in ghee till it is pink in colour. Add milk and sugar and boil till it thickens to consistency of thin porridge. Pour in shallow sweet bowls and when cool decorate with sultanas and slivered almonds and grate a little nutmeg over each bowl.

Coconut Bread Pudding

(KOPRA PATELLI)

4 slices white bread
2½ cups milk
few drops pink colouring
2 tblspn sugar
a good grating of numeg
1 tblsp slivered almonds or pistachios
3 eggs
1 tsp vanilla essence
1 tsp grated rind of lemon
½ cup chopped dates
¼ cup dessicated coconut
butter for smearing over bread

Grease a glass casserole with butter. Smear each slice of bread with butter then cut across into triangles. Arrange slices attractively in casserole.

Beat eggs, sugar, milk, vanilla essence and lemon rind together. Pour half of it over bread and allow to steep for 10 to 15 minutes. Add dates and coconut to rest of milk. Mix well and pour over bread again taking care to distribute dates evenly.

Sprinkle with grated nutmeg and nuts. Place pan in a deep baking tray which is quarter filled with water. Bake in 350°F (180°C) oven for 40 minutes. The water in the pan will assure a steamed effect to pudding.

Coconut Lagan

(KOPRA LAGAN No. 1)

1 heaped cup coconut
2¼ cups milk
1 tblsp full cream of wheat
1½ tblsp ghee
3 eggs
1 tin cream (155g)
1 tin or enough condensed milk to sweeten (397g)
1 tsp rose water
¼ tsp elachi
2 tblsp slivered almonds and pistachios

Braise cream of wheat in ghee till light pink in colour. Mix coconut in milk and let stand for 5 minutes. Add braised cream of wheat to it. Bring to boil and remove from stove when it thickens to consistency of porridge and no moisture is left. Let cool then add beaten eggs and flavourings. Lastly add tinned milk and cream. Mix all well together, grease shallow thalis or casseroles and pour lagan mixture in this. Decorate with slivered almonds. Bake in moderate oven 180°C till set (about 30 minutes). Decorate with rose petals and edible silver leaf paper. Cut in squares or diamond shapes.

Kopra Lagan (Coconut Pudding) Khaas

2¼ cups milk
3 eggs
½ freshly grated coconut
½ tsp elachi
1 tin cream (155g)
½ tsp rose water
Sufficient condensed milk to sweeten
2 slices bread (5mm thick)

Soak bread in milk for 1½ hours. Add beaten eggs, cream and condensed milk with the flavourings. Caramelize 2 tablespoons of sugar by heating it in 1 tablespoon of water and when it is browned, add quickly to above mixture. Grease a pyrex casserole slightly, pour the pudding mixture in it and bake in 180°C oven for over 30 mins.

Decorate the nicely browned top with a handful of finely slivered almonds, pistachios and either serve straight from casserole for dinners or cut in two inch squares as at parties and buffets.

Coconut Pateli
(STEAMED PUDDING) (PHOTO PAGE 84)

VARIATION:

Using same ingredients as above — soak bread and coconut in milk and put through blender to render very fine. Add cream and condensed milk to milk mixture.

Caramalize jelly moulds or baking pans with sugar and few drops of water and when the inside of the moulds are slightly browned pour milk mixture into them. Place moulds in a baking tray containing water and bake for 30 minutes at 350°F (180°C). Unmould and serve cold with cream.

Kopra Lagan with Jalebi
(COCONUT PUDDING)(PHOTO PAGE 196)

Use same ingredients as above but separate white and yolk of eggs. Beat egg yolk well then add to milk. Add cream, condensed milk and flavouring — tint a pale green in colour.

Now beat egg whites till they are stiff. Fold into milk mixture. Grease a casserole and pour pudding mixture into it and put in 350°F (180°C) oven till lagan begins to set. Press 5 or 6 jalebis over top and continue baking till lagan is done. (Lagan should just set and not be allowed to dry out.)

Coconut Lagan
(COCONUT PUDDING)

¼ cup cream of wheat
½ litre milk
Good pinch elachi
1 cup coconut or half fresh coconut, (grated)
3 eggs
¾ cup sugar or to taste
3 tblsp ghee

Boil milk and sugar. When sugar has dissolved, soak the coconut for a while. If using fresh coconut, there will be no need for soaking. Braise soji in ghee and just as it starts to change colour, add coconut and milk and cook till mixture is thick like porridge. Beat eggs and add elachi to it. When milk mixture cools, add eggs and stir vigorously. Grease thali or casserole with butter. Pour in batter and bake in moderate oven till pudding has set and lightly browned. Decorate liberally with slivered almonds and leave in warm oven till serving time.

Coconut Lagan (unusual)

1 fresh coconut
3 white of eggs
½ tsp vanilla essence
½ pint fresh cream
3 tblsp sugar (or to taste)
3 different colour sour ball sweets

Grate coconut and mix together with fresh cream, sugar and vanilla.

Beat white of egg stiff and blend into above mixture.

Put in glass casserole and place in pot of water on stove, bring to boil so that it steams, about 30 minutes.

Crush about a tblsp each of sweets, sprinkle over pudding to form a pattern. Allow to steam a little longer so that the sour ball penetrates into the pudding.

Malido

Malido is made on special festive occasions by all Indians. When the prophet was hurt in a battle he lost some teeth and could not eat solids. To tempt him, his followers made desserts and puddings, and so to this day to mark the occasion, Muslims in India prepare malido as a substitute for those sweets of Arabia.

Malido

1 cup cake flour
½ cup cream of wheat
2 tblsp ghee (solid)
Sufficient milk to make dough of biscuit consistency.

Rub in ghee in flour and cream of wheat. Make dough with liquid.

Roll out on floured board to 5mm thick. Cut out 5cm squares and fry slowly in ghee/oil till light pink in colour. Drain.

Grind through mincer while still hot, rub through wire sieve to get even consistency.

TO THE MALIDO ADD:
½ tsp powdered elachi
1 tblsp dessicated coconut
Sugar to taste
Sprinkle with slivered almonds

Serve dry as above or with milk as follows:

To each sweet bowl half filled with malido, add 2 tablespoons milk and eat as pudding.

Zikar Malido

2½ cups flour
3 cups sugar
1 tblsp ghee
1 tblsp milk
1 cup cream of wheat
½ tsp elachi
2 tblsp sliced pistachios
2 tblsp blanched slivered almonds
Rose water for flavouring

Add ghee to flour and cream of wheat. Sprinkle with little water and form between forefinger and thumb, into little pea-sized balls. Dry balls by keeping them in a heap in a warm place, meanwhile prepare a syrup of 3 cups sugar and 3 cups water. Now fry the heaped pea-sized balls in ghee (frying pan half filled with ghee) till lovely golden pink in colour and dip them in the syrup. The balls should absorb all the syrup.

Sprinkle milk over the balls and replace on stove and simmer over gentle heat till cooked. (Balls will break, but the consistency of malido will be like coarse crushed biscuits). Add rose water and decorate with slivered almonds and pistachios when serving.

Dahi Waras or Daitaras

(YOGHURT BISCUITS)

1 cup flour
½ tsp baking powder
1 desspn ghee
Yoghurt to make dough (¼ cup or more)
Pinch of salt
1 tsp sugar

Mix dry ingredients, rub in ghee and make into dough with sour milk (like a puri dough).

Roll out on floured board to 4mm thickness and cut out into rounds with a biscuit cutter and fry in ghee/oil to a delicate pinkish colour.

Cool on wire rack and dip in Master syrup recipe. Alternatively, the dough may be rolled out like varkhi type samoosas and then fried. For syrup recipes see page 348.

Dahi Waras

2 cups flour
2 tsp baking powder
2 tsp ghee
1 egg
1 cup dahi curd (home made curd, let excess moisture drip out) or yoghurt

Mix together flour and baking powder and rub in ghee. Mix egg and dahi together and make a dough.

Roll out three times and smear melted ghee each time. Finally roll out and cut with cookie cutter into small round puris.

Fry in oil and dip in syrup.

Jardo (Zarda)
(SWEET SAFFRON RICE)

3 tblsp ghee
1 cup rice
1 cup sugar
2 pieces tuj (cinnamon)
¾ cup water
2 whole elachi (bruised open)
½ tsp saffron (optional)
6 sultanas or 4 prunes or
4 aloe boekhara (optional)

boil rice with a pinch of turmeric till well cooked. (Care must be exercised that no hard kernel is left in rice). Drain in colander.

Prepare a syrup with the water, sugar and saffron, (or if not using saffron, tint with egg yellow colouring).

Braise the elachi, tuj and dried fruit in the ghee till the dried fruit swells and is shiny. Now add the syrup to pot with dried fruit and lastly add the cooked rice. Toss and turn lightly till rice is coated with syrup. Allow to cook very slowly till the moisture evaporates and rice is left shiny, and well coated in the syrup (close lid of pot tightly).

Leave in moderate oven for 10 to 15 minutes. Garnish with slivered almonds, thinly sliced or grated fresh coconut.

VARIATION:
Use same ingredients. Boil rice as stated. Braise elachi, tuj and dried fruit in ghee. When fruit swells, add water, bring to boil, then add sugar and simmer till sugar dissolved and syrup forms. Add rice, toss lightly and finish cooking.

Sohla
(SWEET RICE WITH TANGY FLAVOUR)

1 grated pineapple (250g pulp)
1 lemon (juice)
1¾ cup sugar

Prepare as Jardo till the oven stage, but using more sugar than in Jardo. Before putting in oven, add juice of 1 lemon and grated pineapple to the jardo. Mix with a light hand and leave in oven for 15 to 20 minutes.

Safado
(WHITE JARDO)

Cook just like jardo till simmering stage but omit all colouring. Now add ½ cup freshly grated coconut in jardo, turning and tossing lightly till it is well incorporated. Decorate with slivered pistachios and almonds.

Sohla
(SWEET RICE VARIATION)

1 cup rice (cooked soft)
1 tsp rose water
1 cup ghee
Juice of 2 lemons
2 cups sugar
¼ tsp ground elachi
Slivered almonds

Make a thin syrup of sugar with 2 cups of water. To syrup add the lemon juice, elachi and rose water. Add boiled rice and simmer slowly till syrup is absorbed by the rice. Now heat ghee and pour over sohla. Serve hot, decorate with slivered almonds.

Dahi Kurmelo

1 cup rice
Sugar to taste
Slivered almonds
1 carton yoghurt
2 tblsp ghee

Boil rice in salted water till very well done. Drain off water and let cool in colander. Place in casserole then sprinkle with sugar, toss and turn till sugar is absorbed. Heat ghee and pour over rice, again toss and turn. Lastly pour dahi carefully over rice. Decorate with khus-khus, and slivered almonds. Keep in warm oven 150° till serving time. By this time dahi should be absorbed.

Date Halwa Fudge

2 packets dates (500g)
250g almonds
1 tsp saunmf (fennel)
3 dessertspoons ghee
2 tblsp Singhora flour

Clean and pit dates. Stamp with mortar till fairly smooth.

Blanch almonds. Chop half of almonds coarsely and grind remainder.

Heat ghee in pot and braise both the ground and chopped almonds. When almonds just begin to change colour, add singhora flour and braise slightly.

Lastly add dates and saunmf and stir and mash over low heat. When dates are nicely mashed-up tip out mixture in deep baking tray and pat into 2 cm thickness.

When cool cut in squares and serve as fudge.

Ghor Papdi

500g ghor (1½ cups) (Jaggery)
500g ghee (2 cups)
¼ cup cream of wheat (soji)
Elachi (cardomom)
375g almonds (1½ cups ground)
375g coconut
375g brown flour

Braise flour in half of ghee over medium heat — there will be a lovely aroma. Add cream of wheat, coconut and almonds.

In another pot, put rest of ghee with ghor and slowly allow to melt over low heat.

Mix both mixtures well together, then add ½ cup of milk. Return to medium heat.

Keep on stirring till ghee floats to top and sides.

Spread and pat mixture with back of spoon in thali or casserole.

Sprinkle with slivered almonds, charoli, Pistachios.

Cut in diamond or 2" square shapes, set aside to cool and harden.

Tal Papdi
(SESAME SNAPS)

250g ghor (¾ cup)
1½ cups tal (sesame)
2 tblsp ghee

Melt ghor slightly in little ghee. Brown tal separately in frying pan without ghee or oil. Add melted ghor and remove from stove. Mix thoroughly. Put to set in trays or thali to about 1 cm thickness and cut into desired shape while still hot. Let it cool.

Tal Papdi
(VARIATION)

½ cup sesame seeds (or slightly chopped peanuts or
**   other nuts)**
1 cup sugar
1 tsp vinegar
1 tsp butter

Melt sugar and vinegar and add butter — once butter has melted, remove from stove and immediately add tal or nuts and stir in. Pour into a greased tray and start cutting into squares or shapes. Work must be done swiftly before sweet hardens.

Baath or Lapsi
(CRUSHED WHEAT HALWA)

1 cup lapsi
¾ cup sugar
¼ cup ghee
1 piece tuj
2 shelled elachi
2 tblsp dessicated coconut
1 tsp saunmf (fennel)
1 tblsp slivered almonds
Few slices of fresh coconut

Braise baath or lapsi in ghee till golden brown. Add elachi, tuj, and saunmf.

Add 2 cups boiling water and cook very slowly till crushed wheat is soft and cooked.

Add sugar and coconut and cook till it is well absorbed in baath.

Add milk and bake in oven with lid of casserole on, (moderate oven for about 15 mins.).

Decorate with slivered almonds and thin wafers of fresh coconut, before serving.

VARIATIONS:

Substitute for coconut, 4 tablespoons of grated carrots.

Shahi Tukra

4 slices of bread
½ litre milk
½ cup sugar
A pinch saffron
½ cup almonds, blanched and ground
¼ cup water
1 tblsp ghee

Boil milk till consistency is like thick cream.

Soak the saffron in a little boiling milk for an hour.

Add the saffron milk to the kheer. Set aside.

Fry the sliced bread in ghee till golden. Remove from the stove and pour 2 tablespoons of milk over it.

Boil the sugar and water to a thick syrup. Add ground almonds. Take out a tablespoon of the almonds/syrup and set aside.

To the remaining syrup add the thick cream-like milk.

Arrange toasts in a dish. Pour the thick mixture over it and spread a thin paste of almond syrup on it. Sprinkle crushed cardamoms and decorate with silver leaf.

Sikhund
(SOUR/SWEET DESSERT)

1 litre milk
1 dessertspoon dahi (yoghurt)

Heat milk (but do not bring to boil) and add dahi. Remove from stove and leave for a few hours. In the evening spread a clean muslin cloth in colander and pour milk mixture in this. Tie cloth into a bag and keep suspended over draining rack of kitchen. (This is the modern method. In the early days these bags were suspended on verandah rafters).

In the morning, weigh the hard solid lump of cottage cheese milk. To 250g of this soft cottage cheese, add 125g of sugar and mix well with fork in bowl. Spread dry portion of muslin over a deep bowl. Put the mixture in the middle and with back of spoon rub through. After all the milk/-sugar has been sieved through cloth, flavour with a good pinch of powdered elachi and a tablespoon of slivered almonds. Serve in tiny sweet bowls with coffee spoons.

Khajoora

2 tblsp tal (sesame)
½ cup butter
2 cups flour
¼ tsp salt
2 tblsp khus-khus (poppy seeds)
1 cup sugar (please adjust to taste)
½ cup cream of wheat
1 tsp baking powder
Milk (1/3 cup approx.)
½ tsp elachi powder

Sift dry ingredients. Rub in butter and make dough with milk to consistency of rotlas. Roll out to thickness of a rotla (5mm) cut out into finger or diamond shapes. Fry in hot oil. Drain on wire rack.

Dodhi or Pineapple Jam
(DODHI MURABBA)

1 cup dodhi (grated)
1 cup sugar
½ cup boiling water
2 whole cloves
1 tbsp slivered almonds
1 tbsp sultanas
2 sticks cinnamon
2 elachi
1 tbsp ghee

Braise spices and dodhi in ghee. Add water and sugar and bring to boil. Simmer slowly till sugar blended.
Simmer till cooked and jam is shiny.
Substitute pineapple for dodhi, for pineapple murabba.

Gool Goolas
(SWEET FRITTERS)

1½ cups flour
1/3 cup sugar
1 egg
2 tsp saunmf
1½ tblsp ghee
1 tsp baking powder
½ cup milk

Rub ghee in flour, add saunmf, the well beaten egg, sugar and milk.

Make into batter, like chilli bite batter, and leave it for about an hour.

Add baking powder and fry in deep oil over medium heat, fry till a rosy brown.

The amount of batter for each gool goola is about the size of a large marble.

Cool and drain in colander.

NOTE:
Small chunks of fresh pineapple or slices of banana added to batter give a lovely variation.

Dodhi Goolgoolas
(SWEET DUMPLINGS)

1 small dodhi (grated)
1 cup yoghurt
2 eggs
2 tsp baking powder
¼ tsp elachi
2 tblsp ghee
½ cup milk
Cake flour

Beat eggs and to them add liquids, baking powder, elachi, ghee, dodhi and sufficient cake flour to make a thick bhajia batter. Fry marble-sized balls in deep oil over medium heat till goolgoolas are a lovely pink colour. Remove from oil and drain in colander. Whilst they are still warm, dip in syrup and roll in coconut.

Date Biscuits

(KHAJOORAS)

½ cup butter
1 egg
1 tsp baking powder
½ cup chopped dates
3 tblsp sugar
2 cups flour
½ cup chopped almonds

Cream butter and sugar till soft and creamy. Add egg and beat well. Add flour sifted with baking powder. Lastly add almonds and dates. On lightly greased baking sheet, put lumps of batter in rough peaks. Bake in 180°C oven for 25 to 30 minutes.

Jeero Biscuits

(CUMMIN)

2 cups cake flour
1 tblsp lemon juice
1 tsp baking powder
Milk to make dough
4 tblsp butter or ghee
1 tsp crushed jeero
Pinch of salt

Sift dry ingredients together. Rub in butter and lemon juice till flour is like fine breadcrumbs. Add as much cold milk as is required to make a dough that is rollable. Roll out on floured board to thickness of puri. Cut into finger shapes and fry in deep hot oil till crisp and brown.

Plaited Biscuits

(COLOUR PAGE 337)

2 cups flour
3 tsp baking powder
1 egg
4 tblsp butter
4 tblsp sugar

Beat egg in bowl and pour into cup. Add enough milk to egg to make half a cup of liquid.

Sift flour and baking powder in mixing bowl. Add ghee and sugar and rub through palms of hands till flour resembles mealie meal.

Divide flour into two exact halves. To one half add half of egg/milk liquid and knead into dough. To the left over milk/egg liquid add 1 tablespoon of cocoa and mix this into the remaining flour. You will now have two equal amounts of soft White and Brown biscuit dough.

Roll the dough between palms of hand or on floured board into a long thick rope. Cut off 3 inch lengths from each colour dough and plait them together to form a pigtail. Place on baking sheet and bake in 180°C oven for 30 minutes.

Plaits

(CHOTLA)(PHOTO PAGE 337)

2½ cups flour
2 tblsp butter
1 tsp baking powder
1½ cup sugar
2 tblsp golden syrup (mollasses) ⎱
*½ cup ice-cold water   ⎰ mix together
*½ cup milk
pinch of salt
1 cup water

Sift dry ingredients and rub in butter. Make a firm dough with ½ cup water and ½ cup milk. Roll out like thin roti and cut strips of about 1/3 of an inch (8 mm) wide. Make tight plait — cut off in lengths of 2" (5 cm).

Press at both ends to keep the plait in place and fry over low heat until golden coloured.

Drain and cool on wire rack. In a separate pan make syrup with sugar and water. When the syrup is cold add golden syrup to give it a golden colour. Just before serving pour the syrup over the plaits, garnish with almonds and pista and serve.

Fresh Cream Jeero Biscuits

125ml fresh cream
½ cup butter
3 tblsp jeero
3 cups cake flour
6 tsp baking powder
¼ tsp salt

Sift dry ingredients. Rub in butter. Make dough with cream. The dough will be soft like maska biscuit dough. Put large marble-sized balls on greased tray. Bake in hot oven 200°C for 10 minutes. Reduce heat to 180°C and finish baking.

Egg/Coconut Halwa

6 eggs
½ tin condensed milk (200g)
½ cup cake flour
¾ cup sugar (adjust to taste)
1 cup coconut (freshly grated or dessicated)
¼ tsp elachi
¾ cup ghee

Beat eggs, sugar, condensed milk and flour smoothly. Add elachi and coconut and mix well. Heat ghee in large pot and add mixture to it. Stir at regular intervals to prevent scorching. When mixture thickens and ghee starts showing on top the Halwa is done. Garnish with slivered nuts.

Dephla
(SWEET PURIS)

2 cups cake flour
¼ tsp salt
¼ cup ghor mixed with ½ cup water
1 tblsp ghee
1 tblsp oil

Mix all ingredients and if necessary add a little more water to make a pliable dough. Roll out thin and cut in rounds or desired shapes with biscuit cutters. Fry in deep hot oil to a pale golden brown and drain on rack.

Mitha Sakar Pada

500g cake flour
½ tsp elachi
1 cup milk
1 cup sugar
½ cup ghee

Boil milk and sugar till sugar melts and no grains are left. Allow to cool. To flour add elachi and ghee and rub in well through palms. Make dough with sugar/milk.

Roll out to thickness of puri (without using any flour for sprinkling during rolling).

Cut in diamond shapes and fry in deep oil over hot heat.

CAUTION:
Put oil on for frying and then start making dough as this has to be fried immediately after dough is made.

Soji Puri
(CREAM OF WHEAT PURIS)

2 cups of flour
¼ tsp salt
1½ tsp baking powder
½ cup cream of wheat (soji)
1½ tblsp solid ghee
¾ cup milk/water

Sift flour with salt, baking powder and cream of wheat. Rub in ghee and knead into dough with milk/water. (Soft biscuit consistency dough).

Roll out to 3mm thickness, cut into rounds (6cm diameter) and fry in deep hot oil.

Poli
(HINDU FESTIVAL PASTRY)

3 cups flour
2 tblsp ghee
½ tsp salt

Mix salt and flour and rub in ghee and make dough with warm water till a nice soft dough as for puri. Knead the dough thoroughly.

FILLING:
1 fresh coconut
3 tblsp sugar
1 tblsp khus khus (poppy seeds)
1 tblsp tal (sesame seed)
1 tsp fine elachi (cardomom)
¼ tsp nutmeg
oil for frying

Grate 1 whole coconut, roast in pan to tan slightly, add sugar, khus khus, and tal. The khus-khus and the tal must be slightly roasted in separate pan and crushed with a rolling pin before adding to coconut and sugar. Add elachi powder and pinch of nutmeg. Mix thoroughly, and if desired, add slivered almonds.

Make small round puris and put 1 tablespoon of above filling and fold over like jam tarts, pinching edges close, and fry in deep hot oil, till golden colour. Drain on wire racks.

Semolina Balls
(SAFED LAARWA)

1 cup flour
½ fresh coconut
2 tblsp melted ghee
½ tsp elachi (fine)
little milk for mixing
1 tblsp blanched almonds
¼ cup taystee wheat
¼ cup castor sugar
1½ tsp baking powder
1 tblsp sultanas
1 tblsp charoli (chirongee nuts)

Sift flour, taystee wheat and baking powder together. Rub in ghee and using milk form into a stiff dough.

Mould into small balls and fry in hot ghee. Mince together the almonds, charoli, sultanas and coconut and also the fried white balls.

Mix the sugar and elachi into this and form into stiff small balls. The oil, sultanas and moisture from coconut will allow this, but see to it that you mould the balls really hard otherwise they will crumble up.

Boiled Sev
(BOILED VERMICELLI)

1 cup vermicelli
2 tblsp ghee
1 tblsp slivered almonds
½ cup sugar

Boil vermicelli in 5 cups boiling water for a few minutes or till done, drain in colander. Place in pyrex ware or casserole, pour over ghee and sugar and slivered nuts, and place in oven till sugar melts and is absorbed by sev (do not allow to go dry), turn over once or twice. Serve hot with Mango Rus (Manjo juice).

Variation Sev
(VERMICELLI PUDDING)

2 cups sev (fine vermicelli)
½ cup ghee
1 tin condensed milk (397g)
1 cup milk
2 elachi (cardamom) seeded
1 tblsp sultanas
1 tin cream or ¼ pint fresh cream (155g)

Braise vermicelli and sultanas in ghee. Just as vermicelli beings to turn pink and sultanas are swollen, add the milk.

Immediately lower heat, close lid of pot and allow to cook very slowly till milk is absorbed and the vermicelli soft.

Add elachi seeds, fresh or tinned cream and as much of the condensed milk as is required to sweeten.

Allow to cook till dry like thick pudding. Decorate with slivered almonds and serve.

Vermicelli Dessert
(MITHI SEV)

2 cups vermicelli (4 oz)
3 tblsp ghee
Tuj (cinnamon)
2 elachi (seeds of elachi)
1 dozen sultanas
1 cup sugar
½ cup milk

Braise sultanas in ghee, with the tuj and elachi till the vermicelli turns a delicate pink in colour. Add ½ cup of boiling water and simmer slowly till cooked.

Add sugar and simmer on stove with pot closed till it is absorbed by the vermicelli.

Add milk, bake in oven with lid of casserole on till vermicelli is dry and loose. (Some may prefer to tint the milk with a little saffron or yellow egg colouring before adding it).

Decorate with blanched almonds, coconut or pistachios.

Coconut Peach Pie

BASE:
140g coconut
65g sugar
¼ cup butter (melted)
¾ cup flour
1 tsp baking powder
1 large egg

Sift dry ingredients. Mix in melted butter. Make dough with well beaten egg.

Bake at 180°C in ovenproof dish in which pie can be set and served. Remove when lightly browned.

TOPPING:
1 tin clingstone peaches (410g)
250ml fresh cream
125ml sour milk
slivered almonds
2 tblsp sugar

Whip sugar and cream. Add yoghurt and mix. Grate peaches into above mixture, and pour over warm base.

Allow to chill in fridge. Sprinkle slivered almonds on top before serving.

Soji/Peach Pie
(SEMOLINA AND PEACHES)

3 tblsp cream of wheat
2 egg yolks
1 tin canned peaches (small)
1¾ cups milk
30g butter or ghee
2 tblsp brown sugar
2 egg whites
½ cup castor sugar
½ tsp ground cinnamon

Braise cream of wheat in ghee or butter and just as it begins to change colour add milk, brown sugar and cinnamon.

Stir constantly and bring to boil, then allow to simmer very slowly till thick.

Cool slightly. Beat-in egg yolks and cook gently for a minute or two so that the egg cooks-in.

Turn into sponge tin or heatproof casserole and chill. Top with sliced peaches leaving a few for decoration.

Make meringue by beating egg whites till stiff. Then add castor sugar, a tablespoon at a time, beat in till it stands in stiff peaks. When all the sugar has been used up and meringue can stand in peaks, carefully cover pie with peaked up meringue.

Bake in 180°C oven for 15 minutes, reduce heat to 125°C and bake for 10 more minutes. Switch off oven and allow meringue to harden slightly. Best served hot. Garnish with peach slices, and serve with whipped cream.

Plain Soji Halwa
(TAYSTEE WHEAT HALWA)

½ cup taystee wheat (soji)
3 tblsp ghee (solid)
½ cup sugar
½ cup milk
1 tblsp blanched slivered almonds
1 cup hot water
8 sultanas or 6 prunes
1 piece tuj
2 shelled elachi (seeds)
1 tblsp dessicated coconut
1 tblsp butter

Braise taystee wheat with the sultanas or prunes in the ghee till the wheat changes a light pink in colour and the dried fruit is shiny and swollen.

Add boiling water and let simmer very slowly till wheat is cooked.

Now add the sugar and allow to cook till it is well absorbed in the halwa.

Add milk and butter and cook over very low heat or better still, bake in moderate oven with lid of casserole on, for about 15 minutes or till the halwa is fluffy and dry like rice.

Just before serving, sprinkle top with coconut and almonds.

Many people prefer to add the coconut at the milk stage, leaving aside the almonds for decoration.

Beda Soji Halwa
(EGG AND TAYSTEE WHEAT HALWA)

1/3 cup semolina (soji)
3 tblsp ghee (solid)
A few seedless raisins
*Little ground elachi and a few seeds of elachi
1 tblsp slivered almonds
*1 tblsp grated coconut
*3 eggs
*¾ cup milk   *Whisk together
*¾ cup sugar

Braise semolina and raisins in ghee. Add ¼ cup boiling water and cook very slowly till water evaporates.

Whisk eggs, sugar, coconut and elachi with the milk and add to halwa.

Cook very slowly and stir all the time to prevent eggs curdling and lumping.

Bake in moderate oven for about 15 minutes with lid of casserole on and let dry out.

Decorate with slivered almonds and grated coconut before serving.

Soji Halwa
(DELUXE)

½ cup soji (cream of wheat)
2¼ cups milk
1 level tsp elachi seeds
1 tblsp sultanas
¾ cup sugar or sweeten with condensed milk (less than 1 tin)
¾ cup ghee
125g fresh cream
4 large eggs
½ cup freshly ground almonds

Whisk eggs in milk, and add elachi.

Braise cream of wheat and sultanas in ghee till soji is a delicate pink and the sultanas shiny and swollen. Lower heat and add egg/milk liquid. Stir continuously till mixture is thick like kheer (milk pudding).

Now add cream and sugar or condensed milk, whichever is preferred. Condensed milk gives a creamy texture but take care not to over-sweeten.

Lastly add ground almonds (blanched and ground). Stir briskly till smooth and of even texture*.

Leave over low heat, with lid of pot closed. When halwa is dry and resembles damp bread crumbs, garnish with slivered almonds and pistachios. Serve warm, decorated with edible silver paper.

(*) **NOTE:**

At this stage the halwa can be transferred into a heatproof casserole and allowed to finish cooking in 350°F/180°C oven. It can be served straight from oven to table with the addition of almond and silver paper decorations. (Silver paper is optional)

Variation with Masoor (Mithai)

Prepare as above but at cream and sugar stage add 125g masoor (mithai available from sweetmeat shops). The masoor must be coarsely crushed and mixed into halwa.

Page 329

Mango Jardo
(MANGO SWEET DESSERT)

2 cups rice
125ml cream
¼ cup sugar
2 cups mango pulp
2 cups milk
½ tsp rose water
Few strands saffron (optional)
Juice of 1 lemon

Wash mangoes and dry on cloth. Peel and extract pulp in liquidiser or by sieving through wire strainer. Boil milk in enamel pot over low heat. When it begins to thicken, add mango pulp, saffron strands, rose water, lemon and sugar. Stir continuously to prevent scorching. When mixture is thick like pudding, remove from stove, cool and add cream.

Cook rice in salted water and little turmeric till done. Drain in colander. In greased casserole arrange alternate layers of rice and mango pulp, starting with rice and ending with rice. Dot with a little ghee and bake in 180°C oven till pudding has set. Decorate with slivered almonds and pistachios.

Mango Halwa

3 cups mango pulp
2½ cups milk
Pinch of saffron (optional)
1 cup sugar (or condensed milk to taste)
¼ tsp elachi

Put all ingredients in enamel pot over low heat and stir continuously as it is prone to scorch. When mixture starts leaving sides of pot, it is done. Grease a casserole and pour halwa into this. Cut in diamond shapes when cold.

Sweet Potato Lagan

2 tbsp melted butter/ghee
1 cup sweet potato (mashed)
1 cup dessicated coconut
1½ cups milk
¾ cup sugar
2 eggs
2 tsp baking powder
¼ tsp ground elachi

Peel and wash sweet potatoes. Boil soft. Measure 1 cup after mashing. Whip eggs well. Blend in sweet potatoes. Add rest of the ingredients and mix well. Grease a casserole (25 x 20 x 5 cm deep). Spread mixture and sprinkle surface with a little khus-khus (poppy seeds) and slivered almonds. Bake in 180°C oven till pale gold in colour. Serve warm.

Sweet Pumpkin Lagan

2 cups mashed pumpkin
3 tblsp cream of wheat (soji)
1½ tblsp ghee
1 cup sugar
½ cup dessicated coconut (or fresh)
¼ tsp powdered elachi
¼ cup milk
3 eggs
1 tsp baking powder

Braise soji in ghee till pale pink in colour — add mashed pumpkin, sugar and milk and stir till thick and mushy.

Remove from stove, cool slightly then add beaten egg, and rest of ingredients. Mix well and spread in greased casserole.

Sprinkle with poppy seeds and slivered almonds. Bake in 180°C oven for 25 minutes.

Caramel Pudding

½ cup sugar
1½ cups flour
½ cup chopped nuts
¾ cup milk
1 cup sugar
3 tblsp sugar (extra)
2 tblsp butter
2½ tsp baking powder
3 tblsp butter
2 cups hot water

In thick pan caramelize 1 cup sugar over low heat till it is a deep caramel colour.

Add 2 tblsp butter, ½ cup sugar and add the hot water slowly, till it starts to boil. Keep simmering.

Sift flour, baking powder, the 3 tblsp sugar and nuts, then rub in 3 tblsp butter. Mix together, then stir in milk. Drop spoonsful into the boiling syrup. When all the flour mixture has been used up, cover syrup and simmer gently till syrup is absorbed.

Serve with cream.

Pancakes

(GHAWLAS OR DOSAIS)
(SEE COLOUR PAGES 27, 141, 333)

We are introducing a whole new chapter on the very versatile pancake or ghawla or dosai as you may call them.

While the basic method remain the same the smart dosai maker will use unusual stuffings to make her pancakes outstanding. We give you several recipes made with eggs and some without.

Choose your favourite basic recipe then have fun serving them as savouries, sweets or in curry bases.

NOTE ON FREEZING:

Pancakes freeze very well. When stuffed and rolled-up place them side by side in a plastic container. Cover each layer with plastic or foil.

Thaw at room temperature but when they have to be fried after stuffing then it is best to fry them when still slightly stiff and not completely thawed.

Basic Pancake Batter

1 egg
½ tsp bicarb
1 tsp baking powder
2 tblsp melted butter or ghee
1½ cups buttermilk (half milk and half yoghurt)
1¼ cups flour
½ tsp salt

Mix bicarb into buttermilk. Beat egg and add to buttermilk. Add rest of ingredients to mixture and beat well till batter is smooth, and consistency of cream or thin custard.

When a few drops of water are sprinkled on the tava and they start skidding around the tava (griddle) it is ready for use. Greasing of griddle will not be necessary but should this be so then wipe with an oiled cloth.

Pour batter from lipped jug to form pools on the tava. When small ones are required then several pancakes can be made at the same time. As soon as top of pancake bubbles, turn it over and allow other side to brown delicately.

Hot pancakes are delicious served with jam, cream or honey. Basic batter can be used to give interesting variations.

1) Fold-in a cup of rice crispies into batter before making.

2) Fold in chopped nuts.

3) Omit sugar, add more salt. Spice with jeera (cummin) and ground green chillies. Add this to batter together with a grated onion and chopped bhaji. This is delicious for breakfast or tea snacks.

Pancake Desserts

Smear with honey or jam. Fill with whipped cream and sliced banana and roll over. Spread cream over top and sprinkle with coconut, nuts and flaked chocolate.

Ghawla

(INDIAN PANCAKE) (PHOTO PAGE 333)

2 eggs
2 tblsp sugar
2 tblsp flour
1 tblsp milk
1 level tsp baking powder
½ tblsp ghee
vanilla

Put flour in bowl. Make a well in the centre and add all ingredients except the baking powder. Beat well and keep aside in a covered bowl for a few hours. Add baking powder just before making. Beat in well.

Pre-heat heavy skillet or tava with a flat base. Grease with a tablespoon or so of ghee and pour two tablespoons of batter at a time to make thin pancake-like ghawlas. Turn over when underside is done and grill the reverse side in a similar way.

FILLING:

Spread each ghawla lightly with slightly beaten fresh cream. Over every alternate ghawla, sprinkle flaked chocolate and slivered almonds and pile them on one another. Six to seven layers of ghawla make a very attractive dessert. Decorate top-most ghawla with cream, flaked chocolate and nuts and if desired, with tiny specks of edible silver leaf.

ALTERNATELY:

Make ghawlas as above. Smear each with cream, sprinkle with nuts and chocolate and roll up to resemble tiny swiss rolls. (See colour plate 333).

Swiss Roll Dessert

(PHOTO OPPOSITE)

1 lt milk
2 tsp china grass powder (falooda)
½ cup water
¾ cup fresh cream
almonds (slivered)
1 tin Nestlé Cream (155g)
1 tin condensed milk (397g)
1 egg (beaten)
1 chocolate flake
1 tblsp maizena
1 Swiss roll (chocolate spread)
1 Swiss roll (jam spread)

Put milk to boil. Make a paste with egg, maizena and a little extra cold milk.

Boil separately china grass powder in ½ cup water. Add egg and maizena paste to milk which has just begun to boil. Stir until milk comes to boil again.

Remove from stove and add boiled china grass, condensed milk and tinned cream. Beat very well.

Place sliced swiss roll in casserole, alternating the two colours. Pour cream custard over cake and leave in fridge to set.

Decorate with fresh cream, slivered almonds and flake.

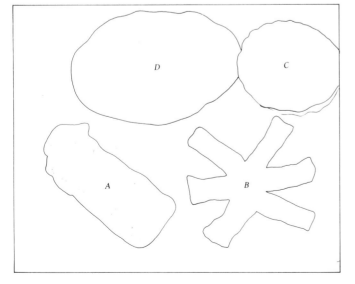

A Cheese Pyramid (334)
B Pancake Delights (331)
C Meringue Torte
D Swiss Roll Falooda Dessert (332)

Pineapple/Honey Tart

1 cup sugar
1 large egg
1 cup margarine (250g)
2½ cups sifted cake flour
2 tsp baking powder
½ tsp salt

SYRUP:
¼ cup butter
½ cup honey

FILLING: (mix together)
2 tins (310g) crushed pineapple (drain off excess
   syrup)
½ cup coconut
½ cup chopped nuts (almonds, pecan or walnuts)

Grease a fireproof baking dish well.

Sprinkle bottom with the mixture of coconut, nuts and
pineapple and spread over the pastry made as follows:

Cream butter and sugar together, beat in the egg and
then the dry ingredients.

Bake for 30 mins in 180°C oven (350°F).

Remove from oven and pour honey syrup over this.

HONEY SYRUP:

Heat butter and honey together and pour over tart while
hot. Decorate with nuts and pineapple rings if desired.

Marie Biscuit Delights
(PAGE 337)

1 pkt marie biscuits
125g butter
1 egg (beaten)
½ cup sugar
250 g dates

Break biscuits in quarters. Chop dates fine. Melt butter
and sugar, then add dates and simmer till dates are soft.

Remove from stove and quickly beat in the beaten egg.
Replace on stove and add biscuits and cook for a few
minutes, till biscuits are coated with date mixture.

Spread out on foil and carefully roll up like a thin swiss
roll. Sprinkle roll all around with dessicated coconut. Chill
for few hours. When cold slice thinly.

Pineapple Dessert
(COLOUR PHOTO 336)

1 pineapple grated
sugar
2 eggs
¾ cup milk
1 tin cream or 1 cup fresh for topping
1 egg white
2 tbsp castor sugar

Grate pineapple — measure and put in pot. Take an
equal measure of sugar, add to pineapple and cook gently
till sugar absorbed. Allow to cool.

Beat two eggs and mix with milk and then mix with
pineapple.

Spread mixture in a greased glass casserole and bake at
350°F (180°C) till set.

Make a meringue by beating egg white stiff with castor
sugar. Spread this over warm pudding and return to oven
till meringue is done.

Beat cream lightly, spread over cool dessert and
decorate with pineapple rings and cherries.

Cheese Cake
(PYRAMID SHAPE)(PHOTO PAGE 333)

125 g butter (½ cup)
1 egg
250 g cream cheese (1 cup)
24 tennis biscuits
½ pint fresh cream (1 cup)
80 g sugar (1/3 cup)
5 ml vanilla essence
15 glacé cherries
1 cadbury flake chocolate
tin foil

Cream butter and sugar. Add egg, vanilla and cheese.
Place 3 rows with 4 biscuits on tin foil (place rows lengthwise — side by side). Spread rest of mixture over biscuits.

Place a row of cherries down the centre.

Lift foil from both sides of the pyramid leaving the
centre 4 biscuits to form the base, close foil. Chill cake for
a few hours. Before serving, spread cake over with
whipped cream and decorate with chocolate flake.

Simple Cheese Pudding

¼ cup milk
1 pkt Marie or Digestive biscuit (crumbed)
½ cup butter
1 box creamed cottage cheese (250g)
½ cup sugar
3 egg whites
1 cup cream lightly whipped
¼ tsp vanilla
1 dsp gelatine dissolved with 2 tblsp water OR
2 tsp faloods grass powder (agar-agar) dissolved in boiling water

Grease a casserole. Melt butter in a pot and add crumbed biscuits.

Mix together and pat half of this mixture into the casserole. Beat cottage cheese, sugar and milk together.

Whisk egg white till stiff and whip cream lightly. Fold cream and egg white into cottage cheese mixture.

Add vanilla essence and either the gelatine or the agar-agar, stir in lightly.

Pile mixture into casserole and sprinkle remainder of the biscuit over the top. Leave in fridge to set.

VARIATIONS:

1. Fold in 1 cup pureed strawberries — add to cottage cheese mixture.
2. 1 cup grated pineapple

Mock Cheese Cake

1 tin Nestles Condensed Milk
4 eggs (separated)
1½ tsp Maizena (level)
½ cup lemon juice
1 pkt Marie Biscuits
⁵/₈ cup Margarine

A spring-form cake tin (loose sides which can be removed) is recommended. Crush biscuits very finely with a rolling pin.

Add the melted margarine or butter, mix thoroughly, line a greased cake tin base with the biscuit mixture.

Leave about ¼ cup mixture. Into the 4 egg yolks stir the maizena, mix well then add the tin of condensed milk, stirring well, then add the lemon juice.

Beat egg whites till they stand in peaks, then very carefully **fold** into the above mixture with a wooden spoon.

Pour this whole mixture onto the prepared biscuit mix. Now sprinkle a ¼ cup of the biscuit crumb mix over the custard looking mixture.

Bake in a medium oven for approx 35 to 40 minutes. Leave in pan till cold, then very carefully lift the outside of the cake pan off after having loosened the sides of the cake with a knife.

Jerusalem Baqlava

2 cups flour
¼ tsp salt
¼ tsp baking powder
1 cup ground nuts (fresh)
2 tblsp lemon juice
2 tblsp oil
2 eggs
1 cup melted ghee
1 cup slivered nuts and pistas
2 tblsp honey
½ cup water

Place sifted flour in basin and make a well in middle. Add eggs, oil and water, and slowly work in the flour from the sides till a dough is formed. Knead and pound dough on board for 15 minutes. It will be smooth and supple. Cover and keep in fridge for 20 mins.

Divide dough in 10 parts. Roll each portion out on floured board till it is paper thin. Grease a large baking tin and put one roti on this. Brush the surface with melted ghee and put on another roti. Brush the surface of second roti with ghee, then sprinkle liberally over it, a mixture of the honey, lemon juice and nuts. Again pile on a double layer of roti and then add nuts over them. When last double layer of rotis are piled on, score through the baqlava in diamond shapes and bake in 180°C-200°C oven for 30 minutes or till baqlava is a beautiful golden colour. Remove from oven and whilst baqlava is still hot, brush with a little melted ghee and sprinkle nuts and pistachios.

When cold make a syrup of sugar and water flavoured with rosewater. Pour this syrup over the baqlava, allowing it to drain off at the sides and between the scored diamond design. Cut out in diamond shapes and serve as a dessert or with tea.

Halwa E Muzaffar
(Extraordinary Halwa)

This halwa is most unusual in that it is made from meat!

It also has a story. Two gentlemen are responsible for my attempt to devise this recipe, and I have named it after the one who first made reference to it.

My late husband and I were invited to the home of an Indian couple in Montreal. While the lady had cooked a delicious meal, it was the husband who enthused over cookery for it was his hobby to collect old Mughal recipes.

Muzaffar Saheb mentioned that he had come across a most unusual formulae for a halwa made from milk and meat. Unfortunately the method was vague and the quantities of the various ingredients not stated! That was years ago!

Recently the eminent lecturer Maulana Akbarabadi was a guest in my home. over lunch he mentioned that the most unsusual desert he had ever tasted was made from milk and meat but that his hostess had refused to divulge the recipe since it was an old family secret coming down from the days of the Mughals.

This recalled our conversation with Muzaffar and I set about experimenting. The result is this recipe which may not be the greatest in the world but it is certainly unusual for who has ever tasted a desert made from meat!

Heat ghee in a separate pan and when it is really hot pour over halwa.

Add mawa and all over ingredients marked with an asterisk to halwa.

Stir frequently over low heat to prevent halwa from scorching.

Steep saffron in 3 tablespoons of boiling milk. Sieve this into halwa.

Now taste for sweetness and adjust sugar according to taste.

When ghee floats free of halwa it is done.

Serve in crystal bowl garnished with slivered nuts and silverwarak.

NOTE: If a more crumbly halwa is desired, then mince the soaked meat — drain off all moisture and add to milk. In this instance the halwa must not be put in the blender and pureed.

A Urad Paad (338)
B Pineapple Dessert (334)
C Pastry Tart
F & D Melting Moments (372)
E Plaits (326)
G Marie Biscuit Delights (374)
H Swedish Tea Ring
I Coconut Date Tart

Serves 20 people:
500 g mutton or chicken breasts (meat only)
2 litres milk
150g mawa (see page 352)
*1 tin condensed milk
Additional sugar to sweeten (up to ½ cup)
*1 cup fresh cream (or tinned)
*½ cup freshly blanched and chopped almonds
*½ cup freshly blanched and ground almonds
*½ cup fresh coconut (grated)
*1 tsp pounded elachi
1 tsp saffron strands
1¼ cups ghee
*1 tsp rose essence
¼ cup slivered almonds and pistachios
Silver Edible Paper (WARAK)

Remove all fat from meat. Chop into cubes and wash thoroughly. Soak meat overnight in cold water.

Put milk and meat to simmer gently over low heat for 2 hours.

Blend very fine in blender till a thin puree results.

Return puree to pot and continue simmering till contents become mushy.

Dodhi Paak
(VARIATION)

2 cups grated dodhi
2¼ cups water
2 cups icing sugar
½ lemon juice
½ tsp crushed elachi

Boil the dodhi in 1½ cups of water, then squeeze through cloth all excess water.

Make a syrup with the icing sugar and remaining water, add the lemon juice. The syrup is done when a bubble will form on the spoon.

Add the dodhi to the hot syrup and add the elachi. Put in casserole to set. Sprinkle with almonds.

Carrot or Dodhee Paak
(CAN BE MADE WITH PUMPKIN AS WELL)

1 litre milk
½ tin condensed milk
¼ cup (or more) sugar
2 tblsp ground almonds
1 tblsp slivered almonds
2 tblsp fresh coconut (ground)
1 cup grated dodhi
small tin of cream (155g)
1/3 cup ghee
½ tsp powdered elachi
1 tsp saffron (optional)
1 tblsp dates or sultanas

Boil milk and add dodhi. Cook till thick. Add sugar and simmer until mixture is like thick porridge. Add condensed milk, flavourings, sultanas, coconut, almonds and dates and stir all the time.

Cook till milk is absorbed. Add cream and keep over very low heat. Meanwhile heat ghee separately and pour over paak.

Keep over heat till mixture is fairly thick. Tip out in casserole and allow to set and cool. Sprinkle with sliced nuts and cut in diamond shape.

Dodhi Halwa Variation

½ litre milk
180g mawa (see page 352
1 tsp rose water
1 cup dodhi
¾ cup sugar
¼ tsp ground elachi

Grate dodhi then measure required amount. Put milk to boil and keep on stirring till it begins to thicken. Now add grated dodhi and keep on stirring till thick and mushy. Add sugar and keep on stirring till thick like porridge. Now add mawa, stirring continuously till a halwa of an even consistency results. Add rose water, elachi and a drop or two of green colouring. Pat in thali and cut in squares when cool. Decorate with slivered pistachios, almonds and edible silver paper. This soft halwa must be stored in fridge if it is meant to keep for longer than a day.

Urad Paak
(COLOUR PHOTO 337)

500g urud flour (black gram flour)
500g castor sugar
125g freshly ground almonds
125g goondar
1½ cups milk
2½ cups ghee

Add small quantities of milk to sifted flour and rub through fingers. Continue till flour is damp.

Add ½ cup ghee, again moisten flour with ghee. Push through wire sieve so that no lumps remain. Take the 2 cups ghee and slowly braise flour mixture till the flour becomes lightly tanned.

Switch off heat and add castor sugar, almonds and goondar. When this is well mixed and incorporated in flour mixture, spread out in trays to set.

Sprinkle top with charoli and slivered almonds, cut in diamond shapes.

Carrot Halwa

A few strands of saffron (optional)
2 cups carrot pulp (or 1½ cups carrot and ½ cup
   dodhi pulp)
2 litres milk
1 cup ghee
2 tblsp cream of wheat
1 tin cream (155g)
Sugar to taste (¼ cup or more)
1 tsp elachi (fine powder)
1 tin condensed milk (397g)
2 tblsp ground almonds
3 tblsp blanched slivered almonds and pistachios
1 tblsp freshly grated coconut or dessicated coconut

Scrape and wash clean the carrots or carrot and dodhi. Mince it through a mincer or grate it very finely. Boil this pulp in milk over low heat carefully watching and stirring at intervals to prevent milk from scorching. If boiled too fast the carrot will not blend in smoothly in the milk.

When mixture is thick and mushy, leave aside and in a separate pot, heat the ghee with the cream of wheat, till latter is golden colour. Add the carrot pulp to this and stir vigorously. Add cream, condensed milk, coconut and ground almonds and sweeten with sugar to taste. Some people prefer halwas very rich and sweet, in which case add more sugar. The ingredients quoted here results in a very eatable and palatable halwa. The halwa must now be stirred vigorously as it will after the sugar stage, scorch very easily. When the halwa is fairly dry and the ghee skims to the top it is done. Before serving sprinkle slivered almonds and pistachios.

Variations of Carrot Halwa

Using same methods and ingredients as above, cook halwa very dry till no moisture is left. Allow to cool on flat shallow trays. When cold, sprinkle with slivered almonds and pistachios and cut in small diamond shapes.

Dodhi Halwa in Klim

1 cup klim powdered milk
1 litre milk
¼ cup freshly ground almonds
1 cup sugar
1½ cups dodhi (250g)
½ tsp ground elachi

Blend klim with ½ cup of milk very carefully, so that no lumps remain. Put grated dodhi in rest of milk to cook slowly till mushy. Add sugar and keep stirring continuously till thick like porridge. Now add the grated almonds and elachi and stir well. Continue cooking till the halwa is made. Cool slightly then pack in thali or casserole. Decorate with edible silver paper and slivered pistachios. Cut in diamonds or squares.

NOTE:

When boiling milk, etc. if the rim of the utensil is greased with a little glycerine, this prevents milk from boiling over.

Dodhi Lagan
(MARROW DESSERT)

1 litre milk
¼ cup khus-khus
¾ cup sugar
¼ cup ghee (2 tblsp)
½ tsp elachi
1 cup grated dodhi
½ cup fresh grated coconut
¼ cup soji
2 eggs

Boil grated dodhi in milk over slow heat till it is well absorbed and thick like milk pudding. Add khus-khus and coconut and simmer slowly for about 10 minutes. Add sugar and continue to simmer slowly. Meanwhile braise cream of wheat in ghee in a frying pan till light pink in colour and add to above mixture. Stir in well and remove from heat.

Beat eggs till frothy, add elachi and mix well into cooled dodhi mixture, taking care that eggs do not cook, which is likely to happen if mixture is not sufficiently cool. Beat briskly.

Spread in greased thali or casserole and decorate with khus-khus and slivered almonds and bake in 180°C oven for 30-40 minutes. Cut in diamond shapes and serve.

Jatka Halwa in Syrup

3 cups cake flour
2 tblsp cream of wheat (soji)
*2 cups sugar
*1½ cups water   for syrup
3 tblsp heaped solid ghee
1 tsp elachi seeds
1 tblsp khus-khus (poppy seeds)
*1 egg
*¾ cup milk   beat together
*¾ cup water
½ cup slivered pista and almonds
2 tblsp coconut (dessicated)

Beat egg, milk and water together.

Mix flour, cream of wheat together and rub in ghee.

Sprinkle small amount of egg/milk mixture over the flour and keep on forming pea-sized balls which must be in 3 different sizes ranging from small peas to larger ones.

Sort out different sized flour balls and keep them in separate heaps.

Make fairly thin syrup with sugar and water, add elachi to it and keep on side of stove away from direct heat.

Fry pea balls in small quantities, using small amounts of ghee at a time, till they are gold in colour. Fry the larger ones first and add to pot of warm syrup. Continue in this way till all the balls are fried (small ones last).

Replace syrup with balls over low heat, sprinkling an additional 1/3 cup milk over them. All the syrup and milk must be absorbed by the balls. Finally, sprinkle coconut, almonds and pistachio and carefully mix into halwa.

Jatka Halwa in Milk

2 cups cake flour
1 tblsp cream of wheat
¼ cup melted ghee
*1½ cups sugar
*½ cup water
1 tsp elachi
1 tblsp khus-khus (poppy seeds)
½ litre milk (for boiling)
¼ cup slivered pistas, almonds
1 tblsp charoli
1 cup milk (for sprinkling)
½ cup ghee   *syrup

Mix cream of wheat and flour and rub in ghee.

Sprinkle small quantities of the one cup of milk over flour and keep on moulding three sizes of balls which range from small size peas to larger ones. Sort out balls and keep each size separately in trays.

Put ½ litre of milk on stove and as soon as it reaches boiling point switch down and keep simmering very gently.

Starting with the larger sized balls, fry them in small quantities of ghee till they are gold in colour and lower into simmering milk

Fry khus-khus in a tablespoon of ghee and pour over balls.

When the fried balls have steeped well in the milk, remove pot from stove.

Tip out contents of pot into a fire-proof casserole. Make syrup with sugar and water, add elachi and pour over casserole. Bake at 180°C for about 1 hour.

When nearly done, sprinkle with slivered nuts and bake till jatka halwa is a lovely pale gold colour. Serve warm.

Cake Flour Halwa

2 cups flour
3 cups milk
½ cup ghee
6 eggs
1¼ cups sugar (adjust according to taste)
6 elachi (seeds of cardomom)

Braise flour in ghee till pink. Meanwhile break eggs in bowl, add milk, sugar, elachi. Beat well and add to braised flour, stirring briskly to avoid any lumpy mixture. Keep on stirring over low heat, till thick like pudding. (Like thick Kheer). Spread in greased casserole, sprinkle with almonds, or serve in small individual bowls. Should be served warm.

Ginger Halwa with Honey and Dates

500g ginger
½ fresh coconut
125g slivered almonds
180g honey (½ cup)
1 cup ghee
250g chopped dates (1 cup)
125g ground almonds (½ cup)

Scrape ginger clean. Wash and drain. Now grate ½ of ginger and grind the other half. Grate the fresh coconut.

Heat ghee and braise both grated and ground ginger slowly in it, till dry and gold in colour. Add coconut and ground almonds and braise for 10 minutes. Add the honey and simmer till fairly dry. Add dates and slivered almonds and cook for 10 to 15 or more minutes. Store in glass casserole and eat 1 tablespoonful of this with morning tea or coffee. Delicious with coffee after dinner.

NOTE:

Try and obtain tender ginger.

Ginger Halwa in Milk

COLOUR PHOTO 160

500g ginger, scraped, washed and minced
2 litres milk
1 tblsp chirongee (or charoli)
½ tsp saffron
2 tblsp sultanas
sugar to taste (approx ¾ cup)
½ cup ground almonds
2 tblsp pistachio
125g dates (finely chopped)
1 cup ghee
¾ tin condensed milk (275g)
2 drops of Kevra essence (optional)

Bring milk to boiling point.

Add ground ginger and simmer gently till a soft solid mass results (like mawa).

Heat ghee and blend mawa into it. Add nuts, fruit and condensed milk, stirring all the time. Taste and add as much of sugar as is necessary. Stir till halwa is fairly dry and ghee floats on top. Serve garnished with slivered almonds.

Batata Puri

(SWEET POTATO PURI)

1 cup mashed sweet potato
60g sugar (¼ cup)
1 walnut-sized lump of butter
1 tsp baking powder
¼ tsp salt
Flour to form dough

Mash sweet potatoes after boiling them soft. Add butter, baking powder, salt and sugar. Mix lightly and add enough flour to form a fairly stiff and rollable dough. (Care must be taken to drain off any moisture from mashed potatoes otherwise it will make a sticky dough).

Roll out to ¼ inch thickness, cut out with biscuit cutter to desired shapes and fry in hot oil like puris. Drain off. Scrumptuous with coffee if eaten hot.

Keeps well in tin.

Fried Dates

Pit dates, stuff each date with an almond. Fry in shallow ghee. Serve as sweets after tea.

Khajoor Paak

(DATE FUDGE)

2 pkts dates (500g)
3 dsp ghee
250g ground almonds and pistachios
3 tblsp freshly ground coconut
1/3 tsp elachi powder
1 tblsp sesame seeds (tal)
a few strands of saffron

Pit dates and grind through mincer. Mix in almonds and coconut. Heat ghee and braise sesame seeds and add the dates when they turn pink in colour.

Braise date mixture in ghee till it is shiny.
Stir in elachi and tip out in tray or casserole. Pat down smoothly.

Sprinkle slivered almonds over surface.
When cool, cut in squares and serve like sweets.

Mithi Roti

(EASY METHOD) (PHOTO PAGE 343)

DHAL FOR FILLING:
2 cups toovar dhal (oil lentils)
2 cups water
¼ tsp elachi powder
2½ cups sugar
2 tblsp ghee

Soak dhal overnight or at least for a few hours in cold water.

Wash off all the skins. Put in pot with water and bring to boil, then reduce heat and allow to simmer slowly till soft and mushy.

Sieve through wire strainer. Return to pot, add sugar and cook till nearly dry.

Stir continuously to prevent scorching. Add ghee and allow to attain a lovely golden colour.

Cool, then form into ping-pong sized balls and leave aside on floured plate or board.

THE DOUGH:
2 cups flour
3 tblsp ghee (solid)

Rub ghee in flour till latter is fine like breadcrumbs. Using just sufficient boiling water, make into dough the consistency of puri dough.

CAUTION:

Do not overknead. The dough will have a porous texture.

Divide dough into balls which are the same size as the dhal balls.

Roll each into a circle, approximately thrice its present size.

Place a ball of dhal in the centre and carefully close over, with dough.

Roll out again in neat even strokes, avoiding breaking of dough till roti is size of a small bread plate.

Braise over tava (griddle) till underside is slightly freckled.

Turn over, and as soon as it balloons up, pour a dessertspoonful of melted ghee carefully over surface. Turn again and spread with ghee on reverse side.

As mithi rotis are braised rather quickly, it would be advisable to roll them all out first, before attempting to braise them. In this event keep the rolled out rotis on a floured board and cover with a slightly damp cloth, lest they dry out.

Variation Batata Mithi Roti

After mashing sweet potato in pot, mix in sugar and butter to make mixture like dhal for mithi rotis. Flavour with elachi.

When cold, take ping pong-sized ball and put in mithi roti dough and proceed as for mithi rotis.

Pumpkin Mithi Roti

Make dhal of mashed pumpkin with sugar and use in mithi rotis. (See colour page 287).

A Jam Pastry (368)
B Mitha Samoosas (347-348)
C Mithi Roti (342)
D Naan Khataay (362-3)

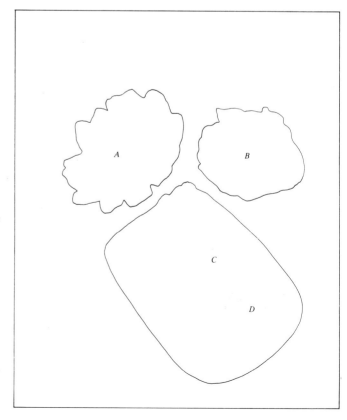

Mitha Samoosas

Though there are many variations of this very delicious Indian pastry, whether baked or fried, whatever the difference in making the dough or whatever the filling used the rolling procedure remains the same.

(a) Dough must be kneaded smooth, it must be pliable and easy to roll without tearing.

(b) Divide dough into number of portions called for in recipe.

(c) Roll each portion out into as large a roti as you can manage — it must be tissue thin.

(d) Smear evenly with whatever oils called for in recipe.

(e) Pile rotis up one on top of the other, taking care that smeared side is put over smeared side of the one below. In this manner only the underside of the first one of the pile, and the topside of the top-most roti will be unsmeared.

(f) Roll slightly over pile to ease out any air pockets.

(g) After this the pile of rotis is either rolled over like swiss roll (in which event top of pile will have to be smeared with oil again) or squares cut out and rolled to size of samoosa required.

(h) If it is intended to make khajas then follow instructions as how to fold and nip back corners.

(i) When frying it is best to fry each samoosa individually since the feather like wafers can break very easily. The best method is to put a samoosa on a large slotted spoon (jara) then lower this in the heated oil and hold it with the left hand — meanwhile with right hand lightly pouring oil from side of pan over the samoosa with a deep ladle.

(j) Drain on wire rack, thereafter line a tin or cardboard box with newspaper covered with a top sheet of brown or tissue paper. Place samoosa on this pile, cover with more tissue, or with thin muslin and leave for a day or two till all oil is absorbed, leaving samoosa delightfully crisp.

FILLING No. 1

1 cup dessicated coconut
1 tblsp ghee
¾ tsp elachi powder
Condensed milk
¼ cup slivered almonds
3 tblsp slivered pistachios
3 tblsp charoli
1 tblsp sultanas

Keep a dish of cold water nearby then braise coconut in ghee till aroma arises, but before it changes colour add sultanas, elachi and almonds — stir quickly then plunge pan in cold water so that coconut does not scorch — when cold sweeten with condensed milk.

FILLING No. 2

60g mawa
4 tblsp fresh coconut
¼ tsp elachi
2 tblsp freshly ground almond
1 tblsp sultanas (optional)
Condensed milk to sweeten

FILLING No. 3

2 tblsp cream of wheat
1½ cups coconut
1 tblsp sultanas (optional)
¼ cup sugar
½ cup slivered almonds and pistachios
Condensed milk to sweeten

Braise cream of wheat in 1 tblsp of ghee.

When it turns pink, add coconut and sugar and braise for a minute. Remove from stove, add almonds, pistachios and condensed milk.

The Oil for Smearing

Melt the ghee and slowly work in the amount of flour or rice flour called for in recipe — when it bubbles remove from stove and plunge it immediately in cold water so that flour does not darken. This thin paste of oil/flour is then brushed over the rotis.

The Photograph shows the balls of dough rolled out like thin tissue paper. The one on the marble slab can hardly be seen for it is virtually transparent.

Alongside on the tray the rolled out rotis have been piled on top of each other after being brushed with melted ghee (in pot).

Mitha Samoosas

THE PASTRY:
3 cups flour
1 tblsp ghee (solid)
1 tsp (heaped) baking powder
Luke warm water to make stiff dough

THE GHEE/FLOUR FOR BRAISING:
3-4 tblsp of ghee (adjustments will have to be made for
hot days and the thickness of ghee when used)
8 tblsp of flour

After pastry has been rolled, (see below) put the ghee and flour in pan on stove to braise. When it bubbles remove from stove and plunge pan in cold water so that flour does not darken.

Divide dough into 8 portions and roll out to paper thin rotis.

Smear with braised flour/ghee mixture as explained above and pile rotis on as in Indian type pastry.

Divide pile of rotis in half and pile the semi-circles together so that you have 16 layers. (See photo page 349).

Cut this into 5cm squares, pinch back each corner about 5mm towards centre of square and place the dough with pinched corners side facing downwards.

Roll with light hand to a little puri sized circle (5mm thick) and fill each circle with a little filling.

Brush edges with white of egg and close over like a jam tart. Fry each samoosa in deep ghee/oil (¼ ghee and ¾ oil) over low to medium heat.

It would be best to fry samoosas individually.

Place each samoosa in a slotted frying spoon inside pan or deep pot, and pour over it continually the heated ghee till samoosa is crisp but has not changed to deep colour.

Cool and drain on wire racks. Line a tin or cardboard box with newspapers, cover with a clean white cloth and place samoosas inside for a day or two so that all excess ghee is absorbed by cloth, leaving samoosas delightfully crisp.

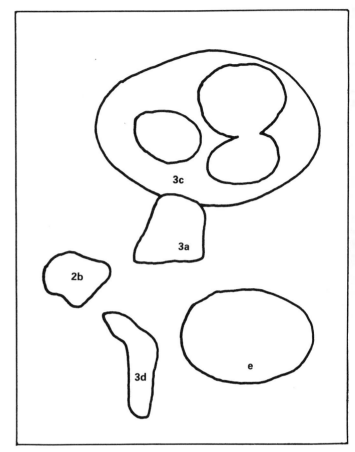

Photograph on Page 347 shows a plate of fried chana puri at far end.

On marble slab the khaja dough (recipe Page 350) is cut into squares.

1. (a) Squares being rolled out.

   (b) Squares then filled with savoury filling and folded over.

2. (a) Squares have been folded with 4 corners meeting in centre to form an envelope shape — it can be fried at this stage, (see diagrams and recipe on page 351)

   OR

   (b)The envelope shape is turned over and again the corner brought to centre to make a smaller envelope.

3 (a) The piled up dough is smeared on top and then rolled up like swiss roll and finger-wide circles are cut.

   (b) The finger-wide circle is rolled out into a circle (e) this gives you pin wheel pastry.

   (c) On silver plate the fried pin wheel pastry filled with sweet or savoury filling can be seen. (See pin wheel pastry — page 192).

   (d) The finger-wide circle is flattened down and rolled into a long shape — this is the shape required for Banana Puris. (Page 351).

Varkhi samoosa rotis thinly rolled, piled one on top of the other then cut into half and the one half put over the other. (Photo opposite)

Baked Mitha Samoosas

1 tin cream (155g)
3 eggs
3 tblsp thick ghee
3 tsp baking powder
Sufficient flour to make dough
Extra ghee (melted) for smearing

Beat ghee, eggs, baking powder and cream till fluffy and creamy. Work in flour to make a soft pliable dough.

Divide dough into 10 rotis and roll out very thin. Smear tops of rotis only, sprinkle with flour and pile one on top of another.

Cut roti into 4 equal quarters and pile these on top of each other. This will ensure you 40 layers.

Divide piled dough into 9 or 10 portions. Roll each out and fill with filling.

Bake in 180°C oven — after 10 minutes pour a tablespoon of melted ghee over each samoosa, then return to oven to finish baking.

NOTE: These samoosas must be filled up well. You will need at least 4 cups of coconut as a start for the filling.

Banana Puri
(FLAKY FRIED WAFERS)

1 tsp ghee
2 cups flour
¼ cup milk
Pinch of salt
½ tsp baking powder
¼ cup water
1 egg
Pinch of salt

Beat milk, water and egg together. Sift flour with salt and baking powder. Rub in ghee and form into fairly stiff dough with milk/water liquid. Proceed to roll as above.

THE SYRUP:

Boil 1½ cups sugar in 1 cup water till thick and syrupy. Add ½ teaspoon of rose water for flavour.

Banana Puri Variation

1½ cups flour
¾ tsp baking powder
1 egg yolk
1 tblsp ghee
Pinch of salt
Yoghurt

Sift dry ingredients. Rub in ghee and egg yolk and make into dough to consistency of puri using just enough sour milk for that purpose. Proceed to roll and fry as for Khajas.

NOTE:

Instead of sprinkling with flour, maizena gives better results.

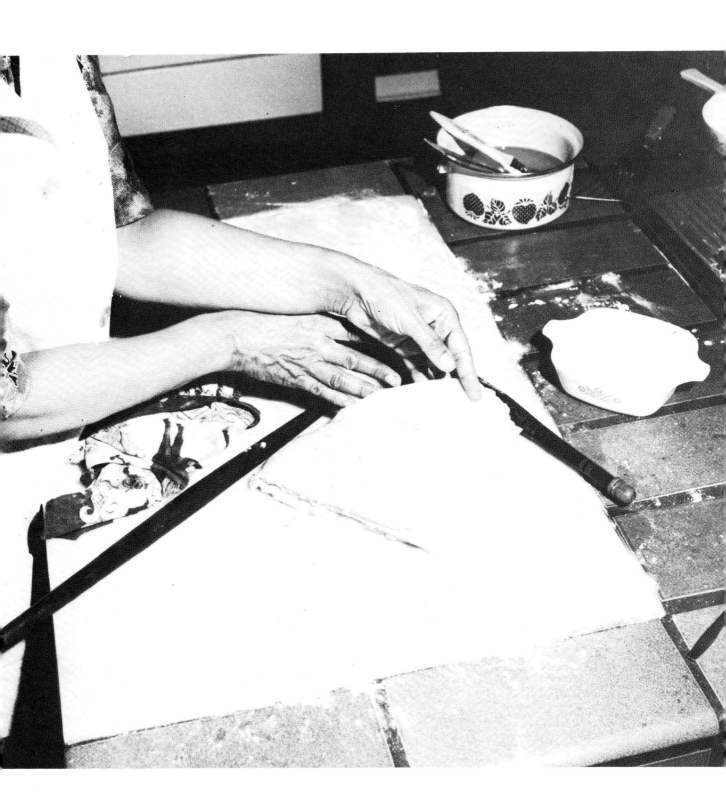

Khajas (BANANA PURI)

Maizena for sprinkling
2 cups flour
60g butter
Pinch of salt
½ tsp baking powder
Few drops lemon juice
1 cups sugar
1 cup water
Rose water or elachi for flavour

Mix flour, salt and baking powder. Rub in butter till flour is like breadcrumbs. Add drops of lemon juice into iced water and knead into a stiff dough. Leave dough for a few hours.

Divide dough into 8 sections and roll each one out into a large thin roti (like tissue paper).

Brush each with melted ghee, sprinkle with Maizena and sandwich together, piling one on top of the other.

Roll out together slightly. Brush top of this large roti with ghee, sprinkle with Maizena and roll up like a swiss roll.

Cut roll into 1cm thick sections. Flatten each one slightly, with the layers showing on the two sides, with roller till it is the length of a man's forefinger.

Fry in deep ghee/oil over slow heat till they are crisp but still in colour.

Drain on wire racks and when cool pour carefully about a tablespoon of syrup over each side.

Dry off on grease proof paper.

Rose Petal Pastry

Maizena for sprinkling
1 egg
1 tsp baking powder
Milk to form dough
2 cups flour
1 tblsp ghee

Rub ghee into flour till it resembles breadcrumbs. Add beaten egg and just enough milk to form a stiff pastry dough. Knead well.

TO ROLL:

Divide dough into 8 portions and roll each out into a large thin roti. Smear 7 of these rotis with melted ghee and sprinkle with Maizena. Pile one on top of the other and put an unsmeared roti on top of pile. Roll out slightly to smoothen.

TO FORM INTO ROSE PETALS:

With sharp knife, cut through piled dough into diamond shapes (8-10cm large). fold each diamond shape at its broadest point (see diagram) and slightly pleat or gather at this line, giving the whole a good twist to form a stem. When all diamonds have been formed, cover with damp cloth and fry as for banana puri (see beginning of section, page 346). Drain on wire rack and when well drained and cold, pour over rose syrup (see page 348).

NOTE:

Any of the other Khaja or banana puri dough may be used to make pastry of this shape.

Banana Puri (Khaja)

(SEE PAGE 347)

3 cups flour
1¼ cups milk
1 egg
2 tblsp ghee (level — solid)
2 tsp baking powder

Banana puri may be frozen after swiss rolling. Cut in 2.5 cm wide slices, flatten tops slightly to give you the length and thickness you want then put in plastic container, lining different layer with plastic sheets.

When required fry in a small deep pan, and when oil is 180ºC (temperature of frying Gulaab Jamboo) lower each banana puri turning frequently and pressing down with spoon to keep puri submerged, as soon as it has filled out and different layers have separated put in another puri and treat it in the same manner as the first — as soon as the first one is crisp remove on to wire rack to drain.

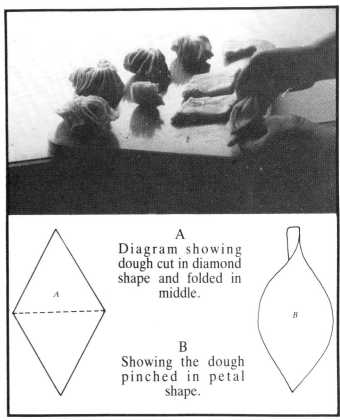

A
Diagram showing dough cut in diamond shape and folded in middle.

B
Showing the dough pinched in petal shape.

1. Cut dough in squares of size below.
2. Fold along AB so that corner 1 falls on E.
3. Similarly fold other solid lines so that corners 2, 3 and 4 all centre on E.
4. Now reverse dough and fold along dotted lines so that they too centre on E.

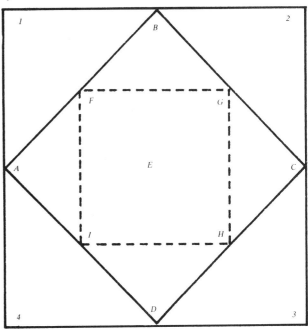

Burfee

(PAGE 166)

Using approximately 3 litres of milk make 500g Mawa.

TO MAKE MAWA:

Using 2 cups of milk at a time, boil rapidly over heat, stirring all the time and taking care that it does not scorch, till a hard lump remains. Remove lump and put aside.

Use up rest of milk like this till you have 500 grams of Mawa.

500g mawa
2 cups water
½ (75g) tin cream
360g sugar (or more)
250g powdered milk (Klim)
elachi powder ½ tsp
2 tblsp freshly ground almonds or pista
rose essence for flavouring

The mawa will be hard and lumpy so cut it up into pieces and put into mixing bowl.

Add cream, almonds and Klim to mawa and mix well together.

Leave aside for a few hours to dry. Put through an almond grinding machine and leave aside again for an hour or two or put through food processor.

Make a syrup by mixing water and sugar till all grains of sugar are well dissolved in the water.

Now put over heat and bring to boil.

Lower heat and continue boiling till only 1½ cups of liquid remains (syrup must be slightly thickened but not sticky).

Add rose water and elachi to syrup. Add the cream/klim mixture to the syrup. Lower heat and stir till syrup is absorbed by the mawa mixture.

Throw out into mixing bowl and leave for a few hours before patting it into burfee shaped blocks.

Decorate with slivered almonds that have been tinted in multicolours.

Burfee Variation

(PHOTO PAGE 360)

500g mawa
1 tblsp ghee
1 tin cream (small)
6 tblsp Klim (150g)
150g sugar (¾ cup)
1 tsp elachi
2-3 tblsp ground almonds
1 cup water

Mix cream and ghee into Klim, add mawa and mix well. Then grind in almond grinding machine.

Put on stove over low heat and continue stirring till mixture is fairly dry. Dissolve sugar in cold water by stirring

well then put over high heat and bring to boil till syrup begins to get sticky.

Pour over mixture. Stir vigorously, then allow to cool.

Leave for a few hours before cutting into blocks and decorate with tinted slivered almonds.

Burfee (with butter)

1 tin Nespray (500g)
1 tin Nestlé cream (155g)

Mix Nespray and cream together and leave for 1½ hours. Put through almond grinding machine or through food processor till evenly blended. This will now resemble mawa.

1 tin condensed milk (397g)
1 tin Nestlé cream (155g)
¼ cup butter (60g)
1 tin Carnation milk (410g)
½ cup sugar

Mix latter ingredients together. Put in pot and bring to boil.

Once it starts boiling, lower the heat but continue to stir vigorously to prevent scorching.

After about 10 minutes the contents will resemble a kheer (thick pudding) mixture.

Remove from stove and add the Nespray mixture in small quantitities at a time till all have been mixed-in.

Now add 1 cup of sifted icing sugar, ½ teaspoon of powdered elachi and 2 tablespoons of either ground almonds or pistachios.

Mix well, allow to cool and set in glass bowl of choice.

Cut in blocks and decorate with slivered tinted almonds etc.

Klim Burfee

500g powdered milk (Klim)
1 tsp elachi
½ pint fresh milk (1 cup)
rose essence
360 g icing sugar
3 tblsp sugar
2 oz butter (60g)
1 cup water

Mix Klim and milk together.

Rub with finger tips till mixture resembles fine bread crumbs. Mix icing sugar, butter and water together in pot and bring to boil.

Allow to infuse twice, then lower heat and add Klim mixture to it. Mix and stir well over heat for about 5 minutes.

Add flavouring, cool and leave in mixing bowl for a day before patting it into burfee shaped blocks and decorating with tinted slivered almonds.

Chana Magaj

(Photo Page 318)

60g Klim
500g chana (gram) flour
1 tblsp ghee
375g icing sugar
500g ghee (in hot weather use 2 tblsp less than specified)
½ cup milk (hot) (4 tblsp)
¼ cup almonds or pecan nuts (chop fine and roast in oven)

(a) Sprinkle 1 tablespoon ghee and milk over gram flour and rub between fingers till flour resembles fine breadcrumbs. Leave for an hour or two to dry completely.

(b) Heat ghee in thick based pan on stove, then add crumbed mixture in it and slowly allow to turn a light beige, but continue stirring all the time to prevent scorching, allow to cool. (30 to 40 minutes)

(c) Now add sifted icing sugar to the cooked gram flour mixture which will be lumpy after the roasting.

(d) Rub mixture with fingers, exercising great care and patience to break down the little globules until fairly uniform fine grains are produced, or put through food processor.

Lastly add and mix in the almonds reserving just a little for decorating the top.

Pack into a 4mm deep tray. When set, cut into blocks and lift out carefully. Sprinkle top with leftover roasted slivered almonds.

Chana Magaj Variation

(Photo Page 160)

500g chana (gram) flour
4 tblsp Nespray Powdered Milk
375g icing sugar
½ cup milk
2 tblsp ghee
½ cup Pecan nuts
500g ghee (in hot weather use 2 tblsp less)

Follow as in above up till stage B. Add sifted icing sugar and klim and proceed again as in above recipe.

Tapioca/Sago Halwa

1 dsspn lemon juice
1 kg sugar
7 cups water
150g tapioca
150g sago
2½ cups almonds, blanched and split or chopped as preferred (375g)
1½ cups ghee
½ bottle egg yellow colouring
½ tsp jelly red colouring
1 tsp crushed elachi seed

Soak tapioca and sago overnight in 3 cups of water. In the morning put through blender and liquidise fine. Push through strainer into pot to ensure that its absolutely fine. Any remaining liquid must also go into pot.

Mix rest of water, sugar, elachi and colouring into pot of tapioca, mix well.

Put on stove to boil and as soon as mixture becomes translucent and begins to jell, then add ghee and nuts.

Mixture will have to be stirred vigorously for well over an hour till it is sticky and gluey. Halwa is done when ghee begins to float on top and whole mass of halwa lifts up with spoon like toffee.

Tip out in deep tray to cool and settle. Cut in blocks on the following day.

> **NOTE:** If you prefer a very sticky halwa, mix in a tblsp of maizena when mixing tapioca mix with sugar/water.

Badam Luddoo

½ cup sugar
1 cup water
500g ground almonds
125g freshly made mawa from milk
½ tsp fine elachi

Mix almonds, mawa and elachi smoothly together.

Mix sugar with water and bring to boil. When syrup is about to spin a thread, test between fingers, and add the almond mixture and stir well for two minutes. Remove from fire and allow to cool.

Mould the mixture into round larwa shapes (ping-pong ball size). Roll in slivered pistas.

Mawa Ghari

White vegetable fat for dipping (Holsum)
1 cup flour
½ cup milk
1 tblsp ghee

Rub ghee in flour. Make dough with milk. This dough, though soft will require much kneading, (5 to 10 minutes). Knead till smooth and shiny. Test with back of thumb and if dough jumps back like elastic, it is done.

FILLING:
Mawa of ½ litre milk
1 tblsp coconut
¼ tsp powdered elachi
Castor Sugar (if filling is not sweet enough, add as much as is required)
2 tblsp ground almonds
½ tin condensed milk (200g)
Handful sultanas (optional)

Strain mawa through sieve. Add rest of the ingredients and mix well. Divide into ping-pong sized balls and keep aside. Divide dough in ping-pong sized balls. Roll each out to a 15cm diameter circle. Put a lump of filling in each circle. the filling must be patted into a thick disc, half the size of the dough. Carefully enclose filling with extended dough, cutting off any extra dough with a pair of scissors. Flatten the dough — press ghari slightly with a roller, to ease out air bubbles.

Heat oil in deep pan (medium heat). Place each ghari on a perforated spoon and lower into oil, keeping it well immersed. To pour oil over ghari with a ladle is not recommended, for that results in bubbly crust. Gently shifting slotted spoon in oil, prevents scorching. Fry over low heat for 5 minutes. Remove when ghari is light cream and drain on wire rack. When cool dip in slightly melted holsum. Dry and cool on wire rack.

Mawa Ghari (Variation)

DOUGH:
1½ cups flour
2 tblsp ghee

Form into dough with cold water.

FILLING:
1 cup cream of wheat
2 cups coconut
1 cup icing sugar
½ tin condensed milk (200g)
2 tblsp ghee
Holsum (white veg. fat) for dipping

Braise cream of wheat in ghee and just as it turns pink, add coconut and sugar. Remove from stove and add condensed milk.

Roll rounds of Ghari and add filling. Pat into shape. Fry very slowly in deep oil by placing on slotted spoon and lowering in oil — do not pour oil over top as this makes crust bubble.

Remove when paste has hardened and is deep cream in colour. Dip each in slightly melted Holsum (125g). Dry on wire rack.

Masoor Paak

Syrup
2 cups water
3 cups sugar

½ tsp elachi powder
1 tsp rose essence
A few drops of egg yellow colouring
500g Ghee/oil (half ghee and half oil)
2 cups chana flour (gram)

Dissolve sugar in water. Add flavourings and just a few drops of egg yellow colouring to tint syrup a pale mustard in colour. Bring to boil and when syrup starts spinning a strong thead, lower heat. The syrup must still be kept warm but not allowed to boil further.

Meanwhile sift chana flour into a bowl and keep it near stove.

Also put ghee/oil on stove and heat until hot.

With a milk ladle pour (about a quarter of a cup) of the hot ghee/oil over the flour and with finger tips rub it in so that flour resembles breadcrumbs.

Add flour mixture to pot of syrup and braise over gentle heat. Keep on stirring and adding ladlesful of ghee/oil, until all the oils have been absorbed by the flour.

After 12 to 15 minutes the mixture will start to turn pinkish at the sides and will fall away from the sides of the pot. This is a sign that the masoor is done. Tip out into a deep tray (5 cm) and allow to cool and set but cut into diamond shaped blocks before it gets hard.

Gulaab Jamun
(INDIAN DOUGHNUTS)

¼ tsp bicarb
½ tin condensed milk (200g)
1 cup flour
1 tsp baking powder
1 tblsp soji (semolina)
1 tblsp ghee
¼ tsp fine elachi (ground)

Put dry ingredients in bowl, add ghee and elachi then add the condensed milk and make into soft dough.

Roll into length and thickness of forefinger and fry in ghee/oil over medium heat (deep frying strongly recommended) and care should be taken that the heat is lowered and the jamboos slowly allow to swell. Remove from ghee when golden brown and drain in colander. Meanwhile prepare a syrup as follows:

SYRUP:
Boil together 1½ cups sugar and 1 cup water. Flavour with 1 tsp of rose water and remove from stove before it starts to get sticky. However syrup must be left over very low heat so that it is warm for dipping. (Caution: the syrup must be thin). Dip the hot jamuns in it. Drain and cool.

Gulaab Jamun
(without cream of wheat)
(Photo Page 318)

1 tin condensed milk (397g)
1 tblsp ghee
2 cups flour (adjust)
3 tsp baking powder
Elachi
Ghee and oil for frying
½ tsp bicarb

Mix milk, ghee and elachi, and beat well. Add baking powder and bicarb, mix. Sift flour and put into dish of milk mixture and make into a nice soft dough. Shape into long finger shapes and fry slowly (180°C temperature). Dip into hot syrup.

Mawa Gulaab Jamun
OIL (Photo Page 196)

125g mawa
1 small tin condensed milk (155g)
1 level tsp baking powder
¼ tsp elachi
1 level tsp ghee
Cake flour to form soft dough

Mix ingredients well together and mould jamuns to size of ladies' forefinger. Over gentle heat in deep ghee/oil, fry to a pale golden brown. Remove and dip into syrup. Dry off on wire rack. May also be moulded round.

Gulaab Jamun
(WITH ALMONDS) (PHOTO PAGE 160)

2½ cups flour (adjust)
1 tin condensed milk
¼ tsp bicarb
1 egg
pinch of salt
2 tblsp ghee
3 tblsp freshly ground almonds
3 tsp baking powder
¼ tsp elachi powder

Sift dry ingredients together. Add almonds. Rub in ghee, add beaten egg and condensed milk and mix into a soft dough.

Mould into forefinger-sized jamuns and fry in deep oil over medium heat. Drain on wire rack.
Dip jamuns in cool syrup.

Gulaab Jamun Variation

1 tin condensed milk
4 tbsp soji (cream of wheat)
4 tsp baking powder
3 cups flour
2 tbsp ghee
2 eggs
1 tsp elachi (cardomom)

Beat ghee, soji and eggs well together. Add milk and elachi and beat again. Lastly add flour and baking powder and mix to form soft jamun dough. Leave in fridge overnight. Fry next day, in deep oil over moderate heat (400°F) till jamuns are a lovely dark tan colour. Dip in syrup.

THE SYRUP:
Mix 1½ cups sugar in 1 cup water and when sugar is dissolved, put on stove and boil till syrup begins to form.

Mawa Gulaab Jamun Dessert

500g mawa (see page 352)
1 tin Nestles cream (155g)
1 tsp baking powder
Flour as needed

Measure off 500g of mawa. Mix in cream till it is of even consistency. Add baking powder and mix sufficient flour to make dough the consistency of goolab jamuns. Fry slowly in ghee or oil as preferred. Cool. Soak in flavoured syrup till serving time and serve in little bowls (two jamuns per person) with a tablespoon or two of the syrup.

Rusgullah
(TRADITIONAL)

2 litres milk
1 tsp alum powder
15 pieces of misri (sugar candy)
*2 cups sugar
*3 cups water
*¼ tsp elachi seeds

NOTE: If alum powder is not available add 2 tblsp of lemon juice.

Bring milk slowly to boil. As soon as it starts boiling, add the alum or lemon which will make milk curdle up in lumpy masses.

Strain off water and hang the lumpy mass in a muslin bag for about 2 hours. This dry mass must be passed twice through a mincer.

Divide this minced mass into fifteen lumps. Mould each lump gently around the small pieces of sugar candy.

Make syrup with water, sugar and elachi seeds, then lower these rusgullahs in a rapidly boiling syrup made from the sugar, water and elachi seeds and keep simmering for 20 minutes.

At intervals of every 4 or 5 minutes, a tablespoon or two of hot water will have to be added to syrup to prevent it from crystallizing.

Cool and serve rusgullahs with a little of the syrup.

RUSGULLAH IN RASMALAAI: (Page 141)
Remove rusgullah from syrup and serve them in rasmalaai made thus:

Boil 2 litres of milk over low heat till it is thick and creamy and measures about ¾ litre.

Add sugar to sweeten, and flavour with a few drops of rose essence and good pinch of elachi powder.

Add the cold rusgullah to this milk base and leave in fridge to get cold.

Serve cold in small glass bowls.

Rusgullah
(VERY EASY)

500g Ricotta cheese
1 tblsp sugar

Mix together, then mould into balls and bake in 180°C oven till firm.

1 carton Ultra Mel Cream
sugar to sweeten
1 tblsp gound almonds
2 tblsp milk

Dissolve sugar in milk and cream. Blend in almonds and bring to boil. Put in Rusgullahs and steep in fridge till needed.

Sprinkle with pistas and serve cold.

Rusgullahs (with Mawa)

1 cup mawa (see page 352)
2 tsp Maizena
½ tsp Baking Powder
1 egg white
few drops rose essence

SYRUP:
Make a thin syrup with 2 cups water and 1½ cups sugar and keep aside.

Break up mawa into bowl and add all other ingredients. Knead into a smooth dough.

Form into small ping pong-sized balls (rather like large marbles) and fry in ghee over slow heat.

Do not allow balls to change colour for they must be snow white or a very light cream in colour.

Soak balls in syrup till most of syrup is absorbed into the balls. Serve in small dessert bowls.

Penda

1 cup mawa (see page 352)
500g icing sugar
2 tsp rose water
Elachi

Grind the mawa through a mincer, add icing sugar, rose water and elachi.

Take dough into hands and rub well until very smooth. Make into round balls.

Flatten slightly, but dome the top side and decorate with almonds.

Badam Halwa

(PHOTO PAGE 318)

1 7/8 cup maizena (250 g)
4 cups white sugar (1 000 g)
3 cups whole almonds (500 g)
1 tsp crushed elachi seeds
Few strands saffron
1 cup ghee (thick) (250 g)
1 tblsp egg yellow colouring (½ bottle)
8 cups water (1 litre)
½ tsp jelly red colouring
2 tsp lemon juice

Blanch almonds and split in two halves.

Mix maizena and sugar with lemon juice and cold water, then add colourings and mix well. Put in flat thick based pot or Indian style keraai and put on stove to boil. Stir and when it starts to jell add the ghee, almonds, elachi and saffron strands. Keep on stirring vigorously taking care that mixture does not stick to pan (approximately 1 hour). By this time it should be a thick sticky mass virtually lifting out of the pan.

Slightly grease 30 x 20 x 5 cm deep casserole or pan and tip out the halwa into it to set. The halwa should be the consistency of toffee but should you have tipped it out too soon, keep it in a warm oven for a little while. Allow to cool and serve the next day. This halwa keeps indefinitely if left in fridge.

VARIATIONS:

Mixed Nuts: Proceed as above but instead of almonds use:

1 cup blanched pistachios (split)
1½ cup blanched almonds (split)
½ cup blanched charoli

Pistachio: Proceed as above but use pistachios only or half pista and half almonds. Use ¼ tblsp green colouring only.

Walnuts: If using walnuts do not use any colouring.

Coconut Paak

1 cup water
500g dessicated coconut
375g sugar
½ tin condensed milk (200g)
1 tin cream (155g)

Mix coconut with milk and cream. Make thick sticky syrup out of sugar (syrup must spin thread). Pour hot syrup over coconut and mix well. Add elachi. Put aside to set. Cut into squares. (If preferred tint to a pale green or pale pink).

Jalebis

Some people like a starter as a rising agent for their jalebis and others again opt for baking powder or yeast. Our basic recipe can be adapted for any of the three agents.

A starter is made by pouring 2 cups of water over a cup of brown unsifted flour. Each evening and morning (for 2 days) drain off top moisture and add fresh water to it.

½ cup starter or ¼ cake yeast (7 g) or ¼ tsp baking
  powder
2 cups cake flour
1¾ cup lukewarm water
1 tblsp rice flour (optional)

Sift flour (if using baking powder then sift with flour.

Yeast must be crumbled and mixed into paste with a little water then added to the flour. The starter must be rubbed into flour). Add rising agent of choice and mix into smooth thickish batter which is of a consistency that is easy to force through a jarra. Keep batter uncovered for 10 hours or overnight.

Heat oil in deep pan (175°C). Put some of the batter into either jalebi machine, a forcing bag with a tube or an empty milk tin with a hole punched into the bottom.

Make jalebi squiggles directly into the hot oil (about three inch wide pretzel shapes) and fry each batch of 4 jalebis for about two minutes or till they are a gold colour on both sides. Dip each jalebi into the syrup (prepared beforehand as stated below) for a minute and leave on wire racks to drain off.

THE SYRUP:
2 cups sugar
Good pinch cream of tartar
Jalebi colouring or egg yellow colouring
1¾ cups water
2 tblsp rose water

To cold water in deep pot add the sugar and cream of tartar. Stir over medium heat till sugar dissolves. Allow to boil rapidly for five minutes without stirring. Remove pan from heat and add colouring and rose water. Keep syrup warm and handy for dipping as soon as jalebis are fried.

Larwa or Luddoo

(PHOTO PAGE 318)

500g sugar (2 cups)
1 cup water
250g chana flour (2 cups)
1½ tsp baking powder
¼ bottle egg yellow colouring
Tinted slivered almonds
½ tblsp ghee (solid)

Make a sticky syrup of water and sugar, removing it to side of stove so that it keeps warm.

CAUTION:

Syrup must not begin to spin threads and must be removed from heat when it begins to thicken.

Sift dry ingredients and rub in ghee. Add 1 cup water and form into thick batter. Press this through larwa making pan or large holed colander held over hot oil. Fry till a golden colour. Steep the bhoondis (which is the term for the worm shaped fried larwa bits) in the hot syrup till all the syrup is absorbed. Cool and set aside for an hour or two, then mould handfuls of bhoondis to form larwa sized balls. Roll these balls in the brightly tinted slivered almonds.

Seerkhomo Cake

250g soft butter
½ cup sugar
2 cups flour
¼ cup sultanas
2 cups coconut
2 tsp ghee
¾ tsp powdered elachi
1½ cups milk
4 eggs
4 tsp baking powder
½ cup slivered almonds
1 tblsp soji
½ cup ground almonds
1 cup sugar

Braise soji in ghee and just as it begins to change colour add the almonds, coconut, sultanas, elachi and ½ cup sugar. Sift flour with baking powder and rub in soft butter. Beat eggs and sugar (1 cup) till thick. Add flour and milk and lastly the seerkhomo mixture (nus/sugar/soji, etc.) Pour in greased pan or casserole and bake for 30 minutes in 180°F oven.

Sutherfeni (COLOUR PHOTO PAGE 99)

Housewives have in the past decade been able to master the art of sutherfeni, which in the past was left to the care of professional mithai makers. We are indebted to a friend who not only gave us her recipe but consented to have the whole process photographed. As will be gauged from the photographs, much proficiency must be gained before one can shred the dough to the flaky hair-thin strings, which is the criteria by which sutherfeni is judged. Most appropriately the children have named this sweet, "granny's hair", because it is as white and fragile as granny's hair. (See photograph on next two pages)

THE DOUGH:
3-4 tblsp oil
6 cups flour
2½ cups water
Oil for frying
125g vegetable fat (Holsum)

BEGINNER'S RECIPE:
2 cups flour
125ml water
Oil for frying
SYRUP:
1¼ cups water
2 cups sugar

Using just as much water as is necessary, make a stiff dough with the flour and water. Leave overnight, covering the dough with a damp cloth.

CAUTION:
Keep dough covered with a damp muslin cloth during all stages of sutherfeni making. Again when handling, keep dipping fingers in a bowl of cooking oil kept on the table for that purpose. This will prevent dough from sticking and make it more pliable.

With a wooden pestle, pound the dough to absolute smoothness. Alternately put it twice through a mincer. The dough should now be stiff but as smooth and pliable as a piece of plasticine.

Manipulate dough between palms of hands so that thick coils of ropes are formed. Continue rolling in this manner, drawing and extending the coiled rope, till a continuous rope (the size of a lady's little finger) forms easily.

NOTE:
Beginners are advised to use the smaller recipe.

ILLUSTRATION "A" (Top photograph Page 360)
When pencil thick strings of even thickness begin to form easily, break off lengths the width of your table (an enamel surface table is best for sutherfeni making) or a large marble or rolling board if you prefer using this.

Place these pencil thick strings of dough alongside each other till all the dough is used up.

ILLUSTRATION "B" (Bottom photo Page 360)
Grate vegetable fat and mix it with 3 or 4 tblspoons oil, so that after much rubbing and creaming with fingers it is of soft, face-cream consistency. Rub this cream evenly over the surface of the strings on the table. Gather the strings together and roll-up like a swiss roll. Leave aside for half an hour.

ILLUSTRATION "C" (Top photo Page 361)
Cut of protruding strings from each end of swiss roll so that it is of even and uniform size. Now commencing from the middle of the swiss roll, once more proceed to draw strings from the dough. It will be noticed that automatically a thinner string (like 6 ply knitting wool) begins to be drawn. Instead of placing them on the table, proceed to wind the string between thumb and extended forefinger, taking care that you wind in such a manner that the pile becomes higher and higher. when the pile is about three inches high, break off and commence another. The piles will resemble miniature bird's nests. From your dough you will be able to manage about 8 birds' nests. Leave for 20 minutes.

ILLUSTRATION "D" (Top photo Page 361)
With gentle pressure of left hand, press at bottom and sides of bird's nest in such a manner that the top widens slightly, and the bottom narrows down. Simultaneously with the right hand (dipping fingers in oil every now and then so that they are perpetually moist) gently pat the top of the nest so that it collapses and instead of a bird's nest you now have something resembling a woman's hair bun which is 5mm thick. Proceed as above till all the buns have been formed.

ILLUSTRATION "E" (Bottom photo Page 361)
In deep oil over high heat, briskly fry the buns with the help of a jara (Indian type of frying spoon with colander type perforations). At intervals of a minute or two, turn the bun over till it is crisp and the hair-like strands are clearly separated and visible. Remove from oil whilst bun is still a light cream in colour. Drain on wire rack that has been placed over a tray which has a rim, for oil will continue to ooze out for a long time. Keep on rack for several hours.

Place sutherfeni over thick layers of newspaper that has been covered with brown or lunch paper. Any excess of oil will be absorbed by the paper, leaving the sutherfenis dry and crisp.

TO SERVE AS MITHAI
Pour thin syrup over sutherfeni and garnish with brightly tinted slivered almonds.

AS AN EXCLUSIVE DESSERT
Serve in individual plates a whole sutherfeni, with slightly whipped cream and garnished with slivered nuts, strawberries, flaked chocolates, etc., or with ice cream.

A

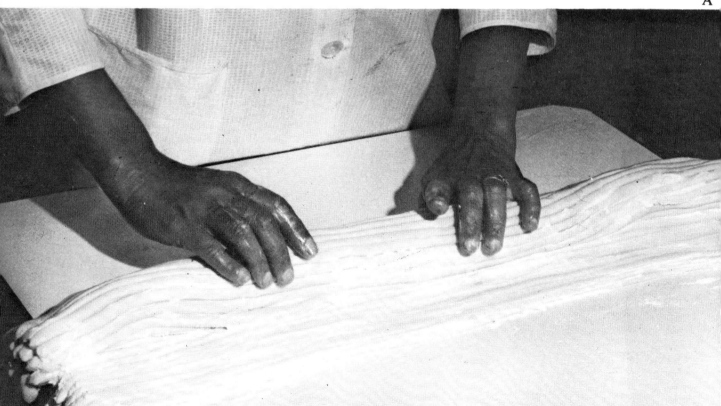

B

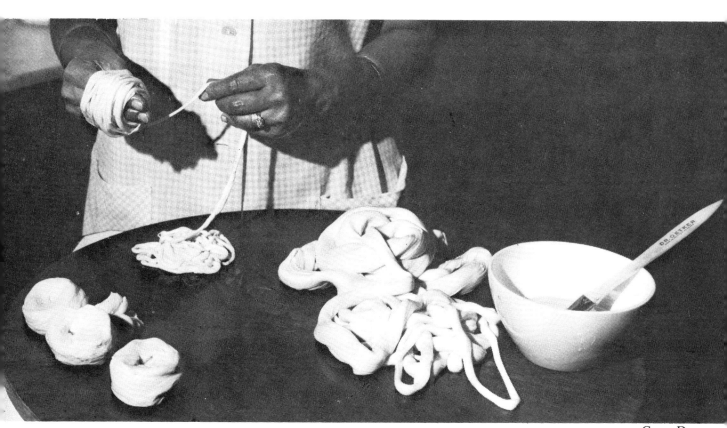

C   D

E

Naan Khataay No. 1

(PHOTO PAGE 343)

¼ tsp crushed elachi
1 cup ghee
¾ cup castor sugar
1 1/3 tsp bicarb
2 tsp baking powder
4 level tblsp cream of wheat (soji)
4 tblsp condensed milk
2 yolks of eggs
2½-3 cups flour (approx. 350g)

Cream ghee and castor sugar well together. Add yolks of eggs and beat in.

Add all other ingredients, except flour and beat till light and creamy.

Add sifted flour carefully to achieve consistency of biscuit dough.

Mould lumps of dough and flatten into naan khataay shapes, (5-6cm in diameter and 1cm thick).

Press down one whole unblanched almond in centre of each naan khataay.

Bake in 190°C oven for 5 minutes, switch down to 150°C and continue baking for 20 more minutes.

Switch off oven, but leave biscuits to get crisp.

Naan Khataay

(PHOTO PAGE 160)

¾ cup castor sugar
1 cup ghee
1 egg
2 tsp baking powder
½ tsp of bicarbonate of soda
¼ tsp elachi or nutmeg
Flour to form dough (2½ cups)

Put ghee in bowl and add baking powder, sugar, and spices. Stir briskly with spoon, add egg and stir till fairly frothy then add in enough flour to form a biscuit-like dough.

Divide dough into ping-pong sized balls. Roll between palms of hands, flatten with finger (½ inch thick) leaving indents and pinches, and finally place a blanched whole almond in the middle.

Bake in 185°C to a pale cream colour like short-bread. Cool in pan before removing, as it is likely to break if removed while still hot.

Naan Khataay with Rice Flour

1 cup ghee
1 egg yolk
1 tsp elachi (powdered cardomom)
¼ tsp nutmeg
1 tbsp rice flour
Flour as required
¾ cup castor sugar
 tsp baking powder
¼ tsp bicarb
1 tbsp cream of wheat (soji)

Beat ghee and sugar together till light and fluffy. Add yolk and beat again. Add all other ingredients except the flour and beat in.

Finally incorporate just as much flour as is needed to make a soft biscuit dough. Form into naan khataay shapes and bake in 400°F (200°C) oven for 10 minutes.

Switch down to 150°F and finish baking till biscuits done.

Naan Khataay with Chana Flour

1 cup ghee
1 cup castor sugar
¾ cup chana flour
dash of nutmeg
dash of elachi powder
½ tsp bicarb
2½ to 3 cups flour

Cream ghee and castor sugar well, add bicarb and beat again. Lastly add sifted dry ingredients.

Bake at 350°F for 20 minutes.

Coconut Naan Khataay

1 cup ghee
1 cup castor sugar
1¼ cup coconut
2½ to 3 cups flour
1 egg yolk
2½ tsp baking powder
½ tsp nutmeg or elachi

Beat ghee, castor sugar, baking powder and spices well together.

Then beat in egg yolk. Mix in coconut and add as much flour as required.

Bake in 200°C oven for 5 minutes, then lower heat to 150°C. Switch off oven. Leave naan khatay in oven till cool.

Butter Naan Khataay
(SHORTBREAD)

50g castor sugar
100g butter
150g plain flour

Pre-heat oven at 170°C (340°F).
Sift flour, rub in butter with fingertips and knead very lightly till smooth.
Press into ungreased baking tin and prick all over with a fork. Flute edge with forefinger and thumb.
Bake in centre of oven for about 35-40 mins or until light brown in colour. Remove from oven. When slightly cool, cut in triangles.

Naan Khataay with Ghee/Oil

½ cup ghee
½ cup castor sugar
Yolk of 1 large egg
½ tsp bicarb
½ cup oil
¼ cup tayssatee wheat
2 cups flour
1/3 tsp baking powder

Boil together ghee and oil. Cool completely. Cream together the above with castor sugar till thick and creamy for 10 minutes.
Stir in taystee wheat, add yolk and beat for another 10 minutes. Sift flour, baking powder and bicarb. Add to creamed mixture to make a soft dough. Shape in rounds.
Place 7 cms. apart on ungreased sheet. Bake for 10 minutes on 350°F to 300°F for another 5 minutes. (180°C)

Bow Tie Delights

1 cup flour
½ cup milk/water (sufficient to make a soft, rollable dough)
1 tsp thick ghee

Rub ghee in flour and make dough with milk/water.
Roll out dough and cut out in circles the size of small saucers. Leaving a centre rib of pencil-thin dough, make slits from opposite edges towards this rib at finger-wide distances.
After slits have been made, gather centre rib together.
Now twist right hand side of rib completely over to form a frilled bow tie shape.
Fry bow ties slowly in deep oil till they are pink and crisp.
Dip in syrup (see page 355).

Muska-na Biscuits
(INDIAN RUSKS)

4 cups flour (full)
1 cake compressed yeast (20g)
1 tsp salt
3 tsp jeero (cummin)
250g butter
1 cup warm water (or more)
2 tsp sugar

Break yeast into warm water, add sugar and stir till finely blended.
Sift flour and salt and rub butter into flour till it is like fine breadcrumbs.
Add jeero and make into dough with the yeast/water mixture. (Dough will be sticky).
Let rise in a warm place for a few hours and when it is about twice the volume, knead a little and form into small marble-sized balls.
Put aside in tray for another half an hour or longer (till it has risen again) and bake in 180°C oven for half an hour then switch the oven down to 100°C and continue to bake for three or four hours. The finished Muska-na biscuit will be shiny and hard outside but scrumptuously crisp inside.

Muska-na Biscuits with Bhugroo
(RESIDUE OF MELTED BUTTER)

2 cups flour
2 tblsp heaped, bhugroo
¾ cup malaai (cream from top of milk)
1½ tsp baking powder
1 tsp jeero (cummin)

Mix bhugroo in flour till fine, like breadcrumbs. Add jeero and baking powder. Make dough with malaai. Very sticky, soft dough will result.
Form in small marble-sized balls. bake in 180°C oven for 30 minutes, then switch down to 125°C and bake till hard like rusks.

Muska
(VARIATION)

2½ cups flour
1 tblsp crushed jeero
½ cup water
2 tsp baking powder
¾ tsp salt
½ cup (cream or malaai)

Western Delights

This section devoted to cakes, biscuits and desserts cannot be termed 'Indian' as it is entirely 'Western' in origin. However they are perhaps as common in our homes as Indian type desserts, which tend to be much richer. Therefore no cookery book purporting to be representative of South African Indian Cooking would be complete without them.

Owing both to shortage of space and the knowledge that so many comprehensive books on this subject are freely available, we have omitted here the better known sweets, and included only those that enjoy overwhelming popularity amongst Indians. It will be noticed that recipes calling for dates, honey, nuts, etc. have been given preference. This reflects the Indian gourmets predilection for these commodities.

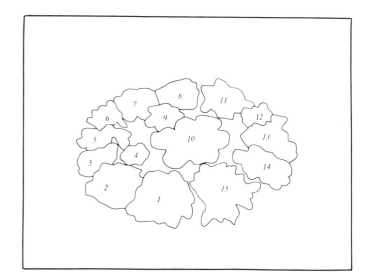

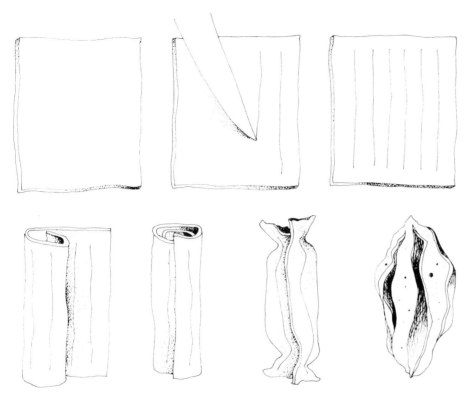

Chinese Lanterns

(PHOTO PAGE 364) (See diagram above)

3 cups flour
¼ tsp baking powder
3 tbsp butter
Salt to taste
1 tsp mangrel (onion-seed)

Sift dry ingredients together. Rub in butter and form into stiff dough with a little cold water.

Make into stiff dough. Roll out thin and cut rectangular pieces. Make lengthwise slits as shown in the diagram. Roll lengthwise and press at both ends. Fry in deep oil.

Mitha Tukra

¼ cup dessicated coconut
¼ cup milk
½ cup sugar
1/8 tsp elachi (ground)
2 tblsp cream of wheat (soji)
½ cup water
2 tblsp ghee
Flour

Boil together, water, milk and sugar. Cool. Add ghee, cream of wheat, coconut, elachi and sufficient flour to make a soft puri-type dough. Roll out on floured board and spread with ghee as you would a roti. Fold like roti and roll out again to thickness of roti. Cut in diamond shapes. Fry in deep hot oil till golden brown. Drain and cool on rack.

Cream Maska-na Biscuits

2 cups flour
4 tsp baking powder
½ tsp salt
½ cup butter
1 tsp jeero (or shah jeero)
1½ cups thin cream

Sift flour with salt and baking powder. Add jeero and rub in butter.

Add cream and make soft maska biscuit dough. (Very soft). Heat oven to 180°C and bake for 12 minutes. Reduce heat to 125°C and bake for 1 hour longer. Leave to dry out in cool oven. When cold, pack in tin, closing lid tightly.

Pastry

In most Indian homes in South Africa, pastry is a firm favourite. Even though the principles of making it are so different from the varkhi type of pastry, many Indian housewives have mastered the art so well, that they could possibly teach it to women from whose country it originated. Many again have become frustrated in their efforts and given up in despair. To such, we feel that if they but understood the basic principles involved they would soon be able to make it successfully.

Most housewives know that the making of pastry on cold and rainy days is more rewarding. With the help of refrigeration and thermostatically controlled ovens however, there is no reason why it should be any the less successful on warmer days as well.

See recipe page 368

COLD INGREDIENTS: Hands, utensils and ingredients must be cold. This prevents butter from melting and oozing out, which results in heavy unappetising pastry.

COLD AIR: In pastry this is your valuable agent. The frequent rollings and foldings are aimed at trapping-in as much atmospheric air as possible, which when put in a hot oven expands and results in the alternate layers of pastry and air, giving the desirable flakiness and lightness.

SIEVING IN AIR is absolutely essential in successful pastry making and it is therefore recommended that you sift dry ingredients at least twice.

DOUGH: The grating of butter and then resting it in the fridge makes it easier to manipulate the dough. After the flour has been sifted finally into the mixing bowl, mix your cold water/lemon or soda-water, and take a quarter or a third of the grated butter from the fridge. Rub butter into flour with finger tips till it resembles breadcrumbs. Dexterity is the key to success and over-handling causes heaviness and toughness to pastry.

FOLDING AND ADDING BUTTER: As the idea of frequent foldings is to incorporate the rest of the butter in manageable quantities, and to wrap-in as much air as possible, care should be taken to keep butter away from edges, and to press down slightly the edges, so that both butter and air do not escape.

RESTING DOUGH IN BETWEEN ROLLINGS gives butter a chance to harden and to form into layers with the dough. Dexterity in rolling is essential to use swift, light pressure and keep a forward direction only instead of rolling backwards and forwards.

BAKING: Remember that the folded-in cold air, will expand in the oven and cause the flour grains to burst and absorb the rapidly melting butter. Thus if the oven is not hot enough the butter will melt and run out instead of being absorbed. Secondly, that if the oven door is opened or heat reduced too quickly, the quickly risen pastry will flop down and nullify the efforts, and lastly, that pastry must be prevented from burning. So for **Initial Expansion** put pastry in hot oven for 5 minutes. **To maintain the rising** reduce heat to 200°C for another 5 minutes, then for **Crispiness** switch down again to 180°C and continue baking for 10 more minutes. Switch off and finish baking.

STORING: Store in airtight tins lined with paper after pastry is absolutely cold. Pastry dough can be left in freezer after rolling — carefully seal in double layer of plastic bags. Thaw at room temperature, then roll out for filling of choice.

IN FREEZER: Baked pastry may deteriorate. If intended to keep for some time, storing in freezer is most successful. Natural thawing at room temperature will leave pastry as crisp as it was at the time of freezing. If required more quickly put in warm oven for 5 minutes.

Basic Pastry Dough
(SIMPLE)

2 cups flour
1 cup iced water
Juice of ½ lemon
¼ tsp salt
½ tsp baking powder
250g butter (1 cup)

Grate butter and leave in fridge. Sift flour with salt and baking powder twice. Use ¼ of butter and rub it coarsely in into flour till it resembles fine breadcrumbs. Add lemon juice to iced water and use just enough to make uneven dough.

Caution: Do not over knead dough. Handle just as much as is necessary to make a rough textured dough.

Roll out on slightly floured board in oblong shape. Dot with ½ of left over grated butter. Fold over 1/3 of dough then bring over the last 1/3. Roll out again and use up left over butter dotting all over dough. Fold in envelope shape and roll again. Leave in fridge for at least 1 hour. Roll out two times in swift, sure strokes. By this time butter should have been evenly absorbed into dough. Leave in fridge for another ½ hour covering with plastic or muslin cloth. Then use as required.

Baking of tartlets, pies and other filled pastry, pre-heat oven to 250°C. Bake for 5 minutes then reduce heat to 200°C. Bake another 5 minutes, once more lower heat to 180°C and bake for 10 more minutes. This ensures a crisp pastry which will not go soggy.

Caution: Avoid opening door of oven within first 10 minutes of baking.

Pastry

(EXCELLENT) (COLOUR PHOTO PAGE 343)

3 cups cake flour
½ cup maizena
½ cup flour
1 tsp cream of tartar & ½ tsp
½ tsp salt
500g butter
1 egg yolk
1 tsp white vinegar
1 cup iced water
1 tsp sugar

Sift together the ½ cup flour and cream of tartar and leave aside in small bowl. (Flour-mix).

Sift together the maizena and ½ tsp of cream of tartar. Keep in separate bowl.

Beat egg yolk and vinegar together and keep aside. Divide butter in 5 equal portions and keep in freezer.

Sift the 3 cups flour with salt and sugar in mixing bowl and cut one portion of butter into it.

Rub through fingers till flour resembles bread crumbs.

To egg yolk, add sufficient water to fill a cup. Add slowly to flour and working very lightly, make into dough which is the consistency of firm but not frozen butter.

Roll out dough on a board sprinkled with a tablespoon of maizena/cream of tartar blend, and sprinkle maizena mix thickly over top of surface.

Grate 2/3 of another portion of butter over dough, sprinkle flour-mix over it and fold 1/3 of dough over. Grate remaining portion of butter over the folded portion, sprinkle with flour-mix and fold over again. Wrap in plastic bag and keep in freezer for 20 minutes.

Repeat process with remaining 3 portions of butter but remember to sprinkle liberally with maizena and flour-mix — leaving dough in freezer in between rollings.

All of the flour and maizena will have been used up in this last rolling. Dough can be kept in freezer, wrapped in double plastic for use when required.

Hot Water Pastry

1 cup boiling water
250g margarine
1 tsp salt
4 level cups sifted flour

Melt margarine in boiling water with salt. (Do not allow to cool). Add flour into boiled water. Mix with spoon at first, then mix in with hands.

On floured board, roll and fold 3 to 7 times.

Fill pies, pattern top with knife, brush with egg yolk, and bake in 180°C oven for ½ an hour.

Date/Nut Pastry Roll

1 cup chopped walnuts or slivered almonds
1 cup chopped dates
Condensed milk
¼ cup dessicated coconut

Divide pastry in two. Roll each out to 3 mm thickness and brush lightly, all over dough, with condensed milk and distribute ½ of nuts, coconut and dates evenly. Roll up like swiss roll. Cut the roll 6 mm deep at finger-wide intervals. Bake in 250°F oven for 5 minutes. Reduce heat to 200°F and bake for 5 minutes. Further reduce heat to 150°F and bake for 20 minutes. Then switch oven till crisp. Allow to cool in oven. This will ensure crispness. Cut through in slices.

NOTE: Above filling can be put between two layers or in individual tarts.

Horse Shoe Pastry

(PHOTO ABOVE)

Prepare basic pastry dough as in pastry recipe on page . After repeated foldings and rollings, finally roll out dough into a large rectangle. Brush with beaten egg white, sprinkle with sugar and roll as indicated in photograph. Cut off in 3 mm inch slices. Sprinkle slices with a little sugar and put on baking sheet. Bake in 250°C oven for 5 minutes. Reduce heat to 180°C and bake for 10 more minutes. Finally switch off oven and allow pastry to cool off in oven.

Pecan Nut Biscuits

(PHOTO ABOVE)

Roll out pastry and cut in 7cm squares. Fold like a horn, filling the centres with halves or quartered walnuts or pecan nuts. Bake as for pastry.

Mille Feuilles
(1 000 LEAF PASTRY)

Using your favourite recipe and method make a pastry dough with half a pound of butter. Roll and fold till dough is ready to use. Leave in fridge for ten minutes then finally roll out to a large ¼" thick rectangle. Divide this rectangle into three equal parts (approximately 9 x 4½").

Place on large baking sheet and bake in 200°C oven for 5 minutes. Switch heat down to 150°C and bake for 10 minutes then switch off oven, and leave pastry inside till oven is cold.

TO SERVE:
Spread top of each pastry piece with apricot jam. Over the jam spread some whipped cream and put the three layers together by piling them one on top of the other. Smear sides and top with either some more whipped cream or with the following frosting.

FROSTING:
Mix a cup of icing sugar with some hot water till it is of a spreadable consistency. Let cool then smear all over mille feuille. This is a lovely dessert to serve after dinner. May be served with tea at parties. It is a firm favourite.

FILLINGS:
(1) Add ½ a cup of mashed strawberries to whipped cream and spread over jam on two bottom layers. Over top most layer and sides spread whipped cream and stud with halved strawberries.

(2) Instead of strawberries add chopped walnuts.

Croissants may also be folded as in diagram alongside. For recipe see overleaf.

Pastry Cigars

Roll out pastry dough into large oblong.

Cut into strips 6cm wide, place strips in freezer for 10-15 minutes. Brush with little beaten egg.

Sprinkle with sugar, coconut and chopped pecans. Chopped pitted dates can also be used.

Cut into squares. roll up like cigars and freeze for 15 minutes.

Bake as for jam tarts.

ALTERNATIVELY:
Enclose a whole pitted date in pastry squares.
Use serrated cutter for fancy edges.

Pastry Tartlets

Line patty pans with your favourite pastry recipe and put a dessertspoon full of mixture made as follows:

Beat 1 egg (small) and ¼ cup castor sugar till creamy.

Beat in ¼ cup of ground almonds or ½ cup dessicated coconut.

Bake in hot oven till pastry done.

When cool spread on top with a teaspoon of strawberry or apricot jam or add jam before putting in coconut filling.

ALTERNATIVELY:
Roll out pastry in two large rectangles. Spread one with aove mixture and cover with the second one. Cut out in finger shapes or small squares. Brush top with white of egg. Bake and when cool spread with jam and decorate with slivered nuts.

Pastry Fingers

Pastry dough
1 egg white
2 tbsp sesame seeds
10 tbsp icing sugar
coconut
chopped nuts

Roll out pastry 23 x 30 cms. Make paste of icing sugar and egg white lightly beaten. Spread over pastry. Sprinkle coconut sesame and nuts. Cut into fingers 2 x 7 cms.

Lift carefully on greased trays. Bake in 200°C for 10 minutes. Lower to 180°C and bake till done (about 10 minutes). Leave in oven which has been switched off until crisp.

Croissants

(COLOUR PHOTO PAGE 287)

½ tsp lemon or orange rind
1 1/8 cup butter (310g) or marge
1 egg and 1 egg yolk
20 g yeast
4 cups flour
1 tsp finely grated orange peel
3 tblsp sugar
1 tblsp water
1 cup milk (lukewarm)
1/8 tsp salt

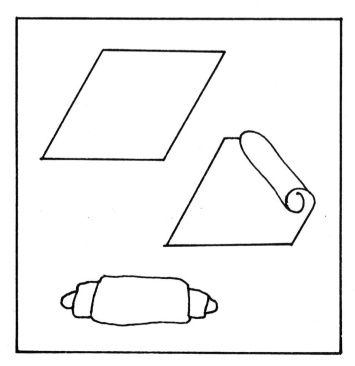

CROISSANTS METHOD

STEP 1:
Take 1 cup butter (250g) and divide into two parts, place each part out on a piece of foil. Pat and spread each part evenly into a 15cm square. Wrap the foil around the squares of margarine and keep in the fridge till required.

STEP 2:
Sift flour and salt into bowl and add rind.
Place yeast in a small bowl with a tsp of sugar, blend then slowly add the milk. Blend smooth then sprinkle a tablespoon of flour over mixture and keep in warm place for 10 minutes. Add remaining sugar to mixture.

STEP 3:
To yeast mixture add left over margarine and a lightly beaten egg. Mix flour with this, and form into a dough. Turn onto floured board and knead well for 5 to 10 minutes. Place dough in a lightly greased bowl and leave to rise till doubled in volume. (20-25 minutes).

STEP 4:
Turn out on floured board and knead for 3 minutes. Roll out dough into a 50 x 20cm rectangle. Place a slab of margarine in centre of rectangle. Bring right side of dough over rectangle and place the other slab of margarine on this. Bring over the left side of dough to cover the second slab of margarine. Seal folds well, then rest dough for 5 minutes.

STEP 5:
Roll dough out into rectangle and fold as before but without margarine this time. Roll out again and repeat folding process.
Freeze dough overnight or till required for use.

STEP 6:
Thaw at room temperature — roll out 3 or 4 times but there will be no need to refrigerate in between rollings. Then divide dough in half. Roll each out to 37 cm sq. Brush lightly with egg yolk mixed with water then divide each rectangle into 8 squares of 12cm each.

STEP 7:
Roll each square starting from one corner to the opposite corner — form into a crescent shape and leave on baking sheet to rise double in volume (about 15-20 minutes). Glaze with egg and bake in 200°C oven for 5 minutes. Reduce to 180°C and bake for 10 more minutes.

OR:
Roll each half portion of dough into an arch, starting from broad side. Roll each triangle piece to point — shape into crescent.

Roll out dough very thin (3mm). Roll over like swiss roll, cut roll in 5cm pieces — cut down halfway through each piece and spread out like butterfly. (Page 370).

Malaai Scones
(CREAM SCONES)

1 to 1½ cups malaai (cream skimmed off boiled milk)
3 tsp baking powder
1 egg
enough flour to form dough
3 tbsp sugar
1 tbsp butter

Cream malaai and butter till well blended in. (If malaai is rich and thick it will not be necessary to add the butter.)

Add sugar and beat well. Add egg and beat well again. Finally add dry ingredients and form into a scone dough. Roll out thickly. Brush with egg yolk.

Cut into squares or rounds or desired shapes and bake in 180°C oven till a light brown. Serve hot with butter or cream.

Sweet Dough for Coffee Cakes, Buns, etc.

4½-5 cups flour
½ cup butter or margarine
1 cup luke warm milk
1 tsp salt
2 eggs
1 cake yeast (20g)
½ cup sugar

Mix sugar, salt and milk together. Crumble the compressed yeast into the milk mixture, and stir till dissolved.

Add eggs and butter to bowl and mix well together. Finally add sifted flour, mix and knead well on floured board. Allow to rise double in bulk. Punch dough down, knead again and allow to rest for 20 minutes, as this will make it easier to handle dough. Roll dough into a large oblong. Soften 2 tablespoons butter and spread all over dough.

Mix ½ cup sugar and 2 teaspoon cinnamon and sprinkle all over surface. Over this strew ½ cup chopped nuts and ½ cup sultanas. Roll up like a swiss roll and bring the two ends together to form a ring.

Join the ends and place the sealed side down on a greased baking sheet. Cut from outer edge of ring towards the inner circle at every two finger wide distances (see sketch). Let rise again. Bake in 375°F (185°C) oven for 30 to 35 minutes.

Remove from baking sheet, but while still warm spread a frosting over it and decorate with nuts and cherries.

Aunty K's Tea Scones

1 cup cream
2 tsp sugar
good pinch salt
2 tblsp margarine or butter
3 tblsp grated cheese
3 eggs
3 tblsp coconut
¼ cup milk
5 tsp baking powder
sufficient flour to make soft dough

Beat eggs and cream in bowl. Add all other ingredients excepting the cheese and the flour.

Mix a little but do not over beat. Add sufficient flour to make soft scone batter.

Drop into greased muffin pans. Sprinkle grated cheese over each and bake in 350°F (180°C) oven for 15 to 20 minutes.

Cream Buns

4 cups flour
2 tbsp powdered milk
2 tbsp castor sugar
1 cup cream
1 tsp salt
¼ cup butter
15g compressed yeast
icing sugar (sifted for sprinkling)

Sift flour and salt.
To the powdered milk, add sufficient cold water to make 1 cup liquid. Place milk in pot with butter and half the sugar, and heat till lukewarm.

Cream yeast with rest of sugar until well blended in and it becomes liquidy.

Make a well in the centre of the dry ingredients, pour in yeast and milk mixture and beat to form an elastic dough.
Knead until smooth and shiny.

Cover with greased plastic and leave in warm place and allow to rise double in size.

Turn onto a lightly floured board and divide into 6 equal portions. Knead and mould each into a nice ball.

Place on greased baking trays and flatten slightly. Leave for 20 minutes.

Bake in top half of oven at 425°F (220°C) for 15-20 minutes. Dust top with icing sugar.

Almond/Coconut Bars

BOTTOM LAYER:
½ cup butter
1 cup cake flour (sifted)
½ cup sugar (white or brown)

Cream butter and sugar well together. Add flour. Mix well with hand. Press in bottom of ungreased pan 30 x 20 cm, and bake for 10 minutes in 180°C oven.

Meanwhile prepare topping.

TOPPING:
2 eggs
1 tsp vanilla
1 tsp baking powder
1 cup fresh grated coconut or dessicated coconut
1 cup brown sugar (or white)
2 tblsp flour
½ tsp salt
1 cup chopped almonds or nuts

Beat eggs well. Stir in sugar and vanilla. Add flour, sifted with baking powder and salt. Lastly add coconut and nuts. Mix well.

Spread over biscuit layer and return to 180°C oven. Bake for 25 to 30 minutes. Cut in bars whilst still hot.

Japanese Biscuits

(Photo Page 364)

1 cup butter
¼ cup oil
flour as required
¾ cup icing sugar
1 cup Maizena

Cream butter, oil and sugar till light and fluffy. Add Maizena and beat in.

Now add as much flour as is required to make a soft biscuit dough. Roll out on waxed paper and cut into squares.

Leave in fridge for half an hour. When cold gently remove from paper and place on baking sheet.

Bake in medium oven (150°C) for 20 minutes. Remove biscuits before they turn brown.

Melt a little jam and brush this diagonally across the little squares. Sprinkle some finely chopped nuts over the jam, or decorate the biscuit with a chocolate or other topping of choice.

Melting Moments (PHOTO PAGE 337)

1 cup butter
1 cup self-raising flour
pinch of salt
½ cup icing sugar
1 cup mazina

Make biscuit dough and press through nozzle. Bake in moderate oven. Stick together with icing or jam.

Coconut Rings

2 cups flour
1/8 tsp salt
½ cup butter (or margarine)
½ tsp vanilla
¼ cup castor sugar
1 tsp Baking Powder
2 eggs
coconut for rolling

Sift dry ingredients together. Rub in butter till flour resembles breadcrumbs.

Beat eggs and vanilla essence.
Add about 2/3 of this egg mixture into flour and form into soft biscuit dough. (Note: dough must be rollable).

Roll out to 5mm thick and cut into rings or strips. Dip rings in remaining egg and then into coconut.

Place biscuits on baking sheet and bake in moderate oven (350°F/180°C) until light brown. (About 10 minutes).

Almond Biscuits (PHOTO PAGE 364)

½ cup butter
1 egg yolk
1½ cups flour
¼ tsp salt
1/3 cup castor sugar
¼ cup ground almonds
½ tsp baking powder

Cream butter and sugar well together. Beat in egg yolk.
Add almonds and lastly sieve in flour, salt and baking powder. Mix into soft dough.
Roll out 5mm thick and cut in small rounds. Bake in 350°F (180°C) oven for 10-15 minutes.
When cold put together with jam and ice tops with vanilla icing.

VANILLA ICING:
To ½ cup icing sugar add ½ teaspoon vanilla and blend to spreading consistency with sufficient cold water.

Quick Savoury and Sweet Scones

(COLOUR PHOTO PAGE 287)

2 cups flour (sifted)
1 tsp salt
¾ cup milk
3 tsp baking powder
5/8 cup butter/margarine (6 tblspns)
2 tsp sugar

DO NOT OVERHANDLE DOUGH.

Sift dry ingredients into bowl. Cut butter into flour and rub till it resembles coarse bread crumbs. Stir in milk and form into soft but lumpy dough.

Gather dough and put on board and knead lightly with heel of hand several times. Roll out about 12mm thick and cut with round cutter.

Brush tops with beaten egg yolk or milk. Bake in 450°F (220°C) oven for 10-12 minutes.
Serve hot with golden syrup, honey, jam or cream.

Variation

2 cups flour
1 tsp salt
3/8 cup milk
¼ tsp bicarb
2 tsp baking powder
6 tblsp butter
3/8 cup yoghurt
1 tsp sugar

Sift dry ingredients together. Mix bicarb into yoghurt and milk. Rub in butter and add yoghurt mixture to form dough. Bake as above.

VARIATION A:

When mixing in butter add ½ cup grated cheese into flour.

VARIATION B:

Add 1 tsp crushed jeera (cummin) and 1/3 tsp black crushed pepper to flour.

Almond Meringue Torte

THE BATTER:
¼ cup butter
¾ cup castor sugar
1 cup flour
3 tblsp milk
4 egg yolks (well beaten)
1 tsp baking powder
¼ tsp salt

Mix together the butter and sugar till creamy. Add beaten egg yolks and beat in well into batter. Sift flour, baking powder and salt and stir into batter. Lastly add milk and mix in. Grease two 20 cm diameter pans and divide mixture equally and pour into pans. Top with the following meringue:

MERINGUE:
4 egg whites
¼ tsp cream of tartar
1 cup castor sugar

Beat cream of tartar and egg whites till frothy. Gradually add (two tablespoons at a time) castor sugar and beat till meringue stands in stiff peaks. Carefully put half of meringue over each of the pans with the batter.
Sprinkle half of following mixture over each meringue: ½ cup slivered almonds (crush up coarsely); and 2 tablespoons sugar. Bake in 160°C oven for 35 minutes. Serve with whipped cream.

Kakra Finska

(FINNISH BISCUITS) (PAGE 364)

¾ cup butter
1 tsp almond essence
¼ cup castor sugar
2 cups cake flour

Beat together thoroughly the butter and sugar. Add essence and mix in the flour with hands. Chill in refrigerator for an hour. Put the biscuit dough on a floured board and pat into a slab of approximately the following size: 5 cm wide, 2 cm high and 30 cm long. Now carefully cut with a sharp knife through slab at distances of not more than 6 mm. Each thin biscuit will have to be placed on a large ungreased baking sheet as it is cut, for it is a very delicate dough.
Brush the top of each biscuit with a lightly beaten white of egg. Sprinkle each biscuit generously with almond mixture made thus: Crush blanched slivered almonds lightly with a rolling pin. To ¼ cup of crushed almonds add a tablespoon of castor sugar.
Bake in 160°C oven for 20 minutes. Biscuits will be crisp but light in colour.

Arum Lily Biscuits

(Photo Page 364)

¾ cup butter
1 egg
¼ tsp salt
½ cup castor sugar
1½ tsp baking powder
3 cups flour

Cream butter and sugar well. Add well beaten egg.

Mix thoroughly, then add sifted dry ingredients and blend to a biscuit dough.

Roll dough out to 5 mm thickness and cut in rounds with fluted cookie cutter.

Fold two sides of bottom half of circle to centre, to resemble a lily.

Bake in moderate oven for 15 minutes.

Coat bottom of biscuit with melted chocolate.

Marie Biscuit/Date Delights

(Photo Page 337)

2 pkts marie biscuits (crushed)
1 cup butter or margarine
1 cup sugar
750 g dates (1½ pkt)
1 egg
2 tblsp coconut

Place butter and sugar in pot and allow to melt. Add chopped dates and simmer gently till mixture is soft and blended. Quickly add egg and beat-in. Finally add crushed biscuits.

Mix well and spread on greased trays. Flatten smoothly and sprinkle top with dessicated coconut. Leave in fridge for about an hour to set. Cut in slices or squares.

Alternatively do not crush biscuits, but spread filling over them in layers. When cool cut in slices.

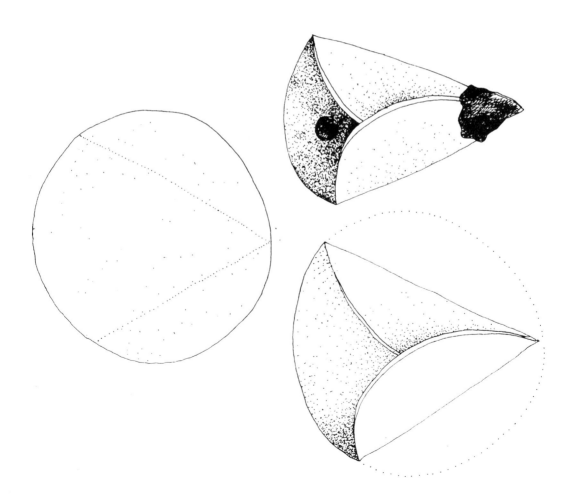

Chocolate Coconut Biscuits

½ cup butter
¼ cup castor sugar
1 tblsp cocoa
1 cup dessicated coconut
1 cup cake flour
¼ tsp baking powder

Cream butter and sugar well together. Work in coconut.
Sift flour, baking powder and cocoa together and work slowly into dough.
Press evenly on an ungreased baking sheet and bake for 20 minutes in 180°C oven.
Cut in bars or squares while hot. Remove from tray when cold.

Honey Oat Fingers

¾ cup flour
¼ level tsp bicarbonate of soda
1 cup rolled oats
1 tblsp honey (or golden syrup)
½ tsp baking powder
Pinch of salt
1 level tsp cinnamon
125g sugar
1 cup coconut
125g butter

Sift the flour, soda, salt and cinnamon. Add the sugar, oats and coconut. Heat the honey and butter together and add to the dry ingredients. Mix into a dry dough. Pack into a greased Swiss roll tin and bake in upper half of a moderate oven for about 15 minutes. Cut into neat finger shapes whilst hot and allow to cool on the tray.

Hazel Coffee Cream Biscuits

(Photo Page 364)
½ cup butter
¾ cup flour
¼ cup castor sugar
½ cup ground hazel nuts

NOTE:
If hazel nuts are not available, use any other nut of choice.
Cream butter and sugar together till light and fluffy. Add flour and ground nuts and knead into soft biscuit dough.
Pat dough in baking tin and bake in 300°F (155°C) oven till done.
After removing from oven spread with topping and leave in fridge to set.

TOPPING:
¼ cup butter
2 tsp coffee powder
¾ cup icing sugar
hot water

Mix coffee in a little hot water. Cream icing and butter till fluffy.
Add coffee and beat in.
Cut in squares or finger shapes.

Mocha Logs Biscuits

(Photo Page 364)
1 cup butter
1 egg
1 tsp vanilla essence
3 tbsp instant coffee
¾ cup castor sugar
¼ tsp salt
¼ tsp baking powder
2½-3 cups flour for dough

Cream butter and sugar well together. Add egg and beat well. Add vanilla, salt, flour, coffee and baking powder and mix into batter. Add just sufficient flour to make a soft biscuit dough.
Use a large icing nozzle or shape into logs with hands. Bake in 180°C oven till biscuits are done. Dip in melted chocolate and decorate with chopped nuts.

Date and Nut Ribbons

2 cups flour
1 cup brown sugar
½ cup margarine or butter
1 egg
½ tsp salt
¼ tsp bicarb
1 tbsp milk

FILLING:
1 cup dates
½ cup sugar
1 tbsp lemon juice
½ cup walnuts
¼ cup water

Chop dates and walnuts. Put in saucepan with sugar, water and lemon juice.
Stir over low heat until dates are soft. Cool slightly before spreading over dough.

DOUGH:
Sift dry ingredients together.
Melt butter, cool slightly and add milk and egg. Add to dry ingredients and mix well.
Cover and refrigerate for an hour. Knead dough slightly to soften, then roll and treat each half portion thus:
Cut dough in four strips (5cm) each 2'' wide.
Spread filling over three strips and pile them one on top of the other.
Finally put plain layer over top of pile. Repeat with the other half of the dough. Refrigerate for an hour.
Cut into narrow ribbon-like slices (6mm). Put on greased tray and bake in 325°F (160°C) oven for 12-15 minutes.

Flaky Wafer Jerkins

(Photo Page 364)

2 cups flour
2 tsp baking powder
1/3 cup milk
2 tblsp sugar
2 eggs
125g butter (½ cup)

Cream butter and sugar. Add eggs and beat well.

Add flour, baking powder and knead to a biscuit dough together with the milk.

Divide dough in six portions and roll out 6 rotis.

Spread each roti with filling (see below) and pile one on top of the other. Put pile of rotis on baking sheet. Brush last roti with egg.

Sprinkle with nuts and bake in 350°F (180°C) oven. Cut in squares

FILLING:

90g butter
1 cup chopped nuts
¼ cup sugar
2½ tsp milk

Mix well together and spread on rotis.

Caramel Wiggles

(Photo Page 364)

1 cup margarine or butter
1 tsp vanilla
¼ tsp salt
½ cup icing sugar
2¼ cups flour
¾ cup finely chopped nuts

Cream thoroughly butter, sugar and vanilla. Work in flour, salt and nuts and form into a soft dough. Shape dough into tiny balls.

Roll on board and form into rings or push through biscuit machine, through star shaped cutter and form into rings.

Bake in 350°F (180°C) oven.

With caramel icing make wiggles through very small icing tube.

CARAMEL ICING:

Boil a tin of condensed milk in water for 2-2½ hours and add 3 tablespoons Orley Whip Cream and beat well.

Coconut Swiss Rolls

(Photo Page 364)

2 cups flour
1/8 tsp salt
125g butter
½ tsp vanilla essence
6 tblsp castor sugar (60g)
1 tsp baking powder
2 eggs
coconut

Sift the flour, castor sugar, salt and baking powder into a bowl. Rub in butter finely. Beat eggs well and add the vanilla.

Add about 2/3 of the egg mixture to the dry ingredients and blend to a softish dough.

Roll out dough to 5 mm thickness.

Cut in small rectangles, fill with coconut filling, and roll up. Dip in well beaten egg, and then roll in coconut.

Place on greased sheets and bake in moderate oven for 10 to 15 minutes.

COCONUT FILLING:

90g butter
1 tsp vanilla
½ cup coconut
1/3 cup icing sugar
¼ cup cut, coloured cherries

Blend together above ingredients in small bowl.
Place onto rectangles.
ALTERNATIVE:
After dipping in egg and coconut, decorate with small red cherry in centre of biscuit and two green cherry pieces on sides of red.

Coconut Nests

(Photo Page 364)

1¼ cups flour
¼ tsp salt
½ cup butter
¼ cup castor sugar
1 egg yolk (separate yolk from white)
1 egg white
Coconut

Sift flour with salt. Cream butter, blend in sugar. Add beaten egg yolk and combine well. Mix the dry ingredients. Roll dough in tiny balls, then roll in egg white (slightly beaten). Finally roll in coconut. Place on greased pan, indent the centre with fingertip. Bake about 20 minutes in 180°C oven. Fill with cherries or jam when cool.
SPECIAL:
Instead of rolling in coconut, roll in crumbed almonds, (blanched, slivered toasted almonds crushed with a rolling pin).

Soji Shortbread (CREAM OF WHEAT)

125g margarine
75g self-raising flour
125g semolina
60g castor sugar

Sift dry ingredients, rub in margarine and knead together.

Grease a round baking tin and press mixture into it.

Make out a pattern with a fork and flute the edges with thumb and forefinger.

Bake at 180°C for about 40-45 minutes. When still warm, cut into triangles and dust lightly with icing sugar.

Coconut Twists

1 cup butter (but keep aside ¼ of it)
4 tsp baking powder
1 egg
¾ cup milk
3 cups flour
   FILLING:
1½ cups coconut
1½ cups sugar
The remaining butter

Rub in butter till flour resembles fine breadcrumbs. Beat egg and milk and add to flour to form soft biscuit dough. Divide dough in 5 portions and roll each out into a large circle. Spread top of four circles with the filling and then pile one on top of the other.

Place last circle over rest and brush it with a little beaten egg. Cut pile into sizes the length and width of a forefinger. Twist each length like a rope and place on lightly greased trays. Bake in 350°F (180°C) oven for 15 to 20 minutes.

To prepare filling, beat the sugar and butter till creamy. Then add coconut and beat in.

Date and Nut Slices
(COLOUR PHOTO 364)

1 cup butter
2 eggs
½ cup chopped almonds
1 tsp vanilla
3 cups flour
½ cup sugar
½ cup chopped dates
½ cup chopped pecans
2 tsp baking powder

Cream butter and sugar till light and fluffy. Add vanilla and eggs and beat well. Add dates and chopped nuts.

Finally add the flour sifted with the baking powder. Cut out in shapes after rolling out. Bake in moderate oven for 25 to 30 minutes.

Butter Nut Fancies

250 g butter
1 cup finely choped almonds or nuts
Enough flour to make soft dough
¾ cup castor sugar
1 cup coconut

Cream butter and sugar till creamy. Add nuts, coconut and then the flour. Roll out ½'' thick. Roughen surface with fork. Cut into fancy shapes. Bake in 350°F (180°C) for 10 minutes. Lower heat to 250°F (125°C) and bake till done.

ECONOMICAL VARIATION:
Instead of nuts add slightly crushed rice crispies.

Swedish Rings

¾ cup butter
1 egg
3 cups flour
1 beaten egg for brushing tops
*½ cup castor sugar
¾ cup castor sugar
1½ tsp baking powder
¼ tsp salt
*½ cup blanched slivered almonds.

Cream butter and sugar well together. Beat egg well and add and blend in. Add sifted dry ingredients and knead into soft dough. Knead well. Rol out to 5 mm thickness and cut into strips the length and thickness of a pencil.

Twist into figure 8's or bow strings. Brush with beaten egg and dip into the granulated sugar* and finely chopped almond mixture.

Bake on very slightly greased baking sheet in hot oven (400°F/200°C) for about 10 minutes.

Coconut Tartlets

250 g pastry
2 egg whites
¾ cup coconut
apricot jam
4 tblsp castor sugar
½ tsp baking powder

Roll out puff pastry fairly thinly. Cut into rounds and line small patty pans. Put a teaspoonful of jam into each. Beat egg whites stiffly and gradually add castor sugar, beating after each addition.

Fold-in coconut and baking powder. Spread a Tbsp or two of this mixture over jam. Bake in hot oven 210°C for 10 minutes. Switch off after 10 minutes and take care that coconut does not brown.

Chocolate Logs

(FOR FILLING SEE PAGE 376)

250g butter
1 cup coconut
2½ cups flour
1 tsp baking powder
4 tblsp cocoa
¾ cup sugar
1 tsp vanilla
2 eggs
Pinch of salt

Cream butter and sugar well.

Add eggs, beat and add all dry ingredients. Mix into biscuit dough.

Roll to 5 mm thickness and cut into rectangles. Fill with coconut filling. Roll up and bake in 180°C oven.

Decorate with plain white butter icing through fine icing tube or leave uncoated.

Use same coconut filling as for coconut swiss roll filling.

Angel Food Dessert

Angel food is an American dessert that is a great favourite amongst our people and we have been especially requested to give this recipe with its Indianised fillings. It is an excellent way to use up left over whites of eggs.

Special baking pans must be used for angel food. 25 cm deep tube pans of thick metal are best. On no account must the pan or any utensil used in the making of angel food be greased.

Angel Food

Carefully separate egg whites and take care that there
**   is no trace of yoke**
Egg whites of 12 eggs
¼ tsp salt
1 tsp vanilla
1½ tsp cream of tartar
½ tsp vanilla or almond extract

Beat the egg white with above till it is foamy and frothy. Then gradually mix in (two tablespoons at a time) ¾ cup castor sugar and continue to beat with rotary beater till meringue stand up in stiff peaks.

When mixture is really stiff then carefully mix in a third at a time of: One cup flour and 1½ cups castor sugar, sifted together three times.

Carefully fold in the flour mixture into meringue batter. Folding it in with a knife, or wire whip. Bake in bottom shelf of 180°C oven for 40 minutes or till it is done. When cake is cool invert on wire rack prising it slightly loose from sides and tube. Cake must be handled gently. When cool prepare and fill with any of following fillings.

Angel Food Fillings

Carefully cut off 1 cm from top of angel food cake. Then carefully scoop out centre, leaving a wall 2 cm thick at outside and inside towards the tube. Scoop out this centre and mix with any filling below, then fill it into, the hollowed out centres. Replace top of cake. Smear thickly sides and top of angel food with stiffly beaten fresh cream tinted with appropriate colour and decorate as suggested with each filling.

(1) BURFEE FILLING

¾ cup of burfee or any appropriate left-over mithai
250 ml fresh cream
¼ cup blanched slivered almonds
The scooped out angel food
½ tsp rose water
2 granadillas (scooped out)

Whip cream very stiff. Add all the other ingredients and mix well. Pack firmly into hollowed out angel food. Replace with top of angel food and ice with fresh cream.

Decorate with coloured slivered almonds and pistachios as for mithai. (Top of cake may be tinted a very pale green). For outside of cake another 250 ml of cream is used after sweetened and beaten stiff.

Twist into figure 8's or bow strings. Brush with beaten egg and dip into the sugar and finely chopped almond mixed together.

(2) PINEAPPLE FILLING

1 cup freshly grated pineapple
250 ml fresh cream
1 peppermint crisp chocolate or any hard centre choco-
**   late (90g)**
½ cup slivered almonds and pistachios (or walnuts or
**   pecan nuts)**
Scooped out angel food
2 granadillas scooped out

Whip cream stiff and fill as No. 1. Decorate top and sides of cake with additional fresh cream, walnut halves and pineapple balls, or small slices of pineapple.

Eclairs, Cream Puffs or Choux Cases

1 cup water
1 cup sifted cake flour
½ cup butter
4 eggs

Bring water and butter in saucepan to boiling point. Stir in flour all at once and stir vigorously till it leaves sides of pan and forms into a lump. Remove from heat. Beat in eggs one at a time and beat till velvety and smooth. Grease baking sheet for cream puffs. drop two tablespoonsful batter at a time. For petit choux 1 tablespoon of batter at a time. For eclairs two tablespoons of batter shaped into long fingers. Heat oven 200°C and bake for 30 minutes. Reduce heat to 150°C and bake for 20 minutes. Switch off oven and bake till dry and crisp.

SWEET FILLINGS for Cream Puffs or Eclairs:-

(1) Stiffly whipped cream (sweetened to taste). Fold-in cut-up fresh strawberries or fruit of choice.

(2) Whipped cream. Fold in diced canned fruits or fruit salad drained dry of syrup. This will not require sweetening as fruits are sweet enough.

(3) Whipped cream, sweetened to taste. Add diced fresh fruit, chocolate bits, and nuts folded-in.

(4) Different coloured and flavoured ice creams in the puff and an ice cream sauce slopped on top.

(5) Long eclairs must be filled with cream and glazed on top with chocolate.

SAVOURY: Bake small petit Choux cases:

(1) Left over cold meats to which add diced pickles and a little cottage cheese.

(2) Left over cold fish. Flaked and dressed with tartare sauce.

(3) Shrimps braised in a little oil. Dress with french dressing. All of above must be served on a bed of fresh vegetable salad with plenty of crisp lettuce, cucumbers, radishes etc.

(4) Left over dry curries such as moong dhal curry, or moong sprout curry or dry karela curry etc., a little chopped dhunia and dicked pickles converts it into a delicious savoury to be served with tea or as a side dish.

Hungarian Tart

125g butter
2 tblsp cooking oil
1 beaten egg
2 tsp baking powder
2 tblsp castor sugar
½ tsp vanilla
2 cups flour
Jam for spreading

Cream butter and sugar. Add cooking oil and vanilla. Beat well. Stir in beaten egg. Lastly add sifted flour and baking powder. Mix altogether into a dough and knead well. Divide dough in two portions and spread half in lightly greased cake tin and prick with fork. Spread with softened jam, then grate the second portion over jam. Bake in 180°C oven for 30 minutes. Dust top with icing sugar whilst hot. Cut in squares.

Scotch Crumpets

2 tblsp Maizena
6 tblsp flour
2 tblsp oil
1 egg (beaten)
¼ tsp salt
1½ tsp baking powder
3 tblsp sugar
½ cup milk

Sieve together the dry ingredients (but not the sugar). Add all the other ingredients and beat well.

Heat a griddle well. Grease it slightly, then drop spoonsful, the size of crumpets.

When bubbles appear, turn and brown on the other side. Keep covered with kitchen towel till all are made.

Serve with butter, jam and cream.

Shortbread

250 g butter (1 cup)
3 cups flour
1 tsp baking powder
¾ cup castor sugar
2 heaped tblsp corn-flour

Sift flours and baking powder together. Cream butter and sugar well together. Add flour and form into biscuit dough. Take all the dough and shape with hands into an oblong block of apprximately 30 cm long by 5 cm wide and 4 cm high. Cut off with sharp knife in 6 mm slices and place on baking sheet. Bake for 20 minutes in 150°C oven.

Koeksusters

4 cups flour
4 potatoes (approx 250 g)
2 eggs
¼ cup oil
¼ cup sugar
1 cup milk (warm)
coconut for rolling
1 tsp salt
2 tbsp butter (1/8 cup)
1 cake yeast (20g)
1 tsp ground nutmeg
½ tsp ground cloves
1½ tsp ground cinnamon
1 tsp ground ginger
1 tbsp grated naartjie peel

Boil potatoes in jacket and mash smooth while hot. Mix yeast in 2 tsp of sugar and keep for few minutes till bubbly— blend smooth.

Sift flour with salt, spices, grated peel and sugar. Cream butter and add beaten eggs and mix well together. Add to mash. Add milk to yeast mixture and add to potatoes etc.

Make soft dough with flour and yeast mixture. Leave in warm place for a few hours and till dough has doubled in size. Roll out thickly and cut out with doughnut cutter or plait or make oblong shape as desired.

Keep on greased surface for 30 minutes allowing koeksusters to rise. Heat oil 350°F (180°C) and fry on both sides to an even gold colour. Drain on wire rack and dip in syrup.

THE SYRUP:

Make a thin syrup with 2½ cups of sugar, 1½ cups water. Keep syrup simmering over low heat while steeping koeksusters, allowing them to absorb syrup before removing.

Roll in coconut. (Optional).

Yoghurt Cake

½ cup butter
2 eggs (separated)
1¼ cups flour
2 tsp baking powder
1 cup castor sugar
125ml yoghurt (½ cup)
pinch of salt
1½ tsp lemon essence

Cream butter and sugar until light and fluffy.

Add egg yolks one at a time, and beat till light and creamy. Stir in yoghurt.

Sift flour, salt and baking powder and fold into mixture with lemon essence.

Beat egg whites until stiff but not dry. Mix 1/3 into batter. Fold in the rest gently into batter.

Turn into greased tube pan and bake in 350°F (180°C) oven for 30-35 minutes. Cover with white of egg frosting or icing.

Chocolate Nut Cake

1¾ cup flour
1/3 cup cocoa
½ tsp salt
½ cup butter
2 eggs
1 tblsp instant coffee
1 tsp baking powder
1 cup castor sugar
1 tsp vanilla essence
1 cup yoghurt

Sift dry ingredients. Cream butter and sugar. Add eggs one at a time, beating well after each addition. Add vanilla. Add sifted ingredients alternately with yoghurt. Bake in 350°F (180°C) oven for 40 to 50 minutes. Take pan out of oven and cool on a wire rack.

TOPPING:

84g butter
2/3 cup brown sugar
walnuts
¼ cup ideal milk (unsweetened tinned)
1 cup coconut

Cream butter, then add sugar and ideal milk. Beat well. Blend in coconut and nuts. When cake is cool, spread topping over and place pan under griller (about 15 cm below element). Allow topping to brown. Let cake cool in pan.

Then turn over on a clean cloth placed over a wire rack, so that topping does not stick. If a darker cake is desired use 2/3 cup cocoa.

3 Minute Date Cake

2 eggs
1¾ cups flour
½ lb dates
1¼ cup brown sugar
¼ tsp nutmeg
Pinch of salt
3½ oz butter
3 tsp baking powder
½ tsp cinnamon

Cream butter and sugar well. Add eggs and beat again.

Sift flour with spices and salt and add to butter mixture.

Stone dates and chop, then heat slightly and add to batter.

Add milk and beat all well together. Grease deep cake tin and bake for 30 minutes in 180°C oven.

When cake has cooled, slice in half and sandwich with whipped cream or coffee icing.

Spice Cake

½ cup butter
¾ cup white castor sugar
2 cups cake flour
1 tsp ground cinnamon
½ tsp cloves
½ cup sour milk (yoghurt)
¾ cup brown sugar
2 eggs
1 tsp bicarb. of soda
½ tsp nutmeg
½ tsp salt
½ cup milk

Sift flour with spices. Add bicarb. to milk and sour-milk.

Beat butter and sugar well till fluffy. Add eggs one at a time and beat till fluffy. Add flour alternately with butter-milk liquid. Grease 30 x 20cm pan, sprinkle with flour and pour in batter. Bake for 30 minutes in 180°C oven. Ice with cocoa or chocolate icing.

Carrot Cake Variation

2 cups grated carrot
1 orange (grate rind off for flavouring)
3 eggs
¾ cup light brown sugar (170g)
2 tblsp grated almond
¼ cup fresh brown bread crumbs (60g)
½ cup self-raising flour
FILLING:
¼ cup butter
1½ cup icing sugar
2 tblsp orange juice

Peel and grate carrots, place in pot with ¼ cup water and stir over low heat for 10 minutes till carrots are cooked and dry.

Add 1 tblsp of grated orange rind to carrot puree. Separate egg yolk and white. Beat yolk with sugar till thick and pale in colour.

To this add carrot puree, grated almonds, bread crumbs and mix well.

Sift flour and fold into puree. Beat egg white till stiff then fold carefully into batter with metal spoon.

Grease two round 16cm in diameter sandwich pans. Line with waxpaper and pour equal quantities of batter into them.

Bake for 30 minutes in 160°C oven, test if done. Cool cake on wire rack and remove paper.

FILLING:

Cream butter well, sift in icing sugar and beat in juice of orange. Sandwich cake and use rest for sides and top.

Decorate with thin carrot curls, using a potato peeler to cut off the strips.

Place in a syrup (sugar and water) for 4 minutes. Drain. Roll up and place over cake for decoration.

Carrot Cake

1 cup butter
2 eggs
1 cup mixed dry fruit (currants etc.)
1 dsp grated lemon peel
3 cups flour
1/3 tsp fine nutmeg
2 cups grated raw carrots
½ cup brown sugar
1 tsp fine cinnamon powder
2½ tsp baking powder
½ cup milk

Cream butter and sugar well together. Beat in egg. Mix together the grated carrot, dried fruit and lemon peel.

Sift together the flour, spices and baking powder. To the creamed butter mixture add the flour, fruit and milk, till they are well incorporated.

Grease baking pan and bake in 350°F (180°C) oven for about 45 minutes.

Rich Fruit Cake

1¼ cups butter (375g)
1¼ cup brown sugar
4 eggs
¼ cup oil
½ cup mixed peel
½ cup cherries
1½ tsp mixed spice
3 cups mixed fruit (raisins, sultanas, currants, dates etc.)
1 cup chopped almond, pecan or other nuts
2½ cups flour
1½ tsp baking powder
1 tsp ground ginger
1 tsp ground cinnamon
1 ground clove

Line the cake tin with a double layer of foil and grease slightly.

Chop dates, nuts, quarter cherries and dust dried fruit with a tablespoon of flour.

Sift flour, baking powder and spices.

Beat sugar and butter till light and creamy.

Add one egg at a time, but beat well after each addition and add oil and beat.

Add flour and spices and fold in with wooden spoon.

Lastly add nuts and fruit and mix the ingredients into the batter.

Pour mixture in prepared cake tin and bake in 350°F (180°C) oven for 30 minutes, then decrease to 300°F (150°C), and bake for another 2 hours.

To prevent over browning on top, cover top of baking tin with foil.

Rich Fruit Cake
VARIATION

1½ cups butter
3 cups flour
2 tsp baking powder
6 large eggs
½ cup orange juice or black coffee
½ cup glace cherries
1¼ cup brown sugar
1/3 tsp salt
1½ tsp mixed spices
250 g currants/sultanas
125 g dates
3/4 cup chopped pecan nuts

Cream butter and sugar till it is light and fluffy. Add eggs one at a time and beat in well into batter. (If it shows sign of curdling add a little of the flour with each egg.)

Sift all dry ingredients together. Dust the dried fruit with a little of the flour. Add rest of flour to batter and mix-in. Now add fruit and nuts and lastly the orange juice or the black coffee. Put in lined, greased tin and bake in moderate oven (350°F — 180°C) for 1½ hours.

Queen Elizabeth Cake

1 cup boiling water
1 cup chopped dates
1 tsp bicarb soda
1 cup castor sugar
¼ cup butter
1 egg
1 tsp vanilla
1½ cups sifted flour
1 tsp baking powder
pinch of salt

Pour boiling water over chopped dates, add 1 tsp bicarb and leave to steep.

Cream sugar and butter, add egg and vanilla and beat well.

Sift dry ingredients and add to above mixture. Add date mixture.

Pour into greased pan or loaf tin.

Bake in 188°C oven for 45 minutes.

ICING

5 tbsp brown sugar
5 tbsp fresh cream
2 tbsp butter

Boil brown sugar, fresh cream and butter together for 15 minutes. Spread over cake and sprinkle with nuts.

Black Boys or Cocoa Ball Icing

ICING:

2 tsp maizena
3 cups sugar
2 tblsp cocoa
1 cup water

Mix all well. Boil for 12 minutes stirring continuously over low heat till icing is sticky. Dip cup cakes in this and roll in dessicated coconut.

Walnut Cake

2 cups flour
Pinch of salt
¾ cup chopped nuts
1 tsp vanilla
¼ cup milk
1 tsp baking powder
¾ cup butter
¾ cup sugar
3 eggs

Cream butter till soft. Add sugar and beat till light. Add eggs one at a time and beat well after each addition. Add vanilla. Sift dry ingredients and add alternately with milk, and at the same time incorporate the chopped nuts but take care not to overbeat at this stage.

Line a loaf pan with paper and grease it generously. Bake in 180°F oven for 30 minutes, switch down to 125°F and bake till cake is done.

Leave in pan for 10 minutes then cool on wire rack and spread with an icing made from:

2 tblsp milk
1 tblsp butter
30 g milk chocolate

Melt above ingredients slowly, then quickly beat in one egg yolk. Add as much icing sugar as is necessary to make icing.

NOTE: For a very light cake, use same recipe as above, but only add egg yolks and leave egg whites till last. After cake has been mixed, beat egg whites stiff, then fold into batter and bake.

Banana Cake

60 g chocolate (optional)
½ cup margarine
1½ cups castor sugar
¼ cup buttermilk (½ milk and ½ yoghurt)
1 cup mashed ripe bananas
½ cup chopped almonds
2 large eggs
2 cups flour
¼ tsp baking powder
¾ tsp bicarb
1 tsp salt

Sift flour, salt, baking powder and bicarb twice.

Cream butter and sugar till light and creamy. Add eggs and beat in till light and fluffy.

Into buttermilk blend in bananas and nuts and stir in alternately with flour mixture into a batter. Grate in chocolate.

Pour in loaf pan which is slightly greased.

Bake at 180°C oven for 35-40 minutes.

For Food Cooked
For Photographs Thanks Are
Due To

ALI LEILA — Tart

ANSARI SAYEDA — Urad Paak

BOBAT ZUBEIDA — Marie Biscuit Delights

COOVADIA FATIMA — Chicken/Macaroni casserole

DADABHAY SHIRIN — Nihari

GANI MAYMUNA — Steak cutlets

GANI HALIMA — Pineapple dessert

HAFFEJEE RAZIA — Pizza

KAJEE AYESHA — Achar, Bhaji and karela lagan

LOCKHAT SHERBANU — Biscuits, bhinda/chicken curry

LOONAT FATIMA — Snoek/vegetable dokra

MAHOMEDY HAFSA — Chicken Casserole, Aaloo chutpatty, Frikkadels, mutton in milk, breadloaf

MAHOMEDY FATIMA — Naan khataay

MALL KHADIJA — Biscuit and pastry tart

MAYAT FATIMA — Wholewheat breadrolls, brinjal/prawn delight, patelli

MOOLA ZULEIKHA — Pancake dessert

MOOSA AMINA — Curries

MOOSA HAFISA — Falooda dessert

MOOSA HAWABIBI — Achars, egg mince paratha, madumbi curry, crayfish curry, roast chicken, puris.

MOOSA KHADIJA — Pyramid cheese dessert

MOOSA ZOHRA — Sev curries

MEHFILE NISA OF POTGIETERSRUS — Hawa Sooliman, Ayesha Laari and Rokayya Bhayed (Biscuits on large tray)

NADVI KHORSED — Murukku, Sev, Shaami Kabaabs, Plaits, Japanese Lanterns

PARUK BARI ISMAIL — Cabbage packet curry, macaroni/cheese casserole

PARUK AYESHA YAKOOB — Bread loaves

PARUK HAWABIBI — Rice ring, mawa goolab jamuns

PARUK CHOTIMA — Bhejo curry, sekta sing curry

RABOOBEE NURJEHAAN — Chabli Kabaab, Dum ka Gosht, Brinjal curry, rasgoola, parathas

SEEDAT ROKAYYA — Whole baked fish and fish in olive oil

SHAIK FAZILA and ZUBEIDA — Melting moments

SHAIK BIFOI — Papdi mootha curry, toovar dhal dokra, tripe curry

VAID KHADIJA — Grilled Prawns, chicken in tomato

MAHOMEDY MARIAM A.H., MAYAT ZULEIKHA, PARUK MARIAM E.E.G., MDLADLA MILDRED — Various fish and prawn curries; Various chicken and meat dishes; Various rice and biryani dishes; Various Lagans (mealie meal, souffle, tortilla bhatura etc.); Various vegetable and meat/vegetable curries; Various soups, sprouts and bhajias; Various sweet and savoury pastries; Various savouries (vadde, stuffed pancakes, kabaabs, banana cutlets); Various Achars and chutneys; Various Frozen foods in tupperware; Various Desserts and halwas; Various Brinjal dishes.

Index of Coloured Photographs

HOW TO USE THE INDEX

For your convenience we have duplicated the index. Persons who are conversant with Indian cuisine should encounter no difficulty in using the General Index which ranges from A to Z. They will simply look up Biryani under B, Kurma under K, Dodhi Halwa under D and so forth. However even supercooks will find it worthwhile to browse through the classified index for many new categories of dishes have been included in this edition.

The classified index is recommended for persons new to Indian cookery. We suggest that they read through WHERE TO FIND IT (Pages 14 and 15) for clues as to which section to look up for the dish they are hunting for. As a general rule Biryanis, Yakhnis Pilaaus etc. will be found under rice dishes but Jarda (Sweet Rice) will be found in the dessert section. For instance Carrot Halwa will be found under C in the general index but in the classified index they must look in the dessert section under Halwas. In other words whereas in the general index the key ingredient controls the indexing, in the classified index the category of dish is the key word to look for.

CLASSIFIED INDEX
SECTION 1
Rice Dishes

SECTION 2
Curries or Tarkaris
Basic Curry, Dhal & Soup

SECTION 2A
Dry Curries, Beef, Mutton, Poultry, Etc.

Venison Or Game

SECTION 7

Chutney, Kachoomer and Pickles

SECTION 8

Papads and Papdums

SECTION 9

Roti, Bread and Naan

SECTION 10

Convalescent and Remedial Foods

SECTION 11

Ice Cream, Juice, Syrup, Milk Drinks

SECTION 12

Sweets and Desserts